Berlin

timeout.com/berlin

Time Out Guides Ltd
Universal House
251 Tottenham Court Road
London W1T 7AB
United Kingdom
Tel: +44 (0)20 7813 3000
Fax: +44 (0)20 7813 6001
Email: guides@timeout.com
www.timeout.com

Published by Time Out Guides Ltd, a wholly owned subsidiary of Time Out Group Ltd.
Time Out and the Time Out logo are trademarks of Time Out Group Ltd.

© **Time Out Group Ltd 2011**
Previous editions 1993, 1996, 1998, 2000, 2002, 2004, 2006, 2009.

10 9 8 7 6 5 4 3 2 1

This edition first published in Great Britain in 20XX by Ebury Publishing.
A Random House Group Company
20 Vauxhall Bridge Road, London SW1V 2SA

Random House Australia Pty Ltd 20 Alfred Street, Milsons Point, Sydney, New South Wales 2061, Australia

Random House New Zealand Ltd 18 Poland Road, Glenfield, Auckland 10, New Zealand

Random House South Africa (Pty) Ltd Isle of Houghton, Corner Boundary Road & Carse O'Gowrie, Houghton 2198, South Africa

Random House UK Limited Reg. No. 954009

Distributed in the US and Latin America by Publishers Group West (1-510-809-3700)
Distributed in Canada by Publishers Group Canada (1-800-747-8147)

For further distribution details, see www.timeout.com.

ISBN: 978-1-84670-249-5

A CIP catalogue record for this book is available from the British Library.

Printed and bound in Great Britain by Butler Tanner & Dennis, Frome, Somerset.

The Random House Group Limited supports The Forest Stewardship Council (FSC®), the leading international forest certification organisation. Our books carrying the FSC label are printed on FSC® certified paper. FSC is the only forest certification scheme endorsed by the leading environmental organisations, including Greenpeace. Our paper procurement policy can be found at www.randomhouse.co.uk/environment

Time Out carbon-offsets its flights with Trees for Cities (www.treesforcities.org).

MIX
Paper from
responsible sources
FSC® C023561

Contents

WHENEVER, WHEREVER YOU NEED MONEY..

BERLIN

WE GET IT THERE IN 10 MINUTES*

CHOICE IS IN YOUR HANDS

1. Arrange for the person sending the money to visit a MoneyGram agent near them. After sending the money, they will give you a reference number.

2. Find your nearest MoneyGram agent at **www.moneygram.com** or anywhere you see the MoneyGram sign.

3. Give the reference number and your ID** to the MoneyGram agent.

4. Fill out one simple form to receive your money.

      **MoneyGram.** *Money Transfer*

00 800 8971 8971 www.moneygram.com

Introduction

If New York is the city that never sleeps, Berlin is the city that never stands still. Turn your back for a year or two – sometimes even a week or two – and it's changed. That little bar you loved has become a Vietnamese supermarket, that gallery you admired has moved house (twice) and the nightclub where you danced until dawn has lost a battle with developers and popped up on the other side of the river. Streets change names, so, even, do metro stations. And remember that neighbourhood where all the cool kids hung out last time you were here? No one goes out there any more. It can be frustrating trying to keep track – but also exactly what makes Berlin such an exciting destination.

For the nine million visitors who come each year, the first task on touching down in the German capital is getting to grips with this slippery, shape-shifting city. The geography does not make life easy. There are next to no hills to climb for a decent vantage point and the scale of some blocks, particularly in the former East, can make for exhausting sightseeing. Plus many of the city's best restaurants and bars pride themselves on being difficult to find, eschewing signage for an unmarked door. Many clubs refuse to advertise, relying instead on word of mouth to spread their reputations.

The first mistake most people make on arrival is to tie themselves up in knots trying to split the city down the middle into East and West. The Berlin Wall wiggled around town, along riverbanks, across the canal and even dividing streets in two. And now, over 20 years since the Iron Curtain fell, the border is ever harder to detect, even for those who were around when it was still up.

Nevertheless, Berlin can never escape its past, and you may stumble across a brass-plated cobble marking the spot where a Jew was rounded up and sent to a concentration camp, a bullet hole from World War II or some Cyrillic graffiti scrawled by a Red Army soldier. Despite its reputation as a decadent party destination, Berlin will never be a place where things are taken lightly. Yet that contradiction is all part of the fun – debauched yet dour, harrowing yet happening. Ugly yet somehow really rather beautiful. Enjoy. Helen Pidd, *Editor*

Berlin in Brief

IN CONTEXT

An overview of the city's turbulent past describes how Berlin emerged from a swamp to play a major role in two world wars and then find itself at the heart of the conflict between East and West in the Cold War. A chapter dedicated to architecture looks at how history has left its mark on the city's buildings, the hodgepodge of styles bearing testimony to the aesthetic battle for Berlin that continues today.
► *For more, see pp15-53.*

SIGHTS

There's more to Berlin than Hitler and the Wall – the moving Jewish Museum, with its stunning annex by Daniel Libeskind, and Hamburger Bahnhof, a modern art gallery housed in an immaculately restored station, to name just two. We take an in-depth look at the world-class galleries on the Museumsinsel as well as more off-beat sights like the old headquarters of the Stasi, the East German secret police.
► *For more, see pp55-107.*

CONSUME

Berlin is a bar-hoppers' paradise and these days the food is more than adequate too, whether you want pork-based local treats, Vietnamese omelettes or a kebab picked up from one of the city's many Turkish restaurants. It's a dream destination for shoppers too, with an array of excellent flea markets and vintage stores as well as all manner of designer boutiques.
► *For more, see pp109-196.*

ARTS & ENTERTAINMENT

Berlin's nightclubs are rated among the best in the world and its reputation for quality (and debauchery) is richly deserved. But the city doesn't just vibrate to the bass of minimal techno – there are three opera houses too. Plus numerous theatres and galleries, and some of the most varied gay life on the planet. And for those seeking cleaner fun, we profile the city's best pools, lakes and saunas.
► *For more, see pp197-270.*

ESCAPES & EXCURSIONS

If you're here for more than a weekend, it's worth getting out of Berlin and exploring the surrounding area. Just half an hour from the centre of town, UNESCO-protected Potsdam is home to the Sanssouci Palace and gardens; while the seaside island of Rügen is an easy train ride north. In summer, the hundreds of lakes in Brandenburg are perfect for exploring by canoe or bicycle.
► *For more, see pp271-286.*

Berlin in 48 Hours

Day 1 From the Wall to the Gate

9AM Have breakfast at **Café Fleury** (*see p139*) or **Nola's** (*see p141*) in Mitte. Stroll over to Bernauer Strasse, where the Berlin Wall once divided the street. Climb the tower at the free **Gedenkstätte Berliner Mauer** museum (*see p99*) and look down over the only remaining section of the Wall to be re-created as it once was, complete with death strip and watchtower. Catch the S-bahn from Nordbahnhof to Brandenburger Tor to admire the bombast of the **Brandenburg Gate** (*see p56*) and the rebuilt **Pariser Platz**. Walk through the Gate from East to West and head to the **Reichstag** parliament building (*see p85*) to visit Norman Foster's dome (you'll need to book in advance).

1PM Depending on the weather, walk through Tiergarten until you reach the lakeside **Café am Neuen See** (*see p170*), which serves fantastic pizzas and cold beer; or take a ten-minute detour east for some top notch sushi at **Ishin Mitte** (*see p140*). Visit the **Denkmal für die ermordeten Juden Europas** (*see p58*), the striking Holocaust memorial with its 2,711 stark concrete slabs. Then it's time for the **Topografie des Terrors** (*see p83*), the old Gestapo HQ, now an outdoor museum charting the rise of Nazism, which runs alongside a stretch of Wall.

1PM Walk along Zimmerstrasse, popping into the free **Stasi Bildungszentrum** (*see p82*). Recharge your batteries with a coffee and a cone at the pun-tastic Kalter Krieg (Cold War) ice-cream parlour at the end of the street – or a hot waffle, if you're visiting in winter. From there it's just a few steps to **Checkpoint Charlie** (*see p80*), which once marked the border between East and West. Skip the expensive museum.

8PM Head to Oranienstrasse in Kreuzberg for a few pre-dinner drinks. **Würgeengel** (*see p169*) has the best cocktails; **Luzia** (*see p168*) is a classic Berlin bar. Head for dinner nearby: **3 Schwestern** (*see p148*) serves modern German dishes in a dramatic old hospital; **Markthalle** (*see p150*) does great schnitzels. **Henne** (*see p149*) has roast chicken and not a lot else.

NAVIGATING THE CITY
Berlin can be hard to get a handle on. It's big, and is not neatly divided into East and West. The city is divided into 12 *Bezirke* (districts) that spread out from central Mitte, where the Fernseheturm (TV tower) stands. Within each district are distinct *Kieze* (neighbourhoods). The River Spree winds through the city more of less from west to east.

There are two kinds of trains in Berlin – the overground S-bahn and the mostly underground U-bahn. Both are usually reliable, and most lines run through the night on weekends. Buses reach parts of the cities the trains bypass and an extensive tram network replaces the U-bahn in much of the former east. There's also a bike hire scheme.

SEEING THE SIGHTS
You shouldn't have to queue long for most sights, with the exception of some of the museums on the Museumsinsel

Day 2 Shopping, History and High Culture

10AM Consider starting your day in the eastern
district of **Friedrichshain**. Around Simon-Dach-
Strasse and Boxhagener Platz there are oodles of
places to choose from for breakfast, though the
all-you-can-eat buffet at **Café 100 Wasser** (*see
p146*) is a local favourite. Weather permitting, hire
a bike and cycle towards the river and along the
East Side Gallery (*see p76*), a long section of the
Wall, before pedalling on to **Alexander Platz** (*see
p69*) where you may or may not decide to pay the
steep fee to catch the lift to the top.

1PM Explore the shops around **Hackescher Markt** – Alte Schönhauser Strasse and
Mulack Strasse have the most interesting selection. Have a quick lunch around there –
the Vietnamese omelettes and sandwiches at **Cô Cô** (*see p139*) are sensational, or, if you
fancy German fodder, try the pizza-esque *Flammkuchen* at **Schwarzwaldstuben** (*see p143*).
While you're in the area, pop into any of the galleries such as **Peres Projects** (*see p216*) or
Galerie Eigen + Art (*see p215*).

3PM Head to the **Museumsinsel** via the Monbijou Brücke, and take your pick of which of the
six museums to visit. To do them all properly would take at least a day – if have time for just
one, choose the revamped **Neues Museum** or the **Pergamon** (for both, *see p64*). If modern
history is more your thing, the **Deutsches Historisches Museum** (*see p61*) is nearby.

6PM Time for a drink. In summer, you get a great view of the TV tower from the garden at
Riva (*see p160*). On a colder day, **Bötzow Privat** (*see p159*) or **Altes Europa** (*see p159*),
both in Mitte, have a cosier vibe. If you want to experience Berlin's heavyweight culture,
try for tickets for the **Philharmonie** (*see p238*) or opera (*see p237*). Alternatively, the
Schaubühne (*see p265*), **Hau** (*see p265*) and **Radial System V** (*see p270*) stage some of the
city's best theatre. And if you want to try some modern German cookery and have a full wallet,
try **Restaurant Tim Raue** (*see p147*) in Kreuzberg or **Reinstoff** (*see p141*) in Mitte.

(especially the newy renovated Neues
Museum, which sells timed entry tickets
in advance) and Schloss Charlottenburg.
Some museums are closed on a Monday
but most keep their doors open late one
night a week, usually Thursday.

PACKAGE DEALS

The Berlin Welcome Card entitles you to
unlimited public transport and 25 or 50
per cent off 160 attractions and tours in
Berlin and Potsdam. It costs €16.90 for

48 hours in zones A and B (note that
Schönefeld Airport is in Zone C), €22.90
for 72 hours. If you're going to visit three
or more museums, it's worth shelling
out for the Museumspass (€19, €9.50
reductions), which gives you access to 70
museums for free on three consecutive
days, including the big hitters on the
Museumsinsel. The Berlin City TourCard is
slightly cheaper but does more or less the
same thing as the Welcome Card – check
the small print for what's included.

Berlin in Profile

MITTE

If Berlin has a centre, then Mitte is it. The name means 'middle' and this bustling district is where the big hitting sights are found. Bisected by the grand street of Unter den Linden, Mitte is home to the Brandenburg Gate, as well as the world class Museumsinsel and the TV tower – plus the swishest bars and restaurants and the swankiest hotels and boutiques.

▶ *For more, see pp56-72.*

PRENZLAUERBERG & FRIEDRICHSHAIN

These two former Eastern districts boast a dizzying number of bars, cafés, restaurants and shops in which to spend time and money. While Prenzlauerberg is artily pretty and a magnet for the yummy mummy brigade, much of Friedrichshain retains the look and feel of its communist past, with wide boulevards lined with Soviet 'wedding cake' style architecture. It's also home to the longest remaining stretch of the Berlin Wall at the East Side Gallery and the legendary Berghain nightclub.

▶ *For more, see pp73-76.*

KREUZBERG & SCHÖNEBERG

The bohemian enclave of Kreuzberg has smartened up since the Cold War days, when its proximity to the Berlin Wall decimated the rents and made it a honeypot for revolutionaries and hedonists. It retains a hint of its radical past, and houses the excellent Jewish Museum and Checkpoint Charlie, as well as many of the city's best bars, plus the nicest stretch of canal around Admiralsbrücke and Paul-Linke-Ufer. Neighbouring Schöneberg is primarily residential, but is also home to Berlin's well-established gay scene.

▶ *For more, see pp77-83.*

TIERGARTEN

Home to Berlin's biggest park and some of the most famous sights, including the Reichstag parliament building, the Holocaust Memorial and Potsdamer Platz – once the beating heart of the roaring twenties and now the rather soulless commercial centre of the city. Most of the embassies are here too, and there is no shortage of upmarket restaurants or sleek bars.

▶ *For more, see pp84-91.*

CHARLOTTENBURG

The impressive Schloss Charlottenburg is this chi-chi district's primary sight, along with the shopping street Kurfürstendamm and the startling Kaiser-Wilhelm Gedächtnis-Kirche, with its war-ravaged steeple left as a permanent reminder of Germany's darkest past. When the Wall was up, this area was the place for upwardly mobile Berliners, and has retained its slightly snooty atmosphere. It's not the place for a wild night out, but boasts countless delightful bars and cafés, particularly around Sevigny Platz.
▶ For more, see pp92-98.

NEUKÖLLN

Not long ago, multicultural Neukölln was considered a no-go area for many Berliners, who had read the headlines about arson attacks and grinding poverty. These days, while it is not without problems, Neukölln – or at least the north of the borough – has now been invaded by the arty party crowd and is a great place for a night out. Weser-strasse is where most of the best bars can be found.
▶ For more, see p106.

TREPTOW

The best things in Treptow are the colossal Soviet War Memorial in Treptower Park, the floating swimming pool and sauna complex on the Badeschiff and the waterside bars and clubs on the border with Kreuzberg.
▶ For more, see pp106-107.

Time Out Berlin

Editorial

Editor Helen Pidd
Deputy Editor Ros Sales
Listings Editors Stephanie Kirchner
Proofreader Mandy Martinez
Indexer Holly Pick

Editorial Director Ruth Jarvis
Editorial Manager Holly Pick
Management Accountants Margaret Wright, Clare Turner

Design

Art Director Scott Moore
Art Editor Pinelope Kourmouzoglou
Senior Designer Kei Ishimaru
Group Commercial Designer Jodi Sher

Picture Desk

Picture Editor Jael Marschner
Picture Desk Assistant/Researcher Ben Rowe

Advertising

New Business & Commercial Director Mark Phillips
International Advertising Manager Kasimir Berger
International Sales Executive Charlie Sokol
Advertising Sales (Berlin) In Your Pocket

Marketing

Senior Publishing Brand Manager Luthfa Begum
Guides Marketing Manager Colette Whitehouse
Group Commercial Art Director Anthony Huggins

Production

Group Production Manager Brendan McKeown
Production Controller Katie Mulhern

Time Out Group

Chairman & Founder Tony Elliott
Chief Executive Officer David King
Chief Operating Officer Aksel Van der Wal
Group Financial Director Paul Rakkar
Group General Manager/Director Nichola Coulthard
Time Out Communications Ltd MD David Pepper
Time Out International Ltd MD Cathy Runciman
Time Out Cultural Development Director Mark Elliott
Group IT Director Simon Chappell
Group Marketing Director Andrew Booth

Contributors

Introduction Helen Pidd. **History** Frederick Studemann (*The All-Seeing Stasi* Kevin Cote; *False Economy* Dave Rimmer; *Making History* Zoe Jewell). **Architecture** Matthew Tempest; Francesca Rogier (*Chipperfield's Neues Museum* Matthew Tempest). **Berlin Today** Helen Pidd (*Grounded for Good* Dave Rimmer). **Sightseeing** Helen Pidd, Zoe Jewell, Dave Rimmer (*Remember, Remember* Dave Rimmer; *Walk: The Wall Remembered* Julie Gregson; *The Turkish Capital* Edmund Gordon; *Walk: Berlin Revived* Dave Rimmer; *Boot Trips* Nicky Gardner; *Tour of the Hour* Dave Rimmer; *Bearpit Karaoke* Helen Pidd). **Hotels** Helen Pidd, Stephanie Kirchner, Neal Wach (*Haven at the Hüttenpalast* Helen Pidd). **Restaurants & Cafés** Helen Pidd (*Profile Tim Raue* Helen Pidd; *Curry, Do Your Wurst* Dave Rimmer). **Bars & Pubs** Helen Pidd (*Brewing Berlin-Style* Helen Pidd). **Shops & Services** Stephanie Kirchner, Jenna Krumminga (*Capital Clothing, Sexy Vintage* Stephanie Kirchner; *Chocolate Confidential* Zoe Jewell). **Calendar** Nickolas Woods. **Children** Helen Pidd, Don Mac Coitir (*Children at Work* Kevin Cote). **Galleries** Andrew Horn (*Starry Nights* Helen Pidd). **Galleries** Helen Pidd, Kimberly Bradley. **Gay & Lesbian** Matthew Fox, Nickolas Woods (*Nina Queer: Queen of Drag* Helen Pidd). **Music** Matthew Tempest, David Canisius, Rachel Doyle. **Nightlife** Mathias Weck, Helen Pidd (*Having A Ball* Kimberly Bradley). **Sport & Fitness** Helen Pidd, Don Mac Coitir (*Cycling & the City, Sauna Culture* Helen Pidd). **Theatre, Cabaret & Dance** Andrew Haydon, Sarah Lewis (*HAU's the Best of Berlin* Andrew Haydon). **Escapes & Excursions** Julie Gregson (*The Wild Side* Helen Pidd). **Directory** Stephanie Kirchner, Helen Pidd.

Maps john@jsgraphics.co.uk

Front Cover Photography Reichstag, Photolibrary.com
Back Cover Photography Elan Fleisher

Photography Elan Fleisher, except pages 7 (top and middle right), 10 (left), 37, 79, 89, 103, 110, 137, 154, 157, 164, 168, 192, 195, 197, 208, 210, 213, 231, 232, 243, 253, 259, 264 Britta Jaschinski; pages 7 (bottom), 11 (top), 271, 272, 275, 276, 280, 281, 285 Shutterstock; page 9 gary718 / Shutterstock.com; page 11 (left), 148 Kei Ishimaru; page 16 Bettmann/Corbis; page 49 Wolfgang Scholvien Photograph; page 65 Staatliche Museen zu Berlin/Maximilian Meisse; pages 71, 109, 172, 178, 179, 279 Jael Marschner; pages 86, 99 Wolfgang Scholvien/Visit Berlin; page 101 Foto Veto; page 135 Reinstoff; page 141 Goetz Schleser; page 147 (top) Wolfgang Stahr; page 147 (bottom) Andrea Thode/Effilee; page 152 Sabine Muench; page 156 Frank Hensel; page 171 visitBerlin.de/Koch; page 198 linerpics; page 199 Bolk / Berliner Philharmoniker; page 203 Pamela B; page 213 Uwe Walter, 2010; page 216 Courtesy the artist and Sprüth Magers Berlin London, photography Jens Ziehe; page 220 Vladimir Wrangel; page 234 Monika Rittershaus/Berliner Philharmoniker; page 236 Reinhard Friedrich/Berliner Philharmoniker; page 239 Matthias Heyde; page 261 Berliner Bäder-Betriebe, Stadtbad Neukölln; page 265 Torsten Elger; page 266 Georg Knoll; page 269 Sebastian Bolesch; page 282 Nikita Starichenko.

The following images were supplied by the featured establishments/artists: pages 46, 93, 111, 115, 122, 127, 128, 129, 131, 132, 165, 167, 174, 204, 207, 209, 227, 258.

About the Guide

GETTING AROUND

The back of the book contains street maps of Berlin, as well as overview maps of the city and its surroundings. The maps start on page 313; on them are marked the locations of hotels (**❶**), restaurants and cafés (**❶**), and pubs and bars (**❶**). The majority of businesses listed in this guide are located in the areas we've mapped; the grid-square references in the listings refer to these maps.

THE ESSENTIALS

For practical information, including visas, disabled access, emergency numbers, lost property, useful websites and local transport, please see the Directory. It begins on page 288.

THE LISTINGS

Addresses, phone numbers, websites, transport information, hours and prices are all included in our listings, as are selected other facilities. All were checked and correct at press time. However, business owners can alter their arrangements at any time, and fluctuating economic conditions can cause prices to change rapidly.

The very best venues in the city, the must-sees and must-dos in every category, have been marked with a red star (★). In the Sights chapters, we've also marked venues with free admission with a **FREE** symbol.

PHONE NUMBERS

The area code for Berlin is 030. You don't need to use the code when calling from within Berlin: simply dial the number as listed in this guide.

From outside Germany, dial your country's international access code (011 from the US) or a plus symbol, followed by the German country code (49), 030 for Berlin (dropping the initial zero) and the number as listed in the guide. So, to reach the Deutsches Historisches Museum, dial + 49 30 203 040. For more on phones, including information on calling abroad from the UK and details of local mobile-phone access, *see p298*.

FEEDBACK

We welcome feedback on this guide, both on the venues we've included and on any other locations that you'd like to see featured in future editions. Please email us at guides@timeout.com.

Time Out Guides

Founded in 1968, Time Out has grown from humble beginnings into the leading resource for anyone wanting to know what's happening in the world's greatest cities. Alongside our influential weeklies in London, New York and Chicago, we publish more than 20 magazines in cities as varied as Beijing and Beirut; a range of travel books, with the City Guides now joined by the newer Shortlist series; and an information-packed website. The company remains proudly independent, still owned by Tony Elliott four decades after he launched *Time Out London*.

Written by local experts and illustrated with original photography, our books also retain their independence. No business has been featured because it has advertised, and all restaurants and bars are visited and reviewed anonymously.

ABOUT THE EDITOR

Helen Pidd spent 2011 in Berlin as Germany correspondent for the *Guardian*, returning to the city she had lived in as a student. She is the author of *Bicycle – The Complete Guide to Everyday Cycling* and co-edited an edition of *Time Out Edinburgh*.

A full list of the book's contributors can be found opposite. However, we've also included details of our writers in selected chapters through the guide.

In Context

Reichstag. *See p85.*

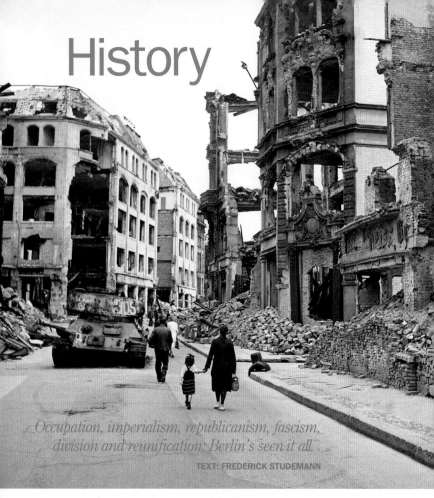

History

Occupation, imperialism, republicanism, fascism, division and reunification: Berlin's seen it all.

TEXT: FREDERICK STUDEMANN

Compared to other European capitals, such as Rome or London, Berlin is just a baby. The area where the city is now was so boggy that nobody bothered to settle there until the 12th century, when German knights wrested the swampland from the Slavs. The name Berlin is believed to come from the Slav word *birl*, meaning 'swamp'. Berlin and its twin settlement Cölln (on what is now the Museumsinsel) were founded as trading posts on the banks of the River Spree, halfway between the older fortress towns of Spandau and Köpenick. Today, the borough of Mitte embraces Cölln and old Berlin, and Spandau and Köpenick are peripheral suburbs. The town's existence was first recorded in 1237, when Cölln was mentioned in a church document. In the same century, construction began on the Marienkirche and Nikolaikirche, both of which still stand.

A MERCHANTS' CITY

The Ascanian family, as Margraves of Brandenburg, ruled over the twin towns and the surrounding region. To encourage trade, they granted special rights to merchants, with the result that Berlin and Cölln – which were officially united in 1307 – emerged as wealthy trading centres linking east and west. Early years of prosperity came to an end in 1319 with the death of the last Ascanian ruler, leaving the city at the mercy of robber barons from outlying regions. Yet, despite political upheaval, Berlin's merchants continued their business. In 1359 the city joined the Hanseatic League of free-trading northern European cities.

The threat of invasion remained, however. In the late 14th century, two powerful families, the Dukes of Pomerania and the brutal von Quitzow brothers, vied for control of the city. Salvation came in the guise of Friedrich of Hohenzollern, a southern German nobleman sent by the Holy Roman Emperor in 1411 to bring peace to the region. Initially, Friedrich was well received by the local people. The bells of the Marienkirche were melted down and made into weapons for the fight against the aggressors. (Echoing this, the Marienkirche bells were again transformed into tools of war in 1917, during the reign of Kaiser Wilhelm II, the last ruling Hohenzollern.)

Having defeated the von Quitzow brothers, Friedrich officially became Margrave. In 1416, he took the further title of Elector of Brandenburg, denoting his right to vote in the election of the Holy Roman Emperor – titular head of the German-speaking states. Gradually, Berlin was transformed from an outlying trading post to a small-sized capital. In 1442, foundations were laid for Berlin Castle and a royal court was established. By 1450, the city's population was 6,000.

With peace and stability came the loss of independent traditions, as Friedrich consolidated power. Disputes rose between the patrician classes and the craftsmen's guilds. Rising social friction culminated in the 'Berlin Indignation' of 1447-48, when the population rose up in rebellion. Friedrich's son, Friedrich II, and his courtiers were locked out of the city and the foundations of the castle were flooded, but it was only months before the uprising collapsed and the Hohenzollerns returned triumphant. Merchants faced new restrictions and the economy suffered.

UNREFORMED CHARACTERS

The Reformation arrived in Berlin and Brandenburg during the reign of Joachim I Nestor (1535-71), the first Elector to embrace Protestantism. He strove to improve Berlin's cultural standing by inviting artists, architects and theologians to work in the city. In 1538, Caspar Theyss and Konrad Krebbs, two master builders from Saxony, began work on a Renaissance-style palace. The building took 100 years to complete, and evolved into the bombastic Stadtschloss, which stood on what is now Museumsinsel in the Spree until the East German government demolished it in 1950.

Joachim's studious nature was not reflected in the self-indulgent behaviour of his subjects. Attempts to clamp down on drinking, gambling and loose morals had little effect. Visiting the city, Abbot Trittenheim remarked that 'the people are good, but rough and unpolished; they prefer stuffing themselves to good science'. After stuffing itself with another 6,000 people, Berlin left the 16th century with a population of 12,000.

THE THIRTY YEARS WAR

The outbreak of the Thirty Years War in 1618 dragged Berlin on to the wider political stage. Although initially unaffected by the conflict between Catholic forces loyal to the Holy Roman Empire and the Swedish-backed Protestant armies, the city was eventually caught up in the war, which left the German-speaking states ravaged and divided for two centuries. In 1626, imperial troops occupied Berlin and plundered the city. Trade collapsed and the city's hinterland was laid waste. To top it all, there were four serious epidemics between 1626 and 1631, killing thousands. By the end of the war, in 1648, Berlin had lost a third of its housing and the population had fallen to less than 6,000.

IN CONTEXT

'On 27 October, Napoleon and his army marched through the Brandenburger Tor. Once again, Berlin was an occupied city.'

LAYING THE FOUNDATIONS

Painstaking reconstruction was carried out under Friedrich Wilhelm, the 'Great Elector'. He succeeded his father in 1640, but sat out the war in exile. Influenced by Dutch ideas on town planning and architecture (he was, after all, married to a Princess of Orange), Wilhelm embarked on a policy that linked urban regeneration, economic expansion and solid defence. New city fortifications were built and a garrison of 2,000 soldiers established as Friedrich expanded his 'Residenzstadt'. In the centre of town, the Lustgarten was laid out opposite the Stadtschloss. Running west from the palace, the first Lindenallee ('Avenue of Lime Trees' or Unter den Linden) was created.

To revive the city's economy, a sales tax replaced housing and property taxes. With the money raised, three new towns were built – Friedrichswerder, Dorotheenstadt and Friedrichstadt. (Together with Berlin and Cölln, these now form the district of Mitte.) In the 1660s, a canal was constructed linking the Spree and Oder rivers, confirming Berlin as an east-west trading centre.

But Friedrich Wilhelm's most inspired policy was to encourage refugees to settle. First to arrive were over 50 Jewish families from Vienna. In 1672, Huguenot settlers came from France. And both groups brought with them vital new skills. The growing cosmopolitan mix laid the foundations for a flowering of intellectual and artistic life. By the time the Great Elector's son Friedrich III took the throne in 1688, one in five Berliners spoke French. Today, French words still pepper Berlin dialect, among them *boulette* (hamburger) and *étage* (floor). In 1701, Elector Friedrich III had himself crowned Prussian King Friedrich I (not to be confused with the earlier Elector).

MILITARY PRECISION

The common association of Prussia with militarism can broadly be traced back to the 18th century and the efforts of two men in particular: King Friedrich Wilhelm I (1713-40) and his son Friedrich II (also known as Frederick the Great). Although father and son hated each other, and had different sensibilities (Friedrich Wilhelm was boorish and mean, Friedrich II sensitive and philosophical), together they launched Prussia as a major military power and gave Berlin the character of a garrison city.

The obsession with all things military did have some positive effects. The King needed competent soldiers, so he made school compulsory; the army needed doctors, so he set up medical institutes. Berlin's economy also picked up on the back of demand from the military. Skilled immigrants arrived (mostly from Saxony) to meet the increased demand. The result was a population boom – from 60,000 in 1713 to 90,000 in 1740 – and a growth in trade.

FREDERICK THE GREAT

Frederick the Great (Friedrich II) took Prussia into a series of wars with Austria and Russia (1740-42, 1744-5 and 1756-63; the last known as the Seven Years War) in a bid to win territory in Silesia in the east. Initially, the wars proved disastrous. The Austrians occupied Berlin in 1757, the Russians in 1760. However, thanks to a mixture of good fortune and military genius, Frederick emerged victorious from the Seven Years War.

When not fighting, the King set about forging a modern state apparatus and transforming Berlin and Potsdam. This was achieved partly through conviction – the King was friends with Voltaire and saw himself as an aesthetically minded Enlightenment figure – but it was also a political necessity. He needed to convince enemies and subjects that even in times of crisis he was able to afford grand projects. So Unter den Linden was transformed into a grand boulevard. At the palace end, the Forum Fredericianum, designed and constructed by the architect von Knobelsdorff, comprised the Staatsoper, Sankt-Hedwigs-Kathedrale, Prince Heinrich Palace (now housing Humboldt-Universität) and the Staatsbibliotek. Although it was never completed, the Forum is still one of Berlin's main attractions. To the west of Berlin, the Tiergarten was landscaped and a new palace, Schloss Bellevue (now the German president's official residence), built. Frederick also replaced a set of barracks at Gendarmenmarkt with a theatre, now called the Konzerthaus.

To encourage manufacturing and industry (particularly textiles), advantageous excise laws were introduced. Businesses such as the KPM (Königliche Porzellan-Manufaktur) porcelain works were nationalised and turned into prestigious and lucrative enterprises. There were also legal and administrative reforms that saw religious freedom enshrined in law and torture abolished. Berlin also became a centre of the Enlightenment. Cultural and intellectual life blossomed around figures such as philosopher Moses Mendelssohn and poet Gottfried Lessing. By the time Frederick died in 1786, Berlin had a population of 150,000 and was the capital of one of Europe's great powers.

A DEBT TO ARCHITECTURE

The death of Frederick the Great marked the end of the Enlightenment in Prussia. His successor, Friedrich Wilhelm II, was more interested in spending money on classical architecture than wasting time debating the merits of various political philosophies. Censorship was stepped up and the King's extravagance sparked an economic crisis. By 1788, 14,000 Berliners were dependent on state and church aid. The state apparatus crumbled under the weight of greedy administrators. When he died in 1797, Friedrich Wilhelm II left his son with huge debts.

However, the old King's love of classicism gave Berlin its most famous monument: the Brandenburger Tor (Brandenburg Gate). It was built by Karl Gottfried Langhans in 1789, the year of the French Revolution, and modelled on the Propylaea in Athens. Two years later, Johann Schadow added the Quadriga, a sculpture of Victoria riding a chariot drawn by four horses. Originally one of 14 gates, the Brandenburger Tor is now Berlin's geographical and symbolic centre.

IN CONTEXT

Brandenburger Tor.

'Things came to a head in 1848, the year of revolutions.'

If the King did not care for intellect, then the emerging bourgeoisie did. Towards the turn of the century, Berlin became a centre of German Romanticism. Literary salons flourished; they were to remain a feature of the city's cultural life into the middle of the 19th century.

THE NAPOLEONIC WARS

In 1806, Berlin came face to face with the effects of revolution in France: following the defeat of the Prussian forces in the battles of Jena and Auerstadt on 14 October, Napoleon's army headed for Berlin. The King and Queen fled to Königsberg and the garrison was removed from the city. On 27 October, Napoleon and his army marched through the Brandenburger Tor. Once again, Berlin was an occupied city.

Napoleon set about changing the political and administrative structure. He called together 2,000 prominent citizens and told them to elect a new administration ('the Comité Administratif'), which ran the city until the French troops left in 1808. Napoleon also ordered the expropriation of property belonging to the state, the Hohenzollerns and many aristocratic families. Priceless works of art were removed from palaces in Berlin and Potsdam and shipped to France. Even the Quadriga was taken from the Brandenburg Gate and sent to Paris. At the same time, the city was hit by crippling war reparations.

When the French left, a group of energetic, reform-minded aristocrats, grouped around Baron vom Stein, moved to modernise the moribund Prussian state. One key reform was the clear separation of state and civic responsibility, which gave Berlin independence to manage its own affairs. A new council was elected (though only property owners and the wealthy were entitled to vote). In 1810, the philosopher Wilhelm von Humboldt founded the university. All remaining restrictions on the city's Jews were removed.

Although the French occupied Berlin again in 1812 on their way home from the disastrous Russian campaign, this time they met with stiff resistance. A year later the Prussian King finally joined the anti-Napoleon coalition and thousands of Berliners signed up to fight. Napoleon was defeated at nearby Grossbeeren. This, together with a later defeat in the Battle of Leipzig, marked the end of Napoleonic rule in Germany.

In August 1814, General Blücher brought the Quadriga back to Berlin, restoring it to the Brandenburg Gate with one symbolic addition: an Iron Cross and Prussian eagle were added to the staff in Victoria's hand.

POLICE AND THINKERS

The burst of reform was, however, fairly short-lived. Following the Congress of Vienna (1814-15), which established a new political and strategic order for post-Napoleonic Europe, King Friedrich Wilhelm III reneged on promises of constitutional reform. Instead of a greater unity among the German states, a loose alliance came into being; dominated by Austria, the German Confederation was distinctly anti-liberal in its tenor. In Prussia state power increased. Alongside the normal police, a secret service and a vice squad were established. The police president even had the power to issue directives to the city council. Censorship increased and the authorities sacked von Humboldt from the university he had created.

With their hopes for change frustrated, the bourgeoisie withdrew to their salons. It is one of the ironies of this time that, although political opposition was quashed, a vibrant cultural movement flourished. Academics like Hegel and Ranke lectured at the university, enhancing Berlin's reputation as an intellectual centre. The period became known as

IN CONTEXT

Biedermeier, after a fictional character embodying bourgeois taste, created by Swabian comic writer Ludwig Eichrodt. Another legacy of this period is the range of neo-classical buildings designed by Schinkel, such as his Altes Museum and the Neue Wache.

For the majority, however, it was a period of frustrated hopes and bitter poverty. Industrialisation swelled the ranks of the working class. Between 1810 and 1840, the city's population doubled to 400,000. But most of the newcomers lived in conditions that would later lead to riot and revolution.

THE INDUSTRIAL REVOLUTION

Prussia was ideally equipped for the industrial age. By the 19th century, it had grown dramatically and boasted one of the greatest abundances of raw materials in Europe. It was the founding of the Borsig Werke on Chausseestrasse in 1837 that established Berlin as the workshop of continental Europe. August Borsig was Berlin's first big industrialist. His factories turned out locomotives for the new Berlin-to-Potsdam railway, which opened in 1838. Borsig also left his mark through the establishment of a suburb (Borsigwalde) that still carries his name. The other great pioneering industrialist, Werner Siemens, set up his electrical engineering firm in a house near Anhalter Bahnhof. The Siemens company also added a new suburb, Siemensstadt, to the city.

THE PEOPLE V FRIEDRICH WILHELM

Friedrich Wilhelm IV's accession to the throne in 1840 raised hopes of an end to repression; and, initially, he appeared to share the desire for change. He declared an amnesty for political prisoners, relaxed censorship, sacked the hated justice minister and granted asylum to refugees. Political debate thrived in coffeehouses and wine bars. The university was another focal point for discussion. In the late 1830s, Karl Marx spent a term there, just missing fellow alumnus Otto von Bismarck. In the early 1840s, Friedrich Engels did his military service in Berlin.

The thaw didn't last. It soon became clear that Friedrich Wilhelm IV shared his father's opposition to constitutional reform. Living and working conditions worsened for most Berliners. Rapid industrialisation brought sweatshops, 17-hour days and child labour. This misery was compounded in 1844 by harvest failure. Food riots broke out on Gendarmenmarkt, when a crowd stormed the market stalls.

Things came to a head in 1848, the year of revolutions. Political meetings were held in beer gardens and in the Tiergarten, and demands made for internal reform and a unification of German-speaking states. On 18 March the King finally conceded to allowing a new parliament, and vaguely promised other reforms. Later that day, the crowd of 10,000 that gathered to celebrate the victory were set upon by soldiers. Shots were fired and the revolution began. Barricades went up throughout central Berlin and demonstrators fought with police for 14 hours. Finally, the King backed down for a second time. In exchange for the dismantling of barricades, he ordered his troops out of Berlin. Days later, he took part in the funeral service for the 'March Dead' – 183 revolutionaries who had been killed – and promised more freedoms.

Berlin was now ostensibly in the hands of the revolutionaries, and the King seemed to embrace liberalism and nationalism. Prussia, he said, should 'merge into Germany'. But the revolution proved short-lived. When pressed on unification, he merely suggested that the other German states send representatives to the Prussian National Assembly, an offer that was rebuffed. Leading liberals instead convened a German National Assembly in Frankfurt in May 1848, while a new Prussian Assembly met in what is now the Konzerthaus to debate a new constitution. At the end of 1848, reforming fervour took over Berlin.

THE BACKLASH

Winter, however, brought a change of mood. Using continuing street violence as the pretext, the King ordered the National Assembly to be moved to Brandenburg. In early

November, he brought troops back into Berlin and declared a state of siege. Press freedom was again restricted. The Civil Guard and National Assembly were dissolved. On 5 December the King delivered his final blow by unveiling a new constitution fashioned to his own tastes. Throughout the winter of 1848-49, thousands of liberals were arrested or expelled. A new city constitution, drawn up in 1850, reduced the number of eligible voters to five per cent of the population. The police president became more powerful than the mayor.

By 1857, Friedrich Wilhelm had gone senile. His brother Wilhelm acted as regent until becoming King on Friedrich's death in 1861. Once again, the people's hopes were raised: the new monarch began his reign by appointing liberals to the cabinet. The building of the Rotes Rathaus (Red Town Hall), completed in 1869, gave the city council a headquarters to match the size of the royal palace. But by 1861 the King was locked in a dispute with parliament over proposed army reforms. He wanted to strengthen his control of the armed forces. Parliament refused, so the King went over its members' heads and appointed a new prime minister: Otto von Bismarck.

THE IRON CHANCELLOR

An arrogant genius and former diplomat, Bismarck was well able to deal with unruly parliamentarians. Using a constitutional loophole to rule against the majority, he quickly pushed through the army reforms. Extra-parliamentary opposition was dealt with in the usual manner: oppression and censorship. Dissension thus suppressed, Bismarck turned his mind to German unification. Unlike the bourgeois revolutionaries of 1848, who desired a Germany united by popular will and endowed with political reforms, Bismarck strove to bring the states together under the authoritarian dominance of Prussia. His methods involved astute foreign policy and outright aggression.

Wars against Denmark (1864) and Austria (1866) brought post-Napoleonic order to an abrupt end. Prussia was no longer the smallest Great Power, but an initiator of geopolitical change. Austria's defeat confirmed Prussia's primacy among German-speaking states. Victory on the battlefield boosted Bismarck's popularity across Prussia – but not in Berlin itself. He was defeated in his constituency in the 1867 election to the new North German League. This was a Prussian-dominated body, linking the northern states, and a stepping stone towards Germany's overall unification.

Bismarck's third war – against France in 1870 – revealed his scope for intrigue and opportunism. Exploiting a dispute over the Spanish succession, he provoked France into declaring war on Prussia. Citing the North German League and treaties signed with the southern German states, Bismarck brought together a united German army under Prussian leadership.

Following the defeat of the French army on 2 September, Bismarck turned a unified military into the basis for a unified nation. The Prussian king would be German emperor: beneath him would be four kings, 18 grand dukes and assorted princes from the German states, which would retain some regional powers. (This arrangement formed the basis for the modern federal system of regional *Länder*.)

On 18 January 1871, King Wilhelm was proclaimed German Kaiser ('Emperor') in the Hall of Mirrors in Versailles. In just nine years, Bismarck had united Germany and forged an empire that dominated central Europe. The political, economic and social centre of this new creation was Berlin.

IMPERIAL BERLIN

The coming of empire threw Berlin into its greatest period of expansion and change. The economic boom (helped by five billion gold francs extracted from France as war reparations) fuelled a wave of speculation. Farmers in Wilmersdorf and Schöneberg became millionaires overnight as they sold off their fields to developers.

During the following decades, Berlin emerged as Europe's most modern metropolis. This period was dubbed the Gründerzeit (Foundation Years) and was marked by a move

IN CONTEXT

away from traditional Prussian values of thrift and modesty towards the gaudy and bombastic. The mood change manifested itself in monuments and buildings. The Reichstag, the Kaiser-Wilhelm-Gedächtniskirche, the Siegessäule (Victory Column) and the Berliner Dom were all built in this period.

Superficially, the Reichstag (designed by Paul Wallot, and completed in 1894) represented a commitment to parliamentary democracy. But in reality Germany was still in the grip of conservative, backward-looking forces. The Kaiser's authoritarian powers remained, as demonstrated by the decision of Wilhelm II to sack Bismarck in 1890 following policy disagreements.

Making History

Every state tells a story.

Confronting the past is a big deal in Germany. *Vergangenheitsbewältigung* is the word for it. For much of the late 20th century, division meant two official versions of history, and it's perhaps no surprise that it took 19 years for what is now the **Deutsches Historisches Museum** (German Historical Museum; *see p61*) to come up with a permanent exhibition on German history that they deemed morally and historically acceptable. The notion of a national history museum in West Berlin was debated in countless committees before finally being given the go-ahead in 1987. It didn't stop the debate, however. Liberal commentators accused more conservative historians of wanting to sanitise the past and take refuge in the classical history of Hegel and Goethe. Helmut Kohl thought it best to ignore the Nazi era as much as possible.

The result of those 19 years of discussion thankfully paid little heed to politicians. Instead, the DHM aimed to contextualise German history within Europe, but at the same time face Germany's difficult past head on. The permanent exhibition in the Zeughaus is super-factual, but the attempt not to make value judgements has created something rather strange in a history museum – at no point in 2,000 years' worth of exhibits does it ever really celebrate history.

The same couldn't have been said for the Zeughaus's previous occupant, the DDR-era **Museum für Deutsche Geschichte** (Museum of German History). That version introduced national history with a 'pre-Marxist' section, beginning with the Reformation. There followed an entire floor devoted to Marx and Engels. Today, Marx and *Das Kapital* are only fleetingly referred to in a box about 19th-century labour movements.

East and West had very different methods for dealing with the past. The DDR exploited history to legitimise the socialist regime. Two traditions of German history were identified, a progressive strand and a reactionary strand, and it's not hard to guess where each one led. While the DDR was the product of the progressive, revolutionary strand, the Federal Republic was the child of Germany's 'feudal', imperial and Nazi past.

In the West, history was ignored more than exploited. The Federal Republic preferred to draw on the more recent *Wirtschaftswunder* (post-war 'economic miracle') for its legitimisation. But when history was presented, it too was interpreted through the lens of the Cold War.

Various tools were used to overcome the day to day difficulties of a divided Germany too. West German brochures used names such as 'the German States Behind The Iron Curtain' or 'the Countryside of Mid- and Eastern Germany Under Communist Tyranny'. DDR maps of Berlin, meanwhile, left the city's western half blank, disdainfully labelling it 'Westberlin', or just 'WB'.

IN CONTEXT

' Political and economic chaos remained. Political assassinations were commonplace, and food shortages led to bouts of famine.'

When Bismarck began his premiership in 1861, his offices on Wilhelmstrasse overlooked potato fields. By the time he lost his job, they were in the centre of Europe's most congested city. Economic boom and growing political and social importance attracted hundreds of thousands of new inhabitants. At unification in 1871, 820,000 people lived in Berlin; by 1890 this number had nearly doubled. The working class was shoehorned into tenements – *Mietskasernen*, 'rental barracks' – that sprouted across the city, particularly in Kreuzberg, Wedding and Prenzlauer Berg. Poorly ventilated and overcrowded, the *Mietskasernen* (many of which still stand) became a breeding ground for unrest.

SEEING RED

The Social Democratic Party (SPD), founded in 1869, quickly became the voice for the have-nots. In the 1877 general election it won 40 per cent of the Berlin vote. Here was born the left-wing reputation of *Rotes Berlin* ('Red Berlin') that persists to the present day. In 1878, two assassination attempts on the Kaiser gave Bismarck an excuse to classify socialists as enemies of the state. He introduced restrictive laws to ban the SPD and other progressive parties. The ban lasted until 1890 – the year of Bismarck's sacking – but did not stem support for the SPD. In the 1890 general election, the SPD dominated the vote in Berlin; in 1912 it won more than 70 per cent of the vote, becoming the largest party in the Reichstag.

BUMBLING BILL

Famed for his ridiculous moustache, Kaiser Wilhelm II came to the throne in 1888, and soon came to personify the new Germany: bombastic, awkward and unpredictable. Like his grandmother Queen Victoria, he gave his name to an era. Wilhelm's epoch is associated with showy militarism and foreign policy bungles leading to a world war that cost the Kaiser his throne and Germany its stability.

The Wilhelmine years were also notable for the explosive growth of Berlin (the population rose to four million by 1914) and a blossoming of cultural and intellectual life. The Bode Museum was built in 1904. In 1912, work began next door on the Pergamonmuseum, while a new Opera House was unveiled in Charlottenburg (later destroyed in World War II; the Deutsche Oper now stands on the site). Expressionism took off in 1910 and the Kurfürstendamm filled with galleries – Paris was still Europe's art capital, but Berlin was catching up. By Wilhelm's abdication in 1918, Berlin had become a centre of scientific and intellectual development. Six Berlin scientists, including Einstein and Max Planck, were awarded the Nobel Prize. But by 1914, Europe was armed to the teeth and ready to tear itself apart. In June, the assassination of Archduke Franz Ferdinand provided the excuse.

WORLD WAR I AND REVOLUTION

No one was prepared for the disaster to come. After Bismarck, the Germans had come to expect quick, sweeping victories. The armies on the Western Front settled into their trenches for a war of attrition that would cost over a million German lives. Meanwhile, the civilian population faced austerity and shortages. After the 1917 harvest failed there were outbreaks of famine. Soon dog and cat meat started to appear on the menu in Berlin restaurants.

The SPD's initial enthusiasm for war evaporated, and in 1916 the party refused to pass the Berlin budget. A year later, members of the party's radical wing broke away to form the Spartacus League. Anti-war feeling was voiced in mass strikes in April 1917 and January 1918. These were brutally suppressed, but, when the Imperial Marines in Kiel mutinied on 2 November 1918, the authorities were no longer able to stop the anti-war movement. The mutiny spread to Berlin, where members of the Guards Regiment came out against the war. On 9 November the Kaiser was forced into abdication and, later, exile. This date is weirdly layered with significance in German history: it's the anniversary of the establishment of the Weimar Republic (1918), the Kristallnacht pogrom (1938) and the fall of the Wall (1989).

On this day in 1918, Philip Scheidemann, a leading SPD parliamentarian and key proponent of republicanism, broke off his lunch in the second-floor restaurant of the Reichstag. He walked to a window overlooking Königsplatz (now Platz der Republik) where a crowd had massed and declared: 'The old and the rotten have broken down. Long live the new! Long live the German Republic!' At the other end of Unter den Linden, Karl Liebknecht, who co-led the Spartacus League with Rosa Luxemburg, declared Germany a socialist republic from a balcony of the occupied Stadtschloss. Liebknecht and the Spartacists wanted a communist Germany; Scheidemann and the SPD favoured a parliamentary democracy. Between them stood those still loyal to the vanished monarchy. All were prepared to fight; street battles ensued throughout the city. It was in this climate of turmoil and violence that the Weimar Republic was born.

THE WEIMAR REPUBLIC

The revolution in Berlin may have brought peace to the Western Front, where hostilities were ended on 11 November, but in Germany it unleashed political terror and instability. Berlin's new masters, the SPD under Friedrich Ebert, ordered renegade battalions returning from the front (known as the Freikorps) to quash the Spartacists, who launched a concerted bid for power in January 1919.

Within days, the uprising was bloodily suppressed. Liebknecht and Luxemburg were arrested, interrogated in a hotel near the Zoo, and then murdered by the Freikorps. A plaque marks the spot on the Liechtenstein Bridge from which Luxemburg's body was dumped into the Landwehr Canal. Four days later, national elections returned the SPD as the largest party: the Social Democrats' victory over the far left was complete. Berlin was deemed too dangerous for parliamentary business, so the government decamped to the provincial town of Weimar, which gave its name to the first German republic.

Germany's new constitution ended up being full of good liberal intentions, but riddled with technical flaws, leaving the country wide open to weak coalition government and quasi-dictatorial presidential rule. Another crippling blow was the Versailles Treaty, which set the terms of peace. Reparation payments (set to run until 1988) blew a hole in an already fragile economy. Support for the right-wing nationalist lobby was fuelled by the loss of territories in both east and west, and restrictions placed on the military led some on the right to claim that Germany's soldiers had been 'stabbed in the back' by Jews and left-wingers.

In March 1920 a right-wing coup was staged in Berlin under the leadership of Wolfgang Kapp, a civil servant from east Prussia. The recently returned government once again fled the city. For four days Berlin was besieged by roaming Freikorps. Some had taken to adorning their helmets with a new symbol: the *Hakenkreuz* or swastika.

Ultimately, a general strike and the army's refusal to join Kapp ended the putsch. But the political and economic chaos in the city remained. Political assassinations were commonplace, and food shortages led to bouts of famine. Inflation started to escalate. There were two main reasons for the precipitate devaluation of the Reichsmark. To pay for the war, the desperate imperial government had resorted simply to printing more money, a policy continued by the new republican rulers. The burden of reparations also led to an outflow of foreign currency.

IN CONTEXT

False Economy

Hyperinflation turned the economy – and society – upside down.

Of all the disasters that have befallen Berlin, nothing was as mad as the hyperinflation of 1923. It wasn't a sudden catastrophe: the German government had been dallying with inflation for years, funding its war effort by printing bonds. In 1914, a dollar was buying 4.2 marks; by late 1922, it was buying 7,000. Then the French occupied the Ruhr and things got really out of hand. By 20 November 1923, the rate was a whopping 4,200,000,000,000 marks to the dollar.

Images from the time are vaguely comic: children using bundles of notes as building blocks, a wheelbarrow of currency for a loaf of bread. At the height of the crisis, over 300 paper mills and 2,000 printing presses worked around the clock to supply the Reichsbank with notes – in denominations of one million, then one billion, then a hundred billion. Some companies paid their employees twice a day, so they could shop at lunch to beat afternoon inflation.

A little hard currency could buy anything – or anyone. Foreign visitors splashed out in an orgy of conspicuous consumption. Entrepreneurs created whole business empires from ever-cheaper marks. And the homes of peasants in nearby villages filled up with Meissen porcelain and fine furniture as Berliners traded valuables for eggs or bread.

People starved as their possessions vanished. The suicide rate shot up, as did infant mortality. Teenagers prostituted themselves after school, often with parental approval. Nothing made sense anymore. And as the fabric of everyday life was seen to unravel, so did people's faith in government. Among the worst hit were those who had most trusted the idea of Germany: the middle-class patriots who had sunk their money into war bonds, only to be paid back in useless paper.

The crisis was eventually brought under control, but the result had been a mass transfer of wealth to a handful of adventurers, big business and government. And as a pauperised people wondered who to blame, the hard right had found a cause. Nothing prepared the ground for Hitler better than the literal and moral impoverishment of the inflationary period.

IN CONTEXT

In 1923, the French government sent troops into the Ruhr industrial region to take by force reparation goods that the German government said it could no longer afford to pay. The Communists planned an uprising in Berlin for October, but lost their nerve.

In November a young ex-corporal called Adolf Hitler, who led the tiny National Socialist Party (NSDAP or Nazi Party), launched an attempted coup from a Munich beerhall. He called for armed resistance to the French, an end to the 'dictatorship of Versailles' and punishment for those – especially the Jews – who had 'betrayed' Germany at the war's end. Hitler's first attempt to seize power came to nothing. Instead of marching on Berlin, he went to prison. Inflation was finally brought down with the introduction of a new currency. But the overall decline of moral and social values that had taken place in the five years since 1918 was not so easy to reverse.

THE GOLDEN TWENTIES

Josef Goebbels came to Berlin in 1926 to take charge of the local Nazi Party. On arriving, he noted: 'This city is a melting pot of everything that is evil – prostitution, drinking houses, cinemas, Marxism, Jews, strippers, negroes dancing and all the offshoots of modern art.' During that decade, the city overtook Paris as Europe's arts and entertainment capital, and added its own decadent twist. 'We used to have a first-class army,' mused Klaus Mann, the author of *Mephisto...* 'Now we have first-class perversions.'

By 1927, Berlin boasted more than 70 cabarets and nightclubs. While Brecht's *Dreigroschenoper* (*Threepenny Opera*) played at the Theater am Schiffbauerdamm, Dadaists gathered on Tauentzienstrasse at the Romanisches Café (which was later one of the victims of the Allied bombing campaign – the Europa-Center mall now stands on the site). There was a proliferation of avant-garde magazines focusing on these exciting new forms of art and literature. But the flipside of all the frenetic enjoyment was raw poverty and glaring social tension, reflected in the works of artists like George Grosz and Otto Dix. In the music halls, Brecht and Weill used a popular medium to ram home points about social injustices.

In architecture and design, the revolutionary ideas of the Bauhaus school in Dessau (it moved to Berlin in 1932, but was closed down by the Nazis a year later) were taking concrete form in projects such as the Shell House on the Landwehr Canal,the Siemensstadt new town, and the model housing project Hufeisensiedlung ('Horse Shoe Estate') in Britz.

STREET-FIGHTING YEARS

The Wall Street Crash and the onset of global depression in 1929 ushered in the brutal end of the Weimar Republic. The fractious coalition governments that had clung to power in the prosperous late 1920s were no match for rocketing unemployment and a surge in support for extremist parties. By the end of 1929, nearly one in four Berliners were out of work. The city's streets became a battleground for clashes between Nazi stormtroopers (the SA), Communists and Social Democrats. Increasingly, the police relied on water cannon, armoured vehicles and guns to quell street fighting. One May Day demonstration left 30 dead and several hundred wounded.

In 1932, the violence in Berlin reached crisis level. In one six-week period, 300 street battles resulted in 70 people dead. In the general election in July the Nazis took 40 per cent of the general vote, becoming the largest party in the Reichstag. Hermann Göring, one of Hitler's earliest followers and a wounded veteran of the beerhall putsch, was appointed Reichstag president. But the prize of government still eluded the Nazis. In November elections they lost two million votes across Germany and 37,000 in Berlin, where the Communists emerged as the strongest party. The election was held against the backdrop of a strike by some 20,000 transport employees protesting against planned wage cuts. The strike had been called by the Communists and the Nazis, who vied with each other to capture the mass vote and

IN CONTEXT

bring the Weimar Republic to an end. Under orders from Moscow, the KPD shunned all co-operation with the SPD, ending any possibility of a broad left-wing front.

As Berlin headed into another winter of depression, almost every third person was out of work. A survey recorded that almost half of Berlin's inhabitants were living four to a room, and that a large proportion of the city's housing stock was unfit for human habitation. Berlin topped the European table of suicides.

The new government of General Kurt von Schleicher ruled by presidential decree. Schleicher had promised President von Hindenburg that he could tame the Nazi Party into a coalition. When he failed, his rival Franz von Papen manoeuvred the Nazi leader into power. On 30 January 1933, Adolf Hitler was named chancellor. That evening, the SA staged a torchlight parade through the Brandenburg Gate. Watching from the window of his house, the artist Max Liebermann remarked to his dinner guests: 'I cannot eat as much as I'd like to puke.'

HITLER TAKES POWER

Hitler's government was a coalition of Nazis and German nationalists, led by the media magnate Alfred Hugenberg. Together their votes fell just short of a parliamentary majority, so another election was called for March, while Hitler continued to rule by decree. Weimar's last free election was also its most violent. Open persecution of Communists began. The Nazis banned meetings of the KPD, closed left-wing newspapers and broke up SPD election rallies. On 27 February a fire broke out in the Reichstag. It was almost certainly started by the Nazis, who used it as an excuse to step up the persecution of opponents. Over 12,000 Communists were arrested. Spelling it out in a speech at the Sportspalast two days before the election, Goebbels said: 'It's not my job to practise justice, instead I have to destroy and exterminate – nothing else.'

The Nazis still didn't achieve an absolute majority (in Berlin they polled 34 per cent), but that didn't matter. With the support of his coalition allies, Hitler passed an Enabling Act that gave him dictatorial powers. By summer Germany had been declared a one-party state. The SS established itself in Prinz Albrecht Palais, where it was later joined by the secret police, the Gestapo. To the north of Berlin near Oranienburg, the Sachsenhausen concentration camp was set up. Along the Kurfürstendamm squads of SA stormtroopers would go 'Jew baiting', and on 1 April 1933 the first boycott of Jewish shops began. A month later, Goebbels, who became Minister for Propaganda, organised a book-burning, which took place in the courtyard of the university on Unter den Linden. Books by Jews or writers deemed degenerate or traitors were thrown on to a huge bonfire. The Nazis began to control public life. Party membership became obligatory for doctors, lawyers, professors and journalists. Unemployment was tackled through public works programmes, conscription to an expanding military and by 'encouraging' women to leave the workplace.

During the Night of the Long Knives in July 1934, Hitler settled old scores with opponents within the SA and Nazi Party. At Lichterfelde barracks, officers of the SS shot and killed over 150 SA members. Hitler's predecessor as chancellor, General von Schleicher, was shot with his wife at their Wannsee home. After the death of President von Hindenburg in August, Hitler had himself named *Führer* ('Leader') and made the armed forces swear an oath of allegiance to him. It had taken the Nazis less than two years to subjugate Germany.

GAMES WITHOUT FRONTIERS

A brief respite came with the Olympic Games in August 1936. To persuade foreign spectators that all was well in the Reich, Goebbels ordered the removal of anti-Semitic slogans from shops. 'Undesirables' were moved out of the city, and the pavement display cases for the racist Nazi newspaper *Der Stürmer* (*The Stormtrooper*) were dismantled. The Games, centred on the newly built Olympiastadion, were not such

IN CONTEXT

'Businesses that had been owned by Jews – such as the Ullstein newspaper group and Jonass department store – were 'Aryanised'.'

a success for the Nazis. Instead of blond Aryans sweeping the field, Hitler had to watch the African-American Jesse Owens clock up medals and records. The Games did work, however, as a public relations exercise. Foreign visitors left with reports of a strident and healthy nation.

As part of a nationwide campaign to cleanse cultural life of what the Nazis considered *Entartete Kunst* (Degenerate Art), works of modern art were collected and brought together in a touring exhibition designed to show the depth of depravity in contemporary ('Jewish-dominated') culture. But Nazi hopes that these 'degenerate' works would repulse the German people fell flat. When the exhibition arrived at the Zeughaus in early 1938, thousands queued for admission. People loved the paintings. After the exhibition, the paintings were auctioned in Switzerland. Those that remained unsold were burnt in the fire station on Köpenicker Strasse. More than 5,000 works were destroyed.

TOTALITARIAN TOWN PLANNING

After taking power, Hitler ordered that the lime trees on Unter den Linden be chopped down to give the boulevard a cleaner, more sanitised form – the first step in Nazi urban planning. Hitler's plans for the redesign of Berlin reflected the hatred the Nazis felt for the city. Hitler entrusted young architect Albert Speer with the job of creating a metropolis to 'out-trump Paris and Vienna'. The heart of old Berlin was to be demolished, and its small streets replaced by two highways stretching 37 kilometres (23 miles) from north to south and 50 kilometres (30 miles) from east to west. Each axis would be 90 metres (295 feet) wide. Crowning the northern axis would be a domed Volkshalle ('People's Hall') nearly 300 metres (1,000 feet) high, with space for 150,000 people. Speer and Hitler also had grand plans for a triumphal arch three times the size of the Arc de Triomphe, and a Führer's Palace 150 times bigger than the one occupied by Bismarck. The new city was to be called Germania.

Little of this was built. The new Chancellery, completed in early 1939, went up in under a year – and was demolished after the war. On the proposed east–west axis, a small section around the Siegessäule was widened for Hitler's 50th birthday in April 1939.

A PEOPLE DESTROYED

Of the half a million Jews living in Germany in 1933, over a third were in Berlin. For centuries, the Jewish community had played an important role in Berlin's development, especially in financial, artistic and intellectual circles. The Nazis wiped all this out in 12 years of persecution and murder. Arrests followed the boycotts and acts of intimidation. From 1933 to 1934, many of Berlin's Jews fled. Those who stayed were subjected to legislation (the 1935 Nuremberg Laws) that banned Jews from public office, forbade them to marry Aryan Germans and stripped them of citizenship. Jewish cemeteries were desecrated and the names of Jews chipped off war memorials. Berlin businesses that had been owned by Jews – such as the Ullstein newspaper group and Jonass department store (now the Soho House hotel, *see p117*) – were 'Aryanised'. The Nazis expropriated them or forced owners to sell at absurdly low prices.

On 9 November 1938, Kristallnacht, a wave of 'spontaneous' acts of vandalism and violence against Jews, was staged in response to the assassination of a German diplomat in Paris by a young Jewish émigré. Jewish properties across Berlin were stoned, looted and set ablaze. A total of 24 synagogues were set on fire. The Nazis rounded up 12,000 Jews and took them to Sachsenhausen concentration camp.

WORLD WAR II

Since 1935, Berliners had been taking part in air-raid drills, but it was not until the Sudeten crisis of 1938 that the possibility of war became real. At that juncture Hitler was able to get his way and persuade France and Britain to let him take over the German-speaking areas of northern Czechoslovakia. But a year later, his plans to repeat the exercise in Poland were met with resistance in London and Paris. Following Germany's invasion of Poland on 1 September 1939, Britain and France declared war on the Reich. Despite the propaganda and early victories, most Berliners were horrified by the war. The first air raids came with the RAF bombing of Pankow and Lichtenberg in early 1940.

In 1941, after the German invasion of the Soviet Union, the 75,000 Jews remaining in Berlin were required to wear a yellow Star of David and the first systematic deportations to concentration camps began. By the end of the war, only 5,000 Jews remained in Berlin. Notorious assembly points for the deportations were Putlitzstrasse in Wedding, Grosse Hamburger Strasse and Rosenstrasse in Mitte. On 20 January 1942 a meeting of the leaders of the various Nazi security organisations in the suburb of Wannsee agreed on a 'final solution' to the Jewish question: genocide.

The turning point in the war came with the surrender at Stalingrad on 31 January 1943. By summer, women and children were being evacuated from Berlin; by the end of 1943, over 700,000 people had fled. The Battle of Berlin, which the RAF launched in November 1943, reduced much of the city centre to rubble. Nearly 5,000 people were killed and around 250,000 made homeless.

THE JULY PLOT

On 20 July 1944 a group of officers, civil servants and former trade unionists launched a last-ditch attempt to assassinate Hitler. But Hitler survived the explosion of a bomb placed at his eastern command post in East Prussia by Colonel Count von Stauffenberg.

In early January 1945 the Red Army launched a major offensive that carried it on to German soil. On 12 February the heaviest bombing raid yet on Berlin killed over 23,000 people in little more than an hour. As the Russians moved into Berlin's suburbs, Hitler celebrated his last birthday on 20 April in his bunker behind Wilhelmstrasse. Three days later Neukölln and Tempelhof fell. By 28 April, Alexanderplatz and Hallesches Tor were in the hands of the Red Army.

The next day Hitler called his last war conference. He then married his companion Eva Braun and committed suicide with her the day after. As their bodies were being cremated by SS officers, a few streets away a red flag was raised over the Reichstag. The city officially surrendered on 2 May 1945.

DEVASTATION AND DIVISION

When Bertolt Brecht returned to Berlin in 1948 he found 'a pile of rubble next to Potsdam'. Nearly a quarter of all buildings had been destroyed. The human cost of the war was as startling – around 80,000 Berliners had been killed, not including the thousands of Jews who would not return from the concentration camps. There was no gas or electricity and only the suburbs had running water. Public transport had broken down. In the first weeks after capitulation, Red Army soldiers went on a rampage of looting, murder and rape. Thousands of men were transported to labour camps in the Soviet Union. Food supplies were used up and later the harvest failed in the land around the city. Come winter, the few remaining trees in the Tiergarten and other parks were chopped down for firewood.

Clearing the rubble was to take years of dull, painstaking work. The *Trümmerfrauen* (rubble women) cleared the streets and created literal mountains of junk – like the Teufelsberg, one of seven hills that now exist as a result. The Soviets stripped factories across Berlin as part of a programme to dismantle German industry and take it back home. As reparation, whole factories were moved to Russia.

Under the terms of the Yalta Agreement, which divided Germany into four zones of control, Berlin was also split into sectors, with the Soviets in the East and the Americans, British and French in the West. A Kommandatura, made up of each army's commander and based in the building of the People's Court in Kleistpark, dealt with the administration of the city. Initially, the administration worked well in getting basics such as public transport back in running order. But tensions between the Soviets and the Western Allies began to rise as civilian government of city affairs returned. In the Eastern sector, a merger of the Communist and Social Democratic parties (both

The All-Seeing Stasi

At least one in 50 were part of the DDR's surveillance operation.

Nobody's exactly sure how many unofficial informers were on the payroll of East Germany's Ministerium für Staatssicherheit, better known as the Stasi. There were something like 90,000 full-time agents, and about 175,000 *Inoffizielle Mitarbeiter* – unofficial informers, that's around 2.5 per cent of those between 18 and 60. One thing's for sure, however: the secret police apparatus was the most pervasive in the history of state-sponsored repression; in its 1940s heyday, the Gestapo only had about 30,000 members.

Though its grip on everyday life in the DDR was exhaustive, the Stasi must go down in history as a flawed institution. In spite of its secret prisons, hidden cameras and microphones, and burgeoning network of IMs, the Stasi ultimately failed to prevent the peaceful revolution of 1989. Still, only a few weeks after the Wall was breached, crowds fell on the Stasi headquarters at Normannenstrasse, venting anger and frustration at their former tormentors.

In the preceding days, Stasi agents were working overtime, using shredders to destroy documents. They barely put a dent in the six million or so files, which are now administered by a special authority charged with reviewing them and making them

available to prosecutors and everyday people who are simply curious to know what the Stasi knew about them.

Not surprisingly, the files contained embarrassing revelations for many politicians, journalists, athletes and other folks trying to get on with life in united Germany. Most of the charges involved people being listed as unofficial informers, a status hard to dispute or verify. Many could have been falsely implicated by over-ambitious Stasi career types, whose rank and pay were pegged to their success at recruiting spies.

There are thousands of Germans who readily own up to their double lives with the Stasi. They have to, in fact, to get their pensions – one major function of the agency minding the Stasi files is to determine who is eligible for retirement payments. One of those qualifying was Erich Mielke, the Stasi supremo, who collected about €400 a month until his death in 2000. His former office is now the centrepiece of the **Forschungs- und Gedenkstätte Normannenstrasse** (*see p106*), otherwise known as the Stasi Museum. You can tour a Stasi prison at the **Gedenkstätte Berlin-Hohenschönhausen** (*see p106*), and there's also the **Stasi Bildungszentrum** (*see p82*), a museum and education centre near Checkpoint Charlie.

IN CONTEXT

'Anyone trying to flee west risked being shot; in the 28 years the Wall stood, nearly 80 people died trying to escape.'

refounded in summer 1945) was pushed to form the Socialist Unity Party (SED). In the Western sector, the SPD continued as a separate party. Events came to a head after elections for a new city government in 1946. The SED failed to get more than 20 per cent of the vote, while the SPD won nearly 50 per cent of all votes cast. The Soviets vetoed the appointment of the SPD's mayoral candidate, Ernst Reuter, a committed anti-Communist.

THE BERLIN AIRLIFT

The situation worsened in spring 1948. In response to the decision by the Western Allies to merge their respective zones in Germany into one administrative entity and introduce a new currency, the Soviets quit the Kommandatura. In late June all transport links to West Berlin were cut off and Soviet forces began a blockade of the city. Three 'air corridors' linking West Berlin with Western Germany became lifelines as Allied aircraft transported food, coal and industrial components to the beleaguered city.

Within Berlin the future division of the city began to take permanent shape as city councillors from the West were drummed out of the town hall. They moved to Rathaus Schöneberg in the West. Fresh elections in the Western sector returned Reuter as mayor. The Freie Universität was set up in response to Communist dominance of the Humboldt-Universität in the East.

Having failed to starve West Berlin into submission, the Soviets called off the blockade after 11 months. The blockade also convinced the Western Allies that they should maintain a presence in Berlin and that their sectors of the city should be linked with the Federal Republic, founded in May 1949. The response from the East was the founding of the German Democratic Republic on 7 October. With the birth of the 'first Workers' and Peasants' State on German soil', the formal division of Germany into two states was complete.

THE COLD WAR

During the Cold War, Berlin was the focal point for stand-offs between the United States and the Soviet Union. Far from having any control over its own affairs, the city was wholly at the mercy of geopolitical developments. Throughout the 1950s the 'Berlin Question' remained prominent on the international agenda. Technically, the city was still under Four-Power control, but since the Soviet departure from the Kommandatura, and the setting up of the German Democratic Republic with its capital in East Berlin (a breach of the wartime agreement on the future of the city), this counted for little in practice. In principle, the Western Allies adhered to these agreements by retaining ultimate authority in West Berlin, while letting the city integrate into the West German system. Throughout the 1950s, the two halves of Berlin began to develop separately as the political systems in East and West evolved.

In the East, Communist leader Walter Ulbricht set about creating Moscow's most hardline ally in Eastern Europe. Work began on a Moscow-style boulevard – called Stalinallee – running east from Alexanderplatz. Industry was nationalised and subjected to rigid central planning. Opposition was kept in check by the new Ministry for State Security: the Stasi (*see p31* **The All-Seeing Stasi**).

West Berlin landed the role of 'Last Outpost of the Free World' and, as such, was developed into a showcase. As well as the Marshall Plan, which paid for much of the reconstruction of West Germany, the US poured millions of dollars into West Berlin to maintain it as a counterpoint to communism. The prominence accorded West Berlin was later reflected in the high profile of its politicians (Willy Brandt, for example) who were received abroad by prime ministers and presidents.

Yet despite the emerging divisions, the two halves of the city continued to co-exist in some abnormal fashion. City planners on both sides of the sectoral boundaries initially drew up plans with the whole city in mind. The transport system crossed between East and West, with the underground network being controlled by the West and the S-Bahn by the East. Movement between the sectors (despite 'border' checks) was relatively normal, as Westerners went East to watch a Brecht play or buy cheap books. Easterners travelled West to work, shop or see the latest Hollywood films. The secret services of both sides kept a high presence in the city. Berlin became the espionage capital of the world.

RECOVERY AND RESTRICTIONS

As the effects of US money and the West German 'economic miracle' took hold, West Berlin began to recover. Unemployment dropped from 30 per cent in 1950 to virtually zero by 1961. The labour force also included about 50,000 East Berliners who commuted over the inter-sector borders.

In the East reconstruction was slower. Until the mid 1950s, East Germany paid reparations to the Soviet Union. To begin with, there seemed to be more acts of wilful destruction than positive construction. The old Stadtschloss, slightly damaged by bombing, was blown up in 1950 to make way for a parade ground, which later evolved into a car park.

In 1952, the East Germans sealed off the border with West Germany. The only way out of the 'zone' was through West Berlin and consequently the number of refugees passing through from the East rose dramatically from 50,000 in 1950 to 300,000 in 1953. Over the decade, one million refugees from the East came through West Berlin.

THE 1953 UPRISING

In June 1953, partly in response to the rapid loss of skilled manpower, the East German government announced a ten per cent increase in working 'norms' – the number of hours and volume of output that workers were required to fulfil each day. In protest, building workers on Stalinallee (now Karl-Marx-Allee) downed tools on 16 June and marched to the government offices on Leipziger Strasse. The government refused to relent, and strikes soon broke out across the city. Crowds stormed Communist Party offices and tore red flags from public buildings. By noon the government had lost control of the city and it was left to the Red Army to restore order. Soviet tanks rolled into the centre of East Berlin, where they were met by stones thrown by demonstrators. By nightfall the uprising was crushed. Officially 23 people died, though other estimates put the figure at over 200.

The 17 June uprising only furthered the wave of emigration. And by the end of the 1950s, it seemed likely that East Germany would cease to function as an industrial state through the loss of skilled labour. Estimates put the loss to the East German economy through emigration at some DM100 billion. Ulbricht increased his demands on Moscow to take action.

In 1958, Soviet leader Nikita Khrushchev tried to bully the Allies into relinquishing West Berlin by calling for an end to military occupation and a 'normalisation of the situation in the capital of the DDR (Deutsche Demokratische Republik – German Democratic Republic, or GDR)', by which he meant Berlin as a whole. The ultimatum was rejected and the Allies made clear their commitment to West Berlin. Unwilling to provoke a world war, but needing to prop up his ally, Khrushchev backed down and sanctioned Ulbricht's alternative plan for a solution to the Berlin question.

IN CONTEXT

THE WALL

During the early summer of 1961, rumours spread that Ulbricht intended to seal off West Berlin with a barrier or reinforced border. Emigration had reached a high point as 1,500 East Germans fled to the West each day. However, when in the early hours of 13 August units of the People's Police (assisted by Working Class Combat Groups) began to drag bales of barbed wire across Potsdamer Platz, Berlin and the world were caught by surprise. In a finely planned and executed operation, West Berlin was sealed off within 24 hours. As well as a fence of barbed wire, trenches were dug, the windows of houses straddling the new border were bricked up, and tram and railway lines were interrupted: all this under the watchful eyes of armed guards. Anyone trying to flee west risked being shot; in the 28 years the Wall stood, nearly 80 people died trying to escape. Justifying their actions, the East Germans said they had erected an 'Anti-Fascist Protection Rampart' to prevent a world war.

Days later, the construction of a wall began. When it was completed, the concrete part of the 160-kilometre (100-mile) fortification ran to 112 kilometres (70 miles); 37 kilometres (23 miles) of the Wall ran through the city centre. Previously innocuous streets like Bernauer Strasse (where houses on one side were in the East, on the other in the West) suddenly became the location for one of the world's most deadly borders.

The initial stunned disbelief of Berliners turned into despair as it became clear that (as with the 17 June uprising) the Western Allies could do little more than make a show of strength. President Kennedy dispatched American reinforcements to Berlin, and, for a few tense weeks, American and Soviet tanks squared off at Checkpoint Charlie. Vice-President Johnson came to show moral support a week after the Wall was built. Two years later Kennedy himself arrived and spoke to a crowd of half a million in front of Rathaus Schöneberg. His speech linked the fate of West Berlin with that of the free world and ended with the now famous statement, 'Ich bin ein Berliner!' (Literally, alas, 'I am a doughnut'.)

In its early years the Wall was the scene of many daring escape attempts. People abseiled off buildings, swam across the Spree, waded through sewers or tried to climb over. But as the fortifications were gradually improved with mines, searchlights and guard dogs, and as the guards were given orders to shoot on sight, escape became nearly impossible. By the time the Wall finally fell in 1989, it had been 'updated' four times to render it more or less completely impermeable.

In 1971, the Four Powers met and signed the Quadrapartite Agreement, which formally recognised the city's divided status. Border posts (such as Checkpoint Charlie) were introduced and designated to particular categories of visitors – one for foreigners, another for West Germans, and so on.

A TALE OF TWO CITIES

During the 1960s, with the Wall an infamous and ugly backdrop, the cityscape of modern Berlin (both East and West) began to take shape. On Tauentzienstrasse in the West the Europa-Center was built, and the bomb-damaged Kaiser-Wilhelm-Gedächtnis-Kirche was given a partner – a new church made up of a glass-clad tower and squat bunker. Hans Scharoun laid out the Kulturforum in Tiergarten as West Berlin's answer to the Museumsinsel complex in the East. The first building to go up was Scharoun's Philharmonie, completed in 1963. Mies van der Rohe's Neue Nationalgalerie was finished in 1968. In the suburbs, work began on concrete mini-towns, Gropiusstadt and Märkisches Viertel. Conceived as solutions to housing shortages, they would develop into alienating ghettos. Alexanderplatz in the East was rebuilt along totalitarian lines, and the Fernsehturm (Television Tower) was finished. The historic core of Berlin was mostly cleared to make way for parks (such as the Marx-Engels Forum) or new office and housing developments. On the eastern outskirts of the city in Marzahn and Hohenschönhausen work started on mass-scale housing projects.

BERLINER

Berlin Wall.

In 1965, the first sit-down was staged on the Kurfürstendamm by students protesting against low grants and expensive accommodation. This was followed by several student political demonstrations against the state in general and the Vietnam War in particular. The first communes were set up in Kreuzberg, sowing the seeds of a counterculture that would make the district famous. The student protest movement came into violent confrontation with the police in 1967 and 1968. One student, Benno Ohnesorg, was shot dead by police at a demonstration against the Shah of Iran. A year later the students' leader, Rudi Dutschke, was shot by a right-winger. Demonstrations were held outside the offices of the newspaper group *Springer*, whose papers were blamed for inciting the shooting. It was out of this movement that the murderous Red Army Faction (also known as the Baader-Meinhof Gang) was to emerge, making headlines in the 1970s with kidnaps and killings.

NORMALISING ABNORMALITY

The signing of the Quadrapartite Agreement confirmed West Berlin's abnormal status and ushered in an era of decline, as the frisson of Cold War excitement and 1960s rebellion petered out. More than ever West Berlin depended on huge subsidies from West Germany to keep it going. Development schemes and tax breaks were introduced to encourage businesses to move to the city (Berliners also paid less income tax), but still the economy and population declined. At the same time there was growth in the number of *Gastarbeiter* (guest workers) who arrived from southern Europe and Turkey. Today there are over 120,000 Turks in the city, largely concentrated in Kreuzberg (*see p79* **The Turkish Capital**).

By the late 1970s, Berlin was in decline. In the West, the city government was discredited by a number of scandals. In East Berlin, where Erich Honecker had succeeded Ulbricht in 1971, a regime that began in a mood of reform became repressive. Some of East Germany's best writers and artists, previously supporters of socialism, emigrated. From its headquarters in Normannenstrasse, the Stasi directed its policy of mass observation and permeated every part of East German society (*see p31* **The All-Seeing Stasi**). Between East and West there were squalid exchanges of political prisoners for hard currency. The late 1970s and early 1980s saw the rise of the squatter movement (centred in Kreuzberg), which brought violent political protest back on to the streets.

IN CONTEXT

THE FALL OF THE WALL

The arrival of perestroika in the USSR had been ignored by Honecker, who stuck hard to his Stalinist instincts. Protest was strong and only initially beaten back by the police. By the spring of 1989, the East German state was no longer able to withstand the pressure of a population fed up with communism and closed borders. Throughout the summer thousands fled the city and the country via Hungary, which had opened its borders to the West. Those who stayed began demonstrating for reforms.

By the time Honecker was hosting the celebrations in the Volkskammer (People's Chamber) to mark the 40th anniversary of the DDR on 7 October 1989, crowds were demonstrating outside, chanting 'Gorby! Gorby!' to register their opposition. Honecker was ousted days later. Honecker's successor, Egon Krenz, could do little to stem the tide of opposition. In a bid to defend through attack, he decided to grant the concession East Germans wanted most: freedom to travel. On 9 November 1989, the Berlin Wall was opened, just over 28 years after it had been built. As thousands of East Berliners raced through to the sound of popping corks, the end of East Germany and the unification of Berlin and Germany had begun.

REUNIFYING BERLIN

With the Wall down, Berlin found itself once again at centre stage. Just as the division of the city defined the split of Europe, so the freedom to move again between East and West marked the dawn of the post-Cold War era. For a year Berlin was in a state of euphoria. Between November 1989 and October 1990, the city witnessed the collapse of communism and the first free elections (March 1990) in the East for more than 50 years; economic unification, with the swapping of the tinny Ostmark for the Deutschmark (July 1990); and the political merger of East into West, with formal political unification on 3 October 1990. (It was also the year West Germany won its third World Cup. The team may have come from the West, but in a year characterised by outbursts of popular celebration, Easterners cheered too.)

Unification also brought problems, especially for Berlin, where the two halves of the city now had to be welded into one whole. While Western infrastructure in the form of roads, telephones and other amenities was in decent working order, in the East it was falling apart. Challenges also came from the collapse of a command economy where jobs were provided regardless of cost or productivity. The Deutschmark put hard currency into the wallets of Easterners, but it also exposed the true state of their economy. Within months, thousands of companies cut jobs or closed down altogether.

Responsibility for restructuring Eastern industry was placed with the Treuhandanstalt, a state agency that, for a while, was the world's largest industrial holding company. The Treuhand gave high-paid employment to thousands of Western yuppies and put hundreds of thousands of Easterners on the dole. Easterners soon turned on the Treuhand, vilified as the agent of a brutal Western takeover. The situation escalated when Detlev Karsten Rohwedder, a Western industrialist who headed the agency, was assassinated in spring 1991 – probably by members of the Red Army Faction. The killing of another state employee, Hanno Klein, an influential city planner, drew attention to another dramatic change brought about by unification: the property boom. With the Wall down and – after a 1991 parliamentary decision – the federal government committed to moving from Bonn to Berlin, a wave of construction and investment swept the city.

DRIFTING TO NORMALITY

The giddy excitement of the post-unification years soon gave way to disappointment. The sheer amount of construction work, the scrapping of federal subsidies and tax breaks to West Berlin, rising unemployment and a delay in the arrival of the government all contributed to dampening spirits. In 1994, the last Russian, US, British and French troops left the city. With them went its unique Cold War status. After decades of being different, Berlin was becoming like any other big European capital.

The 1990s were characterised by the regeneration of the East. In the course of the decade the city's centre of gravity shifted towards Mitte. Government and commercial districts were revitalised. On their fringes, especially around Oranienburger Strasse, the Hackesche Höfe and into Prenzlauer Berg, trendy bars, restaurants, galleries and boutiques sprouted in streets that under communism had been grey and crumbling.

Fast-track gentrification in the East was matched by the decline of West Berlin. Upmarket shops and bars began to desert Charlottenburg and Schöneberg. Kreuzberg, once the inelegantly wasted symbol of a defiant West Berlin, degenerated to near slum-like conditions in places, while a new bohemia developed across the Spree in Friedrichshain. Westerners did, however, benefit from the reopening of the Berlin hinterland. Tens of thousands of them swapped the city for greener suburbs in the surrounding state of Brandenburg.

THE BERLIN REPUBLIC

Having spent the best part of a decade doing what it had done so often during its turbulent past – regenerating itself out of the wreckage left by history – Berlin ended the 20th century with a flourish. Many of the big, symbolic construction projects had already sprouted: the new Potsdamer Platz, a Reichstag remodelled by Lord (Norman) Foster. Other major landmarks such as Daniel Libeskind's Jüdisches Museum and IM Pei's extension to the Deutsches Historisches Museum on Unter den Linden followed.

The turn of the century also saw Berlin return to its position at the centre of German politics. Parliament, the government and the accompanying baggage of lobbyists and journalists arrived from Bonn. From Chancellor Gerhard Schröder down, everyone sought to mark the transition as the beginning of the 'Berlin Republic' – for which read a peaceful, democratic and, above all, self-confident Germany as opposed to the chaos of the Weimar years or the self-conscious timidity of the Bonn era.

In the early 2000s, Berlin's financial problems – brought on by rocketing demands on expenditure, decline in central government handouts and the collapse of traditional industries – grew steadily worse. Matching this was the ineptitude of the city's political establishment, desperate to hang on to old privileges and unwilling to face up to tough, new choices. This was all encapsulated in the collapse of the Bankgesellschaft Berlin, a bank largely owned by the city. In the summer of 2001 it was felled by a raft of dud and corrupt real-estate loans. As well as sparking further deterioration in public

IN CONTEXT

Jüdisches Museum.

finances, the scandal brought down the Senate – a grand coalition of Christian Democrats and SPD that had governed since 1990. The resulting elections went some way towards a new start. Klaus Wowereit, head of the SPD, broke one of the great post-unification taboos and invited the Party of Democratic Socialism – successor party to East Germany's Communists and winners of half the Eastern vote – into a Social Democrat-led coalition.

At national level Schröder's second term was far from happy. A brave attempt at welfare reform saw the chancellor attacked from all sides, including the left of his own SPD. Defeats in regional polls forced Schröder in May 2005 to make one last bold move: early elections. Schröder entered the bitter campaign trailing his opponent Angela Merkel and the Christian Democrats in the opinion polls, but came within a whisker of winning the September general election. The result was a mess. Both the main parties – CDU and SPD – lost votes; neither was able to form its preferred coalition. Instead, they were forced into a CDU-led grand coalition with Merkel as chancellor. As the first woman and first Easterner to hold the chancellorship, Merkel ensured her place in the history books when she took office in November 2005.

BREAKING NEW GROUND

Meanwhile, the final pieces of Berlin's structural reunification puzzle tumbled into place. The following year was to see the colossal new Berlin Hauptbahnhof take a bow as one of Europe's largest stations, while the renovated Olympiastadion would play host to the World Cup Final. Peter Eisenman's Denkmal für die ermordeten Juden Europas (Memorial to the Murdered Jews of Europe) was unveiled with the usual whiff of controversy. The hexagon of Leipziger Platz took final shape as the city centre's reception room. And after years of argument, demolition of the Palast der Republik finally began. The former communist parliament is eventually to be replaced by a reconstruction of the old Stadtschloss that once stood on the site with the Humboldt Forum cultural centre.

The improvement of Germany's international standing was confirmed by the 2006 FIFA World Cup. Berlin was the centrepiece for what was widely judged to be one of the best-organised and – for the fans – most enjoyable competitions in the competition's history. Key to the success was the bold decision to welcome all fans – ticket-holders or not – to Germany to take part in the wider experience of the event. Germany may have failed to scoop the cup at the Olympiastadion, but it proved to the world that it knew how to have a good time.

On the political front, Angela Merkel's relations with the SPD became more strained as the Social Democrats adopted more left-wing positions in a bid to stem a catastrophic collapse in the party's support. When the grand coalition broke down in 2009, fresh federal elections were called. After a hard-fought battle, the CDU remained the biggest party but were forced into a coalition with the pro-business FDP. By 2011, the partnership was still in place, despite a raft of problems.

In Berlin the Social Democrats had more to cheer about. Wowereit and his 'Red-Red' senate was returned to office by elections in 2006 that saw the SPD increase its share of the vote while support for the CDU fell. The Left party, which included the PDS, saw its vote slump by more than nine per cent. At the time of writing, Wowerweit was widely tipped to win another term at the mayoral elections in September 2011.

Relations between Berlin and the federal government remained strained as the two haggled over who should meet the debt-laden city's 'national' costs. Agreement on some issues was matched by bitter wrangling on others such as the ultimate future of the Tempelhof airport site, which was co-owned by local and national governments. The decision to close the airport – in the face of vocal protest – as part of a consolidation of the city's airports at Schoenefeld was made in 2007. Since autumn 2010, it has become a hugely popular park. But for all the wrangling, commentators can agree on one thing: for all its political coalitions and new city landmarks, Berlin hadn't quite settled down yet.

Architecture

The city's many styles reflect a complicated history.

TEXT: MICHAEL LEES, HELEN PIDD

Following its belated, late 19th-century start as a European capital, near obliteration during World War II (from above by the RAF, and on the ground from Soviet forces), and 30 years of straddling the frontline between capitalism and communism, it's hardly surprising that Berlin in 2011 is a barely coherent mish-mash of architectural styles. But while the German capital lacks the consistency (or immediate beauty) of a Paris or an Edinburgh, it is a curate's egg of great individual buildings, from the Baroque to the Stalinist, from DDR-tastic communist follies to elegant masterpieces of 20th century modernism, and bravuro restorations (often by British architects) of ruined landmarks, such as the Norman Foster's Reichstag dome, and now David Chipperfield's supremely subtle resurrection of the bomb-damaged Neues Museum. With the city coffers now empty, a two-decade long building boom which followed the fall of the Wall is over – and sadly much of that legacy is generic office and shopping malls. But Berlin has re-emerged as a cultural and creative metropolis to match its heyday under the Weimar Republic. It always had a long history of architectural development and experimentation. During the 1910s and '20s, Berlin was home to some of the century's greatest architects and designers, such as Peter Behrens, Bruno Taut, Ludwig Mies van der Rohe and Walter Gropius. But the path to modernism had been launched a century earlier by Karl Friedrich Schinkel, perhaps Berlin's greatest builder.

PLAYING CATCH-UP

It wasn't until the late 19th century that Berlin was able to hold its own with grander European capitals, thanks to a construction boom known as the Gründerzeit, triggered by the rapid progress in industry and technology that followed German unification in 1871. The city acquired a massive scale, with wide streets and large blocks. These followed a rudimentary geometry and were filled in with five-storey Mietskaserne ('rental barracks') built around linked internal courtyards. The monotony was partially relieved by a few public parks, while later apartment houses gradually became more humane and eventually got rather splendid. During the 1920s, this method of development was rejected in favour of Bauhaus-influenced slabs and towers, which were used to fill out the peripheral zones at the edge of the forests. The post-war years saw even more radical departures from the earlier tradition in all sectors of the city.

AFTER THE WALL

The post-Wall building boom deposited a new layer, a mixture of contemporary design and historic emulation. The spirit of historic revival has even taken in the city's most famous landmark, the Wall. Speedily dismantled after 1989, it is now commemorated in public art, from the **Gedenkstätte Berliner Mauer** at Bernauer Strasse (*see p99*) to Frank Thiel's portraits of the last Allied soldiers, suspended above **Checkpoint Charlie** (*see p80*). The former line of the Wall is also marked in places by a cobblestone strip, visible just west of the Brandenburg Gate. But its memory is fading. 'Where was the Wall?' is the first question on many visitors' lips, and the answer is surprisingly nebulous, as the course of the Wall twisted and dog-legged at the most convoluted angles. The Wall was rarely straight for long.

EARLY DAYS

Berlin's long journey to world city status began in Berlin and Cölln, two Wendish/ Slavic settlements on the Spree that were colonised by Germans around 1237. Among their oldest surviving buildings are the parish churches **Marienkirche** (*see p72*) and **Nikolaikirche** (*see p72*). The latter was rebuilt in the district known as the Nikolaiviertel, along with other landmarks such as the 1571 pub Zum Nussbaum and the baroque **Ephraim-Palais** (*see p72*). The **Nikolaiviertel**, between Alexanderplatz and the Spree, is the only part of central Berlin to give any idea of how the medieval city might have felt – except it's a clumsy fake, rebuilt by the East Germans in 1987, just a few decades after they had levelled the district.

Little survives of the massive **Stadtschloss** ('City Palace', 1538-1950), other than recently excavated foundations in front of the DDR's now-demolished Palast der Republik. The Schlossbrücke crossing to Unter den Linden, adorned with sensual figures by Christian Daniel Rauch, and the Neptunbrunnen (Neptune Fountain, now relocated south of Marienkirche), modelled on Bernini's Roman fountains, were designed to embellish the palace.

THE RESIDENZSTADT

In 1647, the Great Elector Friedrich Wilhelm II (1640-88) hired Dutch engineers to transform the route to the Tiergarten, the royal hunting forest, into the tree-lined boulevard of Unter den Linden. It led west toward **Schloss Charlottenburg** (*see p96*), built in 1695 as a summer retreat for Queen Sophie-Charlotte. Over the next century, the Elector's 'Residenzstadt' expanded to include Berlin and Cölln. Traces of the old stone Stadtmauer (city wall) that enclosed them can still be seen on Waisenstrasse in Mitte. Two further districts, **Dorotheenstadt** (begun 1673) and **Friedrichstadt** (begun 1688), expanded the street grid north and south of Unter den Linden. Andreas Schlüter built new palace wings for Elector Friedrich Wilhelm III (1688-1713, crowned King Friedrich I of Prussia in 1701) and supervised the building of the Zeughaus (Armoury;

'Restrained historicism gave way to wild eclecticism as the 19th century marched on.'

Nering and de Bodt, 1695-1706; now home to the **Deutsches Historisches Museum**; *see p61*), whose bellicose ornamentation embodies the Prussian love of militarism.

Wilhelm I, the Soldier King (1713-40), imposed conscription and subjugated the town magistrate to the court and military elite. The economy now catered to an army comprising 20 per cent of the population (a fairly constant percentage until 1918). To spur growth in gridded Friedrichstadt – and to quarter his soldiers cheaply – the King forced people to build new houses, mostly in a stripped-down classical style. He permitted one open square, Gendarmenmarkt, where twin churches were built in 1701, one of which now houses the **Hugenotten Museum** (*see p65*).

After the population reached 60,000 in 1710, a new customs wall enclosed four new districts – the **Spandauer Vorstadt**, **Königstadt**, **Stralauer Vorstadt** and **Köpenicker Vorstadt**; all are now part of Mitte. The 14-kilometre (nine-mile) border remained the city limits until 1860.

Geometric squares later marked three of the 14 city gates in Friedrichstadt. At the square-shaped Pariser Platz, Carl Gotthard Langhans built the Brandenburger Tor (Brandenburg Gate) in 1789, a triumphal arch later topped by Johan Gottfried Schadow's *Quadriga* (*see p56*). The stately buildings around the square were levelled after World War II, but have now largely been reconstructed or replaced, including the **Adlon Hotel** (Patzschke, Klotz, 1997; *see p113*), on an expanded version of its original site, and the buildings flanking the gate, **Haus Sommer** and **Haus Liebermann** (Kleihues, 1998).

Even with the army, Berlin's population did not reach 100,000 until well into the reign of Frederick the Great (1740-86). Military success inspired him to embellish Berlin and Potsdam; many of the monuments along Unter den Linden stem from his vision of a 'Forum Fredericianum'. Though never completed, the unique ensemble of neo-classical, baroque and rococo monuments includes the vine-covered **Humboldt-Universität** (Knobelsdorff, Boumann, 1748-53); the **Staatsoper** (Knobelsdorff, Langhans, 1741-43); the **Prinzessinnenpalais** (1733, now the Operncafé) and the **Kronprinzenpalais** (1663, expanded 1732; Unter den Linden 3).

Set back from the Linden on Bebelplatz are the **Alte Bibliothek**, reminiscent of the curvy Vienna Hofburg (Unger, 1775-81, part of Humboldt-Universität), and the pantheon-like, copper-domed **St Hedwigs-Kathedrale** (Legeay and Knobelsdorff, 1747-73; *see p62*). Not long after the Napoleonic occupation, the prolific Karl Friedrich Schinkel became Berlin's most revered architect under Prince Friedrich Wilhelm IV. Drawing on classical and Italian precedents, his early stage-sets experimented with perspective, while his inspired urban visions served the cultural aspirations of an ascendant German state. His work includes the colonnaded **Altes Museum** (1828; *see p63*), regarded by most architects as his finest work, and the **Neue Wache** (New Guardhouse, 1818; *see p61*), next to the Zeughaus, whose Roman solidity lent itself well to Tessenow's 1931 conversion into a memorial to the dead of World War I.

Other Schinkel masterpieces include the **Schauspielhaus** (1817-21, now the Konzerthaus; *see p237*); the neo-Gothic brick **Friedrichwerdersche Kirche** (1830, now the Schinkel-Museum; *see p61*); and the cubic **Schinkel-Pavillon** (1825; *see p98*) at Schloss Charlottenburg. After his death in 1841, his many disciples continued working. Friedrich August Stüler satisfied the King's desire to complement the Altes Museum with the **Neues Museum** (1841-1859 and 1997-2009; *see p64*), mixing new wrought-iron technology with classical architecture. By 1910, Museumsinsel comprised the neo-classical **Alte Nationalgalerie** (also Stüler, 1864; *see p63*) with an open stairway framing an equestrian statue of the King; the triangular **Bode Museum** (von Ihne, 1904; *see p64*); and the sombre grey **Pergamonmuseum** (Messel and Hoffmann, 1906-09; *see p64*). These are a stark contrast to the neo-Renaissance polychromy of the **Martin-Gropius-Bau** across town (Gropius and Schmieden, 1881; see 82).

ERA OF EXPANSION

As the population boomed after 1865, doubling to 1.5 million by 1890, the city began swallowing up neighbouring towns and villages. Factory complexes and worker housing gradually moved to the outskirts. Many of the new market halls and railway stations used a vernacular brick style with iron trusses, such as **Arminiushalle** in Moabit (Blankenstein, 1892; Bremer Strasse 9) and Franz Schwechten's Romanesque Anhalter Bahnhof (1876-80, now a ruin; Askanischer Platz). Brick was also used for civic buildings, like the neo-Gothic **Rotes Rathaus** (1861-69; *see p70*), while the orientalism of the gold-roofed **Neue Synagoge** on Oranienburger Strasse (Knoblauch, Stüler, 1859-66; *see p69*) made use of colourful masonry and mosaics.

Restrained historicism gave way to wild eclecticism as the 19th century marched on, in public buildings as well as apartment houses with plain interiors, dark courtyards and overcrowded flats behind decorative façades. This eclectic approach also reflects in the lavish Gründerzeit villas in the fashionable suburbs to the south-west, especially Dahlem and Grunewald. In these areas the modest yellow-brick vernacular of Brandenburg was rejected in favour of stone and elaborate stucco.

In anticipation of a new age of rationality and mechanisation, an attempt at greater stylistic clarity was made after 1900, in spite of the bombast of works such as the new **Berliner Dom** (Raschdorff, 1905; *see p63*) and the **Reichstag** (Wallot, 1894; *see p85*). The Wilhelmine era's paradoxical mix of reformism and conservatism yielded an architecture of *Sachlichkeit* ('objectivity') in commercial and public buildings. In some cases, such as Kaufmann's **Hebbel-Theater** (1908; now part of HAU; *see p267*), or the **Hackesche Höfe** (Berndt and Endell, 1906-07; Rosenthaler Strasse 40-41, Mitte), *Sachlichkeit* meant a calmer form of art nouveau (or Jugendstil); elsewhere it was more sombre, with heavy, compact forms, vertical ribbing and low-hanging mansard roofs. One of the most severe examples is the stripped-down classicism of Alfred Messel's **Pergamonmuseum**. The style goes well with Prussian bureaucracy in the civic architecture of Ludwig Hoffmann, city architect from 1896 to 1924. Though he sometimes used other styles for his many schools, courthouses and city halls, his towering **Altes Stadthaus** in Mitte (1919; Jüdenstrasse, corner of Parochialstrasse) and the **Rudolf-Virchow-Krankenhaus** in Wedding (1906; Augustenburger Platz 1), then innovative for its pavilion system, epitomise Wilhelmine architecture.

Prior to the incorporation of Berlin in 1920, many suburbs had full city charters and sported their own town halls, such as the massive **Rathaus Charlottenburg** (1905; Otto-Suhr-Allee 100) and **Rathaus Neukölln** (1909; Karl-Marx-Strasse 83-85). Neukölln's Reinhold Kiehl also built the **Karl-Marx-Strasse Passage** (1910, now home of the Neuköllner Oper; *see p239*), and the **Stadtbad Neukölln** (1914; *see p262*), with niches and mosaics evoking a Roman atmosphere. Special care was also given to suburban rail stations of the period, such as the **S-Bahnhof Mexikoplatz** in Zehlendorf, set on a garden square with shops and restaurants (Hart and Lesser, 1905), and the **U-Bahnhof Dahlem-Dorf**, whose half-timbered style aims for a countrified look.

ARCHITECTURAL PIONEERS

The work of many pioneers brought modern architecture to life in Berlin. One of the most important was Peter Behrens, who reinterpreted the factory with a new monumental language in the façade of the **Turbinenhalle** at Huttenstrasse in Moabit (1909) and several other buildings for the AEG. After 1918, the turbulent birth of the Weimar Republic offered a chance for a final aesthetic break with the Wilhelmine style. The humming metropolis gave birth to a new gothic-industrial style known as Brick

Chipperfield's Neues Musuem

A tapestry of textures.

Considering it catapulted David Chipperfield from merely the front-rank of world's architects into the celebrity realm of the 'starchitect', won the 2011 Mies van der Rohe Award for Architecture and saw its mastermind awarded both a knighthood and a RIBA prize, what's surprising about the restoration of Berlin's Neues Museum is how understated and unassuming it is.

While there are glass-and-concrete interventions, there is no single scene-stealing wow factor structure, à la Norman Foster's British Museum Great Courtyard roof, or IM Pei's Louvre pyramid. Indeed, such is the less-is-more aesthetic, the casual visitor simply wanting to see the bust of Nefertiti may wonder what all the fuss was about – especially considering its nine-year gestation period. But wow Berlin it certainly did, with queues of up to six hours for an opening in 2009 merely to see the completed building *before* the exhibits were put in place.

Badly damaged by Allied bombing in World War II, then left to rot under the Communist regime, despite its prominant location on the capital's Museum Island – the Neues (finished in 1855, the 'new' refers to its sister musum next door, the Altes Museum) makeover is breathtakingly elegant, chaste and discreet.

At first, it seems all about a tapestry of textures – mixing and matching exposed brickwork, bullet-pocked columns, and Victorian rococco plasterwork, with new concrete columns, arches and a wooden roof that's half barn-like, half medieval. The biggest single intervention is a gargantuan, blank, modernist staircase, but perhaps the most beautiful space is the top deck of the five-storey concrete 'cage' of slim pillars, inserted into an existing courtyard without touching the sides;

a light-filled atrium containing a handful of Egyptian busts. Or is it the receeding kiln-like chimney space over the statue of Helios in the south-east corner? Of course, if you ever get bored of looking at the architecture, you could look at the exhibits – the building houses one of the world's greatest collections of Egyptian and Roman artefacts. Chipperfield is currently working on a €70 million euro entrance gallery next door to house the ticket office and facilities for all the musuems on Museum Island. He maintains an office in Berlin, and fans of his work should also check out his imposing 10-storey limestone Parkside apartment block, right on the edge of the Tiergarten, behind Potdamer Platz. Its monumental and forbidding grey façade and total absence of ornamentation is undeniably impressive - but only its higgledy-piggledy fenestration and rounded corners subvert the block from being the most Third Reich-esque building in Berlin since the 1930s.

Expressionism, used in electricity power stations (HH Mueller's 1926 **Abspannwerk**, or transformer station, on the canal in Kruezberg at the junction of Ohlauerstr and Paul-Lincke Ufer), breweries (the original **Berliner Kindl brewery**, on Rollbergstr, Neukoelln, closed 2006) and churches (Fritz Hoeger's 1932 **Kirche am Hohenzollerndamm**, 202 Hohenzollerndamm).

A radical new architecture gave formal expression to long-awaited social and political reforms. The Neues Bauen (new buildings) began to exploit the new technologies of glass, steel and concrete, inspired by the early work of Tessenow and Behrens, Dutch modernism, cubism and Russian constructivism. Berlin architects could explore the new functionalism, using clean lines and a machine aesthetic bare of ornament, thanks to post-war housing demand, and a new social democrat administration that put planner Martin Wagner at the helm after 1925. The city became the pioneer of a new form of social housing. The *Siedlung* (housing estate) was developed within the framework of a 'building exhibition' of experimental prototypes – often collaborations among architects such as Luckhardt, Gropius, Häring, Salvisberg and the brothers Taut. Standardised sizes kept costs down and amenities such as tenant gardens, schools, public transport and shopping areas were offered when possible. Among the best-known 1920s estates are Bruno Taut's **Hufeisen-Siedlung** (1927; Bruno-Taut-Ring, Britz), arranged in a horseshoe shape around a communal garden, and **Onkel-Toms-Hütte** (Haring, Taut, 1928-29; Argentinische Allee, Zehlendorf), with Salvisberg's linear U-Bahn station at its heart. Most Siedlungen were housing only, such as the **Ringsiedlung** (Goebelstrasse, Charlottenburg) and **Siemensstadt** (Scharoun et al, 1929-32). Traditional-looking 'counter-proposals' with pitched roofs were made by more conservative designers at Am Fischtal (Tessenow, Mebes, Emmerich, Schmitthenner et al, 1929; Zehlendorf).

Larger infrastructure projects and public works were also built by avant-garde architects under Wagner's direction. Among the more interesting are the rounded U-Bahn station at **Krumme Lanke** (Grenander, 1929), the totally rational **Stadtbad Mitte** (1930; *see p262*), the **Messegelände** (Poelzig, Wagner, 1928; Messedamm 22, Charlottenburg), the ceramic-tiled **Haus des Rundfunks** (Poelzig, 1930; Masurenallee 10, Charlottenburg), and the twin office buildings on the southern corner of Alexanderplatz (Behrens, 1932).

Beginning with his expressionist Einsteinturm in Babelsberg, Erich Mendelsohn distilled his own brand of modernism, characterised by the rounded forms of the **Universum Cinema** (1928; now the Schaubühne; *see p265*) and the elegant corner solution of the **IG Metall** building (1930; Alte Jacobstrasse 148, Kreuzberg).

FASCIST FANTASY

In the effort to remake liberal Berlin in their image, the Nazis banned modernist trademarks such as flat roofs and slender columns in favour of traditional architecture. The Bauhaus was closed down and modern architects fled Berlin as Hitler dreamt of refashioning it into the fantastical mega-capital 'Germania', designed by Albert Speer. The crowning glory was to be a grand axis with a railway station at its foot and a massive copper dome at its head, some 16 times the size of St Peter's in Rome. Work was halted by the war, but not before demolition was begun in Tiergarten and Schöneberg.

Hitler and Speer's fantasy was that Germania would someday leave picturesque ruins. Those ruins came sooner than expected. Up to 90 per cent of the inner city was destroyed by Allied bombing. Mountains of rubble cleared by women survivors rose at the city's edge, such as the Teufelsberg in the West and Friedrichshain in the East. During bombing and reconstruction, many apartment buildings lost their decoration, resulting in the bare plasterwork and blunted lines characteristic of Berlin today.

Fascism also left a less visible legacy of bunker and tunnel landscapes. The more visible fascist architecture can be recognised by its stripped-down, abstracted classicism, typically in travertine: in the West, **Flughafen Tempelhof** (Sagebiel, 1941; *see p78*) and the **Olympiastadion** (March, 1936; *see p98*); in the East, the marblehalled **Reichsluftfahrtministerium** (now the Bundesministerium der Finanzen; Sagebiel, 1936; Wilhelmstrasse 97, Mitte) and the **Reichsbank** (now the Auswärtiges Amt; Wolff, 1938; Werderscher Markt, Mitte).

The **Berlin Wall**, put up in a single night in 1961, introduced a new and cruel reality, and has claim to the be the most iconic structure of the 20th century. Very little of the original actually survives, save for a stretch at Bernauer Strasse, and the East Side Gallery murals. The city's centre of gravity shifted as the Wall cut off the historic centre from the West, suspending the Brandenburger Tor and Potsdamer Platz in no-man's land, while the outer edge followed the 1920 city limits.

Post-war architecture is a mixed bag, ranging from the crisp linear brass of 1950s storefronts to concrete 1970s mega-complexes. Early joint planning efforts led by Hans Scharoun were scrapped, and radical interventions cleared out vast spaces. Among the architectural casualties in the East were Schinkel's Bauakademie and much of Fischerinsel, clearing a sequence of wide spaces from Marx-Engels-Platz to Alexanderplatz. In West Berlin, Anhalter Bahnhof was left to stand in ruins and Schloss Charlottenburg narrowly escaped demolition.

Though architects from East and West shared the same modernist education, their work became the tool of opposing ideologies, and housing was the first battlefield. The DDR adapted Russian socialist realism to Prussian culture in projects built with great effort and amazing speed as a national undertaking. First and foremost was **Stalinallee** (1951-54; now Karl-Marx-Allee, Friedrichshain). The Frankfurter Tor segment of its monumental axis was designed by Herman Henselmann, a Bauhaus modernist who briefly agreed to switch styles.

In response, West Berlin called on leading International Style architects such as Gropius, Niemeyer, Aalto and Jacobsen to build the **Hansaviertel**. A loose arrangement of inventive blocks and pavilions at the edge of the Tiergarten, it was part of the 1957 Interbau Exhibition for the 'city of tomorrow', which included Le Corbusier's Unité d'Habitation in Charlottenburg (Corbusierhaus, just south of S-Bahnhof Olympiastadion).

East and West stylistic differences diminished in the 1960s and 1970s, as new *Siedlungen* were built to even greater dimensions. The **Gropiusstadt** in Britz and **Märkisches Viertel** in Reinickendorf (1963-74) were mirrored in the East by equally massive (if shoddier) prefab housing estates in Marzahn and Hellersdorf.

To replace cultural institutions then cut off from the West, Dahlem became the site of various museums and of the new **Freie Universität** (Candilis Woods Schiedhelm, 1967-79). Scharoun conceived a 'Kulturforum' on the site cleared for Germania, designing two masterful pieces: the **Philharmonie** (1963; *see p238*) and the **Staatsbibliothek** (1976; *see p294*). Other additions were Mies van der Rohe's sleek **Neue Nationalgalerie** (1968; *see p91*) and the **Gemäldegalerie** (Hilmer & Sattler, 1992-98; *see p90*).

The US presented Berlin with Hugh Stubbin's **Kongresshalle** in the Tiergarten (1967, now the Haus der Kulturen der Welt; *see p85*), a futuristic work, which embarrassingly required seven years' repair after its roof collapsed in 1980. East German architects brewed their own version of futuristic modernism in the enlarged Alexanderplatz with its **Fernsehturm** (TV Tower, 1969; *see p71*), the nearby **Haus des Lehrers** (Henselmann, 1961-64; Grunerstrasse, corner of Karl-Marx-Allee, Mitte), with its recently restored frieze, the next-door **Congress Hall** (ICC, and as elegant as anything achieved by Oscar Niemeyer in Brasilia) and the impressive cinemas, **Kino International** (Kaiser, 1964; Karl-Marx-Allee 33, Mitte) and **Kosmos** (Kaiser, 1962; Karl-Marx-Allee 131, Friedrichshain). The 1970s even saw a brief burst of Soviet Sci-Fi architecture, with the bronze-glass and brown marbled **Czech Embassy to the DDR** (Vera & Vladimir Machonin, 1978, 44 Wilhelmstr).

Modernist urban renewal gradually gave way to historic preservation after 1970. In the West, largely in response to the squatting movement, the city launched a public-

IN CONTEXT

Berlin Bunkers

Hard-to-remove relics of war, now repurposed.

Next to the railway lines on the Schöneberg/Tempelhof border (General-Pape-Strasse, corner of Dudenstrasse) stands a huge, featureless cylinder of concrete. Built in 1942 as part of the planning for Germania, the Nazi imperial capital that never was, it's a *Grossbelastungskörper* (heavy load testing body) designed to gauge the resilience of Berlin's sandy geology near the site for a proposed triumphal arch. This artless, seldom-noticed lump is the lone physical trace of the north-south axis whose overblown structures were intended to wow the world. But it's not the only huge hulk of reinforced concrete that the Nazis left behind, and is tiny compared to some of the bunkers, flak towers and air-raid shelters that outlasted the regime they were intended to protect. The question of how to integrate them into the urban landscape has sparked a variety of answers.

Berlin's Zoo flak tower was the biggest bunker in the world when the Royal engineers began trying to blow it up in July 1947. One year and 66,000 tonnes of explosives later, they finally broke the thing open, causing extensive damage to the zoo. It took many further detonations before the last pieces of the foundations were cleared in 1969-70. Given the difficulty of demolition, most of these structures have simply been left where they were. On Pallasstrasse in Schöneberg, an air-raid shelter, formerly part of the otherwise demolished Sportspalast complex, has been used to support one end of an apartment block that bridges the street. After the war, two enormous concrete towers in what is now Volkspark Friedrichshain were blown open, then filled in and covered with rubble from the bombed-out city. Result: the park now has two attractively landscaped hills, and only a few visible segments of balustrade hint at what lies beneath.

A little more can be seen of a similarly blasted and buried Nazi flak tower in Wedding's Humboldthain park. Climbers use its north face as a practice peak, several species of bat dwell in its recesses, a viewing platform on the top offers a panorama of the Berlin skyline, and various guided tours of the interior are offered by the Berliner Unterwelten association (www.berlinerunterwelten.de).

There are two other bunkers you can get inside. Kreuzberg's **Gruselkabinett** (*see p81*) is housed in a five-storey concrete hulk, and includes an exhibition about the structure itself, which was once an air-raid shelter for the long-destroyed Anhalter Bahnhof. A bunker on the corner of Reinhardtstrasse and Albrechtstrasse in Mitte, previously a not-very-convenient air-raid shelter for Friedrichstrasse station, was repurposed as a techno club in the early 1990s and today houses the Sammlung Boros art collection (*see p217*).

But of Berlin's most famous bunker, the one where Hitler spent his last days, there's no longer any trace – it was demolished in the late 1980s. An information board on Gertrud-Kolmar-Strasse (opposite the junction with An Der Ministeriumsgarten) is all that marks its former location.

Sammlung Boros.

private enterprise within the Internationale Bauausstellung (IBA), to conduct a 'careful renewal' of the Mietskaserne and 'critical reconstruction' with infill projects to close the gaps left in areas along the Wall.

It is a truly eclectic collection: the irreverent organicism of the prolific Ballers (Fraenkelufer, Kreuzberg, 1982-84) contrasts sharply with the neo-rationalist work of Eisenman (Kochstrasse 62-63, Kreuzberg, 1988) and Rossi (Wilhelmstrasse 36-38, Kreuzberg, 1988). A series of projects was also placed along Friedrichstrasse. IBA thus became a proving-ground for contemporary architectural theories. (Much of the IBA is explored in Jim Hudson's architectureinberlin blog.)

In the East, urban renewal slowed to a halt when funds for the construction of new housing ran dry; and towards the end of the 1970s, inner-city areas again became politically and economically attractive. Most East-bloc preservation focused on run-down 19th-century buildings on a few streets and squares in Prenzlauer Berg. Some infill buildings were also added on Friedrichstrasse in manipulated grids and pastel colours, so that the postmodern theme set up by IBA architects on the street south of Checkpoint Charlie was continued over the Wall. But progress was slow, and when the Wall fell in 1989 many sites still stood half-finished.

Rejoining East and West became the new challenge, requiring work of every kind, from massive infrastructure to commercial and residential projects. There were two key decisions. The first was to eradicate the Wall's no-man's land zone with projects that would link urban structures on either side. The second was to pursue a 'critical reconstruction' of the old city block structure, using a contemporary interpretation of Prussian scale and order.

The historic areas around Pariser Platz, Friedrichstrasse and Unter den Linden were peppered with empty sites and became a primary focus for this critical reconstruction. The first major commercial project in Friedrichstrasse stuck with the required city scale but took the game rules lightly. The various buildings of the **Friedrichstadt-Passagen** (1996; Friedrichstrasse 66-75, Mitte), despite their subterranean mall link, offer separate approaches. Pei Cobb Freed and Partner's **Quartier 206** (*see p174*) is a confection of architectural devices reminiscent of 1920s Berlin, while Jean Nouvel's **Galeries Lafayette** (*see p173*) is a smooth and rounded glass form. Only the third building, **Quartier 205**, by Oswald Mathias Ungers, uses a current German style, with its sandstone solidity and rigorous square grid.

Good examples of the emerging Berliner Architektur, based on the solidity of the past but with modern detail and expressive use of materials, are to be found in Thomas van den Valentyn and Matthias Dittmann's monumental **Quartier 108** (1998; Friedrichstrasse, corner of Leipziger Strasse, Mitte) and in the **Kontorhaus Mitte** (1997; Friedrichstrasse 180-190, Mitte) by Josef Paul Kleihues, Vittorio Magnago Lampugnani, Walther Stepp and Klaus Theo Brenner.

On both sides of the city, much historic substance was lost in World War II and the sweeping changes that followed. Today, the rebuilding of the former imperial areas near Unter den Linden, the Museumsinsel and Schlossplatz revolve around a choice between critical reconstruction or straightforward replicas of the past. The Kommandenthaus, next to the Staatsoper on Unter den Linden, rebuilt by Thomas van den Valentyn as the **Stiftung Bertelsmann** (2004), is an example of the tendency towards historical replication, as is the mooted reconstruction of Friedrich Schinkel's Bauakademie next door. Thankfully some decisions have been taken in favour of contemporary architecture, particularly the entrance building to the **Auswärtiges Amt** (Foreign Office; Werdescher Markt 1, 1999) by Thomas Müller and Ivan Reimann, and IM Pei's triangular block for the **Deutsches Historisches Museum** (2003; *see p61*), with its curved foyer and cylindrical stair tower.

Berlin's return to capital city status has brought with it a number of interesting new embassies and consulates in and around a revived diplomatic quarter. Notable on

IN CONTEXT

Tiergartenstrasse are the solid red stone **Indian Embassy** by Leon Wohlhage Wernik (2001) and the extension of the existing **Japanese Embassy** by Ryohei Amemiya (2000). There are other intriguing examples around the corner in Klingelhöferstrasse: the monumental, louvre-fronted **Mexican Embassy** by Teodoro Gonzalez de Leon and J Francisco Serrano (2000); and the encircling copper wall of the five **Nordic embassies**, containing work by various Scandinavian architects after a plan by Alfred Berger and Tiina Parkkinen (1999).

There are four main sites now linking East and West: the area around Potsdamer Platz and Leipziger Platz; the government quarter and 'Band des Bundes'; the new Berlin Hauptbahnhof; and the reinstatement of the Reichstag and Pariser Platz, the historical formal entrance to the city. These are mostly stand-alone projects outside the discussion on critical reconstruction; their architecture reflects this in a greater freedom of approach. **Potsdamer Platz** (*see p86*) was the first of the four, designed as a new urban area based on the old geometries of Potsdamer and Leipziger Platz. This former swathe of no-man's land was redeveloped not only to forge a link between Leipziger Strasse to the East and the Kulturforum to the West, but also to supply Berlin with a new central focus in an area that was formerly neither one side or the other.

The twin squares of Potsdamer Platz and Leipziger Platz have been reinstated and five small quarters radiate to the south and west. **Leipziger Platz** has risen again as an enclosed octagonal set-piece, with modern terrace buildings. Potsdamer Platz is by contrast once more an open intersection, entrances to the various quarters beyond staked out with major buildings by Hans Kollhoff, Hilmer Sattler and Albrecht, Helmut Jahn, Renzo Piano and Schweger and Partner (1999-2003). The closed metal and glass block of Helmut Jahn's **Sony Center** (2000) is a singular piece, organised around a lofty central forum with a tented glass and textile roof as its spectacular focus. Offices and apartments look down on to a public space with cinemas, bars, restaurants and the glass-encased remnants of the old Esplanade Hotel.

The **Daimler** (formerly DaimlerChrysler) area on the other side of Potsdamer Strasse is a network of tree-lined streets with squares and pavement cafés. It's also the work of various architects, though Renzo Piano got all the key pieces, notably the **Arkaden** shopping mall, the Debis headquarters, and the **Musicaltheater** and **Spielbank** on Marlene-Dietrich-Platz (all 1999), all in a language of terracotta and glass. The quarter's south-west flank facing on to Tilla-Durieux-Park is a rich architectural mix, with Richard Rogers' two buildings of cylinders, blocks and wedges (1998; Linkstrasse) and Arata Isozaki's concoction of ochre and brown stripes topped with a wavy glass penthouse (Linkstrasse, 1998). It's often said of the Potsdamer Platz project that 'the world's best architects came – and did their worst buildings'. Not quite fair, but not far off, either.

The 'Band des Bundes', the linear arrangement of new government buildings north of the Reichstag, is another project linking East and West. The result of a competition won by Axel Schultes and Charlotte Frank, it straddles the Spree and the former border, resembling a paper clip that binds the two halves of the city. The centrepiece is the **Bundeskanzleramt** (Federal Chancellery; Schlutes and Frank, 2000; Willi-Brandt-Strasse, Tiergarten) flanked by buildings with offices for parliamentary deputies. The arrangement reads like a unity thanks to a common and simple language of concrete and glass.

North of this across the Spree is the new central station, **Berlin Hauptbahnhof** (Von Gerkan Marg, 2006; *see p288*), now Europe's largest rail intersection. The 321-metre (1,053-feet) east–west overground platforms are covered by a barrel vault of delicately gridded glass. This is crossed in a north-south direction by a station hall 180 metres (590 feet) long and 40 metres (131 feet) wide, that gives access to the trains on each intersecting level and to the shopping centre. Each side of the station hall is framed by buildings spanning the east-west vault. The building stands as a functional and symbolic link between East and West Germany, and as a hub of the whole European rail network.

Neue Nationalgalerie. *See p45.*

Finally, there are the historical links. To the south of the Bundeskanzleramt is the **Reichstag** (*see p85*), sitting on the old threshold to the East, gutted, remodelled and topped with a new glass dome by Norman Foster (1999) to bring a degree of public access and transparency to a building with a dark past (although 'temporary' security restrictions imposed in late 2010 meant visits had to be booked in advance, rather than turn up and go). **Pariser Platz** (*see p57*) has been almost entirely built to its old proportions. The US Embassy, long delayed and utterly bland finally unveiled on 4 July 2008 in the south-west corner, completes the set piece. Some of the buildings are a pale blend of modern and historic but there are exceptions such as the **DG Bank** by Frank Gehry (2000; Pariser Platz 3, Mitte) with its witty use of a rational façade in front of the spectacular free forms in its internal court, or Christian de Portzamparc's **French Embassy** (2002; Pariser Platz 5, Mitte), which plays with classical composition but uses contemporary materials. In the opposite corner is the **Akademie der Künste** (Behnisch and Partner; 2005), an exception to its neighbours with a welcoming and open glass façade. Round the corner Michael Wilford's **British Embassy** (2000; *see p292*) also came to terms with the city's strict planning limitations by raising a conformist punched stone façade, which he then broke open to expose a rich and colourful set of secondary buildings in the central court. When the last bits of Leipziger Platz are filled in, all the major symbolic linking projects planned in the reunification period will be complete. While they wait for the urban fabric to gel around them, building on a smaller scale continues.

The last decade has also produced work that had nothing to do with reunification. Daniel Libeskind's **Jüdisches Museum** (1999; *see p82*) in Kreuzberg is a symbolic sculpture in the form of a lightning bolt. Peter Eisenmann's **Denkmal für die ermordeten Juden Europas** (2005; *see p57*), south of Pariser Platz, is a departure from a traditional memorial, with its open and sunken grid of 2,700 steles.

Nicholas Grimshaw's **Ludwig-Erhard-Haus** for the stock exchange (1998; *see p94*) breaks with convention by taking the form of a glass and steel armadillo, though a city-required fire wall obscures the structure. On the corner at Kantstrasse 55, Josef Paul Kleihues' **Kant-Dreieck** (1995) extends the sculptural response with its huge metal weather vane. Dominique Perrault's **Velodrom** (1997; *see p253*) sinks into the landscape in the form of a disc and a flat box of glass, concrete and gleaming steel mesh. Sauerbruch and Hutton's striking headquarters for the **GSW** (1999; Kochstrasse 22A, Kreuzberg), with its translucent sailed top and colourful and constantly changing façade, shows how singular buildings can take the city's urban quality to the next level.

Berlin Today

Berlin's unique past and singular culture informs its present.

TEXT: HELEN PIDD

' I want Berlin to be rich and sexy.' So said Berlin's incumbent mayor, Klaus Wowereit, setting out his vision for the city's future at hustings for the mayoral elections in autumn 2011. It was a neat reversal of his notorious remark at the start of the new millennium that Berlin was 'poor but sexy' – a catchy slogan, soon printed on t-shirts and keyrings, which was typical of Wowereit's talent for getting publicity, rather than investment, for his city. While it's true that Berlin's finances were in a far better shape at the end of his second term than they were when he first took office in 2001, they were still pretty dire. In summer 2011 the city still had more than €62 billion of debts accumulating €2 billion interest annually. And despite torrents of cash streaming continuously into its bank account from other richer German states since reunification in 1990, Berlin is still nowhere near financially independent.

MONEY MAKES THE WORLD GO ROUND

Wowereit – ever the optimist – insists the capital will not be reliant on federal handouts forever. 'The city is not as cheap as it used to be,' he conceded on the election trail in 2011, but that was 'a good thing'. He was irritated by those who saw the price hikes as an out-and-out negative. 'We have to decide whether we want to keep these low standards or take the city forward,' he said, while adding that he didn't want Berlin to become like New York or London, where 'normal' earners can't afford to live near the city centre.

But for many Berliners, rising rents are their biggest bugbear. Foreigners, particularly Britons and Americans, can't believe what they can afford when they move over. Yet an increasing number of locals complain that they are being priced out of the market. Between 2009 and 2011, rents increased by an average of eight per cent – in some of the most popular districts there were price hikes of an astonishing 25 per cent. This being revolutionary old Berlin, the disaffected are not taking things lying down. When the residents of the Liebig 14 alternative house project in Friedrichshain were finally evicted in February 2011, 2,500 police officers in full riot gear were drafted in to quell the protests. Meanwhile estate agents were being terrorised by a group of anti-gentrification campaigners who organised 'naked flashmobs' during property viewings. During open house days at particularly swanky new apartment blocks, the gang would hide in a stairwell and pounce, starkers, on unsuspecting flat viewers, before giving them a lecture on why they should not buy the property and contribute to the yuppification of Berlin.

Commercial rents have also rocketed as foreign investors move in. Some of the city's most popular nightclubs have lost battles with developers in recent years – Bar 25 shut in 2010; Maria am Ostbahnhof followed in 2011. Both were closed to make way for the controversial 'Media Spree' development, which aims to transform the rather desolate post-industrial stretch of the river between Ostbahnhof and Warschauer Strasse into a media hub. The hulking O2 venue was one of the first to move in, along with the headquarters of Universal Music, which relocated from Hamburg – a still relatively rare example of a big firm upping sticks to the capital from elsewhere. They have not been made to feel particularly welcome. Look up as you cross the Schillingbrücke from south to north and you will see an unambiguous message sprayed on to an old factory in gigantic letters: 'FUCK OFF MEDIA SPREE'.

Another popular tactic is to chuck paint bombs at developments deemed overly chi-chi. One block on the Reichenbergerstrasse in Kreuzberg became a favourite target after it emerged the new residents had a car lift to take their vehicles to their front doors, even on the fifth floor. The building was attacked so many times that the inhabitants clubbed together to pay for a full time security guard. One reason the moneyed newcomers were keen to park their cars off the streets is that burning cars – particularly fancy ones – has long been a popular nocturnal sport in Berlin. By the end of August 2011, over 370 cars had been deliberately torched in the capital since the start of the year, with police treating around 40 per cent of the attacks as 'politically motivated'.

A NOT-SO-WARM WELCOME

It's not just BMWs and Porches that incurred the wrath of angry Berliners in recent years: tourists have been getting it in the neck too as the city becomes ever more popular with visitors (a record nine million came in 2010, double the number a decade earlier). With the influx came the griping and the so-called 'anti tourism movement' became a hot topic. If you believed half of what was printed in the local newspapers, Berliners don't want you in their city. They don't want you to drink in their bars, to eat in their cafés, to dance in their nightclubs. 'Berlin doesn't love you' read the stickers stuck on the Admiralbrücke in Kreuzberg, shortly before residents in that particularly gentrified corner of the city wrote to the publishers of a number of guidebooks (though not us), asking to not be included in the listings. Local people were fed up, they said, with drunken tourists yelling on the canal bridge in the early hours, urinating up against

IN CONTEXT

'Though Berlin is Germany's most multicultural city, it is hardly overrun.'

the trees and leaving their rubbish behind. The authorities listened, and ever since there has been a 10pm curfew in the area – though a survey by Visit Berlin tourist board suggested the reprobates were not in fact disrespectful visitors but rowdy residents from the surrounding area.

Then, at the end of February 2011, the Green Party in another area of Kreuzberg, the Wrangelkiez, around Schlesisches Tor u-bahn, held a public meeting under the banner, 'Help! The tourists are coming!'. There was grumbling, too, in the northern reaches of Neukölln – often called Kreuzkölln for its similarity and proximity to neighbouring Kreuzberg. 'Kreuzkotz' read the huge graffitied letters on the top of a roof on the Paul-Linke-Ufer: literally that's 'Kreuz-puke'. Then the owners of Freies Neukölln, one of the first 'scene' pubs on the new party mile of Weser Strasse, made a semi ironic video raging against the hipsters and tourists who pour into the area at night. 'We are very sorry that we kicked off such a bad development... Did it ever occur to you that we are not keen on your parties even though they boost our sales?... You stomp our borough to death with this whole over-educated, self-contended superficiality,' said the rather menacing voiceover.

MORE PROTESTS

Other Berlin protests of late have included widespread opposition to the new flight paths planned for Willy Brandt International Airport (due to open summer 2012), which will, campaigners say, disturb the wildlife in and around former East Berlin's biggest lake, the Müggelsee. Towards the end of 2010 there were also huge demonstrations after the government decided to renew the lives of Germany's 17 nuclear power stations. However, the Fukushima power plant disaster – coupled with worries over a series of key elections in which her party were set for a drubbing – led Angela Merkel to hold a three-month moratorium on the power plant renewals. In May 2011 she announced that Germany was committed to phasing out all of its nuclear power stations by 2022.

The real baddie in many Berliners' eyes in recent years, however, has been Thilo Sarrazin, formerly Berlin's finance minister and recently a bestselling author. When he published *Deutschland schafft sich ab* (*Germany Is Doing Away With Itself*) in 2010, it caused an almighty row. His detractors said he had published a racist tome that suggested that the influx of poor migrants into Germany was making the country more stupid. But for many of the millions who read the weighty book, Sarrazin was the man they had been waiting for: a trailblazer who had no truck with political correctness and who was unafraid to speak the 'truth' about immigration. There is little doubt that Sarrazin's popularity has shaken the government – in October 2010 Merkel gave a speech saying that multiculturalism had 'utterly failed'. The admission came after a survey showed 30 per cent of Germans believed the country was 'overrun by foreigners'.

Though Berlin is Germany's most multicultural city, it is hardly overrun: by the end of 2010, 13.7 per cent of the 3.46 million population came from another country. Turks form the biggest ethic minority – with 104,556 registered, comprising 22.8% of all foreigners in the city. Relations between immigrants and natives are mostly calm, if frosty, though there are occasional suspected neo-Nazi attacks on foreigners. To the relief of the majority, the NPD, Germany's far-right party, has failed to gain a foothold in the city's parliament.

So what's next for Berlin? Is it going to be anything more than a playground for the Easyjet set? Can it keep its cool while attracting investment? Will Wowereit's dream ever become a reality? We'll have to wait and see.

Grounded for Good

Goodbye to Tempelhof Airport.

British architect Lord Norman Foster once described Flughafen Tempelhof as the 'mother of all airports'. It was originally designated in 1923, making it the world's second-oldest airport after Sydney, Australia. At least, that's what it was until 31 October 2008, when the last flight departed and Tempelhof closed for good – a victim of Schönefeld's expansion into the new hub of Berlin-Brandenburg International Airport.

Then began the wrangling over what to do with the enormous site. There were plans aplenty – a high-tech centre, apartments, movie studios, a Formula 1 track, an aviation museum – even a proposal by cosmetics magnate Ronald Lauder to turn the whole thing into a €350 million fly-in clinic and conference centre. In the end, though, the local authorities went for the cheapest option and in autumn 2010 Tempelhofer Park was opened to the public.

Very quickly the park became one of the city's favourite hangouts. It's an incongruous place: completely flat, with the air traffic control tower, runway and terminal building still standing, as well as a US army parachute training facility, shooting range and much more. A typical Sunday will see a softball game in full swing, triathletes time-trialling on the old runway, families enjoying picnics and kites flying high above. At the time of writing, the terminal was only open for trade shows, though that may change in future.

It's worth a visit even to look at the outside. After Lufthansa was founded here in 1926, Tempelhof joined London's Croydon and Le Bourget in Paris as one of Europe's three iconic pre-war airports. It was greatly expanded under the Nazis; when it was finished in 1941, Ernst Sagebiel's eagle-shaped building – its wings two giant, curving terraces of

hangars – was the largest in Europe. Hitler and Albert Speer conceived Tempelhof as integral to their plans for Germania – Berlin rebuilt as overblown fascist showpiece – and the emphatic link of city and air travel was perhaps the Nazis' major contribution to urban planning. The airport remains Berlin's largest structure and the 20th biggest building on the planet.

When the dust settled in 1945, Tempelhof found itself in the American Sector. During the *Luftbrücke* (Airlift) of 1948-49, blockaded West Berlin was kept alive by supplies flown in on Allied aircraft: at its height, one landed at Tempelhof every 90 seconds. At the main entrance, the *Luftbrücke* memorial displays the names of the 39 British and 31 American pilots who lost their lives during 'Operation Vittles'; it was unveiled in 1951 and became Berlin's first major post-war monument.

Tempelhof continued as a civil airport until 1973, and was then used exclusively by the US Air Force until civilian traffic resumed in 1990. But its runways were too short for modern airliners, and usage was dwindling long before the decision to axe both it and Tegel in favour of the new Berlin-Brandenburg International at Schönefeld, scheduled to open in 2012. By the end, the airport was losing €10 million a year.

The airport didn't go down without a fight, but a referendum in April 2007 to force a last-minute reconsideration failed on a low turnout. Analysis of the vote turns the kind of confusion that only Berlin can engender: West Berliners and conservatives were broadly in favour, but most East Berliners, with no sentimental connection to the Airlift, didn't even care enough to vote.

For park opening times, see www.tempelhofer-park.de.

IN CONTEXT

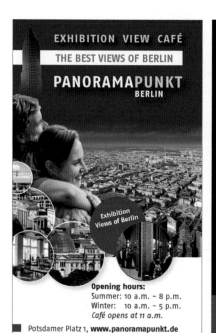

Sights

Brandenburg Tor. *See p56*.

Mitte

The heart of old and new Berlin

Meaning 'middle', Mitte has found itself back in the centre of town since the Wall came down, and is now the life and soul of the party. It hogs many of the biggest sights, including the Brandenburg Gate (**Brandenburger Tor**), TV Tower (**Fernseheturm**) and the magnificent Museum Island (**Museumsinsel**), which includes David Chipperfield's newly renovated **Neues Museum**, as well as the world-famous **Pergamon**. But there's more to this area than tourist fodder: Mitte also boasts some of the best bars, restaurants, shops and clubs in the capital.

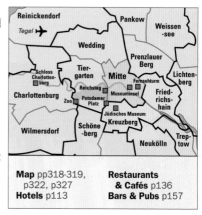

Map pp318-319, p322, p327	**Restaurants & Cafés** p136
Hotels p113	**Bars & Pubs** p157

UNTER DEN LINDEN

From before the Hohenzollern dynasty through the Weimar Republic, and from the Third Reich to the DDR, the entire history of Berlin can be found on or around this celebrated street.

Originally laid out to connect the town centre with the Tiergarten (*see p84*), **Unter den Linden**, running east from the Brandenburger Tor to Museumsinsel (*see p62*), got its name from the *Linden* (lime trees) that shaded its central walkway. Hitler, concerned that the trees obscured the view of his parades, had them felled, but they were later replanted.

During the 18th and 19th centuries, the Hohenzollerns erected no-nonsense baroque and neo-classical buildings along their capital's showcase street. The side streets were laid out in a grid by the Great Elector Friedrich Wilhelm for his Friedrichstadt (*see p18*).

INSIDE TRACK TRABI SAFARI

If you want to see Berlin, GDR-style, take a 'safari' around town in an East German Trabant – you drive an old banger and the sights are ponted out by a guide via radio. Tours set off from the corner of Wilhelmstrasse and Zimmerstrasse. See www.trabi-safari.de.

Brandenburger Tor & Pariser Platz

The focal point of Unter den Linden's western end is the **Brandenburger Tor** (Brandenburg Gate). Constructed in 1791, and designed by Carl Gotthard Langhans after the Propylaea gateway into ancient Athens, the Gate was built as a triumphal arch celebrating Prussia's capital city. It was initially called the Friedenstor (Gate of Peace) and is the only city gate remaining from Berlin's original 18. (Today, only a few U-Bahn station names recall the other city gates, such as Frankfurter Tor or Schlesisches Tor).

The **Quadriga** statue, a four-horse chariot driven by Victory and designed by Johann Gottfried Schadow, sits on top of the Gate. It has had an eventful life. When Napoleon conquered Berlin in 1806 he carted the Quadriga off to Paris and held it hostage until his defeat in 1814. The Tor was later badly damaged during World War II and, during subsequent renovations, the DDR removed the Prussian Iron Cross and turned the Quadriga around so that the chariot faced west. The current Quadriga is actually a 1958 copy of the 18th-century original, and was stranded in no-man's land for 30 years. The Tor was the scene of much celebration while the Wall came down, and after that there had to be further repairs. The Iron Cross was replaced and the Quadriga was turned back to face into Mitte again.

West of the Gate stretches the vast expanse of the **Tiergarten** (*see p84*), Berlin's central park. Just to the north is the reborn **Reichstag** (*see p85*), while ten minutes' walk south is the even more dramatically reconceived **Potsdamer Platz** complex (*see p86*).

Immediately east of the Brandenburger Tor is **Pariser Platz**, which was given its name in 1814 when Prussia and its allies conquered Paris. This square, enclosed by embassies and bank buildings, was once seen as Berlin's *Empfangssaal* – its reception room. Foreign dignitaries would ceremoniously pass through on their way to visit tyrants and dictators in the palaces downtown, and today this remains the area where you'll see enormous limos carting around politicians and diplomats. In 1993, plans were drawn up to revive Pariser Platz, with new buildings on the same scale as the old ones, featuring conservative exteriors and contemporary interiors. Some old faces are back on the historical sites they occupied before World War II: the reconstructed **Adlon Hotel** (*see p113*) is now at its old address, as is Michael Wilford's new **British Embassy**, around the corner at Wilhelmstrasse 70-71.

On the south-west corner of the square – the last building to complete the Pariser Platz puzzle – is the underwhelming **US Embassy**. Since a return to its old address was announced in 1993, construction was delayed first by budgetary miscalculation, then by various problems attendant on new US State Department regulations stipulating a minimum 30-metre (98-foot) security zone around US embassies. The design was adjusted, streets were moved, and America is now securely back on the block. Meanwhile, Wilhelmstrasse is closed to traffic for a block south of the square because of security provisions for the British Embassy.

While outwardly conforming to aesthetic restrictions, many of the straightforward exteriors front flights of fancy within. Frank Gehry's **DG Bank** at No.3 has a huge, biomorphic interior dome hidden behind its regular façade. The **Dresdner Bank** opposite is virtually hollow, thanks to another interior atrium. Next door, Christian de Portzamparc's **French Embassy** features a space-saving 'vertical garden' on the courtyard wall, and 'french windows' extending over two storeys. Nearby is the **Kennedys** (*see p59*), a museum devoted to the famous US dynasty.

Directly to the south of Pariser Platz is the huge **Denkmal für die ermordeten Juden Europas** (Memorial to the Murdered Jews of Europe). Designed by Peter Eisenmann, it's a city-block-size field of concrete slabs, arranged in rows but sloping in different directions on uneven ground. Conceived in 1993, the project became mired in controversy. The winning design of an initial competition was rejected by then Chancellor Kohl, and there was no end of argument over the second competition, including rows over location (the chosen site has no particular link to the Holocaust), function (should such a monument draw a line under history or seek to stimulate debate and discussion?) and content (many feel the memorial should honour all victims of the Holocaust, not only Jewish ones). In

Brandenburger Tor.

SIGHTS

the wake of this one, assorted other victim memorials have been built or are planned (*see below* **Remember, Remember**). The first has already appeared on the other side of Ebertstrasse: Elmgreen and Dragset's **Denkmal für die im Nationalsozialismus verfolgten Homosexuellen** (Monument to the Homosexuals Persecuted during National Socialism). It looks like one of the slabs from the Jewish Denkmal, but contains a video installation.

Between the Denkmal and the Leipziger Platz/Potsdamer Platz complex (*see p86*) is an area filled with representations from Germany's various *Länder*. If you want to visit the site of Hitler's WWII bunker, head to the carpark on the corner of In den Ministergärten and Gertrud-Kolmar-Strasse. There is nothing to see there these days other than an information board detailing in English and German the history of the Führerbunker, but it's chilling nonetheless.

★ FREE **Denkmal für die ermordeten Juden Europas**
Cora-Berliner-Strasse 1 (2639 4336, www. holocaust-denkmal.de). U2, S1, S2, S25 Potsdamer Platz. **Open** *Field of stelae* 24hrs daily. *Information centre* Apr-Sept 10am-8pm daily. Oct-Mar 10am-7pm daily. **Admission** free. **Map** p322/p327 L7.

Remember, Remember

There are many victims to memorialise.

Nowhere is the vexed question of Germany's relationship to its past dramatised more intensely than in the startling proliferation of memorials at the heart of Berlin.

The centrepiece, of course, is the memorial to Jewish Holocaust victims – the **Denkmal für die ermordeten Juden Europas** (*see above*). No debate about the intersection of history, architecture and the form of Berlin's reunified cityscape lumbered on so long or conjured so much controversy as the one that engendered this grid of concrete blocks. The idea of some kind of central memorial had been around since the 1980s opening of the site of the Gestapo headquarters on what is now the **Topographie des Terrors** (*see p83*).

In 1993, the **Neue Wache** (*see p61*), a memorial to the 'victims of fascism and militarism' under the Communists, was recast as one to the 'victims of war and violent rule'. This involved installing an enlarged replica of Käthe Kollwitz's statue, *Mother with Dead Son.* There were immediate protests that this put murdered victims on the same level as dead perpetrators, and memorialised them in a form contrary to Jewish tradition. Chancellor Kohl then promised that a memorial would be erected solely for Jewish victims of the Holocaust.

The winning design of a 1995 competition was a concrete slab the size of two football fields, bearing the names of all 4.2 million identified Holocaust victims. But the cliché of equating the enormity of the crime with the enormousness of the

memorial was widely criticised. Kohl rejected the design. A second competition in 1998 produced a design by Peter Eisenmann and Richard Serra involving 4,000 columns – what eventually got built is a scaled-down version.

Meanwhile representatives of other persecuted groups – Gypsies, gays, the mentally or physically disabled, prisoners of war, political prisoners, forced labourers and blacks – all pointed to the inadequacy of a memorial for Jewish victims alone. Roma groups argued that the extermination of their people should not be separated from that of the Jews, but then refused to share a memorial with homosexuals.

In May 2008, a memorial to gay victims of the Nazis, designed by Michael Elmgreen and Ingar Dragset, was unveiled on the edge of the Tiergarten. It's a lone concrete slab that looks as if it was detached from the Jewish Denkmal over the road, and includes a small window through which a video of two men kissing can be viewed. After criticism by lesbian groups, this will now be rotated every two years with a video of two women.

Disagreements between Roma groups, meanwhile, have delayed construction of a memorial to Gypsy victims of the Nazis. The site that will be home to a fountain designed by Israeli memorial specialist Dani Karavan is on the corner of the Tiergarten closest to the Reichstag, just behind an impromptu memorial to people killed going over the Wall, and not far from the **Sowjetisches Ehrenmal** (Soviet War Memorial; *see p84*). And on another corner of the Tiergarten, in the parking area behind

After many years of controversy, Peter Eisenmann's 'field of stelae' – 2,711 of them, arranged in undulating rows on 19,704 sq metres (212,000 sq ft) of city block – with its attendant information centre to memorialise the Murdered Jews of Europe, was opened in 2005. Each of the concrete slabs has its own foundation, and they tilt at differing angles. The effect is (no doubt deliberately) reminiscent of the packed headstones in Prague's Old Jewish Cemetery. There's no vantage point or overview; to engage with the thing you need to walk into it. It's spooky in places, especially on overcast days and near the middle of the monument, where many feel a sense of confinement. The information centre is at the south-east corner of the site, mostly underground.

It's like a secular crypt, containing a sombre presentation of facts and figures about the Holocaust's Jewish victims.

Kennedys

Pariser Platz 4A (2065 3570, www.thekennedys. de). S1, S2 Unter den Linden. **Open** 10am-6pm daily. **Admission** €7; €3.50 reductions. **No credit cards. Map** p318/p327 L6.

This small museum celebrates the 'special relationship' between Berlin and the Kennedy family, cemented by John F Kennedy's iconic 'Ich bin ein Berliner' speech in June 1963. With photos and memorabilia, the museum tells the history of the family, beginning with immigration to the US from Ireland

Topographie des Terrors

SIGHTS

the Philharmonie, is a memorial to the mentally and physically disabled victims of the Nazis' T4 euthanasia programme – a kind of lobotomised concrete bus. And Ursula Wilms's €23 million Documentation Centre at the Topographie des Terrors opened recently, in May 2010.

There's more to come. The memorial to the workers' uprising of 17 June 1953 – a huge, weatherproofed documentary photo set in the pavement outside the Finance Ministry on Leipziger Strasse – is a reminder that it wasn't only Nazism that left victims to be memorialised. Currently under discussion are memorials for those who died during the expulsion of Germans from Poland and Czechoslovakia after World War II, and for both those who were persecuted for deserting the German army and those who died while serving in the Bundeswehr. A plaque on the north-eastern corner of the Reichstag thanking Hungary for opening its Western border to DDR

citizens in 1989 has inspired Poles to agitate for their own plaque, thanking them for solidarity's role in the downfall of Communism. And conservatives are now asking for a memorial plaque to the victims of 1970s terrorist group, the RAF (AKA the Baader Meinhof gang).

Keen for something positive to stand in this increasingly baleful landscape of segregated victims' memorials, the latest idea is a 'Monument to Germany's Liberty and Unity' – an interactive 'site of joy' that will celebrate German unity. In 2011, after more than a decade of disagreement, Berlin finally settled on an unusual design – a 55-metre, 330-tonne dish-shaped see-saw that can hold up to 1,400 people at any one time. Called *Bürger in Bewegung (Citizens in Motion)* and co-designed by Berlin's star choreographer Sasha Waltz , it is due to be built on the site of the old GDR parliament building on Schloss Platz.

Dalí

DIE AUSSTELLUNG
AM POTSDAMER PLATZ

permanent exhibition

Cultural highlight
Berlin Mitte

opened daily: mon - sat 12 p.m. - 8 p.m.
sun + holidays 10 a.m. - 8 p.m.
(24th december closed)

public transportation: S1/S2/S25 + U2
Potsdamer Platz **entrance:** Leipziger Platz

Hommage á S.Dalí by DaVal

Infos: 0700DaliBerlin (0700 - 325 423 75) | **Tickets:** 01805 - 10 33 23
(0,14 €/Min. from a landline, mobile communications vary, max 0,42 €/Min.)

With more than 450 exhibits from private collections from around the world offers
most comprehensive insight into Salvador Dalí´s virtuoso and experimenting attitude
in almost all artistic techniques right in the pulsating heart of Berlin.

www.DaliBerlin.de

in the late 19th century and ending at the deaths of John and Robert Kennedy. It all looks wonderful in a minimalist setting, but that might also be down to the limits of the subject matter. Don't expect to learn anything new.

East along Unter den Linden

Heading east along Unter den Linden, passing the 1950s Stalinist wedding cake-style Russian Embassy on your right, and, on the next block, the box office of the **Komische Oper** (*see p237*), you reach the crossroads with Friedrichstrasse, once a café-strewn focus of Weimar Berlin.

On the other side of the junction, on the right, housed on the ground floor of a 1920s building now occupied by Deutsche Bank, is the **Deutsche Guggenheim Berlin** (*see right*), a tiddler compared to its big sisters in New York and Bilbao. Facing the art gallery across Unter den Linden stands the **Staatsbibliotek** (it's open to all, and there's a small café), usually filled with students from the **Humboldt-Universität**. The university's grand old façade has been restored, as have the two statues of the Humboldts (founder Wilhelm and his brother Alexander), between which booksellers set up tables in good weather.

Across the street is **Bebelplatz**, site of the notorious Nazi book-burning, commemorated by Micha Ullmann's subterranean monument set into the Platz itself. The glass has become pretty scratched, unfortunately, and it can be hard to see through. Dominating the square's eastern side is the **Staatsoper** (*see p238*), built in neo-classical style by Georg Wenzeslaus von Knobelsdorff in 1741-43. The present building closed for extensive renovations in autumn 2010 and is not expected to reopen until October 2014. Meanwhile, the company is squatting at the Schiller Theatre in Charlottenburg.

Just south of the Staatsoper (and also designed by Knobelsdorff, in 1747) is **Sankt-Hedwigs-Kathedrale** (*see p62*), a curious circular Roman Catholic church, inspired by the Pantheon in Rome. A minute's walk east of here brings you to another church, **Friedrichswerdersche-Kirche**, which now contains the **Schinkel-Museum** (*see right*), a homage to the building's architect.

On the west side of Bebelplatz is Rocco Forte's **Hotel de Rome** (*see p113*), occupying what used to be the East German central bank, and the late 18th-century **Alte Bibliotek**. Alongside that, in the centre of Unter den Linden, stands a restored equestrian statue of Frederick the Great.

On the north side of Unter den Linden, the **Neue Wache** (New Guardhouse), constructed by Schinkel in 1816-18, originally served as a guardhouse for the royal residences in the area. Today, it is a hauntingly plain memorial to the 'victims of war and tyranny', with an enlarged reproduction of a Käthe Kollwitz sculpture, *Mother with Dead Son*, at its centre. Beneath this are the remains of an unknown soldier and an unknown concentration camp victim, surrounded by earth from World War II battlefields and concentration camps.

Next to it to the east is the baroque Zeughaus, a former armoury with a deceptively peaceful pink façade. With renovations completed in 2006, the Zeughaus once again houses the **Deutsches Historisches Museum** (*see below*). The new wing by IM Pei hosts changing exhibitions and has a fine café.

This whole last eastern stretch of Unter den Linden is supposed to undergo further heritage restoration, in line with the eventual rebuilding of the nearby Stadtschloss by the Italian architect Frank Stella.

Deutsche Guggenheim Berlin

Unter den Linden 13-15 (202 0930, www. deutsche-guggenheim.de). U6 Französische Strasse. **Open** 10am-8pm daily **Admission** €4; €3 reductions; free under-12s. Free to all Mon. **Map** p318/p327 M6.

In partnership with the Deutsche Bank (and housed in one of its buildings), this is the least impressive European branch of the Guggenheim, though it has an excellent shop and café.

Deutsches Historisches Museum

Zeughaus, Unter den Linden 2 (203 040, www.dhm.de). U6 Französische Strasse. **Open** 10am-6pm daily. **Admission** €6; free under-18s. **Map** p319/p327 N6.

The permanent exhibition in the Zeughaus finally opened in July 2006 and provides an exhaustive blast through German history from 100 BC to the present day, divided chronologically into significant eras. The museum originally had trouble raising the funds to buy historical objects, but there's enough here now for the exhibits to work on their own, without the need for an overarching narrative. German nationalism becomes the focus once you enter the 19th century and later on more than one room is dedicated to the Nazi era. The DHM has succeeded admirably in looking the past straight in the eye, although the attempt to be impartial means that it is sometimes factual to the extreme. Temporary exhibitions are housed in the gorgeous new Pei building.

FREE Friedrichswerdersche-Kirche/ Schinkel-Museum

Werderscher Markt (266 42 42 42, www.smb.spk-berlin.de). U2 Hausvogteiplatz. **Open** 10am-6pm daily. **Admission** free. **Map** p323/p327 N7.

SIGHTS

Berliner Dom.

This brick church, designed by Karl Friedrich Schinkel, was completed in 1831. Its war wounds were repaired in the 1980s and it reopened in 1987 as a homage to its architect. Inside are statues by Schinkel, Schadow and others, bathed in soft light from stained-glass windows. Pictures of Schinkel's works that didn't survive the war are also displayed.

FREE Sankt-Hedwigs-Kathedrale

Hinter der katholischen Kirche 3 (203 4810, www.hedwigs-kathedrale.de). U2 Hausvogteiplatz or U6 Französische Strasse. **Open** 10am-5pm daily. **Admission** free. *Guided tours* €1.50. **Map** p323/p327 N7.

Constructed in 1747 for Berlin's Catholic minority, this circular Knobelsdorff creation was bombed out during the war and only reconsecrated in 1963. Its modernised interior contains a split-level double altar. The crypt holds the remains of Bernhard Lichtenberg, who preached here against the Nazis, was arrested, and died while being transported to Dachau in 1943.

MUSEUMSINSEL

The eastern end of Unter den Linden abuts the island in the Spree where Berlin was 'born'. The northern part, with its excellent collection of museums and galleries, is known as Museumsinsel (Museum Island), while the southern half (much enlarged by landfill), once a neighbourhood for the city's fishermen (and known as Fischerinsel), is now dominated by a clutch of grim tower blocks.

The five Museumsinsel museums (the Pergamonmuseum, Altes Museum, Alte Nationalgalerie, Bode Museum and Neues Museum) are all now open after undergoing a massive restoration programme, though works are set to continue for some years yet. Such is the importance of the site that it was added to UNESCO's World Cultural Heritage list in 1999.

The **Pergamonmuseum** (*see p64*), one of Berlin's main attractions, is a showcase for three huge and important examples of ancient architecture: the Hellenistic Pergamon Altar (part of a Greek temple complex from what is now western Turkey), the Babylonian Gate of Ishtar and the Roman Market Gate of Miletus. The museum also contains the Museum für Islamische Kunst (Museum of Islamic Art).

Schinkel's superb **Altes Museum** (*see p63*), from 1830, has a small permanent collection, hosts some excellent temporary exhibitions, and for now houses a new exhibition on the ancient world, including sections on the Romans and Etruscans. The renovated **Alte Nationalgalerie** (*see p63*) has once again become home to a wide-ranging collection of 19th-century painting and sculpture.

The **Neues Museum**, rebuilt by British architect David Chipperfield, reopened in 2009 as a home to the Ägyptisches Museum and Charlottenburg's Museum für Vor- und Frühgeschichte (Primeval and Early History Museum). Instead of rebuilding an exact copy, Chipperfield has created new architecture where the old could not be saved.

Dominating the Museumsinsel skyline is the huge, bombastic **Berliner Dom** (*see p63*). It's worth climbing up to the cathedral's dome for fine views over the city. In front of here, bounded on one side by the neo-classical colonnade of the Altes Museum, is the **Lustgarten**, an elegant green square.

Across the main road bisecting the island, is where the DDR's parliament complex Palast der Republik once stood. After lengthy arguments, the asbestos-ridden building was finally demolished in 2009 and at the time of writing, the site was half park, half archaeological site, as experts excavate the foundations of the war-ravaged Stadtschloss, residence of the Kaisers, which was heavily damaged in World War II and demolished by the DDR in 1952. Now the Stadtschloss will be rebuilt, and will eventually house the Humboldt Forum art and cultural centre. Opposite the new development will be the new monument to German unity – a gigantic rocking dish (*see p58* **Remember, Remember**). Temporarily squatting on the site is the ugly and angular blue **Humboldt Box** (Schlossplatz 5, (02131 224 400, www.humboldt-box.com), which houses a tourist information centre, viewing platform and restaurant.

Alte Nationalgalerie

Bodestrasse 1-3 (266 42 42 42, www.alte-national-galerie.de). U6, S1, S3, S2, S25 Friedrichstr., S3, S5, S7, S75 Hackescher Markt. **Open** 10am-6pm Mon-Wed, Fri-Sun; 10am-10pm Thur. **Admission** €10; €5 reductions. **Map** p319/p327 N6.

With its ceiling and wall paintings, fabric wall papers and marble staircase, the Old National Gallery is a sparkling home to one of the largest collections of 19th-century art and sculpture in Germany. Among the 440 paintings and 80 sculptures, which span the period from Goethe to early

Modern, German artists such as Adolph Menzel, Caspar David Friedrich, Max Liebermann and Carl Spitzweg are well represented. There are also some first-rank early Impressionist works from Manet, Monet and Rodin. Although the gallery is worth a visit, don't expect to see any kind of definitive German national collection.

Altes Museum

Lustgarten (266 4242 42, www.smb.museum). U6, S1, S3, S2, S25 Friedrichstr., S3, S5, S7, S75 Hackescher Markt. **Open** 10am-6pm Mon-Wed, Fri-Sun; 10am-10pm Thur. **Admission** €8; €4 reductions. **Map** p319/p327 N6.

Opened as the Royal Museum in 1830, the Old Museum originally housed all the art treasures on Museumsinsel. It was designed by Schinkel and is considered one of his finest buildings, with a particularly magnificent entrance rotunda, where vast neon letters declare that 'All Art has been Contemporary'. Now that the Egyptian galleries have moved into the Neues Museum round the corner, this building now houses a new exhibition on ancient worlds, with an excellent look at the Etruscans and Romans on the top floor. The main floor shows off the collection of classical antiquities, including a world-class selection of Greek art.

Berliner Dom

Lustgarten 1 (2026 9136, guided tours 2026 9119, www.berliner-dom.de). U6, S1, S3, S2, S25 Friedrichstr., S3, S5, S7, S75 Hackescher Markt. **Open** *Apr-Sept* 9am-7pm Mon-Sat; noon-8pm Sun. *Oct-Mar* 9am-7pm Mon-Sat; noon-7pm Sun. **Admission** €7; €4 reductions; free under-18s. **Map** p319/p327 N6.

Hackescher Markt. See p68.

SIGHTS

The dramatic Berlin Cathedral is now finally healed of its war wounds and celebrated its centenary in 2005. Built in Italian Renaissance style, it was destroyed during World War II and remained a ruin until 1973, when extensive restoration work began. It has always looked fine from the outside, but now that the internal work is complete, it is fully restored to its former glory. Crammed with Victorian detail and containing dozens of statues of eminent German Protestants, its lush 19th-century interior is hardly the perfect acoustic space for the frequent concerts that are held here, but it's worth a visit to see the crypt containing around 90 sarcophagi of notables from the Hohenzollern dynasty, or to clamber up for splendid views from the cupola. Call to book a guided tour.

Bode Museum

Monbijoubrücke (266 4242 42, www.smb. museum). U6, S1, S3, S2, S25 Friedrichstr, S3, S5, S7, S75 Hackescher Markt. **Open** 10am-6pm Mon-Wed, Fri-Sun; 10am-10pm Thur. **Admission** €8; €4 reductions. **Map** p319/p327 N6.

Built by Berlin architect Ernst Eberhard von Ihne in 1904, the Bode Museum reopened after a thorough renovation in 2006. It was originally intended by Wilhelm von Bode as a home for art from the beginnings of Christendom, and now contains the Byzantine Collection, Sculpture Collection and the Numismatic Collection. The neo-baroque Great Dome, the Basilica hall and the glorious Cupola have been carefully restored to keep up with modern curatorial standards, but they retain their magnificence. Most impressively, despite one of the world's largest sculpture collections and more than half a million pieces in the coin collection, the museum somehow retains a totally uncluttered feel and the sculptures stand free from off-putting glass cases. In particular, make sure you look out for the wall-length Apse Mosaic from 545 AD and the 14th-century Mannheim High Altar. Both are well worth checking out.

★ Neues Museum

Bodestrasse 1 (266 42-4242, www.neues-museum.de). U6, S1, S3, S2, S25 Friedrichstr., S3, S5, S7, S75 Hackescher Markt. **Open** 10am-6pm Mon-Wed, Sun; 10am-8pm Thur-Sat. Entry by timed ticket. **Admission** €10; €5 reductions. **Map** p327 N6.

Finally reopened in 2009 after extensive remodelling by the British architect David Chipperfield, this stunning building now houses the Egyptian Museum and Papyrus Collection, the Museum of Prehistory and Early History and various artefacts from the Collection of Classical Antiquities. The museum's most famous object is the bust of the Egyptian queen, Nefertiti, which Germany refuses to return to Egypt despite repeated requests, and the skull of the Neanderthal from Le Moustier. The Museum für Vor- und Frühgeschichte (Prehistory &

Early History), which traces the evolution of homo sapiens from 1,000,000 BC to the Bronze Age, has among its highlights reproductions (and some originals) of Heinrich Schliemann's famous treasure of ancient Troy, including works of ceramics and gold, as well as weaponry. Keep an eye out also for the sixth-century BC grave of a girl buried with a gold coin in her mouth. Information is available in English. The Neues Museum has become such a hit that the museum authorities have had to limit visitor numbers by issuing timed tickets – book in advance if you can, and turn up within a half hour of the time you are given. You can sometimes buy tickets at the counter, but don't count on it.

▶ *For more on the renovations, see p43.*

★ Pergamonmuseum

Am Kupfergraben (266 4242 42, www.smb. museum). U6, S1, S3, S2, S25 Friedrichstr., S3, S5, S7, S75 Hackescher Markt. **Open** 10am-6pm Mon-Wed, Fri-Sun; 10am-10pm Thur. **Admission** €12; €6 reductions. **Map** p319/p327 N6.

One of the world's major archaeological museums, the Pergamon should not be missed. Its treasures, comprising the Antikensammlung (Collection of Classical Antiquities) and the Vorderasiatisches Museum (Museum of Near Eastern Antiquities), contain three major draws. The first is the Hellenistic Pergamon Altar, dating from 170-159 BC; huge as it is, the museum's partial re-creation represents only one third of its original size. In an adjoining room, and even more architecturally impressive, is the towering two-storey Roman Market Gate of Miletus (29 m/95ft wide and almost 17m/56ft high), erected in AD 120. This leads through to the third of the big attractions – the extraordinary blue and ochre tiled Gate of Ishtar and the Babylonian Processional Street, dating from the reign of King Nebuchadnezzar (605-562 BC). There are plenty of other gems in the museum that are also worth seeking out, including some stunning Assyrian reliefs.

The museum is also now home to the Museum für Islamische Kunst (Museum of Islamic Art), which takes up some 14 rooms in the southern wing. The collection is wide ranging, including applied arts, crafts, books and architectural details from the eighth to the 19th century. Entrance is included in the overall admission price, as is an excellent audio guide.

▶ *The Pergamonmuseum is currently undergoing renovation, in stages. The museum will remain open while the work is carried out.*

SOUTH OF UNTER DEN LINDEN

What the Kurfürstendamm was in post-war West Berlin, **Friedrichstrasse** had been and is trying to be again: the city's glitziest shopping street. Like Unter den Linden, the north-south street (starting at Mehringplatz in Kreuzberg and ending at Oranienburger

Pergamonmuseum.

Tor in Mitte) was laid out as part of the baroque late 17th-century expansion of the city.

The liveliest, sleekest stretch of the street is that between **Checkpoint Charlie** (*see p80*) and Friedrichstrasse station. A huge amount of money has been poured into redevelopment here, with office buildings and upmarket shops and malls galore, although it's a pretty soulless place.

Look out for the all-glass façade of modernist-style **Galeries Lafayette** (no.75; *see p174*), the acute angles of the expressionist **Quartier 206** (nos.71-74; *see p176*) and the monolithic geometric mass of **Quartier 205** (Nos.66-70). Otherwise there are auto showrooms for Rolls-Royce, Bentley, Volkswagen, Audi and Mercedes-Benz, boutiques for Mont Blanc, Cartier and countless other high-class concerns.

Just to the east of this stretch lies the square of **Gendarmenmarkt**, one of the high points of Frederick the Great's vision for the city. Here, two churches, the **Französcher Dom** ('French Cathedral'; home of the **Hugenottenmuseum**; *see right*) and the **Deutscher Dom** (*see right*), frame the **Konzerthaus** (*see p237*), home to the Deutsches Symphonie-Orchester Berlin.

Just west of Friedrichstrasse on Leipziger Strasse is the **Museum für Kommunikation** (*see pright*). There are many other interesting sights close by over the Mitte border with Kreuzberg. For these, *see pp77-83*.

Deutscher Dom

Gendarmenmarkt, entrance in Markgrafenstrasse (2273 0431). U2, U6 Stadtmitte. **Open** *Oct-Apr* 10am-6pm Tue-Sun. *May-Sept* 10am-7pm Tue-Sun. Guided tours every half hour 11am-5pm; call beforehand for English- or French-speaking guide. **Admission** free. **Map** p322/p327 M7.

Both this church and the Französischer Dom were built in 1780-85 by Carl von Gontard for Frederick the Great, in imitation of Santa Maria in Montesanto and Santa Maria dei Miracoli in Rome. The Deutscher Dom was intended for Berlin's Lutheran community. Its neo-classical tower is topped by a 7m (23ft) gilded statue representing Virtue. Inside is a permanent exhibition on the history of Germany's parliamentary system, from the 1848 revolution through the suspension of parliamentary politics by the Nazis, right up to the present day. The visitor is encouraged to consider the role of parliaments throughout the modern world, but there are no translations so to get much out of this without a guided tour, your German must be up to scratch.

Französischer Dom/ Hugenottenmuseum

Gendarmenmarkt (229 1760, www.franzoesischer-dom.de). U2, U6 Stadtmitte. **Open** noon-5pm Tue-Sat; 11am-5pm Sun. **Admission** €2; €1 reductions. **No credit cards. Map** p322/p327 M7.
Built in the early 18th century for Berlin's 6,000-plus-strong French Protestant community, the church was later given a baroque tower, which offers fine views over Mitte. The tower is purely decorative and unconsecrated – and, therefore, not part of the church, which is known as the Französischen Friedrichstadt Kirche (noon-5pm Mon-Sat; after service-5pm Sun).

An exhibition on the history of the French Protestants in France and Berlin-Brandenburg is displayed within the building (the modest church has a separate entrance at the western end). The museum chronicles the religious persecution suffered by Calvinists (note the bust of Calvin on the outside of the church) and their subsequent immigration to Berlin after 1685, at the behest of the Hohenzollerns. The development of the Huguenot community is also detailed with paintings, documents and artefacts. One part of the museum is devoted to the church's history, particularly the effects of World War II – it was bombed during a Sunday service in 1944 and remained a ruin until the mid 1980s.

Museum für Kommunikation

Leipziger Strasse 16 (202 940, www.mfk-berlin.de). U2 Mohrenstrasse or U2, U6 Stadtmitte. **Open** 9am-8pm Tue; Wed,Thur, Fri 9am-5pm Sat, 10am-6pm Sun. **Admission** €3; €1.50 reductions. Free under-15s. **No credit cards. Map** p322/p327 M7.
A direct descendant of the world's first postal museum (founded in 1872), this collection covers a bit

SIGHTS

Gendarmenmarkt. *See p65.*

more than mere stamps. It traces the development of telecommunications up to the internet era, though philatelists might head straight to the basement and the 'Blue Mauritius', one of the world's rarest stamps.

NORTH OF UNTER DEN LINDEN

The continuation of Friedrichstrasse north of Unter den Linden is less appealing and lively than its southern stretch. Friedrichstrasse station once had an interior notable mostly for its ability to confuse. Its role as the only East–West border crossing point open for all categories of citizen involved a warren of passageways and interior partitions. Today it is open and full of shops.

Following the line of the train tracks east along Georgenstrasse, you come upon the **Berliner Antik & Flohmarkt** (*see p175*) – a succession of antiques stores, bookshops and cafés in the *Bogen* ('arches'), underneath the railway.

The building just to the north of the railway station is known as the **Tränenpalast** ('Palace of Tears'). This was where departing visitors left their Eastern friends and relations who could not follow them through the border. In September 2011, the building reopened as a museum commemorating the division of Berlin (Reichtagsufer 17, open 9am-7pm Tue-Fri, 10am-6pm Sat, Sun, admission free).

Across Friedrichstrasse stands the **Admiralspalast** (*see p241*), a landmark theatre that reopened in 2006 after eight years of darkness. First opened in 1910, a survivor of wartime bombing, the building contains a 1,600-seat theatre used over the decades for everything from Broadway transfers to the Staatsoper. There are also two smaller performance spaces and a restored roman-style bathhouse-turned-21st-century spa.

Crossing the river on the wrought-iron Weidendammer Brücke, a left turn on

Schiffbauerdamm brings you to the **Berliner Ensemble** (*see p265*), with its bronze statue of Bertolt Brecht, who directed the company from 1948 to 1956, surrounded by quotations from his works. *Die Dreigroschenoper* (*The Threepenny Opera*) was premiered here on 31 August 1928. The theatre's canteen, down some steps in the backyard, is open to the public, and is a great place to grab a cheap bite to eat (*see p136*). There are also various congenial bars and restaurants along the riverfront, beyond which this neighbourhood begins to merge into what is now the government quarter.

Back on Friedrichstrasse stands the **Friedrichstadtpalast** (*see p268*), a large variety venue that was an entertainment hotspot during the DDR days, since it took hard currency; it still pulls the crowds today, albeit mostly grannies from out of town. Further north is the **Brecht-Weigel-Gedenkstätte** (*see below*), home to Bertolt Brecht (until his death in 1956) and his wife Helene Weigel. Both are buried in the Dorotheenstädtische Friedhof (open 8am-dusk daily) next door, along with the architect Schinkel, the author Heinrich Mann and the philosopher Hegel.

Two worthwhile museums are five and ten minutes' walk from here: the **Museum für Naturkunde** (Natural History Museum; *see p67*) and the **Hamburger Bahnhof – Museum für Gegenwart** (Hamburg Station Museum of Contemporary Art; *see p67*), which puts on a series of excellent, temporary exhibitions within the atmospheric confines of a former railway station.

Brecht-Weigel-Gedenkstätte

Chausseestrasse 125 (200 571 844). U6 Oranienburger Tor. **Open** *Guided tours* every 30mins 2-3.30pm Tue; 5-6.30pm Thur, 10am-3.30pm Sat, 11am-6pm Sun, and by

SIGHTS

appointment. **Admission** €5; €2.50 reductions. **No credit cards. Map** p318/p326 M5.

Brecht's home from 1948 until his death in 1953 has been preserved exactly as he left it. Tours of the house (phone in advance for an English one) give interesting insights into the life and reading habits of the playwright. The window at which he worked overlooked the grave of Hegel in the neighbouring cemetery. Brecht's wife, actress Helene Weigel, continued living here until her death in 1971. The Brecht archives are kept upstairs.

▶ *The Kellerrestaurant near the exit serves Viennese dishes as cooked by Weigel, see p140.*

★ Hamburger Bahnhof – Museum für Gegenwart

Invalidenstrasse 50-51 (3978 3439 , www. hamburgerbahnhof.de). S3, S5, S7, S75 Hauptbahnhof. **Open** 10am-6pm Tue, Wed, Fri; 10am-6pm Thur; 11am-8pm Sat; 11am-6pm Sun. **Admission** incl temporary exhibitions €12; concession €6 **No credit cards. Map** p318 K5.

The Hamburg Station Museum of Contemporary Art opened in 1997 within a huge and expensive refurbishment of a former railway station. The exterior features a stunning fluorescent light installation by Dan Flavin. Inside, the biggest draw is currently the gradual unveiling of the Friedrich Christian Flick Collection – a staggering 2,000 works from around 150 artists, mostly of the late 20th century. Flick, from a steel family whose fortune was tainted with Nazi-era controversy, has paid for the refurbishment of the Rieckhalle – an adjacent 300m (984ft) warehouse – to accommodate the works from his collection, many of them large-scale, as they are doled out in temporary, themed exhibitions. There are other exhibitions too – Cärsten Höller filled the big hall with real life raindeer for his installation Soma in 2011 – plus one of Berlin's best art bookshops.

INSIDE TRACK AMPELMÄNNCHEN

Wondering why pedestrian traffic lights have much jauntier little red and green men than in other cities? Both are wearing hats and the green man has a very purposeful stride. They are *Ampelmännchen*, a hangover from East Germany, which had different traffic lights from the West. In the euphoria following the collapse of communism, the *Ampelmännchen* started to die out and be replaced by their more straight-laced western counterparts– until Ostalgie struck and a campaign was launched to bring them back. Now, you can see them on both sides of the reunified city.

★ Museum für Naturkunde

Invalidenstrasse 43 (2093 8551, www. naturkundemuseum-berlin.de). U6 Zinnowitzer Strasse. **Open** 9.30am-6pm Tue-Fri; 10am-6pm Sat, Sun. **Admission** €6; €3,50 reductions (including special exhibitions). **No credit cards. Map** p318 L4.

Berlin's recently renovated Natural History Museum is a real treasure trove. The biggest draw is the skeleton of a Brachiosaurus dinosaur, which weighed 50 tons at death and is as high as a four-storey house. Restored to its former glory after years in storage, 'Oliver' – as the dinosaur has been nicknamed – is one of the world's largest known land animals and was discovered in the early 1900s. Four renovated exhibition rooms were reopened in 2007, including the new 'Evolution in Action', although unfortunately a lot of information in the old exhibitions is still in German only. Don't miss the creepy new *Forschungssammlungen* (research collections), which reopened in 2010 to show off the museum's store of over a million pickled animals suspended in jars of alcohol.

The Scheunenviertel

If the area south of Friedrichstrasse station is the new upmarket face of Mitte, the Scheunenviertel (stretching around the north bank of the Spree, running east from Friedrichstrasse to Hackescher Markt) is the face of its moneyed bohemia.

Today, this is one of Berlin's main nightlife districts and art quarters, littered with bars and galleries. Once far enough out of town that it was safe to build the highly flammable hay barns (*Scheunen*) here, this was also historically the centre of Berlin's immigrant community, including many Jews from Eastern Europe. During the 1990s, it again began to attract Jewish immigrants, including both young Americans and Orthodox Jews from the former Soviet Union.

In the 1990s, the Scheunenviertel became a magnet for squatters with access to the list of buildings supposedly wrecked by lazy urban developers, who had ticked them off as 'gone' in order to meet quotas but had actually left them standing. With many other buildings in disrepair, rents were cheap, and the new residents soon learned how to take advantage of city subsidies for opening galleries and other cultural spaces. Result: the Scheunenviertel became Berlin's hottest cultural centre.

The first of these art-squats was **Tacheles**, on the western end of Oranienburger Strasse, the spine of the Scheunenviertel. Built in 1907, the building originally housed an early attempt at a shopping mall. It had stood vacant for years when squatted by artists after the Wall came down. It then became a rather arrogant

SIGHTS

INSIDE TRACK STOLPERSTEINE

Walking around Berlin, particularly in Mitte's Scheunenviertel, you may stumble across a brass plated cobblestone with some writing engraved on it – this is a *Stolpersteine* (literally stumbling block), set down to remember a victim of the Holocaust. The stone will usually tell you a person's name, date of birth and at which concentration camp they were murdered.

SIGHTS

arbiter of hip in the neighbourhood, with studio and performance spaces, a cinema, and several edgy bars and discos and eventually became one of Berlin's most popular tourist attractions. In 2011 it looked as though Tacheles' days were numbered when half the occupants agreed to a €1 million pay-off from developers. At the time of writing, a further 80 loosely grouped artists insisted they were going nowhere, though the bars, restaurants and al fresco art studios had closed down.

Across Tucholskystrasse at Oranienburger Strasse 32 is an entrance to the **Heckmann Höfe** (the other is on Auguststrasse), a series of courtyards that have been delightfully restored to accommodate shops and restaurants. The free-standing building with the firm's coat of arms in the pavement in front of it was once the stables.

A little further down the block stands the **Neue Synagoge** (*see p69*), with its gleaming golden Moorish-style dome. Turning into Grosse Hamburger Strasse, you find yourself surrounded by Jewish history. On the right, on the site of a former old people's home, there's a memorial to the thousands of Berlin Jews who were forced to congregate here before being shipped off to concentration camps. Behind the memorial is a park that was once Berlin's oldest Jewish cemetery; the only gravestone left is that of the father of the German Jewish renaissance, Moses Mendelssohn, founder of the city's first Jewish school, next door at No.27. That the school has heavy security fencing and a permanent police presence, even today, only adds to the poignancy of this place.

Across the street at Nos.15-16 is the **Missing House**, a memorial by Christian Boltanski, in which the walls of a bombed-out house have the names and occupations of former residents inscribed on the site of their vanished apartments. A little further on, the **Sophienkirche**, from which nearby Sophienstrasse gets its name, is one of Berlin's few remaining baroque churches. It is set back from the street behind wrought-iron fences and,

together with the surrounding ensemble, is one of the prettiest architectural sites in the city. The interior is a little disappointing, however. Just north of the synagogue is the new **Ramones Museum** (*see p69*), run by probably the biggest fan of the New York band.

At the end of Oranienburger Strasse, at the corner of Rosenthaler Strasse, is the famous **Hackesche Höfe**. Built in 1906-07, these form a complex of nine interlinking Jugendstil courtyards with elegant ceramic façades. The Höfe symbolise Berlin's new Mitte: having miraculously survived two wars, the forgotten, crumbling buildings were restored in the mid-1990s using the old plans. Today, they house an upmarket collection of shops, galleries, theatres, cafés, restaurants and cinemas and are just about Berlin's top tourist attraction. Try to avoid visiting at the weekend.

A few doors up Rosenthaler Strasse is a tumbledown alley alongside the Central cinema, in which a workshop for the blind was located during World War II. Its owner managed to stock it fully with 'blind' Jews, and helped them escape or avoid the camps. Now it houses alternative galleries, bars and shops. In the same complex is the **Anne Frank Zentrum**, home to a multi-media exhibition which tells the life story of the young Dutch diarist who was murdered in Bergen-Belsen. Across the street from the Hackesche Höfe, and under the S-Bahn arches, there are further bars, restaurants and shops.

There are still more fashionable bars and shops along **Rosenthaler Strasse** and around the corner on **Neue Schönhauser Strasse**, as well as some good sandwich and coffee bars. This area has settled into being Berlin's hip centre with many cool little shops. Most of the original houses have now been renovated and the gaps left by wartime bombing have been filled in by slick new buildings. Even the *Plattenbauten*, the East German prefabs, have been spruced up, although the pavements still have craters.

Leading off Rosenthaler Strasse, **Sophienstrasse** is Mitte's most picturesque street. Built in the 18th century, it was restored in 1987 for the city's 750th anniversary, with craftworkers' ateliers that have replicas of old merchants' metal signs hanging outside them. This pseudo-historicism has now become part of a more interesting mix of handcraft shops. The brick façade of the Handwerker Verein at no.18 is particularly impressive. If you wander into the courtyard (as you can with most courtyards that aren't private), you'll find the **Sophiensaele** (*see p267*), an interesting performing arts space in an old ballroom. The Sophiensaele was also the location of the first German Communist Party HQ.

At Nos.20-21 are the **Sophie-Gips Höfe**, which came into being when wealthy art patrons Erika and Rolf Hoffmann were denied permission to build a gallery in Dresden for their collection of contemporary art. Instead, they bought this complex between Sophienstrasse and Gipsstrasse, restored it, and installed the art here, along with their spectacular private residence (*see right*).

Running between the west end of Oranienburger Strasse and Rosenthaler Strasse, **Auguststrasse** was the original core of Berlin's eastern gallery district; it was here that the whole Mitte scene began almost two decades ago, with such important venues as **Eigen + Art** (*see p215*) and **KW Institute for Contemporary Art** (*see p216*), among many others. This became known as Mitte's 'Art Mile', and the street still makes a good afternoon's stroll, although many of the cutting-edge galleries have moved on.

Anne Frank Zentrum

Rosenthaler Strasse 39 (288 865 610, www.anne frank.de). U8 Weinmeisterstrasse. **Open** 10am-6pm Tue-Sun. **Admission** €5; €2.50 reductions; €10 families; free under-10s. **No credit cards**. **Map** p326/N5.
This permanent exhibition about the life and death of Anne Frank opened in 2006 and is a co-project with the Anne Frank House in Amsterdam. Pictures, collages, films and special objects describe the world of the diarist and her family in the context of National Socialism, the persecution of the Jews and World War II.

Neue Synagoge

Centrum Judaicum, Oranienburger Strasse 28-30 (8802 8316, www.centrumjudaicum.de). S1, S2 Oranienburger Strasse. **Open** *Mar-Oct* 10am-8pm Mon, Sun; 10am-6pm Tue-Thur. *Nov-Feb* 10am-6pm Mon-Thur, Sun; 10am-2pm Fri. **Admission** €3,50; €2,50 reductions. **No credit cards**. **Map** p319/p326 N5.
Built in 1857-66 as the Berlin Jewish community's showpiece (and inaugurated in the presence of Bismarck), it was the New Synagogue that was attacked during Kristallnacht in 1938, but not too badly damaged – Allied bombs did far more harm in 1945. The façade remained intact and the Moorish dome has been rebuilt. Inside is a permanent exhibition about Jewish life in Berlin and a glassed-in area protecting the ruins of the sanctuary.

Ramones Museum

Krausnickstrasse 23 (7552 8890, www.ramones museum.com). S1, S2 Oranienburger Strasse. **Open** noon-10pm daily. **Admission** €3.50. **No credit cards**. **Map** p326 N5.
Run by a German guy who claims to be the Ramones' number one fan, this odd museum houses a vast collection of memorabilia, including childhood photos of the group, gig set lists, fliers from the band's early days and concert t-shirts. There are also movie screenings, acoustic shows, and Ramones-related special events.

Sammlung Hoffman

Sophienstrasse 21 (2849 9121, www.sophie-gips.de). U8 Weinmeisterstrasse. **Open** (by appointment only) 11am-4pm Sat. **Admission** €8. **No credit cards**. **Map** p319/p326 N5.
This is Erika and Rolf Hoffmann's private collection of international contemporary art, including a charming floor installation work by Swiss video artist Pipilotti Rist and work by Lucio Fontana, Frank Stella, Douglas Gordon, Felix Gonzalez-Torres and AR Penck. The Hoffmans offer guided tours through their apartment every Saturday by appointment – felt slippers supplied. Every summer Erika changes the entire display.

ALEXANDERPLATZ & AROUND

Visitors who have read Alfred Döblin's *Berlin Alexanderplatz* or seen the television series by Fassbinder may arrive here and wonder what happened. What happened was that in the early 1970s Erich Honecker decided that this historic area should reflect the glories of socialism, and tore it all down. He replaced it with a masterpiece of Commie kitsch: wide boulevards; monotonous white buildings filled with cafés and shops (though to a degree these took their cue from modernist structures dating from the Weimar era, such as the block between the south-west side of the square and the station); and, of course, the impressive golf-ball-on-a-knitting-needle, the **Fernsehturm** (Television Tower; *see p71* **Tower of the Hour**). The goofy clock topped with the 1950s-style atom design signals the time in (mostly) former socialist lands; water cascades from the Brunnen der Völkerfreundschaft ('Fountain of the Friendship of Peoples').

There were plans to replace most of Alexanderplatz with a dozen or so skyscrapers, among which the Fernsehturm would remain standing, but it seems unlikely they will ever come to fruition. For now, the Kaufhaus department store on the north-west of the square has been expanded and has lost its '70s façade, while the 22,000 square metres of new shopping space going up on the north-east corner at press time have ruined the square's Communist-era sightlines and obscured the view across Grunerstrasse of the domed Kongresshalle and the Haus des Lehrers with its first-floor frieze – two of Berlin's finest examples of DDR architecture. Beyond them is Alexa (*see p175*), a giant new shopping mall that no one likes.

SIGHTS

One of the few survivors from pre-war Alexanderplatz sits in the shadow of the Fernsehturm: the **Marienkirche** (*see p72*), Berlin's oldest parish church, dating from the 13th century. Later 15th-century (the tower) and 18th-century (the upper section) additions enhance the building's harmonious simplicity.

Just south of here stands the extravagant **Neptunbrunnen**, an 1891 statue of the trident-wielding sea god, surrounded by four female figures representing the Elbe, Rhine, Oder and Vistula rivers. It was moved here from the Stadtschloss when the Communists demolished it in 1950. Overlooking Neptune from the south-east is the huge red-brick bulk of the **Berliner Rathaus** (Berlin Town Hall; *see right*), while to the south-west is the open space of Marx-Engels Forum, one of the few remaining monuments to the old boys – the huge statue of Karl and Fred begs you to take a seat on Marx's lap. On Spandauer Strasse behind the Radisson Hotel, is the entrance to the **AquaDom & Sea Life** (*see right*), one of Mitte's more eccentric attractions, and round the corner on the river is the hardly more sensible **DDR Museum** (*see below*).

For a vague impression of what this part of the city might have looked like before Allied bombers and the DDR did their work, take a stroll around the Nikolaiviertel, just south of Alexanderplatz. This is Berlin's oldest quarter, centred around **Nikolaikirche** (dating from 1220; *see p72*). The DDR's reconstruction involved bringing the few undamaged buildings from this period together into what is essentially a fake assemblage of history. There are a couple of historic residences, including the **Knoblauch-Haus** (*see p72*), and the **Ephraim-Palais** (*see p72*). You'll also find Gottfried Lessing's house, restaurants, cafés (including a reconstruction of Zum Nussbaum, a contender for the oldest bar in Berlin) and expensive shops. On the southern edge of the district is the **Hanf Museum** (Hemp Museum; *see p72*).

Long before the infamous Wall, Berlin had another one: the medieval **Stadtmauer** (City Wall) of the original 13th-century settlement. There's almost as much left of this wall (a couple of minutes' walk east of the Nikolaiviertel, on Littenstrasse/Waisenstrasse) as there is of the more recent one. Built along the wall by the junction with Parochialstrasse is the extremely old restaurant Zur Letzten Instanz. It takes its name from the neighbouring law court. There has been a restaurant on this site since 1525, Napoleon among its customers.

Just over the Spree from here is the church-like red-brick **Märkisches Museum** (*see p72*), which houses a rambling, but not uninteresting, collection tracing the history of the city, and the small neighbouring **Köllnischer Park**. The park's bearpit is home to Schnute and Maxi, Berlin's two flesh-and-blood brown bears – and official symbols of the city.

AquaDom & Sea Life

Spandauer Strasse 3 (0180 5666 90101, www.sealife.de).S3, S5, S7,, S75 Hackescher Markt. **Open** 10am-6pm daily. **Admission** €16,95; €11-95-€15,95 reductions. **Map** p319/p327 N6.

Billed as two attractions in one, both involving lots of water and plenty of fish. Sea Life leads you through 13 themed aquaria offering fish in different habitats. The AquaDom is the world's largest free-standing aquarium – a spacey stucture that looks like it might just have landed from some extremely watery planet. You take a lift up through the middle of this giant cylindrical fishtank – a million litres of saltwater that is home to 2,500 colourful creatures, and enfolded by the atrium of the Radisson Hotel (*see p117*).

FREE Berliner Rathaus

Rathausstrasse 15 (guided tours 9026 2411). U2, U5, U8, S3, S5, S7, S9, S75, Alexanderplatz. **Open** 9am-6pm Mon-Fri. Guided tours by appointment. **Admission** free. **Map** p319/p327 O6. This magnificent building was constructed of terracotta brick during the 1860s. The history of Berlin up to that point is illustrated in a series of 36 reliefs on the façade. During Communist times, it served as East Berlin's town hall – keeping its old nickname, Rotes Rathaus ('Red Town Hall'), after the colour of the façade, doubly fitting. West Berlin's city government workers moved here from their town hall, Rathaus Schöneberg, in 1991. Admission is restricted to small parts of the building; bring some ID.

DDR Museum

Karl Liebknecht Strasse 1 (847 123 731, www. ddr-museum.de). S 3, S5, S7, S75 Hackescher Markt. **Open** 10am-8pm Mon-Fri, Sun; 10am-10pm Sat. **Admission** €6; €4 reductions. **Map** p319/p327 O6.

Bright blue neon signage and a Trabant in the window welcome you into 'one of Europe's most interactive museums!' This is 'Ostalgia' in action. Touch screens, sound effects and even the 'DDR Game' mean that the more distasteful aspects of East German life are cheerfully glossed over. The museum is essentially a collection of DDR memorabilia, from travel tickets to Palast der Republik serviettes. Climb inside the Trabi or sit on a DDR couch in a DDR living room where you can watch DDR TV. Information on the Stasi gets the interactive treatment too – you can pretend to be a Stasi officer and listen in on a bugged flat. Take it all with a large pinch of salt.

Tower of the Hour

Berliners have learned to love the Fernsehturm.

Most great cities have their iconic landmarks, the kind of thing film directors work into shot to establish a change of location. Eiffel Tower in the background? Yes, we're in Paris. Big Ben? It's London. Sydney Harbour Bridge? Time for the Australian part of the story. And these days, if the hero's just arrived in Berlin, you'll probably get a shot of the Fernsehturm (television tower).

It was not always so. The Nazis had envisaged a city stuffed with landmarks, with oversized triumphal arches and mountainous meeting halls, but by the late 1940s there was nothing much left to say 'Berlin' save ruins and rubble. In 1950, the East Berlin authorities blew up what was left of the old Prussian Stadtschloss, an act widely regarded as one of cultural barbarism, and started thinking about a new landmark to fill the void at the city's heart. While they pondered, another dilemma arose. The new medium of television demanded that a transmission tower be built in the eastern part of Berlin to provide a service to compete with the powerful signals already emanating from the West.

The winning design came from an architect called Herbert Henselmann, who in 1958 had come up with a plan for a complete overhaul of Berlin's medieval centre: the now-open area between the Spree and Alexanderplatz. It was mostly low-rise stuff, but part of his vision was for a 'tower of signals'. The inspiration for Henselmann's designs was the new mania for space travel that followed the launch of Sputnik, the first artificial satellite, in October 1957. Henselmann's tower would have a tapering shaft, to represent a rocket soaring into the sky; and at the very top would be a bright, socialist-red sphere to represent a satellite.

Construction began in 1965, and the Fernsehturm was finally opened on 7 October 1969 – the 20th anniversary of the founding of the DDR. It marked the very centre of the city in the manner of a medieval church tower, allowed the second DDR TV station to commence broadcasting, and advertised the thrusting virility of socialism in a form visible for miles around, including from all over West Berlin. Equipped with a viewing platform at 203 metres (668 feet) and a revolving restaurant one floor above it (the Telecafe, christened after a naming competition in the party newspaper, *Neues Deutschland*), it was also a handy tourist attraction.

Its simple, ball-on-spike shape was also a boon to East Berlin's graphic designers. At last, the city had a politically neutral but versatile symbol that could be used in myriad ways. Soon it was appearing on tourist brochures and party calendars, commemorative stamps and political posters, city maps and menu covers, shopping bags and official invitations. Easily anthropomorphised with a smiley face added to the ball, and often depicted with garlands of flowers, it was also perfect for literature addressed to socialist youth. In the heyday of East Berlin, it was as inescapable as a graphic icon as it was as a towering landmark.

The Fernsehturm nearly didn't survive Reunification: it was so closely associated with the outgoing communist regime, there were calls to tear it down. But it remains useful and is still a major tourist draw. And now that bananas and free speech are sufficiently plentiful, Berliners have once again learned to love the thing. Today, the Fernsehturm once more appears everywhere, though its use as a graphic icon has become considerably more playful. The spike spears an apple in publicity for an organic greengrocer. Its shape counterposes that of a stretching human body in an ad for a company offering yoga classes. It dominates a tripped-out Berlin skyline on any number of flyers for rock concerts and techno parties. The revolving restaurant, which originally went round just once an hour, today pirouettes in a giddy 20 minutes, and the tower itself is still the fourth-tallest free-standing structure in Europe. What more could you ask of an icon?

SIGHTS

SIGHTS

Ephraim-Palais

Poststrasse 16 (2400 2162, www.stadt museum.de). U2, U5, U8, S5, S7, S9, S75 Alexanderplatz. **Open** 10am-6pm Tue-Sun. **Admission** €3; €1.50 reductions; free to all Wed. *Combined ticket with Knoblauch-Haus & Nikolaikirche* €5; €3 reductions. **No credit cards.** Map p319/p327 O6.

Built in the 15th century, remodelled in late baroque style in the 18th century, demolished by the Communists, and then rebuilt by them close to its original location for the 750th anniversary of Berlin in 1987, the Ephraim-Palais is today home to temporary exhibitions drawn from the city's collection. Soft, chandelier lighting and parquet floors lend a refined touch.

Fernsehturm

Panoramastrasse 1A (242 3333, www.berliner fernsehturm.de). U2, U5, U8, S5, S7, S3, S75 Alexanderplatz. **Open** *Mar-Oct* 9am-midnight daily. *Nov-Feb* 10am-midnight daily. **Admission** €11; €7 reductions; free under-3s. Map p319/p327 O6.

Built in the late 1960s at a time when relations between East and West Berlin were at their lowest ebb, the 365m (1,198ft) Television Tower – its ball-on-spike shape visible all over the city – was intended as an assertion of Communist dynamism and modernity. A shame, then, that such television towers were a West German invention. A shame, too, that they had to get Swedish engineers to build the thing. Communist authorities were also displeased to note a particular phenomenon: when the sun shines on the tower, reflections on the ball form the shape of a cross. Berliners dubbed this phenomenon 'the Pope's revenge'. Nevertheless, the authorities were proud enough of their tower to make it one of the central symbols of the East German capital, and today it is one of Berlin's most popular graphic images. Take an ear-popping trip in the lift to the observation platform at the top: a great way to orient yourself early on a visit to Berlin. The view is unbeatable by night or day – particularly looking westwards, where you can take in the whole of the Tiergarten and surrounding area. If heights make you hungry, take a twirl in the revolving restaurant, which offers an even better view. There are usually queues to get up there, however.

Hanf Museum

Mühlendamm 5 (242 4827/www.hanfmuseum.de). U2, U5, U8, S5, S7, S3, S75 Alexanderplatz. **Open** 10am-8pm Tue-Fri; noon-8pm Sat, Sun. **Admission** €4,50, € 3 reductions; free under-10s. **No credit cards.** Map p319/p327 O6.

The world's largest hemp museum aims to teach the visitor about the uses of the plant throughout history, as well as touching on the controversy surrounding it. The café (doubling as a video and reading room) has cakes made with and without hemp.

FREE Knoblauch-Haus

Poststrasse 23 (240 020 171, www.knoblauch haus.de). U2, U5, U8, S5, S7, S3, S75 Alexanderplatz. **Open** 10am-6pm Tue-Sun. **Admission** free. Map p319/p327 O6.

This neo-classical mid 18th-century townhouse was once home to the influential Knoblauch family and contains an exhibition about some of their more prominent members. However, the real draw is the house's striking haute bourgeoise interior. The first floor contains an exhibition called Domestic Living in the Biedermeier Era, while the second floor hosts temporary exhibitions about 19th-century cultural history.

FREE Marienkirche

Karl-Liebknecht-Strasse 8 (2475 9510, www. marienkirche-berlin.de). U2, U5, U8, S5, S7, S9, S75 Alexanderplatz. **Open** 10am-6pm daily. **Admission** free. Map p319/p327 O6.

Begun in 1270, the Marienkirche is one of Berlin's few remaining medieval buildings. Just inside the door is a wonderful Dance of Death fresco dating from 1485, and the 18th-century Walther organ here is considered his masterpiece. Marienkirche hit the headlines in 1989 when the civil rights movement chose it for one of their first sit-ins, since churches were among the few places where people could congregate without state permission. Guided tours are available.

Märkisches Museum

Am Köllnischen Park 5 (240 020 171, www. stadtmuseum.de). U2 Märkisches Museum. **Open** 10am-6pm Tue-Sun. **Admission** €5; €3 reductions; free to all first Wed of mth. Map p323/p327 O7.

This extensive, curious and somewhat old-fashioned museum traces the history of Berlin through a wide range of historical artefacts. Different sections examine themes such as Berlin as a newspaper city, women in Berlin's history, intellectual Berlin and the military. There are models of the city at different times, and some good paintings, including works by members of the Brücke group. Some sections have captions in English.

Nikolaikirche

Nikolaikirchplatz (240 020 171, www.stadt museum.de). U2, U5, U8, S5, S7, S75 Alexanderplatz. **Open** 10am-6pm daily. **Admission** €5; €3 reductions, free to all first Wed of mth. Map p319/p327 O6.

Inside Berlin's oldest congregational church is an interesting historical collection chronicling the city's development until 1648. Old tiles, tapestries, stone and wood carvings – even old weapons and punishment devices – are on display. The collection includes fascinating photos of wartime damage, plus examples of how the stones melted together in the heat of bombardment.

Prenzlauer Berg & Friedrichshain

Two former East Berlin neighbourhoods make their mark.

Neither of these two former East Berlin districts have many conventional sights, but are worth a visit for their cafés, bars, parks and streetlife. Prenzlauer Berg sits north-east of Mitte, an attractively gentrified district with a great selection of shops and hangouts, not to mention Berlin's liveliest fleamarket at the Mauerpark every Sunday.

Further east, Friedrichshain, stretching out from the Stalinist spine of Karl-Marx-Alle into waterfront and post-industrial quarters, feels more a product of the Communist era. It is home to the East Side Gallery, the longest surviving stretch of the Berlin wall.

Map p319, p325, p328	**Restaurants & Cafés** p143
Hotels p125	**Bars & Pubs** p164

PRENZLAUER BERG

Once a grey, depressing working-class district, in the last two decades Prenzlauerberg has had its façades renovated, its streets cleaned, and its buildings newly inhabited by everyone from Russian artists to office workers. Galleries and cafés have sprouted, and century-old buildings have finally had central heating and bathrooms installed. Alternative types might feel the district has lost its edge, but, for many Berliners, there's no area cooler part of town.

Laid out at the turn of the 20th century, Prenzlauer Berg seems to have had more than its fair share of visionary social planners. It has wider streets and pavements, giving the area a distinctive, open look. Although a few buildings still await restoration, the newly scrubbed and painted streets give the impression of a 19th-century boulevard.

The district's focal point is pretty **Kollwitzplatz**. The square is lined with bars, cafés and restaurants, and hosts an organic market (*see p175*) on Thursday and Saturday. Knaackstrasse, heading south-east from Kollwitzplatz, brings you to one of the district's main landmarks, the **Wasserturm**. This water

tower, constructed by English architect Henry Gill in 1852-75, provided running water for the first time in Germany. During the war, the Nazis used its basement as a prison and torture chamber. A plaque commemorates their victims; the tower has been converted into apartments.

Opposite the Wasserturm on Rykestrasse is the **Synagoge Rykestrasse**, a neo-Romanesque turn-of-the-20th-century structure that was badly damaged during Kristallnacht in 1938. After renovation in 1953, it was the only working synagogue in old East Berlin. Now it stands peacefully in gentrified surrounds. Nearby, to the south-west of Kollwitzplatz, is the **Jüdischer Friedhof** (Jewish Cemetery), Berlin's oldest, and fairly gloomy due to its closely packed stones and canopy of trees. If you want to know more about the district's history, look in at the **Prenzlauer Berg Museum** (*see p74*).

Moving on clockwise to the other side of Kollwitzplatz, Knaackstrasse extends north-west to the vast complex of the **Kulturbrauerei** (*see p242*), an old brewery that now houses a concert space, galleries, artists' studios, a market and cinema. South-west from here, the area around Kastanienallee has plenty of good bars, shops and restaurants. And to the north-east, the so-called 'LSD' area around Lychener Strasse, Stargarder Strasse and Dunckerstrasse, leading up to Helmholzplatz, is another hot spot.

East of here, on the other side of Prenzlauer Allee, is **Ernst-Thälmann-Park**, named after the leader of the pre-1933 German Communist Party. In its north-west corner stands the **Zeiss-Grossplanetarium** (*see right*), a fantastic DDR space that once celebrated Soviet cosmonauts and still runs programmes on space. Over on the

Greifswalder Strasse side of the park, just north of the Danziger Strasse corner, is a giant statue of Ernst Thälmann himself, raising a Communist fist – one of Berlin's few remaining socialist-realist monuments.

FREE Prenzlauer Berg Museum
Prenzlauer Allee 227 (902 953 917). U2 Senefelderplatz/M2 Knaackstrasse. **Open** 10am-6pm Mon-Fri. **Admission** free. **Map** p319/p328 P4.

Walk The Wall Remembered

Once an iconic barrier between Cold War enemies, little of the Wall remains today.

Most of the Berlin Wall was demolished between June and November 1990. What had become the symbol of the inhumanity of the East German regime was prosaically crushed and re-used for road-fill.

This walk sets out to trace the course of a small stretch of the Wall on the northern border of Mitte. Along the way you can see some of the remnants – including the restored segment at the **Gedenkstätte Berliner Mauer** (*see p99*) – and gain an impression of how brutally the border carved its way through the city.

The starting point is Berlin's central station – **Hauptbahnhof**, in former West Berlin. Exit the station into Invalidenstrasse, turning right along the street. Continue eastwards, passing on your left a Wilhelmine building, now a regional court, and the railway station turned art gallery, **Hamburger Bahnhof – Museum für Gegenwart** (*see p67*).

A little further on is the **Sandkrugbrücke**, located on a former border crossing into East Berlin. A stone by the bridge commemorates Günter Litfin, the first person to be shot dead attempting to escape to West Berlin (in 1961). The Invalidenhaus on the eastern side long predates the Cold War. Built in 1747 to house disabled soldiers, it was used in East German times as a hospital, ministry of health and Supreme Court. Today it houses the **Bundesministerium für Wirtschat und Arbeit** (Federal Ministry of Economics and Labour). Keeping this complex on your right, turn down the canalside promenade, continuing along until you get to the **Invalidenfriedhof**.

The Wall once ran straight through this graveyard – and a section remains. Headstones of the graves in the 'death strip' were removed so as not to impair the sightlines of border guards. The graveyard

is a fascinating microcosm of Berlin history. Metres from the splendid 19th-century tombs of Prussian generals, there is a plaque commemorating members of the anti-Hitler resistance. Victims of air raids and the Battle of Berlin are buried in an adjacent mass grave. And it was here in 1962 that West Berlin police shot dead an East Berlin border guard to save a 15-year-old boy who was in the process of escaping.

Just outside the graveyard is a former **watchtower** improbably nestling in front of a new apartment building at the corner of Kieler Strasse. It's closed in winter, but sometimes you can look inside the observation post in summer.

Between here and the corner of Chausseestrasse there are few traces left of the Wall, which ran roughly parallel to the canal before veering right, close to the present helipad. At the end of Boyenstrasse, pavement markings indicating the Wall's former course briefly appear before vanishing under the new corner building.

Looking down Chausseestrasse, note the line of powerful street lights indicating the site of another checkpoint. The **Liesenstrasse Friedhof** is the graveyard where 19th-century writer Theodor Fontane is buried. It was also part of East Berlin's border strip. A short section of the Wall appears before the railway bridge at the junction with Gartenstrasse.

The last leg of the walk takes you up Bernauer Strasse. Desperate scenes took place here in August 1961 as people jumped – three of them to their deaths – from the windows of houses that then stood on the street's eastern side. The buildings were in East Berlin, but the pavement before their doors was in the West. The iconic photo of a border guard leaping over barbed wire into the West was snapped days earlier at the street's northern end.

SIGHTS

A small but interesting permanent exhibit on the history and culture of the district – lots of old photos – with temporary exhibitions too.

Zeiss-Grossplanetarium
Prenzlauer Allee 80 (4218 4512/www.sdtb.de).
S41, S42 S8, S85 Prenzlauer Allee. **Open** 9am-noon, 1-5pm Tue-Thur; 9am-9.30pm Fri; 2.30-9pm Sat; 1.30am-5pm Sun. **Admission** €5; €4 reductions. **No credit cards. Map** p319/p328 Q2.

This vast planetarium was built in the 1980s. Though changing exhibitions are in German only, the shows in the auditorium are entertaining for all.

FRIEDRICHSHAIN

As Prenzlauer Berg and Mitte became gentrified, Berlin's bohemia edged south-east into Friedrichshain. Much of the area remains pretty bleak, dominated as it is by big Communist-era

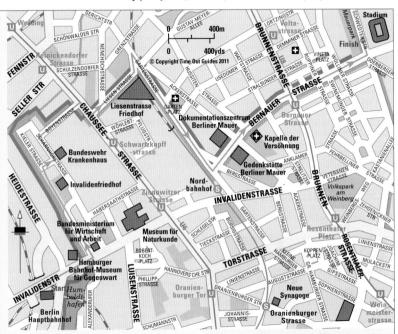

In the 1960s and '70s, a number of tunnels were dug from cellars in this area and dozens escaped this way.

At the **Gedenkstätte Berliner Mauer** you can gain an impression of what the border installation looked like – from below or above. The **Dokumentationszentrum** opposite, an information centre about the Wall, has a viewing platform.

A little further on is the oval **Kapelle der Versöhnung** (Chapel of Reconciliation), built on the site of an older church that was left stranded in the death strip and finally blown up in 1985 by the East German authorities.

The swathe of former borderland beyond lies largely derelict. Redevelopment has been slow because of legal challenges to its appropriation by the Federal Government.

The old patrol road remains in places, as do some of the border illuminations. Note, for instance, the lights on No.20 Swinemünder Strasse. The plasterwork on the building at the corner of Wolliner Strasse also clearly reveals where the eastern side of the Wall abutted existing apartment blocks.

Between Wolliner and Schwedter Strasse, you can still see the turning circle once used by West Berlin buses. On the eastern side, the tram still comes to an abrupt halt in Eberswalder Strasse. Even so, it's hard to believe that this whole area was once part of the world's most heavily fortified border. In the **Mauerpark**, where there is a popular Sunday flea market (*see p175*), you can have one last stroll along the Wall before heading to Eberswalder Strasse U-Bahn.

housing blocks – more than half of its buildings were destroyed during World War II – and slashed through by railway tracks. This was historically an industrial district, and much of its southern part bordering the Spree contains the remains of industrial buildings.

The best way to get a feeling for both Friedrichshain and the old DDR is to walk east from Alexanderplatz down Karl-Marx-Allee – a broad boulevard built in Stalinist style that is now home to the **Computerspiele Museum** (Computer Games Museum). It's from Lichtenberger Strasse onwards that the street truly shows its socialist past, with endless rows of Soviet-style apartment blocks, stretching beyond the twin towers of Frankfurter Tor.

To the south and east of Frankfurter Tor are the bars, clubs and restaurants of **Simon-Dach-Strasse** and the surrounding streets, plus a growing number of fashion and second-hand shops. There's an excellent weekly flea market at **Boxhagener Platz** (*see p175*). This is the lively centre of Berlin's new bohemia, slowly bulging eastwards in the direction of Ostkreuz. North of Frankfurter Allee is another concentration of hangouts in the Rigaer Strasse area.

To the south, on Mühlenstrasse (meaning Mill Street; the old mill is at No.8) along the north bank of the Spree is the **East Side Gallery**, a stretch of former Wall given over to international artists. The industrial buildings hereabouts have been renovated and rechristened **Oberbaum City**, and are now home to loft spaces, offices and studios. Both Universal Music and MTV-Europe have moved their German headquarters here and development of the waterfront continues. This is also now Berlin's main clubbing area, with clubs occupying a variety of post-industrial spaces.

At the district's far north-west corner is the **Volkspark Friedrichshain**. This huge park is scattered with socialist realist art, and has an open-air stage, a fountain of fairy-tale characters and the popular **Café Schönbrunn** (*see p146*). Graves of fighters who fell in March 1848 in the battle for German unity are here too. It's a popular gay cruising zone too.

Computerspiele Museum

Karl-Marx-Allee 93A (6098 8577, www. computerspielemuseum.de). U5 Weberwiese. **Open** 10am-8pm Mon, Wed-Sun. **Admission** €8; €5 reductions. **Map** p325 R6

Bearpit Karaoke

Berliners sing their hearts out.

The place to be in Berlin on a Sunday is the Mauerpark, a scrappy bit of land where the Wall's death strip used to run. During the week, there is not much to see here, but on Sundays the place springs into life. There's a buzzing flea market, dozens of food stalls and impromptu jam sessions from all manner of bands. But the real highlight takes place in the old amphitheatre in the middle of the park: Bearpit Karaoke.

As the name suggests, it's not for the faint-hearted. The set-up is as follows: Irishman Joe Hatchiban rocks up each Sunday at around 3pm on a bike with a trailer-mounted sound system and a laptop filled with backing tracks. Brave singers are then invited to step on to the stage and perform. Joe has a veto if their chosen song doesn't take his fancy.

Some crooners, like the wildly bearded Detlef, are regulars – he tends to shuffle on stage laden down with mysteriously full carrier bags and launch into a German version of 'My Way'. But everybody's welcome. You might get primary-school-aged sisters singing Mariah Carey, a Japanese tourist wailing along to LeAnn Rimes or a drunk group on a hen night murdering 'It's Raining Men'. Meanwhile, enterprising hawkers clamber up and down the stands selling cold beers. Sometimes the crowd – often over a thousand strong – sings and claps along. Other times, they are booing before the chorus. If things aren't going well, Joe suggests ways of bringing a performance back from the brink, whether it's ripping off an item of clothing or attempting the caterpillar. The fun continues until the speakers run out of batteries – usually at 7pm or thereabouts.

Bearpit Karaoke runs most Sundays from 3pm in spring, summer and autumn (weather permitting). See www.bearpitkaraoke.com.

Kreuzberg & Schöneberg

Once Cold War border territory, now gentrified but still alternative.

During the Cold War, Kreuzberg was the end of the Free World. Hemmed in by the Wall on its northern and eastern borders, rents collapsed and so did the houses. The only people who lived there were immigrants, artists and agitators – especially idealistic young West Germans who took advantage of a loophole that excused anyone in the 'island' of West Berlin from military service. More than two decades later, the district has been almost completely gentrified, yet Kreuzberg has retained its role as the centre of alternative politics and lifestyle. It is also still home to much of Berlin's Turkish community, as well as the Jewish Museum, and the area around Schlesisches Tor is the city's latest clubbing nexus.

Map pp322-323, p327

Hotels p126

Restaurants & Cafés p148

Bars & Pubs p170

To Kreuzberg's west lies the wealthier, largely residential Schöneberg. Berlin's long established gay scene is focused in its northern reaches, where a cluster of high-profile galleries have also recently set up shop, fleeing the high prices and commercialisation of Mitte.

KREUZBERG

The ornate **Oberbaumbrücke**, renovated in the 1990s by Santiago Calatrava, is a road bridge crossing the Spree to connect Kreuzberg with Friedrichshain. During the Cold War, it was a more serious crossing place: a border post and spy-exchange venue between East and West Berlin. Kreuzberg, too, is divided quite firmly into two halves according to its old postcodes – Kreuzberg 36 is the eastern part, which is scruffy and hip, great for a night out. Kreuzberg 61 is the west: quieter, prettier, duller after dark but lovely during the day.

East Kreuzberg

In the 1970s and '80s, the eastern half of Kreuzberg north of the Landwehrkanal was right at the edge of inner West Berlin. Enclosed on

two sides by the Wall, on a third by the canal, and mostly ignored by the rest of the city, its decaying tenements came to house Berlin's biggest, and most militant, squat community. The area was full of punky left-wing youths on a draft-dodging mission and Turks who came here because the rents were cheap and people mostly left them alone.

No area of West Berlin has changed so much since the fall of the Wall. This once-isolated pocket found itself recast as desirable real estate. Much of the alternative art scene shifted north to Mitte, and even the May Day Riots – long an annual Kreuzberg tradition – began taking place in Prenzlauer Berg. But gentrification was slow to take off in this end of Kreuzberg, unlike in Prenzlauer Berg, and now the riots have moved back (*see p80* **Inside Track**).

Kreuzberg has regained some of its appeal for young bohemia, and enough of the anarchistic old guard stayed behind to ensure that the area retains a distinct atmosphere. It's an earthy kind of place, full of cafés, bars and clubs, dotted with independent cinemas, and is an important nexus for the city's gay community.

Oranienstrasse is the area's main drag, filled with bars and clubs, and is also home to the quirky **Museum der Dinge**. In recent years, the hideous pre-fab development immediately to the north of Kotbusser Tor u-bahn – Kotti for short – has turned from nighttime no-go area into one of Berlin's most popular nightspots and is home to bars including Möbelölfer, Monarch and the Paloma Bar, as well as the clubs Festsaal Kreuzberg and West Germany. This scruffy area is also the centre of Turkish Berlin (*see right* **Turkish Berlin**) and bustles with kebab shops and Anatolian travel agents.

Rather more gentle these days is **Wiener Strasse**, running alongside the old Görlitzer Bahnhof, where more bars and cafés await. A couple of blocks further south lies the chi-chi **Paul-Linke-Ufer**, a canal-side street lined with smart cafes and restaurants and some stunning houses.

The U1 line runs overhead through the neighbourhood along the middle of **Skalitzer Strasse**. The onion-domed Schlesisches Tor station was once the end of the line, but these days the train continues one more stop across the Spree to Warschauer Strasse. You can also walk across the Oberbaumbrücke into Friedrichshain and the post-industrial nightlife district around Mühlenstrasse. But traffic is also coming the other way. Courtesy of riverside development on the Spree and of an overspill from Friedrichshain, the area around Schlesisches Tor station and along Schlesische Strasse and over the canal towards the next borough of Treptow is Berlin's newest hotspot. Sometimes called the Wrangelkiez, the constantly buzzing area has become such a tourist draw that local residents held a crisis meeting in 2011 complaining about noise.

Museum der Dinge

Oranienstrasse 25 (9210 6311, www.museum derdinge.de). U1, U8 Kottbusser Tor. **Open** noon-7pm Mon, Fri-Sun. **Admission** (*see €4; €2 reductions. **No credit cards. Map** p323 P9.
On the top floor of a typical Kreuzberg apartment block, the 'Museum of Things' contains every kind of small object you could imagine in modern design from the 19th century onwards – from hairbrushes and fondue sets to beach souvenirs and Nazi memorabilia. It's not a musty collection, but a sleek, minimalist room organised by themes such as 'yellow and black' or 'functional vs kitsch', rather than by era or type, so that the 'things' appear in new contexts. It can get a little confused at times, which is

hardly surprising with 20,000 objects, but this is a fascinating diversion and there's a great shop too.

South-west Kreuzberg

The more sedate southern and western part of Kreuzberg contains some of the most picturesque corners of West Berlin, including the 'Cross Hill' ('Kreuzberg') in Viktoriapark after which the borough is named.

Viktoriapark is the natural way to enter the area. In summer it has a cheery, landscaped waterfall cascading down the Kreuzberg, and paths wind their way to the summit, where Schinkel's 1821 monument commemorates victories in the Napoleonic Wars – many of the streets nearby are named after battles and generals of that era. From this commanding view over a mainly flat city, the landmarks of both east and west spread out before you: Friedrichstrasse is dead ahead, the Europa-Center off to the left, the Potsdamer Platz high-rises in between, the Fernsehturm over to the right. The view is clearer in winter, when the trees are bare.

Back on ground level, the streets north of the park lead to one of Berlin's most picturesque courtyard complexes. **Riehmers Hofgarten** is cobbled, closed to traffic and often used as a film location for its 19th-century feel. It's also home to one of Berlin's nicest small hotels, the Hotel Riehmers Hofgarten (*see p126*).

Around the corner on Mehringdamm is the **Schwules Museum** (Gay Museum; *see right*). **Bergmannstrasse**, which runs east from here, is the main hub of local activity. Bucking the tendency for everything to move eastwards, this street of cafés, junk shops, bookstores and record shops is livelier than ever by day, although the area is relatively lacklustre at night time. It leads down to **Marheinekeplatz**, where the old Markthalle has recently been revamped as a sort of small mall full of speciality food stalls. **Zossener Strasse**, north from here, also bustles.

Bergmannstrasse continues east past a large cemetery to Südstern. Here is the entrance to the **Volkspark Hasenheide**, the other of the neighbourhood's large parks, with another good view from atop the Rixdorfer Höhe. The streets just south of Bergmannstrasse are like another movie set. Many buildings survived wartime bombing and the area around **Chamissoplatz** has been immaculately restored. The cobbled streets are lined with houses still sporting their Prussian façades and illuminated by gaslight at night.

South of here, just across the border into the borough of the same name, stands the enormous **Flughafen Tempelhof**. Once the central airport for the city, it opened in the 1920s and was later greatly expanded by the Nazis. It's the largest building in Berlin and one of the largest in the world.

Tempelhof Airport was where Lufthansa started life, but its place in the city's affections was cemented during the airlift of 1948-9, when it served as the base for the American and British 'raisin-bombers', which brought supplies to the blockaded city and tossed sweets and raisins to waiting kids. The monument forking towards the sky on Platz der Luftbrücke commemorates those who flew these missions. In 2010, it was turned into a ginormous public park, retaining the terminal buildings and runway (*see p53* Grounded for Good).

Across Columbiadamm from the airport are the **Columbiahalle** and **Columbiaclub** (or C-Club; for both, *see p241*) concert venues. The latter was built by the US Air Force as a cinema – a classic example of 1950s cinema architecture.

Schwules Museum

Mehringdamm 61 (6959 9050, www.schwules museum.de). U6, U7 Mehringdamm. **Open** 2-6pm Mon, Wed-Fri, Sun; 2-7pm Sat. **Admission** €5; €3 reductions. **No credit cards. Map** p322 M10.

The Turkish Capital

From Gastarbeiter to German citizens.

Turkish food is a Berlin staple, but few realise that the doner kebab is no oriental import. It was actually invented in Kreuzberg, in 1971, by one Mehmet Aygun, today proprietor of the **Hasir** (*see p149*) restaurant chain. And Turkish culture stretches beyond street food. Berlin is home to the world's largest Turkish community outside Turkey, with hubs in Kreuzberg and the increasingly fashionable Neukölln, where one in every three residents is of Turkish origin.

The meeting of cultures has had a difficult history. The quick flow of immigration began in 1961 as a direct consequence of the Berlin Wall. With East German workers cut off from jobs in the West, thousands of *Gastarbeiter* ('guest workers') were recruited from Turkey to provide new cheap labour, and crammed together in purpose-built blocks.

The West German authorities proved ungracious hosts. The 'guest workers' were considered no more than a temporary necessity, and the Nationality Act (or 'Blood Law') of 1913, according to which German citizenship was based on heredity, was rigorously upheld. No person born of Turkish parents could be granted a German passport.

The Turkish community thus remained apart from mainstream society. As recently as 2004, a report found that up to 60 per cent of children in Kreuzberg nursery schools couldn't speak a single word of German. Popular antagonism peaked in 1990, when many feared that large numbers of foreign settlers would destabilise Germany's national identity and hinder a successful reunification. Then-Chancellor Helmut Kohl declared that

Germany was 'not a land of immigration' – dissing the nine per cent of the population who had been born abroad.

But attitudes have softened. The basis of nationality on blood has come to be seen as inappropriate for a Germany that wants to transcend the less savoury aspects of its history. Since 2001, a new law grants citizenship to any child born on German soil, provided their parents have been legally resident for at least eight years.

In Kreuzberg, at least, there's a genuine desire for multiculturalism. Turkish families, living side by side with punks and squatters, have developed into a uniquely indigenous community and culture. The sound of *Turkendeutsche*, the hybrid language of the immigrant population, fills the air around Oranienstrasse, while Turkish-German rappers like Cartel and Azziza-A spit lyrics on bar stereos. The weekly **Turkischer Markt** (*see p177*) on the Maybachufer showcases the Turks' more traditional side, while Turkish gay nights at **SO36** (*see p224*) reveal a corresponding cosmopolitanism. Berlin's Turkish football club, Türkiyemspor, is fêted as a model of integration.

SIGHTS

SIGHTS

The Gay Museum, opened in 1985, is still the only one in the world dedicated to homosexual life. The museum, its library and archives are staffed by volunteers and function thanks to private donations and bequests (such as the archive of DDR sex scientist Rudolf Klimmer). On the ground floor is the actual museum, housing permanent and temporary exhibitions. On the third floor, the library and archives house around 8,000 books (around 500 in English), 3,000 international periodicals, photos, posters, plus TV, film and audio footage, all available for lending.

North-west Kreuzberg

The north-west portion of Kreuzberg, bordering Mitte, is not the prettiest, but it's where you will find most of the area's museums and tourist sights. The most prominent is the extraordinary **Jüdisches Museum** (*see p82*) on Lindenstrasse, an example of architecture at its most cerebral, and a powerful sensory experience. Behind it, on Alte Jakobstrasse, is the **Berlinische Galerie**, the home of Berlin's permanent collection of art, photography and architecture. West of here, close to the Landwehrkanal, is the enjoyable **Deutsches Technikmuseum Berlin** (German Museum of Technology; *see p81*).

Over the canal to the north is the site of Anhalter Bahnhof, once the city's biggest and busiest railway station. Only a tiny piece of façade remains, preserved in its bombed state near the S-Bahn station that bears its name. The **Gruselkabinett** ('Chamber of Horrors'; *see right*) occupies an old air-raid shelter on the Schöneberger Strasse side of the area where platforms and tracks once stood.

On Stresemannstrasse, the Bauhaus-designed **Europahaus** was heavily bombed during World War II, but the lower storeys remain. Nearby, on the north side of the street, Berlin's parliament, the **Abgeordnetenhaus von Berlin** (Berlin House of Representatives), meets in what was formerly the Prussian parliament. Its surprisingly good canteen (*see p149*) is open to the public when parliament is not sitting. Dating from the 1890s, the building was renovated in the early 1990s. Opposite stands

the **Martin-Gropius-Bau** (*see p82*), a venue for major art shows. The building was modelled on London's South Kensington museums – the figures of craftspeople on the external reliefs betray its origins as an applied arts museum.

Next to it is a mostly deserted block that once held the Prinz Albrecht Palais, which the Gestapo took over as its headquarters. In the basement's 39 cells, political prisoners were held, interrogated and tortured. The land was flattened after the war. In 1985, during an acrimonious debate over the design of a memorial to be placed here, a group of citizens staged a symbolic 'excavation'. To their surprise, they hit the Gestapo's basement, and plans were then made to reclaim the site. Today there is an open-air exhibition about the rise of National Socialism and a new documentation centre, the **Topographie des Terrors** (*see p83*) . Along the site's northern boundary on Niederkirchnerstrasse is one of the few remaining stretches of the Berlin Wall, pitted and threadbare after thousands of 1990 souvenir-hunters pecked away at it with hammers and chisels. The stark building opposite is Hermann Göring's fortress-like Luftfahrministerium (Air Ministry), a rare relic of the Nazi past, which survived the allies' bombs and is now the Federal Finance Ministry.

Walking east, Niederkirchnerstrasse turns into Zimmer Strasse, home to the new Stasi education centre (**Stasi Bildungszentrum**, *see p82*) and, at number 19A, an extremely good ice cream and waffle shop, the aptly named Kalter Krieg (Cold War).

Zimmer Strasse intersects Friedrichstrasse, where Checkpoint Charlie once stood and where the **Haus am Checkpoint Charlie** (*see p82*) documents the history of the Wall. Most of the space where the border post once stood has been claimed by new buildings, though there is an outdoor exhibition in the dead space north of the old checkpoint. The actual site of the borderline is memorialised by Frank Thiel's photographic portraits of an American and a Soviet soldier. The small white building that served as gateway between East and West is now in the **Alliierten Museum** (*see p103*) – the one in the middle of the street is a replica.

Just south of Friedrichstrasse is Kochstrasse. In April 2008, the eastern stretch, with the towering headquarters of right-wing media magnate Axel Springer, was renamed Rudi-Dutschke-Strasse in honour of one of Germany's most famous student revolutionaries. Forty years ago, Dutschke was victim of an attempted assassination, shot in the head and chest after various Springer publications had called on their readers to 'eliminate the trouble-makers' and 'stop the terror of the young reds'. He later died of

---

INSIDE TRACK IT'S A RIOT

May Day Riots have been an annual event since 1987, when *Autonomen* of the radical left engaged in clashes with police. Things have got a bit quieter in recent years, but there's usually some action around Kottbusser Tor in Kreuzberg on 1 May.

Haus am Checkpoint Charlie.
See p82.

The Berlinische Galerie collects art from Berlin dating from 1870 to the present day – with both a local and international focus. Founded in 1975, the State Museum reopened in its own building close to the Jewish Museum in 2004, moving into a spacious industrial hall that has been rebuilt to provide 4,600 square metres of exhibition space. Its collections include Dada Berlin, the Neue Sachlichkeit (New Objectivity) and the Eastern European avant-garde. The art of the divided and reunified city of Berlin provides another focus.

▶ *Visitors pay the reduced price if they have a ticket to the Jüdisches Museum, see p82, from the same day or either of the two previous days.*

Deutsches Technikmuseum Berlin
Trebbiner Strasse 9 (902 540, www.sdtb.de). U1, U7 Möckernbrücke. **Open** 9am-5.30pm Tue-Fri; 10am-6pm Sat, Sun. **Admission** €6; €3.50 reductions. **Map** p322 L9.

Opened in 1982 in the former goods depot of the Anhalter Bahnhof, the German Museum of Technology is an eclectic, eccentric collection of new and antique industrial artefacts. The rail exhibits have pride of place, with the station sheds providing an ideal setting for locomotives and rolling stock from 1835 to the present. Other exhibits focus on the industrial revolution; street, rail, water and air traffic; computer technology and printing technology. Behind the main complex is an open-air section with two functioning windmills and a smithy. Oddities, such as vacuum cleaners from the 1920s, make this a fun place for implement enthusiasts. The nautical wing has vessels and displays on inland waterways and international shipping, while another wing covers aviation and space travel. There are models and original designs and electronic information points offering commentaries in English on subjects from the international slave trade to the mechanics of a space station. The Spectrum annex, at Möckernstrasse 26, houses over 200 interactive devices and experiments.

Gruselkabinett
Schöneberger Strasse 23A (2655 5546, www.gruselkabinett.net). S1, S2 Anhalter Bahnhof. **Open** 10am-3pm Mon; 10am-7pm on public holidays falling on a Monday, 10am-5pm Tue, Thur, Fri, noon-8pm Sat 10am-7pm Tue, Thur, Sun; 10am-8pm Fri; noon-8pm Sat. **Admission** €9,50; €5,50-€6,50 reductions. **No credit cards. Map** p322 L8.

This chamber of horrors is housed in the city's only visitable World War II air-raid shelter. Built in 1943, the five-level bunker was part of an underground network connecting various similar concrete structures throughout Berlin, and today houses both the Gruselkabinett and an exhibit on the bunker itself. The 'horrors' begin at ground level with an exhibit on medieval medicine (mechanical figures amputate a leg to the sound of canned screaming). Elsewhere, there's a patented coffin designed to advertise your

complications arising from the injuries. In April 1968, Dutschke's supporters demonstrated outside the Springer building, claiming the publisher was partially responsible for the shooting. The recent name change – in part the result of vigorous campaigning by the *taz*, the left-wing national daily, which is also headquartered on Rudi-Dutschke-Strasse – was bitterly opposed by Springer and local conservatives. There aren't too many of those in Kreuzberg, though, and when it came to a referendum, Kreuzbergers cheerfully voted in favour of the new name. The bust of George Bush Snr, which sits alongside Helmut Kohl and Michail Gorbachev outside the Springer building, provides an amusing contrast to the street's hell-raising namesake.

Berlin Hi-Flyer
Corner of Wilhelmstrasse and Zimmerstrasse (2266 78811, www.air-service-berlin.de). U6 Kochstrasse. **Open** Apr-Oct 10am-10pm daily. *Nov-Mar* 11am-6pm daily. **Admission** €19; €6-€13 reductions. **Map** p322/p327 M8.

This helium balloon has hovered 150 metres (490ft) above Berlin in various guises since 1999 and, somewhat bewilderingly, is now one of the city's top tourist attractions – as well as one of its most expensive. You do get a lovely view from up there, but given that you get almost as good a panorama from the dome of the (free) Reichstag, you might wish to give this one a miss.

Berlinische Galerie
Alte Jakobstrasse 124-128 (7890 2600, www. berlinischegalerie.de). U6 Kochstrasse. **Open** 10am-6pm Mon, Wed-Sun. **Admission** €8; €5 reductions; free under-18s. **Map** p323 N8.

SIGHTS

predicament should you be buried alive. Upstairs is scarier: a musty labyrinth with a simulated cemetery, strange cloaked figures, spooky sounds and a few surprises. Kids love it, but not those under ten.

Haus am Checkpoint Charlie
Friedrichstrasse 43-45 (253 7250, www.mauer museum.de). U6 Kochstrasse. **Open** 9am-10pm daily. **Admission** €12,50; €9,50 reductions. **Map** p322/p327 M8.

A little tacky, but essential for anyone interested in the Wall and the Cold War. This private museum opened not long after the DDR erected the Berlin Wall in 1961 with the purpose of documenting the events that were taking place. The exhibition charts the history of the Wall, and gives details of the ingenious and hair-raising ways people escaped from the DDR – as well as exhibiting some of the actual contraptions that were used, such as a home-made hot-air balloon. *Photo p81.*

★ Jüdisches Museum
Lindenstrasse 9-14 (2599 3300, guided tours 2599 3305, www.juedisches-museum-berlin.de). U1, U6 Hallesches Tor. **Open** 10am-10pm Mon; 10am-8pm Tue-Sun. **Admission** €5; €2.50 reductions. **Map** p323 N8.

The idea of a Jewish museum in Berlin was first mooted in 1971, the 300th birthday of the city's Jewish community. In 1975, an association was formed to acquire materials for display; in 1989, a competition was held to design an extension to house them. Daniel Libeskind emerged as the winner, the foundation stone was laid in 1992 and the permanent exhibition finally opened in 2001. The ground plan of Libeskind's remarkable building is in part based on an exploded Star of David, in part on lines drawn between the site and former addresses of figures in Berlin's Jewish history, such as Mies van der Rohe, Arnold Schönberg and Walter Benjamin. The entrance is via a tunnel from the Kollegienhaus next door. The underground geometry is startlingly independent of the above-ground building. One passage leads to the exhibition halls, two others intersect en route to the Holocaust Tower and the ETA Hoffmann Garden, a grid of 49 columns, tilted to disorientate. Throughout, diagonals and parallels carve out surprising spaces, while windows slash through the structure and its zinc cladding like the knife-wounds of history. And then there are the 'voids' cutting through the layout, negative spaces that stand for the emptiness left by the destruction of German Jewish culture.

The permanent exhibition struggles in places with such powerful surroundings. What makes the exhibit engaging is its focus on the personal: it tells the stories of prominent Jews, what they contributed to their community and to the cultural and economic life of Berlin and Germany. After centuries of prejudice and pogroms, the outlook for German Jews seemed to be brightening. Then came the Holocaust. The emotional impact of countless stories of the eminent and ordinary, and the fate that almost all shared, is hard to convey adequately in print. The museum is a must-see, but expect long queues and big crowds. Last entrance is one hour before closing.

▶ *Visitors pay the reduced price if they have a ticket to the Berlinische Galerie, see p81, from the same day or either of the two previous days.*

Martin-Gropius-Bau
Niederkirchnerstrasse 7 (3025 4860, www.gropius bau.de). S1, S2, S26 Anhalter Bahnhof. **Open** 10am-8pm Mon, Wed-Sun. **Admission** varies. **Credit** AmEx, MC, V. **Map** p322/p327 L8.

Cosying up to where the Wall once stood (there is still a short, pitted stretch running along the south side of nearby Niederkirchnerstrasse), the Martin-Gropius-Bau is named after its architect, uncle of the more famous Walter. Built in 1881, it has been renovated and serves as a venue for an assortment of large-scale art exhibitions and themed shows.

FREE ★ Stasi Bildungszentrum
Zimmerstrasse 90/91 (2324 7951, www.bstu. bund.de). U6 Kochstrasse. **Open** 10am-6pm Mon-Sat. **Admission** free. **Map** p322/p327 M8

This state-run education centre opened in 2011 and gives a good overview of how the nefarious activities of the East German secret police affected ordinary people's lives. The exhibition tells the stories of six victims, including Hermann Josef Flade, who was caught distributing leaflets protesting against the undemocratic elections in the GDR at the age of 18 and found himself facing a death sentence.

Jüdisches Museum.

FREE ★ **Topographie des Terrors**
Niederkirchnerstrasse 8 (2545 0950, www.
topographie.de). S1, S2, S25 Anhalter Bahnhof;
U6 Kochstrasse. **Open** *Outside exhibition* 10am-
dusk daily. *Inside exhibition* 10am-8pm daily.
Admission free. **Map** p322/p327 M8.
Essentially a piece of waste ground that was once the
site of the Prinz Albrecht Palais, headquarters of the
Gestapo, and the Hotel Prinz Albrecht, which housed
offices of the Reich SS leadership. This was the centre
of the Nazi police state apparatus and it was from
here that the Holocaust was directed, and the
Germanisation of the east dreamt up. There is an outdoor exhibition that gives a pretty good chronology
of Hitler's rise to power, as well as a new indoor documentation centre. A surviving segment of the Berlin
Wall runs along the site's northern boundary.

SCHÖNEBERG

Geographically and atmospherically, Schöneberg
lies between Kreuzberg and Charlottenburg. It's
a diverse and vibrant part of town, mostly built
in the late 19th century. Though largely devoid
of conventional sights, Schöneberg is rich in
reminders of Berlin's recent history.

Schöneberg means 'beautiful hill' – oddly,
because the borough is flat. It does have an
'island', though: the triangular **Schöneberger
Insel**, carved out by the two broad railway
cuttings that carry S-Bahn line 1 and lines 2
and 26, with an elevated stretch of lines S41,
42 and 45 providing the southern boundary. In
the 1930s, the area was known as Rote Insel
('Red Island'), because, socialistically inclined
and easy to defend as it was approached mostly
over a handful of bridges, it was one of the last
bits of Berlin to resist Nazification. There's a
fine view from Monumentenbrücke, on the east
side of the island going towards Kreuzberg's
Viktoriapark. On the north-west edge of the
island is **St Matthäus-Kirchhof**, a graveyard
and last resting place of the Brothers Grimm.

West along Langenscheidtstrasse leads you
towards the Kleistpark. Here, Schöneberg's
main street is called Hauptstrasse to the south
and Potsdamer Strasse to the north. The latter
is now home to a cluster of galleries, such
as Arndt + Partner, Blain | Southern and
Klosterfelde (*see p219*). Hauptstrasse leads
south-west in the direction of Potsdam. David
Bowie and Iggy Pop once resided at No.155.
Further south, **Dominicuskirche** is one of
Berlin's few baroque churches.

North-west along Dominicusstrasse is
Rathaus Schöneberg, outside which John F
Kennedy made his famous 'Ich bin ein Berliner'
speech. The square now bears his name. This
was West Berlin's town hall during the Cold
War, and the place where mayor Walter
Momper welcomed East Berliners in 1989.

From here, Belziger Strasse leads back in
the direction of **Kleistpark**. The entrance to
Kleistpark from Potsdamer Strasse is an 18th-
century double colonnade, moved here from
near Alexanderplatz in 1910. The mansion in
the park was originally a law court, and during
the Cold War became headquarters for the
Allied Control Council. After the 1972 treaty
that formalised the separate status of East and
West Germany, the building stood virtually
unused. But there were occasional Allied
Council meetings, before which the Americans,
British and French would observe a ritual
pause, as if expecting the Soviet representative,
who had last attended in 1948, to show up. In
1990 a Soviet finally did wander in and the
Allies held a last meeting to formalise their
withdrawal from the city in 1994. This may be
the place where the Cold War officially ended.

On the north-west corner of Potsdamer
Strasse's intersection with Pallasstrasse stood
the Sportpalast, site of many Nazi rallies and
the scene of Goebbels' famous 'Total War'
speech of 18 February 1943. In its place stands
a shabby block of flats. One part of the complex
straddles Pallasstrasse and rests on the huge
concrete hulk of a Nazi air-raid shelter, which
planners were unable to destroy.

At the west end of Pallasstrasse stands
St-Matthias-Kirche. South from here,
Goltzstrasse is lined with cafés, bars and
interesting shops. To the north of the church is
Winterfeldtplatz, site of bustling Wednesday
and Saturday morning markets, engendering a
lively café life by day that turns into a lively
eating-out nexus by night.

Nollendorfplatz to the north is the hub
of Schöneberg's nightlife. The theatre on the
square has had many incarnations. In the
Weimar era it was home to experimental
director Erwin Piscator; under the Third Reich
Hitler came here to watch Zara Leander shows;
in the 1980s it was the infamous Metropol disco.

Outside Nollendorfplatz U-Bahn, the small
memorial to homosexuals killed in concentration
camps is a reminder of the area's history.
Christopher Isherwood chronicled Berlin from
his rooming house at Nollendorfstrasse 17;
Motzstrasse has been a major artery of Berlin's
gay life since the 1920s. Gay Schöneberg
continues around the corner and straddles
Martin-Luther-Strasse along Fuggerstrasse.

Schöneberg's most famous daughter is screen
icon Marlene Dietrich, buried just over the
district's southern boundary, in the Städtische
Friedhof III on Fehlerstrasse in Friedenau. Nico
grew up around here too, and launched her
career by hanging around long enough to be
'discovered' outside the KaDeWe department
store (*see p174*). She is buried at the Friedhof
Grunewald-Forst in Wilmersdorf.

SIGHTS

Tiergarten

Greenery, diplomacy and high culture.

Berlin's answer to Central Park lends its name to this upmarket district, which is home to dozens of embassies as well as the grand Reichstag parliament building. Tiergarten was once hemmed in on the east by the Wall, but these days it is right at the heart of things again, stretching from the futuristic Hauptbahnhof in the north right to the Zoo in the southeast. South of the park is Potsdamer Platz, Berlin's new commercial centre, as well as the museums and venues of the Kulturforum – including the world famous Philharmonie concert hall. Further south still, Potsdamer Strasse is experiencing something of a revival, as a score of galleries have relocated there in recent years, driven out of Mitte by sharply rising rents.

Map p318, p321,	Restaurants
p322, p327	& Cafés p153
Hotels p127	Bars & Pubs p170

THE PARK & THE REICHSTAG

A hunting ground for the Prussian electors since the 16th century, **Tiergarten** was opened to the public in the 18th century. It was badly damaged during World War II; in the desperate winter of 1945-46, almost all the surviving trees were cut down for firewood, and it wasn't until 1949 that Tiergarten started to recover. Today, though, joggers, nature lovers, gay cruisers and picnickers pour into the park in fine weather. There's no nicer place from which to appreciate it all than the gardens of the **Café am Neuen See** on Lichtensteinallee.

All roads entering the Tiergarten lead to the park's largest monument, the **Siegessäule** (Victory Column; *see p86*), which celebrates the last wars Germany managed to win. The park's main thoroughfare, Strasse des 17 Juni (the date of the East Berlin workers' strike of 1953), is one of the few pieces of Hitler's plan for 'Germania' that actually got built – a grand east-west axis, lined with Nazi lampposts and linking Unter den Linden to Neu-Westend. The Siegessäule was moved here from its original position in front of the Reichstag.

Towards the eastern end of Strasse des 17 Juni, just west of the Brandenburger Tor, stands the **Sowjetisches Ehrenmal** (Soviet

War Memorial). Once the only piece of Soviet property in West Berlin, it was built in 1945-46 out of granite and marble from the ruins of Hitler's Neue Reichskanzlei but posed a political problem. Standing in the British Zone, it was surrounded by a British military enclosure, which was in turn guarded by Berlin police – all to protect the monument and the two Soviet soldiers who stood guard. The tanks flanking it are said to have been the first two Soviet tanks into Berlin, but this is probably just myth.

At the north-eastern corner of the park stands the **Reichstag**. Described by Kaiser Wilhelm II as the 'Imperial Monkey House', it hasn't had a happy history: the scene of Weimar squabblings, it was then left as a burnt-out ruin during the Third Reich, regarded by the Red Army as its main prize, and then stranded for decades beside the Wall dividing the Deutsches Volk whose representatives it was intended to house. But in 1999, Lord Norman Foster's brilliant refitting of the building was unveiled. His crowning achievement is the glass cupola: a trip to the top should be a must-do on any visitor's agenda.

When the decision was made in 1991 to make Berlin the German capital, the area north of the Reichstag was picked as the central location for new government buildings. Designed by Axel

SIGHTS

Berlin Hauptbahnhof.

Schultes and Charlotte Frank, the immense Spreebogen complex, also known as the Band des Bundes, is built over a twist in the River Spree (*Bogen* means 'bend'). It crosses the river twice and the old East–West border once, symbolising the reunion of Berlin. The most notable new building is Schultes and Frank's **Bundeskanzleramt** (Federal Chancellery). Across the river to the north, meanwhile, stands the new **Berlin Hauptbahnhof**. Berlin never had a central station before. Now it has the biggest and most futuristic in Europe.

South of the Bundeskanzleramt's western end is the **Haus der Kulturen der Welt** (House of World Cultures), an impressive piece of modern architecture with a reflecting pool that contains a Henry Moore sculpture. Formerly known as the Kongresshalle and nicknamed the 'pregnant oyster', the HdKdW opened in 1957 and today hosts exhibits from cultures around the world.

Also on the park's northern boundary stands **Schloss Bellevue**, a minor palace from 1785 that's now the official residence of the German President. Across the river, a serpentine 718-apartment residence for Federal employees, nicknamed 'Die Schlange' (the Snake) winds across land formerly used as a goods yard. West of Schloss Bellevue is the **Englischer Garten**, laid out on the theory that the lack of revolutions in England was due to the abundance of green spaces.

Just north of here, the smaller branch of the **Akademie der Künste** (*see p238*) has a varied programme of arts events and classical concerts. The district between the Akademie and the loop of the Spree is known as the **Hansaviertel**, a post-war housing project designed by a who's who of architects as part of the 1957 Interbau Exhibition for the 'city of tomorrow'. It's of great interest to specialists, but others may see only an assortment of modernist slabs.

Haus der Kulturen der Welt

John-Foster-Dulles-Allee 10 (3978 7175, www.hkw.de). S5, S7, S9, S75 Bellevue/bus 100. **Open** 10am-7pm daily. **Admission** varies. **Map** p318 K6.

Set up in 1989 to promote art from developing countries, the 'House of World Cultures' mounts spectacular large-scale exhibitions on subjects such as contemporary Indian art, Bedouin culture and the Chinese avant-garde. Recent events have included a celebration of electronic music from around the globe, and a festival of new cinema from Africa; the programme also involves readings, lectures, discussions, concerts and dance. Housed in Hugh Stubbins' oyster-like building, erected in 1957 as America's contribution to the Interbau Exhibition, this is a unique Berlin cultural institution.

▶ *There's a decent café on the premises.*

★ FREE Reichstag

Platz der Republik (2270, www.bundestag.de). S1, S2, S25, U55 Brandenburger Tor/bus 100. **Open** 8am-midnight daily; last entry at 11pm. **Admission** free. **Map** p318/p327 L6.

The imposing Reichstag was controversial from the beginning. Architect Paul Wallot struggled to find a style that would symbolise German national identity at a time – 1884-94, shortly after Unification – when no such style or identity existed. It was burned on 17 February 1933; the Nazis blamed Dutchman Marius van der Lubbe, and used it as an excuse to suspend basic freedoms. But since its celebrated renovation by Lord Foster, the Reichstag has again housed the Bundestag (the Federal German parliament). Foster conceived it as a 'dialogue between old and new': graffiti scrawled by Russian soldiers in 1945 has been left on view, and there has been no attempt to deny the building's turbulent history.

No dome appeared on Foster's original plans, but the German government insisted upon one. Foster, in turn, insisted that unlike the structure's original dome (damaged in the war and demolished in the 1950s), the new dome must be open to visitors. A lift whisks you to the roof; from here, ramps lead to the top of the dome, which affords fine views of the city. At the centre is a funnel of mirrors, angled so as to shed light on the workings of democracy below but also lending an almost funhouse effect to the dome. An excellent free audioguide points out all the sur-

SIGHTS

SIGHTS

rounding landmarks. A trip to the top of this open, playful and defiantly democratic space is a must, but note that you can't just rock up any more: following a series of terrorist threats in autumn 2010, you must now book in advance by filling in an online form and suggesting three possible time slots at least three working days in advance: www.bundestag.de/besuche/kuppel.html.

Siegessäule

Strasse des 17 Juni (391 2961). S5, S7, S9, S75 Bellevue. **Open** *Summer* 9.30am-6.30pm Mon-Fri; 9.30am-7pm, Sat, Sun. *Winter* 9.30am-5.30pm Mon-Sun; **Admission** €3; €2 reductions, free under 5s. **No credit cards. Map** p321 H7.
Tiergarten's biggest monument was built in 1871-73 to commemorate Prussian campaigns against Denmark (1864), Austria (1866) and France (1870-71). Originally planted in front of the Reichstag, it was moved by Hitler to form a centrepiece for the East–West axis connecting Western Berlin with the palaces and ministries of Mitte. On top of the column is a gilded Goddess of Victory by Friedrich Drake; captured French cannons and cannonballs, sawn in half and gilded, decorate the column itself. It's 285 steps to the viewing platform.

SOUTH OF THE PARK

At the south-east corner of the Tiergarten is the reborn **Potsdamer Platz**, intended as the reunified city's new commercial centrepiece. In the 1920s, Potsdamer Platz was reckoned to be one of Europe's busiest squares. The first ever traffic lights stood here (a replica can be seen today on the south side of the square). Then, though, it was bombed flat in World War II; during the Cold War, it became a no-man's land bisected by the Wall. Fierce debate ensued over whether the redevelopment should adopt the typical scale of a 'European' city or go for an 'American' high-rise approach. The result was a compromise: medium-height development except on Potsdamer Platz itself, where high-rises up to 90 metres (295 feet) were allowed.

Opinions are mixed as to the success of the finished article. In the Cold War, the area was neither East nor West, which makes it sound like a good candidate for a unifying centre. But it's really an isolated island of redevelopment, not yet quite connected to any area around it and still neither one thing nor the other. Even so, it's beginning to feel worn in, a natural part of a long-disjointed urban landscape.

Helmut Jahn's soaring **Sony Center**, surprisingly light in steel and glass, contains the Forum, an urban entertainment complex that in turn holds the **CineStar** multiplex (*see p211*), the more offbeat **Arsenal** cinema (*see p210*) and the **Filmmuseum Berlin** (*see p90*). (There's another multiplex over the road in the Daimler quarter, the **CinemaxX**.) Served also by a clutch of new five-star hotels, including the **Ritz-Carlton** (*see p128*) and the **Grand Hyatt** (*see p127*), Potsdamer Platz is also now the main venue for the **Berlin International Film Festival** (*see p202*). But there's little to recommend in terms of eating, drinking or shopping. It's all franchise culture.

One of only two Potsdamer Platz buildings to survive World War II and the subsequent clearout was once here on the Sony site: the **Kaisersaal Café** from the old Grand Hotel Esplanade, a listed building. When plans for the area solidified, the café was found to be in a bad position, so the whole structure was moved 75 metres (246 feet) to its present location on the building's north side, where it's been integrated into the apartment complex on Bellevuestrasse.

The other major corporate presence at Potsdamer Platz is Daimler (formerly DaimlerChrysler), responsible for most of the development south of the Sony Center. One of the most admired of the area's new buildings is Hans Kollhof's triangular, brick-clad tower at Potsdamer Platz 1, which, together with the curved Deutsche Bahn tower over the road, forms the gateway to the area. It's the tallest building here; the **Panoramapunkt** platform up top (*see p91*) affords fine views.

A few doors down the road at Alte Potsdamer Strasse 5 is **Haus Huth**, the only other building in the area that survives from before World War II. For decades a lonely structure in the middle of overgrown wasteland, it now stands next to the three-storey Arkaden shopping mall. At the top is the **Daimler Contemporary** gallery, which exhibits works from the auto manufacturer's big-name art collection. The company has also positioned various pieces of contemporary sculpture around the quarter, including work by Jeff Koons, Robert Rauschenberg, Keith Haring and Nam June Paik. *See p88* **Walk**.

Immediately west of the Potsdamer Platz development is one of the city's major concentrations of museums, galleries and cultural institutions. Collectively known as the **Kulturforum** and built in anticipation of Reunification, it was based on the designs of Hans Scharoun (1946-57). Scharoun himself designed the **Staatsbibliotek** (State Library) and the gold **Philharmonie** (*see p238*), home to the Berlin Philharmonic. Adjacent is the **Musikinstrumentenmuseum** (Musical Instrument Museum; *see p91*).

One block to the west is a low-rise museum complex. Its biggest draw is the **Gemäldegalerie** (Picture Gallery; *see p90*), but the **Kunstgewerbemuseum** (Museum of Decorative Art; *see p91*) is also worth a peek. Here, too, is the **Kunstbibliotek** (Art Library), and a decent café and shop. Next door is the **Matthäuskirche** (Matthias Church) and, to the south, the bold glass cube of the **Neue Nationalgalerie** (New National Gallery; *see p91*).

Between the north flank of the Kulturforum and the south flank of Tiergarten runs **Tiergartenstrasse**, the main drag of Berlin's revived diplomatic quarter. Part of Albert Speer's plan for 'Germania', the original embassy buildings of Hitler's Axis allies were designed by German architects. Damaged by bombing, they were largely abandoned, and Tiergartenstrasse became an eerie walk past decaying grandeur. But with the land often still owned by the respective governments, embassies were reconstructed at their old addresses during the diplomatic relocation from Bonn, and this area is now embassy row again.

SIGHTS

Walk Berlin Revived

Once it was a no-man's land. Now it's at the heart of the city.

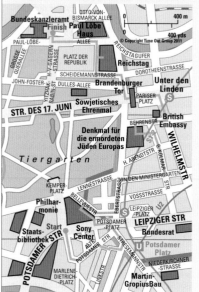

The area around Potsdamer Platz, the Brandenburg Gate and the Reichstag has received special attention in the binding together of the city's two halves. This walk highlights the dramatic changes in what was once a no-man's land.

The walk begins on the corner of Potsdamer Strasse and Eichhornstrasse, which feels like a border. To the west and south is the 1960s **Kulturforum**, home to a variety of cultural institutions that were placed on the edge of West Berlin in anticipation of Reunification. To the east is a new and much denser commercial quarter. Designed and built in the 1990s, it's generally known as **Potsdamer Platz** (*see p86*), although the actual Platz is three blocks. Here stands Keith Haring's sculpture *The Boxers*, part of Daimler Contemporary's collection of art. Comprised of two figures in primary blue and red, conjoined yet in conflict, it's appropriate for Berlin in general and this corner in particular.

From here, walk down Eichhornstrasse, with the **Grand Hyatt** (*see p127*) to your left. Perched on the shoulder of a building

ahead, you'll see a spaceship-like contraption, apparently scanning the streets below but actually another Daimler collection sculpture – Auk de Vries's *gelandet* ('landed'). At the point where this street opens into Marlene-Dietrich-Platz, in front of the Spielbank (casino), there's a third sculpture: Jeff Koons's *Balloon Flower*.

A couple of hundred metres along Alte Potsdamer Strasse on the right is the entrance to the **Arkaden** mall. **Haus Huth** (*see p87*), the old building next to it at No.5, was the only surviving pre-war structure this side of Potsdamer Strasse when Renzo Piano planned the 75,000-square-metre site now known as the Daimler Viertel (quarter) in the early 1990s. Slip through the passage between Haus Huth and the Arkaden, and you'll emerge into Fontaneplatz. The building to the right, with round towers inserted into its corners, is by Richard Rogers. And to the left stands Robert Rauschenberg's *Riding Bikes* – another Daimler-owned sculpture and, like the Haring piece, a symbol of two halves.

Bearing to the left will lead you into Potsdamer Platz itself. The green contraption by the junction is a replica of Europe's first traffic lights, erected here in 1924 when this was supposedly the world's busiest intersection. The borders of the British, American and Soviet occupation zones met at this point, meaning that even among the late 1940s ruins it remained a centre of commerce – no matter which direction the police approached, black market traders were able to escape into another zone. The Wall killed the area for several decades, but with grand new entrances to the sub-surface station and an assortment of high-rises – notably the brick-clad **Kollhoff Tower** and the rounded **Bahn-Tower** that flank Potsdamer Strasse, forming a gateway into Western Berlin – it once more feels like downtown. Ascend to the **Panoramapunkt** (*see p91*) for great views.

Cross Potsdamer Platz and duck left into Helmut Jahn's futuristic **Sony Center** (*see p86*), completely different from the more traditional cityscape of the Daimler Viertel. Taking the exit right of the Café Josty, you'll pass the relocated remains of the 19th-century **Grand Hotel Esplanade** (*see p128*).

The area north of the Sony Center is called the **Lenné Dreieck** (triangle). During the Cold War, this land was politically part of East Berlin but lay west of the Wall, and was left as overgrown wasteland. In 1988, it changed hands as part of an east–west agreement, but not before a squatter's camp had occupied it in order to protest against a planned new road. On the day it formally became West Berlin territory, police moved in to evict the squatters, 182 of whom used ladders to flee into the East. It was the single largest escape across the Wall and possibly the only one in an eastwards direction.

Turn right on Bellevuestrasse and left on Ebertstrasse, and you'll see the line of the Wall is marked by a double row of cobblestones. The buildings on the right

are embassies of the German Länder, constructed on land once occupied by Hitler's Reichskanzlerei. Turn right down In den Ministergarten and, at the junction with Gertrude-Kolmar-Strasse, you'll find an information board about the Führerbunker, which once lay underground here. Turning left along Gertrude-Kolmar-Strasse brings you to Peter Eisenmann's **Denkmal für die ermordeten Juden Europas** (see p59). Get lost among its 2,711 concrete columns, ending up in Behrenstrasse on the other side.

The massive new **US Embassy** is on the corner of Ebertstrasse and Behrenstrasse. Next to it is the anarchistic rear façade of Frank Gehry's **DZ Bank** building. Gehry had to play along with the Pariser Platz conformity rule on the front side, but uses the building's rear quite differently.

Turn left onto Wilhelmstrasse to admire Michael Wilford's much-lauded **British Embassy**. Turning left at the end of the block brings you into Pariser Platz, the square before the Brandenburg Gate. Laid out in 1732, from 1850 it was given a uniform, classical style, but was then destroyed in World War II. In 1993 the Berlin Senate decided to recreate it in classical style; on the left side, Günther Behnisch's glass-fronted **Akademie der Künste** defies those rules. And on the other side of the square, the French Embassy rebels against the statutes with slanted window jambs asymmetrically facing the Brandenburger Tor.

Walk through the **Brandenburger Tor** (see p56). Ahead in the distance is the Siegessäule and to your right the **Reichstag** (see p85). Walk around to the front and queue to visit Norman Foster's wonderful cupola before looking at all the new government buildings hereabouts. Then circumnavigate Platz der Republik to the **Bundeskanzleramt**, Germany's answer to 10 Downing Street, admiring the new Hauptbahnhof on the skyline to the north, and the squat Swiss Embassy that has stubbornly survived war and redevelopment. On the east side of Axel Schultes and Charlotte Frank's Kanzleramt is another piece of public art. A sculpture by Basque artist Eduardo Chillida, with two rusty forms reaching out for each other, it's called *Berlin*.

SIGHTS

The **Gedenkstätte Deutscher Widerstand** (Memorial to the German Resistance; *see below*) lies south on Stauffenburgstrasse, a street named after the leader of the July 1944 plot to kill Hitler. At the corner of Stauffenburgstrasse and Reichpietschufer is **Shell House**, a curvaceous expressionist masterpiece by Emil Fahrenkamp (1932). Five minutes' walk west along the Landwehrkanal sits the gleaming white building of the **Bauhaus Archiv – Museum für Gestaltung** (Museum of Design); a further ten-minute walk leads to the less high-brow attractions of the **Zoologischer Garten & Aquarium** (*see p91*) and the hub of West Berlin around Bahnhof Zoo and the Ku'damm (*see p92*).

Bauhaus Archiv – Museum für Gestaltung

Klingelhöferstrasse 13-14 (254 0020, www.bauhaus.de). Bus 100, 106, 187, M29 Lützowplatz. **Open** 10am-5pm Mon, Wed-Sun. **Admission** *Mon, Sat, Sun* €7; €4 reductions; *Wed-Fri* €6; €3 reductions. **Map** p322 J8.
Walter Gropius, founder of the Bauhaus school, designed the elegant white building that now houses this absorbing design museum. The permanent exhibition presents a selection of furniture, ceramics, prints, sculptures, photographs and sketches created in the Bauhaus workshop between 1919 and 1933, when the school was closed down by the Nazis. There are also first-rate temporary exhibitions, such as a recent show of multidisciplinary work by Max Bill. An interesting gift shop sells design icons such as the Bauhaus lamp by Wilhelm Wagenfeld.

Daimler Contemporary

Alte Potsdamer Strasse 5 (Haus Huth) (2594 1420, www.sammlung.daimler.com). S1, S2, S25, U2 Potsdamer Platz. **Open** 11am-6pm daily. *Guided tours* 4pm 1st Sat of mth. **Admission** free. **Map** p322/p327 L8.
As you'd expect, Daimler's collection is serious stuff. It sticks to the 20th century, and covers abstract, conceptual and minimal art; its collection numbers around 1,300 works from artists such as Josef Albers, Max Bill, Walter de Maria, Jeff Koons and Andy Warhol. The gallery rotates themed portions of the collection, typically 30-80 works at a time, and often stages joint shows in a spirit of dialogue with other private collections.

Dalí – Die Ausstellung am Potsdamer Platz

Leipziger Platz 7 (0700 325 423 7546, www.daliberlin.de). S1, S2,S25, U2 Potsdamer Platz. **Open** noon-8pm Mon-Sat; 10am-8pm Sun. **Admission** €11; €9 reductions; free under-6s. **Map** p322/p327 L7.

There is no obvious reason why Berlin boasts a Salvador Dalí museum, let alone one as good as this. It was opened in autumn 2009 to commemorate 20 years since both the fall of the wall and the artist's death: the somewhat tenuous Berlin theme is that Dalí 'tore down walls in his art'. There are over 400 Dalí originals on show here, drawn from a pool of more than 2,000 works from private collections, including drawings, lithographs, etchings, woodcuts, illustrated books, documents and supporting works, original graphics and complete portfolios.

Museum für Film und Fernsehen

Potsdamer Strasse 2 (300 9030, www.deutsche-kinemathek.de). S1, S2, S25, U2 Potsdamer Platz. **Open** 10am-6pm Tue, Wed, Fri-Sun; 10am-8pm Thur. **Admission** €6; reductions €4.50. **No credit cards**. **Map** p322/p327 L7.
Since 1963, the Deutsche Kinemathek has been amassing a collection of films, memorabilia, documentation and antique film apparatus. In 2000, all this stuff found a home in this roomy, well-designed exhibition space on two floors of the Filmhaus in the Sony Center, chronicling the history of German cinema. Striking exhibits include the two-storey-high video wall of disasters from Fritz Lang's adventure films and a morgue-like space devoted to films from the Third Reich. On a lighter note, there's a collection of clay-mation figures from Ray Harryhausen films, such as *Jason and the Argonauts*. But the main attraction is the Marlene Dietrich collection – personal effects, home movies and designer clothes. Exhibitions are often linked with film programming at the Arsenal cinema downstairs (*see p210*).

Gedenkstätte Deutscher Widerstand

Stauffenbergstrasse 13-14 (2699 5000/www.gdw-berlin.de). S1, S2, S25, U2 Potsdamer Platz. **Open** 9am-6pm Mon-Wed, Fri; 9am-8pm Thur; 10am-6pm Sat, Sun. *Guided tours* Sat, Sun 3pm. **Admission** free. **Map** p322 K8.
The Memorial to the German Resistance chronicles the German resistance to National Socialism. The building is part of a complex known as the Bendlerblock, owned by the German military from its construction in 1911 until 1945. At the back is a memorial to the conspirators killed during their attempt to assassinate Hitler at this site on 20 July 1944. Regular guided tours are in German only, but you can book an English tour four weeks in advance.

Gemäldegalerie

Stauffenbergstrasse 40 (266 42 42 42, www.smb. museum). S1, S2, S25, U2 Potsdamer Platz. **Open** 10am-6pm Tue, Wed, Fri-Sun; 10am-10pm Thur. **Admission** €8; €4 reductions. **Map** p322 K8.
The Picture Gallery's first-rate early European collection features a healthy selection of the biggest names in Western art. Although many fine Italian, Spanish and English works are on display, the highlights are the Dutch and Flemish pieces. Fans of

Rembrandt can indulge themselves with around 20 paintings, the best of which include a portrait of preacher and merchant Cornelis Claesz Anslo and his wife, and an electric Samson confronting his father-in-law. Two of Franz Hals' finest works are here – the wild, fluid, almost impressionistic *Malle Babbe* (*Mad Babette*) and the detailed portrait of the one-year-old Catharina Hooft and her nurse. Other highlights include a couple of unflinching portraits by Robert Campin (early 15th century), a version of Botticelli's *Venus Rising*, and Corregio's brilliant *Leda with the Swan*. Look out, too, for a pair of Lucas Cranach Venus and Cupid paintings and his *Fountain of Youth*. Pick up the excellent (free) English-language audio guide.

Kunstgewerbemuseum

Kulturforum, Matthäikirchplatz 40 (266 42 42 42, www.smb.museum). S1, S2, S25, U2 Potsdamer Platz. **Open** 10am-6pm Tue-Fri; 11am-6pm Sat, Sun. **Admission** €8; €4 reductions. **Map** p322 K7.
The Museum of Decorative Art contains a frustrating collection of European arts and crafts, stretching from the Middle Ages through Renaissance, baroque and rococo to Jugendstil and art deco. There are some lovely pieces on display, particularly furniture and porcelain, but labelling is only in German and the layout of the building is confusing. A recent show was dedicated to the great artist, artists' biographer and art theoretician, Giorgio Vasari.
Other locations Schloss Köpenick, Schlossinsel, Köpenick (266 3666).

Musikinstrumentenmuseum

Tiergartenstrasse 1 (254 810, www.sim.spk-berlin.de). S1, S2, S25, U2 Potsdamer Platz. **Open** 9am-5pm Tue, Wed, Fri; 9am-10pm Thur; 10am-5pm Sat, Sun. **Admission** €4; €2 reductions; free under 17s. **No credit cards**. **Map** p322 J7.
More than 2,200 string, keyboard, wind and percussion instruments dating to the 1500s are crammed into the small Musical Instrument Museum next to the Philharmonie. Among them are rococo musical clocks, for which 18th-century princes commissioned jingles from Mozart, Haydn and Beethoven. Museum guides play obsolete instruments such as the Kammerflugel; on Saturdays at noon, the wonderful Wurlitzer organ – salvaged from an American silent movie house – is cranked into action.

★ Neue Nationalgalerie

Potsdamer Strasse 50 (266 42 42 42, www.neue-nationalgalerie.de). S1, S2, S25, U 2 Potsdamer Platz. **Open** 10am-6pm Tue, Wed; Fri-Sun; 10am-10pm Thur. **Admission** €10; €5 reductions. **Map** p322 K8.
Designed in the 1960s by Mies van der Rohe, the New National Gallery houses German and international paintings from the 20th century. It's strong on expressionism: there are key works by Kirchner, Heckel and Schmidt-Rottluff, as well as pieces by lesser-known expressionist painters such as Ludwig Meidner, whose apocalyptic post-World War I landscapes exert a garish, comic-book power. Cubist pieces cover the likes of Picasso, Gris and Léger. The Neue Sachlichkeit is well represented by paintings from George Grosz and Otto Dix, while the Bauhaus contributes work from Paul Klee and Wassily Kandinsky. Another focus is American Color Field painting, with pieces by Barnett Newman, Morris Louis and Frank Badur. Be warned: the permanent collection is often put into storage to allow for big shows and temporary exhibitions.

Panoramapunkt

Kollhoff Tower, Potsdamer Platz 1, entrance on Alte Potsdamer Strasse (2593 7080, www.panoramapunkt.de). S1, S2, S25, U2 Potsdamer Platz. **Open** 10am-8pm daily in summer; 10am- 5.30pm in winter. **Admission** €5.50; €4 reductions. **No credit cards**. **Map** p322/p327 L7.
What's billed as 'the fastest elevator in Europe' shoots up to the 100m (328ft) viewing platform in the Kollhoff Tower. The building's north-east corner is precisely at the point where the borders of Tiergarten, Mitte and Kreuzberg all meet – and also on what was the line of the Wall. From this vantage point, you can peer through railings and the neighbouring postmodern high-rises at the landmarks of new Berlin. There are good views to the south and west; looking north, the DB Tower gets in the way.

Zoologischer Garten & Aquarium

Hardenbergplatz 8 (254 010/www.zoo-berlin.de). S3, S5, S7, S75, U2, U9 Zoologischer Garten. **Open** *Zoo* Summer 9am-7pm daily; Winter 9am-5pm daily. *Aquarium* 9am-6pm daily. **Admission** *Zoo* €13; €6.50-€10 reductions. *Aquarium* €13; €6.50-€10 reductions. *Combined admission* €20; €10-€15 reductions. **Map** p321 G8.
Germany's oldest zoo was opened in 1841 to designs by Martin Lichtenstein and Peter Joseph Lenné. With almost 14,000 creatures, it's one of the world's largest and most important zoos, with more endangered species in its collection than any in Europe except Antwerp's. It's beautifully landscaped, with lots of architectural oddities, and there are plenty of places for a coffee, beer or snack.

Enter the aquarium from within the zoo or through its own entrance on Olof-Palme-Platz by the Elephant Gate. More than 500 species are arranged over three floors, and it's a good option for a rainy day. On the ground floor are the fish (including some impressive sharks); on the first you'll find reptiles (the crocodile hall is the highlight); while insects and amphibians occupy the second. The dark corridors and liquid ambience, with tanks lit from within and curious aquarian creatures floating by, are as absorbing as an art exhibit.

SIGHTS

Charlottenburg

Culture and the Ku'damm.

The old heart of West Berlin runs all the way from the Tiergarten to Spandau, from Tegel Airport in the north down to Wilmersdorf in the south. Often derided as staid and stagnant in comparison to its edgier eastern neighbours, Charlottenburg is undeniably bourgeois – the fur coat/small dog quotient is high – but it's not boring. As well as boasting some of the city's most charming hotels and loveliest squares, its two main draws are the magnificent Schloss Charlottenburg and the Kurfürstendamm shopping street, home to the KDW, Berlin's answer to Harrods.

Map p316, p321 p328	**Restaurants & Cafés** p155
Hotels p129	**Bars & Pubs** p171

Tauentzienstrasse.

BAHNHOF ZOO & THE KU'DAMM

Hymned by U2 and centrepiece of the film *Christiane F*, **Bahnhof Zoo** (Zoo Station or Bahnhof Zoologischer Garten, to give it its full name) was long the entry point to this part of the city. During the Cold War it was a spooky anomaly – slap in the middle of West Berlin but policed by the East, which controlled the intercity rail system – and a seedy hangout for junkies and winos. In the 1990s, it was spruced up with chain stores and fast-food outlets. Now, since the opening of the new Berlin Hauptbahnhof, it has been downgraded into just another station for local trains: only S-Bahn and RegionalBahn trains stop.

The original building was designed in 1882 by Ernst Dircksen; the modern glass sheds were added in 1934. The surrounding area, with its sleaze and shopping, cinemas and bustling crowds, is the gateway to the Kurfürstendamm, the main shopping street of western Berlin. The discos and bars along Joachimstaler Strasse are best avoided – the opening of the **Beate-Uhse Erotik-Museum** (*see p94*) actually added a touch of class to the area. On the other side of Hardenbergplatz – the square outside Bahnhof Zoo – is the entrance to the **Zoologischer Garten** itself (*see p91*), which lies over the border in Tiergarten. Fans of photography, in particular Helmut Newton, shouldn't miss the

KaDeWe.

new **Museum für Fotografie** (Museum of Photography; *see p95*) behind Bahnhof Zoo.

The most notable nearby landmark is the fractured spire of the **Kaiser-Wilhelm-Gedächtnis-Kirche** (Kaiser Wilhelm Memorial Church; *see p95*) in Breitscheidplatz. Close by is the 22-storey **Europa-Center**, whose Mercedes star can be seen from much of the rest of the city. It was built in 1965 – and it shows. Intended as the anchor for the development of a new western downtown, it was the first of Berlin's genuinely tall buildings; now it's the grande dame of the city's shopping malls. Its exterior looks best when neon-lit at night. The strange sculpture in front was erected in 1983. It is officially called *Weltenbrunnen* (Fountain of the Worlds) but, like almost everything else in Berlin, it has a nickname: *Der Wasserklops* (Water Meatball).

Running along the south of the Europa-Center, **Tauentzienstrasse** is the westernmost piece of the Generalzug, a sequence of streets laid out by Peter Joseph Lenné to link the west end with Kreuzberg and points east. Constructed around 1860, they're all named after Prussian generals from the Napoleonic wars: Tauentzien, Kleist, Bülow, and so on. The tubular steel sculpture in the central reservation along Tauentzienstrasse was commissioned for the city's 750th anniversary and represents the then-divided city.

At the time of writing, Tauentzienstrasse was a mess as an enormous construction project is aiming to return the so-called City West to its former glory. By the end of 2012, the works are supposed to be completed, including a vertiginous tower to be occupied by the five-star Waldorf Hotel, and the renovation of the once legendary Zoo Palast cinema.

The street continues east past **KaDeWe** (*see p174*), the largest department store in continental Europe. Its full title is Das Kaufhaus des Westens (Department Store of the West), and it was founded in 1907 by Adolf Jandorf, acquired by Herman Tietz in 1926 and later 'Aryanised' and expropriated by the Nazis. KaDeWe is the only one of Berlin's famous turn-of-the-century department stores to survive the war intact, and has been extensively modernised over the last decade. Its most famous feature is the sixth-floor food hall.

Tauentzienstrasse ends at Wittenbergplatz. The 1911 neo-classical **U-Bahn station** here (by Alfred Grenander) is a listed building and has been wonderfully restored with wooden kiosks and old ads on the walls. A block further is the huge steel sculpture at An der Urania, with its grim monument to children killed in traffic by Berlin's drivers. This marks the end, or the beginning, of the western 'downtown'.

Leading south-west from the Kaiser-Wilhelm-Gedächtniskirche, the **Kurfürstendamm** (or Ku'damm, as it's universally known), West Berlin's tree-lined shopping boulevard, is named after the Prussian Kurfürst ('Elector') – and for centuries it was nothing but a track leading from the Elector's residence to the royal hunting palace in the Grunewald. In 1881 Bismarck insisted it be widened to 5.3 metres (17 feet).

To the south of the street, many villas were erected, and though few survive today, one sizeable exception contains the **Käthe-Kollwitz-Museum** (*see p95*), the Villa

Savignyplatz.

Griesbach auction house and the Literaturhaus Berlin, with its **Wintergarten am Literaturhaus** café (*see p155*) on Fasanenstrasse. The villas soon made way for upmarket tenement buildings with huge apartments. About half of the original buildings were destroyed in the war and replaced by functional offices, but many bombastic old structures remain.

The ground-level Ku'damm soon developed into an elegant shopping boulevard. It remains so today with cinemas (mostly showing dubbed Hollywood fare), restaurants (from classy to burger joints) and upmarket fashion shops: the Ku'damm is dedicated to separating you from your cash. If you tire of shopping, check out the entertaining **Story of Berlin** (*see p95*).

Side streets to the south are quieter but even more upmarket, and Bleibtreustrasse to the north has more shops and a number of outrageous examples of 19th-century Gründerzeit architecture.

At the north-west corner of the intersection of Ku'damm and Joachimstaler Strasse is the **Neues Kranzler-Eck**, a Helmut Jahn-designed ensemble built around the famous old Café Kranzler, with a 16-storey tower and pedestrian courtyards including a habitat for parrots.

Other notable new architecture in the area includes Josef Paul Kleihues' **Kant-Dreieck** (Fasanenstrasse/Kantstrasse), with its large metal 'sail', and Nicholas Grimshaw's **Ludwig-Erhard-Haus** for the Stock Exchange at Fasanenstrasse 83-84. Back towards the Kurfürstendamm end of Fasanenstrasse

is the **Jüdisches Gemeindehaus** (Jewish Community House), and, opposite, the **Zille-Hof** flea market.

Kantstrasse runs more or less parallel to the Ku'damm at the Zoo end, and contains the grandiloquent **Theater des Westens** and more shops. Since the opening of the **stilwerk** design centre (*see p196*), the stretch between Fasanenstrasse and Savignyplatz has become a centre for designer homeware stores. The environs of leafy **Savignyplatz**, meanwhile, are dotted with chic restaurants, cafés and shops, particularly on Grolmanstrasse and in the Savignypassage. Nearby Knesebeckstrasse includes the excellent **Marga Schoeller Bücherstube** (*see p179*).

Beate-Uhse-Erotik-Museum

Joachimstaler Strasse 4 (886 0666, www.beate-uhse-filialen.de). U2, U9, S5, S7, S9, S75 Zoologischer Garten. **Open** 9am-midnight Mon-Sat; 11am-midnight Sun. **Admission** check website. **Map** p321/p328 G8.

The three floors of this collection (housed above a flagship Beate-Uhse retail outlet offering the usual videos and sex toys) contain oriental prints, some daft showroom-dummy tableaux and glass cases containing such delights as early Japanese dildos, Andean penis flutes, 17th-century chastity belts and a giant coconut that looks like an arse. There's a small, drab exhibit on pioneering sex researcher Magnus Hirschfeld, an inadequate item on Heinrich Zille and a corner documenting the career of Frau Uhse herself, who went from Luftwaffe pilot to annual sex-aid sales of €50 million. It's all oddly respectable, given the subject.

FREE **Kaiser-Wilhelm-Gedächtnis-Kirche**
*Breitscheidplatz (218 5023, www.gedaechtnis
kirche.com). U2, U9, S3, S5, S7, S75 Zoologischer
Garten.* **Open** 9am-7pm daily. *Guided tours*
1.15pm, 2pm, 3pm Mon-Sat. **Admission** free.
Map p321/p328 G8.
The Kaiser Wilhelm Memorial Church is one of
Berlin's best-known sights, and one of its most dramatic at night. The neo-Romanesque structure was
built in 1891-5 by Franz Schwechten in honour of –
you guessed it – Kaiser Wilhelm I. Much of the building was destroyed during an Allied air raid in 1943.
These days the church serves as a stark reminder of
the damage done by the war, although some might
argue it improved what was originally a profoundly
ugly building. Inside the rump of the church is a glittering art nouveau-style ceiling mosaic depicting
members of the House of Hohenzollern going on pil-
grimage towards the cross. Here you'll also find a
cross made from the nails from the destroyed cathedral at Coventry, and photos of the church before
and after the war. Inside the chapel the wrap-around
blue stained-glass in the windows is quite stunning.
At the time of writing the building was undergoing
extensive renovation work, which is due to be finished in summer 2012.

Käthe-Kollwitz-Museum
*Fasanenstrasse 24, Wilmersdorf (882 5210,
www.kaethe-kollwitz.de). U1, U9 Kurfürstendamm.*
Open 11am-6pm daily. **Admission** €6; €3.50
reductions. **No credit cards**. **Map** p321/p328 F9.

Kaiser-Wilhelm-Gedächtnis-Kirche

Käthe Kollwitz's powerful, deeply empathetic work
embraces the full spectrum of life, from the joy of
motherhood to the pain of death (with rather more
emphasis on the latter than the former). The collection includes her famous lithograph *Brot!*, as well as
charcoal sketches, woodcuts and sculptures, all displayed to good effect in this grand villa off the
Ku'damm. Some labelling is in English.

★ **Museum für Fotografie**
*Jebenstrasse 2 (266 424 242, www.smb.museum/
mf). S3, S5, S7, S75, U2, U9 Zoologischer Garten.*
Open 10am-6pm Tue, Wed, Fri-Sun; 10am-10pm
Thur. **Admission** €8; €4 reductions. **Map**
p321/p328 G8.
Shortly before his death in 2004, Berlin-born Helmut
Newton, who served his apprenticeship elsewhere
in Charlottenburg at the studio of Yva (now the Hotel
Bogota; *see p132*), donated over 1,000 of his nude
and fashion photographs to the city and provided
funds towards the creation of a new gallery. The new
Museum of Photography, doubling as a home for
the Helmut Newton Foundation (www.helmut
newton.com), was the result. In a former casino
behind Bahnhof Zoo, it's now the largest photographic gallery in the city. The first two floors are
given over to Newton's work, which is parcelled up
in a series of alternating exhibitions. Six colossal
nudes, modelled on Nazi propaganda photos from
the 1930s, glare down at you on entering the building, and set the tone for the big, garish, confrontational pieces that dominate the exhibits. Further
space is devoted to temporary exhibitions.

Story of Berlin
*Kurfürstendamm 207-208 (8872 0100, www.
story-of-berlin.de). U1 Uhlandstrasse.* **Open** 10am-
8pm daily; last entry 6pm. **Admission** €10; €8
reductions, €5 6-13s. **Map** p321/p328 F8.
If you're interested in the city's turbulent history, the
Story of Berlin is a novel way of approaching it. The
huge floor space is filled with well-designed rooms
and multimedia exhibits created by authors, designers and film and stage specialists, telling Berlin's
story from its founding in 1237 to the present day.
The 20 themed displays are labelled in both German
and English. Underneath all this is a massive nuclear
shelter. Built by the Allies in the 1970s, the low-
ceilinged, oppressive bunker is still fully functional
and can hold up to 3,500 people. Guided tours are
included in the price of the ticket.

SCHLOSS CHARLOTTENBURG & AROUND

The palace that gives Charlottenburg its
name lies about three kilometres (two miles)
north-west of Bahnhof Zoo. In contrast to the
commercialism and crush of the latter, this
part of the city is quiet, wealthy and serene.
Schloss Charlottenburg (*see p86*) was

SIGHTS

Schloss Charlottenburg.

built in the 17th century as a summer palace for Queen Sophie-Charlotte, wife of Friedrich III (later King Friedrich I), and was intended as Berlin's answer to Versailles. It's not a very convincing answer, but there's plenty of interest in the buildings and grounds of the palace – the apartments of the New Wing and the gardens are the main attractions.

In front of the Schloss entrance is the **Museum Berggruen** (*see right*) and the art nouveau and art deco collection of the **Bröhan-Museum** (*see below*). The arrival across the street of the **Sammlung Scharf-Gerstenberg** (*see below*), which is mostly concerned with Surrealism, firmly establishes this corner of town as a centre for early 20th-century art.

There are few eating, drinking or shopping opportunities in the immediate vicinity of the palace, but if you head down Schlossstrasse and over Bismarckstrasse, the streets south of here, particularly those named after philosophers (Leibniz, Goethe) have many interesting small shops selling antiques, books and the fashions worn by well-to-do locals.

Bröhan-Museum

Schlossstrasse 1A (3269 0600, www.broehan-museum.de). U2 Sophie-Charlotte-Platz or U7 Richard-Wagner-Platz. **Open** 10am-6pm Tue-Sun. **Admission** €6; €4 reductions; under 18s free. Special exhibitons vary. **Map** p316 C6.
This quiet, private museum is made up of three well-laid-out levels of international art nouveau and art deco pieces that businessman Karl Bröhan began collecting in the 1960s and donated to the city of Berlin on his 60th birthday. The wide array of paintings, furniture, porcelain, glass, silver and sculptures dates from 1890 to 1939. Hans Baluschek's paintings of social life in the 1920s and '30s and Willy Jaeckel's series of portraits of women are the pick of the fine art bunch; the furniture is superb too. The third floor

hosts special exhibitions, such as a recent one on art deco in Sweden. Labelling is only in German. Good website, though.

Museum Berggruen

Westlicher Stülerbau, Schlossstrasse 1 (266 42 42 42, www.smb.museum/mb). U2 Sophie-Charlotte-Platz or U7 Richard-Wagner-Platz. **Open** 10am-6pm Tue-Sun. **Admission** €8; €4 reductions. **Map** p316 C6.
Heinz Berggruen was an early dealer in Picassos in Paris, and the subtitle of this museum, Picasso und seine Zeit (Picasso and his Time), sums up this satisfying and important collection. Displayed over an easily digestible three circular floors, it's inevitable that Pablo's works dominate; his astonishingly prolific and diverse output is well represented. The highlight is perhaps the 1942 *Reclining Nude*. There are also works by Braque, Giacometti, Cézanne and Matisse, and most of the second floor is given over to wonderful paintings by Paul Klee.

Sammlung Scharf-Gerstenberg

Schlossstrasse 70 (266 42 42 42, www.smb. museum/ssg). U2 Sophie-Charlotte-Platz or U7 Richard-Wagner-Platz. **Open** 10am-6pm Tue-Sun. **Admission** €10; €5 reductions. **Map** p316 C6.
Now housed in the eastern Stüler building and in the Marstall (stables wing) opposite Charlottenburg Palace, the Collection Scharf-Gerstenberg exhibits works by the Surrealists and their forerunners. The exhibition showcases artists such as Piranesi, Goya and Redon to Dali, Magritte and Ernst. The original collection was gathered by Otto Gerstenberg around 1910, and added to by his grandsons Walter and Dieter Scharf.

Schloss Charlottenburg

Luisenplatz & Spandauer Damm (320 911, www.spsg.de). U2 Sophie-Charlotte-Platz or U7 Richard-Wagner-Platz. **Open** *Old palace*

Apr-Oct 10am-6pm Tue-Sun. Last admission 5.50pm. Nov-Mar 10am-5pm Tue-Sun. Last admission 4.30pm. *New Wing* 10am-6pm Mon, Wed-Sun. **Admission** *Old palace* €12; €8 reductions. *New wing* €5; €3. *Belvedere* €3, €1.50 reductions. *Mausoleum* €3; €1.50 reductions. **Map** p316 C6.

Queen Sophie-Charlotte was the impetus behind this sprawling palace and gardens (and gave her name to both the building and the district) – her husband Friedrich III (later King Friedrich I) built it in 1695-9 as a summer home for his queen. Later kings also summered here, tinkering with, and adding to the buildings. It was severely damaged during World War II, but has now been restored, and stands as the largest surviving Hohenzollern palace.

The bafflingly complicated individual opening times and admission prices have many a visitor scratching their heads. The easiest option, therefore, is to go for the combination ticket that allows entrance to all parts of the palace, with the exception of the state and private apartments of King Friedrich I and Queen Sophie-Charlotte in the Altes Schloss (Old Palace), which are only accessible on a guided tour (€8; €5 reductions; in German only). This tour, through more than 20 rooms, some of staggering baroque opulence, has its highlights (particularly the Porcelain Cabinet), but can be skipped – there's plenty of interest elsewhere. The upper apartments in the old palace can be visited without a guided tour, but they are really only of interest to silver and porcelain junkies.

The one must-see is the Neue Flügel (New Wing). Also known as the Knobeldorff Wing (after its architect), the upper floor of the wing contains the State Apartments of Frederick the Great and the Winter Chambers of his successor King Friedrich Wilhelm II. The contrast between the two sections is interesting – Frederick's rooms are all excessive rococo exuberance (the wildly over-the-top Golden Gallery literally drips gilt), while Friedrich Wilhelm's far more modestly proportioned rooms reflect the more restrained classicism of his time. Frederick the Great was a big collector of 18th-century French painting, and some choice canvases hang from the walls, including Watteau's masterpiece *The Embarkation*

Boot Trips

The city by boat.

While Berlin's claims to be 'the Prussian Venice' may meet with deserved scepticism, the German capital is still an engagingly watery place. The Spree meanders through the city on its journey from the Czech Republic to the Elbe. Beyond that, the entire city and its surrounding region is a maze of inter-fingering rivers, lakes and canals. For many parts of the city, boats are the ideal form of transport. Indeed, in northwest Berlin, in and around Tegeler See, there are isolated houses on islands that can only be reached by ferry.

Even the regular BVG local transport tickets include ferry services across various lakes. For visitors on a budget, a normal AB zone ticket is enough to get you on the hourly year-round ferry link from Wannsee to Kladow. There's even a decent pub by the pier in a quasi-rural setting on the other side.

A fine range of city centre tours is offered by **Stern und Kreisschiffahrt** (www.sternundkreis.de), **Reederei Winkler** (www.reedereiwinkler.de), **Reederei Riedel** (www.reederei-riedel.de) and **Star-Line** (www.starlineschifffahrt.de). All four operators offer circular tours, usually lasting three to four hours, which take in the Spree and the Landwehrkanal. Passengers can hop on and off at landing stages en route, and basic food and drink is served on board. For a complete tour, expect to pay around €12 per adult. There are convenient landing stages at the **Schlossbrücke** in Charlottenburg, at the **Haus der Kulturen der Welt** (*see p85*) in Tiergarten, at Märkisches Ufer, at Jannowitzbrücke and in the Nikolaiviertel. Note that many services operate only from mid March to late November.

A short train journey to Wannsee (20 minutes by Regionalbahn from Mitte) offers more opportunities. Stern & Kreis' Seven Lakes Trip (7-Seen-Rundfahrt) gives a chance to ogle some of Berlin's poshest backyards as the cruise slides gently past the handsome mansions surrounding the **Kleiner Wannsee** (*see p104*). The same tour takes in the Glienicker Brücke, cruises the Havel and stops at **Pfaueninsel** (*see p104*). The service runs daily from late March to mid October with departures at 10.30am and hourly thereafter. Boats leave from piers near Wannsee station. Also with Stern & Kreis, a longer trip from Wannsee (daily in summer, less frequently the rest of the year) runs via Potsdam to quaint Werder, one of the most beautiful of Brandenburg villages, with a cluster of fish restaurants around the quay.

SIGHTS

for Cythera. Also worth a look are the apartments of Friedrich Wilhelm III in the New Wing.

By the east end of the New Wing stands the Neue Pavillon (New Pavilion). Also known as the Schinkel Pavilion, it was built by Schinkel in 1824 for Friedrich Wilhelm III – the King liked it so much that he chose to live here in preference to the grandeur of the main palace.

The huge gardens are one of the palace's main draws. Laid out in 1697 in formal French style, they were reshaped in a more relaxed English style in the 19th century. Within them you'll find the Belvedere, a three-storey structure built in 1788 as a teahouse, now containing a collection of Berlin porcelain. Also in the gardens is the sombre Mausoleum, containing the tombs of Friedrich Wilhelm III, his wife Queen Luise, Kaiser Wilhelm I and his wife. Look out for temporary exhibitions in the Orangery. There's a café and restaurant at the front of the palace. Note: the entire palace is closed on Mondays.

ELSEWHERE IN CHARLOTTENBURG

About three kilometres (two miles) north-east of Schloss Charlottenburg is a reminder of the terror inflicted by the Nazi regime on dissidents, criminals and anybody else they deemed undesirable. The **Gedenkstätte Plötzensee** (Plötzensee Memorial; *see right*) preserves the execution shed of the former Plötzensee prison, where more than 2,500 people were killed between 1933 and 1945.

A couple of kilometres south-west of Schloss Charlottenburg, at the western end of Neue Kantstrasse, stands the futuristic International Conference Centre (ICC). Built in the 1970s, it is used for pop concerts, political rallies and the like. Next door, the even larger Messe- und Ausstellungsgelände (Trade Fair & Exhibition Area) plays host to trade fairs ranging from electronics to food to aerospace. Within the complex, the **Funkturm** (Radio Tower; *see right*) offers panoramic views. Nearby, Hans Poelzig's **Haus des Rundfunks** (Masurenallee 9-14) is an expressive example of monumental brick modernism.

Another couple of kilometres north-west is the **Olympiastadion** (*see right*). One of the few pieces of Fascist-era architecture still intact in Berlin, it was extensively renovated to host the 2006 World Cup Final. Immediately south of Olympiastadion S-Bahn station is a huge apartment block designed by Le Corbusier. The **Corbusierhaus**, with its multicoloured paint job, was constructed for the International Building exhibition of 1957. From here, a ten-minute walk along Sensburger Allee brings you to the sculptures of the **Georg-Kolbe-Museum** (*see right*).

Funkturm

Messedamm (3038 1905). U2 Theodor-Heuss-Platz or Kaiserdamm. **Open** *Aug-June* 10am-8pm Mon; 10am-11pm Tue-Sun. **Admission** €4.50; €2.50 reductions. **No credit cards. Map** p320 A8/B8.

The 138m (453ft) high Radio Tower was built in 1926 and looks a bit like a smaller version of the Eiffel Tower. The observation deck stands at 126m (413ft); vertigo sufferers should seek solace in the restaurant, only 55m (180ft) from the ground.

Gedenkstätte Plötzensee

Hüttigpfad (344 3226, www.gedenkstaette-ploetzensee.de). Bus 123. **Open** *Mar-Oct* 9am-5pm daily. *Nov-Feb* 9am-4pm daily. **Admission** free. **Map** p317 F3.

This memorial stands on the site where the Nazis executed over 2,500 (largely political) prisoners. In a single night in 1943, 186 people were hanged. In 1952 it was declared a memorial to the victims of fascism, and a commemorative wall was built. There is little to see today, apart from the execution area, behind the wall, with its meat hooks from which victims were hanged (many were also guillotined), and a small room with an exhibition. Excellent booklets in English are available. The stone urn near the entrance is filled with earth from concentration camps. The rest of the prison is now a juvenile correction centre.

Georg-Kolbe-Museum

Sensburger Allee 25 (304 2144/www.georg-kolbe-museum.de). S3, S75 Heerstrasse/bus X34, M49, X49. **Open** 10am-6pm Tue-Sun. **Admission** €5; €3 reductions. **No credit cards.**

Georg Kolbe's former studio has been transformed into a showcase for his work. The Berlin sculptor, regarded as Germany's best in the 1920s, mainly focused on naturalistic human figures. The Georg-Kolbe-Museum features examples of his earlier, graceful pieces, as well as his later sombre and larger-than-life works that were created in accordance with the ideals of the Nazi regime. One of his most famous pieces, *Figure for Fountain*, is outside in the sculpture garden.

Olympiastadion

Olympischer Platz 3 (2500 2322, www.olympiastadion-berlin.de). U2 Olympia-Stadion or S3, S5, S75 , Olympiastadion. **Open** varies. **Admission** €4, €3 reductions. guided tours €8, €4 reductions, hours vary (see website). **No credit cards.**

Originally designed by Werner March and opened in 1936 for the Olympics, the 74,000-seat stadium underwent a major and long overdue refitting for the 2006 World Cup, including better seats and a roof over the whole lot. Home of Hertha BSC (*see p254*), it also hosts the German Cup Final, plus other sporting events and concerts. There is a visitor centre by the Osttor (eastern gate), where you can book a guided tour.

Other Districts

The best of the rest.

As it consists of two cities – once divided and now fused back together – it's not surprising that Berlin sprawls for miles in every direction. Though most of the key sites are in the main central districts, exploring the outlying boroughs – especially lively Neukölln and the bucolic Grünewald – is well worth the effort. And if the distances look daunting on a map, remember that the capital's expansion into a hinterland of lakes and forests coincided with the age of railways, and public transport will whisk you to most of the city's far-flung neighbourhoods.

Map pp317-318	**Restaurants**
Hotels p133	**& Cafés** p156
	Bars & Pubs p172

NORTH OF THE CENTRE
Wedding

The working-class industrial district of Wedding, formerly on the western side of the Wall, is now politically part of Mitte. Few visitors venture very far into its largely grim fastness. Apart from a couple of low-key attractions – the **Anti-Kriegs-Museum** (Anti-War Museum; *see below*), the Eschenbräu microbrewery (*see p167*) and the **Zucker Museum** (Sugar Museum; *see p100*) – the big draw is one of the few remaining stretches of the Wall at the **Gedenkstätte Berliner Mauer** (Berlin Wall Memorial; *see right*). There is also an increasing number of galleries relocating here now that so many artists are being priced out of Mitte.

FREE Anti-Kriegs-Museum
Brüsseler Strasse 21 (4549 0110, tours 402 8691, www.anti-kriegs-museum.de). U9 Amrumer Strasse. **Open** 4-8pm daily. **Admission** free. **Map** p317 H2.
The original Anti-War Museum was founded in 1925 by Ernst Friedrich, author of *War Against War*. In 1933, it was destroyed by the Nazis, and Friedrich fled to Brussels. There he had another museum from 1936 to 1940, when the Nazis again destroyed his work. In 1982, a group of teachers including Tommy Spree, the grandson of Ernst Friedrich, re-established

this museum in West Berlin. It now hosts films, discussions, lectures and exhibitions, as well as a permanent display including World War I photos and artefacts from the original museum, children's war toys, information on German colonialism in Africa and pieces of anti-Semitic material from the Nazi era. Though admission is free, donations are welcome.
▶ *Exhibitions are only in German; but you can call ahead to arrange a tour in English with Spree.*

FREE Gedenkstätte Berliner Mauer
Bernauer Strasse 111 (4679 86666, www.berliner-mauer-gedenkstaette.de). U8 Bernauer Strasse or S1, S2 Nordbahnhof. **Open** *Documentation centre* Apr-Oct 9.30am-7pm Tue-Sun. Nov-Mar 9.30am-6pm Tue-Sun. **Admission** free. **Map** p318 M4.
Immediately upon unification, the city bought the stretch of the Wall on Bernauer Strasse to keep as a memorial. Impeccably restored, including death strip, watch tower and border fortifications, it's the best place to get a sense of just how brutally Berlin was severed in two. On this particular street, neighbours woke up one morning to find themselves in a different country from those on the opposite side of the road, as soldiers brandishing bricks and mortar started to build what the East German government referred to as the 'Anti-Fascist Protection Wall'. Start off at the new Visitors Centre by Nordbahnhof but don't miss the excellent documentation centre across the street from the Wall, which includes a very good aerial video following the route of the wall in 1990:

SIGHTS

it's the best chance you have of really getting your head around it. From the centre's tower you can look down over the Wall and the Kapelle der Versöhnung (Chapel of Reconciliation). The Gedenkstätte is a work in progress. Eventually, the trustees hope to extend the Wall along 1.4 kilometres of the former border strip.

Further down the road in the old Nordbahnhof is a great exhibition called Border Stations and Ghost Stations in Divided Berlin, which tells the story of how East Germany closed down and then fiercely guarded stations through which West German trains travelled during the Cold War.

FREE Zucker-Museum

Amrumer Strasse 32 (3142 7574, www.dtmb.de). U6 Seestrasse or U9 Amrumer Strasse. **Open** 9am-4.30pm Mon-Thur; 11am-6pm Sun. **Admission** free. **No credit cards. Map** p317 H2.

A museum devoted to the chemistry, history and politics of sugar may not sound like the most entertaining of places to spend an afternoon, but this Zucker-Museum, originally opened in 1904, contains a fascinating collection of paraphernalia. Don't miss the slide show on the slave trade.

WEST OF THE CENTRE

Spandau

Berlin's western neighbour and eternal rival, Spandau is a little baroque town that seems to contradict everything about the city of which it is now, reluctantly, a part. Spandauers still talk about 'going into Berlin' when they head off to the rest of the city. Berliners, meanwhile, basically consider Spandau to be part of West Germany, though travelling there is easy on the U7, alighting at either Zitadelle or Altstadt Spandau, depending on which sights you want to visit. None are thrilling, but they make for a low-key escape from the city.

The **Zitadelle** (Citadel; *see right*) contains in one of its museums Spandau's original town charter, which dates from 1232, a fact Spandauers have used ever since to argue their historical primacy over Berlin. Spandau's old town centre is mostly pedestrianised, with 18th-century townhouses interspersed with burger joints and department stores. One of the prettiest is the former Gasthof zum Stern in Carl-Schurz-Strasse; older still are houses in Kinkelstrasse and Ritterstrasse; but perhaps the best-preserved district is north of Am Juliusturm in the area bounded by Hoher Steinweg, Kolk and Behnitz. Steinweg contains a fragment of the old town wall from the first half of the 14th century; Kolk has the **Alte Marienkirche** (1848); and in Behnitz, at No.5, stands the elegant baroque **Heinemannsche Haus**. At Reformationsplatz, the brick nave

of the **Nikolaikirche** dates from 1410-50; the west tower was added in 1468, and there were later enhancements by Schinkel.

One of the most pleasant times to visit is at Christmas, when the market square houses a life-size Nativity scene with real sheep and the Christmas market is in full swing. The café and bakery on Reformationsplatz are excellent.

Many will know the name Spandau from its association with Rudolf Hess, Hitler's deputy, who flew to Britain in 1940 for reasons that are still disputed, was held in the Allied jail here after the Nuremberg trials, and remained here (alone after 1966) until his suicide at age 93 in 1987. The 19th-century brick building at Wilhelmstrasse 21-24 was then demolished to make way for a supermarket for the British forces. Some distance south of Spandau is the **Luftwaffenmuseum der Bundeswehr Berlin-Gatow** (*see below*).

FREE Luftwaffenmuseum der Bundeswehr Berlin-Gatow

Gross-Glienicker Weg, Gatow (3687 2601, www.luftwaffenmuseum.de). U7 Rathaus Spandau, then bus 135 to Seekorso. **Open** 10am-6pm Tue-Sun. **Admission** free.

You probably need to be a bit of a plane nut to make the journey here. The museum is on the far western fringes of the city at what was formerly the RAF base in divided Berlin; it's a long journey by public transport followed by a 20-minute walk from the bus stop. Then there's a lot more walking to take in more than 100 aircraft scattered around the airfield plus exhibits in two hangars and the former control tower. The main emphasis is on the history of military aviation in Germany since 1945, although there's also a World War I tri-plane, a restored Handley Page Hastings (as used here in the Airlift) and a whole lot of missiles.

Zitadelle

Am Juliusturm, Spandau (354 9440, tours 334 6270, www.zitadelle-spandau.net). U7 Zitadelle. **Open** 10am-5pm daily. **Admission** €4.50; €2.50 reductions. **No credit cards.**

The oldest structure in the citadel (and the oldest secular building in Berlin) is the Juliusturm, probably dating back to an Ascanian fortress from about 1160. The present tower was home until 1919 to the 120-million Goldmark reparations, stored in 1,200 boxes, which the French paid to Germany in 1874 after the Franco-Prussian War. The bulk of the Zitadelle was designed and built between 1560 and 1594, in the style of an Italian fort, to dominate the confluence of the Spree and Havel rivers. Since then it has been used as everything from a garrison to a prison to a laboratory. There are two museums within the Zitadelle: one tells the story of the building with models and maps; the other is a museum of local history.

Meet the Neighbours

Wild boar, racoons and other undomesticated animals are choosing the city life.

Every town has its wildlife, and Berlin is home to all the usual suspects – and more.

The city's symbol is the bear, but outside its two zoos (*see p91* and *p107*), the only place you'll encounter any them is in the small bearpit in Köllnischer Park near the Märkisches Museum (*see p72*) – home to Schnute and her daughter Maxi, the official bears of Berlin.

During the Cold War, Berlin was noted for its rabbits, which hopped happily around no-man's land. But one way or another, Reunification seems to have killed off the bunnies. Meanwhile, the number of foxes has increased: they're now often spotted sauntering around the inner city, and scavenging for discarded sandwiches in playground litter bins.

But the biggest increase has been in Berlin's wild boar population. *Wildschwein* often make the news. A man in Dahlem finds a boar under his dining table, which bites him when he tries to shoo it away. Hertha BSC training sessions are disrupted by wild boar tearing up one of the training pitches. The club brings in a hunter who studies their habits for a week – and then kills them. In 2011, wild boar snuck into a Charlottenburg cemetery and destroyed the turf, causing €25,000-worth of damage. A pair were even seen in Alexanderplatz, nosing around for food.

These are not shy, retiring creatures. These are undomesticated pigs, typically weighing in at somewhere between 90 to 140 kilos (200-300 pounds), with five-inch tusks and a nasty temper – this particularly applies to females with children. If you encounter one, treat it with respect.

Still, many people like them, and leave food out for them. The abundant supply of eats in the city is one reason for the rise in numbers, along with warmer winters. City hunting consultant Derk Ehlert estimates the total population to be upwards of 8,000, bossing the forests, rooting around city parks, and even making themselves at home on overgrown railway embankments.

Wild boar have been here longer than the city itself, but racoons are a more recent arrival. A bunch of them escaped when a stray Allied bomb hit a racoon farm near Berlin during World War II. Half a century later, these small furry aliens have spread across Germany. Racoons have also started leaving their natural habitat near streams or lakes and moving into the city, where food and shelter are easy to find. Unfortunately, shelter often means someone's attic or cellar. Urban racoons shin up drainpipes, jump on to roofs from tree tops, or simply wander in via the cat flap. They can even turn knobs and open latches.

Once racoons have made themselves at home in your garage or gable, it's extremely difficult to get them out again. Studies show that the more of them people trap and kill, the more they breed. Urban racoon experts instead recommend preventative measures: trimming tree branches, covering drainpipes. But whatever does or does not prove effective, there's no escaping the fact that suburban Berliners are on the front line of this furry invasion.

SIGHTS

SOUTH-WEST OF THE CENTRE
Zehlendorf & the Dahlem museums

Berliner Teufelsberg.

South-west Berlin contains some of the city's wealthiest suburbs, and in the days of division was the American sector, from which time assorted landmarks survive. One major draw is the museums at Dahlem, including the world-class **Ethnologisches Museum** (Ethnological Museum; *see below*). In the same building are the **Museum für Asiatische Kunst** (Museum of Asian Art) and the **Museum Europäischer Kulturen** (Museum of European Cultures).

Dahlem is also home to the **Freie Universität**, some of whose departments occupy former villas seized by the Nazis from their Jewish owners. North-west of the U-Bahn station, opposite the Friedhof Dahlem-Dorf (cemetery), is the **Domäne Dahlem** working farm (*see below*) – a great place to take kids.

Ten minutes' walk east from Dahlem along Königin-Luise-Strasse brings you to the **Botanischer Garten & Botanisches Museum** (Botanical Garden & Museum; *see below*), while taking the same street for a kilometre or so west of Dahlem brings you to the edge of the **Grunewald** (*see p103*).

Botanischer Garten & Botanisches Museum
Königin-Luise-Strasse 6-8 (8385 0100, www.botanischergartenberlin.de./BGBM). S1 Botanischer Garten, then 15min walk. **Open** *Botanischer Garten* Nov-Jan 9am-4pm daily. Feb 9am-5pm daily. Mar 9am-6pm daily. Apr 9am-8pm daily. May-July 9am-9pm daily. Aug 9am-8pm daily. Sept, Oct 9-7pm daily. *Museum* 10am-8pm daily. **Admission** *Botanischer Garten & Museum* €6; €3 reductions. *Museum* €2.50; €1.50 reductions. **No credit cards.**
The Botanical Garden was landscaped at the beginning of the 20th century. Today, it is home to 18,000 plant species, 16 greenhouses and a museum. The botanical gardens make for a pleasant stroll. The botanical museum, however, is a bit dilapidated and there's no information in English, but it's the place to come for advice on whether those mushrooms you found in the forest are delectable or deadly.

Domäne Dahlem
Königin-Luise-Strasse 49 (666 3000, www.domaene-dahlem.de). U3 Dahlem-Dorf. **Open** *Museum* 10am-6pm Mon, Wed-Sun. Under 18s free. *Open-air museum* freely accessible. *Farmer's shop* 10am-6pm Mon-Fri; 8am-1pm Sat. **Admission** *Museum* €3; €1,50 reductions. On market days €2, reductions free. *Farmer's shop* free. **No credit cards.**

On this organic working farm, children can see how life was lived in the 17th century. Craftspeople preserve and teach their skills. It's best to visit during one of several festivals held during the year, when kids can ride ponies, tractors and hay wagons. When the weather is nice, there's a garden café as well.

Ethnologisches Museum
Lansstrasse 8 (266 42 42 42, www.smb.spk-berlin.de). U1 Dahlem-Dorf. **Open** 10am-6pm Tue-Fri; 11am-6pm Sat, Sun. **Admission** €6; €3 reductions.
The Ethnological Museum is a stunner – extensive, authoritative, beautifully laid out and lit. It encompasses cultures from Oceania to Central America to Africa to the Far East. Only the true ethno-fan should attempt to see it all, but no one should miss the Südsee (South Sea) room. Here you'll find New Guinean masks and effigies, and a remarkable collection of original canoes and boats – some huge and elaborate. The African rooms are also impressive – look out for the superb carvings from Benin and the Congo, and beaded artefacts from Cameroon. An enlightening small exhibit explores the influence of African art on the German expressionists.

Two other museums are housed in the same building. The Museum für Asiatische Kunst (Museum of Asian Art) features archaeological objects and works of fine art from India, Japan, China and Korea from the early Stone Age to the present. The Museum

SIGHTS

Europäischer Kulturen (Museum of European Cultures) contains exhibits about European everyday culture from the 18th century to the present. One highlight is a mechanical model of the nativity, displayed each year in the Advent period. Audio guides in English are available.

Grunewald

The western edge of Zehlendorf is formed by the Havel river and the extensive Grunewald, largest of Berlin's many forests. On a fine Sunday afternoon, its lanes and pathways fill with walkers, runners, cyclists, horse riders and dog walkers. This is because it's so easily accessible by S-Bahn. There are several restaurants next to the station, and on the other side of the motorway at Schmetterlingsplatz, which are open from April to October.

One popular destination is the **Teufelsee**, a tiny lake packed with bathers in summer, reached by heading west from the station along Schildhornweg for 15 minutes. Close by is the mound of the **Teufelsberg**, a product of wartime devastation – a railway was laid from Wittenbergplatz to carry the 12 million cubic metres of rubble that forms it. There are great views from the summit. There has been talk of replacing the abandoned American electronic listening post on the top with some kind of hotel and conference centre, but for now, you can take tours of the spooky site (*see right*).

South of the station, at the far end of the **Grunewaldsee**, the 16th-century **Jagdschloss Grunewald** (Grunewald Hunting Lodge) is an example of the kind of building that once maintained the country life of the landed gentry, the Prussian Junkers. Here, you can find bathing by the lake in summer, including a nudist section.

A further kilometre south-east through the forest is the **Chalet Suisse**, an over-the-top Swiss-themed restaurant popular with families because of its playground and petting zoo. A further ten-minute walk takes you to the **Alliierten Museum** (Allied Museum; *see right*) on Clayallee. A kilometre north of here is the **Brücke-Museum** (*see p104*), housing a collection of expressionist paintings and prints.

Further south, **Krumme Lanke** and **Schlachtensee** are pleasant urban lakes along the south-eastern edge of the Grunewald, perfect for picnicking, swimming or rowing – and each with its own station.

On the west side of the Grunewald, halfway up Havelchaussee, is the **Grunewaldturm**, a tower built in 1897 in memory of Wilhelm I. It has an observation platform 105 metres (344 feet) above the lake, with expansive views as far as Spandau and Potsdam. There is a restaurant at the base, and another over the road, both with garden terraces. A short walk south along Havelufer leads to the ferry to **Lindwerder Insel** (island), which also has a restaurant. To the north, a little way into the forest, the singer Nico, who grew up in Schöneberg, is buried among the trees in the **Friedhof Grunewald-Forst**.

FREE Alliierten Museum

Clayallee 135, corner of Huttenweg (818 1990, www.alliiertenmuseum.de). U3 Oskar-Helene-Heim/bus 115. **Open** 10am-6pm Mon, Tue, Thur-Sun. **Admission** free.

The Allies arrived as conquerors, kept West Berlin alive during the 1948 Airlift and finally went home in 1994. In what used to be a US Forces cinema, the Allied Museum is mostly about the period of the Blockade and Airlift, documented with photos, tanks, jeeps, planes, weapons and uniforms. Outside is the former guardhouse from Checkpoint Charlie and an RAF Hastings TG 503. Guided tours in English can be booked in advance. It's ten minutes' walk north up Clayallee from the U-Bahn station.

Berliner Teufelsberg

Guided tours 7469 0537, mobile 0163 858 5096, www.berlinsightout.de. **Open** *tours* 1.30pm Sun; meet at the S-bahn station Grunewald. **Tickets** €15 adults; €8 reductions. Under 14s not allowed.

Alliierten Museum.

SIGHTS

During the Cold War, the Allies built this listening station on the top of one of Berlin's highest hills to eavesdrop on what the East Germans were up to on the other side of the Wall. The site was abandoned when the Iron Curtain fell and soon became a favourite spot for urban explorers and stoners looking for a trippy place to smoke a joint. Exploring the site on your own is still illegal, though the tours had just been officially sanctioned at the time of writing – but for how long was unclear. Check the website or call before turning up.

Brücke-Museum

Bussardsteig 9 (831 2029, www.bruecke-museum.de). U3 Oskar-Helene-Heim, then bus 115 to Pücklerstrasse. **Open** 11am-5pm Mon, Wed-Sun. **Admission** €5; €3 reductions. **No credit cards.** This small but satisfying museum is dedicated to the work of Die Brücke ('The Bridge'), a group of expressionist painters that was founded in Dresden in 1905 before later moving to Berlin. A large collection of oils, watercolours, drawings and sculptures by the main members of the group – Schmidt-Rottluff, Heckel, Kirchner, Mueller and Pechstein – is rotated in temporary exhibitions.

Wannsee & Pfaueninsel

At the south-west edge of the Grunewald, you'll find boats and beaches in summer, and castles and forests all through the year. **Strandbad Wannsee** is the largest inland beach in Europe. Between May and September, there are boats and pedalos and hooded, two-person wicker sunchairs for hire, a playground and a separate section for nudists. Service buildings house showers, toilets, cafés, shops and kiosks.

The waters of the Havel (the Wannsee is an inlet of the river) are extensive and in summer warm enough for comfortable swimming; there is a strong current, so don't stray beyond the floating markers.

A small bridge north of the beach leads to Schwanenwerder, once the exclusive private island retreat of Goebbels and now home to the international think-tank, the Aspen Institute.

The town of Wannsee to the south is clustered around the bay of the Grosser Wannsee and is dominated by the long stretch of promenade, Am Grossen Wannsee, scattered with hotels and fish restaurants. On the west side of the bay is the **Gedenkstätte Haus der Wannsee-Konferenz** (*see right*). At this elegant Gründerzeit mansion, now a museum, a January 1942 meeting of prominent Nazis laid out plans for the extermination of the Jews.

A short distance from S-Bahn Wannsee along Bismarckstrasse is a little garden where German dramatist Heinrich von Kleist shot himself in 1811; the beautiful view of Kleiner Wannsee was the last thing he wanted to see.

On the other side of the railway tracks is **Düppler Forst**, a forest including a nature reserve at Grosses Fenn at the south-western end. Travelling three S-Bahn stops to Mexikoplatz, then taking the 629 or 211 bus, brings you to the reconstructed 14th-century village at **Museumsdorf Düppel** (*see p105*).

From Wannsee, bus 218 scoots through the forest to a pier on the Havel, and from there it's a brief ferry ride to **Pfaueninsel**. This island was inhabited in prehistoric times, but isn't mentioned in archives until 1683. In 1685, the Grand Elector presented it to Johann Kunckel von Löwenstein, a chemist who experimented with alchemy but instead of gold produced 'ruby glass', examples of which are on view in the castle.

It was only at the start of the Romantic era that the island's windswept charms began to attract more serious interest. In 1793, Friedrich Wilhelm II purchased it and built a *Schloss* for his mistress, but died in 1797 before they had a chance to move in. Its first residents were Friedrich Wilhelm III and Queen Luise, who spent much of their time together on the island, even setting up a working farm there. A royal menagerie was later developed. Most of the animals were moved to the new Tiergarten Zoo in 1842, and only peacocks, pheasants, parrots, goats and sheep remain. Surviving structures include the Jakobsbrunnen (Jacob's Fountain), a copy of a Roman temple; the Kavalierhaus (Cavalier's House), built in 1803 from an original design by Schinkel; and the Swiss cottage, also based on a Schinkel plan. All are linked by winding paths laid out in the English manner by Peter Joseph Lenné. A walk around the island, with its monumental trees, rough meadows and views over the Havel, provides one of the most complete sensations of escape to be had within the borders of Berlin.

Back on the mainland, a short walk south along Nikolskoer Weg is the **Blockhaus Nikolskoe** (805 2914, www.blockhaus-nikolskoe.de), a huge wooden chalet built in 1819 by Friedrich Wilhelm II for his daughter Charlotte, and named after her husband, the future Tsar Nicholas of Russia. There is a magnificent view from the terrace, where you can sit back and enjoy mid-priced Berlin cuisine or coffee and cakes.

★ FREE Gedenkstätte Haus der Wannsee-Konferenz

Am Grossen Wannsee 56-58 (805 0010, www.ghwk.de). S1, S7 Wannsee, then bus 114. **Open** 10am-6pm daily. **Admission** free. On 20 January 1942, some prominent Nazis, chaired by Heydrich, gathered here to draw up plans for the Final Solution. Today, this infamous villa has been converted into the Wannsee Conference Memorial House, a place of remembrance, with a photo exhibit

Stranbad Wannsee.

on the conference and its genocidal consequences. Call in advance if you want to join an English-language tour, though the information is in both English and German these days.

Museumsdorf Düppel

Clauertstrasse 11 (802 6671/www.dueppel.de). S1 Mexikoplatz, then bus 118, 622. **Open** *Mar-mid Oct* 3-7pm Thur; 10am-5pm Sun. Last entry 1hr before closing. Closed mid-Oct-Feb. **Admission** €2; €1 reductions, children free, different prices for special events. **No credit cards**.

At this 14th-century village, reconstructed around archaeological excavations, workers demonstrate handicrafts, medieval technology and farming techniques. Ox-cart rides for kids. Small snack bar.

Glienicke

West of Wannsee, and only a couple of kilometres from Potsdam, Glienicke was once the south-westernmost tip of West Berlin. The suspension bridge over the Havel here was named **Brücke der Einheit** (Bridge of Unity) because it joined Potsdam with Berlin. After the building of the Wall, it was painted different shades of olive green on the East and West sides and used only by Allied soldiers and for top-level prisoner and spy exchanges – Anatoly Scharansky was one of the last in 1986.

The main reason to come here is **Park Glienicke**. Its centrepiece is **Schloss Glienicke** (not open to the public), originally a hunting lodge designed by Schinkel for Prinz Carl von Preussen, who adorned the garden walls with ancient relics collected on his Mediterranean holidays, and decided to simulate a walk from the Alps to Rome in the densely wooded park. The summer houses, fountains and follies are all based on original Italian models, and the woods and fields around them make an ideal place for a Sunday picnic, since this park is little visited. At the nearby inlet of Moorlake, there's a restaurant in an 1842 hunting lodge.

EAST & SOUTH-EAST OF THE CENTRE

Neukölln

Until recently, there was little in Neukölln to attract visitors from other districts, let alone other countries. Long considered a problem area because of its high concentration of poor immigrants (mainly Turks) and reputation for drug abuse and arson, it was a place most Berliners only ever saw on the news. But as the creep of gentrification forced up rents in Mitte, Kreuzberg and Prenzlauberg, artists and students were forced further out of the city. Many have ended up in Neukölln, where they have opened up galleries, boutiques, bars and restaurants.

The bit of the borough most tourists are likely to want to spend time in is Neukölln's north-western corner, often called **Kreuzkölln** for its proximity and similarity to neighbouring Kreuzberg. It's bordered in the north by the canal, in the west by Kotbusser Tor and in the south by Sonnenallee. There aren't really any conventional sights here, but the bar scene, in particular, is currently the best in the city.

Start exploring Neukölln via the **Maybachufer** on the south bank of the Landwehrkanal (U8 Schönleinstrasse), which is home to the bi-weekly Turkish market as well as the legendary Ankerklause pub (*see p169*). Take a right down Friedelstrasse, wherer you'll find a number of the city's hip restaurants such as Johnny Woo (*see p151*) and Manuela Tapas (Friedelstrasse 34, 5471 5227, www.manuelatapas.com) and carry on until you reach Weserstrasse, the area's nightlife hub.

Lichtenberg & Treptow

Many of the other neighbourhoods in the old East have little to offer the visitor. East of Prenzlauer Berg and Friedrichshain, Lichtenberg isn't very appealing, though it does contain the **Tierpark Berlin-Friedrichsfelde** (Berlin-Friedrichsfelde Zoo; *see p107*) and both the Stasi Museum, more properly known as the **Forschungs- und Gedenkstätte Normannenstrasse** (*see below*), and the **Gedenkstätte Berlin-Hohenschönhausen** (*see right*), a former Stasi prison turned chilling exhibit of state oppression. Further south is the **Museum Berlin-Karlshorst** (*see p107*), documenting the somewhat troubled history of Russian-German relations during the last century.

South of Lichtenberg and bordering Neukölln, Treptow is chiefly of note for **Treptower Park**, containing the massive

Sowjetisches Ehrenmal (Soviet War Memorial). From here, several boats leave in the summer for trips along the Spree.

The park continues to the south, where it becomes the **Plänterwald** and houses a dormant amusement park, complete with frozen ferris wheel and overgrown log flume. You can take tours of the site on weekends via www.berliner-spreepark.de (click on 'Spreepark Führungen').

Forschungs- und Gedenkstätte Normannenstrasse (Stasi Museum)

Ruschestrasse 103 (553 6854, www.stasi museum.de). U5, S41, S42, S8, S85, S9 Frankfurter Allee or U5 Magdalenenstrasse. **Open** 11am-6pm Mon-Fri; 2-6pm Sat, Sun. **Admission** €5; €4 reductions. **No credit cards**. In what used to be part of the headquarters of the Stasi, you can look around what used to be the offices of secret police chief Erich Mielke – his old uniform still hangs in his wardrobe – and see the displays of bugging devices and spy cameras concealed in books, plant pots and car doors, all in the service of what was one of the most thoroughgoing police states in history. Some information is only in German, but tours in English can be booked in advance. At the time of writing, the museum was squatting in the old officers' canteen while Mielke's HQ was being renovated. Works were scheduled to finish in late 2011.

Gedenkstätte Berlin-Hohenschönhausen

Gensler Strasse 66 (9860 8230, www.stiftung-hsh.de). M5 Freienwalder Strasse or M6 Gensler Strasse. **Open** Guided tours German 11am, 1pm, 3pm daily. *English* 2.30pm Wed, Sat. **Admission** €5; €2,50 reductions. **No credit cards**. A sprawling former remand prison run by the Stasi, the building has a dirty history. Originally the site of a canteen for the Nazi social welfare organisation, it was turned into 'Special Encampment No.3' by the Soviets and later expanded by the MfS (Ministerium für Staatssicherheit; Stasi). Excellent and highly personal guided tours by ex-prisoners take 90 minutes. The inmates were all political prisoners, from the leaders of the 1953 workers' uprising to critical students. The experience is gut-wrenchingly bleak, but a potent insight into how the Stasi operated. On one interrogator's office wall hangs a painting of a fairytale castle, underneath which prisoners underwent horrifying psychological interrogation.

FREE Mies van der Rohe Haus

Oberseestrasse 60, Hohenschönhausen (970 006 18, www.miesvanderrohehaus.de). Tram M5 to Oberseestrasse, Tram 27 to Stadion Buschallee/ Suermondtstrasse. **Open** 11am-5pm Tue-Sun. **Admission** free.

German architect Ludwig Mies van der Rohe designed this L-shaped modernist gem in 1933 for Karl Lemke, the owner of a Berlin graphic art and printing firm. Lemke and his wife lived there until 1945 when the Red Army stormed in and used it as a garage. From 1960 until the fall of the wall, the Stasi used the house as a laundry: these days it hosts art exhibitions. It's not as dramatic as the architect's Barcelona Pavilion, but is well worth a visit if you're out this way.

FREE Museum Berlin-Karlshorst

Zwieseler Strasse 4, corner of Rheinsteinstrasse (5015 0810, www.museum-karlshorst.de). S3 Karlshorst. **Open** 10am-6pm Tue-Sun. **Admission** free.

After the Soviets took Berlin, they commandeered this former German officers' club as HQ for the military administration and it was here, on the night of 8-9 May 1945, that German commanders signed the unconditional surrender, ending the war in Europe. The museum looks at the German-Soviet relationship over 70 years. Divided into 16 rooms, including the one where the Nazis surrendered, it takes us through two world wars and one cold one, plus assorted pacts, victories and capitulations. Exhibits include photos, memorabilia, maps, videos and propaganda posters. Buy a guide in English; exhibits are labelled in German and Russian. English tours can be booked in advance.

Tierpark Berlin-Friedrichsfelde

Am Tierpark 125 (515 310, www.tierpark-berlin.de). U5 Tierpark. **Open** *Jan-late Mar, late Oct-Dec* 9am-5pm daily. *Late Mar-mid Sept* 9am-6pm daily. *Mid Sept-late Oct* 9am-5pm daily. **Admission** €12; €6-€8 reductions.

One of Europe's largest zoos, with plenty of roaming space for herd animals, although others are still kept in rather small cages. Resident beasts include bears, elephants, big cats and penguins. In the zoo's north-west corner is the baroque Schloss Friedrichsfelde. One of the continent's biggest snake farms is also here.

▶ *To read about the wild animals that choose to make the city their home, see p101 Meet the Neighbours.*

Köpenick

The name Köpenick is derived from the Slavonic *copanic*, meaning 'place on a river'. The old town, around 15 kilometres (nine miles) south-east of Mitte, stands at the confluence of the Spree and Dahme, and, having escaped bombing, decay and development by the DDR, still maintains much of its 18th-century character. This is one of the most sought-after areas of East Berlin, with handsome shops, cafés and restaurants clustered around the old centre. With its old buildings and extensive riverfront, it's a fine place for a Sunday afternoon wander.

The imposing **Rathaus** (Town Hall) is a good example of Wilhelmine civic architecture. It was here in 1906, two years after the building's completion, that Wilhelm Voigt, an unemployed cobbler who'd spent half his life in jail, dressed up as an army captain and ordered a detachment of soldiers to accompany him into the Treasury, where they emptied the town coffers. He instantly entered popular folklore. Carl Zuckmeyer immortalised him in a play as Der Hauptmann von Köpenick ('Captain of Köpenick') and the Kaiser pardoned him because he had shown how obedient Prussian soldiers were. His theft is re-enacted every June during the Köpenicker summer festival. Close by is **Schloss Köpenick** (*see below*), with medieval drawbridge, Renaissance gateway and baroque chapel.

Schloss Köpenick

Schlossinsel 1 (266 42 42 42, www.smb.museum). S47 Spindlersfeld. **Open** 10am-6pm Tue-Sun. **Admission** €4; €2 reductions.

Overspill from the Kunstgewerbemuseum is presented as 'RoomArt', with furniture and decorative art from the Renaissance, baroque and rococo eras arranged according to period beneath carefully restored ceiling paintings. There's also an exhibition on the history of the island, plus a riverside café.

Friedrichshagen & the Müggelsee

A couple of kilometres east of Köpenick, the village of **Friedrichshagen** has retained its independent character. The main street, **Bölschestrasse**, is lined with steep-roofed Brandenburg houses, and ends at the shores of a large lake, the **Grösser Müggelsee**.

Friedrichshagen is particularly enjoyable when the **Berliner Burgerbräu** brewery, family-owned since 1869, throws open its gates for its annual summer celebration. Stalls line Bölschestrasse, the brewery lays on music, and people lounge about on the lake shore with cold beer. Boat tours are available, and the restaurant Braustubl, next to the brewery, serves good Berlin cuisine.

SIGHTS

Consume

Hotels

Budget, boutique or blow-out.

With an average room price of just €82 per night, Berlin still ranks among the least expensive western cities to stay in – compared, at least, to London at €118 a night, and New York at €150 a night. There are so many places to choose from now that hoteliers are going the extra mile to stand out: the very good-value **Amano** near Hackescher Markt rents out iPods containing audio walking tours and music from Berlin-based bands, while the 304-room **nHow** by the river in Friedrichshain is touting itself as a 'music and lifestyle hotel', complete with two recording studios and a spa – and Gibson guitars on room service. In trendy Neukölln, you can sleep in vintage caravans parked in an old vacuum cleaner factory at the **Hüttenpalast**.

CONSUME

CITY ROUND-UP
A number of chains have responded to Berlin's tourist boom by expanding quickly across the city – there are now three excellent **Adina Apartment Hotels**, centrally located by the Hauptbahnhof, Checkpoint Charlie and Hackescher Markt, and the surprisingly smart budget chain **Motel One** now has eight branches in the city. Perhaps inevitably, given the influx of easyJet weekenders, there is also now a bright orange **easyHotel** on Rosenthaler Strasse.

On the luxury front, the **Adlon**, **Sofitel** and **Hotel de Rome** still steal the show, though the very fashionable **Casa Camper** hotel in Hackescher Markt is snapping at their heels. So too is **Soho House**, which has opened a Berlin outpost in an old Jewish department store, installing a swimming pool on the roof.

At the other end of the scale, there appears to be a new hostel opening up every month, and standards are generally high. We particularly like the new **Grand Hostel** in Kreuzberg and the **Circus**, an old favourite which never sits on its laurels in Mitte. Most now offer single and double rooms as well as old-school dormitories, so are worth considering if you're on a budget.

> ❶ Red numbers given in this chapter correspond to the location of each bar as marked on the street maps.
> *See pp316-328.*

As the guide went to press, the Waldorf Astoria was putting the finishing touches to its 31-storey, 232 room luxury hotel right opposite the Gedächtniskirche in Charlottenburg. And in 2012 the Spanish hotel group Whim was set to open Das Stue (it's Danish for living room, apparently), a five-star boutique place directly by the Tiergarten.

PRICES
Although prices given throughout this chapter were correct as this guide went to press, they should be taken as guidelines, not gospel. Many of the larger hotels now refuse to publish any rates at all, depending instead on direct booking over the internet (often at a discount), which enables them to vary their prices daily. In addition to hotels' own websites, discount specialists such as expedia.com and hotels.com are worth a look too. It's wise to reserve in advance whenever possible: on any given weekend in Mitte or Prenzlauer Berg many hotels are extremely busy. Be wary of cancellation policies too: it's best to ask before you book.

We've indicated where breakfast is included in the room price. Most hotels offer it as a buffet, which can be as simple as coffee and rolls (called *schrippen* in Berlin) with cheese and salami, or the full works, complete with smoked meats, muesli with fruit and yoghurt, and even a glass of sparkling wine.

Hotels are graded according to an official star rating system designed to sort the deluxe from the dumps – but we haven't followed it in this guide, as the ratings merely reflect room size and amenities such as lifts or bars, rather than other important factors such as decor, staff or atmosphere. Instead, we've divided the hotels by area, then listed them in four categories, according to the standard prices (not including seasonal offers or discounts) for one night in a double room with en suite shower/bath. For Deluxe hotels, expect to pay more than €190; for properties in the Expensive bracket, €120-€190; for Moderate hotels, allow €60-€120; while budget rooms go for less than €60. For hotels catering to a predominantly gay clientele, *see p223.*

VisitBerlin
Reservations & information (250 025, www.visitBerlin.de).
This privatised tourist service can sort out hotel reservations as well as tickets for shows and travel arrangements to Berlin.

Booking.com
0180 100 496, www.booking.com.
With offices Europe-wide, this booking service has pre-reserved beds in hotels of all categories in the city, and guest information can be sent directly to the hotel as a confirmed booking. Check for special offers too.

Casa Camper. *See p113.*

CONSUME

MITTE

The city's historic administrative quarter is alive and well, with an ever-growing number of hotels in all price brackets. While many tourists have started to defect towards less trafficked areas, the faded post-Wall charm of one of the city's oldest quarters is still popular with many. You may not find much of the historic *pension* charm of Charlottenburg here, but for shopping and sightseeing it's one of the more exciting parts of Berlin.

Deluxe

Adlon Kempinski Berlin

Unter den Linden 77, 10117 (226 10, www.hotel-adlon.de). S1, S2 Unter den Linden 77. **Rates** from €220 double. **Map** p318/p327 L6 **❶**

Not quite the Adlon of yore, which burned down after World War II, this new, more generic luxury version was rebuilt by the Kempinski Group in 1997 on its original site next to the Brandenburg Gate. Apart from a few original features, you're really paying for the prime location and the superlative service: bellboys who pass you a chilled bottle of water when you return from a jog in nearby Tiergarten; a silver-tongued concierge who can wangle you a table at the best restaurants or tickets to a sold-out opera. You're most likely to get the €220 rate in January or mid July to mid August. If you want to rent out one of the three bulletproof presidential suites from which Michael Jackson once dangled his child, it will set you back around €12,500.

Bar. Disabled-adapted rooms (2). Gym. Swimming pool. Internet (wireless). Parking. Restaurants (2). Room service. Spa. TV.

★ Casa Camper

Weinmeisterstrasse 1 (www.casacamper.com/berlin, 2000 34 11). U8 Weinmeisterstrasse. **Rates** €205-€305 double. **Map** p326 O5 **❷**

In 2011, the Spanish shoe company opened this luxury boutique hotel right in the heart of the Scheunenviertel. Tired shoppers as well as hungry partygoers can take a break and grab some refreshments any time at the hotel's 24-hour snack bar, which is included in the price of the room. Full meals are served at the restaurant, 'Dos Paillos', which specialises in Asian-style cuisine served in tapas-sized portions. But the chief attraction of this stylishly minimalistic joint are the light-flooded showers with their stunning views over the city. *Photo p112. Disabled-adapted rooms. Gym. Internet (wireless). Parking (€20). Restaurant.*

Hotel de Rome

Behrenstrasse 37, 10117 (460 6090, www.hotelderome.com). U6 Französische Strasse. **Rates** from €395 double. **Map** p319/p327 N6 **❸**

THE BEST HOTELS

A charming gem out West
Pension Funk. *See p132.*

Camping – but not as you know it
Hüttenpalast. *See p134.*

Smart value chain that's colonised the best spots in town
Motel One. *See p126.*

Style on a budget
Amano. *See p118.*

1920s sophistication – just like the Duke
The Ellington. *See p129.*

Weird and wonderful with a rock 'n' roll edge
Michelberger. *See p125.*

Clean, airy, and not a bunk bed in sight
Grand Hostel. *See p126.*

In 2006, this 19th-century manse, which was originally built to house the headquarters of Dresdener Bank, was transformed by Rocco Forte into a pretty sumptuous affair; and yet, despite the intimidating grandeur, the young staff are surprisingly friendly. All 146 rooms are state-of-the-art plush, with plenty of polished wood, marble and velvet. The former basement vault now houses a pool, spa and fully equipped gym. The lobby restaurant, Parioli, specialises in upscale Mediterranean cuisine with al fresco dining in the summer, and lighter fare is available in the sleek Bebel Bar & Lounge or the Opera Court, where high tea is served every afternoon. *Bar. Gym. Internet (high-speed). Parking (€20). Restaurant. Room service. Spa. TV.*

Sofitel Berlin Gendarmenmarkt

Charlottenstrasse 50-52, 10117 (203 750, www.sofitel.com). U2, U6 Stadtmitte. **Rates** from €190 double. **Map** p327 N6 **❹**

'Design for the senses' is the motto here. This is a truly lovely hotel, and rooms are often difficult to come by, but it's well worth the fight. So much attention has been paid to detail: from the moment you enter the lobby, with its soothing colour scheme and wonderful lighting, the atmosphere is intimate and elegant. This carries into the rooms, each beautifully styled, with perhaps the best bathrooms in the city. Even the conference rooms are spectacular, and the hotel's 'wellness' area is complete with plunge pools, gym and meditation room. In summer you can wind down on the sun deck high above the surrounding rooftops.

CONSUME

Bar. Business centre. Gym. Internet (wireless). Parking (€18). Restaurants (2). Room service. Spa. TV.

Expensive

Albrechtshof

Albrechtstrasse 8, 10117 (308 860, www.hotel-albrechtshof.de). U6, S1, S2, S3, S5, S7, S75 Friedrichstrasse. **Rates** (incl breakfast) €126-€208 double. **Map** p318/p327 M6 ❺

Located a stone's throw from the Berliner Ensemble and Friedrichstrasse station, the Albrechtshof is a member of Verband Christlicher Hotels (Christian Hotels Association). They don't make a song and dance about it, but it has its own chapel, named after former guest Martin Luther King. The rooms are comfy and clean, if not particularly stylish, and the staff are friendly. The restaurant offers local cuisine, and in summer breakfast is served in the courtyard garden.

Bar. Disabled-adapted rooms. Parking (€15). Restaurant. TV.

Dietrich-Bonhoeffer-Haus

Ziegelstrasse 30, 10117 (284 670, www.dietrich-bonhoeffer-hotel.de). U6, S1, S2, S3, S5, S7, S75 Friedrichstrasse or S1, S2 Oranienburger Strasse. **Rates** (incl breakfast) €129 double. **Map** p318/p326 M5 ❻

Named after the theologian executed by the Nazis for alleged participation in the 1944 Hitler assassination attempt, this hotel sits on the corner of a quiet side street directly behind the Friedrichstadtpalast. It was originally built in 1987 as a meeting place for Christians from East and West; as such, the atmosphere is warm, and the staff helpful – they even post the day's weather forecast in the lift. The rooms are large, the breakfast is pretty good and the location is excellent.

Internet (wireless). Parking (€10). Restaurant. TV.

Gendarm

Charlottenstrasse 61, 10117 (206 0660, www.hotel-gendarm-berlin.de). U2, U6 Stadtmitte. **Rates** €180 double. **Map** p322/p327 M7 ❼

If you fancy a five-star location but don't want to spend a fortune, then this place is just the ticket. Aside from a few pink frills, it doesn't have a lot of extras, but the 21 rooms and six suites are smart and

---

INSIDE TRACK DOUBLE DUVETS

Don't be surprised if your double bed comes with two single duvets. It's a German thing: they think we're crazy for fighting over one between two. And as for why the pillows are so big and square? We've never figured that one out either.

---

comfortable, and it's close to the restaurants of Gendarmenmarkt, shopping on Friedrichstrasse and the State Opera. At rates around half those at the nearby Sofitel or Hilton, you can't really go wrong – unless you bring a car, that is: parking around here can end up costing as much as your room.

Bar. Gym. Internet (free wireless). TV.

Hackescher Markt

Grosse Präsidentenstrasse 8, 10178 (280 030, www.classik-hotel-collection.de). S3, S5, S7, S75 Hackescher Markt. **Rates** (incl breakfast) €133-€208 double. **Map** p319/p326 N5 ❽

This elegant hotel in a nicely renovated townhouse avoids the noise of its central Hackescher Markt location by cleverly having many rooms face inwards on to a tranquil green courtyard. Some have balconies, all have their own bath with heated floor, and the suites are spacious and comfortable. The pleasant, helpful staff speak good English, and, while you don't necessarily get the most atmosphere for the money, you can't beat the address.

Bar. Internet (wireless). Parking (€15). TV.

Honigmond Garden Hotel

Invalidenstrasse 122, 10115 (2844 5577, www.honigmond.de). U6 Oranienburger Tor. **Rates** (incl breakfast) €125-€230 double. **Credit** V. **Map** p318/p326 M4 ❾

Along with its nearby sister Honigmond Restaurant-Hotel (*see p119*), this is one of the most charming hotels in Berlin, and it doesn't cost an arm and a leg. Choose between large bedrooms facing the street, smaller ones overlooking the fish pond and Tuscan-style garden, or spacious apartments on the upper floor. As with all great places, the secret is in the finer detail. The rooms are impeccably styled with polished pine floors, paintings in massive gilt frames, antiques and iron bedsteads. There's also a charming sitting room overlooking the garden. Highly recommended.

Internet (wireless). Parking (€10). TV. ?

Lux 11

Rosa-Luxemburg-Strasse 9-13, 10178 (936 2800, www.lux-eleven.com). U2 Rosa Luxemburg-Platz. **Rates** €109-€220. **Map** p319/p326 O5 ❿

A member of the Design Hotels group, this former apartment house for the DDR secret police is a stylish, no-nonsense apartment-hotel with an emphasis on wellbeing. The cool, modern white-walled apartments are elegant and well appointed, with everything from intercom for visiting guests to microwave and dishwasher in the kitchen, and queen-sized beds in between. The location is perfect for the fashionable sites of Mitte, or a night at the Volksbühne and there's an in-house Aveda salon if you fancy a blowdry before hitting the tiles. Rates drop dramatically the longer the stay.

Bar. Café. Internet (wireless). Parking (€18). Restaurant. Spa. TV/DVD.

CONSUME

Soho House. *See p117.*

Maritim proArte Hotel Berlin

Friedrichstrasse 151, 10117 (203 35, www. maritim.de). U6, S1, S2, S3, S5, S7, , S75 Friedrichstrasse. **Rates** (incl breakfast) from €120 double. **Map** p318/p327 M6 ⑪

Despite the fact that its status as one of Berlin's first 'designer hotels' has been overshadowed by newcomers, this is still popular with businessmen and stewardesses, who congregate in the mall-like lobby and like to soak up the posh bar, restaurants and boutiques. The 403 rooms, apartments and suites each have fax and computer connections, air-conditioning and marble bathrooms. The staff is polite and helpful, and it's just a short walk to the shops on Friedrichstrasse or to the Brandenburg Gate.
Bar. Disabled-adapted rooms. Gym. Internet (dataport, wireless in some rooms). Parking (€22). Pool (indoor). Restaurants (3). Room service. TV (pay movies).

Meliá Berlin

Friedrichstrasse 103, 10117 (2060 7900, www.meliaberlin.com). U6, S1, S2, S3, S5, S7, , S75 Friedrichstrasse. **Rates** €121-€302 double. **Map** p318/p327 M6 ⑫

Just across the street from Friedrichstrasse station, this new corner building on the banks of the Spree is a huge link in the Spanish Sol Meliá chain. All 364 rooms are similarly and tastefully appointed, many with fine views of the river and Reichstag beyond, but the rich wood units and headboards seem a little incongruous. The rooftop Café Restaurant Madrid offers reasonably priced theatre and business lunch menus, while the tapas bar off the lobby provides lighter fare and entertainment. The helpful staff are pleasant, making this an ideal and convenient stopover for the harried business traveller; but for simple folk in search of atmosphere, there's better value for the money elsewhere.
Bar. Internet (wireless). Parking (€20). Restaurant.

Radisson SAS Berlin

Karl-Liebknecht-Strasse 3, 10178 (238 280, www.radissonblu.com/hotel-berlin.com). S3, S5, S7, S75 Hackescher Markt. **Rates** €155-€340 double. **Map** p319/p327 N6 ⑬

With interiors by German designer Yasmine Mahmoudieh (responsible for the cabins of the Airbus A380), the 427 rooms here are fresh, uncluttered and free of the normal blandness typical of big hotel chains. The Radisson's claim to fame, however, is 'the tank' – a 25m- (82ft)- high aquarium with a million litres of salt water housing 2,500 varieties of fish. Many of the bedrooms even have a view of it. If you're tempted to take a dip, though, we suggest the pool in the hotel spa, or dive into a drink in the Atrium Lobby Lounge bar.
Bar. Disabled-adapted rooms. Gym. Internet (wireless, high-speed). Parking (free). Pool (indoor). Restaurants (2). Room service. Spa. TV (pay movies).

★ Soho House

Torstrasse 1 (40 50 440, www.sohohouse berlin.com). U2 Rosa Luxemburg Platz. **Rates** double from €130 (€110 for members). **Map** p319 P5 ⑭

The average Berliner has a healthy scepticism towards everything 'private' and 'exclusive', so eyebrows were raised when Soho House opened its branch in the German capital in summer 2010. But even the toughest critic would have to admit that the building and its history are too special to be dismissed out of hand. The Bauhaus building has an incredible back story: it initially housed a Jewish-owned department store before it was taken over first by the Nazis, then by the communist regime, These days, Soho House occupies eight floors, and has installed a very good spa, a library and its own cinema. In the rooms, beautiful old wooden floors and 1920s furniture form a stylish union with raw concrete walls. There's a touch of Britishness, too, with a kettle and biscuits in each room (unusual in Germany), which together with the beautiful patina of the furniture makes Soho House Berlin much more cosy and home-like than its rivals. A swim in the rooftop pool overlooking East Berlin rounds off the experience. *Photo p115.*
Internet (wireless). Restaurant. Gym. Spa.

Westin Grand

Friedrichstrasse 158-164, 10117 (202 70, www.westingrandberlin.com). U6 Französische Strasse. **Rates** €159-€520 double; €30 breakfast. **Map** p318/p327 M6 ⑮

Despite its East German prefabricated exterior, the Westin Grand is pure five-star international posh (the Stones stay here when they're in town). The decor is gratifyingly elegant, with lots of polished crystal and brass and a grandiose foyer and staircase. The rooms are tastefully traditional, and the 35 suites are individually furnished with period decor themed after their names. There's also a garden and patio, plus a bar and restaurant, and the elegant haunts of the Gendarmenmarkt are just outside the door.
Bar. Business centre. Disabled-adapted rooms (2). Gym. Internet (dataport, wireless in some rooms). Pool (indoor). Restaurants (3). Room service. Spa. TV (pay movies).

Moderate

Adina Apartment Hotel Hauptbahnhof

Platz vor dem Neuen Tor 6 (www.adina.eu, 0800 6649 510). S3, S5, S7, S75 Hauptbahnhof. **Rates** €105-€295. **Map** p.318 L5 ⑯

This might not be the most charming or unique hotel in Berlin, but it's mightily convenient if you're traveling by train. Plus it's a hop, skip and a jump away from the Reichstag and Brandenburg Gate. The rooms are equipped with a washer, dryer and a complete kitchen, making it a perfect option for families

CONSUME

Circus. *See p121.*

or a longer stay. Many rooms also have a balcony. The indoor swimming pool is another plus.
Disabled-adapted rooms (12). Gym. Internet (wireless €14.50 per day). Parking (€18). Restaurant. Room Service. Pool. Sauna.
Other locations Adina Apartment Hotel Berlin Checkpoint Charlie Krausenstrasse 35-36, Mitte (200 76 70); **Adina Apartment Hotel Hackescher Markt** An der Spandauer Brücke 11, Mitte (2096 980).

Amano

Auguststrasse 43 (80 94 15-0, www.hotel-amano.com). U8 Rosenthalerplatz. **Rates** €82-€350 (double). **Map** p326 N5 ⑰
The nice thing about Amano is that it doesn't try too hard – and it doesn't need to, given its perfect location right in the centre of Berlin. Its rooms and apartments are modern and unpretentious, the prices affordable. For €3 guests can rent an iPod complete with Berlin-inspired pop music and an audio guide. Other perks are the backyard garden and a roof-terrace lounge where older hotel guests mingle with young preppy professionals. Bikes are also available to rent.
Disabled-adapted rooms. Internet (wireless). Parking (€15). Restaurant. Room service.

Arte Luise Kunsthotel

Luisenstrasse 19, 10117 (284 480, www.arte-uise.com). U6, S1, S2, S3, S5, S7, S75 Friedrichstrasse. **Rates** €85-€150 double. **Map** p318/p327 L6 ⑱
Housed in a former neoclassical residential palace just a short walk from the Reichstag and Brandenburger Tor, this 'artist home' is one of the city's more imaginative small hotels, with each of its

50 rooms decorated by a different renowned artist. There's graffiti artist Thomas Baumgärtel's 'Royal Suite', a golden room spray-painted with bananas; and Angela Dwyer's 'Room Like Any Other', whose surfaces are covered in stream-of-consciousness scrawlings. Some rooms get a little noise from the S-Bahn trains, but that shouldn't deter you: this is a great place to stay.
Bar. Disabled-adapted rooms. Restaurant.

Art'otel Berlin Mitte

Wallstrasse 70-73, 10179 (240 620, www.artotels.de). U2 Märkisches Museum. **Rates** €100-€210 double. **Map** p323/p327 O7 ⑲
A real treasure on the Spree. This delightful hotel is a creative fusion of old and new, combining restored rococo reception rooms with ultra-modern bedrooms designed by Nalbach + Nalbach. As well as highlighting the artwork of George Baselitz – originals hang in the corridors and all 109 rooms – the hotel's decor has been meticulously thought out to the smallest detail, from the Philippe Starck bathrooms to the Breuer chairs in the conference rooms. The staff are pleasant, and the views from the top suites across Mitte are stunning.
Bar. Disabled-adapted rooms. Internet (wireless). Parking (€16). Pool (indoor). Restaurant. TV (pay movies).

Hotel Pension Kastanienhof

Kastanienallee 65, 10119 (443 050, www.kastanienhof.biz). U8 Rosenthaler Platz or U2 Senefelderplatz/tram M1, 12. **Rates** (incl breakfast) €103-€138 double. **Map** p319/p328 O4 ⑳
Ideally located at the bottom of Kastanienallee – or 'Casting'allee as it's now knonw, in reference to its

fame as a place to see and be seen at – this is a warm, cosy, old-fashioned hotel. The pastel-coloured rooms are generously proportioned and well equipped, and there are three breakfast rooms and a bar. The English-speaking staff are friendly. It's often booked up on weekends, so it's a good idea to reserve ahead. *Bar. Internet (web TV). Parking (€9). TV.*

Honigmond Restaurant-Hotel

Tieckstrasse 12, 10115 (284 4550, www. honigmond.de). U6 Oranienburger Tor. **Rates** (incl breakfast) €89-€199 double. **Map** p318/p326 M4 ㉑

The 40 rooms in this beautiful 1899 building are spacious and lovely, and although some of the less expensive ones lack their own shower and toilet, don't let that put you off: this is probably the best and prettiest mid-price hotel east of the Zoo. The reception area has comfy chairs around a gas fireplace, and breakfast is served in the Honigmond restaurant, open since 1920. The friendly staff speak English, and the hotel is perfectly situated within walking distance of the Scheunenviertel and Hackescher Markt. More affordable luxury would be hard to come by.
Bar. Parking (€10). Restaurant. TV.
▶ *For the Honigmond restaurant, see p140.*

★ Miniloftmitte

Hessische Strasse 5, 10115 (847 1090, www.miniloft.com). U6 Naturkundemuseum. **Rates** €100-€160 apartment. **Map** p318 L5 ㉒

A brilliant alternative to the hotel hustle, these 14 flats – housed in a combined renovated apartment building and award-winning steel-concrete construction – are modern, airy and elegant. Each comes with a queen-sized bed, couch and dining area (the frosted-glass panels separating bath and kitchen are an interesting touch), with warm-coloured fabrics, organic basics in the kitchen, and lots of space and light. The owners/designers/architects are a young, friendly couple who live and work on the premises. Rates are greatly reduced the longer the stay, and free cleaning is provided weekly for long-term visitors. Highly recommended.
Internet (high-speed wireless). TV.

Park Inn Hotel

Alexanderplatz 7, 10178 (238 90, www. parkinn.de). U2, U5, U8, S3, S5, S7, S75 Alexanderplatz. **Rates** €79-€159 double. **Map** p319/p327 O5 ㉓

With 1,012 rooms overlooking Alexanderplatz, Berlin's largest (and tallest) hotel is something of a mixed bag. Although the views are spectacular, and most of the rooms have been renovated with extra windows, the vibe is a little cold and impersonal considering the price. There are special package deals – and a casino – for the convention groups that fill the lobby in busloads, and easy access to public transport for a business stopover, but for the traveller in search of warmth and atmosphere, there are better choices nearby.
Bar. Disabled-adapted rooms. Gym. Internet (wireless). Parking (€20). Restaurants (2). TV (pay movies).

Platte Mitte

Rochstrasse 9, 10178 (0177 283 26 02, www. plattemitte.de).S3, S5, S7, , S75 Hackescher Markt. **Rates** (per person) from €50 double. **Map** p319/p326/p327 O6 ㉔

CONSUME

The smart way of giving

Give the perfect getaway

Browse the full range of gift boxes from Time Out
timeout.com/smartbox

Proudly calling itself a 'No Hotel', these three apartments on the 21st floor of a 1967-built *Plattenbau* are airy and well designed, each with spectacular views of the city around Alexanderplatz. Colourfully decorated and eclectic to say the least, the furnishings mix original pieces of the period with artfully fanciful touches such as poster-plastered walls and mannequins by the bed. Babysitting services are available, as well as a personal Pilates trainer. And as most of the neighbours are original tenants, this is a wonderfully unique way to experience Berlin. The prices listed are for up to two nights only, and are greatly reduced for longer stays. Rates include bedlinen and weekly cleaning.
Internet (wireless). Parking (€11). TV/DVD.

Riverside Hotel & Day Spa
Friedrichstrasse 106, 10017 (284 900, www. tolles-hotel.de). U6, S1, S2, S3, S5, S7, S75 Friedrichstrasse. **Rates** €59-€295 double. **Map** p318/p326/p327 M5 ⑳
Behind the rather tacky mirrored windows lies the campest hotel in town. There are claw-footed bronze bathtubs, a clamshell floatation tank which shuts in bathers like a venus fly trap, and an abundance of scarlet and gold. In truth, the Riverside has seen better days – the carpets are a little worn, and the odd cobweb suggests the cleaners could do with paying more attention – but its location can't be beaten. Nor can its prices, which run on a five-star scale, from one star bargains right up to five star deluxe suites. If you're on a budget, ask for the one star "U" room – you'll have to go out into the hall for your own private bathroom, but you get a balcony and a priceless view of the Bode Museum. There are big discounts in the spa for hotel guests and you can fill your own minibar with beers from reception for just €2.50.
Internet (free wireless in rooms, shared terminal in lobby). Parking (€5-10). Spa. TV.

Cheap

baxpax Downtown Hostel Hotel
Ziegelstrasse 28, 10117 (278 748-80, www.baxpax.de). U6, S1, S2, S3, S5, S7, S75 Friedrichstrasse. **Rates** from €29 single; from €27 per person double; from €10 (per person) dorm; €2.50 bedlinen. **No credit cards**. **Map** p318/p326/p327 M5 ㉖
This new, third addition to the Mittes Backpacker Hostel empire is an excellent place to stay, with a brilliant location. Clean, contemporary and well designed, it has all the usual amenities, from baggage room to darts, with the additional luxury of a fireplace lounge, courtyard and rooftop terrace. There's a dorm just for women, 24-hour reception and keycard access for security, and a friendly, relaxed atmosphere.
Bar. Disabled-adapted rooms. Internet (wireless).
Other Locations baxpax Mitte Hostel Chauseestrasse 102 (283 909 65); **baxpax Kreuzberg** Skalitzer Strasse 104 (695 183 22).

★ Circus
Weinbergsweg 1A, 10119 (2839 1433, www.circus-berlin.de). U8 Rosenthaler Patz. **Rates** from €43, €53 with bathroom, single; from €56 double; from €19 (per person) dorm. **Map** p319/p326 N4 ㉗
Almost the standard by which other hostels should be measured, the Circus is a rarity – simple but stylish, warm and comfortable. And the upper-floor apartments have balconies and lovely views. The laid-back staff can help get discount tickets to almost anything, or give directions to the best bars and clubs, of which there are plenty nearby. Deservedly popular, this place is always full, so be sure to book ahead. Just across the Platz, the owners also run the moderately priced Circus Hotel, whose 63 double rooms, each with private bath, surround a central terraced winter garden and café. Reservations and information are available on the above number. *Photos p118, p119.*
Bar. Café. Disabled-adapted rooms. Internet (wireless in lobby). TV room.

CityStay
Rosenstrasse 16, 10178 (2362 4031, www. citystay.de). S5, S7, S75 Hackescher Markt. **Rates** from €40 single; from €50 double; from €17 (per person) dorm; €2.50 bedlinen. **No credit cards. Map** p327 O6 ㉘
On a small, quiet street, but as central as you can get, this is a great modern hostel for the price. The rooms are clean and simple, and there are showers on every floor. Security is top-notch, with access cards for the video-monitored entrance and floors. The helpful staff are friendly. The breakfast buffet features fresh organic bread, and the kitchen will fix your eggs any way you like 'em.
Café. Internet (shared terminal).

EasyHotel
Rosenthaler Strasse 69 (no phone, www.easyhotel.com). U8 Rosenthalerplatz. **Rates** from €25 double. **Map** p326 N5 ㉙
The 125 rooms at this new hotel are as you would expect from the budget airline – small and cheap. But they are smart and clean, and not aggressively orange as you might imagine. Plus the hotel is brilliantly located for the shops, bars and restaurants of the most excting bit of Mitte. Book far enough in

CONSUME

advance and a room here is a real bargain, though beware that just like flying with a low-cost carrier, the extras soon mount up. It's €8 to get your room cleaned, €3 for 24-hour internet access and €3 for luggage storage.
Internet (wireless). TV.

Heart of Gold Hostel Berlin
Johannisstrasse 11, 10117 (2900 3300, www.heartofgold-hostel.de). U6, S1, S2, S5, S7, S75 Friedrichstrasse. **Rates** (incl bedlinen) €40 single; €50-€60 double; €12 (per person) dorm. **Map** p318/p326 M5 ⓵

The prime location aside (it's only 50m from Oranienburger Strasse), this member of the Backpacker Germany Network (www.backpacker-network.de) is an enjoyable place to stay. Rooms are bright and cheerful, all newly done with parquet floors. Lockers are free, and individual bathrooms and showers and a keycard system guarantee security. The laundry is cheap, as are the €1 shots in the bar, and with free sens-o-matic sunglasses and Squornshellous Zeta mattresses to help you recover, what more could a backpacker need? How about a money-back guarantee? If you don't like it, you don't pay.
Bar. Internet (wireless). TV.

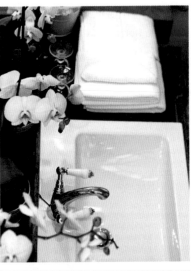

Ackselhaus & Bluehome.

Helter Skelter Hostel

Kalkscheunenstrasse 4-5, 10117 (2809 7979, www.helterskelterhostel.com). U6, S1, S2, S3, S5, S7, S75 Friedrichstrasse. **Rates** (incl bedlinen) from €50 double; from €12 (per person) dorm. **Map** p318/p326 M5 ⑤

Right behind the Friedrichstadtpalast in the historic Kalkscheune ('chalk barn') cultural centre, this centrally located hostel is a wonderful, relaxed place to stay, with amiable and international English-speaking staff. There are apartments available for longer stays, and kitchen facilities in the communal room. The rooms are curiously decorated, but fun – one has a pool table on the ceiling. You're within walking distance of almost everything, and Friedrichstrasse station is handy for anything that isn't on the doorstep. *Internet (free wireless).*

PRENZLAUER BERG

From the cool of Kastanienallee to the funky chic of Helmholzplatz, this neighbourhood just north of Mitte may be charming, but it has a surprising dearth of decent hotels.

Expensive

★ Ackselhaus & Bluehome

Belforter Strasse 21 & 24 (4433 7633, www.ackselhaus.de). U2 Senefelder Platz. **Rates** (incl breakfast) from €150-€220 double. *Bluehome* from €150 single/double. **Map** p319/p328 P4 ㉜

Just doors apart, what ties these two establishments together – aside from their shared reception desk – is a wonderfully realised, luxurious 'modern colonial' style. Each room is lovingly decorated with lots of attention to detail. The delightful Kairo Suite will make you feel like you have been transported away from the hustle and bustle of Prenzlauer Berg right on to the set of *The English Patient.* Decorative themes range from China to Maritime to Movie, so there should be a room for every taste. Bluehome (at No.24), with its blue façade, and balconies overlooking Belforter Strasse, houses the Club del Mar restaurant, which offers a breakfast buffet and open fireplace. There's also a lovely garden out back, complete with lawn chairs in the summer. *Internet (wireless). TV.*

Moderate

Greifswald

Greifswalder Strasse 211, 10405 (442 7888, www.hotel-greifswald.de). Tram M4 Hufelandstrasse. **Rates** €65-€75 double. **Map** p319/328 Q4 ㉝

A hidden gem for those who want some place simple, warm and charming to kick their feet up after a hard day's touring. Tucked away in a quiet rear courtyard just a short distance from both Alexanderplatz and Kollwitzplatz (and the nearby Knaack and Magnet

clubs), this is a favourite among artists and musicians. The rooms are tasteful and cheery without the fluff, the staff friendly and helpful. But the highlight is breakfast, which has to be the best buffet in Berlin… and it's served from 6.30am until noon. During the summer you can have it al fresco in the back. Apartments are also available. Note that parking is limited. Highly recommended. *Internet (wireless). Parking (free). TV.*

Precise Hotel Myer's Berlin

Metzer Strasse 26, 10405 (440 140, www.precisehotels.com.de). U2 Senefelderplatz. **Rates** €82-€112 double. **Map** p319 P4 ㉞

This renovated 19th-century townhouse sits on a tranquil street. There's a garden and a glass-ceilinged gallery, and the big leather furniture seems to beg you to light up a cigar. Plus the beautiful Kollwitzplatz is just around the corner, as are a bunch of decent bars and restaurants, and although the tram stop is just down the street, it's a lovely walk into Mitte. *Bar. Disabled-adapted rooms (3). Internet (dataport). TV.*

Cheap

Lette'm Sleep Hostel

Lettestrasse 7, 10437 (4473 3623, www.backpackers.de). U2 Eberswalder Strasse. **Rates** €40-€49 double; from €11 (per person) dorm. **Map** p319/p328 P2 ㉟

Just off the Helmholzplatz, this small hostel has new floors and bathrooms, and a beer garden in the back for summer barbecues. There's free tea and coffee but no breakfast, which you can either make yourself in the kitchen or enjoy at one of the many decent cafés around the corner. All rooms have hand-basins and hot showers are always available. The three large apartments can sleep up to ten people each, and there are reduced rates for longer stays. *Disabled-adapted rooms. Internet (shared terminal).*

Transit Loft

Immanuelkirchstrasse 14A, 10405 (4849 3773, www.transit-loft.de). Tram M4 Hufelandstrasse. **Rates** (incl breakfast) €59 single; €79 double; €21 (per person) dorm. **Map** p319 Q4 ㊱

This loft hotel in a renovated factory is ideal for backpackers and young travellers. The rooms all have en suite bathrooms and there's a private sauna, gym and billiard room with special rates for hotel guests. The staff is friendly and well informed, and there's good wheelchair access too. *Bar. Disabled-adapted rooms. Internet (shared terminal). TV.*

FRIEDRICHSHAIN

Friedrichshain hasn't quite panned out as the city's new bohemia, but with decent transport connections, a still somewhat

CONSUME

BERLIN · PLAZA
HOTEL

www.plazahotel.de
www.restaurant-knese.de
www.parken-am-kudamm.de
http://blog.plazahotel.de

'Eastie' alternative feel, good cafés and lots of nightlife, it continues to be a great area to stay in, especially if you're on a tight budget.

Moderate

★ Michelberger
Warschauer Strasse 39-40 (29 778 590, www.michelbergerhotel.com). S3, S5, S7, S75, U 1 Warschauer Strasse. **Rates** from €60 double. **Map** p324 S8 ③
With its purposefully unfinished look and effortlessly creative vibe, Michelberger might seem like Berlin in a nutshell to some. While the cheaper rooms are characterised by a stylish simplicity reminiscent of a school gym, the pricier rooms have an air of tongue-in-cheek decadence – decked out in floor to ceiling gold or in the style of a mountain resort – complete with sunken bathtubs and movie projectors. Michelberger might not be as spotlessly clean as other hotels (though it's far from being dirty), but it's much more fun. The downside of the convenient location (right across from U-Bahnhof Warschauer Strasse) is that some of the rooms are quite noisy, so you might want to request a room facing the courtyard.
Internet (wireless).

nhow
Stralauer Allee 3 (www.nhow-hotels.com, 290 2990). S3, S5, S7, S75, U 1 Warschauer Strasse. **Rates** €115-€275 double. **Map** p324 S9 ③
If you're allergic to pink, you're well advised not to check into the nhow. In a huge modern building right by the river Spree, New York designer Karim Rashid has implemented his eye-popping vision of a music and lifestyle hotel. Even the elevators are illuminated by different coloured lights and some are decorated with photos of Rashid and his wife. As you would expect from a music hotel, all rooms are equipped with iPod docking stations and if you're in the mood for a spontaneous jam, you can order a Gibson guitar or an electric piano up to your room. The hotel has a beautiful view on to the river and the breakfast buffet leaves no wish unfulfilled. There's a nice sauna too. *Photos p127.*
Internet (wireless). Parking (€16). Restaurant. Room Service. Disabled-adapted room. Gym.

Cheap

Eastern Comfort
Mühlenstrasse 73-77, 10243 (6676 3806, www.eastern-comfort.com). U1, S3, S5, S7, S75 Warschauer Strasse. **Rates** €45-€64 single; €50-€78 double; €16 (per person) dorm; tent on the upper deck €12; €5 bedlinen & towel (optional). **Map** p324 R8 ③
Berlin's first 'hostel boat' is moored on the Spree by the East Side Hotel, across the river from Kreuzberg. The rooms – or, rather, cabins – are clean and fairly spacious (considering it's a boat), and all have their own shower and toilet. The four-person room can feel a little cramped, but if you need to get up and stretch there are two common rooms, one lounge and three terraces offering beautiful river views. The owners have now done up a second boat, the Western Comfort, which is moored over the river on the Kreuzberg bank.
Internet (wireless in reception). TV room.

Odyssee Globetrotter Hostel
Grünberger Strasse 23, 10243 (2900 0081, www.globetrotterhostel.de). U1, S3, S5, S7, S75 Warschauer Strasse. **Rates** (incl bedlinen) €29-€49 single; €39-€69 double; from €10 (per person) dorm. **No credit cards.** **Map** p324 S7 ④
Down a dark wooden corridor and up the backyard stairs, this is the metal and tat version of a good old-fashioned youth hostel. The place has a little edge to it, with a dimly lit reception area and lounge for a change. The rooms are clean, the showers are good and there's billiards and table football, although the neighbourhood also has lots of alternative clubs and bars. There's also a dormitory with its own kitchen, and discounts, for groups and extended stays, as well as a 5% discount for prepaid bookings.
Bar. Internet (shared terminal). TV room.

OSTEL Das DDR Design Hostel
Wriezener Karree 5, 10243 (2576 8660, www.ostel.eu). S3, S5, S7, S9 Ostbahnhof. **Rates** from €54 double; €15 (per person) dorm. **Map** p324 R7 ④
The four clocks on the wall read: Berlin, Moscow, Peking and Havana. There's a poster of Erick Honecker on the wall. But there's no political message at this budget East German-themed hostel: just a cheap bed for the night. For an additional €3.50, guests are given a *Lebensmittelmarke* (food-ration coupon) for breakfast at the Ossi Hof pub out front. And for those who just can't get enough of the stuff, there's a hotel *Konsum* (state-run market), which sells everything from plaster egg cups to chocolate DDR coins. There's even a rare roll of original toilet paper – but it's not for sale. Just a few streets away at Andreasstrasse 20, is the Ostel's DDR-Ferienwohnung (holiday apartment), 75sq m (807sq ft) of classified two-star lodging that sleeps up to six in DDR style with everything from TV to washing machine, great views and a Trabant-driven tour of the city.
Internet (wireless).

KREUZBERG

The former centre of (West) Berlin's alternative scene, Kreuzberg has some of the city's most picturesque streets, liveliest markets, coolest cafés and most interesting alternative venues. Don't miss the post-Mitte renaissance on Schlesiche Strasse.

CONSUME

Expensive

Riehmers Hofgarten

Yorckstrasse 83, 10965 (7809 8800, www.hotel-riehmers-hofgarten.de). U6, U7 Mehringdamm. **Rates** (incl breakfast) €138-€155 double. **Map** p322 M10 ㊷

In a historic building with one of Berlin's prettiest courtyards, this is a wonderful hotel. The 22 exquisitely styled rooms are airy and elegant (the furniture was custom designed), the staff are charming, and Thomas Kurt, chef at the restaurant, e.t.a. hoffmann, is widely praised. Although the location is somewhat off the beaten track, the neighbourhood has many charms of its own, with Victoria Park and Bergmanstrasse's shops and cafés nearby. If you need to venture further afield, two subway lines stop at the corner. Reasonably priced for what you get, and recommended.

Bar. Disabled-adapted rooms. Internet (wireless). Parking (€10). Restaurant. TV.

Moderate

Johann

Johanniterstrasse 8 (2250740, www.hotel-johann-berlin.de). U1, U6 Hallesches Tor. **Rates** (incl breakfast) €90-€105 double. €15 additional bed for under-12s; €25 for over-12s. **Map** p323 N9 ㊸

This spotlessly clean – if slightly utilitarian – hotel is located in the sleepiest bit of Kreuzberg, one block away from the canal and the great Brachvogel beer garden. It's a ten minute stroll to the Jewish Museum and a pleasant 20-minute walk by the water to reach the restaurants and bars of eastern Kreuzberg. The rooms are big and airy; some (like Room 301 – the pick of the crop) retain original arched ceilings which date back to the building's original use, as army barracks in the 19th century. The simple buffet breakfast can be taken in the lovely courtyard and there's an honesty bar downstairs. The owners Rainer and Katrin provide free cots for babies and most rooms can accommodate a third bed.

Disabled adapted room (1). Internet (free wireless). Parking (€6).

★ *For the Brachvogel beer garden, see p166.*

Cheap

Die Fabrik

Schlesische Strasse 18, 10997 (611 7116, www.diefabrik.com). U1 Schlesiches Tor. **Rates** from €38 single; from €52-€58 double; €18 (per person) dorm. **No credit cards. Map** p324 R9 ㊹

Smack bang in the middle of a newly invigorated Schlesische Strasse, this former telephone factory – hence the name – with turn-of-the-century charm intact, has 50 clean and comfortable no-frills rooms. No kitchen, no TV and no billiards. Just a bed and a locker. But with the café next door for breakfast, and plenty of restaurants, bars and galleries nearby, you don't need much more. It also produces its own solar-powered heating and hot water, and the bedlinen is free. Discounts for children.

Internet (shared terminal).

★ Grand Hostel

Tempelhofer Ufer 14 (200 95 450, www.grand-hostel-berlin.de). U1, U7 Möckernbrücke. **Rates** (per person) from €35 single; €19 twin; €15 triple; €14 4-5 person dorm. Linen (compulsory) €3. **Map** p322 M9 ㊺

This fantastic hostel is situated in an aptly grand 19th-century building with high ceilings and plenty of period character. The rooms are spacious and spotless, and there are no bunks even in the dorms, just comfy real beds with good-quality linen. There are bikes to hire and the cheerful, well informed staff know everything from the best kebab shops in Berlin to where to do karaoke on a Wednesday. The only possible downer is that it's situated in one of the less happening parts of Kreuzberg, albeit with great transport links to the hotspots. *Photos p129.*

Internet (free wireless).

Lekker Urlaub

Graefestrasse 89 (3730 6434, www.lekkerurlaub.de). U8 Schonleinstrasse. **Rates** single €40; double €65; triple €100; 4-person €125. **No credit cards.** **Map** p323 P10 ㊻

This charming bijoux newcomer is in one of the prettiest and buzziest bits of Kreuzberg. Set on the ground floor of a typical Berlin tenement, the rooms are small but clean. Each is unique: the bed in one is only reachable by a ladder, so warn them in advance if you're scared of heights. There's a lovely café attached which serves meals from 9am-6pm, but there are dozens of bars and restaurants within a two-minute radius.

Internet (free wireless).

Motel One Berlin-Mitte

Prinzenstrasse 40, 10969 (7007 9800, www.motel-one.com). U8 Moritzplatz. **Rates** from €64 double. **Map** p323 O8 ㊼

Who'd have thought that such a seemingly anonymous chain could produce such a smart hotel? The 180 rooms, all recently remodelled and refreshed, are basic but done with flair: check out the large dark wood headboards, flat-screen TVs and modern free-standing sinks. Even that appliqué on the curtains and pillows is bearable. Your dog can enjoy it as well for only €5 a night extra. Throw in the bargain rates and top location (in Kreuzberg, despite the name) and you have a winner overall.

Bar. Internet (wireless). Parking (€9.50). **Other locations** throughout the city.

Rock 'n' Roll Herberge

Muskauer Strasse 11, 10997 (61 6236 00, www.rnrherberge.de.de). U Görlitzer Bahnhof.

Rates (incl breakfast & bedlinen) €34-€44 single; €49-€59 double. No credit cards. Map p323 Q9 ⓭

As the name suggests, this budget hotel is aimed particularly at bands on tour and for music lovers to feel at home. It's a great place, with all the trimmings, on a quiet stretch just blocks from the main drags of Kreuzberg. The downstairs rooms are small, but some have bathrooms. The staff are friendly, there's a *Currywurscht* party every Thursday with vegan and vegetarian sausages, and the bar-restaurant is popular with colourful locals.
Bar. Internet (wireless). Restaurant.

Transit
Hagelberger Strasse 53-54, 10965 (789 0470, www.hotel-transit.de). U6, U7 Mehringdamm.
Rates (incl breakfast) €59 single; €69 double; from €21 (per person) dorm. Map p322 M10 ⓭

Located in one of the most beautiful parts of Kreuzberg, this former factory is now a bright and airy hotel with 49 basic but clean rooms, each with a shower and toilet. There's a 24-hour bar on the premises, and the staff speak good English. With Victoria Park around the block and a wealth of bars, cafés and restaurants in the area, it's often full – so it's wise to book ahead. Women-only dorms are also available.
Bar. Internet (shared terminal).

TIERGARTEN

Tiergarten is now officially part of Mitte, but don't tell the locals. There are a few notable establishments dotting the edges of the park that gives the district its name, as well as big modern embassies and a complex of cultural institutions by the New National Gallery – and rising like Oz beyond it, the glitz and glare of Potsdamer Platz.

Deluxe

Grand Hyatt Berlin
Marlene-Dietrich-Platz 2, 10785 (2553 1234, www.berlin.grand.hyatt.com). U2, S1, S2, S26 Potsdamer Platz. Rates from €245 double.
Map p322/p327 K8 ⓭

This is a classy joint, just far enough off the beaten tourist path to keep its cool. The lobby is all matt black and sleek wood panelling – a refreshing change from the usual five-star marble or country villa look. The rooms, which are decorated without a floral print in sight, are spacious and elegant; the internet TV is also a nice touch. The rooftop spa and gym has a splendid swimming pool with views across the city. The sushi restaurant, Vox, is one of the best eateries in the city.
Bars. Disabled-adapted rooms. Gym. Internet (wireless, web TV). Parking (€22). Pool (indoor). Restaurants (3). Spa. TV.

nhow. See p125.

CONSUME

Intercontinental

Budapester Strasse 2, 10787 (260 20,
www.berlin.intercontinental.com). U2, U9,
S3, S5, S7, S75 Zoologischer Garten/bus 200.
Rates from €220 double. **Map** p321 H8 ⑤
The extremely plush and spacious 'Interconti'
exudes luxury. The airy lobby, with its soft leather
chairs, is ideal for browsing the papers, and the
rooms, overlooking the Zoo and western edges of the
new diplomatic quarter, are large and tastefully decorated, right down to the elegant bathrooms.
Thomas Kammeier, Berlin master chef, whips things
up in the Michelin-starred restaurant, Hugo's, while
the huge gym and spa has everything a body could
possibly need to exercise off the meal.
Bar. Gym. Internet (wireless). Parking (€20). Pool
(indoor). Room service. Spa. TV.
▶ *For Hugo's, see p153.*

★ Mandala

Potsdamer Strasse 3, 10785 (590 050 000,
www.themandala.de). U2, S1, S2, S25 Potsdamer
Platz. **Rates** from €270 studio. **Map** p322 L7 ⑤
This privately owned addition to the Design Hotels
portfolio is, given the address, an oasis of calm, luxury and taste. The 144 rooms and suites, most of
which face their glass walls upon an inner courtyard, are perfectly designed for space and light,
decorated in warm whites and beiges, with big
comfortable minimalist furnishings and flat-screen
TVs. A sheltered path through the Japanese garden
on the fifth floor leads to Facil, the world-cuisine
restaurant now vying for its second Michelin star.
The Qiu lounge offers lighter fare, and the rooftop
wellness centre, windowed from end to end, offers
spectacular views of the city. Reduced rates available for longer stays.
Bar. Disabled-adapted rooms. Gym. Internet
(wireless). Parking (€29). Restaurant. Room
service. TV.

Ritz-Carlton

Potsdamer Platz 3, 10785 (337 777,
www.ritzcarlton.com). U2, S1, S2, S26
Potsdamer Platz. **Rates** from €245 double.
Map p322/p327 L7 ⑤
It's flashy, it's trashy, it's Vegas-meets-Versailles.
The Ritz-Carlton is so choc-a-bloc with black marble, gold taps and taffeta curtains that the rooms
seem somewhat stuffy, small and cramped. It's supposedly art deco style but feels more like some
upscale shopping mall. Still, the oyster and lobster
restaurant is deliciously decadent, and the service
is fantastic: the technology butler will sort out the
bugs in your computer connection, and the bath
butler will run your tub. Bring a fat wallet and get
ready to be pampered.
Bars. Disabled-adapted rooms. Gym. Internet
(wireless). Parking (€28). Pool (indoor).
Restaurants (2). Room service. TV (pay
movies, DVD).

Expensive

Grand Hotel Esplanade

Lützowufer 15, 10785 (254 780, www.
esplanade.de). U1, U2, U3, U4 Nollendorfplatz.
Rates from €120 double. **Map** p322 J8 ⑤
With an entry wall of gushing water lit overhead by
glittering lights, this is one of Berlin's better luxury
hotels, overlooking the Landwehr Canal and close to
the Tiergarten. The lobby is equally grand, spacious
and beautifully decorated, while the rooms are tasteful
and gratifyingly free of frilly decor. There's also a fitness centre and a triangular swimming pool, plus
three restaurants to choose from. But just as important is the fact that it's within stumble-back-to-bed
distance of Harry's New York Bar on the ground floor.
Bars (2). Disabled-adapted rooms. Internet
(wireless). Parking (free). Pool (indoor).
Restaurants (3). Spa.

CHARLOTTENBURG

This is the smart end of town, with fine
dining and elegant shopping, and where five-
star luxury hotels sit happily alongside
traditional charms of pensions housed in
grand Gründerzeit townhouses.

Deluxe

Concorde Berlin

Augsburger Strasse 41, 10789 (800 9990,
www.concorde-hotels.com/concordeberlin). U1,
U9 Kurfürstendamm. **Rates** (incl breakfast)
€180-€570 double. **Map** p321/p328 G8 ⑤

Grand Hostel.
See p126.

Designed by Berlin architect Jan Kleihues, this new French-owned five-star is grandly proportioned with a refreshingly minimalist and contemporary approach. Resembling the bow of an ocean liner, its 311 rooms (including 44 huge suites) are each decorated in warm woods and colour tones, with intimate lighting and modern art, to elegant and understated effect. The Restaurant Saint Germain will serve your breakfast, the Brasserie Le Faubourg your French/Med dinner – after cocktails in the Lutèce Bar – and the Club Étoile on the top floors offers a wonderful panorama of the city. The wellness centre may come in handy after all this indulgence.
Bar. Internet (wireless). Parking (€18). Restaurants (2). Spa. TV.

Expensive

Art Nouveau Berlin

Leibnitzstrasse 59, 10629 (327 7440, www. hotelartnouveau.de). U7 Adenauerplatz or S3, S5, S7, S75 Savignyplatz. **Rates** (incl breakfast) €126-€176 double. **Map** p321/p328 E8 ⑤
This is one of the most charming small hotels in Berlin. The rooms are decorated with flair in a mix of Conran-modern and antique furniture, each with an enormous black and white photo hung by the bed. The en suite bathrooms are well integrated into the rooms without disrupting the elegant townhouse architecture. Even the TVs are stylish. The breakfast room has a fridge full of goodies, should you feel peckish in the wee hours, and the folks are sweet.
Internet (dataport). Parking (€5). TV.

Bleibtreu

Bleibtreustrasse 31, 10707 (884 740, www. bleibtreu.com). U1 Uhlandstrasse or S3, S5, S7, S75 Savignyplatz. **Rates** €124-€227 double. **Map** p321/p328 E9 ⑤
The Bleibtreu is a friendly, smart and cosy establishment popular with the media and fashion crowds. The rooms are on the smaller side, but they're all very modern, and decorated with environmentally sound materials. The restaurant is famed for its no-sugar menu, and there's the Deli 31 for a bagel and coffee. The hotel also offers private yoga classes, as well as reflexology. A wonderful choice for the health-conscious, certainly, but good service with lots of pampering and attention means it should appeal to anyone.
Disabled-adapted rooms. Internet (wireless). Restaurant. TV.

★ Ellington

Nürnberger Strasse 50-55, 10789 (6831 50, www.ellington-hotel.com). U1, U2, U3 Wittenbergplatz or U1 Augsburger Strasse. **Rates** €118-€258 double. **Map** p321 G9 ⑤
This hotel is one of the classiest, most sophisticated joint in Berlin. Hidden within the shell of a landmark art deco dance hall, it combines cool contemporary elegance with warmth and ease. The rooms, mostly white with polished wood accents, are brilliantly simple, with modern free-standing fixtures and half-walls, and absolute calm behind the original double windows. The staff are helpful and remarkably cheerful given the daft flat caps they are made to wear. An ambitious menu is served in the Duke restaurant, and there are Sunday jazz brunches in the central

CONSUME

courtyard. All this and KaDeWe around the corner… the Duke would be proud. Highly recommended.
Bar. Business centres (2). Disabled-adapted rooms. Gym. Internet (wireless). Parking (€15). Restaurant.
▶ *For more about the shopping opportunities at KaDeWe, see p174.*

Hecker's Hotel

Grolmanstrasse 35, 10623 (889 00, www.heckers-hotel.com). U1 Uhlandstrasse or S3, S5, S7, S75 Savignyplatz. **Rates** €120-€330 double. **Map** p321/p328 F8 ㊾
This is a sleek, smart, high-quality hotel; stylish, with an air of privacy. The rooms are spacious and comfortable, if not minimally styled, with sparkling marble in the bathrooms, while the suites come with air-conditioning and Bang & Olufsen DVD-TVs. Other highlights include a rooftop terrace and the Cassambalis restaurant, serving Med cuisine.
Bar. Disabled-adapted rooms. Internet (wireless). Parking (€12). Restaurant. TV.

Kempinski Hotel Bristol Berlin

Kurfürstendamm 27, 10719 (884 340, www.kempinskiberlin.de). U1, U9 Kurfürstendamm. **Rates** from €140 double. **Map** p321/p328 F8 ㏿
This famous Berlin hotel was first a celebrated restaurant before being rebuilt in its present form in 1951. While the rooms aren't as plush as you might expect at these prices, the grand atmosphere, friendly staff, original Berlin artwork, wonderful pool and saunas make up for it. A newish restaurant, Reinhard's, has added a regional menu to the proceedings.
Bar. Business centres (2). Gym. Internet (wireless). Parking (€21). Pool (indoor). Restaurants (2). Room service. Spa. TV (pay movies).

Savoy Hotel Berlin

Fasanenstrasse 9-10, 10623 (311 030, www.hotel-savoy.com). U2, U9, S3, S5, S7, S75 Zoologischer Garten. **Rates** €146-€277 double; €19 breakfast. **Credit** AmEx, MC, V. **Map** p321/p328 F8 ㏀
Erected in 1929, and a favourite of author Thomas Mann, this is a smart, stylish hotel with lots of low-key flair. The rooms are elegant and understated, but for a little zing in the suites, such as the white Greta Garbo suite and black marble Henry Miller suite. The Weinrot restaurant serves a well-thought-out modern menu. A further bonus is the location, set back just far enough from the hustle and bustle of Zoologischer Garten to be quiet and convenient.
Bar. Internet (wireless). Restaurant. Room service. TV (pay movies).

Moderate

Berlin Plaza

Knesebeckstrasse 62, 10719 (884 130, www.plaza hotel.de). U1 Uhlandstrasse. **Rates** (incl breakfast) €70-€180 double; free under-13s. **Map** p321/p328 F9 ㏁

Despite a rather plain minimalist decor and colour scheme in the rooms, there's something posh about the Plaza. All double rooms, and even some singles, have both shower and bath. The restaurant and bar serve regional German specialities, and the breakfast buffet is excellent. Children under 13 can stay with parents for free.
Bar. Internet (wireless). Parking (€12). Restaurant. TV (pay movies).

Hotel-Pension Dittberner

Wielandstrasse 26, 10707 (884 6950, www.hotel-dittberner.de). U7 Adenauerplatz or S3, S5, S7, S75 Savignyplatz. **Rates** (incl breakfast) €99-€138 double. **Map** p321/p328 E9 ㏃
From the ride up the 1911 elevator and into the sitting room, this is a grand place, stylish and eclectic, and an obvious labour of love. It's filled with fine original artworks, enormous chandeliers and handsome furnishings. From the beautiful breakfast room to the private rooms, each is airy and elegant, and some of the rooms and suites are truly palatial (one has a winter garden around the courtyard, for example). But the main draw here is comfort. Frau Lange, the owner, is friendly and helpful, and goes out of her way to make her guests feel at home. Truly one of the best pensions in the city.
Internet (shared terminal). TV.

Modena

Wielandstrasse 26, 10707 (885 7010, www.hotel-modena.de). U7 Adenauerplatz or S3, S5, S7, S75 Savignyplatz. **Rates** (incl breakfast) €75-€100 double. **Map** p321/p328 E9 ㏄
Just a floor below the Dittberner (*see above*), this thoroughly unassuming 19-room pension is charming, sweet and cheap. Staff are very friendly, accommodating and speak English, and the atmosphere is relaxed. A top choice if you're travelling as part of a group and want to be in the west end. Added bonus: the price gets lower the longer you stay.
Internet (wireless). TV room.

Cheap

Bogota

Schlüterstrasse 45, 10707 (881 5001, www.bogota.de). S3, S5, S7, S75 Savignyplatz. **Rates** (incl breakfast) €69-€120 double. **Map** p321/p328 E9 ㏅
Though the attractive foyer of this characterful two-star belies rooms more functional than fancy, it's still a wonderful place: terrific value, with a superb atmosphere and friendly staff. The history is remarkable too: there's a bit of ornate parquet near the lobby on which Benny Goodman once tapped his feet at a party. The photographs in the fourth-floor foyer were shot by the fashion photographer Yva, who had her studio on the very spot. Her assistant, Helmut Newton, learned his craft here before fleeing Germany in 1938 (Yva died in the Majdanek concentration

CONSUME

Haven at the Hüttenpalast

Caravans fit for a king.

Berlin is full of surprises, and what's hidden in an old vacuum cleaner factory in a northern Neukölln is one of the most unexpected. The Hüttenpalast (*see p134*; literally, Cabin Palace) is a 150 square metre hall that was once the factory floor. Since summer 2011 it's been home to three vintage caravans and three little cabins, each sleeping two people.

Set out like a mini indoor campsite, there are separate male and female shower rooms and a tree in the middle. Each morning guests emerge from their boltholes to discover the tree has borne fruit – well, little bags containing croissants. There's fresh coffee on hand and the streetfront café does an à la carte menu for those with particularly grumbling stomachs.

Each caravan is different – Kleine Schwester (Little Sister) is decked out with white wood panelling and matching linen; the Herzensbrecher (Heartbreaker) has a domed metal ceiling; the Schwalbennest (Swallow's nest) is big enough to squeeze in a table. The huts, each unique in design and decoration, are perhaps slightly better for anyone prone to claustrophobia.

On the ground floor of another building are six more conventional hotel rooms with en suite showers for those guests who do not consider any kind of camping a holiday.

In the shared courtyard between the café and Hüttenpalast is a charming leafy garden with flowers planted in old bathtubs, oil drums and wine crates. There's a hammock, comfy chairs and the sort of swinging sofa the Germans call a Hollywood-Schaukel.

The Hüttenpalast, surely Berlin's most unusual hotel, is the brainchild of events organiser Silke Lorenzen and Sarah Vollmer, a chef turned fashion and product designer. Like so many creative young Berliners, the thirtysomething pair had moved out to Neukölln in search of cheaper rents and some rough edges that had yet to be smoothed. The area had everything they wanted – interesting neighbours, shops, bars and cheap empty buildings. The only thing it was missing was somewhere to billet friends and family when they came to town. When their spare rooms were full, they had to either send guests down to the boring old Best Western on Hermannplatz or pack them off to another district altogether.

They were already thinking of a new neighbourhood project under the banner Agentur für ALLES (agency for everything) when the lightblub came on: they should set up a hotel. But not just any old hotel. The Hüttenpalast was born.

CONSUME

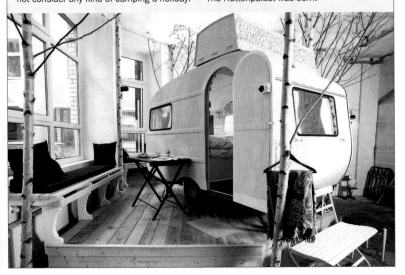

camp four years later). Half the doubles have their own showers and all have at least a sink. Good stuff. *TV (TV room, some individual rooms).*

Hotel Pension Columbus

Meinekestrasse 5, 10719 (881 5061, www. columbus-berlin.de). U1, U9 Kurfürstendamm or U2, U9, S3, S5, S7, S75 Zoologischer Garten. **Rates** (incl breakfast) €60-€90 double. **Map** p321/p328 F8 ⑥⑥

This pension next to the Ku'damm is a charming and unique place, with children in mind. Kids' drawings line the walls, and there are two larger rooms with an optional adjoining two-bed room, perfect for families. Prices are unbeatable for the area, and the owners are extremely kind and friendly. The breakfast room is a quaint place to enjoy a bowl of homemade yoghurt. *TV.*

Hotel Pension Funk

Fasanenstrasse 69 (882 7193, www.hotel-pensionfunk.de). U1 Uhlandstrasse. **Rates** (incl breakfast) €52-€129 double. **Map** p321/p328 F9 ⑥⑦

In the area around Gedächtniskirche, not a lot is left of the charm and glamour that made the Ku'damm the most legendary street of pre-war Berlin. This makes this wonderful pension, which is hidden in a quiet sidestreet, a real gem. The house, built in 1895, used to be home to the Danish silent movie star Asta Nielsen and has been authentically restored. The 14 rooms are decorated with elegant furniture from

before World War I. You might expect dusty corners in a place like this, but everything is pleasantly clean. The owner has done his best to make the bathrooms match modern standards without destroying the overall feel – in one room the bathroom is hidden inside a replica of an antique wardrobe – but some fall slightly short of the standards you would expect from a newer hotel. However, very reasonable prices make up for this. And the breakfast served in the cosy dining room need fear no comparison with much more expensive places. *Internet (wireless). Room service. Parking (€6).*

Pension-Gudrun

Bleibtreustrasse 17, 10623 (881 6462, www.pension-gudrun-berlin.de). S3, S5, S7, S75 Savignyplatz. **Rates** (incl breakfast) €70-€85 double. **No credit cards. Map** p321/p328 E8 ⑥⑧

This simple, tiny pension has huge rooms and friendly, helpful owners who speak English, French, Arabic and German. The rooms are decorated with lovely turn-of-the-century Berlin furniture, and for families or small groups, it's a marvellous deal. *Room service. TV.*

Pension Kettler

Bleibtreustrasse 19, 10623 (883 4949). U1 Uhlandstrasse or S3, S5, S7, S75 Savignyplatz. **Rates** (incl breakfast) €65-€95 double. **No credit cards. Map** p321/p328 E8 ⑥⑨

Amid the collection of art that owner Isolde Josipovici has amassed over the past 35 years, she

Hüttenpalast. *See p134.*

has created the warmest, most eclectic and just plain interesting pension imaginable. Each of the six rooms, five of which have their own shower, is wonderfully decorated as inspired by the historic figure it is named after. There's golden brocade, say, for Goethe. The neighbourhood is fantastic, and public transport is right at hand. Plus breakfast is brought to your room each morning. Highly recommended.

Other districts
WILMERSDORF

Wilmersdorf may not be the most interesting of areas, but it does play host to Berlin's most decadent luxury hotel (**Schlosshotel im Grunewald Berlin**), its most discreet hotel (**Brandenburger Hof Hotel**), its coolest designer hotel (**Ku'Damm 101**), its wackiest hotel (**Propeller Island**) and the world's oldest women-only hotel (**Frauenhotel Artemisia**).

Deluxe

Brandenburger Hof Hotel
Eislebener Strasse 14, 10789 (214 050, www.brandenburger-hof.com). U3 Augsburger Strasse. **Rates** (incl breakfast) €270-€325 double. **Map** p321/p328 G9 ⑩
This discreet, privately owned gem, tucked down a quiet street behind the KaDeWe, is the epitome of modern luxury without the stuffiness. The staff is friendly, and the 72 rooms, all done out in a contemporary-elegant style, are warm and relaxing. There's a beautiful Japanese garden in the middle, surrounded by individually decorated salons available for meetings and special occasions. Chef Bobby Bräuer helms the Michelin-starred Quadriga restaurant. For a real treat, however, avail yourself of the hotel's 'Exquisit Program', which includes limousine service from the airport, flowers, afternoon tea and open bar till 6.30pm. Highly recommended.
Bar. Internet (wireless). Parking (€24). Restaurant. Spa. TV/VCR.

Schlosshotel im Grunewald Berlin
Brahmsstrasse 10, 14193 (895 840, www.schlosshotelberlin.com). S7 Grunewald. **Rates** (incl breakfast) €239-€900 double. **Map** p320 A12 ⑪
Designed down to the dust ruffles by Karl Lagerfeld, this restored 1914 villa on the edge of Grunewald is a luxury that mere mortals can only dream of. There are 12 suites and 54 rooms with elegant marble bathrooms, a limousine and butler service, and a well-trained staff to scurry after you. R&R is well covered too, with a swimming pool, a golf course, tennis courts and two restaurants (with summer dining on the lawn, of course). This is a beautiful place, in a beautiful setting, but so exclu-

sive that it might as well be on another planet. It's worth checking the internet for deals, nonetheless.
Bar. Disabled-adapted rooms. Gym. Internet (wireless). Parking (free). Pool (indoors). Restaurants (2). Spa. TV/VCR.

Expensive

Ku'Damm 101
Kurfürstendamm 101, 10711 (520 0550, www.kudamm101.com). U7 Adenauerplatz or S41, S42, S45, S46 Halensee. **Rates** €119-€250 double. **Map** p320 C9 ⑫
This hotel is a huge hit with style-conscious travellers. The lobby, created by Berlin designers Vogt and Weizenegger, is enjoyably more funk than functional, while the 170 rooms, with lino floors and Le Corbusier, were designed by Franziska Kessler, whose mantra is clarity and calm. There's also a breakfast garden terrace, and the Lounge 101 is good for daytime snacks or a late-night cocktail.
Bar. Disabled-adapted rooms. Internet (wireless). Parking (€14). Spa. TV.

Moderate

Frauenhotel Artemisia
Brandenburgische Strasse 18, 10707 (873 8905, www.frauenhotel-berlin.de). U7 Konstanzer Strasse. **Rates** (incl breakfast) €78-€108 double. **Map** p321 E10 ⑬
Named for the Italian painter Artemisia Gentileschi, the world's oldest women-only hotel has 12 bedrooms, tucked away on the top two floors of a residential apartment building off the Ku'damm. From tiny to palatial, they're all cheerful, clean and functional and each features the work of a different Berlin-based female artist. There's a roof terrace off the breakfast room, communal fridges in the hallways, and a warm, relaxing atmosphere created by its founders, Manuela Polidori and Renate Bühler. There are no mints on the pillows, perhaps, but the diverse clientele has service, respect and comfort assured.
Internet (wireless). TV.

Propeller Island City Lodge
Albrecht Achilles Strasse 58, 10709 (891 9016, www.propeller-island.com). U7 Adenauerplatz. **Rates** from €94 double; €7 breakfast. **Map** p320 D9 ⑮
More than just a hotel, Propeller Island City Lodge is a work of art. Artist-owner Lars Stroschen has created 32 incredible rooms, each themed, and decorated like a jaw-dropping theatre set. The Flying Room, for example, has tilted walls and floors, and a large bed seemingly suspended in air. The Therapy Room, all in white with soft, furry walls, has adjustable coloured lights to change with your mood. While each room has six channels of piped in music, they also have more functional mod cons such as room service and phones. Reservations can

CONSUME

be made via the website, where you can view each room and choose your favourite three. There's also a gallery next door.

NEUKÖLLN

Hüttenpalast

Hobrechtstrasse 65/66, Neukölln (37 30 58 06, www.huettenpalast.de). U7, U8 Hermanplatz.
Rates *Caravans & huts* €60 double. *Rooms* €60 single, €80 double, €110 triple, €130 family room (sleeps four).* **Map** p323 Q10 **⓱**
See p131 **Haven at the Hüttenpalast**.
Photo p132.
Disabled adapted room (1). Internet (free wireless).

CAMPING

If you want to explore the campsites of Berlin or surrounding Brandenburg, ask for a camping map from one of the **VisitBerlin** information offices (*see p299*). With the exception of Tent Station, near the Hauptbahnhof, the campsites are far out of the city, so check timetables for last buses if you want to enjoy the city's nightlife. Prices don't vary much between sites: for tents, you'll pay about €5; for caravans about €8 (plus around €6,50 per person). More information can be obtained from the **Deutscher Camping Club**.

Landesverband des Deutscher Camping Club

Kladower Damm 213-217, Gatow 14089 (218 6071/2, www.dccberlin.de). **Open** 10.30am-6pm Mon; 8am-4pm Wed; 8am-1pm Fri.

Tent Station

Seydlitzstrasse 6, Moabit (3940 4650, www.tentstation.de). S3, S5, S7, S75, U55 Hauptbahnhof. **Rates** per person per night (including pitch) €11 adults; €8 13-17s; €5 5-12s. **No credit cards. Map** p318 J5 **⓯**
Just ten minutes walk north of Hauptbahnhof is this incongruous campsite set in a two hectare area of park land. There's space for up to 125 tents – you can rent one for €4 a night if you don't have your own, plus €1 for a sleeping mat. The highlight is the empty swimming pool, where they sometimes hold swing dancing classes. You can rent out the old pool house too. There's breakfast in the morning from an organic bakery and fairtrade coffee to wash it down with.

YOUTH HOSTELS

The three official youth hostels in Berlin – **Jugendgästehaus-International** (261 1097), **Jugendgästehaus am Wannsee** (803 2034) and **Jugendherberge Ernst Reuter** (404 1610) – all have single-sex dormitories. They're crammed most of the year, so reserve in advance.

You can book online or call the hostels directly. You have to be a member of the YHA to stay in them; to obtain a membership card, go to the Mitgliederservice des DJH Berlin International (also known as the Jugend-Zentrale). Take your passport and a passport-sized photo. Junior membership (under 26s) costs €12.50; family membership is €21. Individual hostels also have a day membership deal – you pay an extra €3.10 per day.

Mitgliederservice des DJH Berlin International

Kluckstrasse 3, 10785 (261 1097, www.jh-berlin-international.de). U1, U7 Möckernbrücke or U1, U2 Gleisdreieck. **Open** 24hrs daily. **Map** p322 L9.

LONGER STAYS

For a longer stay, try calling a *Mitwohnagentur* (flat-seeking agency). Agencies listed below can find you a room in a shared house or furnished flat for anything from a week to a couple of years. Start looking at least a month ahead, especially at holiday times. This is all private accommodation: you will be living in someone's home.

If you're staying for a couple of weeks and find something through a *Mitwohnagentur*, you will probably pay €50-€80 a night. For longer stays, agencies charge different rates. Ask for the total figure, including fees, before booking.

Erste Mitwohnzentrale

Prenzlauer Allee 52, 10629 (324 3031, www.mitwohn.com). Tram M10 Prenzlauerallee/ Danzigerstrasse. **Open** 9am-7pm Mon-Fri; 10am-3pm Sat. **No credit cards. Map** p321/p328 E8.

Fine + Mine Internationale Wohnagentur

Neue Schönhauser Strasse 20, 10178 (235 5120, http://fineandmine.de). U8 Weinmeisterstrasse or S5, S7, S9, S75 Hackescher Markt. **Open** 9am-7pm Mon-Fri; 10am-6pm Sat. **Map** p319/p326 O5.

Freiraum

Wiener Strasse 14, Kreuzberg, 10999 (618 2008, www.frei-raum.com). U1 Görlitzer Bahnhof. **Open** 10am-7pm Mon-Fri; 10am-2pm Sat. **Map** p323 Q9.

HomeCompany

Bundesallee 34-40 Charlottenburg 10717 (194 45, www.homecompany.de). U9 Güntzelstrasse. **Open** 9am-6pm Mon-Thur; 9am-5pm Fri; 9am-1pm Sat. **Map** p321/p328 G8/G9.

Zeitraum Wohnkonzepte

Immanuelkirchstrasse 8, Prenzlauer Berg, 10405 (441 6622, www.zeit-raum.de). Tram M2 Knaackstrasse. **Open** 10am-6pm Mon-Thur; noon-6pm Fri; by appointment Sat. **Map** p319 P4.

Restaurants & Cafés

Berlin's best places to eat.

For a long time, eating in Berlin was more of a necessity than a joy. These days, though, things are looking up, as an increasingly cosmopolitan population has encouraged ethnic variety in the city's eating habits, with a score of new restaurants and cafés serving food from around the world. It's still fair to say that food is unlikely to be the highlight of your trip, but it won't be the nadir either. The breakfast, at least, will probably be very good. Eating out needn't cost much – it's very easy to find lunch for €5 and dinner for €10, though you can also pay €200 a head for the tasting menu with a bit of wine at one of the fancy Michelin-starred joints in town.

EATING IN BERLIN

There has never been a wider choice of places to eat in Berlin. These days, just about every exotic food craving can be satisfied in the city, whether it's Vietnamese omelettes (**Cô Cô**, *see p139*), Korean barbecue (**Kimchi Princess**, *see p149*) or a Californian burrito (**Dolores**, *see p139*).

The local delicacy most tourists are keenest to try remains the *Currywurst*, but there is a lot more to German cuisine than a bland sausage covered with too much ketchup and some curry powder (albeit one with an interesting history – *see p154* **Curry, Do Your Wurst**). Try a plate of *Spätzele*, a southern German speciality that's a cross between a dumpling and pasta – Tirolean restaurant **Wirthaus zum Mitterhofer** (*see p150*) in Kreuzberg does the best. Or if you're feeling carnivorous, a whopping great *Schweinshaxe* (roasted pork knuckle). Still not meaty enough? What about *Eisbein* – a leathery and extremely fatty pig's trotter served with puréed peas. A cheap lunchtime treat is a slab of *Leberkäse*, which despite translating as 'liver cheese', contains neither ingredient, but is instead a mix of corned beef, pork, bacon and onions, ground together into a loaf of meatloaf.

Though *Schnitzels* are more *österreichisch* than *deutsch*, Berlin does them brilliantly – honourable mentions to **Austria** (*see p148*) and **Markthalle** (*see p150*) in Kreuzberg and **Schwarzwaldstuben** (*see p143*) in Mitte. Those who don't like potato salad or sauerkraut could struggle at an old-school German restaurant as they remain the standard side orders.

Vegetarians are pretty well catered for these days. The two branches of über-hip **Chipps** (*see p139*) in Mitte are almost entirely meat-free and **Sing Blackbird** (*see p151*) in Neukölln is an extremely trendy vegan café with a vintage shop attached. Plus the Vietnamese restaurants that have popped up everywhere in recent years always have a good veggie selection – the outrageously cheap **Hamy** (*see p149*) in Kreuzberg is pickof the crop. For reasons unclear, sushi is another Berlin speciality: **Musashi** (*see p151*) on the border between Kreuzberg and Neukölln comes particularly recommended.

Apart from pork and chicken, meat in Berlin tends to be rather disappointing. Beef isn't hung for long enough to make a good steak, and there isn't much of a culture around eating lamb. There is also the tendency to overcook everything.

Unsurprisingly, given Berlin's large Turkish population, there is a lot of Turkish food in the city, most of it in Kreuzberg. But beyond excellent döner kebabs and the *lahmacun* flatbreads better known in Germany as *türkisches Pizza*, most restaurants are much of a muchness, let down again by a generally poor quality of meat. Possibly the best Turkish place in Berlin only serves fish – the very lo-fi **Taka**

> ❶ Blue numbers given in this chapter correspond to the location of each restaurant as marked on the street maps. See pp316-328.

CONSUME

Fish Grill Stube (*see p150*) by Kottbusser Tor u-bahn in Kreuzberg, which does fantastic fresh fish kebabs for under a fiver. If it's meat you want, we recommend an Adana from the **Schlemmerbuffet** (*see p143*) in Mitte, a *Schawarma* from **Imbiss Sanabel** (*see p149*) or the Dürüm Döner from Mustafa's Gemüse Kebap, in east and west Kreuzberg respectively.

On the fancier front, a new generation of homegrown chefs are wowing gastronomes with their take on '*die Neue Deutsche Kuche*' (New German Cookery). **Vau** (*see p143*), TV chef Kolja Kleeberg's swish joint near the Gendarmenmarkt is still packing in high earning punters, Tim Raue is on top form at his eponymous Kreuzberg eaterie (*see p147* **Profile**) and the trio behind **Reinstoff** (*see p141*) seemed to win their Michelin star almost as soon as they opened their doors. For modern German cookery on a budget, head to **Neubau** (*see p150*) in Kreuzberg – it's the new, mid-priced effort from top chef Stefan Hartmann.

But what Berlin does best is cafés, from the classic elegance of the **Café im Literaturhaus** (*see p155*) and **Café Einstein** (*see p154*) to the revolutionary **Kapelle** (*see p140*). Caffeine aficionados swear the best coffee in Berlin is to be found at **Double Eye** (*see p152*) in Schöneberg.

ABOUT THE LISTINGS

All listings have been checked at the time of going to press, but are liable to change. Closing times are particularly nebulous in Berlin. Some restaurants take a break over Easter and August, and many close at Christmas too. Venues have been listed by area and we give a range of prices for main courses listed on the à la carte menu. Budget eateries are marked €. Our favourites are marked with a star. We list restaurants and cafés in this chapter, but bear in mind that many of the bars and pubs in the next chapter (*see pp157-172*) also serve food.

BOOKING

With the exception of well-known, upmarket restaurants, you don't generally need to book more than a day in advance. At many places, you can just turn up.

TIPPING ETIQUETTE

Bills do not include a service charge. Tips are appreciated – 10 per cent is about right, though many stingy locals simply round up to the nearest euro. When the bill comes, the waiter will usually ask '*zusammen oder getrennt?*' – paying together or separately. It is perfectly normal for groups of friends, or even two people on a date, to each pay their own portion of the bill. Give your server the money directly and tell him or her the amount you want to pay,

including the tip. If you are not expecting any change, say '*danke, stimmt so*'. If you want the receipt, ask for '*eine Quittung*'.

MITTE

AlpenStueck

Gartenstrasse 9 (2175 1646/www.alpenstueck.de). S1, S2, S25 Nordbahnhof. **Open** 6pm-1am Tue-Sun. **Main courses** €14.50-€21.50. **Map** p318/p326 M4 ❶ Austrian/German
Ambitious but not over-the-top, artsy but not pretentious, AlpenStueck offers Austrian and south German classics served in a cool ambience. Everything from the strudel crust to the bread is handcrafted; the entrées, including a roast beef smothered in crispy onions and medallions of pork with rösti potatoes and endive salad are at the level where you just can't help talking about flavours and textures. The pasta, including noodles and peas with cherry tomatoes as a starter, is especially memorable. Good wine list and desserts too.

★ Bandol sur Mer

Torstrasse 167 (6730 2051). U8 Rosenthaler Platz. **Open** 6-11pm daily. **Main courses** €22-€25. **No credit cards. Map** p319/p326 N5 ❷ French
Once a kebab stand, this teensy restaurant has space for just 22 diners inside, but Berliners line up for its exquisite entrecôte, innovative seafood (try the swordfish) and an extensive selection of excellent French and German wines. Everything comes fresh from the market and the chefs aren't afraid to add slight twists to the classics, either. The evening's specials are handwritten in chalk on the wall, and reservations are mandatory for the two seatings.

€ Berliner Ensemble Kantine

Bertolt-Brecht-Platz 1, (2840 8117). S1, S2, S25, S3, S5, S7, S75, U6 Friedrichstrasse. **Open** 9am-midnight Mon-Sat; 4pm-midnight Sun. **Main courses** €2.80-€5. **Map** p318/327 M6 ❸ German
Eat hearty, cheap German fare with the cast and crew at the canteen of Brecht's Berliner Ensemble. It's tucked around the back of the theatre, down some steps in the courtyard. The three daily specials are €5 or less, and always include a good veggie option.

★ Bixels

Mulackstrasse 38 (no phone, www.daniel bixel.com). U8 Weinmeisterstrasse, U2 Rosa-Luxemburg-Platz. **Open** noon-9pm Mon-Sat. **Main courses** €5.50-€6.50. **Map** p326 O5. ❹ Café
Ok, so you didn't come all the way to Berlin to have a jacket potato. But there are few better lunchtime treats than one of Daniel Bixel's wondrous creations. Forget boring old tuna mayo or cottage cheese fillings – try beef with tomatoes, olives, carrot and apple salad and red onion; or feta cheese with artichokes, olives and yoghurt sauce.

CONSUME

Understanding the Menu

Getting by in a Berlin restaurant.

USEFUL PHRASES

I'd like to reserve a table for... people. **Ich möchte einen Tisch fur... Personen reservieren.**

Are these places free? **Sind diese Plätze frei?**

The menu, please. **Die Speisekarte, bitte.**

I am a vegetarian. **Ich bin Vegetarier.**

We'd/I'd like to order. **Wir möchten/Ich möchte bestellen.**

We'd/I'd like to pay. **Bezahlen, bitte.**

BASICS

Fruhstuck breakfast. **Mittagessen** lunch. **Abendessen** dinner. **Imbiss** snack. **Vorspeise** appetiser. **Hauptgericht** main course. **Nachspeise** dessert. **Brot/Brötchen** bread/rolls. **Butter** butter. **Ei/Eier** egg/eggs. **Spiegeleier** fried eggs. **Ruhreier** scrambled eggs. **Käse** cheese. **Nudeln/Teigwaren** noodles/pasta. **Sosse** sauce. **Salz** salt. **Pfeffer** pepper. **gekocht** boiled. **gebraten** fried/roasted. **paniert** breaded/battered.

SOUPS (SUPPEN)

Bohnensuppe bean soup. **Bruhe** broth. **Erbsensuppe** pea soup. **Huhnersuppe** chicken soup. **klare Bruhe mit Leberknödeln** clear broth with liver dumplings. **Kraftbruhe** clear meat broth. **Linsensuppe** lentil soup.

MEAT, POULTRY & GAME (FLEISCH, GEFLÜGEL UND WILD)

Boulette meatball. **Ente** duck. **Gans** goose. **Hackfleisch** mince. **Hirsch** venison. **Huhn/Huhnerfleisch** chicken. **Hähnchen** chicken (when served in one piece). **Kaninchen** rabbit. **Kohlrouladen** cabbage-rolls stuffed with pork. **Kotelett** chop. **Lamm** lamb. **Leber** liver. **Nieren** kidneys. **Rindfleisch** beef. **Sauerbraten** marinated roast beef. **Schinken** ham. **Schnitzel** thinly pounded piece of meat, usually breaded and sautéed. **Schweinebraten** roast pork. **Schweinefleisch** pork. **Speck** bacon. **Truthahn** turkey. **Wachteln** quail. **Wurst** sausage.

FISH (FISCH)

Aal eel. **Forelle** trout. **Garnelen** prawns. **Hummer** lobster. **Kabeljau** cod. **Karpfen** carp. **Krabbe** crab or shrimp. **Lachs** salmon. **Makrele** mackerel. **Matjes/Hering** raw herring. **Miesmuscheln**

mussels. **Schellfisch** haddock. **Scholle** plaice. **Seezunge** sole. **Thunfisch** tuna. **Tintenfisch** squid. **Venusmuscheln** clams. **Zander** pike-perch.

HERBS & SPICES (KRAUTER UND GEWÜRZE)

Basilikum basil. **Kummel** caraway. **Mohn** poppyseed. **Nelken** cloves. **Origanum** oregano. **Petersilie** parsley. **Thymian** thyme. **Zimt** cinnamon.

VEGETABLES (GEMÜSE)

Blumenkohl cauliflower. **Bohnen** beans. **Bratkartoffeln** fried potatoes. **Brechbohnen** green beans. **Champignons/Pilze** mushrooms. **Erbsen** green peas. **Erdnusse** peanuts. **grune Zwiebel** spring onion. **Gurke** cucumber. **Kartoffel** potato. **Knoblauch** garlic. **Kichererbsen** chick peas. **Knödel** dumpling. **Kohl** cabbage. **Kurbis** pumpkin. **Linsen** lentils. **Möhren** carrots. **Paprika** peppers. **Pommes** chips. **Rosenkohl** Brussels sprouts. **Rösti** roast grated potatoes. **rote Bete** beetroot. **Rotkohl** red cabbage. **Salat** lettuce. **Salzkartoffeln** boiled potatoes. **Sauerkraut** shredded white cabbage. **Spargel** asparagus. **Tomaten** tomatoes. **Zucchini** courgettes. **Zwiebeln** onions.

FRUIT (OBST)

Ananas pineapple. **Apfel** apple. **Apfelsine** orange. **Birne** pear. **Erdbeeren** strawberries. **Heidelbeeren** blueberries. **Himbeeren** raspberries. **Kirsch** cherry. **Limette** lime. **Zitrone** lemon.

DRINKS (GETRÄNKE)

Bier beer. **dunkles Bier/helles Bier** dark beer/lager. **Gluhwein** mulled wine. **Kaffee** coffee. **Mineralwasser** mineral water. **Orangensaft** orange juice. **Saft** juice. **Tee** tea. **Wein** wine.

CONSUME

Get the local experience

Over 50 of the world's top destinations available.

TIME OUT GUIDES
WRITTEN BY
LOCAL EXPERTS
visit timeout.com/shop

Borchardt
Französische Strasse 47 (8188 6262). U6 Französische Strasse. **Open** 11.30am-late daily. **Main courses** €16-€22. **Map** p322/p327 M7 ❺ **French**
In the late 19th century, the original Borchardt opened next door at no.48. It became the place to be for politicians and society folk, but was destroyed in World War II. Now Roland Mary and Marina Richter have reconstructed a highly fashionable, Maxim's-inspired bistro serving respectable French food. So why not snarf down a dozen oysters and tuck into a fillet of pike-perch or beef after a cultural evening nearby?

★ Café Fleury
Weinbergsweg 20 (4403 4144). U8 Rosenthaler Platz. **Open** 8am-10pm Mon-Sat; 10am-8pm Sun. **No credit cards. Map** p319 ❻ **Café**
This wildly popular French café at the bottom of the hill up to Prenzlauerberg serves both some of the best coffee and breakfasts in town. There are a variety of cakes, tartes, salads and baguettes on offer for lunch.

★ Café Nö!
Glinkastrasse 23 (201 0871, www.cafe-noe.de). U6 Französische Strasse. **Open** noon-1am Mon-Fri; 7pm-1am Sat. **Main courses** €4-€12. **Map** p322/p327 M7 ❼ **German/Mediterranean**
This unassuming but right-on wine bar with simple and wholesome meals is owned by a former DDR rock musician now continuing his family's gastronomy tradition, and given the mostly bland or overpriced restaurants in this neighbourhood, this is a genuine pearl. Snacks include bruschetta and marinated plums baked with bacon; Alsatian *flammkuchen* and lamb ragout are among the dinners. All the food goes well with an intelligent, international wine list.

Chipps
Jägerstrasse 35 (3644 4588, www.chipps.de). U2/U6 Stadtmitte. **Open** 8am-midnight Mon-Fri; 9am-midnight Sat, Sun. **Main courses** €6.50-€9.50. **Map** p318/p327 M7 ❽ **Vegetarian**
This fashionable, airy restaurant is round the back of the Foreign Ministry (Auswärtiges Amt) near the Gendarmenmarkt. There are big windows, and a quiet sun terrace to enjoy in summer. The mostly vegetarian menu offers seasonal soups, salads and a mix and match menu called Chipps Select, in which you compile your own dish from a list of ingredients. The second branch is in a busier part of town. **Other location** Chipps No.2, Friedrichstrasse 120, Mitte (3462 3612).

€ ★ Cô Cô
Rosenthalerstrasse 2 (2463 0595, www.co-co.net). U8 Rosenthaler Platz. **Open** 11am-10pm Mon-Thur, Sun; 11am-midnight Fri, Sat. **Main courses** €4-€6. **Map** p319/p326 N5 ❾ **Vietnamese**
This incredible and popular little café across the street from the easyHotel specialises in *bánh mì* –

Vietnamese baguettes filled with meat or vegetables. The omelette pancakes are pretty sensational too.

Dolores
Rosa-Luxemburg-Strasse 7 (2809 9597, www. dolores-berlin.de). U2, U5, U8, S5, S7, S9, S75 Alexanderplatz. **Open** 11.30am-10pm Mon-Sat; 1-10pm Sun. **Main courses** €3.90-€5.90. **No credit cards. Map** p319/p326 O5 ❿ **Mexican**
For fans of the Northern California-style burrito, this is a true haven. Black beans and lime rice mix with fresh greens and a choice of fillings, such as grilled chicken, marinated beef and tofu. The guacamole is always fresh and perfectly spicy.

Flamingo Fresh Food
Neustädtische Kirchstrasse 8, (832 188 65, www.flamingo-freshfood.de). U6, S1, S2, S5, S7, S25, S75 Friedrichstrasse. **Open** 7.30am-6pm Mon-Fri. **Map** p318/p327 M6 ⓫ **Café**
The streets around Unter den Linden are not blessed with reasonably priced cafés, so hurrah for this newcomer, which serves excellent sandwiches, paninis, soups, salads and pastas in a bright and airy setting right by the Spree.

Grill Royal
Friedrichstrasse 105B (2887 9288, www.grill royal.com). U6, S1, S2, S5, S7, S25, S75 Friedrichstrasse. **Open** 6pm-1am daily. **Main courses** €15-€55. **Map** p318/p326 M5 ⓬ **Bistro**
With its entrance on the promenade by the Spree just down the steps from the north side of Weidendammer Brücke, this comfortably cavernous restaurant is more reminiscent of London or Paris than Berlin, both in scale and colour scheme. In the beginning it seemed full of what pass for celebrities in Germany's capital, but has now settled into a smoothly functioning eatery for a well-heeled but more anonymous crowd. They come to enjoy fine steaks of Irish, French or Argentine provenance, plus a few other meat and fish dishes, and relax to river views and a picture window that turns the kitchen into theatre. Reservations essential.

.HBC
Karl-Liebknecht-Strasse 9 (24 34 29 20, www.hbc-berlin.de). S3, S5, S7, S75 Hackescher Markt. **Open** 7pm-midnight Tue-Sat. **Main courses** €8-€18. **No credit cards. Map** p318/p327 M5 ⓭ **Modern European**
This restaurant, club, bar and cinema hybrid is housed on the first floor of an ugly Socialist towerblock near Alexanderplatz. A whiff of the East still hangs over the starkly modern decor – think concrete spotlights and a deliberately smashed mirror – which can feel a little bleak if the place isn't full, but it is Very Berlin, if that's what you're looking for. The four-course set menu is good value at €30, with highlights including a fois gras terrine and scallop carpaccio starter and a half lobster with

CONSUME

grapefruit for main. This is ambitious cooking that doesn't always hit the high notes, but when the ingredients are in harmony, .HBC is up there with Berlin's best.

Honigmond

Borsigstrasse 28 (2844 5512, www.honigmond-berlin.de). U6 Zinnowitzer Strasse. **Open** 7am-1am Mon-Fri; 8am-1am Sat, Sun. **Main courses** €8.50-€15. **Map** p318/p326 M4 ⓬ **German**

This quiet neighbourhood place serves up traditional German food alongside an innovative menu that ranges from kangaroo to fondue. Noteworthy are the Königsberger Klöpse (East Prussian meatballs in a creamy caper sauce) and a very good Caesar salad. Excellent wine list and remarkable home-made bread (and butter – a rarity in Berlin).

▶ *Honigmond is also a hotel, see p114.*

€ Ishin Mitte

Mittelstrasse 24 (21015707, www.ishin.de). U6, S1, S2, S5, S7, S9, S75 Friedrichstrasse. **Open** 11am-8pm Mon-Fri; 11am-6pm Sat. **Main courses** €5-€14. **No credit cards.** **Map** p318/p327 M6 2 ⓯ **Japanese**

Roomy but crowded, with a constant stream of happy hour-style discounts (starting at €5.50), this is probably the best quality-for-money sushi deal in Berlin. The fish is fresh, with specials offered daily, and portions are generous: when was the last time you actually received more food than the photos on the menu suggested?

Other locations Galleria Steglitz, Schlossstrasse 101, Steglitz (797 1049); Berlinickestrasse 1A, Steglitz (8182 7071).

Kapelle

Zionskirchplatz 22-24 (4434 1300, www.cafe-kapelle.de). U8 Rosenthaler Platz. **Open** 9am-3am daily. **No credit cards.** **Map** p319/p328 N4 ⓰ **Café**

A comfortable, high-ceilinged café-bar across from the Zionskirch, Kapelle takes its name from Die Rote Kapelle, 'the Red Orchestra'. This was a clandestine anti-fascist organisation, and in the 1930s and 1940s the Kapelle's basement was a secret meeting place for the Resistance. The regularly changing menu features organic meat and vegetarian dishes, and the proceeds are donated to local charities and social organisations.

Kellerrestaurant im Brecht-Haus

Chausseestrasse 125 (282 3843, www.brechtkeller.de). U6 Oranienburger Tor. **Open** 6pm-1am daily. **Main courses** €10-€16. **No credit cards.** **Map** p318/p326 M5 ⓱ **German**

Bertholt Brecht got that sleek, well-fed look from the cooking his partner Helene Weigel learned in Vienna and Bohemia. This atmospheric place, crammed with model stage sets and Brecht memorabilia, serves some of her specialities, including

Fleischlabberln (spicy meat patties) and a mighty *Wiener Schnitzel*. In summer, the garden doubles the restaurant's capacity.

Kuchi

Gippstrasse 3 (2838 6622, www.kuchi.de). U8 Weinmeisterstrasse. **Open** noon-midnight Mon-Sat; 6pm-midnight Sun. **Main courses** €7-€16. **Map** p319/p326 N5 ⓭ **Japanese**

It's the quality of the ingredients at this Japanese that makes the food special. And it isn't just fish in the sushi rolls: one *maki* is filled with chicken, mandarin oranges and poppy seeds. Delicate tempura, yakitori chicken hearts or shiitake mushrooms are all excellently served by a young, cool and multinational team. Packed at lunch. The other branch has a takeaway next door that also delivers.

Other location Kantstrasse 30 (3150 7815, delivery service 3150 7816).

★ Lebensmittel im Mitte

Rochstrasse 2 (2759 6130). U2 Weinmeisterstrasse. **Open** 11am-1am Mon-Sat. *Food served* noon-4pm, 5-11pm Mon-Sat. **Main courses** €6.50-€22. **No credit cards.** **Map** p319/p326 O5 ⓳ **German/Austrian**

This deli/restaurant, whose name means 'groceries in Mitte' – is a little journey into the joys of southern German and Austrian cuisine. Up front are fine cheeses, huge loaves of rustic bread, organic veggies, sausage, even Austrian pumpkin seed oil to take away. But guests can also stay, settle into long wooden benches under the antlers on the wall, and dine on high-fat, carb-loaded southern German specialities such as Leberkäse, tongue, rösti and cheese spätzle, accompanied by a broad selection of southern German and Austrian wines or authentic Bavarian beer. The place has a strict no laptop policy.

▶ *For more of Berlin's best food shops, see pp190-191.*

Lutter & Wegner

Charlottenstrasse 56 (202 9540, www.lutter-wegner-gendarmenmarkt.de). U2, U6 Stadtmitte. **Open** noon-midnight daily. **Main courses** €18-€30. **Map** p322/p327 M7 ⓴ **German/Austrian/French**

This place has it all: history (an early Berlin wine merchant, its sparkling wine became known as *Sekt*, now the common German term); a lovely atmosphere

---

INSIDE TRACK TABLE SHARING

At cheaper places it is not unusual to share a table with strangers. If you want to ask someone to move up, say '*könnten Sie vielleicht ein Stück rüber rutschen?*'. To ask if a table or chair is taken, say '*ist hier frei?*'

Reinstoff.

in its airy, elegant rooms; great German/Austrian/ French cuisine; and excellent service. The wine list is justifiably legendary, and if the prices look high, head for the bistro, where the same list holds sway along with perfect salads, cheese and ham plates, plus excellent desserts.

Malatesta

Charlottenstrasse 59 (2094 5072, www.ristorante-malatesta.de). U2, U6 Stadtmitte. **Open** noon-midnight daily. **Main courses** €8.50-€28.50. **Map** p322/p327 M7  **Italian**

This nicely located, first-rate Italian is spread out over two floors. Downstairs there's a small bar for an aperitif or coffee. Starters such as grilled artichoke hearts and antipasto misto, familiar home-made pastas, daily fish specialities and meat dishes such as oxtail filled with truffles are among the reasons to linger upstairs. Service is attentive but not intrusive. The third of Piero de Vetis' restaurants and arguably the best.

▶ *Piero de Vetis's other Berlin restaurants are Osteria No.1 and Sale e Tabacchi. For both, see p150.*

Margaux

Unter den Linden 78 (2265 2611, www.margaux-berlin.de). S1, S2 Unter den Linden. **Open** 7-10.30pm Mon-Sat. **Main courses** €30-€50. **Map** p318/p327 L6 **French**

This top-flight place features Michael Hoffman's slightly avant-garde take on classic French cooking, such as stewed shoulder of venison seasoned with coriander, anise and saffron. The spacious interior is lit by glowing columns of honey-hued onyx, which reflect in black marble floors. The restaurant is named for its extraordinary wine list, which includes some 30 vintages of Château Margaux. Service is first-rate.

€ ★ Monsieur Vuong

Alte Schönhauser Strasse 46 (3087 2643, www.monsieurvuong.de). U8 Weinmeisterstrasse. **Open** noon-midnight daily. **Main courses** €7-€9. **No credit cards.** Map p319/p326 O5 **Vietnamese**

Something of an institution, serving fresh and tasty Vietnamese soups and noodles. A couple of daily specials supplement a handful of regular dishes. Once you've tried the glass noodle salad, you'll understand why less is more. Chic, cheap and cheery, but often packed to the rafters. If you're too hungry to wait, there is similar fare at Manngo, round the corner at Mulackstrasse 29.

Nola's am Weinberg

Veteranenstrasse 9 (4404 0766, www.nola.de). U8 Rosenthaler Platz. **Open** 10am-2am daily. **Main courses** €9-€17. **Credit** MC, V. **Map** p319/p326 N4 **Swiss**

Swiss food in a former park pavilion, with a quiet terrace as well as a spacious bar and dining room. It's hearty fare, such as venison goulash with mushrooms and spinach noodles, or rösti with spinach and cheese with fried eggs. The goat's cheese mousse with rocket starter is big enough for two and it's worth noting that, with a little thought, it's possible to eat quite cheaply here.

Papà Pane di Sorrento

Ackerstrasse 23 (2809 2701/www.papapane.de). U8 Rosenthaler Platz, S1, S2, S25 Nordbahnhof. **Open** noon-midnight Mon-Fri. **No credit cards.** **Main courses** €5-€16.90. **Map** p319/p326 N4 **Italian**

Streetside windows, an open, high-ceilinged dining room, and lots of Italian-restaurant bustle provide a perfect frame for excellent pizzas and pastas. Papà Pane is a lunchtime favourite for gallerists and creative types working nearby on Brunnenstrasse's back courtyards. At night, the art crowd often convenes here in large groups to see and be seen in a casual, open atmosphere. It's also very family-friendly.

Reinstoff

Schlegelstrasse 26C, Edison-Höfe (3088 1214, www.reinstoff.eu). U6 Naturkundemuseum Str. **Open** from 7pm Tue-Sat **Set menus** €64-€124. **Map** p318/p326 M4 **Modern German**

This glamorous and very fashionable restaurant won a Michelin star within months of opening in 2009 and was voted *Liebling des Jahres* (favourite of the year) by the *Frankfurter Allgemeine Zeitung* at the end of 2010. The chef, Daniel Achilles, uses

CONSUME

Bags packed, milk cancelled, house raised on stilts.

You've packed the suntan lotion, the snorkel set, the stay-pressed shirts. Just one more thing left to do – your bit for climate change. In some of the world's poorest countries, changing weather patterns are destroying lives.

You can help people to deal with the extreme effects of climate change. Raising houses in flood-prone regions is just one life-saving solution.

**Climate change costs lives.
Give £5 and let's sort it *Here & Now***

www.oxfam.org.uk/climate-change

Oxfam is a registered charity in England and Wales (No.202918) and Scotland (SCO039042). Oxfam GB is a member of Oxfam International.

Be Humankind Oxfam

regional, mostly organic, ingredients to create what he describes as 'taste adventures'. We prefer to simply describe them as 'delicious'. A typical menu will mix goat's cheese from the Baltic island of Rügen with a salad of melon and strawberries followed by pike caught in National Park of Muritz in Brandenburg, cooked with pig's ears, kohlrabi and radishes. The sommelier can recommend excellent Spanish and German wines to match each course. Note the restaurant is a little tricky to find: it's tucked away in a courtyard near Nordbahnhof.

★ Salumeria Culinario
Tucholskystrasse 34 (2809 6767). S1, S2 Oranienburger Strasse. **Open** 11.30am-11pm Mon-Thur; 11.30am-midnight Fri; 11am-midnight Sat; 11am-10pm Sun. **Main courses** €8-€19. **Map** p318/p326 M5 **㉗** Italian
The daily lunch menu is a great way to recharge after a morning of shopping or gallery hopping. Pick up a bottle of wine, some cheese, olives and salami, or ponder the panettones in the Italian import section, or simply grab a plate to go. There's space for 60 at the busy beer tables on the pavement.

€ Schlemmerbuffet
Torstrasse 125 (no phone). U8 Rosenthalerplatz. **Open** 24hrs daily. **Main courses** €1.30-€7.50. **No credit cards. Map** p319/p326 N4 **㉘** Imbiss (Turkish)
Most people come here for the admittedly very good döner kebabs – veal or chicken: ask for it in the *Durum* flatbread rather than the ordinary *Brot*. But this legendary Turkish joint also does excellent sit-down dishes which can soak up the alcohol you're likely to have consumed if you end up here at five o'clock in the morning.

★ Schwarzwaldstuben
Tucholskystrasse 48 (2809 8084). S1, S2 Oranienburger Strasse. **Main courses** €7-€14.50. **Open** 9am-11pm Mon-Fri; 9am-midnight Sat, Sun. **No credit cards. Map** p318/p326 M5 **㉙** German
Some of the best German cuisine comes from Swabia, but Swabian restaurants tend to be filled with teddy bears and knick-knacks. This place, however, is a casually chic affair, and wears its mounted deer head ironically. The food is excellent. The soups are hearty, standout main courses include the *Schäufele* with sauerkraut and potatoes, and the *Flammkuchen* (a sort of German pizza) is good. Rothaus Tannenzapfle beer on tap.

€ Susuru
Rosa-Luxemburg Strasse 17 (211 1182, www. susuru.de). U2 Rosa-Luxemburg Platz. **Open** 11.30am-11.30pm daily. **Main courses** €6.50-€9. **No credit cards. Map** p319 O6 **㉚** Japanese
This popular restaurant serves amazing udon noodle soups and delicious Japanese 'tapas' such as edamame

beans, *gyoza* filled with shrimp or vegetables and JFC – Japanese fried chicken. Be prepared to share a table.

Vau
Jägerstrasse 54-55 (202 9730, www.vau-berlin.de). U6 Französische Strasse. **Open** noon-10.30pm Mon-Sat. **Set menus** €78-€120. **Map** p322/p327 M7 **㉛** Fusion
Love of innovation and inspiration from all corners of the globe make chef Kolja Kleeberg's menu one of the best in town. His lobster with mango and black olives with tapenade, and braised pork belly with grilled scallops, are complemented by an extensive wine list (bottles from €30). Downstairs, the fake library bar (the 'books' are bricks of coal) is great for special occasions. Booking essential.

★ Weinbar Rutz
Chausseestrasse 8 (2462 8760, www.rutz-weinbar.de). U6 Zinnowitzer Strasse. **Open** 6.30-10.30pm Tue-Sat. **Main courses** €12.50-€34. **Set menus** €105-€180. **Map** p318/p326 M5 **㉜** German
The impressive ground-floor bar has a whole wall showcasing wines from around the globe – the best of the best. There are hearty meals in the bar downstairs (pig's stomach with sauerkraut and mustard seed sauce, anyone?) while the second-floor restaurant serves a limited nouvelle menu from the Michelin starred chef Marco Müller, all of it beautifully presented. Booking essential.

PRENZLAUER BERG

A Cabana
Hufelandstrasse 15 (4004 8508). Tram M4 Hufelandstrasse. **Open** 4pm-late Tue-Sun. **Main courses** €7.90-€14.90. **No credit cards. Map** p319 Q4 **㉝** Portuguese
A bit further east than the fashionable parts of this borough, but convenient for Magnet and the Knaack Club this family-run place is great for relaxing over a big bowl of fresh soup, fish or paella. Home-style cooking is the forte, and the menu changes frequently. Occasional live music.

Anna Blume
Kollwitzstrasse 83 (4404 8749, www.cafe-anna-blume.de). U2 Eberswalder Strasse. **Open** 8am-2am daily. **Map** p319/p328 P3 **㉞** Café
This café and florist rolled into one is named after a poem by Kurt Schwitters. The pastries are expensive but high quality, the terrace is nice in summer, and the interior, not surprisingly, smells of flowers.

Bird
Am Falkplatz 5 (5105 3283, www.thebirdinberlin. com). U2, S8, S41, S42, S85 Schönhauser Allee. **Open** 6-11pm Mon-Thur; 5pm-midnight Fri; noon-midnight Sat, Sun. **Main courses** €9.50-€40. **No credit cards. Map** p319/p328 O2 **㉟** American

CONSUME

The Bird is probably the most authentic American burger and steak joint in Berlin, tucked on a quiet side street across from the Mauerpark. Run by renegades from New York state, it offers freshly ground burgers with a variety of toppings and a plate of hand-cut fries starting at €9.50. There are good steaks and a Caesar salad; the cheesecake is truly homemade; and although there are some OK cocktails and whiskeys (the restaurant's name is bar slang for Wild Turkey bourbon), beer in pitchers is the preferred beverage order here.

Café Anita Wronski
Knaackstrasse 26-28 (442 8483). U2 Senefelderplatz. **Open** 9am-2am daily. **No credit cards. Map** p319/p328 P2 **36 Café**
A friendly café on two levels with scrubbed floors, beige walls, hard-working staff and as many tables crammed into the space as the laws of physics allow. It serves excellent brunches, but there are plenty of other cafés on this stretch if there's no room here. It's quiet in the afternoon and a good spot to sit and read.

Entweder Oder
Oderberger Strasse 15 (448 1382, www. entwederoder.de.vu.de). U2 Eberswalder Strasse. **Open** 9am-late daily. **Main courses** €6-€14. **No credit cards. Map** p319/p328 O3 **37 German**
German food with a light touch: roasts, grilled fish, and the occasional *Schnitzel* cosy up to fresh salads and simple potato side dishes. The menu changes daily and everything is organic. Connected to the underground art scene back in the days of the Wall, this place still rotates new work by local artists.

★ Gugelhof
Knaackstrasse 37 (442 9229/www.gugelhof.de). U2 Senefelderplatz. **Open** 4pm-1am Mon-Fri; 10am-1am Sat, Sun. **Main courses** €7.50-€15. **Map** p319/p328 P4 **38 Alsatian**
A mature Alsatian restaurant that pioneered the Kollwitzplatz scene in the 1990s. The food is refined but filling, the service formal but friendly, and the furnishings are comfortably worn. The choucroute contains the best charcuterie in town, and the *Backöfe* – lamb, pork and beef marinated in riesling and stewed and served in an earthware pot with root vegetables and a bread-crust lid – shows the kitchen at its most characterful. There's also a fine selection of Alsatian *tartes flambées*. Reservations are very much recommended. Breakfast is served until a leisurely 4pm at weekends.

€ I Due Forni
Schönhauser Allee 12 (4401 7333). U2 Senefelderplatz. **Open** noon-midnight daily. **Main courses** €6-€8.40. **No credit cards. Map** p319/p326 O4 **39 Italian**
The punky staff at I Due Forni look more likely to throw you out of a club than tease your tastebuds. But in a city of cheap pizzas baked by Turks or

Palestinians pretending to be Italian, the stone-oven pizza here is authentic and excellent. Sister restaurant of Il Ritrovo – Cucina Casalinga Popolare (*see p146*), it's bit pricier than elsewhere, a meal can still run under €10, and there are also daily pasta specials and a salad that's essentially a head of lettuce you have to chop up yourself. The smaller, sister pizzerias are just as good, though the waiters are a bit less rude. **Other location** Il Casolare, Grimmstrasse 30, Kreuzberg (694 3968);

€ Konnopke's Imbiss
Under U-Bahn tracks, Schönhauser Allee 44b/ corner Danziger Strasse (no phone). U2 Eberswalder Strasse. **Open** 10am-8pm Mon-Fri; noon-8pm Sat. **Currywurst** €1.70-€2. **No credit cards. Map** p319/p328 O3 **40 Imbiss (sausages)**
This venerable sausage stand has been under the same family management since 1930. It reopened after a refurbishment in 2011 and serves probably the most famous – but not the best – *Currywurst* in the city.
▶ *For more on Currywurst, see p154 Curry, Do Your Wurst.*
Other location Romain-Rolland-Strasse 16 (4700 9099).

€ ★ La Focacceria
Fehrbelliner Strasse 24 (4403 2771). U8 Rosenthaler Platz. **Open** 11am-late daily. **Main courses** from €1.50. **No credit cards. Map** p319/p326 N4 **41 Imbiss (Italian)**
Delicious, thin-crust pizzas heated on the spot with fresh toppings such as tuna and rocket, spinach and white cheese, prawns, artichokes and chilli. This bustling *Imbiss* and café is run by old-school Italians who speak little German and pride themselves on classic dishes such as lasagne and a perfect tiramisu.

€ Marien Burger
Marienburger Strasse 47 (3034 0515, www. marienburger-berlin.de). M2 Marienburger Strasse or M4 Hufelandstrasse. **Open** 11am-10pm daily. **Main courses** €3-€5. **No credit cards. Map** p319/p328 P4 **42 American**
Berlin burger bars tend to suffer from some form of pseudo-Americana theming, so this simple but lively neighbourhood hangout is a welcome relief. Grease out with the traditional variations (cheese, chilli, barbecue) or go even further with the deluxe double Marien Burger. Even the singles are pretty big. An extra 90 cents gets you organic beef, and there are also chicken, fish and vegetarian varieties.

November
Husemannstrasse 15 (442 8425, www.cafe-november.de). U2 Eberswalder Strasse/bus N42. **Open** 10am-2am Mon-Fri; 9am-2am Sat, Sun. **No credit cards. Map** p319/p328 P3 **43 Café**
Friendly place that's especially nice during the day when light floods in through picture windows, offering

CONSUME

INSIDE TRACK
INTO THE IMBISS

If you're short of cash, look out for anything in the listings marked *Imbiss*, which means snack bar. Though there are plenty of lousy caravans peddling undercooked sausages and suspiciously cheap kebabs all over town, the standard of fast food is generally so high you never need darken the doors of the city's surprisingly few branches of McDonald's.

views of beautifully restored Husemannstrasse. There's a breakfast buffet until 3pm on Saturdays and 4pm on Sundays.

Oderquelle
Oderbergerstrasse 27 (4400 8080, www. oderquelle.de). U2 Eberswalder Strasse. **Open** times vary. **Main courses** €10-€19.50. **Map** p319/p328 O3 **㊹ Austrian/German**
This simple yet cosy Prenzlauerberg classic might be a tad more expensive than its rivals, but that's because it's better than them. The menu is short but changes regularly. Typical dishes are baked fillet of pork with sauerkraut and parsnip mash or salmon with spinach risotto. It's particularly nice in summer when you can sit outside and watch people go by.

Pasternak
Knaackstrasse 22-24 (441 3399, www.restaurant-pasternak.de). U2 Senefelderplatz or M2 Knaackstrasse. **Open** 9am-1am daily. **Main courses** €12-€21.80. **Map** p319/p328 P4 **㊺ Russian**
Small bar and Russian restaurant that's often crammed, which can be irritating at some tables – try for one in the small side room. The atmosphere is friendly and the food fine and filling. Kick off with borscht or the ample fish plate, then broach the hearty beef stroganoff.

€ Salsabil 2
Wörther Strasse 16 (4404 6073). U2 Senefelderplatz. **Open** noon-midnight daily. **Main courses** €2.80-€6.50. **No credit cards. Map** p319/p328 P3 **㊻ Imbiss (Middle Eastern)**
This Arabic/North African *Imbiss* has all the usual trappings of tabbouleh, falafel, houmous and schwarma, plus lamb sausage, shredded chicken, lots of fried vegetables and some kind of balls made of fried egg and courgette (*Eiji*). It's all very tasty and reasonably priced to eat here or take out. The assorted platter for two is mammoth. Nice choice of desserts too.
Other location Salsabil 1, Göhrener Strasse 6, Prenzlauer Berg (4405 3504).

Sian
Rykestrasse 36 (4050 5775/www.sian-berlin.de). U2 Senefelder Platz or M2 Marienburger Strasse. **Open** noon-midnight daily. **Main courses** €7.80. **No credit cards. Map** p319/p328 P3 **㊼ Vietnamese**
You can tell you're approaching the right address because the Asian decor is literally spilling out into the street, as is the hungry crowd at this popular Vietnamese restaurant. The short but varied menu of tasty noodle-based soups and dishes changes twice weekly. The bad news is that when it's crowded, service can be slow. The good news is that it's slow because dishes are made fresh to order.

Sumo Sushi
Kastanienallee 24 (4435 6130, www.sumosuhi.de). U2 Eberswalder Strasse. **Open** noon-11.30pm Mon-Fri; 3pm-midnight Sat; 2-10.30pm Sun. **Main courses** €6-€21.50. **No credit cards. Map** p319/p328 O3 **㊽ Japanese**
This place stands out for its sashimi, made with very fresh-tasting tuna or salmon, and California maki, rice rolls with crabmeat and avocado rolled in red caviar.

€ Suppen Cult
Prenzlauer Allee 42 (4737 8949, www.suppen-cult.de). M2 Marienburger Strasse or M4 Hufelandstrasse. **Open** 11am-8pm Mon-Fri; 11am-4pm Sat. **Main courses** €3-€5. **No credit cards. Map** p319/p328 P3 **㊾ Imbiss (soups)**
Providing a healthy alternative to fast food for lunch, snacks, or early dinner, this sit-down *Imbiss* offers a wide and tasty assortment of fresh soups and stews to eat in or take away. The menu changes weekly but features the likes of creamed vegetables with ginger and orange or organic lamb stew with coriander and sour cream. Summer brings out chilled soups and various fruit recipes. Home-made desserts and fresh juices are also available.

Trattoria Paparazzi
Husemannstrasse 35 (440 7333). U2 Eberswalder Strasse. **Open** 6pm-1am Mon-Sat; 6-11.30pm Sun (closed Mon summer). **Main courses** €8.60-€18.90. **No credit cards. Map** p319/p328 P3 **㊿ Italian**
Behind the daft name and ordinary façade is one of Berlin's best Italians. Cornerstone dishes are *malfatti* (pasta rolls seasoned with sage) and *strangolapretti* ('priest stranglers' of pasta, cheese and spinach with slivers of ham), but it's worth paying attention to the daily specials too. Booking essential.

FRIEDRICHSHAIN

Alarabi
Krossener Strasse 19 (2977 1995, www. shisha-bar-alarabi.de). U1, S3, S5, S7, S75 Warschauer Strasse or U5 Samariterstrasse.

CONSUME

CONSUME

Open 11am-midnight daily. **Main courses** €8-€16. **No credit cards**. **Map** p324 T7 **61**
Middle Eastern
Arabic restaurant/bar serving vegetarian and meat dishes from Lebanon, Syria and Iraq. Sheeshas (hookah pipes) are the real attraction for the twentysomething crowd: repair to the smoking room and take advantage of the ten flavoured tobaccos at €6 per go (€6.50 after 8.30pm).

Café 100 Wasser

Simon-Dach-Strasse 39 (2900 1356, www.cafe-100-wasser.de). U5 Frankfurter Tor or U1, S3, S5, S6, S7, S75 Warschauer Strasse/bus N5, N29. **Open** 9.30am-late daily. **No credit cards**. **Map** p324 T7 **62** **Café**
The all-you-can-eat brunch buffet (€8.50 Saturday, €10.50 Sunday, coffee and tea included) has a cult following among students and other late risers. Take your time and don't panic as the buffet gets plundered. Just when the food seems to be finished, out comes loads of new stuff.

Café Schönbrunn

Volkspark Friedrichshain (4530 56525, www. schoenbrunn.net). Bus 200. **Open** 10am-late daily. **Map** p319 Q5 **63** **Café**
Not for those afraid to walk in the park at night, but for everyone else it's a favoured hangout. A couple of years ago, this place by the lake sold coffee and snacks to an elderly crowd. With a change of management, the music and food improved dramatically. The unspectacular concrete front was left as it was, and the (new) lounge furniture is pure 1970s. On a sunny afternoon, older park-goers take their first afternoon beer on the terrace next to the in-crowd having breakfast. For your first visit come in daytime – just to make sure you can find it.

Cupcake

Krossener Strasse 12 (2576 8687, www.cupcake berlin.de). S3, S5, S7, S9, S75, U1 Warschauer Strasse. **Open** 1-7pm Mon, Tue; noon-7pm Wed-Sun. **No credit cards**. **Map** p324 T7 **64** **Café**
Dawn Nelson, an American former make-up artist, makes her cupcakes like they're works of art. Swirls of raspberry cream, a cherry perching on the top and Oreo cookie fillings. Some say the cakes are too sweet, others can't get enough. Americanophiles can get their fix of Rice Krispie cakes and New York cheesecake and there's root beer, cream soda and Dr Pepper as well as the usual teas and coffees to drink.

Fliegender Tisch

Mainzer Strasse 10 (297 7648, www.fliegender-tisch.de). U5 Samariter Strasse. **Open** from 5pm-daily. **Main courses** €6-€7. **No credit cards**. **Map** p324 T7 **65** **Italian**
A small and unassuming restaurant away from the hubbub of Simon-Dach-Strasse, the 'flying table' nevertheless fills up with locals of an evening.

Generous helpings of Italian comfort food, including gnocchi, risotto and, of course, the speciality thin crust pizzas, leave you with a warm, fuzzy feeling and a round belly.

Frittiersalon

Boxhagener Strasse 104 (2593 3906, www. frittiersalon.de). U5 Frankfurter Tor. **Open** 5pm-midnight Mon-Thur; 1pm-midnight Fri-Sun. **Main courses** €1.80-€7.80. **No credit cards**. **Map** p324 T7 **66** **Imbiss**
Organic burgers, *bratwurst* and fries are flipped with attitude and served with delicious home-made ketchup, sauces and dips in this 'multikulti' gourmet chip shop. Burgers of the week involve some curious clashes of culture – a Middle-East-influenced 'halloumi burger', for example, where a slab of fried cheese is embellished with yoghurt sauce, sesame dip and salad. For vegetarians there are also soya and camembert burgers, plus a meat-free *currywurst*.

Hot Dog Soup

Grünberger Strasse 67 (no phone, www.hot-dog-soup.de). S3,S5, S7, S9, S75, U1 Warschauer Strasse or U5 Frankfurter Tor. **Open** 11.30am-11pm Mon-Fri; noon-midnight Sat; noon-9pm Sun. **Main courses** €1.80-€3. **No credit cards**. **Map** p324 T7 **67** **Imbiss**
Head here for a quick pick-me-up after scouring the flea market on Boxhagener Platz. Hot Dog Soup serves up a daily changing menu of six tasty soups, including cold ones in summer, and a wide choice of organic Neuland hot dogs in variations such as 'Red Hot Chilli' and 'Hawaii' (with pineapples, chilli sauce and onions). Sausage and soup also come in vegetarian and vegan varieties.
Other location Szredzkistrasse 18 (no phone).

Il Ritrovo – Cucina Casalinga Popolare

Gabriel-Max-Strasse 2 (2936 42130). S3, S5, S7, S9, S75, Uq Warschauer Strasse. **Open** noon-midnight daily. **Main courses** €6-€8.40. **No credit cards**. **Map** p324 T7 **68** **Italian**
The sister restaurant to Il Due Forni (*see p144*), this no-frills Italian has the same hostile approach to customer service but similarly divine pizzas. The bresaola and basil pizza is a particular highlight.

Nil

Grünberger Strasse 52 (2904 7713/www.nil-imbiss.de). U1, S3, S5, S7, S75 Warschauer Strasse or U5 Frankfurter Tor. **Open** 10am-midnight daily. **Main courses** €2-€4.50. **No credit cards**. **Map** p324 S7 **69** **Imbiss** **(Sudanese)**
Sudanese *Imbiss* offering good-value lamb and chicken dishes and an excellent vegetarian selection, including falafel, halloumi and aubergine salad. The peanut sauces are the tasty but sloppy speciality.
Other locations Oppelner Strasse 4 (4881 6414); Kottbusser Damm/Poppstrasse (no phone).

Profile Tim Raue

From Kreuzberg gang to Michelin-starred kitchen.

When 37-year-old Tim Raue opened his eponymous restaurant near Checkpoint Charlie in 2010, he described it as 'a declaration of love to Berlin and its people'. Born and raised in a rough area not far from the Michelin-starred eatery, Raue was member of a notorious Kreuzberg gang, the 36Boys, and seemed destined for a life of crime.

Then, aged 16, he stepped into a professional kitchen for the first time and had an epiphany. Here, he felt, was where he belonged. While his mates carried on raising hell, Raue gorged himself on cookery magazines. In his autobiography *Ich weiss, was Hunger ist* (*I know What Hunger Is*), he describes seeing two star chefs on the cover of one mag – Johannes King and Siegfried Rockendorf. 'Those were the big boys in Berlin,' he wrote. 'I thought: wow, there is another way.'

After setting his sights on the highest echelons of German gastronomy, Raue's rise to become Berlin's restaurant king was stratospheric. His first job was at Die Quadriga in the hotel Brandenburger Hof; he then worked his way through many of the capital's best kitchens until, aged 32, he won his first Michelin star as head chef of Restaurant 44 at Swissotel. By 2008 he had opened an Asian-inspired restaurant, Ma, in the Adlon Hotel, which also won a star.

But in autumn 2010, he decided to go it alone and moved back to his native Kreuzberg. With his wife, Marie, running front of house, Raue nabbed yet another Michelin star just a few months after opening and raised his profile further by appearing as judge on *Deutschlands Meisterkoch*, Germany's *MasterChef*. In 2011, the food magazine *Der Feinschmecker* voted him its chef of the year.

At first glance, the swanky restaurant seems a little out of place in unpretentious Kreuzberg. But little touches play homage to the borough's grimier side – an oil painting on one wall shows black bin bags bulging with rubbish. Raue's cooking uses Asian influences with what he describes as a 'Prussian' twist, which mostly manifests itself in the super precise presentation – sample dishes include giltheaded sea bream with algae butter and asparagus or fillet of beef with beetroot and truffles.

Raue says he wanted the restaurant to reflect its surroundings by being 'anarchic, rule-breaking'. The biggest break with culinary convention is his refusal to include any dairy products or complex carbohydrates on the menu. So no rice, no potatoes, no bread. He wants guests to feel sated without feeling full – a very unGerman idea. At least one critic has quoted back the title of Raue's autobiography in his review, saying that after finishing a dainty six-course menu (€148), he, too, knew what hunger was.

CONSUME

NOW TRY THE FOOD
Listings for Restaurant Tim Raue are on p150.

Prager Hopfenstube

Karl-Marx-Allee 127 (426 7367). U5 Weberwiese.
Open 11am-midnight daily. **Main courses** €7-
€22. **No credit cards. Map** p325 S6 ⓿ Czech
All the favourites from your last Prague holiday
appear here: *svickova* (roast beef), *veprova pecene*
(roast pork), *knedliky* (dumplings) and the lone vegetarian prospect: *smazeny syr* or breaded and deep-
fried hermelin cheese served with remoulade and
fries. Sluice down this heavy fare with mugs of
Staropramen beer; afterwards, a Becherovka herbal
digestif helps thwart indigestion. Fast and friendly
service is a pleasingly inauthentic touch.

Schneeweiss

*Simplonstrasse 16 (2904 9704, www.schneeweiss-
berlin.de). U1, S3, S5, S7, S75 Warschauer
Strasse.* **Open** 8-11pm Mon-Fri; 10am-4pm,
6pm-1am Sat, Sun. **Main courses** €6-€20.
Map p324 T8 ⓷ Alpine
This smart and understated place, done out in minimalist white, offers modern European dishes
described by the establishment as 'Alpine' – essentially a well-presented fusion of Italian, Austrian and
south German ideas. There are daily lunch and dinner
menus, plus a breakfast selection and snacks, shakes
and schnitzels served throughout the day. Although
upmarket for the area, it's great quality for the price
and deservedly popular, so make sure you book.

KREUZBERG

★ 3 Schwestern

*Mariannenplatz 2 (600 318 600, www.3schwestern-
berlin.de). U1 Görlitzer Bahnhof.* **Open** 11am-late
Tue-Sun. **Main courses** €7.80-€18.80. **No credit
cards. Map** p.323 Q9 ⓷ German

This Kreuzberg newcomer is housed in Haus
Bethanien, an old hospital turned art centre on leafy
Mariannenplatz. The airy room has big windows
looking out on to the lovely garden, where you can
sit in summer. Try the *Kässpätzle* (Swabian cheese
dumplings) or the *Schweinsbraten vom Apfelschwein*
– roast pork made from a pig fed on apples – and
accompany it with some excellent Czech beer.
Parties and concerts follow dessert on the weekends.

★ Austria

*Bergmannstrasse 30, on Marheineke Platz
(694 4440). U7 Gneisenaustrasse.* **Open**
6pm-1am daily. **Main courses** €13.50-€18.50.
Map p323 N10 ⓷ Austrian
With a collection of antlers, this place does its best
to look like a hunting lodge. The meat is organic, and
there are also organic wines, Kapsreiter and Zipfer
beer on tap, and a famously over-the-top schnitzel.
Outdoor seating on a tree-lined square makes it a
pleasant warm-weather venue. Literary types may
recall it has a cameo in the Pulitzer prize-winning
novel *Middlesex*, written by a regular diner, Jeffrey
Eugenides, when the narrator declares, 'I don't like
anyone who doesn't like Austria.' Book at weekends
and in summer.

Bar Raval

*Lübbener Strasse 1 (5316 7954, www.barraval.de).
U1 Schlesisches Tor.* **Open** 5-11pm Mon-Thur;
5pm-midnight Fri; noon-midnight Sat; noon-11pm
Sun. **Main courses** €11.50. **Map** p324 R9 ⓷
Spanish
This tapas bar right by Görlitzer Park is co-owned
by the Spanish-German actor Daniel Brühl, (*Good
Bye Lenin!*),and has been a huge hit since it opened
in 2011. It's not particularly cheap, considering the

Knofi.

dainty portions, but the food is good – try the cooked *jamón ibérico* and the *pulpo* – and it does a mean G&T using gin infused with rosemary and thyme.

€ **Baraka**

Lausitzer Platz 6 (612 6330, www.baraka-berlin. de). U1 Görlitzer Bahnhof. **Open** 11am-midnight Mon-Fri; 11am-1am, Sat, Sun. **Main courses** €5-€10. **No credit cards**. **Map** p323 Q9 ⑤ **Imbiss (Middle Eastern)**

North African and Egyptian specialities such as couscous and *fuul* (a traditional fava bean dish) enhance a menu that also includes lots of well-executed standards such as falafel, schwarma and köfte. You can take away your meal or eat in the cavernous restaurant with its cosy seating on embroidered cushions.

€ ★ **Hamy Café**

Hasenheide 10 (6162 5959, www.hamycafe. com/en). U7 U8 Hermannplatz. **Open** noon-midnight daily. **Main courses** €4.90. **No credit cards**. **Map** p323 P11 ⑤ **Imbiss (Vietnamese)**

The best Vietnamese in Berlin and also one of the cheapest, so no wonder it's always packed. Don't panic if there are no tables free when you arrive: either get others to budge up and share their table, or wait. The service is so speedy that it won't take long. Each day there are three specials, all priced at €4.90: glass noodle salad with octopus, perhaps, or a golden chicken curry. Tofu can be substituted for meat or fish. It's licensed, but get a fresh lime juice or a lassi instead of a boring old beer.

Hasir

Adalbertstrasse 10 (614 2373, www.hasir.de). U1, U8 Kottbusser Tor. **Open** 24hrs daily. **Main courses** €9.50-€13.50. **No credit cards**. **Map** p323 P9 ⑥ **Turkish**

You thought the Turks had been chewing döner kebabs since time immemorial? Wrong. They were invented in Germany in 1971 by Mehmet Aygun, who eventually opened this highly successful chain of Turkish restaurants. While you'll get one of the best döners in Berlin here, you owe it to yourself to check out the rest of the menu, which involves various other skewered meats in sauce, and some addictive bread rolls. The place often closes for a couple of hours in the early morning.
Other locations throughout the city.

Henne

Leuschnerdamm 25 (614 7730, www.henne-berlin.de). U1, U8 Kottbusser Tor. **Open** 7pm-midnight Tue-Sat; 5-10pm Sun. **Main courses** €7.90. **No credit cards**. **Map** p323 P8 ⑥ **German**

There is just one thing you should order at Henne: half a roast chicken, milk roasted. The only decisions you need to make after that are whether you want cabbage or potato salad, and which beer you

fancy drinking with it (try the Monchshof). Check the letter over the bar from JFK, regretting missing dinner here. Eating here is not quite the spiritual experience some might claim, but it's worth a visit nonetheless. There's a leafy beer garden that's pleasant in summer.

Kantine im Abgeordnetenhaus

Niederkirchnerstrasse 5 (52325 1945, www.kuk-berlin.de). S1, S2, S25, U2 Potsdamer Platz. **Open** 8.30am-4pm Mon-Thur; 8.30am-3pm Fri. **Main courses** €4.10-€5.60. **Map** p322 L8 ⑥ **German**

The area around Potsdamer Platz is a bit of a gastronomic desert, so if you fancy a bit of an adventure, head a few streets south-west to the Abgeordnetenhaus – the regional parliament for the state of Berlin – and eat lunch with local politicians at their canteen. The food leans towards the hearty – schnitzel with chips and peas or veal gulasch with local asparagus – but there's always a decent veggie option. Note that the canteen is closed to Ordinary Joes between 11.30am and 1.15pm if parliament is in session. Check the website for any closures as well as the full menu for the week ahead.

Kimchi Princess

Skalitzer Strasse 36 (0163 4580203, www.kimchiprincess.com) U1 Görlitzer Bahnhof. **Open** noon-midnight Tue-Sun. **Main courses** €9-€17. **No credit cards**. **Map** p323 Q9 ⑦ **Korean**

This sleek zinc and neon Korean barbecue joint has been choc-a-bloc with customers since it opened in 2010, despite the reliably shoddy service. The owners run two other venues in the same block: the Angry Chicken fried chicken joint and the Soju Bar, named after a kind of Korean schnapps made from sweet potatoes.

€ **Knofi**

Bergmannstrasse 11 (6956 4359, www.knofi.de). U7 Gneisenaustrasse. **Open** 7am-midnight daily. **Main courses** €3-€7. **No credit cards**. **Map** p322 M10 ⑦ **Mediterranean**

Connected to the deli across the street, Knofi is cosy and not much larger than an *Imbiss*, but it boasts a cheap and delicious speciality in the form of crêpe-like *gosses* – both vegetarian or filled with schwarma – and generous portions of soup. It's also a top-notch bakery.

€ **Imbiss Sanabel**

Schlesische Strasse 36 (53000739). U1 Schlesisches Tor. **Open** 11am-1am daily. **Main courses** €3-€7. **No credit cards**. **Map** p324 R9 ⑦ **Middle Eastern**

The best place to head for chicken schwarma, a sandwich-like wrap filled with shaved meat that is basically the Middle Eastern version of a döner kebab. The falafels are great too.

CONSUME

★ Little Otik

Gräfestrasse 71 (5036 2301, www.littleotik.de). U8 Schönleinstrasse. **Open** 7-11pm Wed-Sat. **Main courses** €12-€22. **No credit cards. Map** p323 P10 ❼ **Italian**

This aptly small restaurant in one of the nicest neighbourhoods in Kreuzberg serves imaginative, unusual dishes. Start off with a snack of almonds roasted with brown sugar and sweet paprika before moving on to a starter of fresh ricotta and asparagus crostini. Main courses include slow cooked pork belly with Romano beans, breadcrumbs and purslane leaves; and risotto with nettles, spring onions and herbs. Highly rated by local foodies.

★ Markthalle

Pücklerstrasse 34 (617 5502, www.weltrestaurant-markthalle.de). U1 Görlitzer Bahnhof. **Open** 10am-late daily (food served until midnight). **Main courses** €7.50-€17. **Map** p323 Q8 ❼ **German**

This unpretentious schnitzel restaurant and bar, with chunky tables and wood-panelled walls, has become something of a Kreuzberg institution. Breakfast is served right up until 5pm, salads from noon, and, in the evening, there's a selection of filling and reasonably priced meals. It's also fun just to sit at the long bar and sample the selection of grappas. After dinner, see what's on downstairs at the Privat Club.

€ Mustafas Gemüse Kebap

Mehringdamm 32 (no phone, www.mustafas.de). U6 U7 Mehringdamm. **Open** noon-late daily. **Kebabs** €2.50-€3.90. **No credit cards. Map** p322 M10 ❼ **Imbiss (Turkish)**

This kebab van is permanently stationed right outside Mehringdamm u-bahn station. You can't miss it – just look for the queue. Mustafa's devotees regularly wait half an hour or more for what they insist are the best kebabs in the city. Non meat-eaters rave about the eponymous veggie option, which combines fresh fried vegetables with feta cheese, salad, a squeeze of lemon and a *'geheime Zutat'* (secret ingredient), which is some sort of salty spice mix. Carnivores get the same with added chicken. The high turnover means the food is wonderfully fresh. Bring a book and a beer while you stand in line. If you can't be bothered to hang around, Curry 36 two doors down serves some of the city's better sausages.

★ Neubau

Bergmannstrasse 5 (6273 5120). U6, U7 Mehringdamm. **Open** noon-11pm Mon-Sat. **Main courses** €9.80-€15. **Set lunch** €9.80. **Map** p322 M10 ❼ **German**

This smart bistro opened up in summer 2011 in rather incongruous surroundings in a courtyard behind the Netto supermarket in the chi-chi bit of Kreuzberg. It's the cheaper offshoot of Hartmann's, a Michelin-starred joint over the other side of the district. The €9.80 two-course lunch is a particular bargain for this level of cooking – a typical menu might

be a delicate salad of sugar snap peas with wild celery followed by perfectly poached John Dory fillets with fennel sauce on a bed of creamy mashed potatoes. Homemade rosemary bread comes for free to start proceedings, along with olive oil and crunchy radishes. Dinner takes things up a gear both in price and culinary ambition – three courses are €28; four cost €35. There's great German and Austrian wine too; try a glass of the Weingut Weixelbaum Grüner Veltliner if it's on the list.

Osteria No.1

Kreuzbergstrasse 71 (786 9162, www.osteria-uno.de). U6, U7 Mehringdamm. **Open** noon-2am daily. **Main courses** €8-€19. **Map** p322 M10 ❼ **Italian**

Most of Berlin's best Italian chefs paid their dues at this 1977-founded establishment, learning their lessons from a family of restaurateurs from Lecce. Osteria is run by Fabio Angilè, nephew of the owner of Sale e Tabacchi (*see below*). There's am excellent three-course lunch menu and, in summer, one of Berlin's loveliest garden courtyards. Staff are super-friendly too. Booking is recommended.

★ Restaurant Tim Raue

Rudi-Dutschke-Strasse 26 (2593 7930, www.tim-raue.com). U6 Kochstrasse. **Open** noon-2pm, 7-10pm Tue-Sat. **Set menus** €28-€148. **Map** p322 M8 ❼ **Asian**

See p147 **Profile**.

★ Sale e Tabacchi

Rudi-Dutschke-Strasse 23 (252 1155, www.saletabbi.de). U6 Kochstrasse. **Open** 10am-11.30pm Mon-Fri; 10am-2am Sat, Sun. **Main courses** €9-€28. **Map** p322/p327 M8 ❼ **Italian**

Well known for fish dishes (tuna and swordfish carpaccio or *loup de mer*) and for the pretty courgette flowers filled with ricotta and mint, not to mention its large, impressive selection of Italian wines. The interior design is meant to reflect a time when salt (*sale*) and tobacco (*tabacchi*) were sold exclusively by the state. In summer, enjoy a leisurely lunch or dinner in the garden under lemon, orange and pomegranate trees.

€ ★ Taka Fisch Grill Stube

Adalbertstrasse 97 (no phone). U8/U1 Kottbusser Tor. **Open** noon-midnight Mon-Fri; noon-2am Sat, Sun. **Main courses** €3-€7.90. **No credit cards. Map** p323 P9 ❼ **Imbiss (seafood)**

This tiny, no-frills Turkish place hidden away in the Kottbusser Tor complex serves incredible fresh fish kebabs, grilled to order. It's unlicensed, but copy the regulars by accompanying your meal with a salty Ayran yoghurt drink.

Wirthaus zum Mitterhofer

Fichtestraße 33 (3471 1008, www.wirtshaus-zum-mitterhofer.de). U7 Südstern. **Open**

Jimmy Woo.

CONSUME

5pm-late Mon-Fri; noon-late Sat, Sun. **Main courses** €8.50-€17. **Map** p322 O10 **31** **Austrian**
This friendly neighbourhood Austrian restaurant specialises in hearty fare from the Süd Tirol. It does what is probably the best *späztele* in town, and its immense *Wiener Schnitzel* is pretty historic too. There's great, reasonably priced wine too – the perennially cheery owner will be happy to suggest his reasonably priced favourites.

NEUKÖLLN

Jimmy Woo
Friedlstrasse 24 (017625 356205, www.jimmy-woo.de). U8 Schönleinstrasse. **Open** noon-late Mon-Fri; 1pm-late Sat, Sun. **Main courses** €5-€15. **No credit cards. Map** p323 Q10 **32** **South-east Asian**
This place is more about the vibe than the food – you can soundtrack your meal with whatever music you feel like putting on the stereo and it's where all the Kreuzkölln hipsters hang out. The scran is pretty decent: the spicy lemongrass soup is served in pleasingly big pots and the Southern Laotian Curry has a kick you don't often find in Berlin. All soups and mains are served with a choice of tofu, beef, pork, chicken, fishballs, squid or prawn and the curry. Every Thursday there's a three-course dinner for €18.

★ Lavanderia Vecchia
Flughafenstrasse 46 (6272 2152, www. lavanderiavecchia.de). U8 Boddinstrasse. **Open** noon-2.30pm, 7.30-11pm Tue-Fri;

7.30-11pm Sat. **Main courses** (lunch) €4.50-€12.50. **Set menu** (dinner) €39 (drinks included). **33** **Italian**
It is well worth venturing into deepest Neukölln for this extremely classy, fun and authentic Italian, housed in a former launderette. The lunch menu is cheap but delicious – simple pasta dishes, soups and salads for just €4.50. But it's in the evenings that Lavanderia Vecceria really shines, with its 13-course blow-out. The extravagant culinary adventure is best tackled with a group of good friends because dinner lasts all night. It starts with a vast selection of antipasti, before moving on to a pasta course, then meat or fish, followed by dessert and coffee. Great for a celebration. Reservations are essential in the evening. *Photo p152.*

€ Musashi
Kottbusserdamm 102 (6932 042). U8 Schönleinstrasse. **Open** noon-10.30pm Mon-Sat; 2-10pm Sun. **Main courses** €5-€10. **Map** p323 P10 **34** **Japanese**
It's tiny, it's packed, but Musashi serves some of the tastiest sushi in the city to eat in or take away.

Sing Blackbird
Sanderstrasse 11 (no phone, www.sing blackbird.com). U8 Schönleinstrasse. **Open** 10.30am-8pm daily. **No credit cards. Map** p323 Q10 **35** **Café**
This vegan/vegetarian café has a vintage clothes shop attached and is notable particularly for its breakfasts. Try the Hungry Karl – American style pancakes topped with caramelised apples, berry

Lavanderia Vecchia. *See p151.*

compote or bananas with walnuts and caramel, or the vegan breakfast burrito stuffed with tofu scramble, seasonal veggies, pan roasted potatoes and a lot more besides. The cakes are good too.

SCHÖNEBERG

Double Eye
Akazienstrasse 22 (0179 456 6940, www.double eye.de). U7 Eisenacher Strasse. **Open** 9.30am-6.30pm Mon-Fri; 10am-3.30pm Sat. **No credit cards. Map** p322 J11  **Café**
Double Eye serves the best coffee in Berlin, bar none – and there's a queue out the door to prove it.

Habibi
Goltzstrasse 24, on Winterfeldtplatz (215 3332). U1, U2, U3, U4 Nollendorfplatz. **Open** 11am-3am Mon-Thur, Sun; 11am-5am Fri, Sat. **Main courses** €2.50-€12. **No credit cards. Map** p322 J7 **Middle Eastern**
Freshly made Middle Eastern specialities including falafel, kibbeh, tabbouleh and various combination plates. Wash it down with freshly squeezed orange or carrot juice, and finish with a complimentary tea and one of the wonderful pastries. The premises are light, bright and well run. Deservedly busy – it can get very full.
Other location Akazienstrasse 9, Schöneberg (787 4428).

La Cocotte
Vorbergstrasse 10 (7895 7658, www.lacocotte.de). U7 Eisenacher Strasse. **Open** 6pm-1am daily. **Main courses** €9-€17.90. **No credit cards. Map** p322 J10 **French**
Friendly, gay-owned French restaurant where good cooking is enhanced by a sense of fun and occasional themed events – such as the Beaujolais nouveau being welcomed by a 'rustic chic' buffet and a programme of accordion music and 1980s French

pop. Vegetarians aren't forgotten, there's a nice terrace, and the toilets are absolutely beautiful.

Munch's Hus
Bülowstrasse 66 (2101 4086, www.munchs hus.de). U2 Bülowstrasse. **Open** 10am-1am daily. **Main courses** €6-€17. **Map** p322 K9 **Norwegian**
In a corner of town bereft of good places to eat, Berlin's only Norwegian restaurant is frequented by businessmen and artists from the neighbourhood. Daily specials are reminiscent of the rounded German meal – potatoes and well-dressed greens accompany most dishes – but with a twist that usually involves dill. Creamy soups and fish dishes are the speciality, but light sandwiches and salads are also available.

Petite Europe
Langenscheidtstrasse 1 (781 2964). U7 Kleistpark. **Open** 5pm-1am daily. **Main courses** €8-€15. **Map** p322 J10 **Italian**
You may have to wait for a table in this popular, friendly place, but the turnover's fast. Weekly specials are first-rate, as are the pasta dishes. Salads could be better and none of this is haute cuisine, but it's all well made, hearty and inexpensive.

Renger-Patzsch
Wartburgstrasse 54 (784 2059, www.renger-patzsch.com). U7 Eisenacher Strasse. **Open** 6pm-1am daily. **Main courses** €13-€20. **Map** p322 J11 **German**
The pan-German food – soup and salad starters, a sausage and sauerkraut platter, plus daily varying meat and fish dishes – is finely prepared by versatile chef Hannes Behrmann, formerly of the now defunct Le Cochon Bourgeois. House speciality is Alsatian *tarte flambée*: a crisp pastry base baked and served with toppings in seven variations. Long wooden tables are shared by different parties and in summer there's a nice garden on this beautiful corner.

'IERGARTEN

★ Café Einstein Stammhaus

'urfürstenstrasse 58 (261 5096, www.cafe
instein.com). U1, U2, U3, U4 Nollendorfplatz.
)pen 9am-1am daily. **Main courses** €9-€22.
Iap p322 J8 ㊾ **Austrian/café**
led leather banquettes, parquet flooring and the
rack of wooden chairs all contribute to the old
'iennese café experience at Einstein. Fine Austrian
ooking is produced alongside several nouveau cui-
ine specialities. Alternatively, order *Apfelstrudel*
nd coffee and soak up the atmosphere of this elegant 1878 villa.

Edd's

'ützowstrasse 81 (215 5294, www.edds-thai
estaurant.de). U1 Kurfürstenstrasse. **Open**
.1.30am-3pm, 6pm-midnight Tue-Fri; 5pm-
nidnight Sat; 2pm-midnight Sun. **Main courses**
€14-€21. **No credit cards. Map** p322 J8 ㊿ **Thai**
Known and loved by many, so bookings are pretty
nuch essential for this comfortable, elegant Thai,
vhere a husband and wife team please their guests
vith well-balanced if somewhat spicy creations. Try
he banana flower and prawn salad or duck no.18,
louble cooked and excellent.

Hugo's

Hotel Intercontinental, Budapester Strasse 2 (2602
l 263, www.hugos-restaurant.de). U2, U9, S3, S5,
S7, S75 Zoologischer Garten. **Open** 6-10.30pm
Mon-Sat. **Main courses** €35-€45. **Map** p321 H8
㊿ **German**
)ne of Berlin's best restaurants and with the
Michelin star to prove it. Chef Thomas Kammeier
uxtaposes classic haute cuisine with an avant-garde
new German style. Dishes such as cheek of ox with
beluga lentils and filled calamares, goose liver with
mango, and Canadian lobster salad bring out the
best of a mature kitchen and well-balanced menu.
The beautiful room occupies the entire top floor of
he Intercontinental (*see p128*), with absorbing
views in all directions.

€ ★ Joseph Roth Diele

Potsdamer Strasse 75 (2636 9884, www.joseph-
roth-diele.de). U1 Kurfürstenstrasse. **Open** 10am-
nidnight Mon-Fri. **No credit cards. Map** p322
K8 ㊾ **Café**
A traditional Berlin book café, just a short stroll south
of Potsdamer Platz, which pays homage to the life and
work of inter-war Jewish writer Joseph Roth. It's an
amiable place in ochre tones and with comfy seating,
offering teas, coffees, wines, beers, snacks and stunning value light meals (lunchtime specials from just
€3). There's a limited menu on Friday evenings.

Patio

Helgolander Ufer, corner Kirchstrasse (4030
1700, www.patio-berlin.de). S3, S5, S7, S75
Bellevue. **Open** 10am-1am Mon-Fri; 9am-1am
Sat, Sun. **Main courses** €9-€21. **Map** p317 H5 ㊏
Italian
On the banks of the Spree just above the leafy
Hansaviertel, this designer barge has a sunny terrace on top and light-filled lounge below, both with
extraordinary views of the willows and grand
houses on the bank opposite. The menu features
pretty good Italian classics including stone-oven
pizza (from 6pm), pasta and, unexpectedly, sushi. A
well-stocked bar fuels an extensive cocktail menu
too. Lunch specials are usually under €12.
Reservations recommended.

€ Sushi Express

Potsdamer Platz 2, Passerelle (2575 1863,
www.sushiexpress.de). U2, S1, S2, S26 Potsdamer
Platz. **Open** 11.30am-10pm Mon-Fri; noon-9pm
Sat; 2-8pm Sun. **Main courses** €5-€17.75.
Map p322/p328 K7 ㊐ **Japanese**
Not the easiest place to find, Sushi Express is under
the courtyard of the Sony Center in a passage to the
S-Bahn, accessible from a stairway next to the video
display for the Filmmuseum (*see p90*). But the hunt
is worth it for tasty sushi, sashimi and assorted del-
icacies to be plucked off the conveyor belt running
past you at the counter. The temptation is to just
keep grabbing things, but don't worry, from noon to
6pm Monday to Friday all sushi and rolls are half
price. Hot dishes and lunchboxes are also available,
as is takeaway.

Weizmann

S-Bahnbogen 390, Lüneberger Strasse (394 2057,
www.weizmann.de). S3, S5, S7, S75 Bellevue.
Open noon-11pm Mon-Sat; noon-9pm Sun.
Main courses €5-€15. **No credit cards.**
Map p318 J6 ㊓ **German**
A lovely little place serving the pastas of Swabia,
including *Spätzle* (a dish with *Bratwurst*, lentils or
meatballs), *Käsespätzle* (with cheese), *Maultaschen*
(like giant ravioli) and *Schupfnudeln* (a cross
between pasta and chips). A dark Berg beer makes
the perfect accompaniment. There's a great value
€8.50 buffet on Friday evenings that's well worth
checking out too.

CHARLOTTENBURG & WILMERSDORF

XII Apostel

Savigny Passage, Bleibtreustrasse 49 (312 1433,
www.12-apostel.de). S3, S5, S7, S75 Savignyplatz.
Open 8pm-1am daily. **Main courses** €10-€20.
No credit cards. Map p321/p328 F8 ㊙ **Italian**
It's overcrowded, cramped and pricey, the service
varies from rushed to rude, and the music is irritat-
ing – but the pizzas are excellent and it's open late,
both of which account for its popularity.
Other location S-Bahnbogen 177-180,
Georgenstrasse, Mitte (201 0222).

CONSUME

CONSUME

Curry, Do Your Wurst

Germany's favourite street snack.

Politicians pose with it, pop stars sing songs about it, great cities vie to claim the honour of its invention. The *Currywurst* is more than just a street snack. It's Germany's premier pop culture item. If Warhol had been a Berliner, he would have painted a *Bratwurst* drenched in lurid red ketchup and liberally sprinkled with curry powder.

Germany is proud of its sausages and boasts more than 1,200 different varieties, all prepared and classified in deeply traditional ways. So how on earth did they get around to putting curry powder on them? In Hamburg, where the *Currywurst* is served swimming in a sweet brown sauce, they claim to have invented it in 1947. Germans from the Ruhr area have their own creation myth, in which an Essen sausage seller accidentally drops a can of curry powder into some ketchup. But Berliners know this is nonsense, and there's a commemorative plaque on the corner of Kantstrasse and Kaiser-Friedrich- Strasse in Charlottenburg to prove it. On the afternoon of 4 September 1949 36-year-old Herta Heuwer grew bored with waiting for customers at her humble sausage stand, and began to experiment with spices and seasonings. Some chilli powder in the ketchup... perhaps some worcester sauce, too... pour it all over a skinless pork Bratwurst... scatter curry powder on top... Lo, the *Currywurst* was born! It was also quickly patented under number 721319. Sliced up on a paper plate, often served with chips and mayonnaise, and designed to be consumed standing up with a beer, the *Currywurst* sallied forth in conquest.

In the 1950s, *Currywurstbuden* sprang up on every corner, scenting West Berlin with the aroma of hot fat, warm ketchup and Indian spices. By the time the Wall went up in 1961, the *Currywurst* had already crossed into the East, though to this day it is still often served on that side of town with a skin of pig's intestine, while in western Berlin it is usually skinless. (If you want it without intestine, ask for it '*ohne Darm*').

In East Berlin, the *Currywurst* held its own through the Communist period, most notably at **Konnopke's Imbiss** (*see p144*), serving sausages since 1930 under the U2 tracks south of Eberswalder Strasse station. In West Berlin, the *Currywurst* had to fight a war on two fronts against new-fangled Italian pizza slices and that other Berlin street food invention, the döner kebab. Though beaten back for a time, in today's more conservative climate the *Currywurst* is enjoying something of a comeback, celebrated as classless, authentic and German. Konnopke's is not the only celebrated Currywurst stand. The sausages at **Ku'damm 195** (Kurfurstendamm 195, Charlottenburg) a re pricey but crisp. The perennial queue at **Curry 36** (Mehringdamm 36, Kreuzberg) testifies to the quality of its *Wurst*. If caught in need of a *Currywurst* at the opposite end of Kreuzberg, try **Curry 7** (Schlesische Strasse 7). Perhaps our favourite place of all, however, is the organic vendor **Witty's** (*see p156*), serving classic Currywurst and fantastic chips directly opposite KaDeWe.

Witty's.

Alt Luxemburg

Windscheidstrasse 31 (323 8730, www.alt luxemburg.de). U2 Sophie-Charlotte-Platz. **Open** 5-10.30pm Mon-Sat. **Main courses** €27-€33. **Set menus** €48-€70. Map p320 D8 **100** **Fusion** Karl Wannemacher combines classic German and French flavours with Asian influences in a wonderfully romantic dining room. Sample such wonders as horseradish terrine with smoked eel, or monkfish with a succulent saffron sauce and tomato. The wine list could do with more moderately priced bottles, but here's 15% off all the food from 5pm to 7pm.

€ Ashoka

Grolmanstrasse 51 (3101 5806, www.myashoka.de). S3, S5, S7, S75 Savignyplatz. **Open** 11am-midnight daily. **Main courses** €3.60-€7.50. **No credit cards**. Map p321/p328 F8 **101** **Indian**
Most Indian restaurants in Berlin seem to offer more or less the same menu. This one can be forgiven, as it was the first to open. More than 20 years later, it's still one of the best, offering well-priced, well-prepared dishes in quiet and tasteful surroundings. Plenty of vegetarian options and inventive weekly specials. The branch on Goethestrasse offers vegetarian south Indian cuisine.
Other locations Satyam, Goethestrasse 5 (3180 5111); Ajanta, Grolmannstrasse 15 (310 16116).

★ Café Hardenberg

Hardenbergstrasse 10 (312 2644, www.cafe-hardenberg.de). U2 Ernst-Reuter-Platz. **Open** 9am-1am daily. Map p321/p328 F7 **102** **Café**
Across from the Technical University and usually packed with students drinking coffee. Simple, decent pasta, salads and sandwiches at reasonable prices.

★ Café im Literaturhaus

Fasanenstrasse 23 (882 5414). U1 Uhlandstrasse. **Open** 9.30am-1am daily. **No credit cards**. Map p321/p328 F8 **103** **Café**
The café of the Literaturhaus, which has lectures, readings and a bookshop. The greenhouse-like winter garden or salon rooms are great for ducking into a book over breakfast or a snack.

First Floor

Hotel Palace, Budapester Strasse 45 (2502 1020, www.firstfloor.palace.de). U2, U9, S3, S5, S7, S75 Zoologischer Garten. **Open** 6.30-10.30pm Tue-Sat. **Main courses** from €46. **Set menus** €109-€149. Map p321 G8 **104** **French**
Now under the sway of hot young chef Matthias Diether, this is the place to come for refined French/European cuisine such as Bresse pigeon served with chanterelles and a ragout of potatoes, venison stuffed with foie gras, or *loup de mer* and Breton lobster served with saffron and tomato confit. Three set menus are offered daily. One of Berlin's top tables.

Florian

Grolmanstrasse 52 (313 9184, www.restaurant-florian.de). S3, S5, S7, S75 Savignyplatz. **Open** 6pm-3am daily. **Main courses** €12-€22. Map p321/p328 F8 **105** **German**
Florian has served fine south German food on this quietly posh street for a couple of decades now. The cooking is hearty, the service impeccable. Yes, staff will put you in Siberia if they don't like your looks, but they'll also welcome you back if you're good.

Gabriel

Jüdisches Gemeindehaus, Fasanenstrasse 79-80 (882 6138, www.itsgabriel.de). U1, U9 Kurfürstendamm. **Open** 10.30am-3.30pm, 6.30-10.30pm daily. **Main courses** €14-€22. **No credit cards**. Map p321/p328 F8 **106** **Jewish**
Enter the Jewish Community Centre through airport-style security and head one floor up to this excellent kosher restaurant. Expect a full range of Jewish central and east European specialities, including some of the best *pierogi* in Berlin.

Genazvale

Windscheidstrasse 14 (0176 633 33 659, www.genazvale.de). S3, S5, S7, S75 Charlottenburg. **Open** 3pm-late daily. **Main courses** €8-€21. **Set menu** €28 (per person, min two people). **No credit cards**. Map p320 C8 **107** **Georgian**
A decent, upmarket restaurant that draws a mixed crowd of Georgian and Russian expats, with a few Germans and tourists for good measure. Expect plum sauces, walnuts and coriander as a backdrop to mega-portions of meat. Georgian kitsch abounds, but is easily ignored after a vodka or two. Try the lamb *khinkali* and expect honey and pomegranates aplenty. Small range of first-class Georgian wines.

Julep's

Giesebrechtstrasse 3 (881 8823, www.juleps-berlin.de). U7 Adenauerplatz. **Open** 5pm-1am Mon-Thur, Sun; 5pm-2am Fri, Sat. **Main courses** €9-€26. Map p320 D8 **108** **American**
Julep's gets the fusion flavours of contemporary American cuisine just right with an array of imaginative dishes such as duck prosciutto or quesadillas with rhubarb and apple chutney, teriyaki chicken with lemongrass and basmati rice or Cajun-style red snapper. The caesar salad is a real classic, and pleasingly indulgent desserts include chocolate brownies made with Jack Daniels. Happy hour is 5-8pm and all night Sunday.

Marjellchen

Mommsenstrasse 9 (883 2676, www.marjellchen-berlin.de). S5, S7, S9, S75 Savignyplatz. **Open** 5pm-midnight daily. **Main courses** €10-€20. Map p321/p328 E8 **109** **German**
There aren't many places like Marjellchen around any more. It serves specialities from East Prussia, Pomerania and Silesia in an atmosphere of

CONSUME

old-fashioned *gemütlichkeit*. The beautiful bar and great service are further draws, and the larger-than-life owner recites poetry and sometimes sings.

★ Paris Bar

Kantstrasse 152 (313 8052, www.parisbar.net). S3, S5, S7, S75 Savignyplatz. **Open** noon-2am daily. **Main courses** €10-€25. **Map** p321/p328 F8 ⑩ **Brasserie**

Owner Michel Wurthle's friendship with Martin Kippenberger and other artists is obvious from the art hanging on every available inch of wall and ceiling. Paris Bar, with its old-salon appeal, is one of Berlin's tried and true spots. It attracts a crowd of rowdy regulars, and newcomers can feel left out when seated in the rear. The food, it has to be said, isn't nearly as good as the staff pretend. The adjoining Bar du Paris Bar has yet to gain that settled-in feel. To experience the often rude service and pricey food, you'll need to book.

Restaurant 44

Swissôtel, Augsburger Strasse 44 (220 102 288, www.restaurant44.de). U1, U9 Kurfürstendamm. **Open** 6-10.30pm Mon-Sat. **Main courses** €32-€36. **Map** p321/p328 G8 ⑪ **Fusion**

New chef Danijel Kresovic offers an international menu that fuses European ideas with more exotic flavours in dishes such as monkfish with curry spices, prawn *chiboust* and chanterelle ragout, or halibut with *pata negra*, pistachios and sweet potatoes. There's a fine selection of wines by the glass too.

Sachiko Sushi

Jeanne-Mammen-Bogen 584 (313 2282, www.sachikosushi.com). S3, S5, S7, S75 Savignyplatz. **Open** noon-midnight daily. **Main courses** €3.50-€18. **Map** p321/p328 F8 ⑫ **Sushi**

This was Berlin's first kaiten (conveyor belt) sushi joint. It's invariably packed with upmarket thirtysomethings, plucking the scrummy morsels as they circumnavigate a chrome and black stone bar.

€ Schwarzes Café

Kantstrasse 148 (313 8038, www.schwarzescafe-berlin.de). S3, S5, S7, S75 Savignyplatz. **Open** 24hrs daily (closed 3-10am Tue). **No credit cards. Map** p321/p328 F8 ⑬ **Café**

Open all hours for breakfasts and meals, Schwarze Café was once all black and anarchistically inclined (hence the name), but the political crowd moved on decades ago and the decor has been brightened. Service can get overstretched when it's crowded, such as early on a weekend morning, when clubbers stop for breakfast on their way home.

€ Witty's

Wittenbergplatz (no phone). U1, U2, U3 Wittenbergplatz. **Open** *summer* 11am-midnight; *winter* times vary. **Main courses** €2.80-€3.30. **No credit cards. Map** p321 H8 ⑭ **Imbiss**

There are *Imbiss* stands on every corner of Wittenbergplatz, but this one, on the northwest corner of the square, opposite KaDeWe, is one of the best in the whole city. It's a friendly and courteous operation, serves only Neuland organic meat, and has gorgeous thick-cut chips with a variety of sauces to choose from (chilli, satay, garlic mayo) to go with your *Currywurst*. Get an organic Asgard beer to go with it.

► *For more on Currywurst, see p154 Curry, Do Your Wurst*

OTHER DISTRICTS

Zehlendorf

★ Fischerhütte am Schlachtensee

Fischerhüttenstrasse 136 (8049 8310, www.fischerhuette-berlin.de). U1 Krumme Lanke, S1 Mexikoplatz. **Open** 10am-midnight daily. **Main courses** €14-€30. **German**

Situated in the woods by the Schlachtensee lake, this lovely restaurant and beer garden is the perfect way to round off a day exploring the Grunewald.

Fischerhütte am Schlachtensee

Bars & Pubs

If you like bars, you've come to the right city.

With relaxed licensing laws, generous measures and an absence of identikit chains, Berlin can claim to be a great city for bars. Whether you want to sit on a battered sofa with a beer and a book or drink cocktails in a slick style bar as the sun comes up, the city has somewhere for you. The locals like a drink too – many drinks, in fact, but they handle their booze so well that displays of drunken behaviour are rare. Their secret is simple: they take their time. There's no need to rush. In Berlin bars can stay open as late as they like.

If you're used to a more conservative imbibing climate, it might be wise to pace yourself at first. Here no one is going to shout 'time' in your ear, even though the general tendency is for bars to close earlier these days. If you feel like carrying on when the staff finally do get around to putting the chairs up on the tables and pointedly offering to call you a taxi, there's bound to be somewhere else open nearby. Just ask the bar staff – they're probably going there too.

The archetypal Berlin bar is artfully shabby, with flea market furniture, exposed brickwork, open ended closing times and an open minded clientele – the likes of **Mein Haus am See** (*see p160*) in Mitte, **Hotel** (*see p167*) in Kreuzberg, **Wohnzimmer** (*see p164*) in Prenzlauerberg or **Natanja & Heinrich** (*see p170*) in Neukölln.

For those who like things a little more upmarket, there's no shortage of fashionable style bars, such as **Tausend** (*see p160*) under the Friedrichstrasse rail bridge, **Lebensstern** (*see p171*) above the Café Einstein on the Kurfürstenstrasse or **Solar** (*see p168*) on the 17th floor of a Kreuzberg tower block. Cocktails may sometimes seem expensive at the sleeker establishments, but watch the bartender mix your drink and you'll not feel ripped off: Berliners are far too cool to measure out spirits and if you only get 40ml of each liquor, you're unlucky.

Berlin doesn't do pubs particularly well, notable exceptions being **Alt Berlin** (*see p159*) in Mitte, **Dicke Wirtin** (*see p171*) in Charlottenburg and **Yorkschlösschen** in Kreuzberg, which is also a jazz venue (*see p244*). Despite this, beer remains the main tipple all over town, even though local brews

are a sorry substitute for those of Bavaria and Bohemia (*see p167* **Brewing Berlin-Style**).

There are some lovely beer gardens in the city, however, from **Café am Neuen See** (*see p170*) in the Tiergarten to **Prater** in Prenzlauerberg (*see p163*) and **Brachvogel** (*see p166*) by the canal in Kreuzberg. If you want to meet locals, brave an *Eck-Kneipe*, the determinedly ungentrified and smoky 'corner pubs' you find on most streets. The beer is often ridiculously cheap (the cheapest we've found is 90 cents for a '*kleine Kindl vom Fass*' at Willi Mangler, Hauptstrasse 57 in Schöneberg), but be prepared to be stared at and treated with suspicion.

People tend to pay their own way and drink at their own pace, partly because in many places bills are only totted up as you leave. Exceptions are made for ceremonial rounds of vodka, Jägermeister or tequila.

MITTE

Squatters in Oranienburger Strasse were the first to open cafés after the Wall fell, but these days the Scheunenviertel's main drag mostly caters to the tourist industry. Things are both quieter and funkier up on Auguststrasse, and the corner with Tucholskystrasse bustles of an evening, but Gipstrasse is probably the most happening nexus in this neighbourhood.

> ❶ Green numbers given in this chapter correspond to the location of each bar as marked on the street maps. *See pp316-328.*

1000s of
things to do...

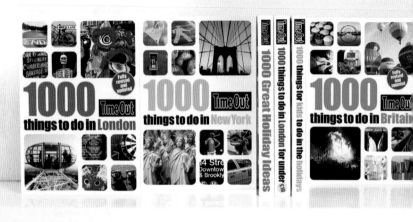

Touristy Hackescher Markt is a bit of a dead loss for bars these days. The restored courtyards across from the S-Bahn station are indeed impressive, but their renovation has chased out the offbeat and left behind rather too many over-designed identikit bars. Torstrasse and the Mitte-Nord area beyond it are happier hunting grounds, especially the quarter around Brunnenstrasse, Veteranenstrasse, Rosenthaler Platz and the beginning of Kastanienallee, which is home to an assortment of eccentric establishments.

Alt Berlin

Münzstrasse 23 (281 9687). U8 Weinmeisterstrasse. **Open** times vary. **No credit cards. Map** p326 O5 ❶

A rare proper pub amid a sea of swish cocktail bars in the Hackescher Markt area. It's very smoky out the front, and the staff have a reputation for surliness, but the place does good beer, the wood-panelled walls have a lovely patina and it's in a very handy location.

★ Altes Europa

Gipsstrasse 11 (2809 3840, www.alteseuropa.com). U8 Weinmeisterstrasse/bus N2, N5, N8. **Open** noon-1am daily. **No credit cards. Map** p319/p326 N5 ❷

The gentle minimalism of the decor – big picture windows, basic furnishings and nothing but a few old maps and prints on the walls – is a relief in an increasingly pretentious neighbourhood, and this spacious place is good for anything from a party to a private conversation. The bar serves light meals, Ukrainian vodka and draught Krusovice in both dark and light varieties to a mixed, youngish crowd.

Amano Bar

Auguststrasse 43 (809 4150, www.bar.hotel-amano.com). U8 Rosenthaler Platz. **Open** *Summer* 4-10pm daily. **Map** p326 M5 ❸

This rooftop bar belongs to the Amano Hotel and is popular with hotel guests and a preppy crowd sipping after-work cocktails. Not the hippest place in the area, but you do get a wonderful view with your drink.

▶ *For more on the Amano Hotel, see p118.*

Bar 3

Weydingerstrasse 20 (9700 5106). U8 Rosa-Luxemburg-Platz. **Open** 9pm-late Tue-Sat. **No credit cards. Map** p319/p326 O5 ❹

Nestled in a cul-de-sac near the Volksbühne, this low-lit bar has wraparound windows, a slick black interior, a spacious U-shaped bar and inexpensive wine and beer. Try the Kölsch brew from Cologne (served in the traditional skinny cylindrical glasses) or small servings of wine that go for €2.50. It's popular with the over-30 art crowd and a great place to both theorise and throw back a few drinks in a sleek but unpretentious atmosphere. It also sells Walkers crisps.

★ Bötzow Privat

Linienstrasse 113 (2809 5390, www.boetzow-privat.de). U8 Rosenthaler Platz. **Open** 9am-late daily. **Map** p326 M5 ❺

Bötzow Privat is a very classy 1920s-style gastropub with wood-panelled walls, above-average food and a classy ambience.

CCCP

Rosenthaler Strasse 71 (www.myspace.com/cccpclub). U8 Rosenthaler Platz. **Open** 6pm-late Tue-Thur; 10pm-late Fri, Sat. **No credit cards. Map** p319/p326 N4 ❻

CCCP is a celebration of all things Russian. This means copious amounts of vodka – straight or mixed – quaffed by locals and a few other shady characters rubbing shoulders in the small, dark space. A crimson colour scheme, seedy vibe and kitsch decorations complete the picture. The doorman might refuse entry to large groups or anyone who looks too much like a tourist.

Eschloraque Rümschrümp

Rosenthaler Strasse 39 (www.eschschloraque.de). U8 Weinmeisterstrasse. **Open** 2pm-late daily. **No credit cards. Map** p326 M5 ❼

Bonus marks if you can pronounce the name of this Mitte classic. More bonus points if you can find it – it's hidden away in one of the courtyards of the Hackescher Höfe. Steel yourself for the eccentric monster-obsessed interior design.

FC Magnet

Veteranenstrasse 26 (0177 291 6707/www.fcmagnet.de). U8 Rosenthaler Platz/bus N2, N8, N84. **Open** 7pm-late daily. **No credit cards. Map** p319/p326 N4 ❽

A few years ago, Berliners began transforming old-style East Berlin social clubs into fancy new bars.

THE BEST BARS & PUBS

For superlative gin and tonics
Tier. *See p170.*

Classy 1920s-influenced cocktail bar for thirtysomething hedonists
Würgeengel. *See p169.*

Wood-panelled gastropub with a rarified air
Bötzow Privat. *See above.*

High ceilings, vintage furniture, cheap drinks
Natanja & Heinrich. *See p170.*

Small but perfectly formed
Rum Trader. *See p172.*

The slacker entrepreneurs behind FC Magnet have taken it a step further, creating a fashionable football bar complete with its own team. Though the drinks aren't exceptional, people pack in at weekends to play Kicker (table football) under a giant photograph of Franz Beckenbauer.

Kim

Brunnenstrasse 10 (no phone, www.kim-in-berlin.com). U8 Rosenthaler Platz. **Open** 9pm-late daily. **No credit cards. Map** p319/p326 N4 ⑨

Minimal, minimal, minimal! This place perfectly captures that unfinished – and inexplicably sexy – look with which Berlin's fashionable set is so enamoured. Kim has been a favourite for twentysomething art-crowders since it opened in February 2007. The door is unmarked; just look for an all-glass façade and crowds of people sporting New Romantic haircuts and skinny jeans. The dimly lit, white-walled space is DIY: under a geometric dropped ceiling handmade by co-owner Oliver Miller are stackable chairs and tables that guests can arrange as they like. Cheap drinks and a rotating roster of neighbourhood DJs add to a don't-give-a-damn aesthetic.

King Kong Klub

Brunnenstrasse 173 (9120 6860, www.king-kong-klub.de). U8 Rosenthaler Platz/bus N8, 52. **Open** 10pm-late Mon, Wed-Sat; 9pm-late Tue. **No credit cards. Map** p319/p326 N4 ⑩

King Kong Klub is unpretentious, with pudgy leather sofas, subdued red lighting and rock 'n' roll and B-movie paraphernalia scattered about. The music policy mainly covers rock and electro; live shows don't happen much here any more, so pick up one of the monthly flyers to see what's going on. Popular with student-types and local eccentrics.

Kingsize

Friedrichstrasse 112b (www.kingsizebar.de). U6 Oranienburger Tor. **Open** 9pm-7am Wed-Sat. **Map** p326 M5 ⑪

The name is a joke – this is one of the tiniest bars in Berlin. It also has some of the pickiest bouncers. But if you get past them, enjoy a drink from a crystal whiskey tumbler and the smug feeling of exclusivity.

★ Mein Haus am See

Brunnenstrasse 197/198 (2388 3561, www.mein-haus-am-see.blogspot.com). U8 Rosenthaler Platz. **Open** 9am-late daily. **No credit cards. Map** p326 N4 ⑫

INSIDE TRACK THE PFAND

Some bars still charge punters a *Pfand* – a refundable deposit on each glass or bottle.

This hugely popular split-level newcomer is situated a stone's throw from busy Rosenthaler Platz. The owners claim 'it's not a bar, it's not a club, it's something sexier in between' – and it's certainly hard to categorise. There are exhibitions, readings, DJs and it almost never closes, so whether you want another beer, a sobering coffee or a panini at 4.30am, this is the place to come. Excellent breakfasts too. It's open pretty much 24 hours a day.

Pony Bar

Alte Schönhauser Strasse 44 (0163 775 6603, www.pony-bar.de). U8 Weinmeisterstrasse/bus N2, N5, N8. **Open** noon-late Mon-Sat; 6pm-late Sun. **No credit cards. Map** p319/p326 O5 ⑬

A good location compensates for some surly staff at this austere watering hole where affordable cocktails are the principal draw, and wines are best avoided. It's quiet as the grave by day but often buzzes deep into the night.

Rivabar

Dircksenstrasse 142 S-Bahnbogen 142 (2472 2688, www.riva-berlin.de). S3, S5, S7, S9, S75 Hackescher Markt. **Open** 6pm-late daily. **Map** p326 N5 ⑭

This bar is housed in one of the railway arches underneath Hackescher Markt station. It would be unremarkable if it weren't for the garden out the back, which has an unexpectedly great view of the TV Tower, and the fantastic cocktails. Staff do the classics very well – try the Old Fashioned – as well as more new-fangled creations like the Basil Gin Smash.

Ständige Vertretung

Schiffbauerdamm 8 (282 3965, www.staev.de). U6, S3, S5, S7, S9, S75 Friedrichstrasse. **Open** 10am-1am daily. **Map** p327 M6 ⑮

The knick-knack-filled Ständige commemorates the highly controversial decision to move the German capital from Bonn to Berlin after Reunification. *Ständige Vertretung* – permanent representation – was the name West and East Germany used to describe the special consulates they kept in each other's countries, not wanting to legitimise the other by calling them an embassy. The place does slightly overpriced old-school German food, and Kölsch on tap. There's a lovely terrace by the river for the summer.

Tausend

Schiffbauerdamm 11 (2758 2070, www.tausendberlin.com). U6, S3, S5, S7, S9, S75 Friedrichstrasse. **Open** 9pm-late Tue-Sat. **Map** p318/p327 M6 ⑯

With an unmarked entrance – look for the iron door under the train overpass – and strict entrance policy, this grown-up bar/lounge is as exclusive as Berlin gets. Here's where the well-heeled see and are seen while sipping innovative drinks in a tubular, steel-ceilinged interior lit by eerily eye-like 3D installations. Try a bracing Wasabi cocktail in summer or a malt

CONSUME

Mein Haus am See.

whisky served with local pine honey in winter. Go late, look sharp. There's also a restaurant called the Backroom Cantina, serving pricey fusion food.

Trust

Torstrasse 72 (no phone). U2 Rosa-Luxemburg-Platz. **Open** 10pm-4am Thur-Sat. **No credit cards. Map** p326 O5 ⑰
If you want a sociable night out, this tiny bar is the place to go. The gimmick is that it only serves whole bottles of Trust-branded spirits and champagne, so you need to club together with other punters to buy one, which you share throughout the night. There's a double bed by the bar for lounging on with your new friends. Note that Trust is too cool to have a sign – the entrance is an unmarked door. Ring the doorbell to be let in.

PRENZLAUER BERG

Kollwitzplatz is a leafy square fringed with cafés and bars. There's more of the same around the Wasserturm, at the junction of Rykestrasse and Knaackstrasse. The cafés near Helmholtzplatz (in the so-called 'LSD' neighbourhood, standing for the initial letters of Lychener Strasse, Schliemannstrasse and Dunckerstrasse) stray a bit further downmarket, stay open later and are somewhat more spontaneous. The Prater beer garden in nearby Kastanienallee is a pleasant place on a warm summer evening, and a good starting point for bar crawls down Kastanienallee and into Mitte.

8mm

Schonhauser Allee 177B (4050 0624, www. 8mmbar.com). U2 Senefelderplatz/bus N2. **Open** 9pm-late daily. **No credit cards. Map** p319/p326 O4 ⑱
This purple-walled dive exists to remind travellers that Berlin isn't Stuttgart. The attractive, young and poor go for that fifth nightcap around 6am, and local scenesters rub shoulders with anglophone expats. There seems to be more hard alcohol consumed here than in your average Berlin hangout but, and contrary to the name, films are rarely shown here these days.

Becketts Kopf

Pappelallee 64 (0162 2379 418). U2 Eberswalder Strasse. **Open** 8pm-late daily. **No credit cards. Map** p319/p328 P2 ⑲
The head of Samuel Beckett stares at you from the window of this intimate spot, which serves expert cocktails and a variety of whiskies. Prices are about average for mixed drinks in Berlin but quality is several notches above. Occasional DJs play avant-jazz.

Dr Pong

Eberswalder Strasse 21 (no phone, www.drpong. net). U2 Eberswalder Strasse/bus N42. **Open** 8pm-late Mon-Sat; 2pm-late Sun. **No credit cards. Map** p319/p328 O3 ⑳

Prater.

Bring your table tennis bat and prepare for ping-pong madness. The action doesn't start until around midnight, but when it does you can expect 30 or so players – some good, some bad – to surround the table. Note that the opening hours are unreliable. If you don't have your own bat, you can hire one for a €5 deposit.

Gagarin

Knaackstrasse 22-24 (442 8807). U2 Senefelderplatz/bus N2. **Open** 9.30am-2am daily. **Map** p319/p328 P4 ㉑

Brought to you by the folks who run Gorki Park and Pasternak, adding a bar to their troika of Russian hospitality. Vogue-ish retro space-age decor (colourful planets and Yuri's likeness adorn the walls) and electronic sounds provide the backdrop for Baltika beer and tasty Russian pub grub.

▶ *For more Russian theming, see p145 for Pasternak and p159 for CCCP.*

Hausbar

Rykestrasse 54 (4404 7606). U2 Senefelderplatz/ bus N2. **Open** 7pm-5am daily. **No credit cards**. **Map** p319/p328 P4 ㉒

Bright red and gold, with a glorious cherub-filled sky on the ceiling, this small pocket of fabulousness seats about 15 people at a push. Hausbar is much more fun than all the pretentious cafés with Russian literary names you'll find around the corner, and it's particularly inviting at three or four in the morning.

Klub der Republik

Pappelallee 81 (no phone). U2 Eberswalder Strasse/bus N42. **Open** 8pm-4am daily. **No credit cards**. **Map** p319/p328 O2 ㉓

Above a music school and accessed via a wobbly staircase in the courtyard, this spacious bar manages to mix the best of the retro design craze with the sort of lively revelry associated with the East in the mid 1990s. Not quite the hotspot it once was, it's nevertheless worth popping in on a night out if you're in the area.

Kohlenquelle

Kopenhagener Strasse 16 (no phone). U2, S41, S42 Schönhauserallee. **Open** 9am-late Mon-Fri; 10am-late Sat, Sun. **No credit cards**. **Map** p319 O2 ㉔

All chipped plaster and mismatched junkyard furniture and as comfy as your gran's sitting room, this typical Berlin bar serves relatively cheap drinks as well as food. The daytime crowd verges on the pretentious (everyone seems to be working on a novel) but night-time patrons are much more lively.

★ Prater

Kastanienallee 7-9 (448 5688, www.prater garten.de). U2 Eberswalder Strasse/bus N42. **Open** 6-11pm Mon-Sat; noon-11pm Sun. **No credit cards**. **Map** p319/p328 O3 ㉕

INSIDE TRACK NO SMOKING?

There has been a smoking ban in Berlin since 2007, but you'd be hard pressed to notice it in most bars and pubs in the city. The current wording of the law – amended in 2009 after a court case launched by the landlord of the **Rum Trader** (*see p172*) – permits smoking in one-room establishments, as long as there is a sign on the door saying *Raucherkneipe* (smokers' pub), and provided no food is served. Any venue bigger than 75 square metres can only allow smoking in a sealed-off room. Officially, anyway. In practice Berliners continue to light up pretty much anywhere they please on a night out, the exception being nightclubs (including the otherwise ridiculously permissive **Berghain**, *see p248*), where the ban is often strictly enforced.

Almost any evening, this huge and immaculately restored swing-era bar, across the courtyard from the theatre of the same name, attracts a smart, high-volume crowd. The beer-swilling lustiness, big wooden tables, and primeval platefuls of meat and veg can almost make you feel like you've been teleported to Munich. In summer, the shady beer garden makes for an all-day buzz. Brunch is served from 10am-4pm on Saturdays and Sundays.

Rakete

Schönhauser Allee 39A (0160 9763 62477, www.rakete-berlin.de). U2 Eberswalder Strasse/ bus N2, N52. **Open** 8pm-late Thur-Sat. **No credit cards**. **Map** p319/p328 O3 ㉖

Small, white and bright, with minimalist furnishings and low-key techno in the background, Rakete has become a casual hangout for local music and film scenesters, though it's as likely as not to have only a handful of people inside. No draught beer, but the bartenders know how to mix a drink.

Razzia in Budapest

Oderberger Strasse 38 (4862 3620, www.razzia-in-budapest.eu). U2 Eberswalder Strasse. **Open** 6pm-late daily. **No credit cards**. **Map** p319/ p328 O3 ㉗

East Berlin not Ost enough? This wood-panelled spot boasts a Hungarian feel that veers from cosy to crazed. There's Böhmisches dark beer on tap, and they pride themselves on their ten house cocktails with names such as Sommer in Budapest and Razzia. Weekend DJs play oldies. *Photo p164.*

Saphire Bar

Bötzowstrasse 31 (2556 2158, www.saphire bar.de). M10 Answalder Platz or M4

CONSUME

Razzia in Budapest. *See p163.*

Dostoevsky with career students over a tepid borscht. Evening light from candelabra reflects on gold-sprayed walls as students and maudlin poets chase brandies with Hefeweizen. Daytimes can be sluggish.

FRIEDRICHSHAIN

Friedrichshain carries the flag for youthful Berlin bohemia. The area around Simon-Dach-Strasse is full of fun bars, cheap cafés and ethnic takeaways, but on a weekend night don't expect to be the only out-of-towners wandering around. Rigaer Strasse and Mainzer Strasse were once hubs of the militant squatting scene, and an element of disgruntled radicalism persists.

Meanwhile, the former socialist showcase boulevard that is Karl-Marx-Allee has begun to develop into a nightlife area, but more as an eastern extension of the Mitte scene than a western annex of the Friedrichshain one.

Bierhof Rüdersdorf
Rüdersdorferstrasse 70 (2936 0215, www.bierhof.info). S3, S5, S7, S75, S9 Ostbahnhof. **Open** 4pm-midnight Mon-Sat; 9am-midnight Sun. **Map** pp324 R7 ③
This industrial beer garden is right next to Berghain, so tends to be full of clubbing casualties looking for their last beer on a Sunday morning. On Sundays it also serves breakfast.
▶ *For more on clubbing at Berghain, see p248.*

Hops & Barley
Wühlischstrasse 22/23 (2936 7534, www.hopsandbarley-berlin.de). S3, S5, S7, S75, S9, U1 Warschauer Strasse. **Open** 5pm-3am daily. **No credit cards. Map** p324 T7 ㉜
This microbrewery in a former butcher's specialises in cider – a rarity in beer-soaked Berlin.
▶ *For more on Berlin's breweries, see p167 Brewing Berlin-Style.*

Habermeyer
Gärtnerstrasse 6 (2977 1887/www.habermeyer-bar.de). S3, S5, S7, S75, S9, U1 Warschauer Strasse. **Open** 7.30pm-late Mon-Fri; 8.30pm-late Sat, Sun. **No credit cards. Map** p324 T7 ㉝
Not a dive, but certainly not fancy, Habermeyer is where local hipsters go for low-key drinks, casual conversation, table football, and a marked absence of the teenagers and tourists who nightly flock to Simon-Dach-Strasse. The decor is unobtrusively '70s, the lighting is dim and reddish, and most nights, the music is delivered by a DJ.

Kaufbar
Gärtnerstrasse 4 (2977 8825, www.kaufbar-berlin.de). S3, S5, S7, S9, S75, U1 Warschauer Strasse. **Open** 10am-midnight Mon, Thur-Sun; 3pm-midnight Tue, Wed. **No credit cards. Map** p324 T7 ㉞

Hufelandstrasse. **Open** 8pm-2am Mon-Thur, Sun; 8pm-4am Fri, Sat. **Map** p319 Q4 ㉘
This sleekly designed bar, a favourite with local creative types, aims for a sophistication more common in cities like New York and Paris. It's worth checking out for the cocktails alone – over 300 of them, with names like Mummies on Ice and the Unbearable Lightness of Being.

Schwalbe
Stargarder Strasse 10 (4403 6208, www.schwalbeberlin.de). U2, S8, S41, S42, S85 Schönhauser Allee. **Open** 6pm-late daily. **No credit cards. Map** p319 P2 ㉙
Unwilling to endure identikit Irish pubs or brave grumpy local *Eck-Kneipen*? Schwalbe is about as chichi as a football bar gets, offering German and Italian league games in a fashionable café environment where you can grab a coffee and cake instead of a beer. Downstairs there are three strangely crowded Kicker (table football) tables and DJs on a Saturday.

★ Wohnzimmer
Lettestrasse 6 (445 5458). U2 Eberswalder Strasse/bus N42. **Open** 9am-4am daily. **No credit cards. Map** p319/p328 P2 ㉚
Immediately behind the door of this shabbily elegant 'living room' is a bar-like structure assembled from kitchen cabinets. Threadbare divans and artsy bar girls make this the perfect place to discuss

A small, stylish bar and café with a neighbourly atmosphere and a gimmick. You can buy the chairs you're sitting on, the table you're eating from, that fork you're holding, the artwork on the walls – just about everything, in fact – hence the name ('Buy-Bar'). Light organic snacks such as salads and soups are served and in summer you can use the pretty garden area.

Kunstliche BEATmung

Simon-Dach-Strasse 20 (www.kuenstliche beatmung.de/7022 0472). U1, S3, S5, S6, S7, S9, S75 Warschauer Strasse. **Open** 7pm-2am daily. **No credit cards.** **Map** p324 S7 ㉟

The low-domed ceiling, plastic furniture and coloured neon are like a cross between cocktail bar and space capsule. Around midnight, the beautiful young things start dribbling in and any oddness is soon swallowed in the crush. The main attraction is an elaborate drinks menu, which provides hundreds of lurid opportunities for ex perimental boozing.

Macondo

Gärtnerstrasse 14 (5473 5943, www.macondo-berlin.de). S3, S5, S7, S9, S75, U1 Warschauer Strasse or U5 Samariter Strasse. **Open** 3pm-late Mon-Fri; 10am-late Sat, Sun. **No credit cards.** **Map** p324 T7 ㊱

This café-bar on Boxhagener Platz brands itself a *Leseplatz* (reading place) and it's perfect for just that. Kitted out, like so many Berlin cafés, with fraying but still trendy vintage furniture, and also offering a good selection of board games, it's more of a chill-out bar than a night-out place. Snacks such as fried yucca and a Latin American brunch on Sundays keep the intellects sated.

Monster Ronson's Ichiban Karaoke

Warschauer Strasse 34 (8975 1327, www.karaokemonster.decom). U1, S3, S5, S7, S9, S75, Warschauer Strasse. **Open** 7pm-midnight daily. **No credit cards.** **Map** p324 S8 ㊲

In 1999, Monster Ronson – aka Ron Rineck – moved to Berlin from Salt Lake City with $7,000 in his pocket. As his savings dwindled, he began sleeping in his car, bought a second-hand karaoke machine, and soon was driving to squat houses all over Europe, throwing karaoke parties and getting paid to do it. Eventually, he saved up enough to open his very own karaoke bar and today Monster Ronson's Ichiban Karaoke is packed with pop star wannabes most nights of the week, belting out songs in one of several different karaoke booths, some small and intimate, others complete with their own stage area.

CONSUME

Saphire Bar. *See p163.*

Paule's Metal Eck

Krossener Strasse 15 (291 1624/www.paules-metal-eck.comde). U5 Frankfurter Tor or U1, S3, S5, S6, S7, S9, S75 Warschauer Strasse/ bus N5, N29. **Open** *Summer* 5pm-late daily. *Winter* 7pm-late daily. **No credit cards.** **Map** p324 S7 ③⑥

Neither a typical heavy metal bar nor remotely typical for this area, the Egyptian-themed Eck attracts a young crowd with relentless metal videos, a decent selection of beers and both pool and table football. Inoperative disco balls, overhead lamps in the shape of mummies and formidable dragon busts deck an interior half designed like a mausoleum, half in gloomy medieval style. A small menu changes weekly and there's live Bundesliga football on weekend afternoons.

Le Petit Laboratoire

Grünberger Strasse 87 (0151 5905 0323, www. myspace.com/lepetitlaboratoire). U5 Samariter Strasse. **Open** 3pm-late Wed-Sat; noon-late Sun. **No credit cards.** **Map** p324 T7 ③⑨

This French bohemian bar, with lots of sofas, bright colours and a comfortingly ramshackle feel, is a new Friedrichshain favourite. The highlight is a selection of delicious, self-invented cocktails. The bar also works as a gallery space and plays host to regular concerts. The Gallic proprietors haven't got the hang of German yet, so English is the working language, as a big sign behind the bar announces.

Supamolly

Jessner Strasse 41 (2900 7294, www. supamolly.de). S41, S42, S8, S85, S9, U5, S4, S8, S10 Frankfurter Allee/bus N5. **Open** 8pm-late Tue-Sat. **No credit cards.** **Map** p324 U7 ④⓪

Having opened in the early 1990s as a semi-legal bolthole fronting a lively squat, Supamolly (or Supamolli) is a miracle of survival. The frequent live punk and ska shows in the club behind the bar dictates only some of the clientele; a healthy mix of young and ageing punks, unemployed activists and music lovers of all types gather in this dim, mural-smeared, candlelit watering hole until the early morning. DJs at weekends.

KREUZBERG

West Berlin's former art and anarchy quarter still offers plenty of alternative life. The fashionable focus is the area around Schlesisches Tor and Kottbusser Tor, though the district around Oranienstrasse is also experiencing a revival.

Although well-supplied with cafés, the increasingly upmarket Bergmannstrasse neighbourhood remains sadly somnolent after dark, though there is a bit of gay life on Mehringdamm.

Barbie Deinhoff's

Schlesische Strasse 16 (www.barbiedeinhoff.de). U1 Schlesisches Tor/bus N29. **Open** 6pm-6am daily. **No credit cards.** **Map** p324 R9 ④①

Run by celebrity drag queen Lena Braun (star of the fashionable documentary *Gender X*), this lively and unusual bar attracts both the more bourgeois members of Berlin's cross-dressing community and the loucher denizens of the Kreuzberg mainstream. The look is pitched somewhere between tacky kitsch and futuristic chic. There are often lectures and art events in the early evening, before the debauchery kicks off.

★ Brachvogel

Carl-Herz-Ufer 34 (6930432, www.brachvogel-berlin.de). U1 Hallesches Tor, U1 Prinzenstrasse. **Open** 9am-late daily. **Map** p323 N9 ④②

This leafy canalside beer garden is particularly popular with families, thanks to the crazy golf course and adventure playground attached. There is an extensive list of wines by the glass and meals on offer throughout the day – on Sunday there is a brunch buffet between 10am and 2pm. If you can, sit in a stripy 'Strandkorb' beach basket and watch the world go by.

Cake

Schlesische Strasse 32 (6162 4610, www.cake-bar.de). U1, U15 Schlesisches Tor/bus N29. **Open** 5pm-late daily. **No credit cards.** **Map** p324 S9 ④③

A diverse crowd in both age and nationality – the hostel across the street lends a youthful international air – mills about in this lounge that comes with old easy chairs, sofas, art-covered walls and a dark red, musty interior. Music gently hums overhead, providing a great atmosphere for relaxing and chatting. There's even a vintage jukebox equipped with a variety of oldies. DJs most weekends for free. Happy hour is 7-9pm daily.

Golgatha

Viktoria Park, entrance via Katzbachstrasse or Dudenstrasse (785 2453, www.golgatha-berlin.de). U6 Platz der Luftbrücke. **Open** Apr-end Sept 10am-late daily. **Map** p322 L11 ④④

This legendary beer garden can do it all – breakfasts under dappled sunlight, hearty lunches and drinking and dancing until the wee small hours. A Kreuzberg institution.

Haifischbar

Arndtstrasse 25 (691 1352, www.haifischbar-berlin.de). U6, U7 Mehringdamm/bus N19. **Open** 7pm-3am Mon-Thur, Sun; 7pm-5am Fri, Sat. **No credit cards.** **Map** p322 M10 ④⑤

Well-run and friendly bar where the staff are expert cocktail-shakers, the music's hip and tasteful in a trancey kind of way, and the back room, equipped with a sushi bar, is a good place to chill out at the

CONSUME

end of an evening. Certainly the most happening place in the Bergmannstrasse Kiez, and with some kind of crowd any night of the week.

Heinz Minki
Vor dem Schlesischen Tor 3 (6953 3766, www.heinzminki.de). U1 Schlesisches Tor. **Open** *Summer* noon-late daily. *Winter* 6pm-late Thur; 9pm-late Fri, Sat; from noon Sun. **Map** p324 S9 ⑯
Massive leafy beer garden by the canal in the far east of Kreuzberg. A more grown-up alternative to Club

der Visionäre (*see p172*) next door. There's coffee and cake on Sundays if you've had enough booze.

★ Hotel
Mariannenstrasse 26a (no phone). U1, U8 Kottbusser Tor. **Open** usually 2pm-late daily. **No credit cards. Map** p323 P9 ⑰
This shabby chic newcomer is not a hotel, but one of the rough-round-the-edges bars Berlin does so well. There are candles on the tables, a decent wine list and an unpretentious clientele. Later on in the evening a club opens in the basement next door.

Brewing Berlin-style

Microbreweries are popping up everywhere.

Considering Germany's reputation for making some of the best beer in the world, Prussian brews have until recently fallen pretty short of the mark. It's worth trying a glass of the classic Berliner Weisse, but few people ask for a second – this slightly sour wheat beer is sweetened with a shot of green woodruff or raspberry syrup – ask for *grün* or *rot* depending on which you feel more confident about stomaching.

A hundred years ago, Berlin was home to just under 130 breweries. These days there's only really one big one left: Schultheiss in Hohenschönhausen, which makes the two most ubiquitous local brews, Berliner Pilsner and Berliner Kindl.

Happily, though, the number of one-man breweries is growing. In Wedding, Martin Eschenbrenner set up a mash tun fermenting vat and storage tank in the old laundry room of his student residence and opened his own brewery: **Eschenbräu**. He now brews 55,000 litres a year, including specialist beers such as Schwarze Molle, Alter Schwede and Roter Wedding; all of which you can sample in his large, leafy beer garden. He also makes Schnapps and apple juice.

Marcus Barkowsky has been brewing his Marcus Bräu Pils and Marcus Bräu Dunkel at 'Germany's smallest brewery' in Mitte for ten years. And in 2009, Philipp Brokamp opened **Hops & Barley** (*see p164*) in Friedrichshain – a pub with its own brewery named after a song by the British punk band, Leatherface.

In Neukölln, Thorsten Schoppe offers guided tours of his **Südstern** brewery. Schoppe set a world record by brewing the strongest beer in the world in accordance with the German Beer Purity Law: viscous, very sweet and with an alcohol content of 27.6 per cent. Also in Neukölln, the **Rollberg** brewery has recently started making highly regarded own-brand beer, which you can sample at some of the city's more discerning drinking dens, such as **Bar Raval** in Kreuzberg (Lübbenerstrasse 1, 5316 7954, www.barraval.de).

The annual Berlin beer festival takes place in August (*see p200*).

The following breweries offer tours and tasting sessions:

Berliner-Kindl-Schultheiss-Brauerei
Indira-Gandhi-Strasse 66-69, Hohenschönhausen (960 9579, www.schultheiss.de/brauerei).

Brauhaus Südstern
Hasenheide 69, Neukölln (6900 1624, www.brauhaus-suedstern.de).

Eschenbräu
Triftstr. 67, Wedding (462 6837, www.eschenbraeu.de).

Microbrauerei Barkowsky
Münzstrasse 1-3, Mitte (247 6985, www.brau-dein-bier.de).

Rollberg
Werbellinstrasse 50, Neukölln (0163 604 6350, www.rollberger.de).

CONSUME

CONSUME

Würgeengel.

★ Luzia

*Oranienstrasse 34 (8179 9958, www.luzia.tc). U1,
U8 Kottbusser Tor.* **Open** *usually noon-late daily.*
No credit cards. Map p323 P8 ㊽
This oddly whimsical bar and café, another one
that's a bit rough around the edges, is the linchpin
of Oranienstrasse's renaissance as a hip destination for young Berliners. The simultaneously
imposing and welcoming ambience is achieved by
a combination of high ceilings, moody lighting,
well-worn second-hand furniture and striking
walls covered in old wallpaper, gold paint and
street art by local talent Chin Chin. There's a small
breakfast menu throughout the day, plus a selection of cakes and coffees and a standard range of
alcoholic drinks.

Matilda

*Graefestrasse 12 (8179 7288, www.myspace.com/
matilda_Berlin). U8 Schönleinstrasse.* **Open** *9am-
late daily.* **No credit cards. Map** p323 P10 ㊾
The cobbles, tree-lined streets and general peace and
quiet make the Graefekiez one of the city's most
pleasant neighbourhoods, and Matilda fits in perfectly. It's small and cosy with plenty of retro furniture: tables and chairs in the front room and squidgy
sofas in the back. Bar staff are on hand to flip records
(mostly 1960s pop and soul) in between serving
drinks. Popular with a young, lazy crowd.

Monarch

*Skalitzer Strasse 134, 1st floor (6165 6003,
www.kottimonarch.de). U1, U8 Kottbusser
Tor.* **Open** *times vary.* **No credit cards.**
Map p323 P9 ㊿

Finding this bar is part of the fun. It's directly above
the Kaisers supermarket in a particularly ugly pre-
fab; you can see it from the overground platform of
the U1 at Kottbusser Tor. To reach it, take the stairs
to the right of Kaisers and follow the sound of the
bass. It's an unpretentious place with table *Fussball*,
pinball and cheap drinks, and dancing as the night
wears on and the booze takes effect. The smaller and
arguably cooler (but less fun) Paloma bar is just next
door at No.135 if you fancy moving on, and the clubs
West Germany and Festsaal Kreuzberg are on the
same stretch of street.

Mysliwska

*Schlesische Strasse 35 (611 4860). U1
Schlesisches Tor/bus N29, N65.* **Open** *7pm-late
daily.* **No credit cards. Map** p324 R9 ㊿
This small, dark bar draws a mixed local crowd and
doesn't get going until late. The spartan interior
boasts old, small, poker-like tables and stiff wooden
chairs. Except for a pistachio dispenser and a frequently unpopulated, disco-balled side room, frills
are kept to a minimum. There's live music once or
twice a month and DJs play most weekends (there's
no entrance fee).

Solar

*Stresemannstrasse 76 (0163 7652700,
www.solar-berlin.de) S1, S2, S25 Anhalter
Bahnhof.* **Open** *6pm-2am Mon-Thur, Sun; 6pm-
4am Fri, Sat.* **Map** p322 L8 ㊿
If you can get past the slightly fussy bouncers
downstairs , take the lift up to the 17th floor and
admire the stunning view over the city from the
glass-walled lounge bar. There's a posh restaurant

on the ground floor, but we prefer a liquid diet of lychee prosecco cocktails and champagne.

★ Würgeengel

Dresdener Strasse 122 (615 5560, www. wuergeengel.de). U1, U8 Kottbusser Tor/bus N8. **Open** 7pm-late daily. **No credit cards. Map** p323 P9 ⑤

Red walls and velvet upholstery convey an atmosphere aching for sin, while well-mixed cocktails and a fine wine list served by smartly dressed waiting staff make this a place for the more discerning drinker. The glass-latticed ceiling and a 1920s chandelier elegantly belie the fairly priced drinks and tapas on offer. Nice in summer, when a canopy of greenery curtains the outdoor picnic tables.

NEUKÖLLN

This working class district used to be known primarily for its high crime and poor immigrants. Now, it's one of the best areas in the city for bar-hopping. Most of the action is concentrated on and around the Weserstrasse, between the junctions with Reuterstrasse and Wildenbruchstrasse. We've only listed a fraction of the bars, and because venues open and close like weekly, treat the listings with extra caution.

Ä

Weserstrasse 40 (306 487 51, www.ae-neukoelln.de). U7 Rathaus Neukölln. **Open** 5pm-late daily. **Map** p324 R11 ⑤

The granddaddy of all the Neukölln hipster bars, the arrival of Ä (pronounce it as if you're expressing disgust) was the first sign the district was changing course. It's remained popular despite the competition, thanks to film screenings, DJs and occasional live bands.

Ankerklause

Kottbusser Brücke, corner of Maybachufer (693 5649, www.ankerklause.de). U8 Schönleinstrasse. **Open** 4pm-late Mon; 10am-late Tue-Sun. **No credit cards. Map** p323 P9 ⑤

Although it looks over the Landwehrkanal, the only thing nautical about this 'anchor den' is the midriff-tattooed, punk-meets-portside swank of the bar staff. A slamming jukebox (rock, sleaze, beat), a ramshackle terrace and good sandwich melts offer ample excuse to dock here from afternoon until whenever they decide to close. Convivial during the week, packed at weekends.

Das Gift

Donaustrasse 119 (www.dasgift.de). U7 Rathaus Neukölln. **Open** 8pm-2am Mon-Thur, Sun; 8pm-late Fri, Sat. **No credit cards. Map** p323 Q11 ⑤

New life has been breathed into a wood-panelled old *Eck-kneipe* by a group of creative foreigners, including Barry Burns from the post-rock band Mogwai. There's an ever-rotating selection of Scottish beers to be sampled, not to mention Irn-Bru, and it's one of the few places in Berlin to sell salt and vinegar crisps.

CONSUME

Das Gift.

CONSUME

INSIDE TRACK
24-HOUR DRINKING DENS

We're not promising they're any good,
but the following will always be open:
Schwarzes Café (*see p156*); **Ohne Ende**
(Dieffenbachstrasse 36, Kreuzberg);
Rote Rose (Adalbertstrasse 90,
Kreuzberg); **Joschi's Bar** (Motzstrasse
34, Schöneberg)

Heartbreaker

*Sanderstrasse 6 (6165 5735, www.heartbreaker-
berlin.com). U8 Schönleinstrasse.* **Open** 8pm-late
Wed-Sat. **No credit cards. Map** p323 P10 ⑤⑦
This funky little bar has minimalist decor and
excellent DJs.

★ Natanja und Heinrich

*Weichselstrasse 44 (624 9114, www.nathanja-
heinrich.de). U7, U8 Hermannplatz.* **Open**
1pm-3am Tue-Sun. **No credit cards.**
Map p323 Q11 ⑤⑧
Of all the artfully shabby drinking dens in the
neighbourhood, this is probably the nicest, with high
ceilings, interesting furniture and a not-too-cool-for-
school clientele.

★ Tier

*Weserstrasse 42 (no phone). U7 Rathaus
Neukoelln.* **Open** 7pm-late daily. **No credit
cards. Map** p324 R11 ⑤⑨
This glass-fronted bar attracts more than its fair
share of posers and it gets horribly smoky in winter.
But the G&Ts make it all worthwhile – splash out
on a monster shot of Hendrick's gin, served with a
little bottle of tonic and a chunk of cucumber.

SCHÖNEBERG

This gentrified borough retains a hint of its
more radical past, and, around Motzstrasse and
Fuggerstrasse, contains possibly the world's
oldest – and certainly the city's largest – gay
quarter. You'll find numerous bars and shops
catering to all tastes and fetishes.

Around Winterfeldtplatz there's a
concentration of lively cafés, and bar life
mingles with the antique shops along
Goltzstrasse to the south.

★ Ex'n'Pop

*Potsdamer Strasse 157 (2199 7470, www.exnpop.
jimdo.com). U2 Bülowstrasse.* **Open** 10pm-late
daily. **No credit cards. Map** p322 J9 ⑥⓪
They say that if you haven't collapsed in the corner
of this legendary pub, you've never had a proper
night out in Schöneberg. Nick Cave's done it, along
with anyone who was anyone in the decadent dying

days of West Berlin, when Schöneberg was a nihilis-
tic hedonist's paradise, rather than the gentle residential district it has become post reunification.
There are regular concerts and readings, and there's
a small cinema out back showing underground
films. Don't dress up.

Green Door

*Winterfeldtstrasse 50 (215 2515, www.green
door.de). U1, U2, U3, U4 Nollendorfplatz.* **Open**
6pm-3am Mon-Thur, Sun; 6pm-4am Fri, Sat.
No credit cards. Map p322 J9 ⑥①
It really does have a green door, and behind it there's
a whole lotta cocktail shaking going on (the drinks
menu is impressively long). There's also a nice long
and curvy bar, perhaps a few too many yuppies and
a good location off Winterfeldtplatz.

Stagger Lee

*Nollendorfstrasse 27 (2903 6158, www.stagger
lee.de). U1, U2, U3, U4 Nollendorfplatz.* **Open**
Winter 6pm-late daily. *Summer* 8pm-late daily.
No credit cards. Map p322 J9 ⑥②
This rock 'n' roll bar is a local legend and serves
excellent, if unusual, cocktails – the house special
Julep mixes bourbon, mint and cherries, and the
Robert Mitchum is simply a full glass of tequila, a
box of matches and a Lucky Strike.

Zoulou Bar

*Hauptstrasse 4 (0172 314 02 07, www.
zouloubar.de). U7 Kleistpark.* **Open** 8pm-5am
Mon-Thur, Sun; 8pm-6am Fri, Sat. **No credit
cards. Map** p322 J10 ⑥③
Small bar with a funky vibe and occasional DJs. It
can get packed between 10pm and 2am; visit later,
when the crowd has thinned out a bit.

TIERGARTEN

The area around Potsdamer Strasse is kind of
a northern Schöneberg, its scene overlapping
with that of the neighbouring borough. Around
Lützowplatz it's rather more upmarket. Alas,
we can find little to recommend among all the
shiny new franchises of Potsdamer Platz.

Bar am Lützowplatz

*Lützowplatz 7 (262 6807, www.baramluetzowplatz.
com). U1, U2, U3, U4 Nollendorfplatz/bus N2,
N5, N19, N26.* **Open** 6pm-2am Mon-Wed; 6pm-
4am Thur-Sat; 6pm-2am Sun. **Map** p322 J8 ⑥④
Long bar with a long drinks list and classy customers in Chanel suits sipping expensive, well-made
cocktails as they compare bank balances.

★ Café am Neuen See

*Lichtensteinallee 2 (2544930, www.cafe-am-
neuen-see.de). S5, S7, S9, S75 Tiergarten.*
Open 8am-late Mon-Fri; 9am-late Sat, Sun.
Map 321 H7 ⑥⑤

Café am Neuen See.

Hidden away by a small lake in the western part of the Tiergarten, this café, beer garden and brasserie rolled into one is among Berlin's most idyllic spots. In summer there are rowing boats for hire and it's a fun and buzzy place to wile away an afternoon, eating excellent stone baked pizza washed down with big jars of Pilsner – or, unusually for Berlin, cider. In the winter months, the candlelit glass pavilion makes for a cosy and romantic setting for tea and cake, or an evening meal.

★ Lebensstern

Kurfürstenstrasse 58 (2639 1922, www.cafe einstein.com). U1, U2, U3, U4 U1, U2 Nollendorf Platz. **Open** 7pm-3am daily. **Map** p322 J8 ⑥⑥
This smart bar is above Café Einstein and became a second home for Quentin Tarantino when he was in the city to film *Inglourious Basterds*. He liked it so much, that some scenes were filmed there. Cocktails are excellent. There are a barely believable 580 sorts of rum to choose from, as well as, 140 gins.

Kumpelnest 3000

Lützowstrasse 23 (261 6918, www.kumpelnest 3000.com). U1 Kurfürstenstrasse/bus N2, N5, N48. **Open** 7pm-late Mon-Thur, Sun; 5pm-late Fri, Sat. **No credit cards. Map** p322 K8 ⑥⑦
This perennially popular and studiedly tacky establishment is at its best at the end of a long Saturday night, when it's crowded and chaotic and everyone is attempting to dance to disco classics.

Schleusenkrug

Müller-Breslau-Strasse, corner of Unterschleuse (313 9909, www.schleusenkrug.de). S3, S5, S7, S9, S75 Tiergarten/bus N9. **Open** *Summer* 10am-1am daily. *Winter* 10am-6pm daily. **No credit cards. Map** p321 G7 ⑥⑧
A bar and beer garden directly on the canal in the Tiergarten, with easy listening, mod and indie pop nights. During the day, Schleusenkrug retains much of its original flavour, hingeing on nautical themes and large glasses of Pils. *Photo p172.*

Victoria Bar

Potsdamer Strasse 102 (2575 9977, www. victoriabar.de). U1 Kurfürstenstrasse. **Open** 6-11pm Mon-Thur, Sun; 6.30pm-3am Fri, Sat. **No credit cards. Map** p322 K9 ⑥⑨
Victoria is a funky, grown-up cocktail bar, serving a relaxed, mixed crowd. The low-key concept – long bar, subdued lighting, muffled funk and staff who work well together and know what they're mixing – is successful enough for this place to feel like it's been here for ever, although it actually opened in 2003.

CHARLOTTENBURG & WILMERSDORF

There is elegant café life to be enjoyed on the Kurfürstendamm, and around Savignyplatz, Ludwigkirchplatz and Karl-August-Platz, but the last decent nightlife checked out a couple of decades ago, and the bars are no match for neighbouring Schöneberg, let alone Mitte.

Dicke Wirtin

Carnerstrasse 9 (3124952, www.dicke-wirtin.de). S3, S5, S7, S75 Savignyplatz. **Open** noon-2am daily. **No credit cards. Map** p321/p328 F8 ⑦⑩
A proper German pub with prices that belie its chichi location. If you get the munchies, try a plate of bread smothered in *Schmaltz* (lard) for €2.60.

Diener

Grolmanstrasse 47 (881 5329). S3, S5, S7, S9, S75 Savignyplatz/bus N27, N49. **Open** 6pm-2am daily. **Map** p321/p328 F8 ⑦⑪
An authentically old-style Berlin bar, named after famous local boxer Franz Diener. The walls are adorned with faded hunting murals and photos of well-known Germans you won't recognise. You could almost be in 1920s Berlin. Almost. There's authentic German *Hausmannskost* on the menu, but for dinner you should book a table.

Gainsbourg

Jeanne-Mammen-Bogen 576-577 (313 7464, www.gainsbourg.de). S3, S5, S7, S75 Savignyplatz. **Open** 4pm-late daily. **Map** p321/p328 F8 ⑦⑫
There are a lot of bars around Savignyplatz, but this classic is arguably the best. Like old Serge himself,

CONSUME

it has an effortless air of cool, with great drinks and superlative service. Not the cheapest, mind.

Galerie Bremer

Fasanenstrasse 37 (881 4908, www.galerie-bremer.de). U1, U9 Spichernstrasse/bus N9. **Open** 8pm-late Mon-Sat. *Gallery* 4-8pm Tue-Fri. **No credit cards. Map** p321/p328 F9 ⑦

In the back room of a tiny gallery, this bar has the air of a well-kept secret. The room is painted in deep, rich colours with a beautiful ship-like bar designed by Hans Scharoun, architect of the Philharmonie and Staatsbibliothek. When the assistant barman takes your coat and welcomes you, it's meant to make you feel at home, and it's also the done thing to make a little conversation with the majestically bearded owner – he'll remember you next time you drop in. Then you can sit back, feel privileged and watch the odd member of parliament entering incognito.

Puro Sky Lounge

Tauentzienstrasse 11 (2636 7875, www.puro-berlin.de). U1, U2 Wittenberg Platz. **Open** times vary. **Map** p321 G8 ⑦

This place on the top of the Europa Centre is a bit of a cheesefest, but it does have a wonderful view over West Berlin. It has a strict dress code, so smarten up or face being locked out.

★ Rum Trader

Fasanenstrasse 40 (881 1428). U3, U9 Spichernstrasse. **Open** times vary. **No credit cards. Map** p321 F9 ⑦

Subtitled the 'Institute for Advanced Drinking', this tiny bar is a Berlin classic, largely thanks to its eccentric owner, Gregor Scholl, who is ever present, smartly dressed in bow tie and waistcoat. There is no menu: Scholl will ask which spirit you like, and whether you want something *süss oder sauer* (sweet or sour). A short while later he will come back with one of the best cocktails you've ever tasted in your life. Don't waste his time (or talent) asking for a caipirinha. You have to ring the bell for access, and it's worth ringing ahead to check there's space.

OTHER DISTRICTS

Club der Visionäre

Am Flutgraben 2, Treptow (6951 8942, www.clubdervisionaere.com). U1 Schlesisches Tor. **Open** 2pm-late Mon-Fri; noon-late Sat, Sun. **No credit cards. Map** p324 S9 ⑦

Set on an inlet off the Spree just over the border from Kreuzberg, this popular timbered bar occupies an old boathouse, along with several floating docks and a decommissioned boat. The totally lo-fi locale is always warm and welcoming, thanks in no small part to its haphazard, DIY decor. For those in the mood to move their feet, DJs spin minimal techno for the small dancefloor (sometimes it's Ricardo Villalobos at the decks). Most people, however, prefer just to sit under the tree canopy enjoying a casual waterside drink, watching the evening dwindle, perhaps, or lounging in the Sunday afternoon sun. Later at night, things get more lively.

Schleusenkrug. *See p171.*

Shops & Services

Get ready to spend, spend, spend.

Like everything else in Berlin, the shopping landscape is a jumble of wildly diverse elements unified by a communal nod to innovation, individualism and experimentation. In the German capital, high- and low-end establishments, conventional and crazy, chic and street, not only co-exist harmoniously, but interconnect, coming together in interesting unions. A quirky independent bookshop can survive on the same block as a mega chain, and a cheap vintage store selling DDR kitsch can nestle comfortably among some of the city's most expensive boutiques. Even with the influx of big-name international brands and the coming-of-age of the local 1990s avant-garde, Berlin's progressives continue to hatch new schemes for keeping things interesting, while a lively independent shopping scene remains strong.

SHOPPING AROUND TOWN

The best thing to do is just start walking: Berlin has no distinctive shopping centre, and some of its treasures can be found in the least expected places – a hidden inner courtyard, an otherwise empty side street – many popping up for only weeks at a time. Conventional shopping can be found on and around **Tauentzienstrasse** and **Kurfürstendamm** in the west, with luxury brands clustered around **Fasanenstrasse** and household goods in the area between the **Ku'damm** and **Kantstrasse**. In the east, **Friedrichstrasse** offers a similarly up-market selection, but with a hipper, younger edge. For cutting-edge local designers, head to the area around Mulackstrasse, where many have opened interesting boutiques. Within walking distance from there, Torstrasse in recent years has become home to many cool concept stores.

For those seeking more economical options, Berlin has vintage stores in abundance, with clusters on **Oderberger Strasse** in Prenzlauer Berg and around **Mehringdamm** in Kreuzberg. Frequent flea markets are also a great place to look for second-hand wares. The areas around **Kastanienallee** in Prenzlauer Berg, **Wühlischstrasse** in Friedrichshain and **Oranienstrasse** and **Bergmannstrasse** in Kreuzberg are particularly resplendent with independent shops selling music, clothes and books, many produced by local artists. The same is true for the area around

Hobrechtsstrasse in Northern Neukölln, a neighbourhood that has been – and still is – undergoing a massive gentrification process.

OPENING HOURS

Since the end of 2006, shops can stay open 24 hours on Monday through Saturday and even sometimes on Sundays. Most stores haven't taken full advantage of the new laws, but opening hours are definitely longer than they used to be. Big stores tend to open at between 9am and 10am and stay open until 8pm, sometimes 10pm (some of the supermarkets even as late as midnight), with smaller shops shaving an hour or two at each end. Sunday is still an extremely quiet day, but big department stores and malls are sometimes open. *Spätis* (late-night corner shops) can be found all across the city. Internet cafés and filling stations are also open late and stock snacks and drinks.

General

DEPARTMENT STORES

Galeries Lafayette

Französische Strasse 23, Mitte (209 480, www.lafayette-berlin.de). U6 Französische Strasse. **Open** 10am-8pm Mon-Sat. **Map** p322/p327 M7. This elegant glass complex designed by French superstar Jean Nouvel offers great clothes, frequent sales on the upper floors, a good selection of accessories and cosmetics at street level and a basement gourmet food hall where you'll feel transported to Paris. For local flair, check out the store's Labo Mode section, which showcases collections from young, up-and-coming Berlin designers.

KaDeWe
Tauentzienstrasse 21-24, Schöneberg (212 10, www.kadewe.de). U1, U2, U3 Wittenbergplatz. **Open** 10am-8pm Mon-Thur; 10am-9pm Fri; 9.30am-8pm Sat. **Map** p321 H9.
The largest department store in continental Europe celebrated its 100th birthday in 2007. It carries name brands, though the merchandise can be hit or miss. KaDeWe is most famous for its extraordinary food hall, which takes up the entire sixth floor.

Kaufhof
Alexanderplatz 9, Mitte (247 430, www.galeria-kaufhof.de). U2, U5, U8, S3 S5, S7, S75 Alexanderplatz. **Open** 9.30am-8pm Mon-Wed, 9.30am-10pm Thur-Sat. **Map** p319/p327 O5.
Once the retail showpiece of communist East Berlin, this busy, utilitarian megastore underwent massive renovation and expansion in 2006. Today, it is the most successful branch of the Kaufhof chain.
Other locations Koppenstrasse 8, Friedrichshain (245 400); Johannisthaler Chausee 289, Neukoelln (6652 600), Frankfurter Allee 115-117, Friedrichshain (408 9980).

Manufactum
Hardenbergstrasse 4-5, Charlottenburg. (24 03 38 44, www.manufactum.de). U2 Ernst-Reuter-Platz. **Open** 10am-8pm Mon-Fri; 10am-6pm Sat. **Map** p321 F7.
When Manufactum was founded in 1988 as a counterpoint to cheap mass production, it resembled a cult and the wittily written catalogue was treated like a bible by its followers. But its focus on traditionally manufactured products hit the German spot for quality and sustainability. Today there are eight Manufactum stores in Germany, selling everything from household goods, clothing and toys, to cosmetics and gardening supplies. The various products produced in monasteries are also great.

Naturkaufhaus
Schlossstrasse 101, Steglitz (797 3716, www.naturkaufhaus-berlin.de). U9 Schlossstrasse. **Open** 10am-8pm Mon-Sat.
Berlin's first department store for organic goods. It's spread over seven floors of the Galleria mall. The stock ranges from the usual foodstuffs you find in local health food shops to a selection of wine, eco-friendly clothes, shoes, cosmetics and even bedding.

Quartier 206
Friedrichstrasse 71, Mitte (2094 6500, www. quartier206.com). U6 Französische Strasse. **Open** 10.30am-7.30pm Mon-Fri; 10am-6pm Sat. **Map** p322/p327 M7.

Galeries Lafayette. *See p173.*

Reminiscent of New York's Takashimaya, this upmarket store offers not just the most lusted-after designers, but the definitive items from those labels. Cult cosmetics and perfumes are on the ground floor; upstairs is devoted to women's and men's fashion, lingerie, jewellery and shoes, plus a home-living section that's stocked with sinfully expensive design items.

MALLS

Alexa
Alexanderplatz 4, Mitte (269 3400, www. alexacentre.com). U2, U5, U8, S3, S5, S7, S75 Alexanderplatz. **Open** 10am-9pm Mon-Sat. **Map** p319 P6.
This (supposedly) art deco monstrosity may not look like much from the outside, but inside it's pleasant enough. And with over 180 stores, it provides some much-needed shopping convenience in East Berlin. Includes all the mid-range fashion staples (H&M, Zara, and so on) as well as Europe's largest MediaMarkt.

Potsdamer Platz Arkaden
Alte Potsdamer Strasse 7, Tiergarten (255 9270, www.potsdamer-platz-arkaden.de). U2, S1, S2, S25 Potsdamer Platz. **Open** 10am-9pm Mon-Sat. **Map** p322 L8.
The glass and steel Arkaden is a useful address for familiar names – Benetton, Body Shop, Mango and over 120 others. Don't miss the delicious Italian ice-cream at Caffé e Gelato on the second floor.

MARKETS
Flea markets

Just about every neighbourhood has its own flea market; for a full list, see www.berlin.de/orte/shop/kategorie/flohmaerkte. From November, the city also hosts Christmas markets, some tacky, most charming. The loveliest is at the **Gendarmenmarkt**, while those at **Kollwitzplatz** in Prenzlauer Berg and the **Gedächtniskirche** in Charlottenburg are also enchanting. For a complete list, go to www.berlin-tourist-information.de/kultur/index.en.

Antik- und Buchmarkt Bodemuseum
Am Kupfergraben (www.antik-buchmarkt.de, 0171 710 1662). U6, S1, S2, S3, S5, S7, S25, S75 Friedrichstrasse. **Open** 11am-5pm Sat, Sun. **Map** p319/p327 N6.
On the riverbank by the Deutsches Historisches Museum, Kunst und Nostalgie Markt is one of the few places in Berlin that you can still find genuine relics of the DDR, with anything from old signs advertising coal briquettes to framed pictures of Honecker. Also paintings, prints, candles, leather-work, books and CDs.

Flohmarkt am Arkonaplatz
Arkonaplatz, Prenzlauer Berg (0171 6010 904, www.troedelmarkt-arkonaplatz.de). U8 Bernauer Strasse. **Open** 10am-4pm Sun. **Map** p319/p328 N3.
A broad array of retro gear ranging from records to clothing, books to trinkets, bikes to coffee tables – all at moderate prices. Best selection in the morning.

Flohmarkt am Boxhagener Platz
Boxhagener Platz, Friedrichshain (0162 2923 066). U1, S3, S5, S7, S75 Warschauer Strasse or U5 Samariterstrasse. **Open** 10am-6pm Sun. **Map** p324 T7.
Many local young artists and T-shirt designers set up stalls at this overflowing market, while punky types and bohemian mothers shop for vintage sunglasses and unusual crockery. Depending on the day, you could snatch some great second-hand finds from students selling their old stuff. This place can be very cheap if you bargain hard enough.

Flohmarkt am Mauerpark
Bernauer Strasse 63-64, Prenzlauer Berg (0176 2925 0021). U8 Bernauer Strasse. **Open** 7am-5pm Sun. **Map** p319.
One of the biggest and busiest flea markets in Berlin, selling everything from cheap fashion to cardboard boxes of black market CDs. Students and residents sell their things here at great prices, and you might just find a treasure trove of awesome second-hand clothing, books, bags and other goods. *Photo p178.*
▶ *This is also the venue for the weekly outdoor singing session, Bearpit Karaoke, see p76.*

Kunst und Trödel Markt
Strasse des 17 Juni, Tiergarten (2655 0096, www.berliner-troedelmarkt.de). U2 Ernst-Reuter-Platz or S5, S7, S9, S75 Tiergarten. **Open** 10am-5pm Sat, Sun. **Map** p321 F7.
Kunst und Trödel Markt lies on the stretch west of the S-Bahn station. Quality, early 20th-century objects with prices to match, alongside a jumble of vintage clothing, old furniture, second-hand records and books. Interesting stuff, but cramped aisles.

CONSUME

World Class

Perfect places to stay, eat and explore.

★ Nowkoelln Flowmarkt
*Maybachufer. (www.nowkoelln.de, no phone). U8
Schönleinstrasse.* **Open** 10am-6pm every 3rd Sun
of the mth. **Map** p323 Q10.
Berlin's hippest flea market. Good for vintage fashion,
organic treats and perfomances by local musicians.

General markets

Berlin's many *Wochenmärkte* usually sell
cheaper, fresher produce than regular shops.
For a good list, see www.hungryinberlin.com/
local-market-schedule.

Farmers' Market at Wittenbergplatz
*Wittenbergplatz, Schöneberg (2363 6360). U1,
U2, U3 Wittenbergplatz.* **Open** 9am-6pm Thur.
Map p321 H8.
Predominantly organic produce, including cheese,
bread, pasta, meat, fruit and veg from local farms.
Also non-edible items such as wooden brushes.

Farmers' Market at Zionskirchplatz
*Zionskirchplatz, Prenzlauer Berg (01577, 893
7884). U2 Senefelderplatz or U8 Rosenthaler
Platz.* **Open** 11am-6pm Thur; 11am-7pm Sat.
Map p319/p328 N4.
Regional growers sell fruit and veggies, fresh fish
and homemade jams, breads and cheeses. Farmers
set up their stands on the cobblestone walkway surrounding one of Berlin's most beautiful churches,
making this a truly picturesque market throughout
the year.

★ Market at Kollwitzplatz
*Kollwitzplatz, Prenzlauer Berg (organic market
4433 9137, farmers' market 0172 3278 238).
U2 Senefelderplatz.* **Open** noon-7pm Thur;
9.30am-5pm Sat. **Map** p319/p328 P4.
The Saturday market is popular with gourmets
stocking up on weekend food supplies or for locals
out for a stroll and a snack. You'll find everything
from organic and non-organic vegetables, cheeses to
amazing fresh pasta and children's toys. A Turkish-
run stand sells the best *Gözleme* in town and another
offers delicious and inexpensive fish soup. The
Thursday market is a little smaller and exclusively
organic.

Türkischer Markt
*Maybachufer, Neukölln (29 77 24 86). U8
Schönleinstrasse.* **Open** noon-6.30pm Tue, Fri.
Map p323 P10.
A crowded market across the canal from Kreuzberg,
designed to meet the needs of the local Turkish com-
munity. Fresh veg, wonderful spices, great prices.

Winterfeldt Markt
*Winterfeldtplatz, Schöneberg (0175 437 4303).
U1, U2, U3, U4 Nollendorfplatz.* **Open** 8am-2pm
Wed; 8am-4pm Sat. **Map** p322 J9.

THE BEST SHOPS

Berlin's answer to Colette.
Corner Berlin. *See p184.*

Sixth-floor food hall of the gods.
KaDeWe. *See p174.*

A goldmine for second-hand shoppers.
Made in Berlin. *See p187.*

Quality household items for
traditionalists.
Manufactum. *See p174.*

Beautiful books for lovers of all things
art and urban.
Pro qm. *See p180.*

Stationery for the aesthete.
RSVP. *See p192.*

On Saturdays, it seems as if all of Berlin is visiting
this jam-packed market, full to the brim with vegetables, cheese, wholegrain breads, *wurst*, meats,
flowers, clothes, pet supplies, toys and more .
Many people come here for their weekly shopping;
others, to meet a friend at one of the many cafés
off the square. A Berlin institution worth experiencing first-hand. *Photo p179.*

Specialist

ANTIQUES

Suarezstrasse in Charlottenburg is lined
with over 30 antique shops, selling everything
from Victorian furniture to art deco clocks.
For 18th- and 19th-century goods, the
dealers on Schöneberg's **Keithstrasse** and
Goltzstrasse are worth a visit, as are the
streets around **Fasanenplatz** in Wilmersdorf.
Charlottenburg's **Bleibtreustrasse** is also
home to a handful of shops. In the east,
you'll find several small, unpretentious
Antiquaritäten on **Grünberger Strasse**
in Friedrichshain and **Kollwitzstrasse**
and **Husemannstrasse** in Prenzlauer
Berg. *See also p175* **Flea markets**.

Bleibtreu-Antik
*Schlüterstrasse 54, Charlottenburg (883 5212,
www.bleibtreu-antik.de). S3,S5, S7, S75
Savignyplatz.* **Open** noon-7pm Mon-Fri; 11am-3pm
Sat; or by appointment. **Map** p321/p328 E8.
This shop has been around since the early 1970s,
offering an impressive array of 19th-century
antiques. Fully restored Biedermeier and Jugendstil

Flohmarkt am Mauerpark. See p175.

furniture, glassware, silver and lamps are the main focus, along with an impressive selection of costume jewellery from 1900 to 1960.

Deco Arts
Motzstrasse 6, Schöneberg (215 8672).U1,
U2, U3, U4, Nollendorfplatz. **Open** 3-7pm
Wed-Fri; noon-5pm Sat. **No credit cards.**
Map p321 H9.
Deco Arts stocks shell-shaped 1930s sofas and other deco furniture at fair prices, the odd piece by Marcel Breuer and Carl Jacobs and some 1950s and '60s treasures. If a sofa's too big to get home, pick up a stylish ashtray or vase.

Radio Art
Zossener Strasse 2, Kreuzberg (693 9435,
www.radio-art.de). U7 Gneisenaustrasse.
Open noon-6pm Thur, Fri; 10am-1pm Sat.
Credit AmEx, MC, V. **Map** p323 N10.
A fine collection of antique radios, ranging from big, wooden, 1930s sitting-room centrepieces to tiny '70s transistors in shocking pink plastic.

BOOKS & MAGAZINES

Berlin still has a lively independent bookshop scene, with hundreds of small, idiosyncratic booksellers catering to specific neighbourhoods, communities and interests. For gay bookshops, *see p220.*

English-language

Another Country
Riemannstrasse 7, Kreuzberg (6940 1160,
www.anothercountry.de). U7 Gneisenaustrasse.
Open 11am-8pm Mon-Fri; noon-6pm Sat, Sun.
No credit cards. Map p322 M10.
An impressive second-hand bookshop mostly used as a library, Another Country is stocked with about 20,000 English-language titles that can be borrowed or bought. The spacious, welcoming premises abound with comfortable nooks and crannies, and the store plays host to a weekly film night, TV night and dinner night.

Books in Berlin
Goethestrasse 69, Charlottenburg (313 1233,
www.booksinberlin.de). S3, S5, S7, S9, S75
Savignyplatz. **Open** noon-7pm Mon-Fri; 10am-4pm
Sat. **Map** p321/p328 E7.
Run by a Bostonian and stocking a dynamic selection of new and used histories and political tracts, classical and modern fiction and reference and travel books, this is something of a Berlin institution.

East of Eden
Schreinerstrasse 10, Friedrichshain (423 9362,
www.east-of-eden.de). U5 Samariterstrasse.
Open noon-7pm Mon-Sat. **No credit cards.**
Map p325 T6.
The owners of this old-school second-hand shop shuttle frequently to London in search of paperback staples and rare editions. Books are also available to borrow at a small fee. Readings and concerts too.

Fair Exchange
Dieffenbachstrasse 58, Kreuzberg (694 4675,
www.fair-exchange.de). U8 Schönleinstrasse.
Open 11am-7pm Mon-Fri; 10am-6pm Sat.
No credit cards. Map p323 P10.
Big selection of second-hand English-language books, with an emphasis on literature. The atmosphere is cosy.

Hugendubel
Tauentzienstrasse 13, Charlottenburg (01801 484
484, www.hugendubel.de). U1, U9 Kurfürstendamm.
Open 9.30am-8pm Mon-Sat. **Map** p321 G8.
This large branch of a chain houses more than 140,000 books, and there's a big English-language section. An in-house café offers drinks and snacks.
Other locations Potsdamer Platz Arkaden, Alte Potsdamer Strasse 7, Tiergarten (0180 148 4484); Wilmersdorfer Strasse 121, Charlottenburg (0180 148 4484) Hermannplatz 1, Neukoelln (0180 148 4484).

Marga Schoeller Bücherstube
Knesebeckstrasse 33, Charlottenburg (881 1112).
S3, S5, S7, S75 Savignyplatz. **Open** 9.30am-7pm
Mon-Wed; 9.30am-8pm Thur, Fri; 9.30am-6pm Sat.
Map p321/p328 F8.

CONSUME

Rated among Europe's best independent literary bookshops by *Bookseller* magazine, this excellent establishment, founded in 1930, includes one of Berlin's most interesting English-language sections.

Mundo Azul International Children's & Youth Bookstore

Choriner Strasse 49. (4985 3834, www.mundo azul.de). U2 Eberswalder Strasse. **Open** 10am-7pm Mon; 10am-6pm Tue-Fri; 10am-4pm Sat (10am-6pm in winter). **No credit cards.** **Map** p328 O3.

A unique selection of books in English, French, Italian, Spanish and German for children aged from 0 to 15 years.

Saint Georges

Wörther Strasse 27, Prenzlauer Berg (8179 8333, www.saintgeorgesbookshop.com). Tram M2 Marienburger Strasse. **Open** 11am-8pm Mon-Fri; 11am-7pm Sat. **Map** p319/p328 P3.

Comfortable leather couches are provided for browsing a decent and reasonably priced selection of English-language books, both old and new. Lots of biographies and contemporary literature, plus a good turnover of dog-eared classics. US dollars and British pounds are also accepted.

Storytime Books & Café

Schmargendorfer Strasse 36-37, Friedenau (8596 7004, www.storytime-books.com). U9 Friedrich-Wilhelm-Platz or S1 Friedenau. **Open** 10am-6pm Mon-Fri; 10am-2pm Sat. **Map** p321 G12.

Owner Diane Pentaleri-Otto specialises in children's books and works hard to make the shop child- and parent-friendly. There are many events for kids, such as a weekly story time in English and sing-alongs in English and German, with coffee for the grown-ups.

Taschen Store Berlin

Friedrichstrasse 180-184, Mitte, (253 25991, www.taschen.com). U6 Französische Strasse. **Open** 10am-8pm Mon-Sat. **Map** p327 M7.

The Philippe Starck-designed Taschen Store is a treasure trove for beautiful but affordable coffee table books

General

25 books

Brunnenstrasse 152, Mitte (4373 5707, www.25 book.de). U8 Bernauer Strasse. **Open** 2pm-7pm Wed, Fri, Sat. **No credit cards.** **Map** p319 N3.

This carefully curated store sells photo books and regularly hosts exhibitions and book presentations as well.

Artificium

Rosenthaler Strasse 40-41, Mitte (3087 2280, www. artificium.com). S3, S5, S7, S9, S75 Hackescher Markt. **Open** 10am-8pm Mon-Thur; 10am-9pm Fri, Sat, noon-7pm Sun. **Map** p319/p326 N5.

Tucked into the Hackesche Höfe, this art bookshop specialises in 20th-century culture, stocking titles on everything from photography to dance, design to film, architecture to theatre.

Berlin Story

Unter den Linden 40, Mitte (2045 3842, www. berlin-story.de). U6 Französische Strasse. **Open** 10am-7pm Mon-Sat; 10am-6pm Sun. **Map** p318/p327 M6.

CONSUME

Winterfeldt Markt. *See p177.*

You won't find a better selection of Berlin-related books in German and English: everything from novels with Berlin settings to non-fiction volumes on the history and culture of the city. Historical maps, posters, videos, CDs, postcards and souvenirs are also available.

Bücherbogen

Savignyplatz Stadtbahnbogen 593, Charlottenburg (3186 9511, www.buecherbogen.com). S3, S5, S7, S75 Savignyplatz. **Open** 10am-8pm Mon-Fri; 10am-7pm Sat. **Map** p321/p328 E8.

The store for all manner of art books. This branch under the Savignyplatz S-Bahn station stocks international magazines and books on painting, sculpture, photography, design and architecture; the branch in the National Gallery specialises in books on 20th-century art, architecture and photography.

Other locations Neue Nationalgalerie, Potsdamer Strasse 50, Tiergarten (261 1090); Schlossstrasse 1, Charlottenburg (3269 5814).

★ Do you read me?

Auguststrasse 28, Mitte (6954 9695, www.doyou readme.de). U8 Rosenthaler Platz. **Open** *Summer* 10am-9.30pm Mon-Sat. *Winter* 10am-7.30pm Mon-Sat. **Map** p319 N5.

This great shop has the best selection of international magazines in the city. Topics include fashion, art, architecture and many others.

Dussmann das KulturKaufhaus

Friedrichstrasse 90, Mitte (2025 1111, www.kulturkaufhaus.de). U6, S1, S2, S3, S5, S7, S75 Friedrichstrasse. **Open** 10am-midnight Mon-Sat. **Map** p318/p327 M6.

Intended as a 'cultural department store', this spacious five-floor retailer has books, CDs, magazines, DVDs and just about everything in between. You can borrow reading glasses (€10 deposit) or a portable CD player (€50 deposit) for the time you're in the store. There's a big English language bookshop on the groundfloor.

Hammett Krimis

Friesenstrasse 27, Kreuzberg (691 5834, www.hammett-krimis.de). U7 Gneisenaustrasse. **Open** 10am-8pm Mon-Fri; 9am-6pm Sat. **Map** p323 N10.

This store stocks a huge selection of new and second-hand crime novels in English and German.

Kochlust

c/o Coledampf & Companies, Prinzenstrasse 85d (www.kochlust-berlin.de, 24 63 88 83). U8 Moritzplatz. **Open** 10am-8pm Mon-Fri; 10am-6pm Sat. **No credit cards**. **Map** p323 O8.

A haven for cooking enthusiasts and foodies. In addition to its huge variety of German books, there are some 300 English titles. Recipes can be tested in the shop's kitchen, where cooking classes are held.

Kohlhaas & Company

Fasanenstrasse 23, Wilmersdorf (882 5044). U1 Uhlandstrasse. **Open** 10am-7.30pm Mon-Fri; 10am-6pm Sat. **Map** p321/p328 F8.

German literature predominates in this elegant little high-brow bookshop under the Literaturhaus.

Modern Graphics

Oranienstrasse 22, Kreuzberg (615 8810, www.modern-graphics.de). U1, U8 Kottbusser Tor. **Open** 11am-8pm Mon-Fri; 10am-8pm Sat. **Map** p323 P9.

A large selection of imported and alternative comics. Modern Graphics also sells T-shirts, graphic novels, anime and calendars.

Other locations Tauentzienstrasse 9-12 in the Europa-Center, Charlottenburg (8599 9054).

Pro qm

Almstadtstrasse 48-50, Mitte (2472 8520, www.pro-qm.de). U2 Rosa-Luxemburg-Platz. **Open** 11am-8pm Mon-Sat. **Map** p319/ p326 O5.

The artist owners here offer a well-informed and cosmopolitan selection of new and used books and mags on architecture, art, design, pop culture, urban life and cultural theory. Good selection of English titles.

Second-hand & antiquarian

There are small antiquarian booksellers all over Berlin, and many have at least a shelf or two of English books. The areas around **Knesebeckstrasse** and **Pestalozzistrasse** in Charlottenburg, **Winterfeldtstrasse** in Schöneberg and **Kollwitzstrasse** and **Husemannstrasse** in Prenzlauer Berg all provide decent literary pickings.

CHILDREN

Wooden toys are a German speciality. Puppets from the Dresdener puppet factory and tiny wooden figures from the Erzgebirge region are distinctive. Stuffed toys are also traditional: Steiff and its rival Sigikid offer beautifully made cuddly animals. **Storytime Books** and **Mundo Azul** (for both, *see p179*) are great children's bookshops. For clusters of cute stores for the little ones, go to **Prenzlauer Berg**, a neighbourhood that sometimes seems to be inhabited solely by young families, especially the area around Helmholtzplatz. **Finkid** on Dunckerstrasse (http://stores.finkid.de/berlin-prenzlauer-berg) sells robust outdoorwear for kids and **Lila Lämmchen** (www.lilalaemmchen.de), also on Duncker, has clothes made from natural and organic materials as well as Rudolf-Steiner-approved toys.

Kwik Shop. *See p183.*

Dollyrocker

Gärtnerstrasse 25, Friedrichshain (5471 9606, www.dollyrocker.de). U1, S3, S5, S7, S75 Warschauer Strasse or U5 Samariterstrasse. **Open** 10am-7pm Mon-Fri; 11am-5pm Sat. **No credit cards. Map** p324 T7.

Designers (and mothers) Gabi Hartkopp and Ina Langenbruch recycle high-quality textiles to create colourful and adorable clothing and accessories for kids up to seven years old. Under their sewing machines, a man's blouse becomes a boy's T-shirt, women's designer jeans become a girl's dress – each piece unique. Hand-made leather shoes are also sold.

Emma & Co

Niebuhrstrasse 2, Charlottenburg (8867 6787). S3, S5, S7, S75 Savignyplatz. **Open** 11am-7pm Mon-Fri; 11am-4pm Sat. **Map** p321/p328 E8.

Melanie Waltje's charming shop offers well-made but thankfully not overly expensive children's wear, bedding, toys and gift items such as name books and terry-cloth teddies.

Toys

Heidi's Spielzeugladen

Kantstrasse 61, Charlottenburg (323 7556). U7 Wilmersdorfer Strasse. **Open** 9.30am-6.30pm Mon-Fri; 9.30am-4pm Sat. **Map** p320 D8.

Wooden toys, including cookery utensils and child-sized kitchens, are the attraction here. Also a good selection of books, puppets and wall-hangings.

Michas Bahnhof

Nürnberger Strasse 24A, Schöneberg (218 6611, www.michas-bahnhof.de). U3 Augsburger Strasse. **Open** 10am-6.30pm Mon-Fri; 10am-6pm Sat. **Map** p321 G9.

Small shop packed with model trains, old and new, and everything that goes with them.

Tam Tam

Knesebeckstrasse 59-61, Charlottenburg (882 1454). S3, S5, S7, S75 Savignyplatz. **Open** 10am-7pm Mon-Fri; 10am-6pm Sat. **Map** p321/p328 F8.

A bright, charming shop filled with stuffed animals and wooden toys, including building blocks, trains, trucks, dolls' houses and child-sized wooden stoves.

v.Kloeden

Wielandstrasse 24, Charlottenburg (8871 2512, www.vonkloeden.de). U7 Adenauerplatz. **Open** 10am-7pm Mon-Fri; 10am-4pm Sat. **Map** p320 D9.

The oldest and friendliest toy store in town stocks children's books in English, toys and reading material from the Montessori and Steiner schools, lovely handmade Käthe Kruse dolls, Erzgebirge wooden figures and all kinds of modern kids' fare.

CONSUME

Zartholz
Knaackstrasse 54, Prenzlauer Berg (451 4747, www.zartholz.de). U2 Senefelderplatz. **Open** 10.30am-6pm Mon-Fri; 10am-4pm Sat. **Map** p319/p328 P4.
A charming two-storey shop full of traditional German toys, with an emphasis on those made of wood. You'll find all the classics of German childhood, including a Käthe Kruse dolls and wooden items from perennial Swedish favourite BRIO.

DESIGNER KIOSKS

These stores, selling everything from locally crafted knick-knacks to high-quality designer items, used to crowd Berlin. That's before Etsy, the e-commerce website for handmade goods, hit the internet and crafting became really big in Germany. Some of them have moved to the internet since, but the remaining shops are a good place to look for original souvenirs.

CONSUME

Capital Clothing

The Berlin fashion industry grows up.

Although Berlin's fashion scene has profited from the capital's cool image and the influx of young creatives from all over the world, the city still has a long way to go if it wants to play in a league with fashion capitals like Paris, Milan or New York. But there's already a lot going on. Every year, Berlin hosts a number of fashion fairs – Berlin Fashion Week, Bread and Butter and Premium being the three most important – and experts count fashion sales as among the city's important economic factors of the future. In the last decade, the fashion industry in Berlin has grown almost 30 per cent and quite a few young designers have gained international attention.

One example is **Reality Studio** (www.realitystudio.de), a label probably best known for its collaboration with Topshop. Its often voluminously cut designs, which are comfortable to wear despite their air of artsy avant-garde, are the epitome of Berlin style. So is **Esther Perbandt**'s androgynous fashion, which can be admired and purchased in her new Mitte showroom (Almstadtstrasse 3, 8853 6791, www.estherperbandt.com).

Lala Berlin's (2576 2924, www.lala berlin.com) stylish and cosy knitwear has become well known across the Atlantic, not least due to famous fans like Claudia Schiffer, Cameron Diaz and Jessica Alba. The label **Wolfen** (442 98 16, www.wolfen germany.de) also started with knitwear and now in addition produces beautifully simple dresses and straight-line skirts, inspired by the GDR workers' milieu and sold at its store on Auguststrasse for – considering quality and labour input – almost socialist prices.

Kaviar Gauche (www.kaviargauche.com, 2887 3562, flagshipstore Linienstrasse 44, Mitte) produces elegant bags and dresses, while the label **Perret Schaad**

(www.perretschaad.com), despite being a relative newcomer, has already been praised as 'the best that happened to German fashion since Jil Sander'.

Not all of the designers have their own showroom, but permanent and semi-permanent concept stores are springing up like mushrooms, the area around Torstrasse being particularly fertile ground for shops such as the wonderfully crazy **Happy Shop** (Torstrasse 67, 0157 7847 3620, www.happyshop-berlin.com). **Voo** (6165 1119, http://blog.vooberlin.com), hidden in a backyard on Oranienstrasse, illustrates how nightlife and fashion in the German capital are often inseparably intertwined. The creative director of the store is also one of the promoters of one of Berlin's best club nights, the Broken Hearts Club at Ballhaus Berlin. Voo sells local and international designers (many Scandinavian), gifts and accessories. **WoodWood** (Rochstrasse 4, 2804 7877), a cool concept store by the Danish label of the same name, is another example of the Scandinavian-German fashion friendship. **Schwarzhogerzeil** (Mulackstrasse 28, 2887 3868) offers beautiful but rather pricey fashion and jewellery. Luckily, just a couple of footsteps down the street, its sister store **Blau** (Mulackstrasse 23, 7544 2210) sells second-season Isabel Marant and other reduced items.

Sustainability is a major trend within the Berlin fashion scene and shops like the **ecoShowroom** (Almstadtststrassen35, 688 120 64, www.ecoshowroom.de) in Mitte, **Wertvoll** (Marienburgerstrasse 35, 255 677 26, www.wertvoll-berlin.de) in Prenzlauer Berg or **De la Reh** in Charlottenburg (Nürnbergerstrasse 23, 0163 1619 595, www.delareh.de) have picked up on it. Berlin may not be Milan, but it's all the better for it.

Kwik Shop

Kastanienallee 44, Mitte (4199 7150, www.kwikshop.de). U2 Senefelderplatz or U8 Rosenthaler Platz. **Open** 11am-7pm Mon-Sat. **Map** p319/p326 O4.

Originally, this quirky little shop had no door, so products had to be sold through a kiosk window; the practice stuck, and today, despite there being a door, all the goods are displayed in the shop window and sold through a hatch. The selection features both wacky gift items and finely crafted household miscellany, much of it self-made by owners Annette Bruns and Oliver Spies. *Photo p181.*

Luxus International

Kastanienallee 101, Prenzlauer Berg (4432 4877, www.luxus-international.de). U2 Eberswalder Strasse. **Open** 11am-8pm Mon-Sat; 11pm-7pm Sun. **Map** p319 O3.

For €7.50 a month, this platform for local talent rents individual shelves to the scores of Berlin designers who can't afford to open their own shops. The stock is always changing and usually off-beat; it includes everything from earrings to ashtrays, handbags to T-shirts, lamps to notebooks. These Berlin originals make excellent souvenirs and fabulous gifts.

SupaLifeKiosk

Raumerstrasse 40, Prenzlauer Berg (4467 8826, www.supalife.de). U2 Eberswalder Strasse. **Open** noon-7.30pm Mon-Sat. **Map** p319 O3.

SupaLifeKiosk is a store, a gallery and design firm all in one. It's a platform for local designers selling handmade and limited-edition objects including silk-screened prints, cards, books, clothing and other random items. Young Berlin-based designers feature heavily, and rotating monthly exhibits keep things interesting.

ELECTRONICS & PHOTOGRAPHY

Well known electronics chains, with branches around the city in addition to those listed here, include **Saturn** (Alexanderplatz 8, Mitte, 263 9970, www.saturn.de) and **Media Markt** (Grunerstrasse 20, Mitte, 240 8840, www.mediamarkt.com).

Everyday developing can be done at branches of **Rossmann** (www.rossmann.de) and **Schlecker**; branches of **Saturn** (at Alexanderplatz and Potsdamer Platz, among others; www.saturn.de) also provide processing services.

Fix Foto

Kurfürstendamm 209, Charlottenburg (882 7267, www.fixfoto.de). U1 Uhlandstrasse. **Open** 9am-8pm Mon-Sat; **Map** p321/p328 F8.

One-hour developing, enlargements, CD-Rom and other fast services.

Other locations Kurfürstendamm 142, Wilmersdorf (892 32 29); Teltower Damm 3, Zehlendorf (811 30 64).

Fotoimpex

Alte Schönhauser Strasse 32B, Mitte (2859 9081, www.fotoimpex.de). U8 Weinmeisterstrasse. **Open** noon-8pm Mon-Sat. **No credit cards.** **Map** p319/p326 O5.

A positive mecca for all things to do with black-and-white, analogue photography, including one-day, by-hand developing and printing. Hundreds of film varieties, high-quality equipment and all manner of cameras and accessories are sold at very reasonable prices. No wonder this is where local photographers go to stock up.

Sofortbild Shop

Brunnenstrasse 195, Mitte (9395 5342, www.sofortbild-shop.de). U8 Rosenthaler Platz. **Open** noon-8pm Mon-Fri; noon-6pm Sat. **Map** p319/p326 O5.

In a world where digital photography has taken over, do you ever feel nostalgic for the haptic pleasure of the good old polaroid? Then this shop is for you. It sells original Polaroid cameras, as well as various instant picture films. Books, prints and postcards are also on offer.

FASHION

In the last two decades, the Berlin fashion scene has exploded, with international brands opening flagship stores, local designers selling innovative collections out of studio shops, and guerrilla stores keeping things on the move. High-end department stores and big, mid-market chains are clustered on **Kurfürstendamm** and **Friedrichstrasse**. Traditional luxury brands are focused on **Fasanenstrasse** off the Ku'damm, while fancy, avant-garde boutiques and flagship stores abound in the area around Mulackstrasse and **Alte Schönhauser Strasse**. Smaller local talents have set up shop on **Kastanienallee** in Prenzlauer Berg, **Wühlischstrasse** in Friedrichshain, **Oranienstrasse** in Kreuzberg and in Northern Neukölln on and around Hobrechtstrasse.

Designer: international

Acne Jeans

Münzstrasse 23, Mitte (2804 4870, www.acnejeans.com). U8 Weinmeisterstrasse. **Open** noon-8pm Mon-Sat. **Map** p319/p326 O5.

This young Swedish brand has a huge following. Its Berlin flagship store is the first outside Scandinavia and features the label's complete collections of men's and women's fashion, shoes, bags, accessories and jewellery.

CONSUME

Apartment

Memhardstrasse 8, Mitte (2804 2251, www.
apartmentberlin.de). U2, U5, U8, S5, S7, S9,
S75 Alexanderplatz. **Open** noon-7pm Mon-Fri;
noon-7pm Sat. **Map** p319/p327 O5.
Unmarked and entirely empty, Apartment's huge
white-box storefront is easy to miss. But head down
to the basement and you'll find clothing, accessories
and shoes from hot local and international designers,
from Bernard Wilhelm to Jeremy Scott. Next door,
its sister store Cash sells second-season items and
vintage fashion (open 2-7pm Mon-Fri).

A.P.C.

Mulackstrasse 36, Mitte (2844 9192,
www.apc.fr). U2 Rosa-Luxemburg-Platz or
U8 Weinmeisterstrasse. **Open** 11.30am-7.30pm
Mon-Fri; noon-6pm Sat. **Map** p319/p326 O5.
Tucked away in a side street, this flagship store from
the French cult brand offers mens- and womenswear
in classic Paris styles, own-label CDs and gadgets.

Corner Berlin

Französische Strasse 40, Mitte (2067 0940,
www.thecornerberlin.de). U6 Französische Strasse.
Open 10.30am-7.30pm Mon-Fri; 10am-7pm Sat.
Map p322/p327 M7.
This impeccably designed store offers a select mix
of men's and women's fashion, accessories, electronics, books, music, art and even vintage furniture for
the stylish set with money to spend. Featured
designers include Alexander McQueen, Stella
McCartney and Christian Louboutin. There's also an
in-house bar and restaurant.

Herr von Eden

Alte Schönhauserstrasse 14 (2404 8682,
www.herrvoneden.com). U8 Weinmeisterstrasse.
Open 10.30am-8pm Mon-Fri; 10am-7pm Sat.
Map p326 O5.
Proving that men's suits don't have to be boring, this
Hamburg label sells dandyish fashion that manages
to be tongue-in-cheek and elegant at the same time.

Lena Hoschek

Neue Schönhauserstrasse 1A, Mitte. (2787 6985,
www.lenahoschek.com).U8 Weinmeisterstrasse.
Open 11am-8pm Mon-Sat. **Map** p319/326 O5.
Austrian fashion designer Lena Hoschek made a
name for herself by re-inventing the traditional
dirndl dress, giving it a fresh Rockabilly look. Not
everybody's cup of tea, for sure. But the designs are
imaginative and her store is worth a visit, even if
you're not on your way to the Octoberfest.

Lil*Shop

Brunnenstrasse 184, Mitte (2804 5338, www.lil-
shop.com). U8 Rosenthaler Platz. **Open** noon-7pm
Tue-Fri; noon-6pm Sat. **Map** p319 N4.
Once upon a time, a series of Comme des Garçons
guerrilla stores popped up around Berlin and then

disappeared, one by one. But the Japanese brand was
such a hit here that the women who ran the series
decided to open this little (permanent) gem, which
carries vintage CDG and Junya Watanabe clothing,
accessories and perfumes in addition to the label's
current collection.

Mientus

Wilmersdorfer Strasse 73, Charlottenburg
(323 9077, www.mientus.com). U7 Wilmersdorfer
Strasse or S3, S5, S7, S75 Charlottenburg.
Open 10am-7pm Mon-Sat. **Map** p321/p328 E8.
Clean cuts for sharp men from a range of well-known
collections including Dsquared, D&G, Prada, Miu
Miu and Paul Smith.
Other locations Kurfürstendamm 52,
Charlottenburg (323 9077); Bleibtreustrasse 24,
Charlottenburg (8823 786); Weinmeisterstrasse
12, Mitte (8823 786).

Veronica Pohle

Kurfürstendamm 64, Charlottenburg (883 3731,
www.veronicapohle.de). U7 Adenauerplatz. **Open**
10.30am-7.30pm Mon-Fri; 11am-6.30pm Sat.
Map p321 E9.
A large boutique with womenswear from top inter-
national labels such as Anna Sui, Vivienne
Westwood, Matthew Williamson, Diane von
Fürstenberg and Seven for all Mankind and Paul
Smith.

Designer: local

Andreas Mukurdis

Potsdamer Strasse 77-78, Haus E Tiergarten
(3088 1945, www.andreasmurkudis.net). S1,
S2, S25, U2 Potsdamer Platz. **Open** 10-8pm
Mon-Sat. **Map** p319/p326 O5.
In summer 2011, Andreas Murkidis, brother of the
well-known German fashion designer Kostas
Murkurdis, gave up his backyard shop on the busy
Mitte shopping mile and moved his concept store to
the up-and-coming gallery district of Potsdamer
Strasse. In the former home of the local Tagesspiegel
newspaper he now sells a variety of exclusive goods
–bags, jewellery, porcelain, as well as clothes by Dries
van Noten and, of course, his famous brother.

Fetish

For quality rubber and latex clobber, visit
Black Style (*see p232*); **Leathers** (*see p233*)
produces excellent leather and SM gear.

Schwarze Mode

Westfaelische Strasse 30, Wilmersdorf (8904 4568,
www.schwarzemode.de) S41, S42, S46 Halensee.
Open 11am-7pm Mon-Sat. **Map** p.320 P9.
Leatherette, rubber and vinyl are among the delica-
cies stocked here for fetish fashionistas. A selection
of erotic and SM books, mags and toys is also sold.

Sports gear

Karstadt Sporthaus

*Joachimstaler Strasse 5-6, Charlottenburg
(880240, www.karstadtsport.de). U2, U9, S3, S5,
S7, S75 Zoologischer Garten.* **Open** 10am-8pm
Mon-Sat. **Map** p321/p328 G8.
Four-level megastore with a wide selection of both
name brands and cheaper alternatives in international sportswear, German football paraphernalia
and children's clothes.

MontK

*Kastanienallee 83, Prenzlauer Berg (448 2590,
www.mont-k.de). U2 Eberswalder Strasse.*
Open 10am-8pm Mon-Fri; 10am-6pm Sat.
Map p319/p328 O3.
If you're a serious camper, skier, canoeist or climber,
MontK can kit you out with all the proper equip-
ment, outerwear and footgear.

Niketown Berlin

*Tauentzienstrasse 7B-7C, Schöneberg (25 070,
www.nike.com). U1, U2, U3 Wittenbergplatz.*
Open 10am-8pm Mon-Thur; 10am-9pm Fri, Sat.
Map p321 G8.
The monster outlet for the monster US company is
housed in a state-of-the-art glass and neon building,
and sells everything bearing the famous swoosh.

Street/clubwear

Despite an influx of some of the biggest names
in international streetwear, Berlin has managed
to retain an unusually strong contingent of
streetwear labels operating independently and
under some charmingly idealistic business
philosophies, as well as attracting a flood of
higher-end urbanwear labels, particularly
from Scandinavia and Japan. Friedrichshain,
Kreuzberg and Neukölln are particularly good
areas for the former, while Mitte is the place
for the latter.

Big Brobot

*Kopernikusstrasse 19, Friedrichshain (7407 8388,
www.bigbrobot.com). U5 Frankfurter Tor.* **Open**
11am-8pm Mon-Fri; 11am-6pm Sat. **Map** p324 S7.
The first German home for British label Fenchurch.
Big Brobot also stocks Boxfresh, Stüssy and X-
Large, among others. There are all sorts of cultish
accessories, as well as comics and small-edition publications. The refreshingly unpretentious staff are
friendly and helpful.

Eisdieler

*Kastanienallee 12, Prenzlauer Berg (2839 1291,
www.eisdieler.de). U2 Eberswalder Strasse.* **Open**
noon-8pm Mon; noon-7pm Sat. **Map** p319/p326 O3.
A group of young Berlin designers pooled their
resources to transform this former ice shop into an
urban streetwear collective, and each of them manages a label under the Eisdieler banner.

Été-clothing

*Bergmannstrasse 18, Kreuzberg (3289 5543,
www.ete-clothing.de). U7 Gneisenaustrasse.*
Open 11am-8pm Mon-Sat. **Map** p322 M10.
Été-clothing stocks a wide range of street fashion –
including Billabong, Hurley, Roxy and local label
IrieDaily – as well as a good selection of skate- and
surfboards. The owners are boarders themselves, so
they know what's what.

Firmament

*Linienstrasse 40, Mitte (4980 8674, www.am-
firmament.com). U8 Rosa-Luxemburg Platz.*
Open noon-8pm Mon-Sat. **Map** p319/326 O5.
Offering high-end Japanese and local streetwear
brands like Visvim, Supreme and Wtaps, this is
also the only shop in Berlin to showcase the entire
collection of Munich-based label Acronym. The
store's savvy owners are also the driving force
behind the online street magazine *Beinghunted*
(www.beinghunted.com) and the online shop The-
Glade (www.the-glade.com).

IrieDaily

*Depot 2, Oranienstrasse 9, Kreuzberg (611 4655,
www.iriedaily.de). U1 Görlitzer Bahnhof.* **Open**
11am-8pm Mon-Sat. **Map** p323 P9.
Eastern earthiness combined with a skater/hip hop
aesthetic has made IrieDaily one of the most popular
local brands. This is the company's flagship. Girls'
tops and trousers are flattering and edgy, the hood-
ies slinky and cosy; men's cargo pants are classy and
velvety. Innovative accessories include belts and
bags.

JR Sewing

*Hobrechtstrasse 18, Neukölln (7640 3759,
www.jr-sewing.de). U7, U8 Hermannplatz.*
Open 11am-7pm Mon-Fri; noon-6pm Sat.
Map p323 Q10.
Shop owner and designer Jana Reiche's most successful creation is a T-shirt with a slogan that seems
to resonate not only with the city's many creatives
(and wannabe creatives): '*Is mir egal, ich lass das
jetzt so*' (roughly translated: 'I don't care, I'll just
leave it that way.'). Apart from her own designs,
Reiche sells other labels from the store's Neukölln
neighbourhood as well as beanies, cotton tote bags
and jewellery – all for really reasonable prices.

Wood Wood

*Rochstrasse 4, Mitte (2804 7877, www.wood
wood.dk). U2, U5, U8,S3, S5, S7, S75
Alexanderplatz.* **Open** noon-8pm Mon-Sat.
Map p319 O6.
An avant-garde design collective from Copenhagen,
Wood Wood offers beautiful, electric and sometimes
outrageous street fashion, sneakers and accessories

CONSUME

by higher-end designers such as Cheap Monday, Maharishi and Kim Jones. Almost half the stock is Wood Wood's own, an explosion of prints, stitching and bright colours tempered by clean, classic cuts.

Used & vintage

Calypso

Rosenthaler Strasse 23, Mitte (2854 5415, www.calypsoshoes.com). U8 Weinmeisterstrasse. **Open** noon-8pm Mon-Sat. **Map** p319/p326 O5.
Hundreds of stilettos, wedges and platforms in vivid shades and exotic shapes from the 1930s to the '90s, almost all in fine condition.
Other location Oderberger Strasse 61, Prenzlauer Berg (281 6165).

Colours

Bergmannstrasse 102, Kreuzberg (694 3348, www.kleidemarkt.de). U7 Gneisenaustrasse. **Open** 11am-7pm Mon-Fri; noon-6pm Sat. **Map** p322 M10.
Rows of jeans, leather jackets and dresses, including party stunners and fetching Bavarian dirndls, plus the odd gem from the 1950s or '60s.

Das Neue Schwarz

Mulackstrasse 37 (2787 4467, www.dasneue schwarz.de). U2 Rosa-Luxemburg Platz, U8 Weinmeisterstrasse. **Open** 11am-8pm Mon, Thur-Sat. **No credit cards**. **Map** p319/326 O5.
Hidden in a backyard between the trendy and expensive designer stores of Mulackstrasse, Das Neue

---

Sexy Vintage

Real glamour, second-hand.

Granted, the phrase coined by Berlin's long-serving mayor Klaus Wowereit about the city being poor but sexy has been somewhat overused. But the truth is that majority of Berliners don't have sufficient funds to dress head to toe in designer gear. So in order to feel sexy on the cheap – and to display the individual sense of style that is en vogue in the city – vintage fashion is often the way to go for the fashion conscious. The result can lead to fierce competition for the best gear: that if you don't get up early to make a steal at the

flea market (*see p175*), the best finds might be snatched from under your nose. Fortunately, there are a number of great vintage stores with a never ceasing assortment of hand-picked, affordable items. In the area around Kastanienallee you'll find an abundance of colourful vintage stores that are certainly fun to look at, but chances that you find something you'll actually want to wear are slight (unless you have a thing for wild '70s patterns and polyester). An exception is **Goo** (4403 3737, www.paulsboutiqueberlin.de),

Soeur.

schwarz (which translates as 'the new black') is a great alternative for the more adventurous shopper. Just ring the doorbell and you'll be welcomed by friendly staff. Vintage items by high-end designers are to be found here, as well as an interesting selection of shoes and jewellery.

Garage

Ahornstrasse 2, off Einemstrasse, Schöneberg (211 2760). U1, U2, U3, U4 Nollendorfplatz. Open 11am-7pm Mon-Fri; 11am-6pm Sat. Map p322 J9.

Garage sells cheap second-hand clothing priced by the kilo. The large selection at this barn-like locale is well-organised, making it easy to root out last-minute party gear.

Garments

Linienstrasse 204/205, Mitte (2847 7781, www garments-vintage.de). Open noon-7pm Mon-Sat. No credit cards. Map p.319/326 O5.

Garment's two branches, one in Mitte and one Prenzlauer Berg, both offer a great selection of stylish and high quality vintage clothing, shoes and original jewellery. The shop on Stargarder Strasse sells some men's fashion as well.

Other location Stargarder Strasse 12a (7477 9919).

Made in Berlin

Neue Schönhauser Strasse 19, Mitte (2123 0601). U8 Weinmeisterstrasse. Open 11am-8pm Mon-Sat. Map p319/p326 O5.

a tiny store on Oderbergerstrasse that can be easily overlooked, but sells pretty no-name basics and pieces by labels such as WoodWood or Berlin's own Wolfen with potential to become everyday-favourites. A little bit further up the road **Calypso** (2854 5415, www.calypsoshoes.com) sells vintage shoes in all shapes and sizes. **Soeur** (3289 1520), on Marienburgerstrasse, is worth a detour. The clothes aren't cheap, but carefully selected, and you can find pieces by Stella McCartney and Prada as well as local designers and high-street brands. Soeur also sells new A.P.C items. If you fancy matching glasses, just a few footsteps away is **Lunettes Brillenagentur** (*see 193*) with an amazing selection of vintage specs.

Some of the best vintage shops in terms of quality, however, can still be found Mitte. Stores such as **Garments** (*see above*), **XVII-dix-sept** (*see p188*) or **Das Neue Schwarz** (*see p186*) sell stylish and idiosyncratic fashion and accessories.

If you only have time to visit one vintage store in the city, head to **Made in Berlin** (*see avove*). The colourful store has a huge selection of jackets, shoes and dresses. Even if not every item is of the best quality, the place is great for playing dress-up.

A more glamorous experience is **Sterling Gold** (*see p188*). Tucked away in the historic Heckmann Höfe, it's crammed full with beautiful ball gowns and cocktail dresses dating from the1940s to the 1990s. Just the place to go for ladies who are fed up with the whole poor-but-sexy-business and would like to feel like a princess for once.

Lunettes Brillenagentur.

CONSUME

Sister store of Garage (*see p187*), where the 'better stuff' supposedly goes – vintage Adidas, Burberry and Lacoste, for example. It's still pretty cheap, though, and offers a ton of great no-name 1980s gear. Every Tuesday between noon and 3pm you get a 20% discount.

Other location Friedrichstrasse 114a, Mitte (2404 8900).

No.34

Mulackstrasse 34, Mitte (no phone). U2 Rosa Luxemburg Platz, U8 Weinmeisterstrasse. **Open** noon-8pm Mon-Sat. **No credit cards**. **Map** p319/326 O5.

This very special shop is not only to be recommended for its small but exclusive selection of rare high-end vintage pieces, but also for its beautiful textiles from various parts of the world. Designer pieces by labels such as Bless or Cosmic Wonder and other diverse items, most sharing a certain ethno-touch, complete the shopping experience. Because it neither has a real name nor a sign, the place is easy to overlook, but it's definitely one of Berlin's most interesting concept stores.

Sterling Gold

Oranienburger Strasse 32, Mitte (2809 6500, www.sterlinggold.de). S1, S2 Oranienburger Strasse. **Open** noon-8pm Mon-Fri; noon-6pm Sat. **Map** p319/p326 N5.

Michael Boenke couldn't believe his luck when he was offered a warehouse full of prom dresses during a trip to America. He shipped them to Berlin, and this shop in the Heckmann Höfe was the result. The fabulous ball- and cocktail gowns – in every conceivable shade and fabric, and dating from the 1950s to the '80s – are in terrific condition. Prices start at €80, and labels range from big designers to total no-names.

XVII-dix-sept

Steinstrasse 17, Mitte. (5448 2882, www.XVII-store.com). **Open** 11am-7pm Mon-Fri; 11am-5pm Sat. **No credit cards**. **Map** p319/326 O5.

The stylish owners of this small shop used to work in the fashion industry, so they know what's hot. They also collaborate with the German publisher Suhrkamp and sell paperbacks of German classics that perfectly match the store's decor.

FASHION ACCESSORIES & SERVICES

Jewellery

OONA

Auguststrasse 26, Mitte (2804 5905/www.oona-galerie.de). S1, S2, S25 Oranienburger Strasse or U8 Rosenthaler Platz. **Open** 2-6pm Tue-Fri; 1-6pm Sat. **Map** p319/p326 N5.

In addition to its permanent collection, this 'gallery for contemporary jewellery' features the work of innovative young jewellery artists from Europe, Japan and Australia. For these frequent exhibitions, the gallery and artists choose a special theme and work together with architects, photographers and interior designers to develop a concept. A mix of precious and non-precious materials means there's a corresponding mix of price tags.

Scuderi

Wörther Strasse 32, Prenzlauer Berg (4737 4240, www.scuderi-schmuck.de). U2 Senefelderplatz. **Open** 11am-7pm Mon-Fri; 11am-4pm Sat. **Map** p319/p328 P3.

Bettina Siegmund and Daniela Nagi work magic with gold, silver, pearls, stones and hand-rolled glass, creating lightweight ornaments that make a strong statement.

TomShot

Szredzkistrasse 56, Prenzlauer Berg (4403 8350, www.tomshot.com). U2 Eberswalderstrasse. 11am-7pm Mon-Fri; 11am-4pm Sat. **Map** p.319 P3.

Fashionable custom jewellery, hand-manufactured in Berlin.

Other location Alte Schönhauser Strasse 25 (4005 4984).

Bags, hats & buttons

Bag Ground

Gipsstrasse 23B, Mitte (2758 3177, www.bag-ground.com). U8 Weinmeisterstrasse. **Open** noon-8pm Mon-Sat. **Map** p319/p326 N5.

This colourful shop is full of handbags hip and bright, plain or clubby, with prices starting at €50.

Knopf Paul

Zossener Strasse 10, Kreuzberg (692 1212, www.paulknopf.de). U7 Gneisenaustrasse. **Open** 9am-6pm Tue, Fri; 2-6pm Wed, Thur. **No credit cards**. **Map** p323 N10.

A Kreuzberg institution stocking buttons in every shape, colour and style you can think of. Whatever you're seeking, Paul Knopf ('Button') will help you find it. His patient and amiable service is remarkable considering most transactions are for tiny sums.

Rike Feurstein

Rosa-Luxemburg Strasse 25, Mitte (9225 9669, www.rikefeurstein.com). U2 Rosa-Luxemburg Platz. **Open** noon-7pm Mon-Fri; noon-6pm Sat. **Map** p319/326 O5.

Rike Feurstein's original but extremely wearable and stylish designs will make you want to wear a different hat every day.

Lingerie

Blush

Rosa-Luxemburg-Strasse 22, Mitte (2809 3580, www.blush-berlin.com). U2 Rosa-Luxemburg-Platz

or U8 *Weinmeisterstrasse*. **Open** noon-8pm
Mon-Fri; noon-7pm Sat. **Map** p319/p326 O5.
Beautiful lingerie in lace and silk. Imports from
France and Italy, as well as German brands.

Les Dessous

Fasanenstrasse 42, Wilmersdorf (883 3632, www.
les-dessous.de). U3, U9 Spichernstrasse. **Open** 11am-
7pm Mon-Fri; 10am-3pm Sat. **Map** p321/p328 F8.
A beautiful shop featuring lingerie, silk dressing
gowns and swimwear by Eres, Dior and La Perla.

Fishbelly

Friedelstrasse 25, Neukölln (2804 5180, www.
fishbelly.de). U8 Schönleinstrasse. **Open** noon-7pm
Mon-Fri; 1pm-7pm Sat. **Map** p323 O10.
Often compared to Agent Provocateur, this shop is
licensed to thrill with extravagant undergarments
by big-name designers and an own-brand line of
imaginative lingerie.

Shoes

There's some truth to the sock-and-sandal
cliché: when it comes to shoes, Germans tend to
appreciate comfort and it seems no coincidence
that Birkenstocks were invented here. A major
chain selling comfortable shoes by quality
brands is **Aktiv Schuh** (www.aktiv-schuh.de,
branches all over town). There are several
other big chains selling affordable footwear,
such as **Leiser** or **Görtz**, with branches
scattered all over Berlin, particularly in the
main shopping areas around Gedächtniskirche,
Friedrichstrasse or Hackescher Markt. But
there are smaller shops selling more individual
styles, as well.

Budapester Schuhe

Kurfürstendamm 43, Charlottenburg (886 24206,
www.budapester-schuhe.net). U1 Uhlandstrasse.
Open 10am-7pm Mon-Fri; 10am-6pm Sat.
Map p321/p328 F8.
This is the largest of four Berlin branches, offering
the latest by the likes of Prada, D&G, Sergio Rossi
and Miu Miu. At Kurfürstendamm 199, across the
street, you'll find a conservative range for men, and
at the Bleibtreustrasse branch, prices are slashed by
up to 50% for last year's models, remainders and
hard-to-sell sizes.
Other locations Bleibtreustrasse 24,
Charlottenburg (886 29500); Kurfürstendamm
199, Charlottenburg (881 707).

Massschuhmacherei

Sophienstrasse 28-29, Mitte (4004 2861,
www.massschuhmacherei.de). S3, S5, S7, S75
Hackescher Markt. **Open** noon-5pm Tue-Fri.
Map p319/p326 N5.
Handmade shoes for men and women in classic,
understated designs. The shop also does repairs.

★ Shusta

Rosenthaler Strasse 72, Mitte (7621 9780,
www.shusta.de). U8 Rosenthaler Platz.
Open 11am-8pm Mon-Sat. **Map** p.319 N4.
In this beautiful, high-ceilinged store, you'll find
unique, stylish, good-quality shoes, imported from all
over the world by Tedros and Fidel, the shop's very
cool and friendly owners. A separate door leads up
the stairs to another room with classic, smart men's
shoes as well as some women's clothing. The store
can get pretty crowded on Saturday with passers-by
and local hipsters coming by in search of the perfect
pair or just to have a chat with the proprietors.

Solebox

Nürnberger Strasse 16, Charlottenburg
(9120 6690, www.solebox.de). U1, U2, U3
Wittenbergplatz. **Open** noon-8pm Mon-Sat.
Map p321 G8.
The place for rare and collectable limited-edition
Pumas, Nikes or Adidas, Solebox stocks a massive
selection of exclusive sneakers as well as a small
offering of clothing and gear to wear them with.
Friendly and well-informed staff.

Trippen

Rosenthaler Strasse 40-41, Mitte (2839 1337,
www.trippen.com). S3, S7, S75 Hackescher
Markt. **Open** 11am-8pm Mon-Fri; 10am-8pm
Sat. **Map** p319/p326 N5.
In this sunny, minimalist store in the Hackeschen
Höfe, Berlin designers Michael Oehler and Angela
Spieth present avant-garde shoes and bags in wood,
leather and rich colours. Parents will be pleased to
know that a children's line is also available at the
'family' branch on Knaackstrasse.
Other locations Alte Schönhauser Strasse 45,
Mitte (2463 2284); Knaackstrasse 26, Prenzlauer
Berg (4050 0392).

FOOD & DRINK

The proliferation of reasonably priced and
pleasantly designed organic food shops in
Berlin has prodded otherwise complacent
supermarket chains such as Kaiser's and Extra
into stepping up their game. But those in need
of discount groceries will find the omni-present
Lidl and Aldi chains unchanged and as cheap
as ever. There are also hundreds of speciality
stores, ranging from ethnic to gourmet,
American to Asian. And there are the great
department-store food halls, most notably
at the **Galeries Lafayette** (*see p173*) and
KaDeWe (*see p174*).

Bonbonmacherei

Oranienburger Strasse 32, Mitte (4405 5243,
www.bonbonmacherei.de). S1, S2, S25
Oranienburger Strasse. **Open** noon-8pm
Wed-Sat. **No credit cards. Map** p319/p326 N5.

Nostalgic candy shop that offers sweet, sour and everything in between. You can watch Katja Kolbe and Hjalmar Stecher produce the sweets in their on-site workshop using vintage equipment and old recipes. High quality at reasonable prices.

Broken English

Körtestrasse 10, Kreuzberg (691 1227, www.brokenenglish.de). U7 Südstern. **Open** 11am-6.30pm Mon-Fri; 11am-4pm Sat. **Map** p323 O10.
Caters to homesick British expats with a range of teas, biscuits, crisps, sweets and extras. This is the place to find chocolate digestives, Oxo cubes, Marmite and Heinz baked beans. There's also a selection of cheeses and deep-frozen pies, and a gift section. Pricey, though.
Other locations Leonhardtstrasse 23, Charlottenburg (28599307); Lepsiusstrasse, Steglitz (72011606).

Fresh 'n' Friends

Kastanienallee 26, Prenzlauer Berg (4171 7250, www.freshnfriends.com). U2 Eberswalder Strasse. **Open** 24hrs daily. **No credit cards**. **Map** p319/p326 O3.
This store is open 24/7 – practically unheard of in Berlin. What's more, it's actually good. With its offering of fresh, healthy organic foods at standard '*Bio-markt*' prices, this supermarket-meets-organic-deli is a lifesaver for night owls.

Getränke Hoffmann

Kleistrasse 23-26, Schöneberg (2147 3096, www.getraenke-hoffmann.de). U1, U2, U3 Wittenbergplatz. **Open** 9am-8pm Mon-Fri; 8am-8pm Sat. **No credit cards**. **Map** p321 H9.
Branches all over town offer a wide range of every-day booze at everyday prices. Call 0800 440 22 00 to place an order for delivery anywhere in Berlin.
Other locations throughout the city.

Chocolate Confidential

Sweet delights.

Beautifully designed interiors, packaging to savour and, above all, bitter, sweet and surprising chocolate. Berlin may be Germany's rebel city, but when it comes to chocolate, the locals are perfectionists.

Fassbender & Rausch (Charlottenstrasse 60, Mitte, 2045 8443, www.fassbender-rausch.com) specialises in superlatives: 'the most delicious chocolate since 1863', 'the biggest chocolate house in the world' and 'Europe's first chocolate restaurant'. In fact, the two families began separately – Fassbender in 1863 and Rausch seven years later – and only teamed up in 1999. It's hard to avoid the tourist crush in the world's largest chocolate store, but still a joy to see such extravagant celebration of the cocoa bean, with giant edible models of the Brandenburg Gate and other local landmarks. The upstairs restaurant serves wacky seasonal dishes that all contain chocolate, and offers 'chocolate-dinner-shows' with tacky historical themes.

Orthodox chocoholics should make their way to much more self-effacing old-timer, **Erich Hamann Bittere Schokoladen** (Brandenburgische Strasse 17, Wilmersdorf, 873 2085). The shop front looks more like a deserted department store than a revered *confiserie* and retains its original 1928 design by Johannes Itten of the Bauhaus. Inside are stacks of dark, bitter chocolate in the original packaging that make little concession to newfangled

chocolate types. In the factory behind the shop, the third generation of Hamanns are keeping faithful to the recipe.

At **Ritter Sport Schokowelt** (Französische Strasse 24, Mitte, 2009 5080/www.ritter-sport.de) chocolate lovers of all ages can create their own chocolate from dozens of different ingredients, learn some interesting facts about how chocolate is made or enjoy a chocolate breakfast at the store's upstairs Schokolounge.

Go to the tiny **Nibs** café (Bleibtreustrasse 46, Charlottenburg, 347 26 300, www.nibs cacao.de) for Spanish *churros* to dunk in hot chocolate, as well as a good selection of chocolate-related gifts, if at Savignyplatz prices. You can even sign up for a year's chocolate subscription here and get a package of chocolate 'surprises' every month.

Olivia (Wühlischstrasse 30, Friedrichshain, 6050 0368, www.olivia-berlin.de) is a cutesy boutique of a chocolaterie run by an all-woman team and has the best-looking cakes of all. The *Chilli Schokoladen Torte* is pure chocolate heaven. You can watch the elegant *tartes* being created nearby on Gärtnerstrasse. Queues stretch out of the tiny shop on market days, so if it's too full, choose from a lengthy list of hot chocolates at the friendly **Karvana** (Gabriel-Max-Strasse 4, 0178 343 3256, www.karvana.de) around the corner.

★ Kadó

Graefestrasse 75, Kreuzberg (6904 1638,
www.kado.de). U8 Schönleinstrasse. **Open**
9.30am-6.30pm Tue-Fri; 9.30am-3.30pm Sat.
No credit cards. Map p323 P10.
A mind-boggling selection of liquorice from all over
the world is beautifully presented in rows of glass
jars. All shapes, sizes and varieties are available.

Königsberger Marzipan

Pestalozzistrasse 54A, Charlottenburg (323
8254). U7 Wilmersdorfer Strasse. **Open** 11am-
6pm Mon-Fri; 10am-1pm Sat. **No credit cards.**
Map p320 D8.
Irmgard Wald and her late husband arrived from
Kaliningrad after the war and began their confec-
tionery trade anew. With her smiling American-born
granddaughter, Frau Wald still produces fresh, soft,
melt-in-your-mouth marzipan.

Leysieffer

Kurfürstendamm 218, Charlottenburg (885 7480,
www.leysieffer.de). U1 Uhlandstrasse. **Open** 9am-
7pm Mon-Sat; 10am-5pm Sun. **Map** p321/p328 F8.
The beautifully packaged jams, teas and handmade
chocolates from this German fine food company
make perfect gifts.

Vinh-Loi

Ansbacher Strasse 16, Schöneberg (235 0900).
U1, U2, U3 Wittenbergplatz. **Open** 9am-7pm
Mon-Sat. **No credit cards. Map** p321 G8.
Asian groceries arrive at this supermarket fresh
from the airport two or three times a week. There
are teas and tofu, Thai fruit and vegetables, and
every kind of noodle, spice mix and bottled sauce.
Also woks, rice steamers and Chinese crockery.
Other locations Gutmuthstrasse 23, Steglitz (no
phone); Muellerstrasse 40, Wedding (no phone).

Weichardt-Brot

Mehlitzstrasse 7, Wilmersdorf (873 8099,
www.weichardt.de). U7, U9 Berliner Strasse.
Open 7am-6pm Tue-Fri; 7am-1pm Sat.
No credit cards. Map p321 G11.
Perhaps the best bakery in town, Weichardt-Brot
grew out of a Berlin collective from the 1960s. Stone-
ground organic flour and natural leavens make this
a mecca for bread lovers.

Wine & spirits

Absinthe Depot Berlin

Weinmeisterstrasse 4, Mitte (281 6789, www.ers-
tesabsinthdepotberlin.de). U8 Weinmeisterstrasse.
Open 2pm-midnight Mon-Fri; 1pm-midnight Sat.
No credit cards. Map p319/p326 O5.
This place stocks the best and most potent absinthes
from across the world – including, of course, the good
Czech stuff. If you're lucky the owner might even
invite you for a sampling session and history lesson.

Planet Wein

Mohrenstrasse 30 (entry Charlottenstrasse), Mitte
(2045 4118, www.planet-weinhandel.de).U2, U6
Stadtmitte. **Open** noon-8pm Mon-Fri; noon-6pm
Sat. **Map** p.322 M7.
Planet Wein offers over 1,000 different wines from
a various countries, ranging from cheap to pricey.

Weinhandlung Hardy

Thielallee 29, Dahlem (8312 598, www.hardy-
weine.de). U3 Thielplatz. **Open** noon-8pm Mon-Sat.
This little Dahlem shop has a big selection of rare
vintage wines.

Klemke Wein & Spirituosenhandel

Mommsenstrasse 9, Charlottenburg (8855 1260).
S3, S5, S7, S75 Savignyplatz. **Open** 9am-7pm
Mon-Fri; 9am-2.30pm Sat. **No credit cards.**
Map p321/p328 E8.
Respected specialists in French and Italian wines
from the tiniest vineyard to the grandest château.
This mom-and-pop shop offers good wines at
good prices, as well as digestifs, whiskies and free
delivery in Berlin.

Whisky & Cigars

Sophienstrasse 8-9, Mitte (282 0376, www.
whisky-cigars.de). S3, S5, S7, S75 Hackescher
Markt. **Open** 11am-7pm Mon-Fri; 11am-6pm
Sat. **Map** p319/p326 N5.
Two friends with a love of single malts are behind
Whisky & Cigars, which stocks 450 whiskies and
cigars from Cuba, Jamaica and Honduras, among
other sources. The shop holds regular tastings and
will deliver.

GIFTS, SOUVENIRS & STATIONERY

Ach Berlin

Markgrafenstrasse 39, Mitte (9212 6880,
www.achberlin.de). U2, U6 Stadtmitte. **Open**
10am-7pm Mon-Sat. **Map** p327 M7.
The Berlin-themed books, knick-knacks and design
items on sale at this shop right are of better quality
than at your average Berlin souvenir store.

Ampelmann Galerie Shop

Rosenthaler Strasse 40-41, Mitte (4404 8801,
www.ampelmann.de). S3, S5, S7, S75 Hackescher
Markt. **Open** 9.30am-8pm Mon-Sat (summer until
10pm); 10.30am-7pm Sun. **Map** p319/p326 N5.
Sells a huge variety of stuff emblazoned with the old
East's enduring symbol, the jaunty red and green
traffic-light men – these days weirdly proliferating
in West Berlin too.
Other locations Karl-Liebknecht-Strasse 1,
in the DomAquarée, Mitte (2758 3238); Alte
Potsdamer Strasse 7, in the Potsdamer
Platz Arkaden, Tiergarten (2592 5691);
Markgrafenstrasse 37, Mitte (4003 9095).

CONSUME

CONSUME

Ausberlin
Karl-Liebknecht-Strasse 17, Mitte (4199 7896, www.ausberlin.de). U2, U5, U8, S3, S5, S7, S75 Alexanderplatz. **Open** 11-7pm Mon-Sat. **Map** p319/p327 O5.
A very cool shop for any and everything 'aus Berlin'. Innovative and design-happy like the city itself, this place sells everything from flashy books to Berlin-themed plasters, from postmodern stickers to progressive fashion. All items are made in Berlin, and prices range from €1 to €200.

Berliner Zinnfiguren
Knesebeckstrasse 88, Charlottenburg (315 7000, www.zinnfigur.com). S3, S5, S7, S75 Savignyplatz. **Open** 10am-6pm Mon-Fri; 10am-3pm Sat. **Map** p321/p328 F8.
Home to armies of handmade tin soldiers, farm animals and historical characters, all painted in incredible detail. You could take home an entire battalion of Prussian Grenadiers, if you should wish to.

Grüne Papeterie
Oranienstrasse 196, Kreuzberg (618 5355). U1 Görlitzer Bahnhof or U1, U8 Kottbusser Tor. **Open** 10am-7pm Mon-Fri; 10am-4pm Sat. **No credit cards. Map** p323 P9.
Grüne stocks eco-friendly stationery, wrapping paper, wooden fountain pens and small gifts and toys.

Leporello Papeterie
Rykestrasse 46, Prenzlauer Berg (4435 6912, www.leporello-berlin.de). U2 Senefelderplatz. **Open** 11am-7pm Mon-Fri; 10am-6pm Sat. **Map** p319/p328 P4.
This wonderful little shop on a beautiful cobbled street houses a well-presented collection of journals, pens and paper in amazing colours and patterns, plus a wide variety of trinkets, gifts and other stationery items. Good quality, big selection, and reasonable prices.

Ostkost
Lychener Strasse 54, Prenzlauer Berg (4465 3623). S41, S42, S8, S85, S9 Prenzlauer Allee, U2 Eberswalder Strasse. **Open** 8am-8.30pm Mon-Fri; 8am-7.30pm Sat. **Map** p319/p328 P3.
This nostalgic 'Eastern foods' shop sells almost-forgotten brands from the DDR, once available on every street corner in East Berlin. Othello chocolate biscuits, Spreewald pickles and Werder ketchup are just some of the many products offered alongside more modern fare from today's East.

RSVP
Mulackstrasse 14, Mitte (2809 4644, www.rsvp-berlin.de). U8 *Weinmeisterstrasse.* **Open** noon-7pm Mon-Sat. **Map** p319/p326 O5.
Stationery for the aesthete: art deco scissors, exotic erasers, paper from Italy, Polish notebooks, G Lalo boxes and Caran d'Ache pens.

RSVP.

HEALTH & BEAUTY
Hairdressers & barbers

There are plenty of so-called 'no-name salons', where you take a number and wait your turn for a hip, cheap haircut. Many are clustered on and around Kastanienallee, where the local favourite is **Notaufnahme** (Nos.29-30, 3011 2460, www.notaufnahme-berlin.de, closed Sun).

Beige
Auguststrasse 83, Mitte (2759 4051/www.salon-beige.de). U6 Oranienburger Tor. **Open** noon-9pm Tue-Sat. **No credit cards. Map** p326 M5.
An exclusive salon on the garden level of a private apartment building in Mitte. The waiting room doubles as a gallery space, and two client rooms are decorated in 1960s and baroque styles. Hair designer Oliver Weidner specialises in modern colours and cuts.

★ Heidelbeerzeiten
Hobrechtstrasse 19 (6290 0188, www. heidelbeerzeiten.de). U7, U8 Hermannplatz. **Open** 10am-9pm Tue-Fri; 10am-6pm Sat. **No credit cards. Map** p323 Q10.
Don't let the unpretentious atmosphere fool you, hairdresser Thomas Ewert and his young team know exactly what they're doing. Opposing the cut-and-go-mentality of many hairdressers in the city, they take a lot of time to provide each customer with

a beautiful, modern cut that doesn't cost a fortune. Word has spread, so it's best to make an appointment at least one week ahead.

JonnyCut

Yorckstrasse 43, Schöneberg (217 0941, www. jonnycut.de). U7, S1, S2, S26 Yorckstrasse. **Open** 11am-8pm Tue-Sat. **Map** p322 K10.
Jonny Pazo is a versatile stylist who shuttles from magazine shoots and record covers to appointments in his small and pleasingly eccentric salon, decked out with pictures of angels and buddhas.

Salon Sucré

Görlitzer Strasse 32A, Kreuzberg (612 2713, www.salonsucre.de). U1 Schlesisches Tor. **Open** *Salon* 10am-6pm Wed-Sat. *Pastry shop* 10am-6pm Thur-Sun. **No credit cards. Map** p324 R9.
What happens when a French pâtissier and a Brazilian hairdresser open a shop together? You get Salon Sucré, where good coffee, delicious homemade pastries and quality haircuts are all offered under one roof at reasonable prices.

Shift

Neue Schönhauser Strasse 8, Mitte (2809 9777, www.shift-friseure.de). U8 Weinmeisterstrasse. **Open** 9am-8pm Mon-Wed, Fri; 9am-9pm Thur; 9am-7pm Sat. **Map** p319/p326 O5.
Shift is popular with a young, designery crowd who come here for its personalised service. Remember the face of your stylist: you'll probably meet him or her, a few years later, in one of the higher-end salons, here or elsewhere.
Other location Grolmanstrasse 36, Charlottenburg (341 8545).

Udo Walz

Kempinski-Plaza, Uhlandstrasse 181-183, Charlottenburg (882 7457, www.udo-walz.de). U1 Uhlandstrasse. **Open** 9am-6pm Mon-Fri; 9am-2pm Sat. **Map** p321/p328 F8.
Udo Walz is the darling of the Berlin hair brigade, and likes to have his picture taken with the likes of Claudia Schiffer. As you'd expect, his stylists are well-trained and imaginative. Perhaps not so predictable is their friendliness.
Other locations Hohenzollerndamm 92, Wilmersdorf (826 6108); Schlüterstrasse 48, Charlottenburg (8872 7905); Knesebeckstrasse 68, Charlottenburg (88 14 455); Friedrichstrasse 185, Mitte (20 62 3994).

Vokuhila

Kastanienallee 16-17, Prenzlauer Berg (4434 2513, www.friseur-vokuhila-berlin.de). U2 Eberswalder Strasse. **Open** 10am-8pm Mon, Wed, Fri; 10am-6pm Tue, Sat; 10am-10pm Thur. **No credit cards. Map** p319/p326 O3.
Immerse yourself in Berlin's 20th-century history: this salon is decorated entirely in East German kitsch, a homage to the fact that hair has been washed, cut and styled here for over 70 years.
Other locations Fehrbellinerstrasse 87, Mitte (922 18188)

Opticians

Brille 54

Friedrichstrasse 71, Mitte (2094 6060, www.brille 54.de). U6 Französische Strasse. **Open** 10am-7pm Mon-Fri; 10am-6pm Sat. **Map** p322/p327 M7.
Brille 54 is a small but sleek space in Quartier 206, designed by hot young local architects Plajer & Franz. All the international names can be found here, including Armani, Gucci and Oliver Peoples.
Other locations Rosenthaler Strasse 36, Mitte (2804 0818); Kurfürstendamm 54, Charlottenburg (882 6696).

ic!

Max-Beer-Strasse 17, Mitte (2472 7200/www.ic-berlin.de). U8 Weinmeisterstrasse. **Open** 11am-8pm Mon-Sat. **Map** p319/p326 O5.
This is probably the hippest eyewear store for adults and children in Berlin, with a diverse range of designer prescription glasses and sunglasses.

★ Lunettes Brillenagentur

Marienburger Strasse 11, Prenzlauer Berg (4373 9465, www.lunettes-brillenagentur.de). M2 Marienburger Strasse or M4 Hufelandstrasse. **Open** noon-8pm Mon-Fri; noon-6pm Sat. **Map** p319/p328 P4.
Owner Uta Geyer has a knack for getting her hands on hard-to-find vintage frames, ranging from sleek 1920s pieces to rockabilly cateyes, from cool aviators to elegant Jackie Os. Prices range from €20 to €200, and most items are also available for rental.

Mykita

Rosa-Luxemburg-Strasse 6, Mitte (6730 8715, www.mykita.com). U2, U5, U8, S5, S7, S9, S75 Alexanderplatz. **Open** 11am-8pm Mon-Fri; noon-6pm Sat. **Map** p319/p326 O5.

INSIDE TRACK
OSTALGIE SOUVENIRS

Communist relics and alleged Wall chunks are sold at stalls near Checkpoint Charlie and the Museumsinsel. The **Haus am Checkpoint Charlie** (*see p82*) sells key rings, lighters and mouse pads with a 'You Are Leaving The American Sector' theme. Most flea markets (*see p175*) have stalls devoted to old DDR artefacts. **Berlin Story** (*see p179*) has a big selection of toy Trabants, historical maps, mounted Wall chunks and other souvenirs.

CONSUME

Since 2004, this young Berlin label has been designing and selling top-quality glasses – and winning praise and acclaim across the world. Creators Philipp Haffmans and Harald Gottschling present their handmade prescription frames and sunglasses on simple, industrial shelves in this beautifully lit, ultra-minimalist store. A fine selection from other brands is also available, but beware: this place isn't cheap.

Shops

Belladonna
Bergmannstrasse 101, Kreuzberg (6904 0333, www.bella-donna.de). U7 Gneisenaustrasse. **Open** 10am-7pm Mon-Fri; 10am-6pm Sat. **Map** p322 M10.
Belladonna stocks beauty and skin care products from Lavera, Dr Hauschka and Weleda, among others, as well as a selection of hair accessories, aromatherapy products and gift items. At the in-house cosmetic studio, experienced aestheticians offer a range of beauty therapies, including Dr Hauschka treatments.

★ Frau Tonis Parfum
Zimmerstrasse 13 (2021 5310, www.frau-tonis-parfum.com). U6 Kochstrasse. **Open** noon-8pm Mon-Fri, 11am-7pm Sat. **No credit cards.** **Map** p327 M8.
Take the smell of 'Berlin Summer' home with you (smells like lemons and fresh mint, apparently) or create your own individual scent at this lovely little perfume manufacturer.

Jacks Beauty Department
Sredzkistrasse 54, Prenzlauer Berg (4426 906, www.jacks-beautydepartment.de). U2 Eberswalderstrasse. **Open** 11am-8pm Mon-Fri; 11am-6pm Sat. **No credit cards.** **Map** p319/328 P3.
This cheerfully decorated shop is run by a professional make-up artist and offers everything that makes a beauty fanatic's heart beat faster. You can also get your hair and make-up done.

Spas & salons

Beate Kahlcke
Rosa-Luxemburg-Strasse 11-13, Mitte (2809 1918, www.beatekahlcke.de). U2 Rosa-Luxemburg-Platz. **Open** noon-8pm Mon; 11am-8pm Tue, Wed; 11am-10pm Thur, Fri; 10am-6pm Sat. **Map** p319/326 O5.
The interior design at Beate Kahlcke is a study in cool, clean-lined sophistication – perfect for a salon that operates in conjunction with Aveda and the design hotel Lux 11 next door (*see p114*). Its internationally trained hairdressers and stylists are personable and savvy; the therapists offer body wraps, massage and skin and nail care. What's more, it's all offered at reasonable prices.

Susanne Kaufmann Spa Berlin
Monbijouplatz 4, Mitte (2345 5973, www.susanne kaufmann.com). S3, S5, S7, S75 Hackescher Markt. **Open** 9am-9pm Mon-Fri; 10am-8pm Sat; by appointment Sun. **Map** p319 N5.
Susanne Kaufmann Spa offers a wide range of luxurious relaxing and beautifying treatments. All products used are purely organic and suitable even for very sensitive skin.

Wax in the city
Alte Schönhauser Strasse 33/34. (2345 6761, www.wax-in-the-city.de). U8 Weinmeisterstrasse. **Open** 11am-8pm Mon-Fri; 10am-6pm Sat. **No credit cards.** **Map** p319/326 O5.
The place to go to get rid of unwanted body hair quickly. The atmosphere is pleasant and professional and staff do their best to make the procedure as painless as possible. No appointment necessary.

HOUSE & HOME

In 2006, UNESCO named Berlin a City of Design, and it's not hard to tell why. Take a stroll around any area in the city, and you're sure to come across several design stores, with goods ranging from antique to DDR to ultra-modern, from plastic to ceramic to steel. In Mitte, **Rosenthaler Strasse** and **Alte** and **Neue Schönhauser Strasse** are home to lots of cool eastern and western items from the 1950s to 1970s. **Oderberger Strasse** in Prenzlauer Berg is good for DDR furniture, and **Grünberger Strasse** in Friedrichshain features well-kept second-hand goods.

DIM
Oranienstrasse 26, Kreuzberg (2850 30121, www.blindenanstalt.de). U1, U8 Kottbusser Tor. **Open** 10am-7pm Mon-Fri; 11am-4pm Sat. **Map** p323 P9.
An initiative of Berlin designers Oliver Wogt and Hermann Weizenegger, the 'Imaginary Factory' offers witty, high-style brushes and wicker items, all handmade by blind craftspeople at Berlin's Institute for the Blind.

Glenk and Hansen
Keithstrasse 13, Tiergarten (2362 7217). U1, U2, U3, U4, U12 Wittenberg Platz. **Open** 3-6pm Thur, Fri; 11am-2pm Sat. **Map** p.321 H8.
Only a few steps away from the Ku'damm, this store both sells and rents out 20th-century design classics by names such as Charles Eames, Verner Panton, Luigi Colani and Egon Eiermann.

Green Living
Schönhauser Allee 36 (Kulturbrauerei), Prenzlauer Berg (8061 4800, www.green-living-berlin.de). U2 Eberswalderstrasse. **Open** noon-8pm Mon-Fri; 11am-4pm Sat. **Map** p319/328 O3.

Ruby Designliving.

All furniture, floors and textiles presented in the Green Living showroom, are environmentally friendly and sustainably produced.

KPM

Wegelystrasse 1, Tiergarten (390 090, www. kpm-berlin.de). S3, S5, S7, S75, Tiergarten. **Open** 10am-6pm Mon-Sat. **Map** p321 G7.
Founded in 1763 by Frederick the Great to encourage the development of a domestic ceramics industry, the Königliche Porzellan-Manufaktur is still making high-quality vases, bowls and other porcelain wares today. The pieces that it produces are beautiful, but expensive.

Laden Schönhauser

Alte Schönhauser Strasse 28, Mitte (281 1704, www.schoenhauser-design.de). U8 Weinmeisterstrasse. **Open** noon-8pm Mon-Fri; 11am-8pm Sat. **Map** p319 O5.
'Retrofuturism' is the name of the game at this jam-packed second-hand shop, which offers brightly coloured plastic 1970s furniture and accessories alongside classics from the likes of Mies van der Rohe and Arne Jacobsen.

Moebel Horzon

Torstrasse 106 (no phone, www.modocom.de). U8 Rosenthaler Platz. **Open** varies. **No credit cards.** **Map** p326 N4.
Artist? Writer? Businessman? It's hard to define what Rafael Horzon really does. But the fact is that he invented simple shelves that are easy on the eye and can be admired in his Mitte showroom.

★ OK Versand

Alte Schönhauser Strasse 36/37 (2463 8746, www.okversand.com). U8 Weinmeisterstrasse. **Open** noon-8pm Mon-Fri; noon-4pm Sat. **Map** p.319/326 O5.
This fantastic store imports colourful and exceptional everyday household goods from Asia, Africa, Latin America and Eastern Europe. Some are made from recycling materials, such as a bowl made of discarded flipflops or a stool made from old bike tires. The focus is more on unusual aesthetics than quality, but all items are fully functional.

Ruby Designliving

Oranienburger Strasse 66, Mitte (2838 6030, www.ruby-designliving.de). S1, S2, S25 Oranienburger Strasse. **Open** 11am-8pm Mon-Fri; 11am-6pm Sat. **Map** p318/326 M5.
Ruby Designliving is a small shop with an astonishingly large and diverse offering of furniture, lamps, glass, rugs, fabrics and household goods from many of the world's most prominent and innovative designers.

Stilwerk

Kantstrasse 17, Charlottenburg (315 150, www.stilwerk.de). S3, S5, S7, 75 Savignyplatz. **Open** 10am-7pm Mon-Sat. **Map** p321/p328 F8.
This huge, glassy, design marketplace offers high-end products from an array of retailers, purveying modern furnishings and kitchens, high-tech lighting and bathroom fittings, as well as an assortment of interior items. There's also a fourth-floor showcase for the work of local craftspeople and designers.

CONSUME

CONSUME

VEB orange
Oderberger Strasse 29, Prenzlauer Berg (9788 6886, www.veborange.de). U2 Eberswalder Strasse. **Open** 11am-8pm Mon-Sat. **Map** p328/p319 O3.
A wide range of original 1960s and '70s furniture and decor from the DDR is stocked here.

MUSIC & ENTERTAINMENT

Berlin is a mecca for vinyl collectors and indie and electronic music junkies. **Kastanienallee** in Prenzlauer Berg, **Boxhagener Strasse** and **Grünberger Strasse** in Friedrichshain, and **Bergmannstrasse** and **Zossener Strasse** in Kreuzberg are the main veins. **Dussmann das KulturKaufhaus** (*see p180*) also has a good selection, and the weekend flea markets are usually full of cheap second-hand records in good condition.

Asphalt Tango Music Store @ Galerie Kai Dikhas
Aufbau Haus am Moritzplatz, Prinzenstrasse 85 D, Kreuzberg, (285 8528, www.asphalt-tango-shop.de). U8 Moritzplatz. **Open** 11am-6pm Tue-Fri. **Map** p323 O8.
This label, artist management office and record store specialises in Gypsy and other music from Poland, Romania, Serbia, Turkey, Bulgaria and elsewhere. One of the best places for Balkan music in Berlin.

Da capo
Kastanienallee 96, Prenzlauer Berg (448 1771, www.da-capo-vinyl.de). U2 Eberswalder Strasse. **Open** noon-7pm Tue-Fri; 11am-6pm Sat. **Map** p319/p326 O3.
Da capo offers a pricey but wide selection of used vinyl, releases on DDR label Amiga plus rare 1950s ten-inch records and jazz singles. Second-hand books and sheet music are available too.

Gelbe Musik
Schaperstrasse 11, Wilmersdorf (211 3962). U3 Augsburger Strasse. **Open** 1-6pm Tue-Fri; 11am-2pm Sat. **Map** p321 G9.
One of Europe's most important avant-garde outlets has racks of minimalist, electronic, world, industrial and extreme noise. Rare vinyl and import CDs, music press and sound objects make for absorbing browsing.

Hard Wax
Paul-Linke Ufer 44a (courtyard, 3rd floor), Kreuzberg (611 301 11, www.hardwax.com). U8, U12 Kottbusser Tor. **Open** noon-8pm Mon-Sat. **No credit cards**. **Map** p323 P9.
Hidden in a Kreuzberg courtyard, this store has been attracting the international dance music scene for over 20 years. It specialises in reggae, dubstep, Detroit techno and anything else involving vinyl and a thumping bass.

Mr Dead & Mrs Free
Bülowstrasse 5, Schöneberg (215 1449, www.deadandfree.com). U1, U2, U3, U4, U12 Nollendorfplatz. **Open** noon-7pm Mon-Fri; 11am-4pm Sat. **Map** p322J9.
Long Berlin's leading address for independent and underground rock, Mr Dead & Mrs Free has bucket loads of British, US and Australian imports, a large vinyl section and a staff that knows and loves its music. Small but choice selection of books and magazines as well.

Musikalienhandlung Hans Riedel
Uhlandstrasse 42, Wilmersdorf (882 7394, www.bauer-hieber.com). U1 Uhlandstrasse. **Open** 9.30am-6.30pm Mon-Fri; 10am-3pm Sat. **Map** p321/p328 F9.
Probably the best address for classical music in Berlin, this huge, old-fashioned shop has been stocking string and brass instruments since 1910 and has one of the largest selections of sheet music in Europe. A good selection of CDs is also available.

Pigasus – Polish Poster Gallery
Torstrasse 62, Mitte (2849 3697, www.pigasus-gallery.de). U2 Rosa-Luxemburg-Platz. **Open** 2-7pm Mon-Sat. **No credit cards**. **Map** p319/p326 O5.
A wide range of Polish, Russian and Ukrainian disco and classical music, plus a wonderful selection of old Polish film and propaganda posters.

Space Hall
Zossener Strasse 33, Kreuzberg (694 7664, www.space-hall.de). U7 Gneisenaustrasse. **Open** 11am-8pm Mon-Sat. **Map** p323 N10.
Space Hall holds a huge range of new and second-hand CDs and vinyl. Techno, house and electronica are the emphasis, but there's also lots of hip hop, indie and rock. Prices are competitive, and the employees know their stuff. The shop on Zossener 35 specialises in vinyl.

Vopo Records
Danziger Strasse 31, Prenzlauer Berg (442 8004, www.vopo-records.de). U2 Eberswalder Strasse. **Open** noon-8pm Mon-Fri; 11am-6pm Sat. **No credit cards**. **Map** p319/p328 P3.
Vopo stocks every type of rock, from punk to metal, from indie to hardcore, from garage to classic. Selected merchandise, second-hand items and Berlin concert tickets are also available.

TICKETS

Theaterkassen (ticket agencies) provide the easiest means of buying theatre and concert tickets, but commissions can run as high as 17 per cent. **Hekticket** (*see p237*) is probably the best bet, offering discounts of up to 50 per cent, or you can try www.ticketonline.de.

Calendar

Highlights of the Berlin year.

There is no day in the year when there isn't some sort of do on in Berlin – whether it's the twice-yearly fashion week, the rowdy May Day riots, (Kreuzberg's very own rite of spring), the flag-waving bank holiday commemorating German Reunification or one of the '*Lange Nacht der…*' (Long night of…) events, which see museums, theatres and opera houses open extra late for the evening. In summer, the multicultural Karneval der Kulturen and the Christopher Street Day parade celebrate the city's cultural diversity, while the Berlinale film festival sprinkles a little stardust over the wintery city each February.

SPRING

MaerzMusik – Festival für aktuelle Musik
Organisers: Berliner Festspiele (254 890, www.berlinerfestspiele.de). **Tickets** vary. **Date** 10 days in mid-Mar.
A holdover from the more culture-conscious days of the old East Germany, this annual contemporary music festival invites international avant-garde composers and musicians to present new works.

Zeitfenster – Biennale für alte Musik
Konzerthaus, Gendarmenmarkt 2, Mitte (203 090, www.zeitfenster.net). U2, U6 Stadtmitte. **Tickets** vary. **Map** p322/p327 M7. **Date** 1wk in Apr.
The Biennial Festival of Early Music focuses on works from the 16th and 17th centuries.

FREE Gallery Weekend
Various venues (2844 4387, www.gallery-weekend-berlin.de). **Date** Last weekend in April.
Around 40 galleries time their openings for the same weekend, making for an arty extravaganza attended by leading dealers as well as ordinary art lovers.

Lange Nacht der Opern und Theater
Various venues (www.berlin-buehnen.de/langenacht). **Tickets** €15. **Date** last Sat in Apr.
Most of the theatres and opera houses in the city stay open until 1am for one night only. A €15 ticket buys you as much culture as you can squeeze into six hours.

Deutschland Pokal-Endspiele
Olympiastadion, Olympischer Platz 3, Charlottenburg (300 633). U2 Olympia-Stadion or S3, S5, S75 Olympiastadion. Information & tickets: Deutscher Fussball-Bund (tickets@dfb.de). **Tickets** vary. **No credit cards**. **Date** late Apr/early May.
The domestic football cup final has been taking place at the Olympiastadion every year since 1985. It regularly attracts some 65,000 fans and tickets are very hard to come by.

May Day Riots
Around Kottbusser Tor, Kreuzberg. U1, U8 Kottbusser Tor. **Map** p323 P9. **Date** 1 May.
An annual event since 1987, when Autonomen engaged in violent clashes with police. The riots have quietened in recent years, but Kreuzberg is still lively on May Day.

Theatertreffen Berlin
Various venues. Organisers: Berliner Festspiele, (254 890, www.berlinerfestspiele.de). **Tickets** vary. **Date** 3wks in May.
A jury picks out ten of the most innovative and controversial new theatre productions from companies across Germany, Austria and Switzerland, and the winners come to Berlin to perform their pieces in May.

FREE Karneval der Kulturen
Kreuzberg (6097 7022, www.karneval-berlin.de). **Date** 4 days in May/June.
Inspired by the Notting Hill Carnival and intended as a celebration of Berlin's ethnic and cultural diversity, the long and popular weekend (always Pentecost)

centres on a 'multi-kulti' parade involving dozens of floats, hundreds of musicians and thousands of spectators. The route changes annually: check the website.

In Transit
Haus der Kulturen der Welt, John-Foster-Dulles-Allee 10, Tiergarten (3978 7175, www.hkw.de). **Bus 100. Tickets** vary. **Map** p318 K6. **Date** around 5 days in May/June.
Dance and performance from beyond Europe. Audiences can watch artists prepare their pieces, or wait for the resulting evening performances.

SUMMER

Yoga-Festival Berlin
Shanti-Park, Alt-Moabit 141, Mitte (3810 8093, www.yogafestival.de). Haupbahnhof S5, S7, S75, S9. **Tickets** *Day* €3-€18. *Weekend* €25-€39. **Date** weekend in June. **Map** p318 K6.
Om-tastic annual event now in its fifth year. A full weekend programme at the Shanti-Park offers practice sessions in the various yoga forms with teachers of note from many different countries. There is also music, a market and special events for children.

Berlin Philharmonie at the Waldbühne
Waldbühne, Am Glockenturm, Charlottenburg (administration 810 75230, box office 0180 533 2433, www.berliner-philharmoniker.de). S3, S75 Pichelsberg, then shuttle bus. **Tickets** €15-€65. **Date** 1 day in June/July.
The Philharmonie ends its season with an open-air concert that sells out months in advance. Over 20,000 Berliners light the atmospheric 'forest theatre' with candles once darkness falls.

International Aerospace Exhibition & Conference
Selchow (3038 2014, www.ila-berlin.de). S9, S45 Flughafen Berlin-Schönefeld. **Tickets** vary. **No credit cards. Date** 11-16. Sept 2012.
This popular biennial event, also known as the Berlin Air Show, is held at Schönefeld airport. It features around 1,000 exhibitors from 40 countries, with aircraft of all kinds, and a serious focus on space. The next events are scheduled for 2012 and 2014.

FREE Fête de la Musique
Various venues (4171 5289, www.fetedela musique.de). **Tickets** free. **Date** 21 June.
A regular summer solstice happening since 1995, this music extravaganza of bands and DJs takes place across the city. The music selection is mixed, with DJs playing everything from heavy metal to Schlager.

Deutsch-Französisches Volksfest
Zentraler Festplatz am Kurt-Schumacher-Damm, Kurt-Schumacher-Damm 207-245, Reinickendorf (213 3290, www.deutsch-franzoesisches-volksfest.de). U6 Kurt-Schumacher-Platz. **Tickets** €2. **No credit cards. Date** 4wks in June/July.
A survivor from the days when this area was the French Sector, the German-French Festival offers fairground rides, French music and cuisine, and Bastille Day fireworks.

FREE Lesbisch-Schwules Stadtfest
Nollendorfplatz/Motzstrasse, Schöneberg (2147 3586, www.regenbogenfonds.de). U1, U2, U3, U4 Nollendorfplatz. **Tickets** free. **Date** weekend before Christopher Street Day (3rd weekend in June). **Map** p322 J9.

Berlin Philharmonie at the Waldbühne.

The Lesbian & Gay Street Fair takes over the Schöneberg area every year, filling several blocks in West Berlin's gay quarter. Participating bars, clubs, food stands and musical acts make this a dizzying, non-stop event that also serves as kick-off for the following week's Christopher Street Day Parade.

FREE Christopher Street Day Parade

2362 8632, www.csd-berlin.de. **Date** Sat in late June.

Originally organised to commemorate the 1969 riots outside the Stonewall Bar on Christopher Street in New York, the fun and flamboyant parade has become one of the summer's most enjoyable and inclusive street parties, attracting straights as well as gays. In 2008, the parade took a new route, starting on Karl-Liebknecht-Strasse and ending, 4 miles (6.5km) later, at the Seigessäule.

Berlin Fashion Week

Various venues (399 800, www.fashion-week-berlin.com). **Date** 6 days in early July & late Jan.

OK, so it's not quite Paris (or Milan. Or New York. Or even London). But Berlin's twice-yearly style shindig is slowly being taken a little more seriously. Interesting locations compensate for the lack of star designers: in summer 2011 models strutted their stuff down the Strasse des 17 Juni boulevard towards the Brandenburg Gate. Bread & Butter, an international trade fair for street and urban wear, takes place at the same time in the former Tempelhof Airport.

Classic Open Air

Gendarmenmarkt, Mitte (Media On-Line 3157 5413, www.classicopenair.de). U6 Französische Strasse, U2, U6 Stadtmitte or U2 Hausvogteiplatz. **Tickets** €13-€89.50. **Map** p322/p327 M7. **Date** 4-7 days in early July.

Big names usually open this concert series held in one of Berlin's most beautiful squares.

Deutsch-Amerikanisches Volksfest

Heidestrasse 30, Tiergarten (0163 3900 930 www.deutsch-amerikanisches-volksfest.de). U6 Reineckendorferstrasse or S3, S5, S7, S75, U55 Hauptbahnhof, then shuttle bus. **Tickets** €2; free children under 14. **No credit cards.** **Date** 2-3wks in July/August.

Established by the US forces stationed in West Berlin, the German-American Festival offers a tacky but popular mix of carnival rides, cowboys doing lasso tricks, candy floss, hot dogs and Yankee beer.

Tanz im August

Various venues. Organisers: HAU, Hallesches Ufer 32, Kreuzberg (2590 0427, www.tanzim august.de). **Tickets** vary. **Date** 2-3wks in Aug.

Tanz im August is Germany's leading modern dance festival, with big-name participants and an international reputation. An annual showcase for global dance trends.

FREE Internationales Berliner Bierfestival

Karl-Marx-Allee, from Strausberger Platz to Frankfurter Tor, Friedrichshain (6576 3560, www.bierfestival-berlin.de). U5 Frankfurter Tor. **No credit cards.** **Map** p325 R6/S6.

Berlin's International Beer Festival showcases hundreds of beers from over 60 countries, bringing conviviality to the city's premier Stalinist boulevard.

Young.euro.classic

Konzerthaus, Gendarmenmarkt 2, Mitte (1805 568 100, www.young-euro-classic.de). U6 Französische Strasse. **Tickets** €12. **No credit cards.** **Date** 2wks in Aug. **Map** p322/p327 M7.

This annual summer concert programme brings together youth orchestras from around Europe.

Lange Nacht der Museen

Various venues (2474 9888. www.lange-nacht-der-museen.de). **Tickets** €15; €12 reductions. **Date** last Sat Jan & Aug.

Twice a year, around 100 of Berlin's museums, collections, archives and exhibition halls stay open into the early hours of the morning with special events, concerts, readings, lectures and performances for the 'Long Night of the Museums'. A ticket gets you free travel on special shuttle buses and regular public transport.

Musikfest Berlin

Various venues. Organisers: Berliner Festspiele (254 890, www.berlinerfestspiele.de). **Tickets** vary. **Date** 2-3 wks in early Sept.

The Berlin Symphony Orchestra collaborates with the Berlin Philharmonic and its conductor, Sir Simon Rattle, in a week of orchestral and chamber music, plus some musical theatre. Orchestras from London, New York and around Europe also participate.

AUTUMN

For the **Berlin Marathon**, *see p255*.

Berlin Music Week

Various venues (2474 9830, www.berlin-music-week-de). **Tickets** vary. **Date** 2nd wk Sept.

This week-long shindig is really several large music-related events rolled into one: the international trade fair Popkomm; All2gethernow, a 'new musci and culture convention'; two multi-venue clubbing festivals (Club Nacht and ClubSpreeBerlin); and the biggie – the two-day indie extravaganza known as the Berlin Festival.

Internationales Literaturfestival Berlin

Various venues (2787 8620, www.literatur festival.com). **Tickets** vary. **Date** 2wks in Sept.

A major literary event, with readings, symposiums and discussions attended by both well-known authors and rising stars from around the world.

Berlin International Film Festival

The stars come out.

For more than 60 years, the **Internationale Filmfestspiele Berlin** (www.berlinale.de) has been the city's biggest cultural event, as well as one of the world's three most prominent film festivals. Born out of the Cold War, it developed from a propaganda showcase, supported by the Allies, into a genuine meeting place – and frequent collision point – for East and West. Whether it was the 1959 French boycott over Stanley Kubrick's indictment of war, *Paths of Glory*, the jury revolt over the pro-Vietnamese film *OK* in 1970 or the 1979 Eastern Bloc walkout over the depiction of Vietnamese people in *The Deer Hunter*, the festival's drama was never confined to the screens. The years following the fall of the Berlin Wall were particularly exciting: the mood and energy of the festival reflected the joy and chaos of the changing city.

Now settled comfortably into Potsdamer Platz, the festival has taken on more of the glamour and celebrity of its two major rivals, Cannes and Venice. At the same time, Festival director Dieter Kosslick has concentrated on creating a more open and energetic atmosphere to the proceedings.

What remains the same, however, is the chance to see arguably the widest and most eclectic mix of any film festival anywhere. Every February, it seems like the entire city turns out to see hundreds of films, presented in eight sections, the most important of which are as follows:

THE INTERNATIONAL COMPETITION

Recent years have seen a rise in the glamour quotient and star attendance. The downside to this is that the selection is becoming more conservative. Concentrating on major, big-budget productions from all over the world, with a heavy (and often heavily criticised) accent on the US, these films often make it to general release. Entries compete for the Gold and Silver Bears, announced at the closing night gala.

THE INTERNATIONAL FORUM OF YOUNG CINEMA

Some devotees claim this is the real Berlin festival, the place where discoveries are made. Born out of the revolt that dissolved the Competition in 1970, the Forum provides challenging and eclectic fare that you won't see elsewhere.

PANORAMA

Originally intended to showcase films that fell outside the guidelines of the Competition, the Panorama shines a spotlight on world independent movies, gay and lesbian and political films.

PERSPEKTIVE DEUTSCHES KINO

Perspektive reflects the festival's increased focus on the latest in German cinema. The newest of the festival's sections, it has emerged as a big audience favourite, helped by the fact that all films are shown with English subtitles. If you think German cinema has a bad rep, this is where to break down the stereotypes.

RETROSPECTIVE

Perhaps the festival's best bet for sheer movie-going pleasure. The Retrospective often concentrates on the mainstream, but it's an opportunity to experience classics and rarities on the big screen. Themes have ranged from great directors such as Louis Buñuel, Fritz Lang and William Wyler, to subjects like 1950s glamour girls, production design, Hollywood mavericks and even Nazi entertainment films.

TICKETS

Tickets can be bought up to three days in advance (four days for Competition repeats) at the main ticket office in the **Arkaden am Potsdamer Platz** (Alte Potsdamer Strasse, Tiergarten, 259 2000), and at Kino, International and Urania. Tickets are also available for online booking. On the day of performance they must be bought at the theatre box office and last-minute tickets are often available. Queues for advance tickets can be long and online tickets can go fast, so plan ahead. Daily screening listings and film reviews can be found in industry dailies put out by *Variety*, *Hollywood Reporter* and *Screen International*, available free at most of the surrounding hotels.

Films are usually shown three times. Prices range from €8-€20. Berlinale Palast is cheaper during the day and all films showing on the last day – Berlinale Kinotag – play at reduced prices. From January onwards, check for updates and programme information on the website at www.berlinale.de.

ARTS & ENTERTAINMENT

Spielzeit'europa

Various venues. Organisers: Berliner Festspiele (254 890, www.berlinerfestspiele.de). **Tickets** vary. **Date** autumn.

This forum for theatre and dance from around Europe showcases work that incorporates new political and aesthetic ideas from a specifically European perspective. It's supplemented by German co-productions. Shows run on and off for five months.

Tag der deutschen Einheit

Date Oct 3.

A bank holiday commemorating the day two Germanies became one, back in 1990. Head to the Brandenburg Gate to join the party.

JazzFest Berlin

Various venues. Organisers: Berliner Festspiele (254 890, www.berlinerfestspiele.de). **Tickets** vary. **Date** 1st weekend Nov.

A wide spectrum of jazz from an array of internationally renowned artists, and a fixture since 1964. The concurrent Fringe Jazz Festival (organised by JazzRadio) showcases less established acts.

Berliner Märchentage

Various venues (2809 3603, www.berliner-maerchentage.de). **Tickets** vary. **Date** 2-3wks in mid Nov.

The Berlin Fairytale Festival celebrates tales from around the world each year with some 400 storytelling and music events in a carnival atmosphere.

Worldtronics

Haus der Kulturen der Welt, John-Foster-Dulles-Allee 10, Tiergarten (3978 7175, www.hkw.de). *Bus 100.* **Tickets** vary. **Date** 4 days in Nov/Dec. **Map** p318 K6.

A festival showcasing the world of electronic music in a city that loves the stuff. Guest musicians come from all over.

WINTER

See also p198 **Lange Nacht der Museen**.

Christmas Markets

Kaiser-Wilhelm-Gedächtniskirche, Breitscheidplatz, Charlottenburg (213 3290, www.weihnachtsmarkt-deutschland.de). U2, U9, S3, S5, S7, S9, S75 Zoologischer Garten. **Open** 11am-10pmpm daily. **Map** p321 G8.

Traditional markets spring up across Berlin during the Christmas season, offering toys, mulled wine and gingerbread. This is one of the biggest.

Berliner Silvesterlauf

Grunewald (3012 8820, www.berlin-marathon.com/events/index.php). S5, S75 Messe Süd. **Entrance fee** €7.50-€15, €5-€10 reductions;. **Date** 31 Dec.

A local Berlin tradition for decades, the New Year's Eve Run (aka the 'pancake run') starts off in Grunewald at the intersection of Waldschulallee and Harbigstrasse.

Silvester

Date 31 Dec.

Given Berliners' enthusiasm for tossing firecrackers and launching rockets out of windows, New Year's Eve is always going to be vivid, noisy and hazardous. Thousands celebrate at the Brandenburger Tor. Thousands more trek up to the Teufelsberg at the northern tip of Grunewald or the Viktoriapark in Kreuzberg to watch the fireworks across the city.

Grüne Woche

Messegelände am Funkturm, Messedamm 22, Charlottenburg (3038 2267, www.gruene woche.de). U2 Kaiserdamm, S3, S5, S75 Messe Süd or S41, S42, S46, U2 Messe Nord S3, S41, S42, S46, S5, S7, S75 Westkreuz. **Tickets** €12. **No credit cards.** **Date** 10 days in Jan. **Map** p320 A8.

Dedicated to food, agriculture and horticulture, the best thing about this show is the opportunity to eat and drink from the far corners of Germany and across the planet.

UltraSchall

Various venues. Organisers: Deutschlandradio Kultur (850 30, www.dradio.de/ultraschall). **Tickets** €8-€18. **Date** 10 days in mid Jan.

New music presented in high-profile venues by some of the world's leading specialist ensembles. Concerts are often broadcast live by the stations Deutschlandradio and Kulturradio.

Transmediale

Haus der Kulturen der Welt, John-Foster-Dulles-Allee 10, Tiergarten (2474 9761, www.transmediale.de). Bus 100. **Tickets** vary. **Date** 5 days in late Jan/early Feb. **Map** p317 H6.

One of the world's largest international festivals for media art and digital culture, with exhibitions and screenings from artists working with video, television, computer animation, internet and other visual media and digital technologies.

Berlin International Film Festival

Potsdamer Platz, Tiergarten & other venues (259 200, www.berlinale.de). S1, S2, S25, U2 Potsdamer Platz. **Tickets** €7-€16. *Festival pass* €100. **Date** 1-2wks in mid Feb.

Now over 60 years old, the Berlinale is one of the world's major cinema festivals, featuring over 300 movies from all five continents. It is centred at the Potsdamer Platz cinemas and attended by international stars, providing this normally glamour-proof city with a bit of glitz in the dead of winter. *See also p201.*

Children

The kids are all right, as far as Berlin is concerned.

Despite its reputation for grown-up hedonism, Berlin is a remarkably child-friendly city. So few locals can afford the luxury of a garden that there are parks all over town – most with the usual swings and roundabouts, some with fantastic adventure playgrounds. At all of Berlin's national museums, under-19s enjoy free admission. Many have decent children's sections, and tickets to one kids' attraction often include a discount voucher for another. There are also superb indoor and outdoor swimming pools to cool off in during the summer months and cosy cafés with dry play areas for rainy days.

GETTING AROUND

Children under six travel free on Berlin's excellent public transport system. That's the good news. The bad news is that a lot of the stations still don't have lifts, so you'll either need to carry buggies upstairs yourself or rely on the kindness of strangers – and Berliners are not known for their altruism. Luckily, most U- and S-bahn stations are not buried very far underground, so you'll never have to do too much heavy lifting. Plus there are no barriers, so you don't have to worry about getting stuck in a turnstile with a pram.

Buses, however, are a breeze. They are designed to tilt towards the pavement at each stop, making it easy to get on with a pushchair or pram, and all vehicles have a designated parking area for *Kinderwagen*. The No.100 and No.200 buses are usually double-decker and run right through all the key tourist destinations. Kids love sitting on the top deck and parents love the price – just the cost of a normal single transport ticket.

For older children, cycling is an option. There are cycle lanes all over town and numerous off-road paths weaving through the city's parks. **Fat Tire Bikes** (Panoramastrasse 1a, Alexanderplatz, 2404 7991, www.berlinfahrr adverleih.com) rents out children's bikes of all shapes and sizes, as well as children's bike seats and even bike trailers to pop your sprogs in.

BABYSITTERS

The bigger hotels sometimes have a babysitting service, but there are a number of English speaking agencies operating in Berlin.

Babysitter-Express Berlin

4000 3 400, www.babysitter-express.de.
This firm operates a 24-hour hotline for all your babysitting emergencies.

Kinderinsel

Eichendorffstrasse 17, Mitte (4171 6928/38, www.kinderinsel.de/en).
This 'children's hotel' offers round-the-clock child-care for children aged 0-14. Drop off your darlings for a few hours or a few days.

WHAT'S ON

To find out what's on, pick up *Tip* or *Zitty*, Berlin's fortnightly listings magazines, and look under the 'Kinder' or 'Familie' section.

MITTE

There's no problem keeping children busy in Mitte. **Museumsinsel** (*see p62*), with its museums and weekend flea market, is a lively spot to visit. The **Bode Museum** (*see p64*) is

INSIDE TRACK KIDS' CLUB

Once a month, one of Berlin's coolest club impresarios, Cookies, puts on a kids' event under the banner Kidz Want Cookies (www.kidzwantcookies.com). Previous shindigs have included Halloween face painting, cookery courses, and arts and crafts sessions:

Mount Mitte.

particularly good for kids – it houses a special interactive children's museum (Kindermuseum) aimed at four- to ten-year-olds. Nearby **Monbijou Park** on Oranienburger Strasse – just over the pedestrian bridge by the Bode Museum – has playgrounds and, in summer, a great wading pool, the Kinderbad Monbijou. For a different perspective, try a boat tour, many of which operate from the Museumsinsel and nearby (*see p97* **Boot Trips**). For a bird's-eye view, scan the city from the **Fernsehturm** (TV Tower; *see p71*) on Alexanderplatz. Down below, children cool off in the **Neptunbrunnen** (*see p70*) during the summer months. Also on the 'Alex', in the Alexa Shopping Centre, is **Loxx Miniature Welten** (4472 3022, www.loxx-berlin.de, open 10am-8pm daily) featuring a working miniature railway that chugs around a scale model of Berlin.

Children will enjoy the dinosaur skeletons and new multimedia displays at the **Museum für Naturkunde** (Museum of Natural History; *see p67*), the mummies at the **Ägyptisches Museum** in the Neues Museum (*see p64*) and the interactive exhibits at the **Museum für Kommunikation** (*see p65*). For a pricier treat, there's **Legoland** in the Sony Center at Potsdamer Platz (*see p207* **Children at Work**). Children aged seven and over will enjoy **MountMitte**, an outdoor rope course strung up by Nord Bahnhof.

AquaDom & Sea Life (*see p70*) has 13 aquaria and plenty of hands-on gadgetry. Its centrepiece is the mighty AquaDom itself, a cylindrical saltwater tank with a glass lift rising through the centre, from which you can view some of the thousands of exotic fish.

Many restaurants in Mitte have children's menus, but the area around Hackesche Höfe and Rosenthaler Strasse offers the richest pickings, with cafés and restaurants of every type.

PRENZLAUER BERG & FRIEDRICHSHAIN

Prenzlauer Berg has enjoyed something of a baby boom in recent years, although it has few specific attractions for kids. There are, however, plenty of cafés, restaurants, squares and playgrounds, particularly around Kollwitzplatz and Helmholtzplatz. **Das Spielzimmer** (Schliemannstrasse 37, 4403 7635, www.das-spielzimmer.net) is a very successful combination of indoor playground and café complete with slides and a dressing-up box. North of Schönhauser Allee station is **Café Milchbart** (Paul-Robeson-Strasse 6, 6630 7755, www.milchbart.net), a family-oriented place with ballpond, climbing frame and excellent healthy food options.

Friedrichshain is slightly less kiddie-tastic, though there are plenty of family-friendly cafés – art centre-cum-café **Amitola** (Krossener Strasse 35, Friedrichshain (2936 1871, www.amitola-berlin.de) comes highly recommended. **Paul & Paula** (Richard-Sorge-Strasse 25, 4208 9440, www.paul-und-paula.de), a café and shop rolled into one, is particularly geared up for babies. Older children will love the **Raw Tempel** (Revaler Strasse 99), a sports and arts complex housed in a dilapidated set of old factories that includes Der Kegel climbing centre (www.derkegel.de) and the Skatehalle indoor skateboarding centre (www.skatehalle-berlin.de). The **Computerspielemuseum** (Computer Games Museum; *see p76*) on Karl-Marx-Allee is fun for teenagers.

Die Schaubude (Greifswalder Strasse 81-84, 423 4314, www.schaubude-berlin.de, closed Mon) is a high-quality puppet theatre used by local and visiting troupes. **Machmit**! (Senefelderstrasse 5, 7477 8200, www.machmitmuseum.de) is a modern children's museum with arts and crafts sessions. **Volkspark Friedrichshain**

(*see p76*) has half-pipes and skater routes for skaters, and the Märchenbrunnen ('fairy tale fountain') features figures from stories by the Brothers Grimm.

KREUZBERG

This vibrant borough has lots to offer kids. Older children will enjoy the **Haus am Checkpoint Charlie** (*see p82*), which displays the old cars and balloons that people used to circumvent the Wall. And they'll love the **Grusel Kabinett** (*see p81*), a spooky chamber of horrors in an old World War II bunker. For an expensive but novel vertical adventure, there's the **Hi-Flyer** (*see p81*), a hot-air balloon that, weather permitting, floats 150 metres (500 feet) above ground near Checkpoint Charlie. Along Zimmer Strasse is the Stasi education centre, a good introduction for teenagers and adults into the nefarious machinations of the East German secret service. The **Deutsches Technikmuseum Berlin** (*see p81*) has vintage locomotives and cars, computers and gadgets, and a maritime wing with boats. Entrance tickets include access to the superb Spectrum and its fantastic hands-on experiments.

Neue City Bowling Hasenheide (*see p257*) has 12 lanes for children and is open from 10am daily. The Hasenheide park next door has a great adventure playground, crazy golf course and small zoo. The little vale in the middle of the park is ideal for tobogganing when it snows.

Leafy **Viktoriapark** (*see p78*) is a landscaped hill with fine views, and another good place for tobogganing when weather permits. In summer, a waterfall cascades down to street level. The park also has playgrounds and a tiny zoo. The best ice-cream in Berlin is just a few blocks north at **Max & Marille** (Hagelbergerstrasse 1, www.vanille-marille.de). Stroll down nearby Bergmannstrasse for a wide choice of food options. Close by is the huge supervised indoor playground **Jolo** (Am Tempelhofer Berg 7D, 6120 2796, www.jolo-berlin.de). Facilities include an inflatable mountain, mini bumper cars and a snack

bar. One of the nicest children's cafés in Berlin is not far away – **Cafe Kreuzzwerg** (Hornstrasse 23, 9786 7609, www.cafe-kreuzzwerg.com) has fantastic coffee and loads to keep little ones amused.

A walk along the south bank of the canal on Carl-Herz-Ufer will take you to the **Brachvogel** beer garden (*see p166*), which has a crazy golf course and a playground next door. On the other side of the river is the slightly anarchic **Sommerbad Kreuzberg** lido complex (*see p263*) with a big children's pool and slide. Further east, on the north bank, is **Statthaus Böcklerpark** with its small petting zoo. It organises a monthly children's flea market as well as other events. Further east again and back on the south side is the child-friendly **Casolare** (Grimmstrasse 30, 6950 6610), which does great pizzas. For dessert, cross the road to **Isabel's Eiscafé** (Böckstrasse 51).

At the east end of the borough is **Görlitzer Park**, with playgrounds and another petting zoo to keep the little ones happy. Also in the park, the glow-in-the-dark mini golf at Schwarzlicht (*see p259*) is a good option for older children, especially on a rainy day.

SCHÖNEBERG

Winterfeldplatz is a pleasant focal point at the northern end of this huge district, with lots of cafés, restaurants and fast food around the square and along Maassenstrasse to the north and Goltzstrasse to the south. There are plenty of parks and playgrounds here.

In the south of the borough, **Natur-Park Schöneberger Südgelände** (www.gruen-berlin.de) is an old railway shunting yard left for nature to reclaim. There's lots for the kids to explore – and no dog mess or crazy cyclists.

Nearby is the **Planetarium am Insulaner** (Munsterdamm 90, 790 0930, www.wfs.be. schule.de), which has programmes for children.

The **Volkspark Wilmersdorf** has several good playgrounds (including one with a ski lift ride). Near the park's eastern end is **Stadtbad Schöneberg** (*see p263*), a swimming pool that's ideal for kids. Inside the Schöneberg Museum is the **Jugendmuseum** (Hauptstrasse 40/42, 902 776 163, www.jugendmuseum.de), a hands-on children's exhibition which offers small visitors the chance to play with everything from a Germanic sacrificial cow to a Barbie doll.

There are child-friendly restaurants all over Schöneberg. Try hearty pasta at **Petite Europe** (*see p152*). Café A-ngels (Motz Strasse 52, www.cafe-angels.de) is a great place to hang out with children and babies – there's free Wi-Fi if you manage to get them to sleep.

ARTS & ENTERTAINMENT

INSIDE TRACK
TODDLER TRAPEZE

By Görlitzer Park in Kreuzberg is the Cabuwazi Zirkus (Wiener Strasse 59, 5446 9094, www.cabuwazi.de), a big top where children can learn circus skills. There are also performances by a young theatre troupe.

ARTS & ENTERTAINMENT

TIERGARTEN

The major draw in Tiergarten is the park itself, with its playgrounds and open spaces. Pedaloes and rowing boats can be hired near the **Café am Neuen See** (*see p170*), which has a great beer garden in summer. Meanwhile, along Strasse des 17 Juni, the main road through the park, there's an interesting flea market at weekends (*see p175*).

In the park's south-western corner is Berlin's beautiful **Zoo** (*see p91*), which used to be the home to the abandoned polar bear Knut (RIP). On rainy days, head for the Zoo's sizeable **Aquarium**. The excellent **Gemäldegalerie** (*see p90*) in Matthäikirchplatz runs Sunday afternoon tours for children.

CHARLOTTENBURG

Away from the bustle of Zoologischer Garten and the Ku'damm, the atmosphere is pleasant, with good restaurants, shops and markets. The Saturday market at Karl-August-Platz is a gathering point for families, with a playground and plenty of cafés. If the sun's out, check out **Zwergenland** (Mommsenstrasse 48), a Snow White and the Seven Dwarves-themed playground or **Piratenspielplatz** (Tegeler Weg 97 & corner of Bonhoeffer Ufer, www.piraten restaurant.de), a pirate-inspired playground with pirate ship and pirate restaurant.

Fifteen minutes' walk west is the pretty **Lietzenseepark**, with a lake, playgrounds, cafés (open Apr-Oct) and sports areas. If the weather's not great, take the kids to **Pingulino** indoor playground (Wintersteinstrasse 22, 3454 0346, www.pingulino.de). There are child-friendly restaurants all over Charlottenburg, particularly to the east. The kids will be welcome for Italian food at **La Cantina** (Bleibtreustrasse 17, 883 2156) or **Totò** (corner of Bleibtreustrasse & Pestalozzistrasse, 312 5449, www.trattoria-toto.de). At **Charlottchen** (Droysenstrasse 1, 324 4717, www.charlottchen-berlin.de), parents eat in the dining room (the

international food is nothing special) while kids let their hair down in a rumpus room. There are theatre performances on Sundays (11.30am, 3.30pm, €5). The most child-friendly museum in the area is the **Story of Berlin** (*see p95*), probably the only history museum they won't tire of after ten minutes.

OTHER DISTRICTS

The **ufaFabrik** cultural centre (Viktoriastrasse 10-18, 755 030, www.ufafabrik.de), in the southern district of Tempelhof, has a farm, several cafés and restaurants, a circus and a variety of courses and workshops. It's right by U-Bahn Ullsteinstrasse (U6).

In the wilds of Neukölln, **Britzer Garten** (www.gruen-berlin.de) is perfect for small children. The immaculately manicured gardens with their once-futuristic architecture look like something out of the *Teletubbies*, and there are farm animals, playgrounds, a narrow-gauge railway, a working 19th-century windmill and plenty of food and drink options.

South-west of the city, the vast **Grunewald** woods (*see p103*) are perfect for long walks, and the Kronprinzessinnenweg, which runs through the middle, is ideal for rollerblading and cycling. On a breezy day, fly a kite and enjoy the view from the **Teufelsberg** (*see p103*); on a sunny day, take a dip in the **Teufelsee** (*see p103*) or any of the area's numerous lakes. **Strandbad Wannsee** (*see p104*) is Europe's largest inland beach; there's a playground, cafés and pedalos. The 204-step climb up the **Grunewaldturm** (Havelchaussee, 300 0730) is rewarded with a beautiful view of the Havel river and surroundings, and there's a restaurant and beer garden too.

To the east of the Grunewald, **Domäne Dahlem** (*see p102*) is a 1600s-style working farm featuring demonstrations by blacksmiths, carpenters, bakers and potters, plus ponies, tractors and hay wagons to ride. **Museumsdorf Düppel** (*see p105*) is a reconstructed 14th-century village around archaeological excavations near the Düppel forest. From April to October, kids can ride ox carts or witness medieval technology, crafts and farming techniques.

To avoid summer crowds on the Havel and Wannsee, try the **Tegeler See** to the north-west of the centre. In bad weather, take refuge at **Jack's Fun World** (Miraustrasse 38, 4190 0242, www.jacks-fun-world.de, closed Mon). Be warned: the extra fees for the best attractions at this indoor playground can add up. North-east of Tegel, in the quaint village of Alt Lübars, is **Jugendfarm Lübars** (415 7027, www.jugend-reinickendorf.de/jugendfarm, closed Oct-Mar & Mon), with farm animals and traditional crafts.

South-east of the centre, the **Mellowpark** in Köpenick (Friedrichshagener Strasse 10-12, 652 603 771, www.mellowpark.de) offers supervised play for older children. Activities, daily from 2pm in summer, include skateboarding, basketball and BMX on the banks of the Spree.

Also to the east is the **Tierpark Berlin-Friedrichsfelde** (*see p107*), a lovely park and zoo, with playgrounds, a petting zoo and snack stands. Still further east, the **Müggelsee** (*see p107*) is another beautiful sailing and swimming area. There are day trips by boat from Mitte in the summer.

Out in Marzahn, the **Erholungspark** (Eisenacher Strasse, www.gruen-berlin.de) has oriental gardens, a 'garden of stones' with ponds, fountains and boulders, and a 'rhododendron grove' with statues of characters from Hans-Christian Andersen and the Brothers Grimm. It's dotted with playgrounds, kiosks and cafés.

Children at Work

Everybody loves Lego.

The kids waited patiently as you queued for 45 minutes to get into the Reichstag. And they were absolute angels as the family traipsed around the Bauhaus Archiv looking at chairs. When they've been so good, reward them with the **Legoland Discovery Centre Berlin** (Sony Center, Potsdamer Platz, Tiergarten, www.lego landdiscoverycentre.com/berlin).

The entrance is on ground level behind the giant Lego giraffe outside the Sony Center. The facility itself is in the basement, divided into seven themed areas featuring things to do with Lego bricks, and startling displays made from them. It's focused on kids aged three to ten, who can easily spend a few hours here, unwinding from sightseeing and reconnecting to the familiar build-and-dream world that is Lego.

The Discovery Centre is more of an indoor playground than an educational experience. There's a bit of subtle branding going on – kids can 'discover' how Lego bricks are made in a hokey mock-up of an assembly line, for example. But, no matter how, the appeal is old-fashioned open space, piles of soft, oversized Lego bricks, well-stocked tables where kids can build, and nobody telling them what to do.

Boys tend to gravitate to a couple of ramps where they can race the Lego vehicles they've put together on the workbenches. Close by is a corner where girls are quietly engineering Lego families to inhabit Lego doll's houses. A concession serves reasonably priced drinks and snacks.

In the Modellbau Workshop, small groups of adults and their children receive step-by-step instructions on how to build customised Lego models. Fascinating how a handful of bricks can be swiftly ordered into a pretty convincing Brandenburg Gate; frustrating, though, that you can't keep it as a souvenir.

The Dschungel Expedition is a dark grotto and pastiche of the Indiana Jones films, with jaw-snapping alligators and a giant Lego spider with LED eyes. There's a ride called the Drachenberg in which gondolas that look like dragons whisk you on a spooky tour of a castle. Many of the Lego figures here are actually quite scary in an *Alice in Wonderland* kind of way, and the giant red Lego dragon at the end is lost on the very youngest kids, most of whom have already screwed up their eyes in fear.

Upstairs, Miniland is an expansive, animated cityscape of Lego Berlin landmarks, with the towers of Potsdamer Platz, the Victorian brickwork of Hackescher Markt station and the imposing Berliner Dom all built from the bobbly bricks.

In front of the mini Reichstag is a blinking stage where the Berlin reggae band Seed is playing to a spellbound Lego crowd. For adults, the fascination of Miniland is the discovery of a truth our kids knew all along: with a little imagination and a bunch of Lego bricks, there is nothing you cannot build.

ARTS & ENTERTAINMENT

Film

A world-class festival, historic cinemas and cheap tickets.

The first cinema opened in Berlin in 1895 and the city was soon full of movie palaces such as the Marmorhaus, with its huge white marble façade; the Lichtburg, which looked like a futuristic light sculpture; and the grandest of them all, the Ufa Palast Am Zoo. The latter had an ever-changing façade designed to reflect whatever premiere it was hosting – sweeping searchlights for Fritz Lang's *Spione*, illuminated Nazi banners for Leni Riefenstahl's *Olympia*; or a spaceship flying across the starlit exterior for Lang's *Frau Im Mond*.

THE CINEMAS

That was then. Now, like almost everywhere, the glory days of cinema-going in Berlin are over. While the city still has an impressive 280-plus screens, most of them show big blockbuster fodder.

But a burgeoning alternative film-going scene does exist. Indie mainstays such as **Eiszeit** and **Central** have recently got their groove back, the **Moviemento** is better than ever, and **Babylon-Mitte** has shaken off its stodgy mindset and spiced up its schedule. And all seem to have English programming more in evidence.

For monophones, traditional all-English venues **Odeon** and **Babylon Kreuzberg** are also still there, and all eight screens at the **Cinestar Potsdamer Platz** show English language-fare.

One surviving Berlin phenomenon is the city's fascination with silent films, often presented with live musical accompaniment, ranging from simple piano to full orchestra with the occasional hardcore band for variety. Favourites include historical hits such as *Metropolis* and *The Cabinet of Dr Caligari*. Babylon-Mitte now has a regular silent film programme and films tend to show up at the **Arsenal**, or any of the outdoor cinemas (*see right* **Starry Nights**).

There are five film museums in and around the city – the **Museum für Film und Fernsehen** (*see p90*) on Potsdamer Platz, which includes a special exhibition about Berlin's favourite daughter, Marlene Dietrich, and the **Filmpark Babelsberg** (*see p277*), near Potsdam. Since 2010, Berlin even has its own answer to the Hollywood Walk of Fame, the rather underwhelming Boulevard der Stars on Potsdamer Strasse.

FESTIVALS

The **Berlin Film Festival**, or Berlinale (*see p201*), is the biggest and most prominent of the international film festivals, but it's far from the only game in town.

The **Fantasy Film Festival** (www.fantasyfilmfest.com) shows the latest in fantasy, splatter, horror and sci-fi from the US, Hong Kong, Japan and Europe. Films are often premieres, with occasional previews, retrospectives and rarities. Most shows are in English or with English subtitles. The festival takes place at the Cinemaxx in Potsdamer Platz around mid August.

Mid August also offers the **Globian World & Culture Documentary Film Festival** (www.globians.com) in Potsdam, a week-long event featuring documentaries from world filmmakers shown in English or with English subtitles. It has a real DIY spirit of sharing movies and information, and with an admission price of €3 per show or €30 for the whole week's packed programme, it's definitely worth the trip out to Potsdam.

Along similar lines is the **One World Berlin Festival** (www.oneworld-berlin.de), which takes place in November, an extension of an event in Prague. Nominally centred around human rights issues, the festival casts a wide net to include films on politics, religion, theatre, music, art and culture. At least half of the programme is in English or with English subtitles.

Starry Nights

Berlin's open-air screens are a perfect summer treat.

During winter, Berlin's cinemas are a welcome retreat from the bitter wind and cold. But come summer, few people want to spend their evenings gobbling popcorn in a dark, windowless room – which is where Berlin's *Freiluftkino* (open-air cinemas) come in. On a clement night, it's one of the most enjoyable – and quintessentially *Berlinerisch* – things to do in the capital. Tickets cost €6-€7 and if it rains, the show goes on, so you're well advised to bring warm clothes and a brolly. Most places have plastic chairs or deckchairs, but bring something to sit on just in case.

The films tend not to start until after 9.45pm, when it gets dark, so you have plenty of time to go out for dinner first. Tickets are generally on sale half an hour before showtime. It's worth getting there early, or calling up to reserve tickets in advance, as screenings often sell out very quickly in good weather.

The majority of films shown are dubbed into German, but there are often English originals shown at the **Freiluftkino Kreuzberg** (Mariannenplatz 2, Kreuzberg, www.freiluftkino-kreuzberg.de), set in the leafy garden of the Haus Bethanien cultural centre, which is also home to the elegant 3 Schwestern restaurant (*see p148*). Open from June to August, it offers a mix of past blockbuster hits, cult films and independent movies.

There are two al fresco cinemas in Friedrichshain. The **Freiluft Kino Insel im Cassiopedia** (Revalerstrasse 99, Friedrichshain, 5471 3247, www.freiluft kino-insel.de) has free blankets and umbrellas for hire. The **Freiluftkino Friedrichshain** in the Volkspark (Landsberger Allee, Friedrichshain, www.freiluftkino-berlin.de) has 300 seats, or you can just bring a blanket and picnic and lounge on the grass. Both sell cold drinks, popcorn and free-range sausages. Buggies and prams are welcome.

The **Freiluft Kino Hasenheide** (Volkspark, Neukölln, 283 4603, www.freiluftkino-hasenheide.de), on the border between Kreuzberg and Neukölln, shows a mix of dubbed and original versions of both blockbusters and indie hits. It's next to a petting zoo, so don't be surprised if a goat breaks the tension during a particularly nail-biting scene.

Rather ritzier is the **Sommerkino Kulturforum/Potsdamer Platz** (Matthäikirchplatz 4/6, Tiergarten, www.yorck.de), in between the Philarmonie and Neuer Nationalgalerie, where up to a thousand people can lounge in deckchairs and enjoy classics in their original language.

If you have wheels and want the outdoor experience without the risk of getting wet, check out the **AutoKino Berlin-Mitte** (Kurt Schumacher Damm 207, Reinickendorf, www.das-autokino.de). Yes, it's a real drive-in and while the films are typical Hollywood dubbed into German, it's still a fun, quirky night out.

ARTS & ENTERTAINMENT

Şommerkino Kulturforum.

The **InterFilm Short Film Festival** (www.interfilm.de), also in November, is 23 years old and has grown from a DIY affair into an international event with big buck prizes. It shows over 500 short films from 88 countries, organised into themes such as Miniature Cinema, Love and Insanities, Films by Children, and a programme of midnight movie madness called Eject. Its current home is the Babylon-Mitte with events and parties at the nearby Volksbühne. InterFilm is also responsible for Going Underground, a mini festival of 14 short silent films shown on LCD screens on the U-Bahn in the first week of February. They claim to have Berlin's largest attendance – a (captive) audience of over 1.5 million passengers.

In the spring it's **Britspotting**, the British Independent Film Festival (www.brit spotting.de), an annual compilation of the freshest new (and occasionally mainstream) cinema from the UK and Ireland. Organised by the British Council, it appears in April/May.

Gay and lesbian films are put under the spotlight at **Verzaubert: The International Queer Film Festival** (www.verzaubert filmfest.com), which takes place in April at Kino International (*see p212*). Also check out the year-round MonGay series at Kino International for weekly Queer Cinema premieres and specials.

Transmediale (www.transmediale.de) is an international five-day programme of digital presentations, installations and performances that currently finds a home at the Haus der Kulturen der Welt (*see p85*) and leaves a month-long exhibition in its wake. There are also events and parties at various Berlin clubs.

INFORMATION

Check listings in *tip* and *Zitty*, as well as *(030)*, available free in many bars. An alphabetical overview of cinemas can be found online at www.berlinien.de/kino/kinoprogramm.html.

Watch for the notation OV or OF ('original version' or '*Originalfassung*'), OmU ('original with subtitles') or OmE ('original with English subtitles'). But watch out, OmU could just as easily be a French or Chinese movie with German titles. The cinemas listed here are those most likely to be showing films in English. Various combinations of Monday, Tuesday and Wednesday are known as *Kinotag*, offering reduced admission, and some cinemas offer deals on pre-paid ticket bookings. Even full-price tickets are generally cheaper than in London or New York.

CINEMAS

Arsenal

Potsdamer Strasse 2, Tiergarten (2695 5100, www.arsenal-berlin.de). U2, S1, S2, S25 Potsdamer Platz. **Tickets** €6.50; €5 reductions. **No credit cards. Map** p322 L7.

ARTS & ENTERTAINMENT

Odeon. *See p212.*

Berlin's own cinematheque continues to offer brazenly eclectic programming, ranging from classic Hollywood to contemporary Middle Eastern cinema, Russian art films to Italian horror movies, Third World documentaries with live accompaniment. Also check out its perpetually running series, The History of Film in 365 Films. The Arsenal shows plenty of English-language films and some foreign films with English subtitles. Its two state-of-the-art screening rooms in the Sony Center make it a welcome corrective to its multiplex neighbours.

▶ *The Arsenal is one of the core venues for the Berlin International Film Festival (see p201).*

Astor Film Lounge

Kurfürstendamm 255, Charlottenburg (883 8551, www.astor-filmlounge.de). U1, U9 Kurfürstendamm. **Tickets** €10-€18. **Map** p321 G8.

The first 'premium cinema' in Germany offers a luxury cinematographic experience complete with a welcome cocktail, doorman and valet parking. The building dates from 1948, when a café was converted into a small cinema called the KiKi (Kino im Kindl). It was later redesigned and renamed the Filmpalast, and become one of West Berlin's classiest *Kinos*. After thorough renovations and another name change, it's still a grand example of 1950s movie-going luxury with an illuminated glass ceiling, comfortable seats and a gong to announce the show.

Babylon Kreuzberg (A&B)

Dresdener Strasse 126, Kreuzberg, 10999 (6160 9693, www.yorck.de). U1, U8 Kottbusser Tor. **Tickets** €5.50-€8. **No credit cards**. **Map** p323 P9. Another Berlin perennial, this twin-screen theatre runs a varied programme featuring indie crossover and UK films. Formerly a neighbourhood Turkish cinema, its programme is now almost all English-language and it offers a homey respite from the multiplex experience.

★ Babylon-Mitte

Rosa-Luxemburg-Strasse 30, Mitte (242 5969, www.babylonberlin.de). U2, U5, U8, S3, S5, S7, S75 Alexanderplatz or U2 Rosa-Luxemburg-Platz. **Tickets** €6.50; €3 reductions. **No credit cards**. **Map** p319 O5.

Housed in a restored landmark building by Hans Poelzig, the former Filmkunsthaus Babylon recently reinvented itself with a much more active programming policy. While it nominally focuses on new German independent cinema, English-language fare is on the up, particularly in its regular Schräge Filme (Weird Films) programme; and its foreign film series tend to have English subtitles. Tuesdays are silent film nights, with live musical accompaniment.

Central

Rosenthaler Strasse 39, Mitte (2859 9973, www.kino-central.de). U8 Weinmeisterstrasse or S3, S5, S7, S75 Hackescher Markt. **Tickets** €5.50-€6.50. **No credit cards**. **Map** p319 N5.

Still hanging in there with a programming attitude that's uniquely its own, this place is worth a look for its various series spotlighting pop/trash culture and all forms of exploitation film. In summer, there's an outdoor cinema in the back courtyard.

CineStar Sony Center

Potsdamer Strasse 4, Tiergarten (2606 6400, www.cinestar.de). U2, S1, S2, S25 Potsdamer Platz. **Tickets** €6-€10; €9-€11 for 3D movies. **No credit cards**. **Map** p322 L7.

CineStar has eight screens showing films exclusively in their original language, mostly English. Despite a few random sparks of creativity, it is basically mainstream fare and all major releases tend to show up here. Counteract the high prices by buying the Five-Star ticket – five films for €32.50.

▶ *This is another major venue for the Berlin International Film Festival (see p201).*

Colosseum

Schönhauser Allee 123, Prenzlauer Berg (440 19 200, www.uci-kinowelt.de/berlin_colosseum). U2 S8, S42, S41 Schönhauser Allee. **Tickets** €5.20-€7.80; €4.30-€5 reductions. Off the map. Built in 1924 from a stable for the horses that pulled the first trams, the Colosseum was restored by the Soviets to become the finest cinema in East Berlin. Although it was turned into a multiplex in the late 1990s, the original auditorium is still in use, restored to 1950s splendour. In the lobby you can see the brick walls of the stables, complete with the rings used to tie up the horses.

Delphi Filmpalast am Zoo

Kantstrasse 12a, Charlottenburg (312 1026, www.delphi-filmpalast.de). U1 Uland Strasse. **Tickets** €5.50-€9. **Map** p321 F8. The Delphi was originally a 1920s dance palace. Bombed out during the war, it was rebuilt as the Delphi Filmpalast and became a major Cinemascope

ARTS & ENTERTAINMENT

and 70mm venue where films such as *Ben Hur* and *My Fair Lady* would run for up to a year. It has the city's last working balcony.

Eiszeit
Zeughofstrasse 20, Kreuzberg (611 6016, www.eiszeit-kino.de). U1, U15 Görlitzer Bahnhof. **Tickets** €5-€7; €6 reductions. **No credit cards.** **Map** p323 Q9.
Eiszeit offers a wide range of alternative cinema – with a recent accent on pop music films – and a good amount of English-language programming. It also hosts readings, performances and live music, and is home to a number of small film festivals.

Filmtheater Am Friedrichshain
Bötzowstrasse 1-5, Friedrichshain (4284 5188, www.yorck.de). Bus 200. **Tickets** €5.50-€8; €8.50-€11 for 3D films; €4.50 children's films. **Map** p319 Q4.
This charming five-screen cinema is right on the park in Friedrichshain and has a lovely beer garden open during the summer months.

FSK
Segitzdamm 2, Kreuzberg (614 2464, www.fsk-kino.de). U1, U8 Kottbusser Tor or U8 Moritzplatz. **Tickets** €5.50-€7. **No credit cards.** **Map** p323 O9.
Named after the state film rating board, this two-screen cinema is deep in the heart of Turkish Kreuzberg. It shows a lot of foreign films, mostly with German subtitles, but occasionally has American or British indie films and documentaries.

Hackesche Höfe Filmtheater
Rosenthaler Strasse 40-41, Mitte (283 4603, www.hackesche-hoefe.org). U8 Weinmeisterstrasse or S3, S5, S9, S75 Hackescher Markt. **Tickets** €6.50-€8; €5 reductions **No credit cards.** **Map** p319 N5.
Being a four-storey walk up hasn't stopped this place from becoming one of the area's best-attended cinemas. It shows mostly foreign films, with documentaries and occasional indie features in English.

INSIDE TRACK SILVER SCREEN

Construction has begun to bring the legendary **Zoo Palast** cinema on Hardenberg Platz back to life as a luxurious 'Kino Lounge'. During the Cold War, West Berlin premières were always held in the striking 1950s building, which in a different reincarnation during the Nazi era was the venue for some of Albert Speer's most spectacular light shows. When it reopens in 2012 after a €4m facelift, the listed cinema will boast seven screens and supremely comfy seats.

★ Kino International
Karl-Marx-Allee 33, Mitte (2475 6011, www.yorck.de). U5 Schillingstrasse. **Tickets** €5.50-8.50. **No credit cards.** **Map** p319 P6.
The monumental post-Stalinist architecture of Kino International belies a modest 551-seat auditorium, but the real reason to come here is for the lobby, with its crystal chandeliers and upholstered seating. A first-class example of 1960s DDR chic, it overtook the Colosseum as East Berlin's premier cinema, and became a common venue for Party functions and socialist shindigs.
▶ *Kino International is also the home of the gay and lesbian Club International, which shows LGBT films every Monday (or Mongay, as it calls it) at 10pm.*

Moviemento
Kottbusser Damm 22, Kreuzberg (692 4785, www.moviemento.de). U7, U8 Hermannplatz, U8 Schönleinestrasse. **Tickets** €5-€7.50. **No credit cards.** **Map** p323 P10.
This cosy upstairs cinema in Kreuzberg is one of the last bastions of Berlin's original alternative cinema scene. The new management has put some fresh energy into the programming, and films in English are on the increase.

Odeon
Hauptstrasse 116, Schöneberg (7870 4019, www.yorck.de). U4, S42, S46 Innsbrucker Platz, S1, S41, S42, S46 Schöneberg. **Tickets** €5.50-€8. **No credit cards.** **Map** p321 D6.
The Odeon is a last hold-out of the big, old, single-screen neighbourhood cinema and should be supported just for that. Deep in the heart of Schöneberg, it's exclusively English-language, providing a reasonably intelligent, though increasingly mainstream, selection of Hollywood and UK fare. *Photo p210.*

Xenon
Kolonnenstrasse 5/6, Schöneberg (7800 1530, www.xenon-kino.de). U7 Kleistpark. **Tickets** €4-€6. **No credit cards.** **Map** p322 E6.
Only in Berlin would a dedicated gay cinema also be a multiple award-winner for children's programming. Those who have come of age can find gay and lesbian programming, largely but not exclusively from the US and UK.

Zeughaus Kino
Unter den Linden 2, Mitte (2030 4770, www.zeughauskino.de). U6 Französische Strasse or S3, S5, S7, S75 Hackescher Markt. **Tickets** €5. **No credit cards.** **Map** p327 N6.
The Zeughaus Kino, at the Deutsches Historisches Museum, has a variety of interesting series and often hosts travelling retrospective shows. It makes a concerted effort to get the original versions of movies, and foreign films sometimes appear with English subtitles. The entrance is on the Spree river.

Galleries

Berlin's nomadic art scene has moved on once more.

Things change very quickly in Berlin and perhaps speediest of all in the art world. Half the galleries we raved about in the last edition of this guide have already closed down or relocated, and many of the hotspots we plugged are now dead. That's not to say Berlin's art scene is in ill-health, merely that the capricious gallerists have moved on yet again. Mitte is no longer the epicentre of the art world. Even Brunnenstrasse, which as recently as 2008 was being touted as the best bet for talent-spotting emerging art, is almost a gallery-free zone just three years later – with the honourable exception of **Kow** at No.9, **Martin Mertens** at No.185, and **Klemm's** in the courtyard of No.6.

Gone too are many of the satellites of established names from major art hubs such as New York and London – Goff + Rosenthal, Curators Without Borders and Haunch of Venison have all shut up shop after making the costly discovery that while Berliners might appreciate art, they are too broke to pay for it. But not all foreigners are deterred: London's **Sprüth Magers** is now having a crack at Berlin, and in the heart of pricey Mitte to boot.

Others, like **Blain|Southern** (the new project from the Haunch of Venison founders), have chosen to set up their Berlin stalls in Schöneberg, which has emerged as the liveliest new gallery hub. You could easily spend a day gallery-hopping around Kürfurstenstrasse and Potsdamerstrasse. As this guide went to press, nine galleries in the area had joined together to put on the Schöneberger Art Walk on the last Saturday of every month (www.schoeneberger artwalk.de).

Rents are relatively cheap around this part of town, which in recent years has been better known for its prostitutes and sex shops than its cultural riches. One of the first to arrive was **Giti Nourbakhschs** (now resident at Kurfürstenstrasse 12), who put her move down to 'Mittemüdigkeit', being tired of Mitte, its high rents and tourists. Plus it makes sense in a way for galleries to be here: the Neue Nationalgalerie (*see p91*) is only up the road and it's very near the money of the KuDamm. A lot of artists also now have studios in the area – many are in the Maltfabrik, the old malt plant which used to be part of the Schultheiss Brewery in Bessemerstrasse 2-14 (www.malzfabrik.de) in southern Schöneberg.

Other clusters can be found in the working-class industrial district of Wedding – **Galerie Max Hetzler** and **Galerie Guido W Baudach** are next door to each other on Oudenarderstrasse – and around Rudi-Dutschke-Strasse in north-west Kreuzberg. Charlottenburg, long written off as a snoozefest with no eye for fresh talent, is now attracting new galleries such as **Galerie Daniel Buchholz**, as well as remaining a showplace for established dealers to display and deal pre-1990s art.

It's not just galleries that have disappeared. As of 2011, the Berlin Art Forum, the city's top art fair, is no more, thanks to some rather childish, not to mention parochial, in-fighting. The Forum had struggled in recent years after the start-up of a rival, Art Berlin Contemporary (ABC). The two had discussed a merger, but, alas, it wasn't to be. Whether ABC will troop on alone beyond 2011 was unclear at press time. At least there is still the **Berlin Biennale**, which is next set to hit town in 2012. There is also the annual April **Gallery Weekend**, when 40-odd spaces in the city coordinate their openings to entice the increasingly high-heeled parade of foreign buyers into opening their wallets.

Berlin itself may still lack collectors with deep pockets, but there is no shortage of artists working in the city. Residents currently making a splash in the art world are Parisian Cyprien Gaillard, who makes videos and photographs dealing with architecture and the ruins of modernism, and the German artist Thomas Zipp.

LISTINGS AND INFORMATION
Index Berlin (www.indexberlin.de) is the most complete art guide for Berlin and its environs. **Berlin Art Link** (www.berlin artlink.com) is another listings website, which also carries features on the latest exhibitions. If you want to hold a guide in your hand, get **Artery** (www.artery-berlin.de). It's published every two months and sold at galleries, bookstores and some newsstands. *Zitty* and *tip*, the two Berlin listings fortnightlies, cover most current showings throughout the city. Nearly all galleries have English-language websites; if you read German, you should check out www.art-in-berlin.de or the Berlin section of www.artnews.org for current 'what's on' information.

This chapter features commercial galleries. Institutions, state-run art museums and private art collections include:
Alte National Galerie 19th century art and sculpture. *See p63.*
Berlinische Galerie the state of Berlin's permanent collection of art, photography and architecture. *See p81.*
Brücke Museum expressionism. *See p104.*
Daimler Contemporary big-name 20th-century artists from Koons to Warhol. *See p90.*
Deutsche Guggenheim modern art. *See p61.*
Gemäldegalerie early European art. *See p90.*
Hamburger Bahnhof modern art, mostly 20th century. *See p67.*
Martin Gropius Bau hosts high-profile temporary exhibitions. *See p82.*
Museum für Fotografie Helmut Newton's photography museum. *See p95.*
Museum Berggruen Picasso. *See p96.*
Neue National Galerie 20th-century art from Germany and abroad. *See p91.*
Sammlung Hoffman international contemporary art. *See p69.*
Sammlung Scharf-Gerstenberg surrealism. *See p96.*

MITTE

BüroFriedrich
Holzmarktstrasse 15-18, S-Bahn arches 53/54 (2016 5115, www.buerofriedrich.org). S3, S5, S7, S75, U8 Jannowitzbrücke. **Open** times vary. **No credit cards. Map** p323 P7.
Dutch expat Waling Boers began this non-profit venue as a place to house internationally collaborative projects with an interesting cultural studies bent. Opening hours are irregular, so call ahead.

C/O Berlin
Corner Oranienburger Strasse & Tucholsky Strasse (28091925, www.co-berlin.info). U6 Oranienburger Tor or S1, S2 Oranienburger Strasse. **Open** 11am-8pm daily. **Admission** €10; €5 reductions. **No credit cards. Map** p318/p326 M5.
Co-founded by photographer Stephan Erfurt, this organisation has exhibited internationally known photographers such as Alfred Eisenstaedt, André Rival, James Nachtwey and Anton Corbijn. In late 2007, it moved into the Postfuhramt, a vast 1870s building that was once a transfer station for the German post system. At the time of writing, C/O's future was uncertain after foreign investors bought the building to turn into luxury flats.

Contemporary Fine Arts
Am Kupfergraben 10 (288 7870, www.cfa-berlin.com). U6, S1, S2, S3, S5, S7, S75 Friedrichsstrasse. **Open** 11am-6pm Tue-Fri; 11am-4pm Sat. **No credit cards. Map** p319/p327 N6.
One of Berlin's highest-shelf galleries lives in swish digs across from famous Museum Island in collector Heiner Bastian's David Chipperfield-designed building. The museum-like space is a slicker-than-slick backdrop for major stars such as Georg Baselitz, and YBA luminaries like Cecily Brown and Chris Ofili. Daniel Richter and Jonathan Meese are other well-known names on display.

DAADGalerie
Zimmerstrasse 90-91 (2613 640, www.daad-berlin.de). U6 Kochstrasse. **Open** 11am-6pm Mon-Sat. **Map** p322/p327 M8.
A shopfront gallery designed to feature works resulting from the 40-year-old artists-in-residence programme, which continues to invite important and aspiring artists to Berlin. Rachel Whiteread and Damien Hirst count among the alumni.

Duve
Invalidenstrasse 90 (7790 2302, www.duve berlin.com). U6 Naturkundemuseum, S1, S2 Nordbahnhof. **Open** noon-6pm Tue-Sat. **No credit cards. Map** p318 L5.
The mission of this space, founded by Alexander Duve in September 2007, is to represent artists who've never been repped by a gallery before.

Young talents Iris Touliatou and Dave McDermott produce works that run across all media; the gallerists also host concerts and readings.

Galerie Eigen + Art
Auguststrasse 26 (280 6605, www.eigen-art.com). S1, S2 Oranienburger Strasse. **Open** 11am-6pm Tue-Sat. **Credit** MC, V. **Map** p319 N5.
This small yet stalwart anchor gallery of the old Auguststrasse art strip is where man-about-town Gerd Harry 'Judy' Lybke continues his long-standing relationship with New Leipzig School star painters Neo Rauch and Matthias Weischer. He also shows thought-provoking works by Christine Hill, Birgit Brenner and Yehudit Sasportas. A far cry from Lybke's Leipzig living room gallery in the early 1980s.

Galerie Eva Poll
Anna-Louisa-Karsch-Strasse 9 (261 7091, www.poll-berlin.de). S3, S5, S7, S75 Hackescher Markt. **Open** 11am-6pm Tue-Fri; 11am-4pm Sat. **No credit cards**. **Map** p319 N6.
Opened in 1968 with her collection of critical realists from the '60s, Eva Poll's beautiful gallery includes, among others, Sabina Grzimek, Peter Sorge and Peter Chevalier.
Other location Kunststiftung Poll, Gipsstrasse 3, Mitte (2849 6250).

Galerie Capitain Petzel
Karl-Marx-Allee 45 (2408 8130, www.capitain petzel.de). U5 Schillingstrasse. **Open** 11am-6pm Tue-Sat. **Map** p319 P6.
This gallery is housed in one of the city's most interesting landmarks, a glass-encased modernist building perfectly preserved from the socialist era. In GDR times, the pavilion was used to showcase socialist art from the Eastern bloc. These days, Cologne gallerist Gisela Capitain and her partner Friedrich Petzel show contemporary artists such as Sarah Morris, Stephen Prina and Wade Guyton.

Galerie Thomas Schulte
Charlottenstrasse 24 (2060 8990, www.galerie thomasschulte.de). U6 Stadtmitte. **Open** noon-6pm Tue-Sat. **No credit cards**. **Map** p322/p327 M7.
New Yorker Thomas Schulte and Swiss-born Eric Franck opened their doors in 1991, hoping to breathe new life into the art market. They recently moved their upmarket, high-quality offerings to a glassed-in storefront space on the edge of Mitte, where their exhibitions of Alice Aycock, Alan McCollum and others can glitter even more brightly.

Klemm's
Brunnenstrasse 7 (4050 4953, www.klemms-berlin.com). U8 Rosenthaler Platz. **Open** 11am-6pm Tue-Sat. **No credit cards**. **Map** p319/p326 N4.
This space features Sebastian Klemm's line-up of young photographers, installation artists and painters such as Peggy Buth, Falk Haberkorn and Sven Johne, most of whom were trained in East German art academies. Openings here turn into some of the best parties in town.

★ Kow Berlin
Brunnenstrasse 9 (311 66 771, www.kowberlin. info). U8 Rosenthaler Platz. **Open** noon-6pm Wed-Sun. **Map** p319 N4.
This starkly beautiful modern building has gathered as many compliments as its contents. It's the new gallery from architect Arno Brandlhuber, the chair of architecture and urban research at the

KW Institute for Contemporary Art. *See p216.*

Andrea Zittel, *Pattern of Habit*. **Sprüth Magers**.

Academy of Fine Arts in Nuremberg. The façade is made from clear glass and polycarbonate panels; inside, there are raw untreated concrete walls and banisters made of iron pipes. Recent exhibitions have showcased Santiago Sierra, Barbara Hammer and Franz Erhard Walther.

KW Institute for Contemporary Art

Auguststrasse 69 (243 4590, www.kw-berlin.de). U6 Oranienburger Tor or S1, S2 Oranienburger Strasse. **Open** noon-7pm Tue, Wed, Fri-Sun; noon-9pm Thur. **Map** p319 N5.

Housed in a former margarine factory and sporting a social event-friendly courtyard designed by Dan Graham, KW has been a major non-profit showcase since the early 1990s. It co-hosts the Berlin Biennale and puts on culturally themed exhibits of contemporary artists – Fassbinder's Berlin Alexanderplatz, for instance. *Photo p215.*

Kunstraum Céline und Heiner Bastian

Am Kupfergraben 10 (2067 3840). U6, S1, S2, S5, S7, S75 Friedrichsstrasse. **Open** 11am-5pm Thur, Fri; 11am-4pm Sat. **Map** p319/p327 N6.

Perched atop the sleek David Chipperfield building he built for himself and other art lovers, this brand-new showcase for local collector Heiner Bastian's private collection opened in November 2007 with a stunning show by Damien Hirst. Contemporary Fine Arts (*see p214*) is housed in the same building; the Kunstraum covers the third floor.

Martin Mertens

Courtyard, Brunnenstrasse 185 (4404 3350, www.martinmertens.com). U8 Rosenthaler Platz. **Open** noon-6pm Tue-Sat. **No credit cards.** **Map** p319/p326 N4.

Martin Mertens moved into this ultra-slick, airy and sociable back courtyard gallery in spring 2008. It's slightly difficult to find, but it's worth the hunt and features high-concept work by a roster of international artists.

Mehdi Chouakri

Schlegelstrasse 26 (2839 1153, www.mehdi-chouakri.com). U6 Naturkundemuseum. **Open** 11am-6pm Tue-Sat. **No credit cards.** **Map** p318/p326 M4.

Chouakri's sharp eye picks emerging artists and established names like Sylvie Fleury, John M Armleder, Gitte Schäfer and Gerwald Rockenschaub and sets their work in sleek, spacious surroundings.

Neugerriemschneider

Linienstrasse 155 (2887 7277). U6 Oranienburger Tor or S1, S2 Oranienburger Strasse. **Open** 11am-6pm Tue-Sat. **No credit cards.** **Map** p318/p326 M5.

Founded by duo Tim Neuger and Burkhard Riemschneider, this elegant courtyard space showcases international art by blue chip talent like the brilliant curry-cooking artist Rirkrit Tiravanija and weather man Olafur Eliasson. In 2011, it put on a show by the Chinese dissident artist Ai Weiwei.

Peres Projects

Grosse Hamburger Strasse 17 (275 950 770, www.peresprojects.com); S3, S5, S7, S75 Hackescher Markt. **Open** 11am-6pm Tue-Sat. **No credit cards.** **Map** p319 N5.

Californian impresario Javier Peres has a talent for putting on shows everyone talks about. He hit the headlines in 2011 by coaxing Hollywood actor James Franco into making his European art world debut; and in 2007, with the Bruce LaBruce and Terence Koh show Blame Canada, a live installation of 'degenerate art' consisting of horizontal glory holes, with real (Viagra-assisted) penises poking down from the ceiling and up from the floor like stalactites and stalagmites. **Other location** Schlesische Strasse 26 (6162 6962).

Program

Invalidenstrasse 115 (3950 9316, www.programonline.de). U6 Naturkundemuseum, S1, S2 Nordbahnhof. **Open** 2-7pm Tue-Sat. **Map** p318/p326 M4

Since opening in September 2006, Program has established itself as a non-profit gallery that links art and architectural concepts in cutting-edge inter-disciplinary shows by mostly international artists. Canadian expat Carson Chan and partner Fotini Lazaridou-Hatzigoga also run a small residency programme, studio spaces and a reading room; the space occasionally hosts concerts too.

★ Sammlung Boros
Reinhardtstrasse 20 (www.sammlung-boros.de). U6 Oranienburger Tor. **Open** by appointment only. **No credit cards. Map** p318/p327 L5.
More like a museum than a gallery, this concrete World War II bunker has been transformed into 80 stunning spaces totalling over 3,000sq m and containing the formidable collection of advertising mogul Christian Boros. Works on view include contemporary greats such as Olafur Eliasson and Sarah Lucas. Tours are on weekends by appointment only; book well in advance through the website.

★ Sprüth Magers
Oranienburger Strasse 18 (2888 4030, www.spruethmagers.com). S1, S2 Oranienburger Strasse. **Open** 11am-6pm Tue-Sat and by appointment. **No credit cards. Map** p319/p326 N5
Probably the most important art opening in Berlin in recent years, this outpost of the famous London Gallery represents big names including Cyprien Gaillard, Peter Fischli and David Weiss. The space was once a dancehall and now also houses Image Movement, a high-concept film and record store with interiors designed by artists Rosemarie Trockel and Thea Djordjadze, both represented by the gallery.

PRENZLAUER BERG

Aedes Pfefferberg
Christinenstrasse 18-19 (282 7015, www.aedes-arc.de). U2 Senefelderplatz. **Open** 11am-6.30pm Tue-Fri; 1-5pm Sat, Sun. **No credit cards. Map** p319/p326/p328 O4.
Founded in 1980 as Europe's first gallery for architecture, Aedes has a history of showing 'starchitects' long before they become well known. Berlin architecture stars GRAFT and Japanese SANAA have both been on show here.

Akira Ikeda Gallery Berlin
Pfefferberg, Schönhauser Allee 176 (4432 8510, www.akiraikedagallery.com). U2 Senefelderplatz. **Open** 11am-6pm Tue-Sat. **No credit cards. Map** p319/p326 O4.
Akira Ikeda is hidden at the back of the Pfefferberg, a dilapidated 19th-century brewery turned cultural centre. This magnificent third branch of the gallery (other outposts are in Taura, Japan, and New York) specialises in work post-1945.

KREUZBERG

Carlier/Gebauer
Markgrafenstrasse 67 (2400 8630, www.carliergebauer.com). U6 Kochstrasse. **Open** 11am-6pm Tue-Sat. **No credit cards. Map** p323/p327 N8.
Now in a new, sprawling location, Ulrich Gebauer and co-director Marie Blanche Carlier present a varied programme of larger-scale installations and work in different media by international and politically minded contemporary artists such as Rosa Barba, Michel François, Mark Wallinger and Paul Pfeiffer.

Galerie Berinson
Lindenstrasse 34 (2838 7990, www.berinson.de). U6 Kochstrasse. **Open** 11am-6pm Tue-Sat. **No credit cards. Map** p323 N8.
Hendrik Berinson's gallery is best known for exhibits by such 20th-century masters as Hans Bellmer, George Grosz, Raoul Hausmann, Man Ray and Friedrich Seidenstücker.

Galerie Crone
Rudi-Dutschke-Strasse 26 (2592 4490, www.cronegalerie.com). U6 Kochstrasse. **Open** 11am-6pm Tue-Sat. **Map** p327 N8.
This big-hitting space is in a courtyard behind Restaurant Tim Raue in the uppermost reaches of Kreuzberg. In summer 2011, the gallery put on a mini-blockbuster exhibition featuring works from Joseph Beuys, Norbert Bisky, Anselm Kiefer, Martin Kippenberger, Sigmar Polke and Andy Warhol.

Galerienhaus
Lindenstrasse 34-35 (www.galerienhaus.com). U6 Kochstrasse. **Open** 11am-6pm Tue-Sat. **Map** p323 N8.
This building near the Jewish Museum houses 13 different galleries, including a space run by the Dane Niels Borch Jensen and the Lehmann brothers, two well regarded painters from Dresden.

Johann König
Dessauerstrasse 6-7 (2610 3080, www.johannkoenig.de). U2 Gleisdreieck. **Open** 11am-6pm Tue-Sat. **No credit cards. Map** p322 L8.
König (half-brother of New York gallerist Leo and son of museum-man Kaspar) presents a mixed bag of emerging and mid-career artists and exhibitions in a wide range of media. The line-up includes artists such as Jeppe Hein and Tatiana Trouvé, showing works designed to make viewers and collectors think hard.

Künstlerhaus Bethanien
Kottbusserstrasse 10 (616 9030, www.bethanien.de). U1, U8 Kottbusser Tor or U8 Schönleinstrasse. **Open** 2-7pm Tue-Sun. **No credit cards. Map** p323 P9.
This Berlin institution began as an art squat in the 1970s and has since developed a major studio resi-

dency programme for foreign artists staying in the city. With open studios and three full galleries offering frequently 'different' shows, it remains a lively endeavour, despite the threat of budget cuts.

NGBK
Oranienstrasse 25 (616 5130, www.ngbk.de). U1, U8 Kottbusser Tor. **Open** noon-7pm Mon-Wed, Sun; noon-8pm Thur-Sat. **No credit cards.** **Map** p323 P9.
Begun in the smoky haze of the late 1960s, the NGBK is still confrontational and energetic, continuing its group-based projects with a social conscience. The gallery entrance is through the bookshop.

Nordenhake
Lindenstrasse 34-35 (206 1483, www.nordenhake. com). U6 Kochstrasse. **Open** 11am-6pm Tue-Sat. **No credit cards.** **Map** p323 N8.
Longtime Swedish gallerist Claes Nordenhake opened his first Berlin gallery on Zimmerstrasse in 2000. Now he has purchased an entire former department store and set up shop there, along with several other galleries. He's known for featuring new artists such as Walter Niedermayr and Esko Männikkö.

VW (VeneKlasen/Werner)
Rudi-Dutschke-Strasse 26 (8161 60418, www. vwberlin.com) U6 Kochstrasse. **Open** 11am-6pm Tue-Sat. **Map** p322/p327 M8.
This new space is run by legendary Berlin gallerist Michael Wener, along with Gordon VeneKlasen. Alongside more conventional exhibitions, the space specialises in film work – highlights in 2011 included screenings of *The Invisible Frame* and *Cycling the Frame* by British filmmaker Cynthia Beatt, who worked with the actress Tilda Swinton on both films.

TIERGARTEN

Esther Schipper
Schönberger Ufer 65 (374 433 133, www. estherschipper.com). S1, S2, S25, U2 Potsdamer Platz or U2 Mendelssohn-Bartholdy-Park. **Open** 11am-6pm Tue-Sat. **No credit cards.** **Map** p322 K8.
Since beginning her gallery endeavours in the early 1990s with partner Michael Krome, Esther Schipper has always had a penchant for heady projects and cutting-edge greats, and the tradition continues with shows featuring works by stars Liam Gillick and Carsten Höller, among others.

SCHÖNEBERG

401 Contemporary
Potsdamer Strasse 81B (473 777 83, www.401 contemporary.com). U1 Kurfürstenstrasse. **Open** 11am-6pm Wed-Sat & by appointment. **No credit cards.** **Map** p322 K8.

Berlin outpost of the London gallery representing artists such as Stuart Bailes, Bianca Brunner and Peter Weibel.

Arndt + Partner
Potsdamer Strasse 96 (2061 3870, www.arndt berlin.com). U1 Kurfürstenstrasse. **Open** 11am-6pm Tue-Sat. **No credit cards.** **Map** p322 K8.
One of the city's earliest western German dealers in the post-Wall East, Matthias Arndt has moved his gallery to the Potsdamerstrasse cluster and runs a tightly professional gallery that shows top international examples of experimental yet somehow accessible work. Among his line-up are French star Sophie Calle as well as Thomas Hirschhorn, Gilbert & George, white-hot Josephine Meckseper and Erik Boulatov.

★ Blain|Southern
Potsdamer Strasse 77-87 (0162 232 5864, www.blainsouthern.com). U1 Kurfürstenstrasse. **Open** 11am-6pm Tue-Sat. **Map** p322 K8.
The Berlin outpost of this London/NYC gallery opened in April 2011. Among the artists are Bill Viola, Mat Collishaw and Jonas Burgert. Blain|Southern is the latest project from the founders of Haunch of Venison, which closed down in Berlin in 2010, three years after the brand was sold to Christie's.

Giti Nourbakhsch
Kurfürstenstrasse 12 (4404 6781, www. nourbakhsch.de). U1 Kurfürstenstrasse. **Open** 11am-6pm Wed-Sat. **Map** p322 K9.
This is a favourite gallery of Mario Testino, who said of Nourbakhsch: 'She has this ability of constantly foreseeing the next generation of artists.' Tomma Abts, Ida Ekblad and Spartacus Chetwynd are represented here.

Haus am Lützowplatz
Lützowplatz 9 (261 3805, www.hausam luetzowplatz-berlin.de). U1, U2, U3, U4 Nollendorfplatz. **Open** 11am-6pm Tue-Sun. **No credit cards.** **Map** p322 J8.
Exhibitions were held in this building as early as 1949, and the non-profit society that has occupied it since the early 1960s maintains a pledge to present works by both unknown Berlin artists and guests such as Mario Merz, Rebecca Horn and the British sculptor Tony Cragg.

Kit Schulte Contemporary Art
Winterfeldtstrasse 35 (2100 5237, www.kitschulte. com). U1, U2, U3, U4 Nollendorfplatz. **Open** noon-6pm Wed-Fri. **Map** p322 J9.
Formerly Cain Schulte Contemporary Art, this gallery shows works by emerging and established artists from Europe and the US. Kit Schulte is interested in starting an intercultural dialogue about art, and so collaborates with other galleries and cultural institutions in Germany, Holland, Israel and the US.

Klosterfelde

Potsdamerstrasse 93 (283 5305, www.klosterfelde.de). U1 Kurfürstenstrasse . **Open** 11am-6pm Tue-Sat. **Map** p322 K9.
Young gallerist Martin Klosterfelde shows a wide variety of sometimes offbeat art, ranging from the conceptual musings of 1970s artists like Hanne Darboven to drawings and installations by Jorinde Voigt and Christian Jankowski's filmic and photographic work.

Tanya Leighton

Kurfürstenstrasse 156 (221607770, www.tanya leighton.com). **Open** noon-6pm Wed-Sun & by appointment. **Map** p322 K9.
This British curator opened her Berlin outpost in 2008 with the aim of developing a cross-disciplinary, trans-generational gallery programme with off-site projects.

CHARLOTTENBURG

Camera Work

Kantstrasse 149 (310 0773, www.camerawork.de). S5, S7, S75 Savignyplatz. **Open** 11am-6pm Tue-Sat. **No credit cards. Map** p321/p328 F8.
Named after the magazine started by Alfred Stieglitz, this magnificent courtyard space offers prime viewing of some of the 20th century's most important photographic work, including Irving Penn, Leni Riefenstahl, Peter Beard and Man Ray.

Galerie Anselm Dreher

Pfalzburger Strasse 80 (883 5249, www.galerie-anselm-dreher.com). U1 Hohenzollernplatz. **Open** 2-6pm Tue-Fri. **No credit cards. Map** p321 F9.
Since opening his gallery in 1967, Anselm Dreher continues the lonely task of championing works by international pioneers of conceptual art, such as John M Armleder, Heimo Zobernig and Lawrence Weiner.

Galerie Daniel Buchholz

Fasanenstrasse 30 (8862 4056, www.galerie buchholz.de). U2, U3, S5, S7, S75 Zoologischer Garten or U1, U9 Kurfürstendamm. **Open** 11am-6pm. **No credit cards. Map** p321 F9.
The Cologne gallerist represents artists such as 2006 Turner Prize winner Tomma Abts, Wolfgang Tillmans and Richard Hawkins.

Galerie Georg Nothelfer

Corneliusstrasse 3 (881 4405, www.galerie-nothelfer.de). U1, U2, U3 Wittenbergplatz. **Open** 11am-6.30pm Tue-Fri; 10am-2pm Sat. **No credit cards. Map** p321 H8.

Long-time doyen Nothelfer quietly and importantly pursues his love of Informel and Tachist work, best exemplified by artists such as Walter Stöhner, Henri Michaux and Jan Voss.
Other location Grolman 28, Charlottenburg.

Galerie Springer & Winckler

Fasanenstrasse 13 (315 7220, www.springer-winckler.de). U2, U3, S5, S7, S75 Zoologischer Garten or U1, U9 Kurfürstendamm. **Open** 10am-6pm Tue-Fri; noon-3pm Sat. **No credit cards. Map** p321/p328 F9.
Originally the gallery of Rudolph Springer (one of post-war Berlin's seminal gallerists), this space is now run by his son and partner Gerald Winckler. The young pair show many of the now-huge artists their father knew well, such as Georg Baselitz, Sigmar Polke and Gerhard Richter.

Galerie Volker Diehl

Niebuhrstrasse 2 (2248 7922, www.galerie volkerdiehl.com). S3, S5, S7, S75 Savignyplatz. **Open** 11am-6pm Tue-Sat. **No credit cards. Map** p323/p327 N8.
One of the original organisers of the now-defunct Berlin Art Forum, Diehl has long been a prominent member of the international art world, concentrating his efforts on international talents such as Olga Chernysheva and Martin Assig.

Raab Galerie Berlin

Fasanenstrasse 72 (261 9217, www.raab-galerie.de). U1 Uhlandstrasse. **Open** 10am-7pm Mon-Fri; 10am-4pm Sat. **No credit cards. Map** p321/p328 F9.
Since her monumental first show of the Wild Bunch in 1978, Ingrid Raab has been a grand champion of young talent such as street artist El Bocho and playful painter Nina Maron, as well as stalwarts like Lüpertz, Fetting and the wonderful Odd Nerdrum. Two gallery spaces later, her enthusiasm remains contagious.

WEDDING

Galerie Guido W Baudach

Oudenarderstrasse 16-20 (2804 7727, www.guid owbaudach.com). U9 Nauener Platz. **Open** 11am-6pm Tue-Sat. **Map** p318 J1.
This massive space is like more like a museum than a commercial gallery. In 2011, it hosted shows by Erwin Kneihsl, Andy Hope and Thilo Heinzmann.
Other location Carmerstrasse 11, Charlottenburg.

Galerie Max Hetzler

Oudenarderstr 16-20 (229 2437, www.max hetzler.com). U9 Nauener Platz. **Open** 11am-6pm Tue-Sat. **No credit cards. Map** p322/p327 M8.
This wonderful gallery (which was in business long before its Berlin days began in 1994) represents an amazing roster of talent, including Christopher Wool, Kara Walker and Toby Ziegler.

ARTS & ENTERTAINMENT

Gay & Lesbian

Our picks of the city's huge scene.

'I am gay, and that's good the way it is!' ('*Ich bin schwul, und das ist auch gut so!*') declared Berlin mayor Klaus Wowereit in 2001. Berlin's queer scene is one of the world's best. Over his decade as mayor, Wowereit – or 'Wowi,' as he's known here, who won a further term in state elections in September 2011 – has come to personify the permissive attitude of a city that has long cared more about a good party than labels like 'gay' and 'straight.' Nothing is going to change that attitude. But as a slogan for the city's gay scene, his words constitute a vast understatement.

BERLIN'S GAY HISTORY

Historically, Berlin has acted as a tolerant, catchall city for people of different religions, races and sexual orientations – even when the rest of Germany wasn't quite on-board. Berlin was the capital of a kingdom whose 18th-century king, Frederick the Great, was rumoured to discuss and delve into homoerotic activities (just check out some of the art at his men-only summer retreat **Sanssouci**, *see p274*). Later, in 1897, the first institution in the world with an emancipatory homosexual agenda was founded in Berlin – the Wissenschaftlich-Humanitäres Komitee (Scientific-Humanitarian Committee).

The 1920s accelerated and cemented Berlin as Europe's gay capital. The Weimar era (1918-1933) brought an anything-goes spirit to the city: gay and lesbian bars flourished, drag performances were popular and a lax sexual culture, not to mention a depressed national currency, attracted homosexual tourists from across the globe. The scene was the world's first glimpse at what we might recognise as a modern gay community, and was frequented by Marlene Dietrich, Anita Berber and Christopher Isherwood. This freewheeling period ended with election of the Nazis in 1933, after which homosexuals, especially in saucy Berlin, were persecuted by the state. Thousands of gay men were forced to wear a pink triangle in concentration camps, many perishing in the bloody years of World War II. The gay victims of National Socialism are commemorated in a striking, €600,000 memorial in the Tiergarten that was unveiled in 2008.

During the occupation and the Cold War (1945-1989), gay culture existed on both sides of the Berlin Wall, though mostly underground. West Berlin in particular saw a surge in its gay ranks, as many young men were attracted to the only city in West Germany where citizens were exempt from military service. In 1994, the notorious Paragraph 175, which had criminalised homosexual contact in Germany since 1871, was repealed by the newly unified nation. Civil partnerships between same-sex couples have been legal throughout the country since 2001. Unsurprisingly, it is Berlin's politicians who are now leading the charge for full gay marriage.

After such dramatic swings in acceptance, Berlin has adapted never-again stance towards gay intolerance. There is a strong and open sense of pride here, and alternative lifestyles of all stripes are considered normal – even celebrated on giant pro-tolerance billboards in the U-bahn.

THE CITY TODAY

The gay and lesbian scenes are bold and integrated seamlessly into almost every part of the city. **Schöneberg** has the highest concentration of gay stores, bars, restaurants and organisations. But roving monthly parties and a constant turnover of gay bars have resulted in a diffusion of the scene into **Kreuzberg**, **Mitte**, **Prenzlauer Berg** and **Friedrichshain**. Even traditionally Turkish **Neukölln** has its share of go-to spots.

Summer is the most exciting time of year, when all contingents come together to play, party and protest. The **Lesbisch-Schwules Stadtfest** (*see p199*) on Nollendorfplatz in mid-June is followed by the **Christopher**

Street Day (*see p200*), Germany's version of Pride, which includes a flamboyant annual parade through the Tiergarten. Alternative parades in other parts of town celebrate every shade of the queer rainbow.

The scene includes much more than the venues listed here, especially in terms of cultural events: there are plays, drag performances and the Gay Teddy award for the best gay film at the **Berlin International Film Festival** (*see p201*). Queer films can be seen on Mondays at **Kino International** (Karl-Marx-Allee 33, Mitte, 2475 6011). Gay art and history are documented at the **Schwules Museum** (*see p79*), which also has an archive. And, of course, the Berlin scene offers sex parties for every taste and perversion, as well as gay saunas, cruising parks and stigma-free darkrooms in many bars.

Tens of thousands men have profiles on the wildly popular gay social- and sex-networking site Gay Romeo (gayromeo.com), which provides excellent opportunities to learn about the latest gay happenings in the city and allows visitors to communicate to gay Berliners in English or any other language.

Gays making contact in public is rarely of interest to passers-by, but bigots do exist and so does anti-gay violence. In the West it tends to be by gangs of Turkish teenagers, in the East by right-wing skinhead Germans. But violence is rare and, compared to other cities, Berlin is an easy-going place.

INFORMATION AND PUBLICATIONS

For gay and lesbian helplines, information and counselling services, *see p294*. The best way to find one-off events, parties and festivals are *Blu* (www.blu.fm) and *Siegessäule* (www.siegessaeule.de), free monthly magazines that can be picked up at most LGBT venues. Apart from a 'what's on' calendar, the latter lists all gay and lesbian venues and pinpoints them on a map. *Siegessäule* also publishes *Kompass* (www.siegessaeule-kompass.de), a classified directory in German of everything gay or lesbian. You can find English information in pocket-sized Gay City Guides for individual districts and on the Gaymap website (www.gaymap.info/berlin/index.html).

Mixed

In West Berlin's Schoneberg district, gays and lesbians trod separate paths for decades. Across the wall in East Berlin, though, homosexuals of both sexes shared bars and clubs, making common cause under the Communists. These traditions can still be felt today. With the expansion of the gay scene into other parts of the city over the past ten years, mixed venues now predominate, although most places tend to lean one way or the other. Many one-nighters target both gays and lesbians, and even more don't target homosexuals in particular. Below, we list a selection of mixed cafés, bars and clubs, where just about anyone will feel comfortable. In addition, **November** (Husemannstrasse 15, 442 8425, www.cafe-november.de), in Prenzlauer Berg is a popular mixed bar.

CAFÉS & BARS
Friedrichshain

Freundeszone
Proskauer Strasse 8 (9651 6680, www. freundeszone.de). U5 Samariterstrasse. **Open** 7pm-late daily. **No credit cards.** **Map** p325 T6
Board games, vinyl records and minimalist white décor charactarise this relaxed bar located in the rapidly gentrifying area north of Karl-Marx Allee. A mid-30s crowd sips cocktails before pushing on to wilder destinations to the west and south.

Himmelreich
Simon-Dach-Strasse 36 (2936 9292). U5 Frankfurter Tor, U12, S3, S5, S9, S75 Warschauer Strasse. **Open** from 6pm Mon-Fri; from 2pm Sat, Sun. **No credit cards. Map** p324 S7.
A colourful and comfortable lounge, serving snacks and coffee during the day, as well as drinks.
▶ *Tuesday is women-only night, although men in drag are welcome. See p233.*

Kreuzberg

Barbie Deinhoff's
Schlesische Strasse 16 (no phone, www.barbie deinhoff.de). U1 Schlesisches Tor/bus N29. **Open** 6pm-6am daily. **No credit cards. Map** p324 R9 U
Sure, this is a queer performance space, but most people come to its casual, colorful rooms for the young, pan-sexual crowd, the top-notch local DJs and the hilarious art on the walls. 2-4-1 Tuesdays are popular, attracting a particularly skint Kreuzberg crowd.

Café Melitta Sundström
Mehringdamm 61 (no phone). U6, U7 Mehringdamm. **Open** noon-late daily. **No credit cards. Map** p322 F5.
Daytimes, this place serves as a cosy café for students; in the evenings, it's full of gays too lazy to go to Schöneberg and lesbians who wouldn't go to Schöneberg anyway. At weekends, it's the entrance to SchwuZ (*see p227*) and is hectic and fun.

Drama

Mehringdamm 63 (6746 9562, www.drama bar.de). U6, U7 Mehringdamm. **Open** 1pm-late daily. **No credit cards. Map** p322 M10.

A schizophrenic but stylish café-bar on two floors: the pink palace at street level could only attract the unashamedly camp while rowdy lesbians roll around on leopard-skin cushions amid jungle colours upstairs. Small terrace in summer.

Möbel-Olfe

Reichenberger Strasse 177, corner of Dresdner Strasse (2327 4690, www.moebel-olfe.de). U1, U8 Kottbusser Tor. **Open** 6pm-late Tue-Sun. **No credit cards. Map** p323 P9.

It's an odd location for a gay bar, wedged among Turkish snack bars in a down-at-heel 1960s housing development, but this unpretentious place has been packed since the day it opened, mainly with gay and lesbian beer lovers, thanks to the good range on offer. Thursdays are particularly hopping, though lesbians may prefer the vibe on lady-heavy Tuesdays.

Roses

Oranienstrasse 187 (615 6570). U1, U8 Kottbusser Tor. **Open** 10pm-5am daily. **No credit cards. Map** p323 G4.

Whatever state you're in (the more of a state, the better), you'll fit in just fine at this boisterous den of glitter. It draws customers of all sexual preferences, who mix and mingle and indulge in excessive drinking amid the plush, kitsch decor. No place for uptights, always full, very Kreuzbergish.

Tante Horst

Oranienstrasse 45 (3950 9022, www.tante horst.de). U1 Moritzplatz. **Open** 6pm-2am Tue-Sun. **Map** p323 O8

This adorable, relaxed co-op bar and café has a manifesto in the menu promising an open atmosphere and an embrace of queer culture, making it an excellent place to warm up for a night out no matter where you fall on the sexuality spectrum. At this end of bustling Oranienstasse, both the prices and the noise level drop considerably.

Schöneberg

Café Bilderbuch

Akazienstrasse 28 (7870 6057, www.cafe-bilderbuch.de). U7 Eisenacher Strasse. **Open** 9am-midnight Mon-Sat; 10am-midnight Sun. **Map** p322 11

Quaint and cosy, this venue has many purposes: café, restaurant, gallery and library. Eclectic touches – a dollhouse, vintage chairs, antique tables – tempt people to sit out an afternoon people-watching and tinkering on your laptop or iPhone (there's free Wi-Fi). Crowded at lunch and breakfast thanks to a stand-out menu of classics.

Neues Ufer

Hauptstrasse 157 (7895 7900). U7 Kleistpark. **Open** 11am-2am daily. **No credit cards. Map** p322 E5.

Established in the early 1970s, this is the city's oldest gay café and is located off the beaten Schoneberg track. The former name Anderes Ufer ('The Other Side') was changed to Neues Ufer ('The New Side'), symbolising a new beginning. Relaxed daytime scene.

Other Districts

★ Silver Future

Weserstrasse 206 (7563 4987, www.silver future.net). U7 U8 Hermannplatz. **Open** 2pm-2am Sun-Wed; 2pm-3am Thur-Sat. **Map** p323 Q11

Neukölln is the new frontier of cool in Berlin, and this is its main queer destination. 'You are now leaving the heteronormative zone,' announces a playful sign above the bar – and it's not kidding. Fun for groups of any sexual or gender definition, this neighbourhood bar is welcoming, witty and charmingly rough around the edges.

TortenheBär

Zauritzweg 9 (3454 0304). U2 Deutsche Oper. **Open** noon-9pm Tue-Fri; 3-9pm Sat, Sun. **Map** 321 E7.

A sedate but loveable coffee and wine bar in Charlottenberg. It's not explicitly gay, but its linen-draped tables can often be filled with older, understated opera fans eating yummy tarts and discussing the latest production at the nearby Deutsche Oper.

Möbel-Olfe.

CLUBS & ONE-NIGHTERS

Mitte

Spy Club at Cookies
Friedrichstrasse/Unter den Linden (2809 5396, www.spyclub.de). U6 S3, S5, S7 Friedrichstrasse. **Open** from 11pm last Sat of mth. **Admission** varies. **No credit cards. Map** p318 M6

On the last Saturday of every month, one of Berlin's biggest clubs goes gay. Cookies is a wild dance party with a twist: every edition is hosted by a different fashion personality. The mixed crowd is encouraged to dress up, so the place is often thronged with boys in hipster suits and girls with boas (or vice versa). Expect locals and tourists on the pull, house music, lots of English, steep drink prices and a long, fun night that's not as demanding as a session at Berghain.

ZMF
Brunnenstrasse 10 (zurmoebelfabrik.de). U8 Rosenthalerplatz. **Open** varies. **Admission** varies. **No credit cards. Map** p319 N4.

Head directly through to the second backyard and into the basement to find one of Berlin's premier electro clubs. The hotspot features a rotating set of DJs and a crowd of alterna-gays, young lesbians and straight party people more likely looking for a good beat than a darkroom or one-night stand. Particularly popular among the city's homo set is Saturday's party, Meschugge (literal translation: bonkers), that can go late into the night. The former furniture factory setting provides loads of dance space and plenty of dark corners for canoodling.

Friedrichshain

Berghain/Panorama Bar
Am Wriezener Bahnhof (no phone, www.berghain.de). U5 Weberwiese, S3, S5, S75 Ostbahnhof. **Open** midnight-late Fri, Sat. **Admission** varies. **No credit cards**.

The hippest and hardest electronic music club in Berlin, if not Europe. The building is a Communist-era power station transformed into a concrete cathedral of techno on two floors, with the mixed Panorama Bar upstairs and Berghain below. Saturday nights see Berghain awash with pumped-up, shirtless gay men sweating it out on the dancefloor (or in the darkroom at the back) well into Sunday afternoon. In summer, the party pours over into the garden chill-out area, bar and dance floor. Arrive after 6am to avoid the massive queues. Once on Am Wriezener Bahnhof, just follow the stream of taxis to reach the door. Cameras are prohibited and taken at the door and returned later. But you won't need photos to remember it.

Die Busche (formerly Haus B)
Warschauer Platz 18 (296 0800, www.dashausb.de). U1, S3, S5, S75 Warschauer Strasse. **Open** from 11pm Fri, Sat. **Admission** €3.50-€6. **No credit cards. Map** p323 H4.

Die Busche is an East German relic. Loud, tacky, mixed and packed, this is one of East Berlin's oldest discos and is full of loutish lesbians, gay teens and their girlfriends. The Friday and Saturday parties are musts for kitsch addicts and mainstream pop fans; definitely a no-go area for guys who like a masculine atmosphere.

Kreuzberg

★ S036

Oranienstrasse 190, Kreuzberg (tickets 6110 1313/6140 1306, www.so36.de). U1, U8 Kottbusser Tor. **Open** 8pm-late daily. **Admission** €3-€20. **No credit cards. Map** p323 P9

A key venue for both gays and lesbians. Monday's Montech party (from 11pm) is not completely gay, but the hard techno sounds draw a largely male following. Last Saturday in the month is Gay Oriental Night (Gayhane – House of Halay, from 10pm), with belly dancing, transvestites and Turkish hits. Sunday is Café Fatal, where gays and lesbians get into ballroom dancing with a lesson from a professional thrown in at the start of the evening. The last Friday of every month is gay-friendly My Ugly X, a blissfully trashy combo of pop and drink specials. Roller Skate Disco (one undetermined Friday or Saturday per month, from 10pm) brings in boys and girls to hustle and shimmy to '70s and '80s pop. S036 even makes bingo fun with its brash Super Sexy Bingo night (every second Tuesday from 7pm).

Südblock

Admiralstrasse 1-2, Kreuzberg (609 418 53, www.suedblock.org). U8, U12 Kottbusser Tor. **Open** 10am-closing times vary. **Admission** varies. **No credit cards.**

A former beer-slinger from Möbel-Olfe (*see p222*) opened this bar for Kreuzberg's increasingly large gay population in 2010. Located under the round-about housing development at Kottbusser Tor, the mixed (but girl-heavy) crowd enjoy nightly drinks and dancing, as well as many one-off rock parties. The Kottywood party is a popular go-to for gays and lesbians looking to cap a Friday night grinding to Latin, retro and pop music. Südblock also serves food, ranging from breakfast to midnight snacks.

Gay

You don't need to look for the gay scene in Berlin. It'll find you in about ten minutes. Though events are spread throughout the city, some areas are gayer than others. This is particularly true of the tourist-friendly concentration around Schöneberg's **Motzstrasse** and **Fuggerstrasse**, and the area around **Schönhauser Allee** S-Bahn and U-bahn stations in Prenzlauer Berg. Here, bars, clubs and shops are so numerous it's impossible to take them all in on one visit.

The scene is always shifting, so places listed here may have changed or new ones might have sprung up by the time you read this. *Siegessäule* and *Blu* are the best sources of current information.

CAFÉS, BARS & RESTAURANTS

Mitte

Betty F★★★

Mulackstrasse 13 (www.bettyf.de). U8 Weinmeisterstrasse. **Open** *Summer* from 10pm Mon-Sat; from 9pm Sun. *Winter* varies **No credit cards. Map** p319 O5.

A quirky basement space near Hackescher Markt that offers everything from transsexual theatre performers to surprisingly adept live classical music. Mostly, though, homosexuals of all ages gather here after 9pm for an anything-goes atmosphere that strikes a good balance between edgy and casual.

Prenzlauer Berg

Flax

Chodowieckistrasse 41 (4404 6988, www.flax-berlin.de). S8, S41, S42, S85 Greifswalder Strasse. **Open** 5pm-2am Tue-Thu; 5pm-4am (open end), 10am-1am Sun. **No credit cards. Map** p319 Q4.

It may be on the edge of the Prenzlauer Berg gay scene, but Flax has developed into one of the most popular café/bars in the district, mainly pulling a young, mixed crowd. Excellent Sunday brunch from 10am-5pm for €6.90 per person.

Greifbar

Wichertstrasse 10 (444 0828, www.greifbar.com). S41, S42, S8, S85, S9, U2 Schönhauser Allee. **Open** 10pm-late daily. **No credit cards. Map** p319 P2.

A thirty- to fortysomething Prenzlauer Berg crowd populates this cruisy bar looking for adventure and pleasure, either by picking someone up or by roaming about in the large darkrooms. There's also a decent retro-80s atmosphere if you just want to drink and nibble on the free popcorn.

★ Marietta

Stargarder Strasse 13 (4372 0646, www.marietta-bar.de). S41, S42, S8, S85, S9, U 2 Schönhauser Allee. **Open** 10am-2am Mon-Thur; 10am-4am Sat, Sun. **No credit cards. Map** p319 P2.

Hot hipster bartenders and a large room done up like a GDR office waiting room circa 1979 draw local gay boys and women to Marietta every night of the week. On Wednesday evenings, however, the place is crammed with sexy young men gossiping, laughing and boozing.

Perle

Sredzkistrasse 64 (498 534 50, www.bar-perle.de) U2 Eberswalderstrasse. **Open** 7pm-late Tue-Sat. **Map** p319 P3.

Delicious beverages abound at this small, austerely designed cocktail bar on Prenzlauer Berg's eastern fringe. Most nights, gay men line the bar gripping martinis or gather around the large table in the elevated back room. On Thursday nights, English is the predominant language as Perle becomes a hobnobbing party for gay ex-pats and the Germans that love them. A street-side patio doubles the capacity in summer.

Stiller Don
Erich-Weinert-Strasse 67 (0176 5013 3676).
S41, S42, S8, S85, S9, U2 Schönhauser Allee.
Open 8pm-late daily. **No credit cards.**
Map p319 P1.
Formerly home to the East Berlin avant-garde, now attracting a mixed crowd from all over the city, this place is set up like a cosy café, but it gets high spirited at weekends and on Mondays. An older crowd, mostly over 35, enjoys the periodic jazz and swing music nights.

Kreuzberg

Golden Finish
Wrangelstrasse 87 (no phone, www.golden finish.de). U1 Schlesisches Tor. **Open** from 6pm daily. **No credit cards. Map** p324 R9.
A fun, if mercurial, bar near the growing party zone of Schlesisches Tor. The crowd is a potpourri of Kreuzberg gays – punks, hipsters, bears-in-training – most under the age of 40. Take a whirl as the music maker on do-it-yourself DJ night, usually Saturdays. The name, in case you're wondering, has nothing to do with dirty sex play.

Rauschgold
Mehringdamm 62 (7895 2668, www.rauschgold-berlin.de). U6, U7 Mehringdamm. **Open** 8pm-late daily. **No credit cards. Map** p322 M10.
This plush and somewhat tacky bar is a good place for those who feel like prolonging their night into morning or for taking a first drink on an evening out. The occasional cabaret performances are generally not to be recommended.

Schöneberg

Café Berio
Maassenstrasse 7 (216 1946, www.cafeberio.de)
U1, U2, U3, U4 Nollendorfplatz. **Open** 8am-midnight Mon-Thur, Sun; 8am-1am Fri, Sat.
No credit cards. Map p322 J9.
One of the best daytime cafés in Berlin, this Parisian style café is full of attractive, trendy young men (including the waiters), with a good people-watching terrace in summer.

Hafen
Motzstrasse 19 (211 4118, www.hafen-berlin.de).
U1, U2, U3, U4 Nollendorfplatz. **Open** 8pm-open end daily. **No credit cards. Map** p321 D5.
A red, plush and vaguely psychedelic bar in the centre of Schöneberg's gay triangle. It's popular

with the fashion- and body-conscious, especially at weekends, when it provides a safe haven from nearby heavy cruising dens. It is usually very crowded, especially for the pub quiz, Quizz-o-Rama, which is held in English from 10pm on the first Monday of the month.

★ Heile Welt
Motzstrasse 5 (2191 7507). U1, U2, U3,
U4 Nollendorfplatz. **Open** 6pm-4am daily.
No credit cards. Map p321 H9.
A stylish café, lounge and cocktail bar for the fashion-conscious: the front has a '70s disco feel complete with furry wall; the back lounge offers plush leather seating. It's a good place to kick off an evening, practise some chat-up lines and decide whether to go clubbing or not. Packed by 11pm on Friday and Saturday.

Mutschmanns
Martin-Luther-Strasse 19 (2191 9640,
www.mutschmanns.de). U1, U2, U3, U4
Nollendorfplatz. **Open** 11pm-late Wed;
10pm-late Fri, Sat. **Admission** varies.
No credit cards. Map p321 D5/6.
This well-frequented hardcore bar, with a large and hard darkroom in the basement, is suitable for cruising or just hanging out, but with a dress code of leather, rubber or uniform. Rubber Night is the first Saturday of the month.

Prinzknecht
Fuggerstrasse 33 (2362 7444, www.
prinzknecht.de). U1, U2, U3, Wittenbergplatz.
Open 3pm-2am Mon-Thur, Sun; 3pm-3am Fri,
Sat. **No credit cards. Map** p321 D5.
With a large but under-used darkroom out back, this huge, open bar draws in gays from the neighbourhood as well as leathermen and other hardcore customers. The place is somewhat provincial in feel, but nice for a chat and a beer. The crowd moves outside in summer.

Tom's Bar
Motzstrasse 19 (213 4570, www.tomsbar.de). U1,
U2, U3, U4 Nollendorfplatz. **Open** 10pm-6am daily. **No credit cards. Map** p321 D5.
Once described by *Der Spiegel* as the climax of the night, Tom's is something of a cruising institution. The front bar is fairly chatty but the closer you get to the steps down to the darkroom the more intense things become. Very popular with men of all ages and styles, especially on Monday when you can get two drinks for the price of one.

Tramps
Eisenacher Strasse 6 (no phone). U1, U2, U3, U4
Nollendorfplatz. **Open** 24 hours daily. **No credit cards. Map** p321 H9.
The name says it all. This back alley of a bar, complete with crazy paving on the walls, is the only gay venue

ARTS & ENTERTAINMENT

in the district to open its doors 24/7. Expect a random crowd of local soaks, rent boys and horny bucks looking for easy fun in the darkroom at the back.

Woof

Fuggerstrasse 37 (2360 7870, www. woof-berlin.com). U1, U2, U3 Wittenbergplatz. **Open** 10pm-4am Mon-Sat; 9pm-2am Sun. **No credit cards. Map** p321 H9.

Bears, daddys and leather lovers coagulate around the bar or wonder the sex rooms out back, especially on Tuesdays when drinks are two-for-one. The body-conscious and hairless should tipple elsewhere.

Friedrichshain

Grosse Freiheit 114

Boxhagener Strasse 114 (no phone, www.gay-friedrichshain.de/grosse-freiheit-114). U5 Frankfurter Tor. **Open** from 10pm Tue-Sun. **No credit cards. Map** p324 T7.

The name promises 'big freedom', and the bar delivers with a distinctly open policy to all kinds of gay fellows looking for a good time either at the bar or in the darkrooms. It is particularly popular with older locals, although the changing nature of the neighbourhood is slowly bringing in the under-40 crowd. Note that the name only applies to men: no women are allowed.

★ Zum Schmutzigen Hobby

Revaler Strasse 99 (www.ninaqueer.com). U1, S3, S5, S75 Warschauer Strasse. **Open** from 6pm daily. **No credit cards. Map** p324 T8.

In 2010, famed drag queen Nina Queer moved her popular watering hole from Prenzlauer Berg to this developing (and oh-so-Berlin) party zone of reclaimed buildings next to the Spree. And it's better than ever. The new place is intensely fun, especially later in the night when loud US pop hits fill the air. There is a large outside patio that hosts viewing parties for *Germany's Next Top Model*, *Eurovision* and other TV events of gay interest.

► *For more about Nina Queer, see p227.*

CLUBS & ONE-NIGHTERS

With only a few real clubs – **Die Busche** (*see p223*), **SchwuZ** (*see p227*) and **Connection** (*see p227*) – one-nighters are all the rage. Some come and go, others run and run. Check *Siegessäule* or *Blu*, or look out for flyers in bars, cafés and shops.

Mitte

GMF

Week End, Am Alexanderplatz 5 (2809 5396, www.gmf-berlin.de). U5 U8 S3, S5, S7, S75 Alexanderplatz. **Open** 10pm-late Sun. **Admission** €10. **No credit cards. Map** p319 P5

Berlin's ultimate and long-standing Sunday tea dance is spread over two floors of an office building, with muscled, tank-topped operators delivering partiers from one to the other. Upstairs is the sociable pop floor, rammed with twinks and gym-goers, and providing some cool views of the perpetual construction at Alexanderplatz. Downstairs, there's an intense techno scene, complete with shirtless dancers and cruisiy bathrooms. Both are packed with a stylish, young, energetic crowd.

Horse Meat Disco

Tape Club, Heidestrasse 14 (www.tapeberlin.de). S3, S5, S7, S75 Hauptbahnhof. **Open** from midnight 1 Sat in the mth. **Admission** varies. **No credit cards. Map** p318 K4.

This DJ group may have been born in London's Vauxhall, but Horse Meat Disco has matured in Berlin. Once a month, the city's hottest bearded, beefy men descend on the Tape Club to dance the night away to the group's signature disco-garage sound. Popular, packed and sexy.

★ Klub International

Kino International, Karl-Marx-Allee 33 (2475 6011, www.klub-international.com). U5 Schillingstrasse. **Open** 11pm-late 1st Sat of mth. **Admission** €7-€10. **No credit cards. Map** p319 G3.

In a landmark 1950s DDR cinema, this one-nighter is worth a look for the interior alone. It's one of the biggest parties in town, regularly attracting up to 1,500 youngish guests in their tightest T-shirts. There are two dancefloors and DJs play a mix of house and mainstream music.

Prenzlauer Berg

Chantal's House of Shame

Bassy Club, Schönhauser Allee 176A (www.myspace.com/chantalshouseofshame). U2 Senefelderplatz. **Open** 11pm-7am Thur. **Admission** €7-€10. **No credit cards. Map** p319/p326 O4.

A popular, friendly, electro dance night hosted by well-known local drag queen Chantal. The party has exchanged some of its underground cred for a larger space, but still packs in the party set for an early weekend warm-up. You'll find a cross-section of Berlin's gay scene here, including some attractive transvestites and performers that put on a show around 1am.

★ Irrenhaus

GeburtstagsKlub, Am Friedrichshain 33 (www.geburtstagsklub.de). M4 Am Friedrichshain. **Open** 11pm-late 3rd Sat of month. **Admission** €8-€10. **No credit cards. Map** p319 H2.

This popular one-nighter is true to its name: 'Madhouse'. Hostess Nina Queer attracts a bizarre mixture of party kids, trashy drag queens and other

Nina Queer: Queen of Drag

The hostess with the mostest.

Berlin doesn't have a First Lady, but if it did, she would be Nina Queer. This self-declared 'most famous and successful drag queen in Germany' is at the centre of much that is fun and outrageous in the city's gay scene. One part Jodie Harsh, one part Grace Jones, Nina – or 'die Qveer' as her fans call her – claims to have been born in 1985 in a small mountain village in Carinthia, Austria. In 2000, so the story goes, she – then very much a he, called Daniel – escaped to Berlin and has been attracting attention here ever since. 'The last Austrian empress in Prussian exile' is another of her favourite taglines.

Whether upstaging Hollywood stars on the red carpet during the Berlin Film Festival, saying the unsayable on her Radio Energy show or climbing the pop charts with songs like 'Ficki Ficki Aua Aua' (fuck fuck ouch ouch), she is hard to ignore. In 2011 she even released an autobiography, *Dauerläufig* (*Long Running*), which quickly became a bestseller.

To meet the woman herself, just head to her Friedrichshain bar, **Zum Schmutzigen Hobby** (Dirty Hobby, *see p226*). Exhibitionists love playing Nina's favourite game: *Zeig was Du hast und trink was Du willst* (Show what you've got and drink what you like), in which a punter is given free drinks in return for getting their tackle out under the venue's blinding spotlight: Nina, naturally, will commentate the impromptu strip show. Look out, too, for her weekly Glamour Quiz. Nina also runs the **Irrenhaus** club night (*see p227*) at the Geburtstagsklub, which has been packing in the punters since 2003. It's the place VIPs tend to show up looking for some harmless Berlin debauchery: Justin Timberlake was here once and Nina has the photo to prove it.

flotsam of the night to dance to house and chart music under even more bizarre video installations. Popular and shrill, with candy distributed for free all night and a darkroom out back.

Shade Inc.

NBI, Schönhauser Allee 36. (6730 4457, www.shade-inc.de). U2, S8, S41, S42, S85 Schönhauser Allee. **Open** from 10.30pm Wed. **No credit cards. Map** p319 O3.
Taking the place of wildly popular Berlin Hilton, Shade Inc. holds its own with a random selection of DJs playing electro, pop, mash-ups, house and funk. The music can be hit-and-miss, but the cool venue (a bar in a former brewery now called the Kulturbrauerei, *see p242*), breezy patio, Kate Bush hits and alluring, androgynous crowd remain a constant. Always busy, always fun.

Kreuzberg

★ SchwuZ

Mehringdamm 61 (629 0880, www.schwuz.de). U6, U7 Mehringdamm. **Open** varies. **Admission** varies. **No credit cards. Map** p322 M10.

Saturday is the main disco night at the Schwulen Zentrum ('gay centre'), Berlin's longest-running dance institution. The club attracts a mixed crowd. There are two, sometimes three, dancefloors and much mingling between the three bars and Café Melitta Sundström (*see p221*) upstairs. Friday hosts an assortment of one-nighters, among them the wildly popular London calling on the first Friday of the month, with independent and pop music; on the last Friday of the month there is L-Tunes for lesbians and their friends (*see p233*), with music ranging from all-time favourites to electronica. The line-up for Saturdays includes Bump!, a night of retro party and disco hits on the first Saturday of the month.

Schöneberg

Connection

Fuggerstrasse 33 (218 1432, www.connection-berlin.com). U1, U2, U3, Wittenbergplatz. **Open** 10am-1am Mon-Thur, 11pm-5am;Fri, Sat, 2pm-1am Sun. **Admission** €5 **Map** p321 D5.
Popular men-only club on Saturdays, with DJs playing mainly electronic sounds. The dancefloor is

usually packed, and if you're bored with that you can cruise the vast flesh dungeons of Connection Garage on two floors below. The first Friday of the month is mixed, and it's open the night before public holidays.

Propaganda
Goya Club, Nollendorfplatz 5 (419 939 000, www.propaganda-party.de). U1, U2, U3, U4 Nollendorfplatz. **Open** 11pm-late every 2nd Saturday. **Admission** €10. **No credit cards**. **Map** p322 J9.
Directly across from the Nollendorfplatz U-bahn station sits a legendary 100-year-old building, revamped with designer decor to host events like this untamed dance night. Friendly boy-next-door types crowd onto an oval dancefloor beneath chandeliers for a night of feel-good commercial house and dance music that techno/electro fans would probably wish to avoid.

Friedrichshain

Cocktail D'Amore
Chez Jacki. An Der Schilling Brücke (0176 382 30 322, http://cocktaildamore.tumblr.com). **Open** 1 Sat in the mth (check website). **Admission** varies. **No credit cards**. **Map** p323 Q7
Finding the venue is tough, located as it is at the end of a dirt path along the Spree, but the payoff is great. Sexy boys in their 20s and 30s come here from across the city to dance to minimalist house well past dawn. The vibe can be a bit snobby at first, but as the night wears on, it gets easier to befriend patrons on the dancefloor or in the outdoor chillout space with a soothing view of the river.

LEATHER, SEX & FETISH VENUES

The hardcore and fetish scene in Berlin is huge. These days, leather gays are outnumbered by a younger hardcore crowd and skinhead types who prefer rubber and uniforms. Places to obtain your preferred garb are plentiful, as are opportunities to show it off, including the eternally crowded **Leather Meeting** over the Easter holidays, the annual **Gay Skinhead Meeting**, and various fetish parties and events. Most of the parties are men-only affairs and have a strict dress code.

Mitte

Kit Kat Club
Sage Club, Köpenicker Strasse 76 (2789 830 , www.kitkatclub.org). U8 Heinrich-Heine-Strasse. **Open** 11pm-late Fri-Sun. **Admission** €10-€15. **No credit cards**. **Map** p323 P7.
This legendary mixed/straight sex and techno party club has moved out of Schöneberg to take up residence every weekend at the Sage Club, the nightclub

with its own swimming pool. The fourth Friday of the month is Piepshow; Saturday nights feature the club's flagship CarneBall Bizarre, with the Afterhour event to follow. All nights are listed in the gay press, so make sure the crowd is the one you're looking for. Most parties have a fetish dress code; the least you have to do is take off your shirt.

Prenzlauer Berg

Darkroom
Rodenbergstrasse 23 (no phone, www.darkroom-berlin.de). U2, S8, S41, S42, S85 Schönhauser Allee. **Open** varies. **Admission** free-€2.50. **No credit cards**. **Map** p319 P1.
Yes, there is a darkroom in this small bar. In fact, it's more darkroom than bar. With the help of camouflage netting and urinals, the place pulls in a slightly hardcore clientele, but be warned that on less busy nights things can feel a bit desperate. The Naked Sex Party on Friday and Saturday's Golden Shower Party are particularly popular. Wednesday has an Underwear Sex Party from 6pm.

Stahlrohr 2.0
Paul-Robeson Strasse 50 (0170 803 769, www.stahlrohr-bar.de). U2, S8, S41, S42, S85 Schönhauser Allee. **Open** 10pm-6am Mon, Wed, Thur-Sat; 9pm-6am Tue; 6pm-6pm Sun. **Admission** varies. **No credit cards**. **Map** p319 O1.
A small cruisy pub in front and a large darkroom in back. There are sex parties here for every taste, including the Underwear Party (first and third Fridays), Slave Market (second and fourth Fridays), Topless Wednesdays and Thursdays, Naked Sex Party (Saturdays), Oben-oder-Unten-Ohne party (Naked Top or Bottom; Mondays). There's also the Youngster Party for those aged 18-26 (Tuesdays).

Friedrichshain

★ Lab.oratory
Am Wriezener Bahnhof (no phone, www.lab-oratory.de). U5 Weberwiese, S3, S5, S7 , S75 Ostbahnhof. **Open** 10pm-midnight Thur-Sat; 4-6pm Sun. **Admission** varies. **No credit cards**. **Map** p324 R7.
In the same building as Berghain nightclub, this sprawling hardcore sex den – complete with all the props: slings, beds, cages, pissoir, military zone, mock jail cells, and son on – takes the sexual perversion on offer in Berlin to another level. In addition to the regular and hugely popular Naked Sex Party on Thursdays and the Friday Fuck with two drinks for the price of one, the venue also organises Saturday and Sunday night specials ranging from the relatively soft core Office Slut (suits and ties), Gummi (rubber outfits), Athletes (sports gear) and Fausthaus (oral deep throat), to harder stuff, like Yellow Facts (watersports) and Scat (shit play). Check the website for dates.

ARTS & ENTERTAINMENT

Kreuzberg

Bodies in Emotion Erotik Party

*AHA, Monumentenstrasse 13 (8962 7948 ,
www.aha-berlin.de). U7 Kleistpark.* **Open** 9pm-
5am 2nd Fri of mth. **Admission** €5. **No credit
cards. Map** p322 F5.

This sex party is popular with guys under 30 or
who look it (you won't find many hairy chests here).
What you wear is your business, but most put on
shorts, which they then take off in the sex area,
where mattresses and slings invite you to join in
the fun. The rooms can get so packed that it's difficult to move (which can be good or bad, depending on your outlook).

Club Culture Houze

*Görlitzer Strasse 71 (6170 9669, www.club-
culture-houze.de). U1 Görlitzer Bahnhof.* **Open**
varies. **Admission** €7.60. **No credit cards.
Map** p323 Q9.

Diverse sex parties (some of them mixed), ranging
from Naked to SM and Fetish. Exclusive gay nights
on Monday (Naked Sex), Thursday and Sunday
(Naked and Underwear Sex Party), Friday (Fist
Factory) and Saturday (Gay Sex Party). Mostly
body-conscious night owls visit these kitsch rooms.
Mattresses invite people to lie down, but most
attendees hardly need encouragement.

Ficken3000

*Urbanstrasse 70 (6950 7335, www.ficken
3000.com). U7 U8 Hermannplatz.* **Open** 10pm-
late daily. **Admission** varies. **No credit cards.
Map** p323 P10.

A small, plucky sex club on the border with
Neukölln, Ficken3000 ('Fuck 3000') has both a sense
of humour and an extensive basement cruising dungeon. On Sundays, young ex-pats and hipsters pack
the place for Pork, a night of fun pop remixes, pole
dancing and sex. Porn is shown alongside old Joe
Dallesandro movies.

Quälgeist

*4th backyard, ground floor, Mehringdamm 51
(788 5799, www.quaelgeist-berlin.de). U6, U7
Mehringdamm.* **Open** varies. **Admission** €8-€15.
No credit cards. Map p322 M10.

First institution established solely to organise SM
parties, which include SM for beginners, bondage,
slave markets and fist nights. Pick up flyers at any
leather bar. There's usually a dress code.

Triebwerk

*Urbanstrasse 64 (6950 5203, www.triebwerk-
online.de). U7, U8 Hermannplatz.* **Open** 10pm-late
Mon, Thur-Sat; 9pm-late Tue, Wed; 4pm-late Sun.
Admission free €8 minimum consumption.
Map p323 P10..

This small, comfortable bar with a huge video
screen and a darkroom maze in the basement

attracts Kreuzberg gays of every denomination. On
Mondays there are two-for-one drinks; Naked and
Underwear Parties feature on Tuesdays, Fridays,
Saturdays and Sundays; Wednesdays is After
Work Sex, and it's Cruising Night on Thursdays.

Schöneberg

Ajpnia

*Eisenacher Strasse 23 (2191 8881,
www.ajpnia.de). U1, U2, U3, U4 Nollendorfplatz.*
Open from 7pm Wed; 9pm Sat. **Admission**
€5-€6. **No credit cards. Map** p322 D5.

A two-storey, intimate sex club frequented by men
of all ages. Every first and third Saturday is
Positihv Verkehr, a party by and for HIV-positives;
every second and fourth Saturday is Nachtverkehr
(Night Traffic) and Wednesday is Feierabend-
verkehr (After Work Traffic). Note that Verkehr
also means 'intercourse'. Check the website to
ensure it's not one of the club's occasional women-
only nights.

Angel's

*Courbierestrasse 13 (2362 4700, www.angels
berlin.de). U1, U2, U3, U4 Nollendorfplatz.*
Open 8pm-5am daily. **Admission** varies.
No credit cards. Map p321 H9.

An all-boys strip club in the classic style. The strippers are drawn from the predictable porntastic
stereotypes – sporty athletes, barely legals, hot-
blooded Latinos – and offer both public and private
shows. VIP parties can be arranged for birthdays,
bachelor parties and other special events.

Böse Buben

*Sachsendamm 76-77, Schöneberg
(6270 5610, www.boesebuben-berlin.de).
S1, S41, S42, S46 Schöneberg.* **Open** 4pm-
midnight Wed; 9pm-late Fri, Sat. **Admission**
€6. **No credit cards. Map** p322 J12..

Fetish sex party club with imaginatively furnished
and decorated rooms. Tiled piss room, sling room,
bondage cross and cheap drinks make this quite a
grotto of hedonism. Wednesday is the After Work
Sex Party; weekends have different parties such as
hard SM, fist, bondage and spanking.

CDL-Club

*Hohenstaufenstrasse 58. (32 66 78 55, www.
cdl-club.de). U1, U2, U3, U4 Nollendorfplatz.*
Admission *minimum spend* €9; €6 18-29s.
Map p321 H10.

One of Schoneberg's newest gay sex clubs brings
some original elements to the scene, like a special
treatment for the well endowed (there's cock and
arse measuring; Fridays), a mandatory-mask party
(white for tops, black for bottoms; Thursdays) and
periodic gangbang events (check the website). The
approach seems to be working: the place pulls in a
decent crowd from across the age spectrum.

New Action

Kleistrasse 35 (no phone, www.newaction berlin.de). U1, U2, U3, U4 Nollendorfplatz. **Open** 10pm-5am Mon-Thur; 10pm-7am Fri-Sat; 5pm-5am Sun. **No credit cards**. **Map** p321 D5.

Recently re-opened, this fetish venue has a hardcore atmosphere. Early mornings, the custom-designed bar and small darkroom can become quite a gathering of eccentrics who either don't want to go to bed yet or else just got up. Leather, rubber, uniform, jeans, but also the odd wool pullover creates a casual atmosphere. Don't be sober. Tuesday is 'Big Dick Nite' – a free drink for the well hung.

Scheune

Motzstrasse 25 (213 8580, www.scheune-berlin.de)., U2, U3, U4 Nollendorfplatz. **Open** from 9pm daily. **Admission** free. **No credit cards**. **Map** p321 H9.

Small, welcoming and cheap leather bar. Action in the cellar is late and heavy. There's a Naked Sex Party Sunday afternoon (entrance 5.30-9pm), plus occasional rubber nights. Very popular.

SAUNAS

Saunas are not as popular as they used to be in Berlin, most frequented after work. In-house bills are run up on your locker or cabin number and are settled on leaving. No open cabins, only personal ones.

Apollo Splash Club

101, Schöneberg (213 2424, www.apollosplashclub.com). U1, U2, U3, U12 Wittenbergplatz. **Open** 1pm-7am Mon-Thur; 1pm Fri-7am Mon. **Admission** varies. **No credit cards**. **Map** p321 H8.

This huge labyrinth of sin with 250 lockers and 80 cabins has been given a major revamp in recent years – at least on the first floor. Upstairs has a spa feel, while downstairs retains elements of the place's former Brazillian theme. There is a bar, cinema, dry and steam saunas, a massage area, pool, plunge bath and jungle-style cruising area. Check the website for regularly changing theme nights, such as foam parties and a fantasy do called Splash Dreams.

Treibhaus Sauna

Schönhauser Allee 132, Prenzlauer Berg (448 4503, www.treibhaussauna.de). U2 Eberswalder Strasse. **Open** 1pm-7am Mon-Thur; 1pm Fri-7am Mon. **Admission** €14-€19.80 (incl locker & €4-€6 drink ticket); €5.50 cabin. **No credit cards**. **Map** p319 O2.

Tucked in the first courtyard (buzz for entry), this has become a big favourite, especially with students and youngsters, and, on Sunday afternoon, those P'bergers who failed to pick up on Saturday night. Facilities include dry sauna, steam room, whirlpool,

cycle jet, solarium, a shop stocked with toys and lubricants, and cabins equipped with TV and VCR on a first-come, first-served basis. Internet access, too. During the week, there's a variety of medicinal and therapeutic massage treatments on offer.

CRUISING

Cruising is a popular and legal pursuit in Berlin. Most action takes place in the parks, in the daytime often just metres away from the general public, who don't seem to care. And don't panic or jump into a bush when encountering the police – they are actually there to protect you from gay bashers and they never hassle cruisers. One way or another, it's actually very safe to go roaming about at night. Summer brings out all of the city's finery and there is no taboo about nudity in parks.

Grunewald

S7 Grunewald.

Go to the woods behind the car park at Pappelplatz. Walk 500m (1,640ft) along Eichkampstrasse until it passes under the Autobahn, then turn to the right into the woods. From there it's about another 50m (164ft) to the car park. This is a popular daytime spot but it's also well frequented at night, when bikers and harder guys mingle among the trees.

Tiergarten

S3, S5, S7, S75 Tiergarten. **Map** p321 H7.

The Löwenbrücke (where the Grosser Weg crosses the Neuer See) is the cruising focal point – but the whole corner south-west of the Siegessäule becomes a bit of a gay theme park in summer, when daytime finds hundreds of gays sunning themselves on the Tuntenwiese ('faggot meadow') and taking periodic sex breaks in the woods.

Volkspark Friedrichshain

U2, U5, U8 or S3, S5, S75 Alexanderplatz, then Tram,M4 Am Friedrichshain. **Map** p319 Q5.

Offering friendlier, younger and more relaxed cruisers than Berlin's other hunting grounds, this popular outdoor sex patch was traditionally behind the Märchenbrunnen, but has now moved further east, to the slopes right off Friedenstrasse (just walk into the bushes behind the war memorial). Particularly active on sunny afternoons in the summer, when boys stroll over from nearby meadow.

Wannsee

See p104.

Europe's largest inland beach is home to a patch of sand traditionally occupied by gay men – just walk all the way to end of the beach and through to the far reaches of the FKK zone. Sun-kissed men lounge here on their towels and use the nearest loos and shower rooms to cruise and have fun. Watch for children.

SHOPS

Books & art

Bruno's

Nollendorfplatz, corner of Bülowstrasse 106, Schöneberg (6150 0385, www.brunos.de). U1, U2, U3, U4, U12 Nollendorfplatz. **Open** 10am-10pm Mon-Sat; 1-9pm Sun. **Map** p322 J9.

Large and rather plush shop with extensive selection of reading and viewing material, plus cards, calendars, videos, condoms, lube and other paraphernalia. **Other locations** Schönhauser Allee 131, Prenzlauer Berg (6150 0387).

Prinz Eisenherz

Lietzenburger Strasse 9A, Schöneberg (313 9936, www.prinz-eisenherz.com). U1, U2, U3, U12 Wittenbergplatz. **Open** 10am-8pm Mon-Sat. **Map** p321 H9.

One of the finest gay bookshops in Europe, including, among its large English-language stock, many titles unavailable in Britain. There's a good art and photography section, plus magazines, postcards and news of book readings and other events.

Fashion

Boyz 'R' Us

Maassenstrasse 8, Schöneberg (2363 0640, www.boyz-r-us.de). U1, U2, U3, U4 Nollendorfplatz. **Open** 11am-8pm Mon-Sat. **No credit cards. Map** p322 J9.

Classy clobber for discerning gays who like to be noticed and don't mind paying for it. Think G-Star, Diesel, Calvin Klein. Ladies store Goldelse is accessed through the back.

Laden 114

Eisenacher Strasse 114, Schöneberg (2363 9373). U1, U2, U3, U4, U12 Nollendorfplatz. **Open** noon-7pm Mon-Sat. **No credit cards. Map** p321 H9.

Gay designer fashion with a tougher edge, although there are also second-hand clothing racks with items from €3 upwards to mix and match.

LadeRaum

Mehringdamm 55, Kreuzberg (6953 2798). U7, U8 Mehringdamm. **Open** noon-8pm Mon-Sat. **No credit cards. Map** p322 M10.

Walls full of tight Ts and tops for day and night, many at bargain prices and with clever images. You can design your own with a print from €6.

Waahnsinn

Rosenthaler Strasse 17, Mitte (282 0029, www.waahnsinn-berlin.de). U8 Rosenthaler Platz or Weinmeisterstrasse. **Open** noon-8pm Mon-Sat. **Map** p319 N5.

Men's sequinned hot pants and tank tops are among the stand-out items in this stylish and theatrical 1950s-'70s second-hand clothes shop. Well worth a look, if only for the novelty factor.

Toys & Fetish

Black Style

Seelower Strasse 5, Prenzlauer Berg (4468 8595, www.blackstyle.de). S41, S42, S8, S85, S9, U2, Schönhauser Allee. **Open** 1-6.30pm Mon-Wed; 1-8pm Thur, Fri; 11am-6pm Sat. **Map** p319 O1.

From black fashion to butt plugs, if it's made out of rubber or latex, Black Style has got it. High quality, reasonable prices and big variety. Mail order too.

ARTS & ENTERTAINMENT

Boyz 'R' Us.

ARTS & ENTERTAINMENT

Butcherei Lindinger

Motzstrasse 18, Schöneberg (2005 1391,
www.butcherei-lindinger.de). U1, U2, U3,
U4, Nollendorfplatz. **Open** 2-8pm Mon-Sat.
No credit cards. Map p321 H9.
A smart workshop producing tailor-made leather
clothing, sportswear, kinky keks and chain mail. It also
offers a fantastic range of toys and rubber gear, including some of the biggest dildos on the market.

Connection Garage

Fuggerstrasse 33, Schöneberg (218 1432,
www.connection-berlin.com). U1, U2, U3
Wittenbergplatz. **Open** 10am-1am Mon-Sat; 2pm-
1am Sun. **Map** p321 H9.
Connection Garage stocks a huge selection of leather
novelties, clothing, SM accessories and magazines.
The cruising area comes alive at weekends when it
amalgamates with Connection club (*see p227*).

Jaxx

Motzstrasse 19, Schöneberg (213 8103, www.the
jaxx.de). U1, U2, U3, U4 Nollendorfplatz. **Open**
noon-3am Mon-Sat; 1pm-3am Sun. **Admission**
€8; €6 Tue. **Map** p321 H9.
Jaxx stocks a good selection of toys and videos, plus
there are video cabins and a cruising area.

Leathers

Schliemannstrasse 38, Prenzlauer Berg (442
7786, www.leathers.de). U2 Eberswalder Strasse.
Open noon-8.Mon-Sat. **Map** p319 P2.
This workshop produces leather and SM articles of
the highest quality. There's no smut here – just a range

of well-presented products and friendly, helpful staff.
Extensive online shop for the lazy kinkster.

Mr B

Motzstrasse 22, Schöneberg (2199 7704,
www.misterb.com). U1, U2, U3, U4
Nollendorfplatz. **Open** noon-8pm Mon-Fri; 11am-
8pm Sat. **Map** p321 H9.
The Berlin outpost of this Dutch chain has everything for the hardcore crowd. It's known particularly
for its leather and rubber outfits, metal accessories
and toys, SM articles, lubricants and clothing. Mr B
also hosts the occasional art exhibition.

RoB Berlin

RoB, Fuggerstrasse 19, Schöneberg (2196
7400, www.rob-berlin.de). U1, U2, U3, U4
Nollendorfplatz. **Open** noon-8pm Mon-Sat.
Map p321 H9.
Like the RoB locations in other European capitals,
Berlin's offers top-notch leather regalia and fetish
items made uniquely for this chain in its own workshops. There are themed apartments for rent
upstairs, and loads of information about upcoming
events in the leather community.

Lesbian

Few cities can compete with Berlin's network of
lesbian institutions, but there are few lesbian-
only bars. For mixed bars and club nights,
check *Siegessäule* or *L-mag* (www.L-mag.de),
a quarterly free lesbian magazine. *Blattgold*

www.blattgold-berlin.de, in German), is another lesbian mag, published every other month. There are also relatively reliable listings at www.youngandlesbian.de/szene.html, part of a support group for young lesbians. Many young lesbians favour mixed venues such as **SchwuZ** *(see p227)*, **SO36** *(see p224)*, **Möbel Olfe** *(see p222)* and **Die Busche** *(see p223)*.

CAFÉS & BARS

Mitte

Café Seidenfaden
Dircksenstrasse 47 (283 2783, www.frausucht zukunft.de). U8 Weinmeister Strasse; S3, S5, S7, S75 Hackescher Markt. **Open** 10-6pm Mon-Fri, noon-6pm Sat. **No credit cards. Map** p319 O5.
Run by women from a therapy group of former addicts. There are readings and exhibitions, but absolutely no drugs or alcohol. Packed at lunchtime, quiet at night.

Friedrichshain

Frieda Frauenzentrum
Proskauer Strasse 7 (422 4276, www.frieda-frauenzentrum.de). U5 Samariterstrasse. **Open** 9am-8pm Tue, Thur; 9am-6pm Wed; 2-8pm Fri; 11am-2pm 4th Sat of mth. **No credit cards. Map** p325 T6.
Centre for women's wellbeing and interests, with a full programme of lesbian, mothers' and seniors' events.

Schöneberg

Begine
Potsdamer Strasse 139 (215 1414, www.begine.de). U2 Bülowstrasse. **Open** 5pm-late Mon-Fri; from 7pm-late Sat. **No credit cards. Map** p322 J9
This venerable women-only café frequented by lesbians is part of the 'Meeting point and Culture for Women' centre.

Charlottenburg

Neue Bar
Knesebeckstrasse 16 (3150 3062). S5, S7, S9, S75 Savignyplatz. **Open** 6pm-late Tue-Sat. **No credit cards. Map** p321 C4.
There's a talkative atmosphere at this small pub for women and lesbians.

CLUBS & ONE-NIGHTERS

Freidrichshain

Women's Lounge
Himmelreich, Simon-Dach-Strasse 36 (www.gay-friedrichshain.de/himmelreich). **Open** 10pm-late Tue.

Drink specials attract a casual crowd of Friedrichshain lesbians to this popular joint every Tuesday. Expect more socialising than dancing.
▶ *For more about Himmelreich, see p221.*

Kreuzberg

Girls' Dance
Serene Bar, Friesenstrasse 14 (enter on Schwiebusserstrasse), (690 41 580, www.serene bar.de). U6 Platz der Luftbrücke. **Open** 10pm-late Sat. **No credit cards. Map** p323 M11.
Every Saturday, the girls come out to dance and play together at this long, narrow, amiable bar off the beaten track, near what used to be Tempelhof Airport. 'DJ(ane)s' play for the ladies, who take full advantage of the spacious dancefloor.

L-Tunes
SchwuZ, Mehringdamm 61 (693 7025, www.megadyke.de). U6, U7 Mehringdamm. **Open** 10pm-late 4th Fri of mth. **Admission** €6/€7. **No credit cards. Map** p322 M10.
L-Tunes holds dance and electronica nights on two floors with a chill-out zone every fourth Friday of the month. This is primarily for young Kreuzberger girls, but the crowd varies in both age and demeanour.

SHOPS & SERVICES

La Luna
Dunckerstrasse 90, Prezlauer Berg (4432 8488, www.laluna-toys.de). U2 Eberswaldestrasse. **No credit cards. Open** 2pm-8pm Mon-Fri; noon-6pm Sat.
Men and couples are welcome in this high-end sex shop, but the focus is on women. Vibrators, lingerie and plenty of books, as well as a helpful staff, make for a solid and sexy shopping experience.

Playstixx
Waldemarstrasse 24, Kreuzberg (6165 9500, www.playstixx.de). U1, U8 Kottbusser Tor. **Open** *Women & transvestites* 2-7pm Wed; 2-7pm Fri. *All* 2-7pm Thur and by appointment. **No credit cards. Map** p323 P8
The dildos on offer at this workshop, run by sculptress Stefanie Dörr, are more likely to come in the form of bananas, whales, fists and dolphins than phalluses. Most are made of non-allergenic, highly durable silicon.

Sexclusivitäten
Laura Mérrit, Fürbringerstrasse 2, Kreuzberg (693 6666, www.sexclusivitaeten.de). U7 Gneisenaustrasse. **Open** noon-8pm Fri and by appointment. **No credit cards. Map** p323 N10.
Laura Mérrit calls herself a feminist linguist and sexpert, offering sex counselling, conflict mediation and a big selection of sex toys. Shop for a variety of dildos, vibrators and other items.

ARTS & ENTERTAINMENT

Music

A rich seam of musical life runs through the city.

It can sometimes feel impossible to walk down a street in the capital without seeing musicians lugging cellos on their bicycles, or hearing the sound of someone rehearsing piano scales floating down from a balcony window. It's hardly surprising that there are a lot of musicians around: in the classical arena, Berlin has three state-sponsored opera houses and a vibrant orchestral scene. Meanwhile, in the popular music arena, Berlin is nothing less than legendary as a one-time residence for David Bowie, Iggy Pop and Nick Cave, and as the home of electronica.

Classical & Opera

The posters on the U-bahn proclaim Berlin *Opernhauptstadt* (Opera Capital) – and they aren't kidding. Not only does Germany have one-seventh of the world's opera houses, but Berlin itself can count on three state-subsidised opera houses – a record not matched even in Italy.

Indeed, no city in the world can compete with Berlin when it comes to sheer number of orchestras and opera houses. The former include the Berliner Philharmoniker, Deutsches Symphonie-Orchester Berlin, Rundfunk-Sinfonieorchester Berlin and Konzerthausorchester Berlin, while the latter comprises the Deutsche Oper, Staatsoper Unter den Linden and the Komische Oper. And that's before you get to the smaller companies and venues. And that's not to mention the star names attached – Sir Simon Rattle and Daniel Barenboim, to name just two.

This cultural richness is not only a legacy of the city's long artistic heritage but also of its Cold War division. East and West Berlin were both awash with state subsidies in a bid to demonstrate the cultural supremacy of communist and capitalist philosophy.

After reunification there was twice the amount of everything, and, as a result, Berlin now boasts enough classical music for two (or maybe three) cities. It's not just quantity, but quality too: the Berlin Philharmonic is arguably the world's finest symphony orchestra, and there are several top-notch performances of one kind or another to choose from here virtually every night of the year.

Naturally, in more belt-tightening times, the question of funding, and internecine rivalry between the three houses, is a perennial thorny subject. At the time of the fall of the Wall, the (West) Berlin Deutsche Oper was receiving double the subsidy of its (East) Berlin rival, the Staatsoper.

That situation is now reversed, with the Staatsoper receiving around €3 million a year more in funding. Not only that, but the ornate Staatsoper building on Unter den Linden is currently enjoying a €240-million refurbishment. The Staatsoper, under the baton of Barenboim since 1992, is currently performing at the more utilitarian **Schiller Theatre** on Bismarckstrasse whilst those renovations take place – ironically, just a couple of hundred metres down the street from the Deutsche Oper.

The three opera houses (including the Komische Oper) are now incorporated into one foundation, the Opernstiftung, after some initial push to amalgamate entirely, but co-ordination of their programmes is still an issue, as is their simultaneous closure during summer.

Knowing that the cultural industries are a major powerhouse in Berlin's tourist and intellectual attractions, Berlin's mayor, Klaus Wowereit, in office since 2001 and winning another term in state elections in September 2011, has made a big play of the city being 'poor, but sexy'.

OPERA COMPANIES
The **Deutsche Oper** still lives under the shadow of its former long-time intendant Götz Friedrich, who died in 2000. Kirsten Harms,

who took over the role in 2004 and was due to step down in 2011, has been struggling to provide the house with a distinct artistic profile. Luck hasn't always been on her side, however. In summer 2007, the controversy following the Danish cartoons about Mohammed brought the international spotlight on to the Deutsche Oper's *Idomoneo*, a production unremarkable save for the appearance of a head of the Prophet Mohammed. In an unfolding scandal of operatic proportions, the production was cancelled; however, after a national and international protest, *Idomoneo* eventually re-appeared on the programme. This was followed by the unexplained disappearance of the head of Mohammed, the production's essential prop. In the end, several performances took place under unprecedented security measures and international media scrutiny. As if that wasn't enough, the appointment of Italian Renato Palumbo as new musical director came to a premature end after both audiences and critics loudly voiced their discontent. The Scot Donald Runnicles has been in the hot seat since then.

The **Staatsoper Unter den Linden** moved to the Schiller Theatre in October 2010 for three years, while its home on Unter den Linden is expensively refurbished. (The Schiller itself benefited from a recent €24,000 000 makeover.) The debut at its new home – the world premier of Jens Joneleit's *Metanoia* – was unfortunately jinxed when the director, Christopher Schlingensief, died six weeks before the curtain was due to go up.

In 2011 Barenboim signed another ten-year contract with the Staatsoper. His presence ensures that performances are of the highest quality, even if they have sometimes been overshadowed by spectacular staging – something unlikely to be a problem in the Schiller. Its orchestra, the Berliner Staatskapelle, founded in 1570, is regarded as Berlin's finest opera orchestra.

The **Komische Oper**, under intendant Andreas Homoki, prides itself on contemporary, even controversial, productions, and an outreach programme that includes Turkish subtitling. It doesn't shy away from sex and

violence either, with Richard Strauss's *Salome* in 2011 having a woman wrap her legs around Jesus' waist as he is crucified.

Although the Komische Oper makes do with the smallest budget of the three opera houses, it outshone the other two by winning the prestigious Opera House of the Year award in 2007. Patrick Lange took over from Carl St Clair as general music director in 2010.

For more independent operatic fare, don't neglect the down-at-heel but charming **Neuköllner Oper**, which puts on witty and imaginative productions. Other companies worth checking out are the **Neue Opernbühne**, **Zeitgenössische Oper Berlin** (www.zeitgenoessische-oper.de), the **Berliner Kammeroper** (www.berlinerkammeroper.de) and **Novoflot** (www.novoflot.de), which usually performs at the Sophiensaele. Expect innovative music and theatre of surprising quality despite low budgets.

ORCHESTRAS

Berlin's orchestral scene is as vibrant as ever. The **Deutsches Symphonie-Orchester Berlin** (www.dso-berlin.de) still boasts fairly healthy subsidies and remains one of the finest places in town to hear avant-garde compositions and unusual programmes. Chief conductor Ingo Metzmacher resigned early in 2010 after disputes over financing, with Tugan Sokhiev appointed to take over in 2012 as principal conductor and artistic director.

Groundbreaking 20th-century composers, from Hindemith to Prokofiev and Schönberg to Penderecki, have conducted their own work with the Rundfunk-Sinfonieorchester Berlin (www.rsb-online.de). The orchestra, founded in 1923 to provide programming for the new medium of radio, looks set to continue with its tradition of drawing attention to contemporary works under musical director Marek Janowski. The orchestra has started playing concerts in new locations, such as the Schlüterhof in the Deutsches Historisches Museum (*see p61*),

Fans of the old masters are still well served by the **Konzerthausorchester Berlin** (www.konzerthausorchester.de), previously known as the Berliner Sinfonie-Orchester, which plays at the splendid Konzerthaus. The feisty group – founded after the building of the Wall as the East's answer to the Philharmonic – has a loyal following, but one that prefers more familiar works. Lother Zagrosek, widely recognised for his interpretations of contemporary music, has broadened the musical scope and direction of the orchestra to include the genre, but is due to be suceeded by Hungarian conductor Ivan Fischer from the beginning of the 2012 season.

THE BEST MUSIC FESTIVALS

For classical music
Musikfest Berlin in September. *See p198.*

For free partying all over town
Fête de la Musique in June. *See p199.*

For big-name bands
Berlin Festival in September. *See p200.*

Berlin's chamber orchestras also offer a steady stream of first-rate concerts. One of the finest groups is **Ensemble Oriol Berlin** (www.ensemble-oriol.de), which has a strong emphasis on contemporary music. The **Kammerorchester Berlin** (www.koberlin.de) remains popular but predictable, with works ranging from Vivaldi to Mozart and back again. The **Deutsches Kammerorchester Berlin** (www.dko-berlin.de), founded in 1989, has acquired an excellent reputation for working with rising star conductors and soloists, and for offering innovative yet audience-friendly programmes.

Last but not least, there's the mighty **Berliner Philharmoniker** (www.berliner-philharmoniker.de), which goes from strength to strength under Sir Simon Rattle, appointed in 2002 to succeed Claudio Abbado who was joined by intendant Pamela Rosenberg in 2006. Rattle promised to bring adventure to the programme and attract younger audiences, and has introduced an emphasis on contemporary composers such as Thomas Adès and Marc Anthony Turnage. He has also worked with jazz musicians and improvisers. At the same time, Rattle has put the ensemble through more traditional paces. He has also launched a new education programme with projects that aim to integrate youths from different backgrounds and get them hooked on classical music. He went through a rocky patch around 2005 and 2006, when he came in for criticism from some of the highbrow German press, suggesting he was not filling the shoes of his illustrious predecessors, and Rattle himself has admitted his relationship with musicians had been 'turbulent' as he pressed them away from their Germanic comfort zones. However, in 2008 the orchestra voted to keep him in post until 2018.

FESTIVALS

Music festivals pepper Berlin's calendar. **MaerzMusik – Festival für aktuelle Musik** (*see p198*) takes place in March at various venues, and showcases trends in contemporary music. The **UltraSchall** (*see p202*) festival of new music, organised by DeutschlandRadio and Rundfunk Berlin-Brandenburg every January, features many of the world's leading specialist ensembles. The biennial **Zeitfenster – Biennale für alte Musik** (*see p198*) at the Konzerthaus focuses on 17th-century baroque music for one week in April. Popular programmes, orchestras and soloists often kick off the **Classic Open Air** concert series (*see p199*) on Gendarmenmarkt in July. There's less focus on food, drink and socialising at the **Young.euro.classic**

Philharmonie. *See p238.*

(*see p200*), which assembles youth orchestras from all over Europe in August.

During the second half of September, 60 talented amateur pianists from around the world take part in the biennial **International Piano Amateur Competition** (www.ipac-berlin.com) at the Philharmonie, which is next held in 2012. The **Berliner Festspiele** (www.berlinerfestspiele.de) organises the annual **Musikfest Berlin** (*see p200*) in August and September, which brings some of the world's finest orchestras to Berlin.

TICKETS

Getting seats at the Philharmonie can still be difficult (although the website is easy to navigate), especially when it's for a big-name star or when the Berlin Phil itself is in residence; tickets for concerts by visiting performers are often easier to come by.

Otherwise, it's worth scanning the listings in daily papers or *tip* and *Zitty*, and phoning venues or checking their websites to see what's available. If all else fails, try standing outside the venue with a sign reading '*Suche eine Karte*' ('seeking a ticket'), or chatting up arriving concert-goers ('*Haben Sie vielleicht eine Karte übrig?*' means 'Got a spare ticket?'). You may also see people with extras for sale ('*Karte(n) zu verkaufen*'), but beware of ticket sharks. Some of the former East Berlin venues remain more affordable than their western counterparts, but the days of dirt-cheap tickets are long gone. Standing-room at the top of the Konzerthaus gives a decent view, but before buying cheap seats for the Staatsoper ask how much of the stage you can see.

Most venues offer student discounts. The ClassicCard (www.classiccard.de) is also worth considering: it's €15 if you're under 30, is valid for one year and entitles the holder to excellent seats for a mere €8 for concerts and €10 for opera and ballet. Participating institutions include the Deutsche Oper, Komische Oper, Konzerthaus, Deutsches Symphonie-Orchester Berlin and the Staatsoper Unter den Linden. It can be purchased at these venues and over the internet.

TICKET AGENCIES

Tickets are sold at concert hall box offices or through ticket agencies, called *Theaterkassen*. At box offices, seats are generally sold up to one hour before the performance. You can also make reservations by phone, except for concerts by the Berlin Phil. Theaterkassen provides the easiest means of buying a ticket, but commissions can run as high as 17 per cent. Hekticket is probably the best bet, or you can try www.ticketonline.de. For the 50 or so other agencies around the city, look in the *Gelbe Seiten* (*Yellow Pages*)

under '*Theaterkassen*'. Note that many Berlin venues do not accept credit cards.

Hekticket

Hardenbergstrasse 29D, Charlottenburg (230 9930/www.hekticket.de). U2, U9, S3, S5, S7, S9, S75 Zoologischer Garten. **Open** 10am-8pm Mon-Sat; 2-6pm Sun. **Map** p321/p328 G8.
Hekticket offers discounts of up to 50% on theatre and concert tickets. For a small commission, staff will sell you tickets for the same evening's performance. Tickets for Sunday matinées are available on Saturday. You can check ticket availability online, though not everything is listed. The Mitte branch, in a kiosk just south of the S-Bahn bridge, is closed on Sundays.
Other location Karl-Liebknecht-Strasse 12, Mitte (2431 2431).

MAJOR VENUES

Deutsche Oper

Bismarckstrasse 35, Charlottenburg (343 8401, tickets 3438 4343, www.deutscheoperberlin.de). U2 Deutsche Oper. **Box office** *Performance days* 11am-before performance Mon-Sat; 10am-2pm Sun. *Non-performance days* 1-7pm. **Tickets** prices vary. **Map** p320 D7.
With roots dating back to 1912, the Deutsche Oper built its present 1,900-seat hall in 1961, just in time to carry the operatic torch for West Berlin during the Wall years. Since reunification it has lost out in profile to the more elegant Staatsoper, but retains a reputation for productions of the classics. Discount tickets available half an hour before performances.

Komische Oper

Behrenstrasse 55-57, Mitte (202 600, tickets 4799 7400, www.komische-oper-berlin.de). S1, S2, S25, U55 or U6 Französische Strasse. **Box office** *In person* 11am-7pm Mon-Sat. *By phone* 9am-8pm Mon-Sat; 2-8pm Sun. **Tickets** €8-€93. **Map** p318/p327 M6.
Despite its name, the Komische Oper puts on a broader range than just comic works, and, after its founding in 1947, made its reputation by breaking with the old operatic tradition of 'costumed concerts' – singers standing around on stage – and putting an emphasis on 'opera as theatre', with real acting skill demanded of its young ensemble. Most of its productions are sung in German. Discounted tickets are sold immediately before performances.

Konzerthaus

Gendarmenmarkt 2, Mitte (2030 92101, www.konzerthaus.de). U6 Französische Strasse. **Box office** noon-7pm Mon-Sat; noon-4pm Sun. **Tickets** €10-€99; some 25% reductions. **Map** p322/p327 M7.
Formerly the Schauspielhaus am Gendarmenmarkt, this 1821 architectural gem by Schinkel was all but

THE BEST MUSIC VENUES

For stadium sounds
Olympiastadion. See p253

For al fresco listening
die Waldbühne. See p199.

For reliving the roaring twenties
Admiralspalast. See p241.

destroyed in the war. Lovingly restored, it was reopened in 1984 with three main spaces for concerts. Organ recitals in the large concert hall are a treat, played on the massive Jehmlich organ at the back of the stage. The Konzerthausorchester (*see p235*) is based here, presenting a healthy mixture of the classic, the new and the rediscovered. The Rundfunk-Sinfonieorchester Berlin and the Staatskapelle Berlin also play here. There are also occasional informal concerts in the cosy little Musik Club in the depths of the building.

★ Philharmonie

Herbert-von-Karajan Strasse 1, Tiergarten (254 880, tickets 2548 8999, www.berliner-philharmoniker.de). U2, S1, S2, S25 Potsdamer Platz. **Box office** 9am-6pm daily. **Tickets** €7-€220. **Credit** AmEx, MC, V. **Map** p322 K7.

Berlin's most famous concert hall, home to the world-renowned Berlin Philharmonic Orchestra, is also its most architecturally daring; a marvellous, puckish piece of organic modernism. The hall, with its golden vaulting roof, was designed by Hans Scharoun and opened in 1963. Its reputation for superb acoustics is accurate, but it does depend on where you sit. Behind the orchestra the acoustics leave plenty to be desired, but in front (where it is much more expensive) the sound is heavenly. The structure also incorporates a smaller hall, the Kammermusiksaal, about which the same acoustical notes apply.

The unique Berliner Philharmoniker (www.berliner-philharmoniker.de) was founded in 1882 by 54 musicians keen to break away from the penurious Benjamin Bilse, in whose orchestra they played. Over the last 120 years, it has been led by some of the world's greatest conductors, as well as by composers such as Peter Tchaikovsky, Edvard Grieg, Richard Strauss and Gustav Mahler. Its greatest fame came under the baton of Herbert von Karajan, who led the orchestra between 1955 and 1989, and was succeeded by Claudio Abbado. Since 2002, it has been under the leadership of Sir Simon Rattle. The Berlin Phil gives about 100 performances in the city during its August to June season, and puts on another 20 to 30 concerts around the world. Some tickets are available at a discount immediately before performances. *Photo p236.*

★ Staatsoper Unter den Linden

Schiller Theatre, Bismarckstraße 110, Charlottenburg until 2013 (203 540, tickets 2035 4555, www.staatsoper-berlin.de). U2 Ernst-Reuter-Platz. **Box office** noon-7pm. **Tickets** prices vary. **Map** p321 E7.

The Staatsoper, which is currently closed until 2013 for a €240 million refurbishment, was founded as Prussia's Royal Court Opera for Frederick the Great in 1742 and designed along the lines of a Greek temple. Although the present building dates from 1955, the façade faithfully copies that of Knobelsdorff's original, twice destroyed in World War II. Until the renovations are complete, performances take place at the Schiller Theatre. Unsold tickets are available for €10 half an hour before the performance.

OTHER VENUES

Many churches offer organ recitals, as do castles and museums in summer. Phones are often erratically staffed, so check *tip* or *Zitty* for information.

Akademie der Künste

Pariser Platz 4, Mitte (200 571000). S1, S2, S25, U55 Br (200571000/www.adk.de). S1, S2, S25, U55 Brandenburger Tor. **Open** 10am-10pm daily. *Exhibitions* 10am-8pm Tue-Sun. **Tickets** €5-€10. **No credit cards. Map** p327 L6.

The Akademie der Künste was founded by Prince Friedrich III in 1696, and is one of the oldest cultural institutions in Berlin. By 1938, however, the Nazis had forced virtually all of its prominent members into exile. It was re-established in West Berlin in 1954, in this fine new building by Werner Duttmann, to serve as 'a community of exceptional artists' from around the world. Apart from performances of 20th-century compositions, its programme offers a variety of other events, from jazz and poetry readings to film screenings and art exhibitions. Although most of the now-reunified Akademie have moved into a new building at its pre-war address on Pariser Platz, some performances and exhibitions are still held at the Hanseatenweg venue.
Other Location Hanseatenweg 10, Tiergarten.

Ballhaus Naunynstrasse

Naunynstrasse 27, Kreuzberg (tickets 307 545 3725 /www.ballhausnaunynstrasse.de). U1, U8 Kottbusser Tor. **Box office** 5.30-8pm on performance days. **Tickets** €12; €7 reductions. **No credit cards. Map** p323 P8.

Don't expect to hear anything ordinary at this Kreuzberg cultural centre. A varied assortment of western and oriental music is on the programme here, with drinks and snacks served in the café out front. The long, rectangular hall, which seats 150, plays host to the excellent Berlin Chamber Opera, among others.

Neuköllner Oper.

Nikolaisaal Potsdam

Wilhelm-Staab Strasse 10-11, Potsdam (0331 288 8828, www.nikolaisaal.de). S-Bahn Potsdam. **Box office** 10am-5pm Mon-Fri; 10am-2pm Sat. **Tickets** €22-€45.

Worth a trip out to Potsdam simply for the auditorium: behind a conventional baroque façade, the space-age sci-fi white rubber with protruding ovals on the walls and the white seating is certainly eye-catching, even distracting, but provides super acoustics. The concert hall hosts performances for the Potsdam Chamber Academy, Brandenburg State Orchestra, Brandenburg Symphony Orchestra and German Film Orchestra Babelsberg, as well as one-off art-house indie gigs, such as Lambchop playing along to FW Murnau's silent film *Sunrise*.

Neuköllner Oper

Karl-Marx-Strasse 131-133, Neukölln (6889 0777, www.neukoellneroper.de). U7 Karl-Marx-Strasse. **Box office** 3-7pm Tue-Fri, weekend performance days. **Tickets** €9-€24. **Map** p324 R12.

No grand opera here, but a constantly changing programme of chamber operas and music-theatre works much loved by the Neuköllners who come to see lighter, bubblier, cheaper and much less formal works than those offered by Berlin's big three opera houses. Shame about the acoustics, though.

St Matthäus Kirche am Kulturforum

Matthaeikirchplatz, Tiergarten (2035 5311 office, 2621 206 church, www.stiftung-stmatthaeus.de). U2, S1, S2, S25 Potsdamer Platz. **Box office** noon-6pm Tue-Sun. **Tickets** prices vary. **No credit cards. Map** p322 K8.

Concerts here might be anything from a free organ recital to a chorus of Russian Orthodox monks. Exquisite acoustics.

Universität der Künste

Hardenbergstrasse 33, corner of Fasanenstrasse, Tiergarten (318 50/31852374 box office, www.udk-berlin.de). U2, U9, S3, S5, S7, S9, S75 Zoologischer Garten. **Box office** 3-6pm Tue-Fri; **Tickets** prices vary (often free). **No credit cards. Map** p321/p328 F7.

This place may be grotesquely ugly, but it is nonetheless a functional hall, hosting both student soloists and orchestras, as well as performances by lesser-known professional groups.

Berliner Dom

Lustgarten 1, Mitte (2026 9136 tickets, www.berliner-dom.de). S3, S5, S7, S75 Hackescher Markt. **Box office** *Apr-Sept* 9am-8pm Mon-Sat; noon-8pm Sun. *Oct-Mar* 9am-7pm Mon-Sat; noon-7pm Sun. **Tickets** prices vary. **Map** p319/p327 N6.

Berlin's cathedral holds some recommendable concerts, usually of the organ or choral variety.

Musikhochschule Hanns Eisler

Charlottenstrasse 55, Gendarmenmarkt, Mitte (688 305 700, 688 305 842 tickets, www.hfm-berlin.de). U2, U6 Stadtmitte. **Box office** 10.30am-2.30pm Mon; 2-5pm Wed; 2-4pm Fri. **Tickets** prices vary (usually free). **No credit cards. Map** p322/p327 M7.

This musical academy was founded in 1950 and named after the composer of the East German national anthem. It offers students the chance to learn under some of the stars of Berlin's major orchestras and operas. Rehearsals and master classes are often open to the public for free, and student performances, some of them top-notch, are held in the Konzerthaus across the street. Other events are held at the new Krönungskutschensaal in the Marstall, a 300-seat venue blessed with perfect acoustics.

Other locations Marstall, Schlossplatz 7, Mitte (9026 9700).

Rock, World & Jazz

Berlin has always been a magnet for musicians – from the decadent Weimar years portrayed in *Cabaret*, to the Cold-War-paranoia exile of Bowie, Iggy Pop, Nick Cave and the Bad Seeds, through the corporate career-reinventions of U2 (*Achtung Baby!*) and REM (*Collapse Into Now*), both recorded in the city, to West Berlin's adopted heroine Nico (buried in Grunewald cemetery) and East Berlin's Nina Hagen (who even composed the official club anthem of FC Union) – the city seems to both like playing host to musicians, and be a city bands like playing.

As well as the rich musical history, there is also the array of grungy and idiosyncratic venues, and reputation for debauchery. With all-night public transport, and many gig-goers arriving by bicycle, headline acts at the smaller venues often do not appear on-stage until after midnight, no matter what it says on the ticket.

But not everything is rosy in the garden. The live music scene is not immune to the every-increasing gentrification of the city, as developers and rocketing rents reclaim venues in Kreuzberg, Friedrichshain and Prenzlauer Berg for more corporate ends.

The year 2011 saw the closure of such famous, and previously integral, venues as Maria am Ostbahnhof (swallowed up by the ever-encroaching Media Spree redevelopment project) and Knaack (redeveloped as apartments).

Attempts to host the first music festival in the disused Tempelhof airport ended in disarray in summer 2010, as inadequate logistics and ramped-up security (in the wake of the Duisenberg Love Parade fatal crush) led to huge queues and the all-night licence being revoked.

Meanwhile, alternative music icons of the '80s, '90s or last decade are now either heading towards pensionable age (Blixa Bargeld) or have achieved semi-establishment status (Peaches), or both. In addition, black music – reggae, hip-hop, jazz – perhaps isn't quite as well represented as in London or Paris, reflecting Berlin's fairly white racial mix, but that often means you get to see big-name acts at slightly smaller, more intimate venues than elsewhere on their tours. On the other hand, other musical styles long out of fashion in other capitals – such as goth and punk – steadfastly survive, even thrive, in Berlin.

One field in which Berlin is still definitely leading the field is electronica. The capital is synonymous with the genre, which is now reinventing itself again as a result of the influx of foreign talent. Electroclash is a distant memory, and genres like electrodreck have given way to less confrontational electronic sounds, ranging from Ben Klock's minimal techno, to the more experimental electronica of Brit expats Chris Clark and Planning to Rock. Many of Berlin's current electronic pioneers are regulars at Berghain's legendary Leisure System parties.

VENUES

On the plus side, ticket prices are still relatively cheap, and – while the gargantuan warehouse techno parties of the 1990s may be fading into

mythology – new venues are opening up, most notably **Astra Kulturhaus** (latest hip indie acts), and the refurbished **Huxley's** (hard rock, indie). The huge US acts play the monolithic **02 Arena** on the Spree (still a controversial building among hardcore Kreuzberg crusties), whilst the old **Admiralspalast** theatre, reopened in 2006, now has an eclectic gig policy (PJ Harvey, Arctic Monkeys) in among the theatrical productions.

Holding out against the internet MP3 tide, Berlin still has lots of good record shops, which are as good a place as the listings mags for finding out what's going on via flyers, posters and word-of-mouth.

Most importantly, keep your ears peeled – for all the doom-and-gloom peddled by those locals always mourning for a bygone golden era, this is still a city where an art gallery opening can transmogrify into an impromptu gig, or a sunny evening and a patch of grass by the canal be the spur for someone to set up some decks and speakers for an unofficial rave.

It's not uncommon for normally mild-mannered Berliners to carry on demanding an encore long after the lights have gone up. Every concert has a DJ afterwards and every bartender considers themselves a DJ, even if all they do is slip on Can's Flow Motion while they go and smoke a cigarette.

BUSKERS

Even if gigs in obscure, edgy locations are becoming more the exception that the norm, those seeking some spontaneous, al-fresco musical action should head to the Admiralbrücke, the Mauerpark or Görlitzer Park on a warm summer evening, popular locations for buskers of all musical bents. The large number of wannabe musicians in the city means that some of the buskers are more than competent. They get a chance to really shine during the Fête de la Musique, a one-day music festival in June, when amateur musicians are officially allowed to perform in public at sites all over Berlin, and the city becomes one giant jamming session.

FESTIVALS

Each September, the city hosts **Berlin Musik Week** (*see p200*), which includes trade show PopKomm and the Berlin Festival at the old Tempelhof Airport. In July, *Vice* magazine presents an annual festival largely dedicated to dance-rock, while an 80-minute train ride away in Gräfenhainichen, the **Melt! Festival** (www.meltfestival.de) presents indie-rock and electronica. And if you have an unquenchable desire to discover the Berlin backdrop to David Bowie's *Low*/'Heroes' period or see the bar where Iggy Pop once ended a *Rolling Stone* interview by rolling around on the pavement, the Fritz Music Tour (www.musictours-berlin.com) is for you.

ROCK

The sports venues **Max-Schmeling-Halle**, **O2 World** and **Velodrom**, (for all, *see p253*) also host occasional music events.

Admiralspalast

Friedrichstrasse 101 (4799 7499 tickets, www.admiralspalast.de). S1, S2, S25, S3, S5, S7, S75, U6 Friedrichstrasse. **Open** *Box office* 11am-7pm Mon-Sat; 11am-5pm Sun; also 1hr before performances. **Tickets** vary. **Map** p327 N6.
Reportedly Hitler's favourite theatre, it set the record straight (and exorcised some ghosts) in 2009 by becoming the first venue in Germany to stage Mel Brook's Nazi-lampooning *The Producers*. Restored and reopened in 2006 (after being threatened with demolition in the late 1990s) when not hosting theatre or cabaret, the Admiralspalst, right next to Friedrichstrasse station, has sell-out gigs by the likes of PJ Harvey and Emmylou Harris, and has become the classy-but-cool venue of choice for big names who want to keep an atmospheric, or good acoustic, vibe.

Arena Berlin

Eichenstrasse 4, Treptow (533 2030, www.arena-berlin.de). S41, S42, S8, S85, S9 Treptower Park. **Open** *Box office* 10am-6pm Mon-Fri. **Admission** varies. **No credit cards**. **Map** p324 S9.
Inside a converted bus garage, Arena Berlin presents A-list artists such as Bob Dylan and Björk. A movable stage means it can also put on smaller acts. The surrounding entertainment complex includes the Badeschiff, a swimming pool anchored in the Spree river, and the party boat *MS Hoppetosse*.

★ Astra Kulturhaus

Revaler Stasse 99, Friedrichshain (2005 6767, www.astra-berlin.de). U1 Warschauer Strasse. **Open** varies. **Tickets** vary. **Map** p324 S8.
The new hip indie/dance venue, part of a large complex on old industrial warehouse/sidings grounds somewhat reminiscent of Christiania in Copenhagen. With the demise of Maria am Ostbahnhof, it's likely to become Berlin's premier alternative venue, only let down by poor sightlines, due to eight pillars. The likes of Bill Callahan, God Speed You! Black Emperor, Death Cab for Cutie and Iron and Wine have played here.

Ausland

Lychener Strasse 60, Prenzlauer Berg (447 7008, www.ausland-berlin.de). U2 Eberswalder Strasse. **Open** varies. **Admission** €3-€5. **No credit cards**. **Map** p319/p328 P2.
A small bohemian basement staging free jazz, avant-folk and live electronica as well as films and art

installations. Be aware that shows usually begin an hour later than the posted time (on principle, apparently). Nights usually close with guest DJs whose tastes may not always inspire you to move your dancing feet.

Barbie Deinhoff's

Schlesische Strasse 16, Kreuzberg (no phone, www.barbiedeinhoff.de). U1 Schlesisches Tor. **Open** 6pm-6am daily. **Admission** varies. **No credit cards**. **Map** p324 R9.
With its clutter of mirror balls, salvaged airplane and car seats, this bar, alternative art gallery and indie-rock venue embodies some of the most fun aspects of Berlin living. It's especially partial to electro-poppers with names like Sue & the Unicorn, and its discerning DJs are ace.

Bassy Cowboy Club

Schönhauser Allee 176A, Prenzlauer Berg (281 8323, www.bassy-club.de). U2 Senefelderplatz. **Open** 9pm-late Tue, Fri; 10pm-late Sat. **Admission** from €3. **No credit cards**. **Map** p319/p328 O4.
A move from Hackescher Markt to new premises in Schönhauser Allee and a more diverse music programme has done wonders for Bassy's reputation. These days the venue is a champion of local bands of all genres, so expect a bluegrass act one night and electro-rock the next. There are readings on Tuesday nights.

C-Club

Columbiadamm 9-11, Tempelhof (tickets 8099 8715, www.c-club.de). U6 Platz der Luftbrücke. **Open** *Box office* (phone only) 10am-7pm Mon-Fri. **Tickets** vary. **Map** p323 N11.
Once you get past its old-fashioned box office, this former US Forces cinema is a little characterless. It showcases mid-size acts of every genre, from John Cale to Franz Ferdinand. Bigger draws usually play the Columbiahalle next door.

Columbiahalle

Columbiadamm 13-21, Tempelhof (tickets 6110 1313, www.c-halle.com). U6 Platz der Luftbrücke. **Open** varies. **Tickets** vary. **No credit cards**. **Map** p323 N11.
A roomy venue with a reputation for the best sound in town, Columbiahalle promotes larger acts that haven't made it to stadium status, such as Bon Iver Manu Chao. Drinks are a little expensive, but it's a good-sized place to catch hip hop superstars such as Jay-Z and Snoop Dogg, who would most likely be playing amphitheatres in other cities.

Festsaal Kreuzberg

Skalitzer Strasse 130, Kreuzberg (tickets 6110 1313, www.festsaal-kreuzberg.de). U1, U8 Kottbusser Tor. **Open** varies. **Tickets** vary. **No credit cards**. **Map** p323 P9.

With its eclectic booking policies and location in the heart of grungey-Kreuzberg, the Festsaal has become one of the city's most popular venues, importing indie acts such as Billy Childish and DJs as different as Detroit noise gods Wolf Eyes and Miss Kittin.

Frannz Club
Schönhauser Allee 36, Prenzlauer Berg (7262 7930, www.frannz.de). U2 Eberswalder Strasse. **Open** from 9pm daily. Parties from 10pm. **Tickets** vary. **No credit cards. Map** p319/p328 O3.
A former DDR youth club, Frannz is a black box with decent sound, pricey drinks and unsmiling doormen. Musically, it's heavy on German acts that don't really translate culturally, though it has occasionally booked rockabilly stars such as Wanda Jackson.

Fritzclub im Postbahnhof
Strasse der Pariser Kommune 8, Friedrichshain (698 1280, www.fritzclub.com). S3, S5, S7, S75 Ostbahnhof. **Open** varies. **Tickets** vary. €3-€6 for parties. **No credit cards. Map** p324 R7.
This restored industrial building is relatively young in comparison to other venues, but its association with Radio Fritz gives it the clout to stage the likes of Arcade Fire, Luka Bloom and Fun Lovin' Criminals.

★ Huxley's Neue Welt
Hasenheide 107-112, Neukoelln, (780 99 810, www.huxleysneuewelt.com). U7, U8 Hermannplatz. **Open** *Box office* (phone only) 10am-7pm Mon-Fri. **Tickets** vary. **Map** p323 P11.
Early 20th-century ballroom, renovated for gigs, on the corner of Hasenheide Park, now somewhat incongruously situated inside a modern retail park. There's a slightly Wild West atmosphere and aesthetic: it hosts poker championships and tattoo expos when not showcasing gigs by the likes of Elbow and Kasabian.

Junction Bar
Gneisenaustrasse 18, Kreuzberg (694 6602, café 6981 7421, www.junction-bar.de). U6 Gneisenaustrasse. **Open** *Café* 5pm-2am Mon-Fri; 2pm-2am Sat, Sun. *Bar* 8pm-5am daily. **Admission** €3-€6 (plus €3 drink voucher). **No credit cards. Map** p323 N10.
Originally opened in 1993, Junction Bar is a Kreuzberg landmark that arranges 365 concerts a year of everything from jazz and swing to rock, with DJs keeping the party going into the early hours.

Kulturbrauerei
Schönhauser Allee 36, Prenzlauer Berg (443 150, www.kesselhaus-berlin.de). U2 Eberswalder Strasse. **Open** *Box office* noon-6pm daily. **Tickets** €5-€30. **No credit cards. Map** p318/p326 O3.

With its assortment of venues, outdoor bars and barbecues, this cultural centre, housed in an enormous former brewery can resemble a cross between a medieval fairground and a school disco. The three operations linked to the Kulturbrauerei proper (unlike the nbi; *see below*) are Maschinehaus, Palais and, the largest, Kesselhaus, where reggae concerts are the biggest draws. Jazz and German acts also feature.

Lido
Cuvrystrasse 7, Kreuzberg (6956 6840, tickets 6110 1313, www.lido-berlin.de). U1 Schlesisches Tor. **Open** varies. **Admission** varies. **No credit cards. Map** p324 R9.
Built as a cinema in 1951, Lido recently became Kreuzberg's premier indie-rock and late night dance party venue. Its excellent outdoor area and feelgood vibe make it especially popular in summer. Saturday night 'Balkan Beats' DJ sets are extremely popular.

★ Magnet
Falckensteinsteinstrasse 48, Kreuzberg (4400 8140, www.magnet-club.de). U1 Schlesisches Tor. **Open** 8pm-late daily. **Tickets** €2-€20. **No credit cards. Map** p324 R9.
Recently transplanted from Prenzlauerberg to Kreuzberg, this venue has become one of the biggest bookers for the kind of up-and-coming indie bands featured in the *NME*. Catch them here before they hit the stadium circuit.

nbi
Kulturbrauerei, Schönhauser Allee 36, Prenzlauer Berg (6730 4457, www.neue berlinerinitiative.de). U2 Eberswalder Strasse. **Open** 8pm-late daily. **Admission** varies. **No credit cards. Map** p319 O3.
Now at the Kulturbrauerei, the latest home for this electro club pioneer is a pink box with scattered furniture in the current Wohnzimmer style and an excellent sound system. Labels and promoters such as Monika and RepeatRepeat take over several nights a month, encouraging surprise visits by the likes of Einstürzende Neubauten. The space doesn't lend itself to dancing, but its programmes remain interesting, if less electronics-orientated. Sometimes there's ping-pong.

Passionskirche
Marheinekeplatz 1-2, Kreuzberg (tickets 6959 3624, 6940 1241, www.akanthus.de). U7 Gneisenaustrasse. **Open** varies. **Tickets** vary. **No credit cards. Map** p323 N10.
The likes of Beck, Ryan Adams and Marc Almond have graced the stage of this deconsecrated church – the best place to hear artists whose amplifiers don't go past four. But it's best to get there early, as it's the only church in Berlin whose pews regularly overflow.

ARTS & ENTERTAINMENT

SO36

Oranienstrasse 190, Kreuzberg (tickets 6110 1313, 6140 1306, www.so36.de). U1, U8 Kottbusser Tor. **Open** 8pm-late daily. **Admission** €3-€20. **No credit cards.** **Map** p323 P9.

Berlin's legendary punk club continues to present the heaviest alternative rock, from Bolt Thrower to Killing Joke, as well as pop-rap crossover with attitude from the likes of the Streets. Plus reggae nights, gay parties and more.

Soul Cat Music Club

Reichenberger Strasse 73, Kreuzberg (www. soulcat-berlin.de/no phone) U1 Gölitzer Bahnhof. **Open** from 8pm Tue-Sat. **Admission** usually free. **No credit cards.** Map p323 Q10.

Two-room bar in Kreuzberg doing nightly gigs of soul, blues, folk and jazz. Also has a small record shop selling tapes and vinyl. Gigs usually start around 10pm or 10.30pm.

Tempodrom

Möckernstrasse 10, Kreuzberg (747 370/tickets 01805554111, www.tempodrom.de). S1, S2, S25 Anhalter Bahnhof, U7 Möckernbrücke. **Open** Box office 1hr before performance. **Admission** varies. **Map** p322 L9.

Descendant of the legendary circus tent venue that was pitched in various West Berlin locations, this permanent space in tented form provides a beautiful setting for more upmarket/middle-of-the-road acts such as Janet Jackson and the Pet Shop Boys. Plus there are sports events, comedy, musicals, classical concerts and the Liquidrom.

Volksbühne/Roter Salon

Rosa-Luxemburg-Platz, Mitte (4171 75412, www.roter-salon-berlin.de). U2 Rosa-Luxemburg-Platz. **Open** varies. Concerts/readings from 9pm; parties from midnight. **Tickets** from €5. **No credit cards.** Map p319/p326 O5.

Two or three times a month, East Berlin's leading avant-garde theatre presents art music by the likes of Animal Collective and Brazilian dada songster Tom Zé. And sometimes it even turns over its wood-panelled stage to such curator-friendly DJs as Aphex Twin. The same complex contains the hospitable Roter Salon, where you can hear a broad array of DJs and indie acts.

Wabe

Danziger Strasse 101, Prenzlauer Berg (902 953 850, www.wabe-berlin.de). S8, S41, S42, S85 Greifswalder Strasse. **Open** varies. **Tickets** vary. **No credit cards.** Map p319 Q3.

A DDR-era community centre in Ernst-Thälmann-Park, Wabe's octagonal space encourages young local groups with 'battle of the bands' contests and MTV co-presentations. Plenty of German folk, nostalgia acts and some community events.

Kulturbrauerei.

ARTS & ENTERTAINMENT

Wild at Heart

Wiener Strasse 20, Kreuzberg (610 74701,
www.wildatheartberlin.de). U1 Görlitzer Bahnhof.
Open 8pm-late daily. **Tickets** €3-€12. **No credit**
cards. Map p323 Q9.
The only thing possibly louder than the music here
are the trinkets scatter-blasted across the walls.
Wild at Heart imports artists and DJs from all over
Europe to satisfy its enthusiastic tattooed rock,
punk, rockabilly and ska regulars. It also has a
jukebox to help you down one last shot of whiskey
at daybreak while you ponder why your shirt is the
only one with sleeves.

WORLD

Berlin doesn't have quite the multicultural vibe
of a London or New York – but it tries. Late
spring brings the **Karnival der Kulturen** (*see*
p198), a four-day festival of multiculturalism.
World music artists also play at the Kesselhaus
or Maschinehaus in the **Kulturbrauerei**
complex (*see p242*).

Haus der Kulturen der Welt

John-Foster-Dulles Allee 10, Tiergarten
(3978 7175, www.hkw.de). S3, S5, S7, S75,
Hauptbahnhof, U55 Bundestag, Bus 100.
Open *Box office* 10am-9pm Tue-Sun. **Tickets**
vary. **No credit cards. Map** p318 K6.
Berlin's largest world music venue is a sort of global
cultural centre, housing several auditoriums and
exhibition spaces devoted to themed events.

Havanna

Hauptstrasse 30, Schöneberg (784 8565, www.
havanna-berlin.de). U7 Eisenacher Strasse. **Open**
9pm-late Wed; 10pm-late Fri, Sat. **Admission**
€2.50 Wed; €6.50 Fri; €7 Sat. **No credit cards.**
Map p322 J11.
Three dancefloors with salsa, merengue and R&B.
It's a popular place with expat South Americans and
Cubans. An hour before opening you can pick up a
few steps at a salsa class for €4.

El Sur Bar

Albertstrasse 4, Schoenberg (7676 5614,
www.el-sur-bar.com). **Open** 6pm-late Tue-Sat.
Admission free. **No credit cards. Map** 322 K9.
The upbeat El Sur Bar offers Iberian culture à la
carte – a decent range of tropical cocktails, tapas and
great wines are spiced up with live Spanish and
Portuguese sounds.

Werkstatt der Kulturen

Wissmannstrasse 32, Neukölln (609 7700, www.
werkstatt-der-kulturen.de). U7, U8 Hermannplatz.
Open varies. **Tickets** vary. **No credit cards.**
Map p323 P11
This intimate venue presents trad ethnic music or
local fusions blending jazz, trance or folk elements.

JAZZ

November boasts two fantastic overlapping
jazz festivals: the larger **Berlin JazzFest**
(*see p200*), and the free-rooted **Total Music**
Meeting (www.fmp-online.de). For historical
reasons, jazz venues tend to be clustered on
the old West Berlin. But rather than sticking
to the jazz clubs, it's worth searching out
galleries, artist-run venues, social clubs
and cultural houses. The famed DDR-era
JazzKeller Treptow (www.jazzkeller69.de)
continues to promote interesting shows in a
variety of small spaces. Berlin also features
Germany's only 24-hour jazz radio (101.9 FM).

A-Trane

Bleibtreustrasse 1, Charlottenburg (313 2550,
www.a-trane.de) S5, S7, S9, S75 Savignyplatz.
Open 9pm-2am Mon-Fri, Sun; 9pm-5am Sat.
Performances 10pm daily. Late night jam
session 12.30am Sat (except June, July, Aug).
Admission €10-€20, except special performances.
No credit cards. Map p321/p328 E8.
A-Trane usually lands at least one top-flight act a
month for an extended run. Free entry on Mondays,
except when there's a special performance. Late-night
jam sessions are popular with students and tourists.

B-Flat

Rosenthaler Strasse 13, Mitte (283 3123,
www.b-flat-berlin.de). U8 Rosenthaler Platz.
Open from 9pm daily. **Admission** free-€10.
No credit cards. Map p319/p326 N5.
B-Flat pulls in a decent local hero once in a while,
but its strongest nights tend to feature singers. Free
Wednesday night jam sessions from 9pm.

Quasimodo

Kantstrasse 12A, Charlottenburg (312 8086,
www.quasimodo.de). U2, U9, S5, S7, S9, S75
Zoologischer Garten. **Open** *Performances*
10pm Tue-Sun (doors open 1hr before start
of performance). **Admission** €5-€25.
No credit cards. Map p321/p328 F8.
Privileging the 'jazzy' over jazz, this basement spot
appears close to irrevocably severing connections to
the music for which it was once noted. Yet it still promotes some good homegrown or international acts,
such as American singer Terry Callier.

Yorckschlösschen

Yorckstrasse 15, Kreuzberg (215 8070,
www.yorckschloesschen.de). U6, U7
Mehringdamm. **Open** 5pm-3/4am Mon-Sat, 10am-
3/4pm Sun. **Admission** free-€8. **Map** p322 L10.
A century-old *Eck-Kneipe*, Yorckschlösschen offers a
faintly ridiculous mix of German Dixieland and vintage beat music. But in its old-world environment, it
can get pretty groovy (after a few Weizenbiers). On
Sundays there's breakfast and live music at 2pm.

Nightlife

Berlin deserves its reputation as one of the world's best party cities.

World War II and the Berlin Wall aside, most people's clearest image of Berlin is of impossibly cool young people dancing moodily in some legendarily decadent nightclub. It's a reputation that has been dutifully fed by cinema over the years, whether it's Sally Bowles oozing sex in the KitKat Club in *Cabaret* or sullen hipsters nodding their heads as Nick Cave thrashes his guitar in the classic Berlin flick *Wings of Desire*. The good news is, it's all true. Sort of. Every taste is catered for here, all night long, in every kind of venue, from desperate dives in temporary locations to swanky  premises where mirror balls make the world go round. There's even a KitKat Club (currently domiciled at **Sage**, *see p249*) that makes its celluloid namesake seem staid indeed. And while Berlin might no longer star Liza Minnelli, there's certainly no shortage of young Americans imagining that they're in some kind of movie.

BERLIN BY NIGHT

The landscape of the night is built on shifting sands as the cityscape continues to change. Mitte has seen the biggest number of casualties of late: the Scala has died a death, along with the Rodeo. Over towards Friedrichshain, two legendary haunts have lost battles with developers: Maria am Ostbahnhof and Bar 25, the incredibly popular after-party spot by the Spree. Happily, though, their spirit lives on – **Chez Jacki** (*see p250*) welcomes a lot of the old Maria crowd and half of the Bar 25 crew have now opened the bar/restaurant **Kater Holzig** (*see p248*) on the other side of the river. At the time of writing, Maria was sneakily still holding parties in the original venue under the name ADS, but how long it would continue to get away with this was unclear. And for Kiki Blofeld, a great outdoor party spot next to Kater Holzig, the summer of 2011 was to be its last.

Meanwhile, Berlin's partygoers continue trekking further east in search of a good night out. Around Ostkreuz the irritatingly punctuated **://about blank** (*see p252*) has established a reputation as a cool place to party, along with the ramshackle **Salon zur wilden Renate** (*see p252*). Northern Neukölln is also becoming a party mecca, though there are more late bars than proper clubs in this residential area – a particularly popular late joint in the area is **Pigalle** (*see p252*), which is wrenching the well-heeled set away from Mitte.

The area around Kottbusser Tor in Kreuzberg remains popular, but two stops east along the U1 around Schlesisches Tor is where most of the action is these days. As well as stalwarts like the riverside **Watergate** (*see p251*) and a relocated **Magnet** (*see p251*), a €4 taxi ride up Köpenickerstrasse will take you to **Tresor** (*see p249*), **Sage** and **Kater Holzig**. Across the Oberbaumbrücke into Friedrichshain is **Suicide Circus** (*see p250*), flying the flag for good, old fashioned techno. On the other (western) side of Kreuzberg, converted warehouse **Ritte Butzke** (*see p251*) is touted by some as the underground **Berghain** (*see p250*).

Apropos Berlin's most famous club, surely it needs no more purple prose; it's easy enough to find and the best advice is just to dive in and formulate your own opinion of the city's highest-profile nightspot. But at least it's not content to rest on its reputation. A new sound system has been installed and the owners have even opened a restaurant, Kreuz Friedrichs, to complement the in-house ice-cream parlour, as well as a gallery space on the ground floor called Kubus.

One thing remains the same in this sleepless city: techno still rules, and electronic beats of one kind or another remain the dominant sound of the city. But somewhere or other you can find any type of music you like.

There is no clear boundary between some bars and clubs – in this guide we've listed places like

Trust, Tausend and Kingsize in Mitte and Solar and Monarch in Kreuzberg under Bars, but they could just as easily sit in this chapter.

WHEN TO GO

Despite the fact that many Berliners seem to coast through the week doing nothing more stressful than wondering where to have brunch, they are madly possessive of their weekends and make the absolute most of them. It's not unusual to head off to a party on Friday night and stumble into bed at some point on Sunday afternoon. The real party animals go out during the week too. While this approach is pretty hardcore, the general attitude to clubbing is incredibly laid-back; no dressing up, no forward planning. Berliners let themselves go with the flow. It's usual not to head to clubs until 2am at the earliest, so don't make the mistake of hitting the bars at 7pm – not only will there be next to no one there, but you'll more than likely be too wasted by midnight to last the distance.

GETTING IN

An irritating and increasing number of Berlin clubs now operate some sort of door policy. The brutal phrase *Gesichtskontrolle* (face control) is often bandied about. At peak times outside Berghain on a Saturday night, at least a third of people in the queue don't get past the scary bouncer with a tattoo on his face – you'll know you're in if he nods; if he points to his left, hard luck. Argue the toss if you're feeling brave. But if you want to increase your chances of getting in, there are a few simple rules. Don't be too loud. Don't be obviously off your face. Don't take pictures of each other in the queue. Don't have this guide in your hand. Use English sparingly. Learn the answer to '*wie viel?*' (how many? *Eg ein, zwei, drei, vier*). Some clubs don't like people to try too hard; others will turn punters away who haven't made enough effort. Wear whatever you like, but bear in mind that Berliners tend not to dress up in a British sense – short frocks and high heels might be better left at home. Try not to take rejection personally. The next place will let you in.

LISTINGS

To find out what's on where, pick up a copy of *Zitty* or *tip*, Berlin's two fortnightly listings magazines. Discerning websites include www.bangbangberlin.de, www.iloveberlin.de and http://berlin.unlike.net

Just remember that nothing stays the same for very long. These listings were as correct as we could make them at the time of going to press. But before setting out, it's worth checking that places are still in business.

MITTE

Acud

*Veteranenstrasse 21 (449 1067, www.
acud.de). U8 Rosenthaler Platz or S1, S2, S25
Nordbahnhof.* **Open** varies. **Admission** varies.
No credit cards. Map p319/p326 N4.
A massive complex, containing a cinema, theatre and gallery, operated by a friendly Berlin arts collective. There's also a party floor with a playlist mostly devoted to reggae, breakbeat and drum 'n' bass; the dingy bar is a popular spot for the city's stoners. The cinema programme is interesting, consisting mostly of independent and low-budget films. There's something going on here most nights of the week, and start times and prices vary accordingly. Best to check the website for details first.

Asphalt

*Mohrenstrasse 30 (www.asphalt-berlin.com). U2,
U6 Stadtmitte, U6 Hausvogteiplatz.* **Open** *Bar*
from 8pm Thur, Fri, Sat. **Admission** €10.
Map p327 M7.
This chic newcomer is a favourite with moneyed visitors thanks to its prime location right underneath the Hilton Hotel. It is run by near royalty of the Berlin hospitality world: Roland Mary also heads up the restaurant Borschardt, as well as the lakeside Café am neuen See. Operated under the motto 'advanced urban klubbing', expect a laidback vibe during the week and a big party on Fridays and Saturdays, with the queue to prove it. If you're hungry, there's a pricey sushi restaurant of the same name, operated by bad boy TV chef Tim Raue (*see p147*).

Bohannon

*Dircksenstrasse 40 (6950 5287, www.bohannon.de).
U2, U5, U8, S5, S7, S9, S75 Alexanderplatz or
S5, S7, S9, S75 Hackescher Markt/bus N2, N5,
N8, N65, N84/tram M4, M5.* **Open** 10pm-late
Mon, Thur-Sat. **Admission** €6-€10. **No credit
cards. Map** p319/p326 O5.
The club's name, a nod to funk legend Hamilton Bohannon, indicates its driving musical principle. Billed as offering 'soulful electronic clubbing', this basement location features two dancefloors and regular sets by the likes of dancehall DJ Barney Millah and excellent Friday night soul parties.

Clärchen's Ballhaus

*Auguststrasse 24, Mitte (282 9295, www.
ballhaus.de). S1, S2 Oranienburger Strasse.*
Open 10am-late daily. **No credit cards.
Map** p319/p326 N5.
See p247 **Having a Ball.**

★ Cookies

*Westin Grand Hotel, Friedrichstrasse 158 (2808
806, www.cookies.ch). S1, S2, S25, S3, S5, S7,
S75, U6 Friedrichstrasse.* **Open** 10.30am-6pm
Tue, Thur. **Admission** €8. **No credit cards.**

Having a Ball

Dancing for all.

For nearly 20 years, Berlin has been famous for its substance-fuelled, all-night techno parties in cavernous raw spaces. But in the heart of Mitte, a decidedly old-school venue is giving the rave a run for its money in terms of popularity and downright fun.

And it's actually nothing new. In 2005, **Clärchen's Ballhaus** (*see p246*), a dancehall frequented by nimble Berliners since Clara Haberman established it in 1913, reopened after nearly a year of closed doors. Under new management – the rakish duo of David Regehr and Christian Schulz – Clärchen's is more popular than ever.

'People come here to find the love of their lives,' Schulz has said. These people can range from twentysomething hipsters to 75-year-old Ballhaus veterans to celebrities (such as German actress Heike Makatsch, or even Charlotte Rampling) who've stopped in to cut the rug during Berlin Film Fest parties. Best of all, as the night wears on, these drastically divergent demographics start mixing. It's not unusual to see a geriatric Fred Astaire teaching a young pink-haired artist how to tango or foxtrot.

The Ballhaus actually has two ballrooms. The vast ground-floor space is lined with silver tinsel streamers. Its spacious dancefloor is ringed by wooden tables bedecked with white tablecloths and candles, while a huge disco ball spins overhead. But upstairs is another room that never fails to elicit gasps of awe from first-time visitors. Smaller but with high ceilings and a fin-de-siècle vibe, the chandeliered Mirror Salon has huge cracked mirrors, ornate moulding work and candlelight, transporting guests straight back to the 1920s.

In fact, very little has really changed since then. When Clärchen's was turned over to its new owners, Berliners who'd loved to dance here for decades feared that it would fall prey to the homogenisation that 'renovation' in Berlin often brings. But Schulz and Regehr left the interior almost exactly as it was – both upstairs and downstairs have vintage details, fixtures, even wallpaper... as well as a heady smell of history that's hard to pin down. Is it all DDR, or is it the Weimar era?

Most regulars don't care (and more than a few were actually around during the DDR era). They're here to tango on Tuesdays, learn to swing on Wednesdays, attend the 'pasta opera' nights in the Mirror Salon, or yes, find the love of their lives on weekend nights. Some initially come to have an inexpensive oven-baked pizza, inside or in the beautiful front garden. But the magic never fails: sometime after midnight, both ballrooms teem with all types in a free-for-all that begins with live music and then segues into Michael Jackson, the Beach Boys, old German *schlager* music, or all of the above. It's more cheesy than chic, but that's part of the charm.

ARTS & ENTERTAINMENT

Clärchen's Ballhaus

Weekend.

Aimed squarely at what they call *Profiausgänger* ('professional clubbers'), Cookies tests the mettle of the most hardcore party people. A catacomb of concrete passageways eventually opens up on to a vast concert room resembling a cross between a school gym and a bingo hall, complete with huge, ostentatious chandeliers. A somewhat understaffed island bar serves all manner of drinks – eventually. Music can vary but anything with a thumping bass and an electro slant goes. There's an upmarket vegetarian restaurant, Cookies Cream, in the same complex (the entrance is round the corner on 55 Behrenstrasse).

Golden Gate

Dircksenstrasse/corner of Schicklerstrasse (62900155, www.goldengate-berlin.de). S3, S5, S7, S75 Jannowitzbrücke. **Open** midnight-late Thur-Sat; 11pm-late Sun. **Admission** varies. **No credit cards. Map** p319/p326 O5.

Housed in a ramshackle former bike shop beneath the S-Bahn Arches, Golden Gate's popularity is enjoying something of an upswing these days. Once home to a rather hit-and-miss music policy, with the occasional live show, this grimy little club has now settled firmly on a series of all-weekend techno parties. The venue is almost a scaled-down version of Berghain (and quite possibly an overflow venue for people turned away from that techno mecca), and boasts a refreshingly intimate atmosphere. People either jam into the small dancefloor room or lounge around the bar or the upstairs toilets. It's an anything goes location with a chilled-out crowd. The backyard garden is nice in summer.

Kaffee Burger

Torstrasse 60 (2804 6495, www.kaffeeburger.de). U2 Rosa-Luxemburg-Platz. **Open** 10pm-late Mon-Thur; 9pm-late Fri, Sat; 7pm-late Sun. **Admission** €1-€5. **No credit cards. Map** p319/p326 N5.

Best known as home of the popular twice-monthly Russendisko, Kaffee Burger's programme runs the cultural gamut. Early evenings may see readings, lectures, film screenings or live music. Later on, local and expat DJs play anything from old-school country to something called 'sexabilly', as well as Balkan beats, indie-rock, soul and Britpop fare. The club's decor has been left intact from GDR days, and the relatively bright lighting facilitates interaction with strangers. To go with the eclectic programming, Burger draws a mixed, international crowd, and drinks are cheap.

★ Kater Holzig

Michaelkirchstrasse 22. (restaurant reservations only 5105 2134, www.katerholzig.de). S3, S5, S7, S75, U 8 Jannowitzbrücke. **Open** varies. **Admission** varies. **No credit cards. Map** p323 P7.

When Bar 25 closed in 2011, its devotees didn't have long to wait – or far to go – for its successor. Kater Holzig is right across the river from the old haunt, a hedonistic adventure playground set in and around an old soap factory. There is no sign: look out for the neon cats painted on a wooden fence on the right-hand side of the road as you approach the river. If you can get past the infuriatingly capricious bouncers, you're in for a treat. The sprawling complex is far more than just a nightclub – there's an upmarket restaurant, Katerschmaus, on the third floor of the graffiti covered main building, a daytime café called Obendrauf, as well as space to show films, theatre and art. The actual club is on the ground floor in a classic warehouse space, though the outside area by the Spree is arguably more fun, with a ramshackle wooden hut serving as a bar and decking to lounge on by the water as the sun comes up. At the time of writing, the soap factory was due to be developed into yet more luxury flats come 2013, so call in before the bulldozers arrive.

King-Kong Club

Brunnenstrasse 173 (2859 8538, www.king-kong-klub.de). U8 Rosenthaler Platz. **Open** 10pm-late Mon, Wed-Sat; 9pm-late Tue. **Admission** €0-€5. **No credit cards. Map** p319/p326 N4.

Resolutely down to earth, this small, dark club plays new-wave, glam, post-punk, electro and indie – a good, unpretentious option if you can't stomach house or techno and want to have a pose-free flail about on the dancefloor.

Sage Club

Köpenicker Strasse 76 (no phone, www.sage-club.de). U8 Heinrich-Heine-Strasse. **Open** 10pm-late Thur; 11pm-late Fri-Sun. **Admission** varies. **No credit cards. Map** p323 O7.

A labyrinthine complex of half a dozen or so dancefloors accessed via the north-side entrance to Heinrich-Heine-Strasse U-Bahn station make up the Sage Club, which caters to a relatively young, rock-oriented crowd. It is only reliably open on Thursdays for rock night – a chilled-out, unpretentious night out, where skinny jeans and leather jackets tend to be the uniform of choice. At weekends you'll have better luck with some fetish gear, as Sage is the current home of the notorious KitKat Club (www.kitkatclub.de. Further up Köpenicker Strasse, at No.18-20, the owners also operate Sage restaurant, serving tapas and pizza, as well as an outdoor beach bar in summer. And did we mention the indoor swimming pool?

Tresor

Köpenicker Strasse 70 (no phone, www.tresor berlin.de). U8 Heinrich-Heine-Strasse or S5, S9, S7, S75 Jannowitzbrücke. **Open** midnight-late Wed, Fri, Sat 11pm-late Mon. **Admission** €5-€12. **No credit cards. Map** p323 P7.

Berlin's original techno club is now housed in what was formerly the main central-heating power station for East Berlin. The colossal location is breathtaking, and since only a tiny portion of its 28,000sq m (300,000 sq ft) is in use, there's plenty of room for future development in what is intended to be not just a club, but a huge centre of alternative art and culture. The experience of the basement floor is one you'll not forget; a black hole occasionally punctuated by flashing strobes with some of the loudest, hardest techno you are likely to hear.

Weekend

Alexanderplatz 5, 12th floor (2463 1676, www.week-end-berlin.de). U2, U5, U8 or S3, S5, S7, S75, S9 Alexanderplatz . **Open** 11pm-late Thur-Sat. **Admission** €8-€15. **No credit cards. Map** p319/p328 O5.

Situated right in the middle of former East Berlin, Weekend's home is way up at the top of one of Alexanderplatz's many Communist-era tower blocks. While the interior of the club itself is nothing impressive, the roof terrace is a big draw – a perfect summer location combining often excellent music with spectacular cityscape views. Alas, it's lost its cool and these days it's mostly populated by tourists – apart from on Sundays when the legendary gay party GMF takes up residence (*see p226*).

★ ZMF (ZurMoebelFabrik)

Brunnenstrasse 10 (2nd backyard) (no phone, www.zurmoebelfabrik.de). U8 Rosenthaler Platz or S3,S5,S75 Hackescher Markt/tram M1. **Open** varies. **Admission** varies. **No credit cards. Map** p319/p326 N4.

The initials stand for 'ZurMoebelFabrik', and a furniture factory is what this building originally housed before this cosy club took over use of the basement. It's operated by an arts collective and while there's often a variety of cultural events taking place, the location is starting to make a name for itself as a hot party spot. A bare-brick and concrete dancefloor leads into a spacious lounge with a liberal supply of comfy beaten-up sofas. A highlight at ZMF is the Neon Raiders party, a monthly event with a solid queer following and a sexy, open-minded crowd cutting up the dancefloor to an impressive line-up of international Djs.

PRENZLAUER BERG

Duncker

Dunckerstrasse 64 (445 9509, www.duncker club.de). U2 Eberswalder Strasse or S8, S41, S42, S85 Prenzlauer Allee. **Open** 9pm-late Mon; 10pm-late Wed, Thur; 11pm-late Fri, Sat. **Admission** €5. **No credit cards. Map** p319 P2.

Duncker does have a reasonably varied line-up of events but it definitely operates within a very dark sphere. It's perfectly located in a neo-Gothic church in a non-descript Prenzlauer Berg side street. While the tail end of the week focuses mainly on new wave, dark wave and indie, it's the Dark Monday goth party that is the club's bread and butter. Surprisingly, for a city the size of Berlin, venues catering for our friends in black are few and far between here, making this a precious gem for fans of the genre.

Icon

Cantianstrasse 15 (4849 2878, www.icon berlin.de). U2 Eberswalder Strasse tram M10. **Open** 11pm-late Tue; 11.30pm-late Fri, Sat. **Admission** varies. **No credit cards. Map** p319 O2.

INSIDE TRACK
TECHNO-PHOBES

Allergic to techno? Prefer Richard Wagner to Richie Hawtin? Then check out the **Yellow Lounge** (www.yellowlounge.de), a sporadic classical music club night that brings world-class musicians to some of Berlin's world-famous clubs, including **Berghain** (*see p250*) and **Cookies** (*see p246*).

ARTS & ENTERTAINMENT

A tricky-to-locate entrance in the courtyard just north of the junction with Milastrasse leads to an interesting space cascading down the levels into a long stone cellar. It's a well-ventilated little labyrinth, with an intense dancefloor space, imaginative lighting, good sound and a separate bar. Music here occasionally takes in techno, reggae and hip hop – and it appears to be expanding its tastes by hosting Kitsuné and Ed Banger artists – yet the fact remains that for fans of the genre this is Berlin's premier drum 'n' bass club. Best when the core crowd of locals is augmented by a wider audience for some special event, but this is not usually a spot for the in-crowd.

Roadrunner's Paradise
Saarbrückerstrasse 24 (448 5755, www.road runners-paradise.de). U2 Senefelderplatz. **Open** varies. **Admission** €8-€20. **No credit cards.** **Map** p319/p326 O4.
Navigate your way through to the third courtyard of the former Koenigstadt brewery and you'll find Roadrunner's tucked away in the corner next to a motorcycle repair shop, a suitably greasy location for this butch venue. On offer is a tasty but irregular mixture of live shows and DJ sets, primarily focusing on garage, blues-rock, rockabilly and surf. The tiny stage may seem a little bit lost in the wide-open concert room but there's plenty of room to dance and the sound system is surprisingly up to scratch. Alternatively pull up a bar stool and marvel at the array of 1950s American kitsch while sinking a cold beer.

FRIEDRICHSHAIN

★ Berghain/Panorama Bar
Am Wriezener Bahnhof (no phone, www. berghain.de). U5 Weberwiese, S3, S5, S75 Ostbahnhof. **Open** midnight-late Fri, Sat. **Admission** €10. **No credit cards.** **Map** p324 R7.
A strong contender for best club in the city, if not Europe; words can't really do the place justice. In basic terms, it's a techno club in a former power station, but it has to be experienced to be fully understood. Even non-fans of the genre fall head over heels in love with the relaxed atmosphere, interesting mix of eccentrics, well-thought-out design details, fantastic sound system and sexually liberal attitude. Tip for newbies: Berghain's anything-goes approach extends only so far as what they don't see you doing. If you're searched at the door, an amnesty box gives you the opportunity to surrender anything illegal you may have before being cleared for entry. The club's reputation for a difficult and random door policy is not entirely undeserved. Panorama, with its smaller dancefloor and Wolfgang Tillmans art work, is open all weekend; the more intense Berghain part of the venue, complete with darkrooms, is only open on Saturdays.

INSIDE TRACK
BERGHAIN BLUES

Where should you go if you don't get into Berghain (or don't want to risk getting turned away)? For techno, try **Tresor** (*see p249*), **Horst Krzbrg** (*see p251*) or **Suicide Circus** (*see p250*). For electro, try **Watergate** (*see p251*) or **Ritter Butzke** (*see p251*). For a grope in the dark, try KitKatKlub at **Sage** (*see p249*).

Chez Jacki
An der Schillingbrücke, (0176 382 30 322, www.chezjacki.com). S3, S5, S75 Ostbahnhof. **Open** Thur-Sun, times vary. **Admission** varies. **No credit cards.** **Map** p323 Q7.
Situated at the back of the old Maria am Ostbahnhof club, Chez Jacki picks up where its now defunct neighbour left off: Expect DJs from labels like Kompakt and Ninja Tune as well as live acts. The future of this joint was slightly precarious at the time of writing, so definitely check the website before heading out.

K17
Pettenkofer Strasse 17a (4208 9300, www.k7-berlin.de). S41, S42, S8, S85, S9, U 5 Frankfurter Allee.. **Open** 10pm-late Fri,Sat. **Admission** f€6. **No credit cards.** **Map** p325 U6.
Goth, EBM, industrial and metal are undead and well in this three-floor club. Parties have names such as Dark Friday and Schwarzer Donnerstag and the occasional live earaches feature hardcore, nü-metal and crossover bands. There's also a Dark Hostel within the same complex, offering goth-friendly accommodation.

★ Rosi's
Revalerstrasse 29 (no phone, www.rosis-berlin.de). S3, S41, S42, S5, S7, S75, S8, S85, S9 Ostkreuz. **Open** 11pm-late Thur-Sat. **Admission** €2-€7. **No credit cards.** **Map** p324 T8.
If you were asked to think of the typical Berlin club then something like Rosi's would no doubt spring to mind. It's a tumbledown, DIY affair; all bare bricks and mismatched flea market furniture. The atmosphere is very relaxed and the club tends to attract a young, studenty crowd. Live acts are a regular feature, DJs mainly spin electro and rock, and Karrera Klub hosts parties from time to time. The beer garden is a popular hangout on summer nights.

★ Suicide Circus
Revalerstrasse 99 (no phone, www.suicide-berlin.com). S3, S5, S7, S75, U1 Warschauer Strasse. **Open** 11pm-late Wed, Thur, Sun; midnight-late Fri, Sat. **Admission** €5-€10. **No credit cards.** **Map** p 324 S8.
Situated right by the Warschauer Brücke, Suicide Circus is bringing back Berlin's old-school techno

spirit. The parties on Wednesday are legendary – walk over the bridge on a Thursday morning and you'll both hear and feel the bass pumping out of the excellent sound system. The Sunday daytime afterparties are well regarded too. Over-21s only.

KREUZBERG

Festsaal Kreuzberg

Skalitzer Strasse 130 (6165 6003, www.festsaalkreuzberg.de). U12, U8 Kottbusser Tor. **Open** varies. **Admission** varies. **No credit cards.** **Map** p323 P9.

Festsaal means 'ballroom' and this venue near Kottbusser Tor has quite a refined edge despite the shabbiness of the interior, reinforced by a regular programme of literary and cultural events such as readings and poetry slams. The big hall and good sound system are often put to use for gigs or DJ sets. A special highlight is provided by the two tiny cellar rooms – a great location for small but intense electro parties such (as DJ Emma Eclectic's You're My Disco.)

Horst Krzbrg

Tempelhofer Ufer 1 (www.horst-krzbrg.de). U1, U6 Hallesches Tor; U7 Mehringdamm. **Open** Thur-Sun, times vary. **Admission** varies. **No credit cards.** **Map** p322 M9.

This former post office specialises in Dubstep, house and electro and is often taken over by local labels to showcase their acts. At least once Saturday a month there are swing dance classes from 7pm, followed by a party. The crowd can sometimes be a little

Berghain/Panorama Bar.

cooler-than-thou, but it's an interesting space with an impressive light installation, fairly priced beer and a BBQ outside in summer.

Lido

Cuvrystrasse 7 (6956 6840, www.lido-berlin.de). U1 Schlesisches Tor. **Open** varies. **Admission** varies. **No credit cards.** **Map** p324 R9.

Lido is the HQ of famed Berlin indie-rocksters Karrera Klub, who have been champions of new music in the city for over ten years now. This former theatre is a suitably spacious location to present upcoming new live acts and so far artists such as Friendly Fires, MGMT, Shitdisco and The Horrors have all graced the stage. Lido has one of the best sound systems in the city and what was once a rear courtyard now has a canopy so even in inclement weather you can take a break from the heat of the dancefloor.

Magnet

Falckensteinstrasse 47 (www.magnet-club.de). U1 Schlesisches Tor. **Open** varies. **Admission** varies. **No credit cards.** **Map** p324 R9

Recently reborn in the old 103 club, Magnet is specialises in rock and indie and, along with Lido (*see above*), regularly hosts the Karrera Klub. It's a friendly, down-to-earth place that is as much of a gig venue as a disco, having played host to all manner of bands including Death Cab For Cutie, Ganjaman, Glasvegas and LDC Soundsystem.

★ Ritter Butzke

Ritterstrasse 24 (no phone, www.ritterbutzke.de). U8 Moritzplatz. **Open** midnight-late Fri, Sat. **Admission** varies. **No credit cards.** **Map** p323 O8.

This enormous old factory is one of Berlin's current party hotspots thanks to its reliable booking policy (expect Djs like Pyonen or Gianni Vitello) and imaginative decor. It held illegal parties for years but has now gone legit and even deigns to allow its parties to be promoted in listings mags from time to time. Some tout it as an underground Berghain, but it's far easier to get past the bouncers (even if they are occasionally dressed as knights, *Ritter* meaning 'knight' in German). Just brace yourself for a massive queue if you arrive between 1am and 3.30am.

Soju Bar

Skalitzer Strasse 36 (no phone, www.soju-bar.com). U12 Görlitzer Bahnhof. **Open** 11pm-late Wed-Sat. **Admission** varies. **No credit cards.** **Map** p323 Q9. Owned by the same gang who operate the Kimchi Princess restaurant (*see p149*), this late bar is popular with hip diners working off their Korean BBQ feast on the dancefloor. Try a glass of Soju – a dangerously drinkable South Korean spirit made from sweet potato.

★ Watergate

Falckensteinstrasse 49 (no phone, www.watergate.de). U1 Schlesisches Tor. **Open** 11pm-late

ARTS & ENTERTAINMENT

Wed, Fri, Sat; check website for occasional Tue, Thur events. **Admission** varies. **No credit cards. Map** p324 R9.

This two-floor, riverside club has a slick feel, a great view of the Spree and a better-than-average sound system. The two best-known features here are the panorama windows above the river and the flash, ceiling-mounted lighting display, plus the floating lounge on the Spree. Both floors are open on weekends and usually host two different sets of acts. Music policy is in the electro, house and minimal techno area – (Ricardo Villalobos and Richie Hawtin often play – although artists such as Booka Shade and Digitalism occasionally appear.) House veterans M.A.N.D.Y. (Get Physical) have a residency.

NEUKÖLLN

Pigalle
Sanderstrasse 17, (2463 1676). U8 Schönleinstrasse. **Open** Thur-Sat, times vary. **Admission** varies. **No credit cards. Map** p323 Q10

This small and surprisingly elegant (for Neukölln) bar in a former brothel is run by Marcus Trojan, who has had big hits with Weekend (*see p249*) and Trust (*see p162*). The place has leather banquettes, a small dancefloor and a very intimidating door policy – knock and a face will peer out from the sort of window prison officers use to check inmates are alive in their cells. You are then lead into a grey concrete ante-chamber before being allowed into the dark and sexy bar itself. Gay night Jailbait on a Saturday is very popular.

TIERGARTEN

2BE
Klosterstrasse 44 (8906 8410, www.2be-club.de). U2 Klostestrasse. **Open**varies. **Admission** varies. **No credit cards. Map** p318 K5.

The roster of in-house DJs at 2BE tends to focus mainly on hip hop, with the odd reggae and dancehall tune thrown in for good measure, and there's also usually a live act or two playing each month. Big name DJs from the genre such as Grandmaster Flash and LTJ Bukem have been known to put in an appearance. It's a spacious location with an outside seating area and several bars. The crowd tends to be young and enthusiastic if not verging ever so slightly on chav.

Adagio
Marlene-Dietrich-Platz 1 (258 9890, www. adagio.de). U2, S1, S2, S25 Potsdamer Platz. **Open** 11pm-late pm Fri, Sat. **Admission** €10. **Map** p322 K8.

Spin-off of a swanky Zurich disco, Adagio's 'medieval' decor and Renaissance-style frescos are jarringly at odds with the Renzo Piano-designed theatre whose basement it occupies. Pricey drinks, abundant members-only areas and a music policy of disco, polite house and oldies cater to fortysomething tourists and after-work crowds willing to shell out for an illusion of exclusivity. There's a dress code (no jeans or sports shoes). Friday night is ladies night – complete with male strip show.

Tape
Heidestrasse 14 (2848 4873, www.tapeberlin.de). S3, S5, S7,, S75 Hauptbahnhof. **Open** varies. **Admission** €8-€15. **No credit cards. Map** p318 K4.

You've really got to want to go to Tape. Its location on a rather desolate industrial estate means it's not the kind of venue you'd just happen across. That said, this cavernous warehouse venue has plenty to make the tiresome trip worthwhile. The huge main hall has a superior sound and lighting rig making it the club of choice for multi-media live shows, while things get sweaty on the smaller, neighbouring dancefloor. Expect the likes of Modeselektor, Whomadewho and Santogold to turn up here. They also have an annual art exhibiton 'Tape modern', where 'art meets nightlife'.

FURTHER EAST

★ ://about blank
Markgrafendamm 24c (no phone, http://about party.net). S3, S41, S42, S5, S7, S75, S8, S85, S9 Ostkreuz. **Open** midnight-late Thur, Fri, Sat. **No credit cards. Map** p324 T8

Particularly famed for its open air parties, this club near Ostkreuz station has rapidly become a favourite with the city's more adventurous hedonists.

Glashaus
Eichenstrasse 4, Treptow (5332 0340, www.arena-berlin.de). U1 Schlesisches Tor or S8, S9, S41, S42 Treptower Park. **Open** varies. **Admission** varies. **No credit cards. Map** p324 S9.

Part of the riverside Arena complex. The bare brick walls and sparse lighting of this dingy and intimate location make it look more like a dungeon than a club. It has an adequate sound system for its size, but does tend to get a bit sleazy towards the early hours. The place also transforms into a theatre, while there are club-type events on the *Hoppetosse* and *Badeschiff*, both moored just nearby on the Spree.

Salon zur Wilden Renate
Alt-Stralau 70, Friedrichshain (25041426, www.renate.cc). S3, S41, S42, S5, S7, S75, S8, S85, S9 Ostkreuz. **Open** varies. **Admission** varies. **No credit cards. Map** p324 T9.

This knackered old house is perennially at risk of being torn down and turned into – of course – trendy flats. Parties here are sporadic and often only promoted by word-of-mouth, but if you hear of one, make the trek. Students and wasted ravers press up against refugees from Mitte in the reliably crowded rooms which are still set up like the flats they once were - complete with the odd bed.

Sport & Fitness

Swimming pools, saunas, football and more.

At first glance, Berlin may not seem a particularly sporty place, especially in winter when the mercury hovers around zero for months on end and it seems to make more sense to pile on the blubber than work it off. But underneath all those layers, many Berliners like to keep in shape and there are countless venues, organisations and clubs. The city boasts a particularly fine selection of swimming pools, both indoor and outdoor, many with fantastic saunas attached – a visit to the beautiful Stadtbad Neukölln with its Grecian sauna complex is a must. There is no shortage of

teams to support either – at the last count, Berlin was home to 145 top-flight clubs in pretty much every sport imaginable, including two decent football teams, Hertha and FC Union. A lot of the amateur sides practise on the old airfield at Tempelhof Airport, which is now a gigantic park. Those who prefer to watch than take part are well catered for too: matches tend to be reasonably priced and you can often just show up and pay at the door.

MAJOR STADIUMS & ARENAS

Max-Schmeling-Halle
Am Falkplatz, Prenzlauer Berg (443 045, tickets 4430 4430, www.max-schmeling-halle.de). U2 Eberswalder Strasse or U2, S41, S42, S8, S85, S9 Schönhauser Allee. **Map** p319/p328 O2.
Named after the German boxer who knocked out the seemingly invincible Joe Louis in 1936 (Louis settled the score two years later in only 124 seconds), this 11,900-capacity indoor arena faces an uncertain future. It was built as part of Berlin's abortive bid for the 2000 Olympics, and its anchor tenants, basketball side ALBA Berlin, have moved to the O2 World. Its main attraction now is the up-and-coming Olympic handball club, Berliner Füchse, though at press time the SCC volleyball team were also thinking of moving in. With practically no public parking, it's got its back to the wall against the new, bigger kid in town.

O2 World
Mühlenstrasse 12-30, Friedrichshain (2060 7080, tickets 2060 7088 99, www.o2world.de). S3, S5, S7, S75 Ostbahnhof. **Map** p324 R8.
O2 World, Berlin's latest glitzy multi-purpose arena, has a capacity of 17,000 and state-of-the-art technology that allows it to be converted from sports arena to rock venue in just a few hours. It's the new

sporting headquarters of the Eisbären ice hockey team and Bundesliga basketball champions ALBA.

★ Olympiastadion
Olympischer Platz 3, Charlottenburg (3068 8100, www.olympiastadion-berlin.de). U2 Olympia-Stadion or S3, S5, S75 Olympiastadion.
Designed as the centrepiece for the 1936 Olympics, the Olympiastadion is one of the best surviving examples of Nazi monumentalism. After years of neglect, and despite its status as a protected building, the 74,000-seater was given extensive renovations and a new roof before hosting the 2006 FIFA World Cup Final – in 2011 it was also the venue for the opening game of the Women's World Cup. This huge bowl hosts Berlin's top football club, Hertha BSC (*see p254*), the German football cup final and the ISTAF annual athletics meeting (*see p254*), as well as rock concerts and sundry other events. *Photo p254.*

Velodrom
Paul-Heyse-Strasse 26, Prenzlauer Berg (443 045, tickets 4430 4430/www.velomax.de). S41, S42, S8, S85, S9 Landsberger Allee. **Map** p325 S4.
Opened in 1997, this multifunctional sports and entertainment venue was designed by Dominique Perrault for the annual six-day cycling race, and boasts a cycling track made from Siberian spruce. It also holds equestrian and super-cross events.

ARTS & ENTERTAINMENT

SPECTATOR SPORTS

Athletics

ISTAF Athletics Meeting
301 118 666, www.istaf.de. **Tickets** €6.75-€39;
25% less for reductions.
First held in 1937, this international one-day summer
meet at the Olympiastadion (*see p253*) is the last of
four events in the International Association of
Athletics Federations' Golden League. The $1m
prize money is shared between athletes who win
their disciplines at all four Golden League meetings.
The crowd is often treated to world records.

Basketball

ALBA
300 9050, www.albaberlin.de. **Tickets** €10-€55.
Berlin's representatives in German basketball's top
flight take their name from their sponsors, a waste
disposal and recycling firm. ALBA wiped the floor
with the opposition in the late 1990s and early 2000s
and are again back to winning ways. They used to
pack them into the Max-Schmeling-Halle (*see p253*)
but have now moved to the flashier, bigger O2
World (*see p253*).

Football

Germany hosted both the 2006 FIFA World
Cup Finals and the women's version in 2011,
wowing visitors and observers with a carnival
atmosphere and great home teams to boot.
Berlin's biggest club, Hertha BSC, makes
occasional but usually abortive forays into
Europe (*see right*) and were promoted to the

1. Bundesliga (Germany's premiership) for the
2011/2012 season. The only other team even
vaguely in the picture is the Eastern club FC
Union, although Turkish side Türkiyemspor
enjoys healthy support among Berlin's large
immigrant community.

Hertha BSC
0180 518 9200, www.herthabsc.de.
Tickets €12-€48.
Berlin's top team have repeatedly been touted as title
contenders at the beginning of the season only to dis-
appoint with hot-and-cold performances and mid-
table placings in the Bundesliga. They play at the
Olympiastadion (*see p253*) in the city's far west.

1. FC Union
*Stadion an der Alten Försterei 263, Köpenick
(6566 880, www.fc-union-berlin.de). S3 Köpenick.*
Tickets €9.50-€23. **No credit cards**.
Having withstood the pressures of communism,
'Iron Union' came close to buckling under the stress
and strain of capitalism, slipping to the third division and flirting with bankruptcy. But true to their
name, they've stuck it out, and work has begun
upgrading the club's cosy stadium to meet the official requirements should they ever get promoted
again. No strangers to novel fund-raising efforts,
fans also donated hours, days or even weeks of their
labour on the construction site.

Türkiyemspor
*Jahnstadion, Friedrich-Ludwig-Jahn-Sportpark,
Cantianstrasse 24, Prenzlauer Berg (www.
tuerkiyemspor.info). U2 Eberswalder Strasse.*
Tickets €10; €6 reductions. **No credit cards**.
Map p319/p328 O3.

Olympiastadion. *See p253.*

This amateur Turkish side now plays at the Jahnstadion in Prenzlauerberg, having outgrown its base in Kreuzberg. The club was set up in 1978 and despite sporadic shows of promise, has never quite made it into the Bundesliga. They will play the 2011/12 season in the NOFV-Oberliga Nord.

Horse racing

Galopprennbahn-Hoppegarten
Goetheallee 1, Dahlwitz-Hoppegarten (0334 238 930, tickets 030 780 111, www.hoppegarten.com). S5 Hoppegarten. **Tickets** €9-€45; €6 reductions. Thoroughbred races are held between April and October. The betting is run along the lines of the British tote system: all money bet on a race goes into a 'pot', which is shared between those who have placed winning bets.

Harness racing (Trotting)

Pferdesportpark
Treskowallee 129, Karlshorst (5001 711, www.pferdesportpark-berlin-karlshorst.de). S3 Karlshorst. **Tickets** free weekdays; €2 Sun; €1 reductions. **No credit cards**. Trotting events are held all year round.

Trabrennbahn Mariendorf
Mariendorfer Damm 222-298, Mariendorf (740 1212, www.berlintrab.de). U6 Alt-Mariendorf, then bus M76, 179. **Tickets** free Mon-Fri; €3 Sat, Sun.
Meetings take place irregularly (check the website for exact days and times) on Sundays at 1.30pm and Tuesdays at 6pm. Derby Week in August is a major international event.

Ice hockey

Since German ice hockey clubs set up a private national league in 1994, the sport has become big business. For now, Berlin's **Eisbären** ('polar bears'), the old Eastern club, have seen off their Western rivals, the **Capitals**.

EHC Eisbären Berlin
971 8400, tickets 9718 4040, www.eisbaeren.de. **Tickets** €17-€45.
Having survived both the hot and cold showers of communism and the ice bath of capitalism, EHC Eisbäre, the 2011 all-German champions, have moved to the O2 World.

Olympic handball

This niche sport has been enjoying a renaissance since Germany hosted the 2007 World Championships and the national team got one up on their limelight-hogging football friends by netting gold.

INSIDE TRACK
ANYONE FOR BOULES?

The hipsters of Kreuzberg and Neukölln spend their Sundays playing boules by the Landwehrkanal. Walk east down Paul-Linke-Ufer until you hear the 'tonk'. In the west, boules is played halfway down Schlossstrasse in Charlottenburg

---

Füchse Berlin
495 6009, tickets 4430 4430, www.fuechse-berlin.de. **Tickets** €8-€60. **No credit cards**.
The wily Foxes bear testimony to handball's resurgence, and have now taken up residence at the Max-Schmeling-Halle, with occasional high-profile sorties to the O2 World.

ACTIVE SPORTS & FITNESS

Berlin is a dream for the DIY athlete. This chapter only covers a fraction of what's on; if you don't find what you're looking for, contact one of the organisations listed. *Verbände* are the umbrella 'associations' that co-ordinate sports.

Landes Sportbund Berlin (LSB)
Jesse-Owens-Allee 2, Charlottenburg (300 020, www.lsb-berlin.net). U2 Olympia-Stadion or S3, S5, S75 Olympiastadion. **Open** 9am-3pm Mon-Thur; 9am-2pm Fri.
The Berlin Regional Sports Association's central office provides general information and co-ordinates other offices in charge of specific sports. The Landesausschuss Frauensport, Regional Committee for Women's Sport, is at the same address.

Turngemeinde in Berlin 1848
Columbiadamm 111, Neukölln (611 0100, www.tib1848ev.de). U7 Südstern or U8 Boddinstrasse.
The city's oldest sports club is also perhaps its most diverse, with a list of activities almost as long as its history. As the archaic name suggests (it translates as 'Gymnastics Community in Berlin'), it was founded in 1848. It's based beside the Hasenheide park, where Friedrich Ludwig Jahn, the man known as 'the father of German gymnastics', established the country's first physical education facility in 1811. It offers outdoor and indoor tennis courts, badminton courts, beach volleyball and a profusion of other facilities.

Athletics

Berlin Marathon
Organisers: Berlin-Marathon SCC Running Events GmbH, Hanns-Braun-Strasse/Adlerplatz, Charlottenburg (3012 8810, www.berlin-marathon.com). S3, S5, S75 Olympiastadion. **Entrance fee** €60-€100. **Date** last Sun in Sept.

ARTS & ENTERTAINMENT

ARTS & ENTERTAINMENT

Cycling and the City

Berlin loves cyclists and cyclists love Berlin.

Berlin is the ideal cycling city, with wide boulevards, 650km of bike paths and almost no hills. The forests and lakes surrounding the capital are also perfect for touring, thanks to well-marked paths and generally excellent road surfaces.

The 28km jaunt to the lake of Wannsee in Potsdam is one of the most well-planned routes: just follow the signs starting at Schlossplatz in Mitte, where the East German parliament building once stood. The ride goes through the Gendarmenmarkt and Checkpoint Charlie, past the Jewish Museum and then via Kreuzberg's Viktoriapark. It then heads to Schöneberg Town Hall, where John F Kennedy declared 'Ich bin ein Berliner' in 1963, before winding its way to leafy Dahlem and Potsdam. If you're too tired to pedal back, just hop on the S-bahn. Bikes are allowed on most routes at all but the busiest times. Note you'll have to buy your bike a special ticket too.

Those with stronger legs could pedal from Berlin to Copenhagen: the 630km route is marked all the way (www.bike-berlin-copenhagen.com). Or, for the really ambitious, there's always the European Cycleway R1 (www.euroroute-r1.de). Covering a distance of 3,500km, it links Calais in France with the Russian city of St Petersburg, passing through Berlin en route. Amateur cyclists flock to Berlin in June for the annual Velothon (www.skoda-velothon-berlin.de), a closed road event that takes place on 60km and 120km routes.

The website of the Berlin senate lists lots of great rides in English, including the Wannsee trail and a number of routes following the path of where the Berlin Wall once stood. Search for cycling on www.stadtentwicklung.berlin.de. The basic but useful English language forum Bikes Berlin (www.bikesberlin.com) answers many questions about cycling in Berlin and beyond.

There are bike hire places all over town and many hotels now have their own fleet of bicycles, so you shouldn't have a problem finding two wheels for a weekend. Expect to pay around €10 per day, less if you rent for more than one day. Some of the best hire companies are listed in the directory at the back of this guide (*see p288*). Fahrrad Station (www.fahrradstation.de) rents out more unusual models, such as the very sociable conference bikes that are operated by seven people at once, and Buddy Bikes (www.buddybike.de) offers quirky tandems that allow lovebirds to pedal along side by side. Beautifully restored vintage racers are available from Finding Berlin (www.findingberlin-tours.com).

In summer, Berlin's public bike-sharing scheme, Call A Bike, is in operation. Run by German railways, it's much less ambitious than its Paris and London equivalents, and not nearly as good, especially for tourists. Registering is a bit of a hassle: there is a €12 sign-up fee and it then costs 0.08 cents per minute (up to a maximum of €15 per day). Bikes have to be returned to one of the 80 or so docking stations dotted around the centre of town. The website (in German) is www.callabike-interaktiv.de

Guided bicycle tours are becoming increasingly popular. Fat Tire Bike Tours (2404 7991, www.fatbiketoursberlin.com) organises an assortment of tours, including a four- to five-hour tour along the former line of the Wall. Fahrradstation (0180 510 8000, www.fahrradstation.com) offers themed city tours, including one through East Berlin and another through Kreuzberg and increasingly trendy Neukölln. Berlin On Bike (4373 9999, www.berlinonbike.de) runs various guided outings, including one at night.

Over 40,000 people take part, making it one of the world's biggest marathons. It's spread over two days to accommodate runners, wheelchair athletes and in-line skaters. Because Berlin is flat and the weather moderate in September, world records are often under threat. The less ambitious can try the Berlin Half-Marathon in early April or 'City Night' in August, a 10km (six-mile) trot up and down the Ku'damm. There's also the New Year Fun Run every 1 January, when Berliners work off their hangovers. It starts at the Soviet War Memorial near the Brandenburg Gate.

Beach volleyball

Land-locked Berlin is, strangely, a major centre for beach volleyball and one of four cities that host a grand slam tournament. The **Volleyball-Verband Berlin** (3199 9933, www.vvb-online.de) is the sport's umbrella organisation. Its website lists all permanent beach volleyball facilities in Berlin.

Beach Mitte
Caroline-Michaelis-Strasse, Mitte (0177 280 6861, www.beachmitte.de). S1, S2, S86 Nordbahnhof. **Open** 10am-midnight daily. **Rates** €12/hr Mon-Fri 10am-5pm; €16/hr from 5pm & Sat/Sun. **No credit cards. Map** p318 M4.
This new facility boasts outdoor courts and a beach bar atmosphere with cocktails and a bonfire at night.

City Beach am Friedrichshain
Kniprodestrasse, corner of Danziger Strasse, Prenzlauer Berg (0177 247 6907, www.city-beach-berlin.de). Tram 20 Kniprodestrasse/Danziger Strasse. **Open** call for details. **Rates** €11/hr. **No credit cards. Map** p325 R4.
Nine-court outdoor facility with a beach bar on the Spree in the summer, plus an indoor facility. Call in advance to book a court.

Bowling

BowlingCenter am Alexanderplatz
Rathausstrasse 5, Mitte (242 6657, www.bowling-am-alex.de). U2, U5, U8, S3, S5, S7, S75 Alexanderplatz. **Open** times vary. **Rates** €11.40-€19.20/hr; €1.70 shoes. **No credit cards. Map** p319/p327 O6.
This DDR relic now boasts all mod cons: 18 lanes, pool tables, darts, pinball machines and a restaurant.

Neue City Bowling Hasenheide
Hasenheide 107-109, Kreuzberg (622 2038, www.bowling-hasenheide.de). U7, U8 Hermannplatz. **Open** times vary. **Rates** €1.50-€3.50/person/game. **Map** p323 P11.
Top international bowling competitions are hosted at this 28-lane facility, which also has 12 lanes for children, a bar/restaurant and two rooms reserved for those who fancy a smoke.

Canoeing & kayaking

Der Bootsladen
Brandensteinweg 8, Spandau (362 5685, www.der-bootsladen.de). Bus 149. **Open** *mid Mar-mid Oct* noon-7pm Tue-Fri; 9am-7pm Sat, Sun. **Rates** €6-€7.50/hr.
This is a good place for canoe and kayak tours of the western river and canal system. You'll save money by booking for a whole day.

Kanu Connection
Soltauerstrasse 26-30, Reinickendorf (612 2686, www.kanu-connection.de). U1 Schlesisches Tor. **Open** 10am-7pm Mon-Fri; 9am-1pm Sat. **Rates** €22-€30/person/day; €49-€65/wknd; €95-€117/wk. **No credit cards.**
Kreuzberg itself is a nice area to paddle through, or you could head east to the forests. This outfit can provide you with maps and guides.

Climbing

Climbers can either go to one of the commercial halls or join a club; the latter offer good-value introductory courses and access to some fantastic outdoor venues such as the World War II-era flak tower in Humboldthain or the bonkers MountMitte. The website www.klettern-in-berlin.de lists official and unofficial climbing venues in Berlin.

Deutscher Alpenverein
Markgrafenstrasse 11, Kreuzberg (251 0943, www.dav-berlin.de). U6 Kochstrasse. **Open** 2-7pm Mon, Wed; 9am-1pm Fri. **Admission** *Membership* €80; €36-€43 reductions. **No credit cards. Map** p323 N8.
The DAV offers information, courses and access to cool climbing venues.

Magic Mountain
Böttgerstrasse 20-26, Wedding (8871 5790, www.magicmountain.de). U8, S1 Gesundbrunnen. **Open** noon-midnight Mon-Wed, Fri; 10am-midnight Thur; 11am-10pm Sat, Sun. **Admission** €12-€14; €10-€12 reductions. **Map** p318 L2.
Indoor climbing hall, featuring a range of walls and a 'donut boulder' for experts.

★ MountMitte
Caroline-Michaelis-Strasse 8, Mitte (555 77 8922, www.mountmitte.de). S1, S2, S25 Nordbahnhof or U6 to Naturkundemuseum. **Open** 2pm-30mins before nightfall Mon-Fri; 10am-30mins before nightfall Sat, Sun. Last admission 2hrs before close. **Admission** €19; €14-€17 reductions.
This wacky aerial assault course, featuring such unusual obstacles as flying Trabants, bicycles and gondolas, as well as more workaday rope bridges and beams, is strung up right by Nordbahnhof. The

ARTS & ENTERTAINMENT

Liquidrom.

concept will be familiar to anyone who has visited a GoApe! centre in the UK – everyone is given a helmet and harness and is firmly attached to the steel ropes as they make their way around the course. Note that children have to be over 1.3m tall to take part.

Cricket

It might come as something of a surprise to hear the smack of leather on willow and bellowed 'Howzats!' in Germany, but cricket has been played in Berlin since the mid 19th century. Six teams currently play competitively; in summer there are games starting at 11am every Saturday and Sunday at one of the most beautiful grounds in mainland Europe (Körner Platz, Hanns-Braun-Strasse, Charlottenburg; U2 Olympia-Stadion).

If you want a game yourself, the **Berlin Cricket Club** (6950 9065, www.berlincc.de,), nicknamed 'the Refugees', is a multinational, English-speaking team of expats and locals who are always on the lookout for new members. They're also, as you might expect, the best source for general information about cricket in Berlin. The club was threatened with eviction in 2011, but after a high-profile media campaign managed to win a reprieve. However, the club's long-term future remains in doubt.

Cycling

Cycling is an ideal method of getting around Berlin, as the city is flat and well supplied with cycle lanes. For bike rental, *see p291*. For more information on cycling in Berlin, *see p256* **Cycling & the City**.

Allgemeiner Deutscher Fahrrad-Club

Brunnenstrasse 28, Mitte (448 4724, www.adfc-berlin.de). U8 Bernauer Strasse. **Open** noon-8pm Mon-Fri; 10am-4pm Sat. **Map** p319 N3.
This place has an information and meeting point for cyclists and a do-it-yourself repair station. Contact them for a copy of their Berlin cycle path map.

Berliner Radsport Verband

Paul-Heyse-Strasse 29, Prenzlauer Berg (4210 5145, www.berlin-radsport.de). S41, S42, S8, S85, S9 Landsberger Allee. **Open** 9am-1pm Tue, Fri; 2-7pm Thur. **Map** p325 S4.
Information on clubs, races and events. The Tour de Berlin, a five-stage, 600km (375-mile) race, takes place in May.

Disabled

There are dozens of clubs and organisations for disabled athletes in Berlin. Call **Behinderten-Sportverband Berlin** (3009 9675) for details or visit its website at www.bsberlin.de.

Fitness centres

There are hundreds of health and fitness clubs in Berlin – everything from sweaty body-building basements to luxurious spa-like penthouses. There are also branches of chains such as Kieser, Swiss Training and Gold's.

Aspria

Karlsruher Strasse 20, Wilmersdorf (890 688 810, www.aspria.de). S41, S42, S46 Halensee. **Open** 6am-11pm Mon-Fri; 8am-10pm Sat, Sun. **Rates** from €80/mth. **Map** p320 C9.

Luxurious five-floor complex with a health and beauty centre, 25m pool, saunas, steam room, ice room, restaurants, bars, sun terrace with solariums and a view of central Berlin. The club offers massages, beauty treatments, fitness courses and customised workouts.

Club Olympus Spa & Fitness

Grand Hyatt Berlin, Marlene-Dietrich-Platz 2, Tiergarten (2553 1890, www.berlin.grand.hyatt.com). U2, S1, S2, S25 Potsdamer Platz. **Open** 6am-11pm daily. **Rates** €60/day. **Map** p322 K8.
Luxurious, expensive fitness centre on the hotel roof.

Fitness First Ladies Club Berlin

Tauentzienstrasse 13A, Charlottenburg (2145 9442, www.fitnessfirst.de). U9 Kurfürstendamm or U1, U2, U3 Wittenbergplatz. **Open** 7am-11pm Mon-Fri; 10am-8pm Sat, Sun. **Rates** from €40/mth. **Map** p321 L4.
Fitness First has 19 branches all over Berlin, not all of which are women only. Check the website for more details.

Liquidrom

Möckernstrasse 10, Kreuzberg (258 007 820, www.liquidrom-berlin.de). S1, S2, S25 Anhalter Bahnhof or U7 Möckernbrücke. **Open** 10am-midnight Mon-Thur, Sun; 10am-1am Fri, Sat. **Admission** €19.50/2hrs; €24.50/4hrs; €29.50/day. **No credit cards. Map** p322 L9.
Part of the Tempodrom complex, this is a stylish oasis of watery leisure pursuits, with pools, saunas, steam baths, cold dips, an open-air Japanese Onsen pool, massage facilities and a terrace and bar. One of the highlights is 'liquid sound', a domed, circular pool with lighting and underwater speakers. On Friday evenings, it's all candle-lit.

Gay & lesbian sports

The rift in international GLBT sports that led to the creation of the Outgames as well as the Gay Games also affected Berlin's efforts to host a major event. Berlin's gay mayor saw no option but to withdraw official backing for both factions. The Outgames 2009 went to Copenhagen, and Cologne got the 2010 Gay Games. Berlin, meanwhile, is out in the cold and the gay sporting community is split. But you can still visit www.vorspiel-berlin.de for details of local sports.

Go-karting

Kartland

Miraustrasse 62-80, Reinickendorf (4356 6841, www.kartland.de). **Open** 3-10pm Mon-Thur; 2pm-midnight Fri, Sat; 10am-10pm Sun. **Tickets** €19; €15 children. **No credit cards.**

Golf

As well as conventional golf courses and driving ranges, in Kreuzberg you can play crazy golf at the lovely **Brachvogel** beer garden (*see p166*) or glow-in-the-dark mini golf at **Schwarzlicht**.

Golfpark Schloss Wilkendorf

Am Weiher 1, OT Wilkendorf, Gielsdorf (0334 133 0960, www.golfpark-schloss-wilkendorf.com). S5 Strausberg Nord, then walk/taxi. **Open** *Nov-Mar* 9am-5pm daily. *Apr-Oct* 9am-6pm. **Rates** *Westside Platz* (18 holes) €35 Mon-Fri; €45 Sat, Sun. *Sandy-Lyle-Platz* (18 holes; members only) €50 Mon-Fri; €70 Sat, Sun. *Public course* (six holes) €10 Mon-Fri; €15 Sat, Sun.
The only 18-hole course in the area open to non-members: at weekends, you'll need a *Platzreife* (German golf certificate), which is obtainable with any golf membership or by taking a course and/or test. Call for details.

Schwarzlicht

Görlitzer Strasse 1, Kreuzberg (6162 1960, www.indoor-minigolf-berlin.de). U1 Görlitzer Bahnhof. **Open** noon-10pm Mon-Fri; 10am-10pm Sat, Sun. **Tickets** €4.50; €3.50 reductions.
Good for rainy winter days, this glow-in-the-dark 18-hole mini golf course is in the basement of Café Isa Mitz in Görlitzer Park.

Ice rink, Alexanderplatz. *See p260.*

ARTS & ENTERTAINMENT

Ice skating

The Christmas market at Alexanderplatz
has a small outdoor rink, and you can try
your hand at curling in the Sony Center
at Potsdamer Platz from late November
to early January.

Erika-Hess-Eisstadion-Mitte
*Erika-Hess-Stadion, Müllerstrasse 185, Wedding
(469 079 55). U6 Reinickendorfer Strasse.*
Open *Oct-mid Mar* 9am-noon, 3-5.30pm Mon;
7.30am-noon, 3-5.50pm Tue; 9am-noon, 3-5.30pm,
7-9.30pm Wed; 7.30am-noon, 3-5.50pm, 7.30-10pm
Thur; 9am-noon, 3-5.30pm, 7.30-10pm Fri, Sat.
Admission €3.30; €1.60 reductions. **No credit
cards. Map** p318 K3.
This is the cheapest public rink in town. The venue
also holds important skating competitions.

Horst-Dohm-Eisstadion
*Fritz-Wildung-Strasse 9, Wilmersdorf
(2903 1136, www.horst-dohm-eisstadion.de).
S4 Hohenzollerndamm.* **Open** *Oct-mid Mar*
9am-6pm, 7.30-10pm Mon-Fri; 9am-10pm
Sat; 10am-6pm Sun. **Rates** €3.30/2hrs;
€1.60 reductions. **No credit cards.**
Map p320 D11.
This rink boasts an outer ring for speed skating and
an inner field for figure skaters. Skate rental too.

Sailing & motor boating

There's a lot of water around Berlin. The city
boasts 50 lakes and a 200-kilometre (125-mile)
network of navigable rivers, estuaries and
canals. The city is bordered on the west by
the Havel river and to the south by the Dahme,
while the Spree forms an east–west axis

Sauna Culture
Feel the sweat, then take the plunge.

If you fancy a sauna while you're here,
you're going to have to get your kit off.
Keeping your swimming costume on is
strictly *verboten* – Germans consider it to
be highly unhygienic to sweat in anything but
a clean towel. The towel, incidentally, is for
sitting or lying on, and not to protect your
modesty. If any bit of your body touches
the wood, even your feet, you'll get told
off. There are almost always signs saying
'*Kein schweiss auf's holz!*' (no sweat on
the wood). And you know the saunas are
mixed here, right?

Sauna-going is a serious activity for
Berliners, and they will not be afraid to
tell you if you contravene their (generally
unspoken) rules. The main thing you need
to know concerns the semi-spiritual *Aufguss*,
the water-pouring ritual performed by the
Saunameister usually once an hour on the
hour. This can involve all sorts of high jinks,
but essentially revolves around some bloke
with a teatowel around his waist putting
fragrant water on the hot coals to raise
the temperature to as ridiculous a level
as possible. He will usually follow each
round of pouring (*Aufguss*) by whirling a
towel around his head to circulate the heat,
perhaps wafting it right in your face until
you feel certain you are going to pass out.

Before he starts, the *Saunameister* will
open the door to let some fresh air in, before
putting a go-away sign on the door and then
launching into a little speech. This varies,
but will generally consist of him telling you

his name, what flavour water he is using
and how many rounds he is going to inflict
on you (usually three). He will probably say
something about how you mustn't worry if
you feel you need to leave halfway through,
but he doesn't really mean it. Leaving or
arriving mid *Aufguss* is one of the twin sauna
sins, along with talking during the act.

Anyone even vaguely sensitive to heat
should sit on the lowest rung of the sauna:
only the most macho of *Saunagäste* can
hack it on the upper tier. After the final
Aufguss, it is customary to clap, before
leaving as quickly as possible, ducking
under a shower for a few seconds to wash
off the sweat and then plunging into the
cold water pool. Cooling down is an
essential part of the process. If you can't
hack the plunge pool, at least go outside for
a bit. In Neukölln you can go up on the roof.
At the Saunalandschaft in Lichterfelde Ost
you can have a nudey swim in the outdoor
pool. Then you are supposed to have a little
lie down in the *Ruheraum* (quiet room),
reading or dozing, before it's time to do it
all over again. If the sauna has foot baths,
use them first. It'll get you in the mood.

Most saunas in Berlin have more than
one actual sauna – many have a *Dampfbad*
(steam room), which usually requires visitors
to sit on enormous sheets of clingfilm torn
from an industrial roll, and a selection of
saunas of different temperatures. Berlin's
best sauna, upstairs at the **Stadtbad
Neukölln** (*see p262*), has five: a *Dampfbad*,

through the centre. The **Berliner Segler-Verband** (3083 9908, www.berlinersegler verband.de) has information on sailing in and around Berlin.

If you're planning a longer stay, you might want to join a local sailing club. The **American International Yacht Club Berlin** (8040 3630, www.aiycb.de) has an English website and is a good first port of call. There's also the **German-British Yacht Club** (365 4010, www.dbyc.de). But there are also opportunities for the short-term visitor. The **Wassersportzentrum Berlin** (6418 0140, www.wassersport zentrum.de) runs two sailing/diving/motor boat centres with marinas at the Müggelsee in south-east Berlin. You need a licence for boating and sailing, so if you have one, bring it. Boat rental places may then issue you a charter pass for sailboats or motor boats.

Sauna & Turkish baths

Many of Berlin's public baths have cheapish saunas and massage services, all with their own rules and rituals (*see below* **Sauna Culture**).

Hamam Turkish Bath

Schoko-Fabrik, Naunynstrasse 72, Kreuzberg (615 1464, www.hamamberlin.de/en). U1, U8 Kottbusser Tor. **Open** 3-11pm Mon; noon-11pm Tue-Sun. **Rates** €14/3hrs; €21/5hrs. **No credit cards. Map** p323 P9.
Under the glass cupola of the main hall, women sit in alcoves soaking in warm water. It's a friendly and laid-back place, attracting a mixed clientele. Enjoy Turkish tea and a reviving massage afterwards. Children are not permitted on Tuesdays and Fridays, but Thursday is kids' day (women only, but boys up to the age of six are allowed in).

Stadtbad Neukölln.

a *Kräutersauna* (herbal sauna), a lukewarm *Caldarium*, a mid-temperature *Sanarium* with special lights and the big daddy *Finnische Sauna*, which is where the Saunameister performs his *Aufguss*. Outside Berlin, the lake sauna at the Fontane Thermen in Neu Ruppin, is a real treat: the sauna is situated on a pontoon jutting out into the lake and includes one wall made entirely of glass, as well as two wooden swings big enough for two people to lie on.

Leave at least two hours for a proper sauna session, and shower first unless

you want an earful from anyone who notices. Take a dressing gown if you can, plus flipflops, and leave your blushes at the door. To reach Neu Ruppin, catch the direct train from Berlin Spandau to Rheinsberger Tor – journey time is an hour and a half.

Fontane Therme Neuruppin

An der Seepromenade 21,16816 Neuruppin am See (03391, 4032 400, www.fontane-therme.de). **Open** 10am-10pm daily. **Day ticket** €29 (€33 weekends). **Three-hour ticket** €21 (€25 weekends).

ARTS & ENTERTAINMENT

Sultan Hamam
*Bülowstrasse 57, Schöneberg (2175 3375, www.
sultan-hammam.de). U2 Bülowstrasse.* **Open** *Oct-
Mar* 9.30am-11pm daily. *Apr-Sept* noon-11pm
daily. **Rates** €16/3hrs; €13 peel; €18 massage.
No credit cards. Map p322 J9.
Traditional massages and peelings, as well as more
modern cosmetic treatments. Monday is men's day,
Sunday is family day; otherwise it's women only.

Thermen am Europa-Center
*Europa-Center, Nürnberger Strasse 7,
Charlottenburg (257 5760, www.thermen-
berlin.de). U1, U2, U3 Wittenbergplatz.*
Open *June-Aug* 10am-11pm Mon-Sat;
10am-9pm Sun. *Sept-May* 10am-2pm Mon-Sat;
10am-9pm Sun. **Rates** *June-Aug* €15.90/day.
Sept-May €18.80/day; €16.50/3 hrs; €161/10
admissions . **Map** p321 G8.
Big, central, mixed facility offering Finnish saunas,
steam baths, hot and cool pools, and a garden (open
until October). There is a pool where you can swim
outside on to the roof and back, even in the depths
of winter. Other facilities include a café, pool-side
loungers, table tennis, billiards and massage.

Skateboarding, in-line skating & BMX

Berlin is a skater-friendly city, with small
facilities dotted across town, plus several bigger
complexes; all are listed at www.skatespots.de.
The city's in-line skaters occasionally disrupt
street traffic by holding demonstrations for
equal rights. Routes vary; check www.berlin
parade.de for dates and starting points.

Erlebniswerkstatt des Projektes Erlebnisräume
*Sterndamm 82, Treptow (631 0911,
www.erlebnisraeume.de). S4, S6, S8, S9, S10
Schöneweide.* **Open** call for appointment.
Admission free.
Trial track with jump ramps and a good place to connect with what's on. Projekt Erlebnisräume builds
and maintains skateboarding, skating and climbing
facilities and organises competitions.

Skatehalle Berlin
*Revaler Strasse 99, Friedrichshain (2936 2966,
www.skatehalle-berlin.de). U1, S3, S7, S9, S75
Warschauer Strasse.* **Open** *Oct-Apr* 2-8pm Mon;
2pm-midnight Tue-Fri; noon-midnight Sat; noon-
8pm Sun. *May-Sept* 2-10pm Tue; 2pm-midnight
Wed, Fri; 2-8pm Thur; noon-midnight Sat;
noon-8pm Sun. **Rates** €5; €4 reductions.
Map p324/G8.
This hall houses Germany's biggest halfpipe, as well
as a mini-ramp and street parcours. BMXers are
allowed in on Tuesdays and Saturday evenings and
there are courses on the weekends.

Squash

Many tennis clubs (*see p263*) have squash
courts too.

Sport Oase, Ladyline & Himaxx
*Stromstrasse 11-17, Moabit (390 6620,
www.sportoase.de). U9 Turmstrasse.* **Open**
9am-10.45pm Mon-Thur; 9am-10pm Fri; 10am-
8pm Sat; 9am-9pm Sun. **Rates** vary (see website).
No credit cards. Map p317 H5.
This impressive complex, housed in a former brewery, has badminton and squash courts, saunas, a
mixed fitness room, a women-only fitness centre
called Ladyline, and Himaxx, a high-altitude training centre. There's also a pleasant pub/restaurant.

Swimming (indoor)

Every district has an indoor pool. Check the
phone book under *Stadtbad* or visit
www.berlinerbaederbetriebe.de for the nearest.
Be warned that despite the German reputation
for efficiency, many pools, even sporty ones, do
not have lanes, so swimming at busy times can
be a rather anarchic experience.

SSE Europa-Sportpark
*Paul-Heyse-Strasse 26, Prenzlauer Berg (4218
6120, www.berlinerbaederbetriebe.de). S41, S42,
S8, S85, S9 Landsberger Allee.* **Open** times vary
(check website). **Admission** €4; €2.50 reductions.
No credit cards. Map p325 S4.
One of the largest swimming pools in Europe, this
immense facility next to the Velodrom (*see p253*)
often hosts international swimming competitions.

Stadtbad Mitte
*Gartenstrasse 5, Mitte (3088 0910). S1, S2, S25
Nordbahnhof/Tram M10, 12.* **Open** 6.30am-10pm
Mon, Wed, Fri; 10am-4pm Tue; 6.30am-8pm Thur;
2-9pm Sat; 10am-6pm Sun. **Admission** €4; €2.50
reductions. **No credit cards. Map** p318/p326 M4.
This impressive place, which dates from 1928, has
a 50m pool.

★ Stadtbad Neukölln
*Ganghoferstrasse 3, Neukölln (6824 9812,
www.berlinerbaederbetriebe.de). U7 Rathaus
Neukölln.* **Open** times vary (check website).
Admission €4; €2.50 reductions. **No credit
cards. Map** p324 R12.
Described as 'Europe's most beautiful baths' when
it opened in 1914, the Stadtbad Neukölln survived
the 20th century unscathed and remains beautiful.
Built in Greco-Roman style, the complex features
two splendid pools flanked by Ionic columns, with
original tiling and mosaics, wood panelling and
stained-glass windows.
► *The venue also has the loveliest sauna in
Berlin, see p260 Sauna Culture.*

Stadtbad Schöneberg

*Hauptstrasse 39, Schöneberg (780 9930,
www.berlinerbaederbetriebe.de). U7 Eisenacher
Strasse.* **Admission** €4-€9; €3-€7 reductions.
No credit cards. Map p322 J11.
Great mixture of old and new. Kids can play on the
water slide or in the wave pool while you swim laps
or recharge your batteries in the sauna. It can get
very busy at peak times.

Swimming (open-air)

Before setting out to a pool, check first to
make sure it's open as the city's financial
woes affect opening times. Details of almost
all of Berlin's public pools can be found at
www.berlinerbaederbetriebe.de. Usually the
outdoor swimming season doesn't start until
May, though hardy swimmers could join the
Berliner Seehunde, Berlin's cold water
swimming club, who swim throughout the
winter at the often frozen Orankeesee in
Hohenschönhausen (www.berliner-seehunde.de).
There is also plenty of lake swimming in Berlin:
Schlachtensee and Krumme Lanke in the
West are clean, set in attractive woodland
and easily reachable by public transport.
For more on wild swimming in and around
Berlin *see p279* **The Wild Side**.
   Of the following swimming spots, only the
Badeschiff is open in winter.

★ Badeschiff Berlin

*Eichenstrasse 4, Treptow (533 2030, www.arena-
berlin.de). S9, S41, S42 Treptower Park/bus 265.*
Open 8.30am-midnight daily. **Admission** €4;
€3 reductions. **No credit cards.**
This popular commercial operation features a former barge converted into a heated swimming pool,
docked on the banks of the Spree. It belongs to the
Arena Berlin (*see p241*) cultural centre, and also
boasts two saunas and a bar.

Sommerbad Kreuzberg

*Prinzenstrasse 113-119, Kreuzberg (616 1080).
U1 Prinzenstrasse.* **Open** times vary (check
website). **Admission** €4; €2.50 reductions.
No credit cards. Map p323 O9.
This popular outdoor complex for swimming and
sunbathing, known as Prinzenbad, has a 50m pool
and one for non-swimmers. There's disabled access,
a nudist area and refreshments.

Strandbad Wannsee

*Wannseebadweg, Nikolassee (7071 3833, www.
berlinerbaederbetriebe.de). S1, S7 Nikolassee.*
Open times vary (check website). **Admission**
€4; €2.50 reductions. **No credit cards.**
Strandbad Wannsee is Europe's largest inland
beach, with sand, sunbeds, water slides, pedalos,
snack stalls and beer garden. It makes for the

complete seaside experience, only without the salty
water. It's very shallow, so good for children.

Strandbad Grünau

*Sportpromenade 9, Köpenick (2509 0683,
www.strandbad-gruenau.de). S46, S8 to Grünau
then tram 68 to Strandbad Grünau.* **Open** times
vary (check website). **Admission** €5; €3
reductions. **No credit cards.**
More charming than Wannsee but not nearly as popular, this east Berlin bathing spot on the Spree river
near Köpenick boasts 100 *Strandkorb* beach chairs
for rent and is great for serious swimming and dip-
ping alike. There's a nudist section, for those into
that sort of thing.

Tennis

Tennis is an expensive sport to play in Berlin.
The cheapest time is in the mornings and
even then it can cost €15-€30 an hour for
an indoor court. The **Tennis-Verband
Berlin-Brandenburg** (8972 8730, www.
tvbb.de) has information about local leagues
and clubs.

TC City Sports

*Brandenburgische Strasse 53, Wilmersdorf
(873 9097, www.citysports-berlin.com). U7
Konstanzer Strasse.* **Open** 8am-midnight daily.
Rates *Tennis* €14-€19/45 mins. *Squash* €12.50-
€19.50/45 mins. *Badminton* €10.50-€17.50/45
mins. *Sauna* €5. **Credit** cards accepted.
Map p321 E10.
Tennis, squash and badminton courts, plus a sauna,
solarium, restaurant and beer garden. Coaching is
available for all three sports, along with aerobics and
classical dance. If you've been playing a racquet
game, the sauna comes free.

Tennis Center Weissensee

*Roelckestrasse 106, Weissensee (927 4594,
www.tcwsports.com). S41, S42, S85, S9
Greifswalder Strasse.* **Open** 7am-midnight daily.
Rates €14-€20/hr singles; €23-€36/hr doubles.
No credit cards.
Tennis, badminton and fun ball courts, all indoors.
Prices include use of the sauna (10am-10pm).

Windsurfing, water-skiing, wakeboarding & surfing

The **Müggelsee** in the south-east of Berlin
is a popular lake for water sports, as are the
Wannsee in the south-west and the **Tegeler
See** in the north-west. Useful (but German-
only) websites include:
www.fss-berlin.de/index_content.html (surfing);
www.wakeboard-berlin.de (wakeboarding);
www.wsev.de/wsev.jsp (windsurfing)
www.wasserskiclub-berlin.de (water-skiing).

Theatre, Cabaret & Dance

Theatre thrives in Berlin.

Berlin has one of the most exciting theatre cultures anywhere in the world. The city has five generously funded, multi-stage state theatres, surrounded and supplemented by a huge, thriving off-scene. The blessing and curse of the 'Big Five' – the **Berliner Ensemble**, **Deutsches Theater**, **Maxim Gorki Theater**, **Schaubühne** and **Volksbühne** – is that they run all their productions in an ever-changing, unpredictable repertory system. So if you want to catch a specific show, check the theatre's website before booking your flights to make sure it's on. The

upside of all this for real theatre junkies is that even in a short stay you can catch several of any theatre's productions, including classic stagings that have been running (usually with the original casts) sometimes for over a decade. Conversely, off-scene shows, especially at main venues like the **HAU** and **Sophiensaele**, tend to have quite short runs, although revivals are not uncommon.

INFORMATION

While it is sometimes possible to catch performances with English surtitles (most frequently at the **Schaubühne**), it is equally possible to get a lot out of a show without speaking German, thanks to the frequently astonishing visual aspect of productions. It's also worth noting that a lot of the repertoire – especially at the state theatres – includes much of the same Greek, Shakespeare and Chekhov that English audiences are used to, albeit presented with a radically different approach.

Berlin also has a West End's worth of commercial theatres (*We Will Rock You*

and *Blue Man Group* were here at the time of writing), mostly situated in the city's Westend, along with *Hinterem Horizont*, a jukebox musical based on the songs of German 1980s rock veteran Udo Lindenberg.

FESTIVALS

It sometimes feels like Berlin never stops holding theatre festivals, be it a new, seemingly ad hoc umbrella for a huge range of fringe shows or a prestigious, jury-selected showcase of the best stagings nationally or internationally.

Perhaps the most important festival of the year is **Theatertreffen** at the Berliner Festspiele (www.berlinerfestspiele.de), which invites the ten productions that have been judged best of the season from the whole of Germany. Tickets are a bit pricey, and it's more of an industry shindig than a tourist attraction, but it's a great opportunity to see the best of the best in one place. Running alongside it is the **Stückemarkt** new plays festival, which offers a series of readings (in German) of the best new national and international scripts.

**INSIDE TRACK
SUMMER SHUTDOWN**

Pretty much all of Berlin's theatres close at some point in July and don't reopen until September. If you want to see some theatre in Berlin, don't come in August.

Berliner Festspiele also hosts the international festival **Spielzeit'Europa** from October to January, offering a showcase of the usual international festival suspects – the 2011/2012 edition, for example, includes veteran director Peter Sellars collaborating with Toni Morrison on *Desdemona* and a production by Societas Raffaello Sanzio and DV8.

On the off-scene, perhaps the most ambitious festival is **100° Berlin – Das Lange Wochenende des Freien Theaters**, which, as the name suggests, is a long weekend in February during which Sophiensaele and HAU throw open their doors to all kinds of performance groups, and a daily ticket (under €20) can get you admission to upwards of six hours of different performances across four sites with a choice of late after-show bars.

In mid November, there is the **Sehnsucht – Festival Politik im Freien Theater** (www.politikimfreientheater.de). The Schaubühne's **Festival for International New Drama** (FIND) in March showcases new works from Germany and abroad.

STATE THEATRES

Berliner Ensemble

Bertolt-Brecht-Platz 1, Mitte (2840 8155, www.berliner-ensemble.de). U6, S1, S2, S5, S7, S75 Friedrichstrasse. **Box office** 8am-6pm Mon-Fri; 11am-6pm Sat, Sun. **Tickets** €5-€30; €7 reductions. **Map** p318/p327 M6.
Probably Berlin's most famous theatre, thanks largely to its historical association with Bertolt Brecht. Under current artistic director Claus Peymann, it is regarded by Germans as a little too comfortable and touristy, a place where older, formerly radical directors go to work. You can still see the late Heiner Müller's 16-year-old staging of *The Resistable Rise of Arturo Ui* along with productions by Robert Wilson and Peter Stein.

Deutsches Theater

Schumannstrasse 13A, Mitte (284 410, tickets 2844 1225, www.deutschestheater.de). U6, S1, S2, S5, S7, S9, S75 Friedrichstrasse. **Box office** 11am-6.30pm Mon-Sat; 3-6.30pm Sun. **Tickets** €4-€45; €9 reductions. **Map** p318 L5.
Of all the theatres in Berlin, the Deutsches Theater behaves most like a state theatre in any other German city, offering a *Spielplan* of new interpretations of works by Goethe and Schiller alongside Shakespeare, Aeschylus and a smattering of new plays. Productions vary enormously, from the intensely exciting and innovative to somewhat more stately fare, depending on the director.

Maxim Gorki Theater

Am Festungsgraben 2, Mitte (2022 1115, www.gorki.de). U6, S1, S2, S5, S7, S75 Friedrichstrasse. **Box office** noon-6.30pm Mon-Sat; 4-6.30pm Sun. **Tickets** €10-€34. **Map** p319/p327 N6.
This jewel of a theatre is slightly off the beaten tourist track. Back in 2006, author and director Armin Petras became the Maxim Gorki's intendant, and with a young and new ensemble he has breathed life into this landmark. The programming features new interpretations of classical and modern dramas, as well as adaptations from films and novels, with the result that the atmosphere alone is often enough to transcend the language barrier.

★ Schaubühne am Lehniner Platz

Kurfürstendamm 153, Charlottenburg (890 023, www.schaubuehne.de). U7 Adenauerplatz or S5, S7, S75 Charlottenburg. **Box office** 11am-6.30pm Mon-Sat; 3-6.30pm Sun. **Tickets** €7-€43; €9 reductions. **Map** p320 D9.
Of the Big Five, the Schaubühne is probably the most popular with English audiences and has a long history of anglophile collaboration. It was the theatre that essentially established Brits Mark

ARTS & ENTERTAINMENT

Schaubühne am Lehniner Platz.

Ravenhill and Sarah Kane as Germany's favourite playwrights. Under current artistic director Thomas Ostermeier, the house production style treads a happy medium between German radicalism and British realism, which, coupled with the frequent surtitling of performances in English, makes it an ideal starting point for anyone looking for an introduction to German theatre.

Volksbühne

Rosa-Luxemburg-Platz, Mitte (2406 5777, www. volksbuehne-berlin.de). U2 Rosa-Luxemburg-Platz. **Box office** noon-6pm daily. **Tickets** €10-€30; €6-€15 reductions. **Map** p319/p326 O5.
Built in 1914, the Volksbühne is certainly Berlin's most imposing theatre, and its austere exterior is well suited to the current regime under artistic director Frank Castorf, whose own productions seem to enrage as much as delight. That said, his immense four-hour interpretation of Chekhov's *The Three Sisters, Nach Moskau! Nach Moskau!*, was a critical

hit. Also worth looking out for is work from the idiosyncratic associate director René Pollesch, which might best be described as a kind of knockabout farce of critical theory wrapped up in dazzling stagecraft.

FRINGE

Ballhaus Ost

Pappelallee 15, Prenzlauer Berg (4799 7474, www.ballhausost.de). U2 Eberswalder Strasse. **Box office** *Phone* 9am-8pm Mon-Sat; 2-8pm Sun. **Tickets** €13; €8 reductions. **Map** p319/p328 P2.
This somewhat dilapidated former ballroom hosts art, performance art, dance productions and concerts, offering a unique and authentic cultural evening. There's also a lounge and bar populated by a very cool crowd.

★ Ballhaus Naunynstrasse

Naunynstrasse 27, Kreuzberg (7545 3725, www.ballhausnaunynstrasse.de). U1, U8

HAU's the Best of Berlin

Three old theatres have come together to make some of the city's best drama.

The most innovative programming in the city today is coming from the amalgamation of the century-old former Hebbel Theater (HAU1), Theater am Hallesches Ufer (HAU2) and Theater am Ufer (HAU3). Since 2003 it has been run by Matthias Lilienthal, Frank Castorf's former *Dramaturg* at the Volksbühne, and in that time it has gained an incredible reputation for hosting the most extraordinary programme of radical international work.

The venue's programmes frequently read like a *Who's Who* of international performance, including groups like the Nature Theater of Oklahoma, Alain Platel, Bruce la Bruce, Alvis Hermanis, Jerome Bel and Peaches, as well as long-standing HAU regulars Gob Squad and Rimini Protokoll.

The Hebbel Theater itself is worth a visit for the auditorium alone, which manages to combine scale with intimacy in a large, old-fashioned wood-panelled traditional theatre. Interestingly, much of the glass at the back of the theatre building was replaced by old gin bottles following damage in the war when there was a shortage of glass in the city.

Theater am Hallesches Ufer has an even more interesting past, having served as the former site of both the Zodiak Free Arts Lab – credited as the birthplace of Krautrock and home to bands such as Tangerine Dream and Ash Ra Tempel – and as the

first Schaubühne theatre before it moved to its current home in the Kino Universum. It's also worth noting that it's home to the very serviceable WAU café – an excellent place for late post-show drinks that also serves excellent pizzas.

Lilienthal hands over artistic directorship of the venues at the beginning of the 2012 season, but his successor, highly regarded Belgian Annemie Vanackere, is likely to continue the venue's success.

For listings, *see right*.

Kottbusser Tor. **Box office** 5.30-8pm performance days. **Tickets** €12; €7 reductions. **No credit cards. Map** p323 P8.

Thanks to the inclusion of artistic director Nurkan Erpulat's *Verrücktes Blut* in 2011's Theatertreffen, Ballhaus Naunynstrasse is now *the* fringe theatre to visit. Located in the largely Turkish Kreuzkölln district, the company is gaining a strong reputation for investigating issues surrounding the immigrant experience and identity in Germany.

Brotfabrik

Caligariplatz 1, Weissensee (471 4001, www. brotfabrik-berlin.de). Tram M2, M13 Prenzlauer Allee/Ostseestrasse. **Box office** *By phone* 9am-8pm Mon-Sat. **Tickets** €12; €8 reductions. **Map** p319 Q1.

Far from the centre of town, this former bread factory houses a cinema, gallery, café and small experimental theatre where productions by visiting companies are performed in a variety of languages. The café has a congenial summer courtyard.

English Theatre Berlin

Fidicinstrasse 40, Kreuzberg (691 1211, www.etberlin.de). U6 Platz der Luftbrücke. **Box office** 1hr before performance. **Tickets** €8-€18. **No credit cards. Map** p322 M11.

Under directors Günther Grosser and Bernd Hoffmeister, F40 (formerly known as Friends of Italian Opera) boasts a high-quality programme. Expect house productions, international guest shows and co-productions with performers from Berlin's lively international theatre scene. Theater Thikwa, one of Europe's most renowned companies working with disabled actors, is also based here.

★ HAU

Main office: HAU2 (Theater am Hallesches Ufer) Hallesches Ufer 32, Kreuzberg (box office 2590 0427, information 2590 040, www.hebbel-am-ufer.de). U1, U7 Möckernbrücke or U1, U6 Hallesches Tor. **Box office** noon-7pm daily (other locations 1hr before performance). **Tickets** €11-€18; €7 reductions. **Map** p322 M9.

See left **Hau's the Best of Berlin.**

Other locations HAU1 (Hebbel Theatre), Stresemannstrasse 29, Kreuzberg; **HAU3** (Theater am Ufer), Tempelhofer Ufer 10, Kreuzberg.

Sophiensaele

Sophienstrasse 18, Mitte (information 2789 0030, tickets 2835 266, www.sophiensaele.com). U8 Weinmeisterstrasse or S5, S7, S9, S75 Hackescher Markt. **Box office** 1hr before performance. **Tickets** €15; €10 reductions. **No credit cards. Map** p319/p326 N5.

Hidden on a quiet side road near Hackescher Markt and set back from the road behind a little courtyard, it would be quite easy to miss Sophiensaele. But it's well worth seeking out – here, over four floors, you are likely to see some of the most cutting-edge performances in Berlin, and in some of the most atmospheric performance spaces the city has to offer.

Theater am Schokohof

Ackerstrasse 169-170, Mitte (441 0009, www. tisch2000.de). U8 Rosenthaler Platz. **Box office** 1hr before performance. **Tickets** €12; €8 reductions. **No credit cards. Map** p319/p326 N4.

In the back courtyard of the Schoko-Laden, a former squatted house turned cultural centre, lurks a hard-core East German theatre company – one of the few left untarnished by globalisation. Independent, tiny and grungy: a true Berlin experience.

Theaterdiscounter

Klosterstrasse 44, Mitte (2809 3062, www.theaterdiscounter.de). S1, S2 Oranienburger Strasse. **Box office** 1hr before performance. **Tickets** €13; €8 reductions. **No credit cards. Map** p319/p326 N5.

Opened in 2003 in an old telegraph office, this is where an intense group of ten actors and various directors perform new and experimental work. It's anti-illusion theatre with interactive possibilities – very casual and fresh.

Theater unterm Dach

Kulturhaus im Ernst-Thälmann-Park, Danziger Strasse 101, Prenzlauer Berg (902 953 817, www.theateruntermdach-berlin.de). S8, S41, S42, S85 Greifswalder Strasse/tram M4, M10. **Open** *By phone* 7pm until performance daily. **Tickets** €8; €5 reductions. **No credit cards. Map** p319 Q3.

In the large attic of a converted factory, situated well off the beaten path, Theater unterm Dach is the place to see new German fringe groups. Productions are always full of energy and can be quite inspiring. Small but surprisingly exciting programme.

CABARET

Although cabaret in today's Berlin bears little resemblance to the classic cabaret of the Weimar years, there are some great performers here who can re-create an entire era in one night. The town is teeming with acts that can be more sexually adventurous (or ambiguous) than most other places and still manage to titillate the cool Berlin audiences. Some good ones to watch out for include **Die O-Tonpiraten** (clever drag musical theatre that montages famous film dialogues into irreverent storylines), the charming American entertainer **Gayle Tufts** ('denglish' stand-up comedy with pop) and **Bridge Markland** (gender-bending dance and poetry).

Don't confuse cabaret with *varieté*; the latter is more of a circus-like show, minus the animals but with lots of dancing girls.

ARTS & ENTERTAINMENT

Kabarett is different again – a unique kind of German entertainment with a strong following in Berlin. It's basically political satire sprinkled with songs and sketches, sometimes intellectual and sometimes crass. It can be found at venues such as Stachelschweine, Wühlmäuse, Mehringhof Theatre, Kartoon or Kneifzange (check local listings for details), but most of it will be over your head if you don't have perfect German and a thorough understanding of local politics.

When it comes to *travestie* – drag revue – Berlin has some of the best on offer, from fabulous to tragic, and in places where you might not expect it. For the more progressive and intelligent drag acts, the **BKA** (*see right*) is a safe bet. Venues come in all sizes and styles, from small and dark to huge and glittery. Remember that the look and price of a venue is not always an indication of the quality of the show.

Varieté & revue

Chamäleon

Hackesche Höfe, Rosenthaler Strasse 40-41, Mitte (tickets 400 0590/www.chamaeleonberlin.de). S5, S7, S9, S75 Hackescher Markt. **Box office** 10.30am-8pm Mon-Fri; 10.30am-10pm Sat; noon-8pm Sun. **Performances** 8pm Tue-Fri (July, Aug 9pm); 7pm, 10pm Sat. **Tickets** €24-€45. **Map** p319/p326 N5.

This beautiful old theatre with a touch of decadence is located in the courtyards of the Hackesche Höfe. The focus is on stunning acrobats combined with music theatre. As Hackesche Höfe becomes increasingly commercialised and touristy, there's a risk this club may become a sort of Wintergarten (*see below*). For now, though, it attracts a diverse audience and is the most comfortable and affordable revue house.

Friedrichstadtpalast

Friedrichstrasse 107, Mitte (2326 2326, www.show-palace.eu). U6, S1, S2, S5, S7, S75 Friedrichstrasse. **Box office** 10am-6pm Mon, Sun; 10am-5.30pm Tue; 10am-6.30pm Wed-Sat. **Performances** times vary. **Tickets** €16.90-€104.90. **Map** p319/p326 M5.

An East Berlin institution in a building originally designed to be the opera house in Damascus, this is the city's biggest revue theatre. Since Reunification it has mainly featured big, Vegas-style musical revues with Vegas-style prices to match. Mostly packed with coachloads of German tourists.

Wintergarten Varieté

Potsdamer Strasse 96, Tiergarten (tickets 588 433, www.wintergarten-berlin.de). U1 Kurfürstenstrasse. **Box office** opens 4hrs before performance. **Performances** times vary. **Tickets** prices vary. **Map** p322 J8.

Prussia meets Disney with shows that are slick, professional and a little boring. Excellent acrobats and magicians, but some questionable comedy acts. Fancy decor and more busloads of tourists.

Cabaret

Bar jeder Vernunft

Spiegelzelt, Schaperstrasse 24, Wilmersdorf (883 1582, www.bar-jeder-vernunft.de). U3, U9 Spichernstrasse. **Box office** noon-7pm Mon-Fri; 3-6pm Sat; 3-7pm Sun. **Performances** daily (usually 7pm or 8pm). **Tickets** €15-€30. **Map** p319/p328 F9.

Some of Berlin's most celebrated entertainers perform in this snazzy circus tent of many mirrors – the programme includes shows, comedy, cabaret, literature and theatre. You can order a €29 menu on top of the ticket price. It's not the cheapest night out in Berlin, but it'll be worth it if the place revives its much-lauded production of *Cabaret*.

BKA Theater

Mehringdamm 34, Kreuzberg (202 2007, www.bka-theater.de). U6, U7 Mehringdamm. **Box office** 10am-9pm Mon-Fri; noon-9pm Sat. **Performances** 8pm Mon-Fri; 7.30pm Sun (8.30pm in summer). **Tickets** €9-€24. **Map** p322 M10.

With a long tradition of taboo-breaking acts, BKA still features some of the weirdest and most progressive performers in town: intelligent drag stand-up, freaky chanteuses and power-packin' divas. The theatre is filled with private tables and arena seats overlooking the stage. Fresh performances and good theme parties.

Café Theater Schalotte

Behaimstrasse 22, Charlottenburg (341 1485, www.schalotte.de). U7 Richard-Wagner-Platz. **Box office** 1hr before performance. **Performances** usually 8pm, days vary. **Tickets** €15; €12 reductions. **No credit cards. Map** p316 D6.

Nice café, dedicated staff and some excellent shows. The O-Tonpiraten, a very clever drag theatre troupe, often plays here. The theatre hosts some brilliant acts in November during its annual international a cappella festival.

Kleine Nachtrevue

Kurfürstenstrasse 116, Schöneberg (218 8950, www.kleine-nachtrevue.de). U1, U2, U3 Wittenbergplatz. **Performances** 9pm, 11.30pm Wed-Sat. **Tickets** €20-€30. MC, V. **Map** p321 H8.

Used as a location for many films, this is as close as it gets to real nostalgic German cabaret – intimate, dark, decadent but very friendly. Nightly shows consist of short song or dance numbers sprinkled with playful nudity and whimsical costumes. Special weekend performances at 9pm vary from erotic opera or a four-course meal served to songs sung by the male 'reincarnation' of Marlene Dietrich.

Radialsystem V. *See p270.*

Scheinbar

Monumentenstrasse 9, Schöneberg (784 5539, www.scheinbar.de). U7 Kleistpark. **Box office** 1hr before performance. **Performances** 8.30pm most days. **Tickets** €7-€12. **No credit cards.** **Map** p322 K11.

Experimental, fun-loving cabaret in a tiny club exploding with fresh talent. If you like surprises, try the open-stage nights, where great performers mix with terrible ones, creating a surreal night for all.

Tipi am Kanzleramt

Grosse Querallee, between Bundeskanzleramt & Haus der Kulturen der Welt, Tiergarten (3906 6550, www.tipi-am-kanzleramt.de). Bus 100, 248 Platz der Republik. **Box office** noon-7pm Mon-Sat; 3-6pm Sun. **Performances** 8pm Tue-Sat; 3pm, 7pm Sun. **Tickets** €12.50-€59.50. **Map** p318 K6.

A circus tent in the Tiergarten, near the Federal Chancellery, with cool international performers presenting various comedy, dance and cabaret shows. Similar fare to Bar jeder Vernunft (*see p268*), except everything's twice the size.

Travestie

Theater im Keller

Weserstrasse 211, Neukölln (4799 7477, www.tikberlin.de.de). U7, U8 Hermannplatz. **Tickets** *By phone* 10am-10pm daily. **Performances** 8pm Fri, Sat. **Tickets** €27. **Map** p323 Q11.

With seating for 43 people, this cosy neighbourhood drag club has a passable revue show.

DANCE

In the past decade, Berlin has become home to a dynamic dance scene that cultivates fresh ideas while continuing to nurture the strong traditions of German dance theatre. Throughout the year, the city's theatres are filled with dance events, including international festivals and co-productions for international choreographers; among the latter are Meg Stuart, recently appointed resident director at the **Volksbühne**. Sasha Waltz is another key figure in European dance, whose fame has essentially put Berlin on the contemporary dance map. The city's dance scene is constantly evolving and expanding, making it an exciting place to witness the art form. Those wanting more accessible entertainment can often find touring productions by DV8 or Pina Bausch here. At the other end of the spectrum, there is a huge amount of highly experimental work on show, often attracting large audiences. In addition to daring programming in major houses, alternative spaces have popped up across the city, offering a more intimate connection with dance.

For information on upcoming performances, pick up a copy of *TanzRaumBerlin* (www.tanzraumberlin.de), a Berlin newspaper specifically dedicated to dance.

Venues & festivals

There are many possibilities for young artists to integrate themselves into Berlin's thriving and unconventional dance scene, both by participating in festivals and by making use of the professional training on offer, particularly in Prenzlauer Berg and Kreuzberg. **Dock 11** (www.dock11-berlin.de) is now the city's most recognised dance school, providing training and rehearsal and production space. **Tanzfabrik** (www.tanzfabrik-berlin.de) is another reputable institution that not only houses training and rehearsal space, but also holds international workshops and offers an innovative residency programme for dance makers.

LaborGras (www.laborgras.com), by the canal in Kreuzberg, is a small performance

ARTS & ENTERTAINMENT

venue offering professional training. It frequently invites well-respected teachers from across the world to teach and perform.

The **Tanz im August** festival, hosted by HAU (*see p267*), is one of Europe's leading dance festivals, attracting people from all over Europe. The three-week festival keeps a keen eye on current trends, showing the most influential and cutting-edge choreography of the season coupled with workshops for the public and lectures from both artists and critics. Its success has allowed it to expand into performance venues around town, including **Radialsystem V** (*see below*), **Sophiensaele** (*see p267*), and **Ballhaus Ost** (*see p266*).

Since 2004, the Sophiensaele has hosted **Tanztage** (*see p202*), a dance festival held in the first two weeks of January. Here, young local dance artists present their work, in some cases for the first time. The festival is becoming increasingly well recognised across Europe.

The **Lucky Trimmer** dance series (www.luckytrimmer.de) is another mini festival, held at the theatre at the **Tacheles Arts Centre** (Oranienburgerstrasse 54-56A, Mitte, 282 6185, www.tacheles.de). Ten short performances are staged in one evening, enabling an easy exchange between artists and their audiences. It has been a roaring success, frequently selling out. Productions tend towards the experimental, although they maintain a light and playful spirit.

The performance venue **Radialsystem V** was opened in 2006 by Jochen Sandig, the partner of choreographer Sasha Waltz. This warren of rooms in a former pumping station by the river provides an impressive setting for her work, although the programme is generally heavier on music than on dance. Together with high ticket prices, the venue tends to cater to the upper echelons of Berlin society, with programming more conservative than most other dance venues.

★ Radialsystem V

Holzmarktstrasse 33, Friedrichshain (288 788 588, www.radialsystem.de). S3, S5, S7, S75 Ostbahnhof. **Box office** 10am-7pm Tue-Sun. **Tickets** prices vary. **No credit cards. Map** p323 Q7.
Radialsystem V is a 'new space for the arts' and a base for Sasha Waltz's dance company, and also home to the early music ensemble Akamus (www.akamus.de). A former pumping station by the river, it promotes a variety of one-off performance events, and attracts a well-heeled crowd. *Photo p269.*

Choreographers

Following a similar tradition to her predecessor Pina Bausch, Sasha Waltz, Berlin's foremost choreographer, has contributed enormously to the aesthetic continuum of postmodern German dance theatre. Her often heavily dramatic dance works, always visually stunning, are performed internationally in the biggest theatre houses in Europe and Asia. The hole left at the Schaubühne after Sasha Waltz departed, meanwhile, has been partially filled by Argentinian choreographer Constanza Macras.

Less obviously crowd-pleasing than the dance spectacles of Waltz and Macras, but also attracting big audiences, is the work of award-winning choreographer Meg Stuart. Since moving to Berlin from Brussels, the American has developed a cult following with her sparse yet rigorous and often provocative productions at the **Volksbühne** (*see p266*). Her induction into the theatre world has put her at the top of her game, attracting commissions from all over the world.

Other younger and less established choreographers to look out for include Christoph Winkler, whose success with *Tales of the Funky B-Boys and Break Girls* and commitment to investigating societal problems and phenomena have made him one of the leaders of the new dance wave.

Thomas Lehmen, another lesser-known yet notable figure in the dance world, produces highly conceptualised works that often reflect upon the form itself. His presence in Berlin has been greatly influential on current and future dance makers.

The Practicable collective, comprising five French collaborators (Alice Chauchat, Frédéric de Carlo, Frederic Gies, Isabelle Schad and Odile Seitz), is also noteworthy. It recently gained attention for its feminist work, *The Breast Piece*, in which the culturally loaded symbol of the breast is dissected and re-examined. The collective also continues to develop new works and research projects coupled with workshops for the public.

Ballet

In 2004, what had been three main companies became one, when half of the Deutsche Oper dancers and all but one at the Komische Oper lost their jobs. Those who were left joined the existing Staatsoper Ballet to form the **Staatsballett Berlin** (www.staatsballett-berlin.de). Thankfully, 'dancer of the century' Vladimir Malakhov remains at the helm and, with his roots in the Russian academic tradition, continues to uphold the reputation of Berlin ballet. Malakhov's 88-member company performs from September to June at the **Deutsche Oper** and the **Staatsoper Unter den Linden**.

Escapes & Excursions

Rügen. *See p280.*

Escapes & Excursions

Bucolic landscapes and historic cities, a stone's throw from Berlin.

There is enough in Berlin to occupy a lifetime, let alone a weekend visit, but a trip beyond the city limits is more than worthwhile. Travel less than an hour out of town on the S-bahn and you're in Brandenburg: a whole new world where fields, lakes and dense woods are interrupted by a sparse scattering of little-visited towns and villages (*see p284* **Getting Nowhere Fast**). This chapter is divided into excursions (day trips) and escapes (destinations further afield). By far the most popular day trip from Berlin is to **Potsdam** (*see below*), which is to Berlin what Versailles is to Paris. Still only a few hours away, the seaside resort of **Rügen** is a popular holiday destination, and the cities of **Leipzig** and **Dresden** are perfect for a weekend break.

TRAVELLING BY TRAIN

Trains to all destinations depart from **Berlin Hauptbahnhof**, Europe's biggest and most futuristic train station. Depending on where they're going, trains will also stop at the Gesundbrunnen in the north, the new Südkreuz station (formerly Papestrasse) and also at Berlin-Spandau out west.

Regionalbahn trains – the red, double-decker ones – serve Berlin's hinterland, including many of the destinations in this chapter. They stop at larger stations such as Zoologischer Garten, Friedrichstrasse, Alexanderplatz and Potsdamer Platz, as well as Hauptbahnhof.

Deutsche Bahn has an excellent timetable search facility in English at www.bahn.com.

Excursions

POTSDAM & BABELSBERG

Potsdam is capital of the state of Brandenburg and, just outside the city limits to the south-west, Berlin's most beautiful neighbour. Known for its 18th-century baroque architecture, it's a magnet for tourists. The summer weekend crowds can be overwhelming; visit outside peak times if you can.

For centuries, Potsdam was the summer residence of the Hohenzollerns, who were attracted by the area's gently rolling landscape, rivers and lakes. Despite the damage wrought during World War II and by East Germany's socialist planners, much remains of the legacy of these Prussian kings. The best-known landmark is **Sanssouci**, the huge landscaped park created by Frederick the Great, one of three royal parks flanking the town.

Potsdam has changed considerably since Reunification. In East German times its associations with the monarchy were regarded with suspicion; the lack of political will and economic means led to much of the town's historic fabric falling into disrepair or being destroyed. In 1990, however, Potsdam was assigned UNESCO World Heritage status and some 80 per cent of the town's historic buildings have since been restored.

The end of East Germany also marked the end of Potsdam's historic role as a garrison town. Until the Soviet withdrawal, some 10,000 troops were stationed here. With their departure, vast barracks and tracts of land to the north of the town were abandoned. The area is currently being redeveloped for civilian use, including the BUGA or Volkspark, with its nature museum, the **Biosphäre**.

THE OLD TOWN

One of the most dominant – if not the prettiest – buildings of historical interest in the old town is the 19th-century **Nikolaikirche**. It's hard to miss the huge dome, inspired by St Paul's in London. Rather more graceful is the mid 18th-century **Altes Rathaus**, diagonally opposite, whose tower was used as a prison until 1875. Nowadays, the former town hall is used for exhibitions and lectures. Both the Nikolaikirche and the Altes Rathaus were badly damaged in the war and rebuilt in the 1960s. The two buildings are all that remain of the original Alter Markt, once one of Potsdam's most beautiful squares.

The **Stadtschloss**, in the centre of town, was substantially damaged during the war and the East German authorities demolished the rest of it in 1960. There are plans to rebuild it, but funding problems mean this is unlikely to happen soon. Private sponsors have already paid for the reconstruction of the Fortunaportal, one decorative former entrance to the palace, in the Alter Markt. To get an impression of this square before 1945, take a look at the model in the foyer of the Altes Rathaus.

The area behind the gargantuan Hotel Mercure was once part of the palace gardens. Later, Friedrich Wilhelm I, the Soldier King, turned it into a parade ground. Now it has become a park. If you walk up Breite Strasse, you can see all that is left of the old Stadtschloss. The low red building that now houses the **Filmmuseum Potsdam** is the former *Marstall*, or royal stables. Dating from 1685 and originally an orangery, it is one of the oldest buildings in the town.

The nearby Neuer Markt survived the war intact. At number 1 is the house where Friedrich Wilhelm II was born. The *Kutschstall*, originally a royal stables, now houses the new **Haus der Brandenburgisch-Preussischen Geschichte**, with its exhibition charting 800 years of Brandenburg history.

THE BAROQUE AND DUTCH QUARTERS

Potsdam's impressive **baroque quarter** is bounded by Schopenhauerstrasse, Hegelallee, Hebbelstrasse and Charlottenstrasse. Some of the best houses can be found in Gutenbergstrasse and Brandenburger Strasse, the city's pedestrianised shopping drag. Note the pitched roofs with space to accommodate troops – the Soldier King built the quarter in the 1730s. Just around the corner is **Gedenkstätte Lindenstrasse**, once the house of a Prussian officer, later a Stasi detention centre (you can now tour the cells).

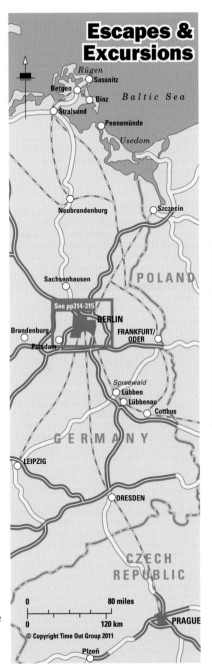

Three baroque town gates – the **Nauener Tor**, **Jäger Tor** and **Brandenburger Tor** – stand on the northern and western edges of the quarter. On its east, two churches bear witness to Potsdam's cosmopolitan past. The Great Elector's 1685 Edict of Potsdam promised refuge to Protestants suffering from religious persecution in their homelands, sparking waves of immigration. The **Französische Kirche** on Hebbelstrasse was built for the town's Huguenot community, while **St Peter & Paul's** in Bassinplatz was built for Catholic immigrants who came to this Protestant area in response to the Prussian kings' drive to bring in skilled workers and soldiers.

The **Holländisches Viertel**, or Dutch Quarter, is the most attractive part of Friedrich Wilhelm I's new town extension. As part of a failed strategy to lure skilled Dutch immigrants to the town, the king had Dutch builders construct 134 gable-fronted houses. In the **Jan Bouman Haus** on Mittelstrasse you can see an original interior. Today this area is filled with upmarket boutiques and restaurants.

THE RUSSIAN INFLUENCE

Another Potsdam curiosity is the Russian colony of **Alexandrowka**, 15 minutes' walk north of the town centre. The settlement consists of 13 wooden clad, two-storey dwellings with steeply pitched roofs laid out in the form of a St Andrew's Cross. There's even a Russian orthodox church with an onion dome. Services are still held in the Alexander-Newski-Kapelle.

Alexandrowka was built in 1826 by Friedrich Wilhelm III to commemorate the death of Tsar Alexander I, a friend from the Wars of Liberation against Napoleon. The settlement became home to surviving members of a troupe of Russian musicians given into Prussian service by the Tsar in 1812. Two of the houses are still inhabited by the descendants of these men. Russian specialities are served by waitresses in folkloric costume at the **Teehaus Russische Kolonie** (Alexandrowka 1, 0331 200 6478, closed Mon, mains €8-€14). Nearby is the tiny **Alexandrowka Museum** (Russische Kolonie 2, 0331 200536, www.alexandrowka.de, closed Mon) with films and exhibits about the colony.

The area around and to the north of **Alexandrowka** became the focus of a different Russian presence during the Cold War. The late Wilhelmine villas served as offices to the Soviet administration or as officers' homes. Soviet forces took over buildings used by the Prussian army in the 19th century and later by the Nazis. One such is the castle-like **Garde-Ulanen-Kaserne** in Jäger Allee, close to the junction with Reiterweg.

The recently restored **Belvedere**, at the top of the hill to the north of Alexandrowka, is the town's highest observation point. It fell into disuse after the Wall went up in 1961, when people were banned from enjoying views over West Berlin.

POTSDAM'S ROYAL PARKS

Back towards the town centre is Potsdam's biggest tourist magnet, **Park Sanssouci**. It's beautiful, but be warned: its main avenues can become overrun and it is not always easy to get into the palaces (guided tours are compulsory and numbers limited).

The park is a legacy of King Frederick the Great, who was attracted to the area by its fine views. He initially had terraced gardens built here before adding a palace. *Sans souci* means 'without worries' and reflects the king's desire for a sanctuary where he could pursue his philosophical, musical and literary interests. Voltaire was among his guests. His nearby Bildergalerie was the first purpose-built museum in Germany.

After victory in the Seven Years' War, Frederick the Great built the huge **Neues Palais** on the park's western edge. Friedrich II's sumptuous suite, as well as the Grottensaal (Grotto Room), Marmorsaal (Marble Room) and Schlosstheater (Palace Theatre), are worth a visit. Parts of the Palais are being renovated for Frederick the Great's 300th birthday in 2012, as are portions of the surrounding park.

Attractions in the park include the Orangery; the Spielfestung, or toy fortress, built for Wilhelm II's sons, complete with a toy cannon that can be fired; the Chinesisches Teehaus (Chinese Teahouse), with its collection of Chinese and Meissen porcelain; and the Drachenhaus (Dragonhouse), a pagoda-style café. In the park's south-west corner lies **Schloss Charlottenhof**, with its blue-glazed entrance and copper-plate engraving room, built in the 1830s on the orders of crown prince Friedrich Wilhelm IV. Outside Sanssouci in the Breite Strasse is the Dampfmaschinenhaus that pumped water for Sanssouci's fountains, but was built to look like a mosque.

North-east of the town centre is another large park complex, the **Neuer Garten**, designed on the orders of Frederick the Great's nephew and successor to the throne, Friedrich Wilhelm II. In the neo-classical **Marmorpalais** the king died a premature death, allegedly as a result of his dissolute lifestyle. At the park's most northern corner is **Schloss Cecilienhof**, the last royal palace to be built in Potsdam. This incongruous, mock-Tudor mansion was built for the Kaiser's son and his wife. Spared

Sanssouci. *See p277.*

wartime damage, in summer 1945 it hosted the Potsdam Conference, where Stalin, Truman and Churchill (later replaced by Clement Attlee) met to discuss Germany's future. Inside, you can see the round table where the settlement was negotiated.

During the conference, the Allied leaders lived across the Havel in one of Babelsberg's secluded 19th-century villa districts. Stalin stayed in Karl-Marx-Strasse 27, Churchill in the Villa Urbig at Virchowstrasse 23, one of Mies van der Rohe's early buildings, and Truman in the Truman-Villa in Karl-Marx-Strasse 2. These buildings can be viewed from the outside only.

Potsdam's third and most recent royal park, **Park Babelsberg**, also makes for a good walk. In East German times this fell into neglect because it lay so close to the border. **Schloss Babelsberg**, a neo-Gothic extravaganza inspired by Windsor Castle, nestles among its wooded slopes. Another architectural curiosity is the Flatowturm, an observation point in mock medieval style close to the Glienicker See.

Also on the east side of the Havel, not too far south of Potsdam's main station, is the Telegraphenberg – once the site of a telegraph station. In 1921, it became the site of Erich Mendelsohn's Expressionist **Einsteinturm**, commissioned to house an observatory that could confirm the General Theory of Relativity. A wonderfully whimsical building, it was one of the first products of the inter-war avant-garde.

On the nearby Brauhausberg, there is one last reminder of Potsdam's complex, multi-layered past. The square tower rising up from the trees is the present seat of Brandenburg's state parliament. In East German days, the building was known as the 'Kremlin' because it served as local Communist party headquarters. Originally, it was the Kriegsschule – 'the war school' – where young men trained to be officers in the German imperial army.

HOLLYWOOD BABELSBERG

The main attraction in Potsdam's eastern neighbour, **Babelsberg**, is the film studio complex, sections of which are open to the public in theme-park form. In the 1920s, this was the world's largest studio outside Hollywood and it was here that Fritz Lang's *Metropolis*, Josef von Sternberg's *The Blue Angel* and other masterpieces of the era were produced. During the Nazi period it churned out thrillers, light entertainment and propaganda pieces such as Leni Riefenstahl's *Triumph of the Will*. More than 700 feature films were made here in the Communist era.

The studios were privatised after Reunification and now there are modern facilities for all phases of film and TV production, and offices for all manner of media and production companies. The **Filmpark Babelsberg** has an assortment of attractions, ranging from themed restaurants and rides to set tours and stunt displays, but it's all pretty tacky stuff.

Schloss Cecilienhof.

FREE Potsdam Museum

*Benkertstrasse 3 (0331 289 6821, www.potsdam.
de/potsdam-museum). Tram 92, 96 Nauener Tor.*
Open 1pm-5pm Thur-Sun. **Admission** free.
From August 2012: *Am alten Markt. Tram 91,
92, 93, 96, 98, 99 Alter Markt.* **Admission**
check website when museum is open.

Potsdam's city hall is being renovated until summer
2012. The status quo of the renovations as well as
future permanent exhibitions are currently documented by a temporary exhibition. In August 2012,
the new museum will be opened with a temporary
show on Frederick the Great. It will also house a permanent exhibition on the history of the city, with
artifacts, paintings, photographs and sculptures.

Biosphäre

*Georg-Hermann-Allee 99 (0331 550 740, www.
biosphaere-potsdam.de). Tram 96 Volkspark.*
Open 9am-6pm (last entry 4.30pm) Mon-Fri; 10am-
7pm (last entry 5.30pm) Sat, Sun. **Admission**
€9.50; €6.50-€8 reductions. Free under-5s.

Filmmuseum Potsdam

*Breitestrasse 1A (0331 271 8112, www.film
museum-potsdam.de). Tram X98, 90, 92, 93,
96 Alter Markt.* **Open** 10am-6pm Tue-Sun.
Admission €4.50; €3.50 reductions. *Guided
tours* €1. **No credit cards.**

The permanent exhibition explores nearly a century
of film-making at the Babelsberg studios, focusing
on DEFA, East Germany's sole film-making company. The onsite cinema regularly shows films, and
guided tours are available in English.

Filmpark Babelsberg

*entrance on Grossbeerenstrasse (0331 721 2750,
www.filmpark.de). S7 Babelsberg, then bus 601,
619, 690 to Filmpark/RE1 Medienstadt.* **Open**
10am-6pm daily. Closed Halloween to Easter.
Admission €21; €17 reductions.

Gedenkstätte Lindenstrasse

*Lindenstrasse 54 (0331 289 6136, www.
potsdam.de/potsdam-museum). Tram 91, 94,
96 Dortusstrasse.* **Open** 10am-6pm Tue, Thur,
Sat. **Admission** €1.50. **No credit cards.**

Haus der Brandenburgisch-Preussischen Geschichte

*Kutschstall, Am Neuen Markt (0331 620 8550,
www.hbpg.de). Tram X98, 90, 92, 93, 96 Alter
Markt.* **Open** 10am-6pm Tue-Fri; 10am-5pm
Sat, Sun. **Admission** €5; €4 reductions.
No credit cards.

Jan Bouman Haus

*Mittelstrasse 8 (0331 280 3773). Tram 92, 96
Nauener Tor.* **Open** 1-6pm Mon-Fri; 11am-6pm
Sat, Sun. **Admission** €2; €1 reductions. Free
under-12s. **No credit cards.**

INSIDE TRACK CAR-SHARING

If you haven't got a car and want to travel
to another city on the cheap, it's worth
investigating the car-sharing service
Mitfahrzentral. Drivers with space in their
cars make their offers via an easy-to-
navigate website, listing their destination,
when they're going and how much they
want you to chip in. You have to sign
up to the (German-language) website,
www.mitfahrgelegenheit.de, but it's free
– and much safer than hitching.

Marmorpalais

*Im Neuen Garten (0331 9694 200, www.spsg.de).
Tram 92, 96/bus 603 Reiterweg/Alleestrasse.*
Open *May-Oct* 10am-6pm Tue-Sun (last entry
half an hour before closing). *Nov-Apr* as guided
tour only, 10am-4.30pm Sat, Sun. **Admission** €5;
€4 reductions. **No credit cards.**

FREE Nikolaikirche

*Am Alten Markt (0331 270 8602, www.
nikolaipotsdam.de). Tram 91, 92, 99 Alter Markt.*
Open *Jan-Mar, Nov, Dec* 9am-5pm Mon-Sat. *Apr,
May, Sept, Oct* 9am-7pm Mon-Sat. *June-Aug* 9am-
9pm Mon-Sat. *Service* 10am Sun; sightseeing after
11.30am Sun. **Admission** free.

★ Sanssouci

(0331 9694 200, www.spsg.de). Bus 606, 695.
Open *Palace & exhibition buildings* Apr-Oct 9am-
6pm Tue-Sun. Nov-Mar 9am-4.30pm daily. Last
entry half an hour before closing. **Admission**
Palace & exhibition buildings €12; €5-€8
reductions. *Park* free.

Each of the various palaces and buildings within the
complex has its own closing days each month and
some are only open mid May to mid October. Phone
or check the website for full details. *Photo p275.*

★ Schloss Cecilienhof

*Im Neuen Garten (0331 9694 200, www.spsg.de).
Bus 603.* **Open** *Apr-Oct* 9am-6pm Tue-Sun. *Nov-
Mar* 9am-4.30pm Tue-Sun. Last entry half an hour
before closing. **Admission** €6; €5 reductions.

Where to eat & drink

B-West (Zeppelinstrasse 146, 0331 9792013,
mains €5-€10) attracts a lively, young crowd
and serves simple German cuisine. **Café
Heider** (Friedrich-Ebert-Strasse 29, 0331
270 5596, mains €3-€17) offers excellent coffee
and cake, plus a wide range of main dishes.
Backstoltz (Dortusstrasse 59, 0177 326 7253,
mains €3-€15) is a cosy croissanterie, good for
a light breakfast or lunch. **Matschkes Galerie**

Café (Alleestrasse 10, 0331 2800 359, mains €4-€10) serves good simple German and Russian cooking and has some outdoor seating. There's also an assortment of cafés, pubs and restaurants along pedestrianised Brandenburger Strasse, most of which have tables outside in summer, and on nearby Lindenstrasse and Dortusstrasse.

Nightlife

Lindenpark (Stahnsdorfer Strasse 76-78, 0331 747 970, www.lindenpark.de) in Babelsberg has a range of regular club nights and gigs. **Theaterschiff** (Lange Brücke, 0331 972302, www.theaterschiff-potsdam.de), moored close to the Hans-Otto-Theater, is a vessel hosting a theatre, cinema, cabaret and discos. **Waschhaus** (Schiffbauergasse, 0331 271 560, www.waschhaus.de), a large club just outside Potsdam centre, has both DJs and live acts.

Getting there

By train
Both Potsdam and Babelsberg can be reached via the S7 S-Bahn line. It takes just under an hour from Mitte and you will need a ticket that covers the C zone. From some parts of Berlin it's easier to take the S1 to Wannsee, and change to the S7 there. There is also a direct, hourly Regionalbahn train (RE1) to Medienstadt Babelsberg that takes just 20 minutes from Mitte, and a number of Regional trains to Potsdam Haupbahnhof. The station is across the river from the centre of town.

Getting around

Potsdam is small compared to Berlin, but it's still too big and spread out to do everything on foot. The tram and bus network covers everything, however, and the routes aren't difficult to figure out. A **Potsdam Card** (from €9.50), available from the tourist office, provides free public transport as well as discounted entry to most attractions.

Tourist information

Potsdam Tourismus Service
Brandenburger Strasse 3 (0331 275 58899, www.potsdamtourismus.de). Tram 91, 94/bus X98, 695 Luisenplatz. **Open** *Apr-Oct* 9am-7pm Mon-Fri; 9am-2pm Sat, Sun. *Nov-Mar* 10am-6pm Mon-Fri; 9am-2pm Sat.

SACHSENHAUSEN

Many Nazi concentration camps have been preserved and are open to the public as memorials and museums. KZ Sachsenhausen is the one nearest camp to Berlin.

Immediately upon coming to power, Hitler set about rounding up and interning his opponents. From 1933 to 1935 an old brewery on this site was used to hold them. The present camp received its first prisoners in July 1936. It was designated with cynical euphemism as a *Schutzhaftlager* ('Protective Custody Camp'). The first *Schutzhaftlagern* were political opponents of the government: Communists, social democrats, trade unionists. Soon, the variety of prisoners widened to include anyone guilty of 'anti-social' behaviour, gays and Jews.

About 6,000 Jews were brought here after Kristallnacht alone, many later sent to Auschwitz. It was here that some of the first experiments in organised mass murder were made: thousands of Russian POWs from the Eastern Front were killed at the camp's 'Station Z'.

The SS evacuated the camp in 1945 and began marching 33,000 inmates to the Baltic, where they were to be packed into boats and sunk in the sea. Some 6,000 died during the march before the survivors were rescued by the Allies. Another 3,000 prisoners were found in the camp's hospital when it was captured on 22 April 1945.

After the German capitulation, the Russian secret police, the MVD, reopened Sachsenhausen as 'Camp 7' for the detention of war criminals; in fact, it was filled with anyone suspected of opposition. Following the fall of the DDR, mass graves were discovered, containing the remains of an estimated 10,000 prisoners. On 23 April 1961, the partially restored camp was opened to the public as a national monument and memorial.

The parade ground, where morning roll-call was taken, and from where inmates were required to witness executions on the gallows, stands before the two remaining barrack blocks. One is now a museum and the other a memorial hall and cinema, where a film about the history of the camp is shown. Next door stands the prison block.

There are another couple of small exhibitions in buildings in the centre of the camp (no English labelling), but perhaps the grimmest site here is the subsiding remains of Station Z, the small extermination block.

A map traces the path the condemned would follow, depending upon whether they were to be shot (the bullets were retrieved and reused) or gassed. All ended up in the neighbouring ovens.

Note: it's a good idea to hire an audio guide (€3; available in English) at the gate.

FREE KZ Sachsenhausen
Strasse der Nationen 22, Oranienburg (03301 2000, www.stiftung-bg.de. **Open** *Mid Mar-mid Oct* 8.30am-6pm Tue-Sun. *Mid Oct-mid Mar* 8.30am-4.30pm Tue-Sun. **Admission** free.
The grounds of the camp are open on Mondays too, but the museum is closed.

Getting there

By train
Oranienburg is at the north end of the S1 S-Bahn line (40mins from Mitte). From the station follow signs to 'Gedenkstätte Sachsenhausen' `(20mins walk).

Escapes

SPREEWALD

This filigree network of tiny rivers, streams and canals, dividing patches of deciduous forest and farmland, is one of the loveliest excursions from Berlin. Author Theodor Fontane described the Spreewald as how Venice would have looked 1,500 years ago. It gets crowded in season, compromising its claim as one of the most perfect wilderness areas in Europe. Still, out of season, you can have the area to yourself.

The Wild Side

Wild swimming within easy distance of Berlin.

Pretty much all of the hundreds of lakes in Berlin and Brandenburg are swimmable, but these are some of the nicest and easiest to reach without a car.

Bötzsee
near Strausberg (35km east of Berlin).
Altlandsberger Chaussee 102, Eggersdorf.
S5 to Strausberg and then the Bus 391 to Eggersdorf Mittelstrasse. The lake is a kilometre walk; follow the signs to the Hotel Seeschloss – the lake is behind the hotel.

The waters of this lovely little lake are crystal clear. The directions given lead to the *Strandbad* (beach), where you sometimes have to pay a small entry fee.

Flakensee
near Erkner (30km southeast of Berlin).
Take the S3 to Erkner. From there it's a 3.5km walk or cycle to the lake. Alternatively, get off the S3 at Rahnsdorf and take the historic tram 87 to Woltersdorfer Schleuse.
There are lots of little bathing spots around this lake, which is pretty clean given the number of motor boats using it.

Helenesee
near Frankfurt/Oder (110km southeast of Berlin).
Take the RE1 train from Berlin Hauptbahnhof to Frankfurt/Oder. From there it's either 8km by bike, or a short ride on the 984 bus to the Strandbad.
This big lake near the border with Poland is known by locals as the *kleine Ostee* (little Baltic sea) because of its kilometre-long white sandy beach and cooling clear water. There's a campsite and a youth hostelr.

Schermützelsee
near Buckow (50km east of Berlin)
Take the S5 to Strausberg and then bus 926 to Buckow.
This dreamy little lake right in the middle of the Märkische Schweiz nature park is 42 metres deep. In summer, it's a great way to cool off after a long walk or a visit to Bertolt Brecht's summer house, now a museum (Bertolt-Brecht-Strasse 30, Buckow, 033433 467, www.brechtweigelhaus.de).

Spreewald

About 100 kilometres (60 miles) south-east of Berlin, the Spree bisects the area into the **Unterspreewald** and Oberspreewald. For the former, Schepzig or Lübben are the best starting points; for the latter, go 15 kilometres (nine miles) further on the train to Lübbenau.

The character of both sections is very similar. The **Oberspreewald** is perhaps better, for its 500 square kilometres (190 square miles) of territory contain more than 300 natural and artificial channels, called *Fliesse*. You can travel around these on punts – rent your own or join a larger group – and also take out kayaks. Motorised boats are forbidden. Here and there in the forest are restaurants and small hotels. The tourist information centre in Lübbenau provides maps and walk routes.

The local population belongs to the Sorbish minority, a Slav people related to Czechs and Slovaks. Their own language is found in street names, newspapers and so on. This adds an air of exoticism, unlike the folk festivals laid on for tourists in the high season.

Where to eat & drink

There are plenty of eating and drinking options in Lübben and Lübbenau, and little to choose between most of them. Follow your nose.

Getting there

By train

There are regular trains to Lübben and Lübbenau. Journey time is around an hour to Lübben and

an extra 15 minutes to Lübbenau. Check www.bahn.co.uk for the timetable.

Tourist information

Tourist websites www.spreewald-info.com and www.spreewald-online.de are good sources of information about the area and allow you to book hotel rooms online.

Haus für Mensch & Natur

Schulstrasse 9, Lübbenau (03542 89210).
Open *Apr-Oct* 10am-5pm daily. Closed Nov-Mar.
Set in an old schoolhouse, the 'House for Mankind & Nature' is the visitor centre for the Spreewald Biosphere Reservation. It has an exhibition about the environmental importance of the Spreewald.

Spreewald Information

Ehm-Welk-Strasse 15, Lübbenau (035 423 668, www.luebbenau-spreewald.com). **Open** *May-Sept* 10am-6pm Mon-Fri; 9am-4pm Sat; 10am-4pm Sun. *Oct, Apr* 10am-6pm Mon-Fri; 9am-4pm Sat. *Nov-Mar* 10am-4pm Mon-Fri.

RÜGEN

The Baltic coast was the favoured holiday destination of the DDR citizen; post-Reunification it is still the most accessible stretch of seaside for Berliners. The coast forms the northern boundary of the modern state of Mecklenburg-Vorpommern. Bismarck famously said of the area: 'When the end of the world comes, I shall go to Mecklenburg, because there everything happens a hundred years later.'

The large island of Rügen is gradually resuming its rivalry with Sylt in the North Sea – both islands claim to be the principal north German resort. The island is undoubtedly beautiful, with its white chalk cliffs, beechwoods and beaches. Most people stay in the resorts on the east coast, such as **Binz** (the largest and best known), **Sellin** and **Göhren**. In July and August, Rügen can get crowded (don't go without pre-booked accommodation), and the island's handful of restaurants and lack of late-night bars mean visitors are early to bed and early to rise. Go out of season for some peace.

Where to stay & eat

Most accommodation on Rügen is in private houses. Your best bet is to contact the local tourist office (*see right*), which will help you find a room. Camping is very popular on Rügen. Binz offers the best selection of places to eat.

Getting there

By train

There are some direct trains to Bergen on Rügen, but the journey usually involves changing trains at Stralsund. Journey time is between 3 and 4hrs. Check www.bahn.co.uk for timetable.

Tourist information

The head office in Bergen provides information, but cannot book hotel rooms; try the other offices for bookings. Visit www.ruegen.net for general information.

Bergen *Am Markt 25 (03838 807 70, www.ruegen.de)*. **Open** *mid Aug-June* 8am-6pm Mon-Fri. *July-mid August* 8am-6pm Mon-Fri; 8am-7pm Sat; 9am-4pm Sun.

Kurverwaltung Göhren *Postrasse 9 (03830 866 790, www.ostseebad-goehren.de)*. **Open** *Summer* 9am-6pm Mon-Fri; 9am-noon Sat. *Winter* 9am-noon, 1-4.30pm Mon, Wed, Thur; 9am-noon, 1-6pm Tue; 9am-noon, 1-3pm Fri.

Kurverwaltung Sellin *Warmbadstr.4 (03830 3160, www.ostseebad-sellin.de)*. **Open** *Jul, Aug* 10am-6pm daily. *Sept-June* 8.30am-6pm Mon-Fri; 10am-2pm Sat, Sun.

Ostseebad Binz *Heinrich-Heine-Strasse 7 (03839 314 8148/www.ostseebad-binz.de)*. **Open** *Summer* 10am-6pm Mon-Fri; 10am-6pm Sat, Sun. *Winter* 9am-4pm daily.

DRESDEN

Destroyed twice and rebuilt one and a half times, the capital of Saxony – 100 kilometres (60 miles) south of Berlin – boasts one of Germany's best art museums and many historic buildings. The most recent wave of rebuilding – including the restoration of the Frauenkirche – was completed in time for the city's 800-year anniversary in 2006.

Rugen.

Zwinger.

Modern Dresden is built on the ruins of its past. A fire consumed Altendresden on the bank of the Elbe in 1685, and the city was subsequently reconstructed. On the night of 13 February 1945, one of World War II's largest Allied bombing raids caused huge firestorms that killed between 25,000 and 40,000 people. After the war, Dresden was twinned with Coventry, and Benjamin Britten's *War Requiem* was given its first performance in the Hofkirche by musicians from both towns. Under the DDR, reconstruction was erratic, but a maze of cranes and scaffolding sprang up in the 1990s – Dresden has been making up for lost time.

Its major attractions are the buildings from the reign of Augustus the Strong (1670-1733). The Hofkirche and the **Zwinger** complex are fine examples of the city's Baroque legacy. Dresden's main draw for art lovers is the **Gemäldegalerie Alte Meister** in the Zwinger, a superb collection of Old Masters, particularly Italian Renaissance and Flemish. There is also porcelain from nearby Meissen, and collections of armour, weapons, clocks and scientific equipment.

There's more art at the newly refurbished **Albertinum**, which holds major works of painting and sculpture from the Romantic period to the present day.

Building was continued by Augustus's successor, Augustus III, who then lost to Prussia in the Seven Years' War (1756-63). Frederick the Great destroyed much of the city during the war, though not the lovely riverside promenade of the Brühlsche Terrasse in the old part of town. A victorious Napoleon ordered the demolition of the city's defences in 1809.

By the Zwinger is the **Semperoper** opera house (1838-41), named after its architect Gottfried Semper. It was fully restored in 1985.

The industrialisation of Dresden heralded a new phase of construction that produced the **Rathaus** (Town Hall, 1905-10) at Dr-Külz-Ring, the **Hauptbahnhof** (1892-95) at the end of Prager Strasse, the **Yenidze cigarette factory** (1912) in Könneritzstrasse, designed to look like a mosque, and the **Landtagsgebäude** (completed to plans by Paul Wallot, designer of Berlin's Reichstag, in 1907) at Heinrich-Zille-Strasse 11. The finest example of inter-war architecture is Wilhelm Kreis' **Deutsches Hygiene-Museum** (1929) at Lingner Platz 1, housing the German Institute of Hygiene.

The **Neue Synagoge** was dedicated in Rathenauplatz in November 2001, 63 years after its predecessor (built by Semper in 1838-40) was destroyed in the Nazi pogroms.

Reconstruction of the domed **Frauenkirche** at Neumarkt was completed and the restored cathedral reconsecrated in October 2005. The Communists had left it as a heap of rubble throughout the Cold War period as a reminder of Allied aggression. In the end its restoration was funded partly by private donations from the UK and US. The golden orb and cross that top the dome were built by goldsmith Alan

Smith, son of one of the British pilots who took part in the 1945 bombings.

The **Striezelmarkt**, founded in 1434, is the oldest Christmas market in Germany. It is held on Altstädtermarkt every December and is named after the savoury pretzel you will see everyone eating. Dresden is also home to the best Stollen, the German yuletide cake.

The Neustadt – on the north bank of the Elbe – literally means 'new town', although it is over 300 years old. Having escaped major damage during the war, the Neustadt has much of its original architecture intact. When Augustus the Strong commissioned the rebuilding of Dresden in 1685, he pictured a new Venice. The Neustadt doesn't quite measure up, but the 18th-century townhouses in Hauptstrasse and Königstrasse are charming.

To avoid the tourist spillover from the Altstadt, head north and east of Albertplatz. Recently, a wealth of boutiques, cafés and bars has sprung up here in the cobblestone streets.

Albertinum
Brühlsche Terrasse (0351 4914 2000. www.skd.museum). **Open** 10am-6pm Tue-Sun. **Admission** €8; €6 reductions.

Gemäldegalerie Alte Meister
Zwinger, Theaterplatz (0351 4914 2000, www.skd. museum.de). **Open** 10am-6pm daily. **Admission** €10; €7.50 reductions. **No credit cards**.

Semperoper
Tickets: Schinkelwache, Theaterplatz (0351 491 10/www.semperoper.de). **Open** *Box office* 10am-6pm Mon-Fri; 10am-1pm Sat, Sun; also 1hr before performances. **Tickets** vary.

Where to stay

The **Artotel Dresden** (Ostra-Allee 33, 0351 49220, www.artotel.de, €99-€164 double) is decorated with 600 works by local artist AR Penck. **Bastei/Königstein/Lilienstein** (Prager Strasse, 0351 4856 2000, www.ibis-dresden.de, €65-€105 double) are three functional tower-blocks on Prager Strasse between the rail station and Altstadt. The **Hotel Bayerischer Hof Dresden** (Antonstrasse 33-35, 0351 829370, www.bayerischer-hof-dresden.de, €117-€132 double) has comfy rooms and a personal feel. The **Hotel Taschenbergpalais Kempinski** (Taschenberg 3, 0351 49 120, www.kempinski-dresden.de, €165-€245 double) provides slightly stuck-up luxury in a baroque palace. Over in the Neustadt, the **Hostel Mondpalast** (Katharinenstrasse 11-13, 0351 563 4050, www.mondpalast.de, from €14 per person) is a decent budget option. **Hotel Smetana**

(Schlüterstrasse 25, 0351 256 080, www.hotel-smetana.de, €79-€109 double) is a pleasant three-star, east of the centre.

Where to eat & drink

Caroussel (Bülow-Residenz, Königstrasse 14, 0351 80030, closed Sun, Mon, mains €30-€40), a contemporary German restaurant, offers fine cooking and has a leafy courtyard that's nice in summer. **Piccola Capri** (Alaunstrasse 93, 0351 801 4848, closed Sun, mains €6.50-€15.50) is one of the best Italians in the Neustadt. In the same part of town, there are plenty of good bars and cafés on and around Alaunstrasse in the area north-east of Albertplatz.

Getting there

By train
Regular direct trains take about 2hrs from Berlin. Check www.bahn.co.uk for the timetable.

Tourist information

Dresden Tourist-Information
Kulturpalast, Schlossstrasse 2 (0351 50160160, www.dresden.de/tourismus). **Open** *Apr-Dec* 10am-7pm Mon-Fri; 10am-6pm Sat; 10am-3pm Sun. *Jan-Mar* 10am-6pm Mon-Fri; 10am-2pm Sat.

LEIPZIG

One of Germany's most important trade centres and former second city of the DDR, Leipzig is a centre of education and culture and the place where East Germany's mass movement for political change began. It's also synonymous with Bach, who lived here for 27 years. The city, once one of Germany's industrial strongholds, has also been famed for its fairs for centuries; trade fairs (*Messen*) are still its bread and butter. Its pedestrianised, recently restored old centre is another attraction: with its Renaissance and baroque churches, narrow lanes, old street markets and the ancient university, it's hard to believe that it was bombed to bits during World War II. The area

---

INSIDE TRACK
SUPER-CHEAP GROUP TRAVEL

If you are travelling in a group on a Saturday or Sunday, the Schönes Wochenende ticket is worth investigating. Up to five people can travel on one €39 ticket all around Germany. The only proviso is you have to stick to the slower (S-Bahn, RB, IRE, RE) trains.

is also crammed with enough sights, bars and restaurants to fill a visit of a day or two.

In Saxony, around 130 kilometres (80 miles) south-west of Berlin, Leipzig traces its origins back to a settlement founded by the Sorbs, a Slavic people who venerated the lime tree, some time between the seventh and ninth centuries. They called it *Lipzk* (Place of Limes).

Most visitors arrive at **Leipzig Hauptbahnhof**, the huge, renovated central train station (largest in Europe before Berlin Hauptbahnhof was opened). The station stands on the north-east edge of the compact city centre, and is surrounded by a ring road that follows the course of the old city walls. Much of the ring road is lined with parks; most of the city's attractions can be found within its limits.

The first place to head is the Leipzig Tourist Service office, diagonally left across tram-strewn Willy-Brand-Platz from the front of the train station. Pick up a guide to the city in English (which includes a map) and head for Markt, the old market square, to get your bearings. The eastern side of the square is occupied by the lovely Renaissance **Altes Rathaus** (Old Town Hall), built in 1556-57. It now houses the **Stadtgeschichtliches Museum** (Town Museum). On the square's south side are the huge bay windows of the Könighaus, once a haunt of Saxony's rulers when visiting the city (the notoriously rowdy Peter the Great also once stayed here).

The church off the south-west corner of Markt is the **Thomaskirche**, where Johan Sebastian Bach spent 27 years as choirmaster of the famous St Thomas's Boys Choir; the

Getting Nowhere Fast

It's the journey as well as the destination.

No other European capital is surrounded by such a sparsely populated landscape as Berlin. This is a region of rare and delicate beauty, often ignored by visitors. Flat it may be, but the Land of Brandenburg deserves more attention than it gets. Forests and lakes are interspersed with water meadows and low gravelly ridges that speak of glaciers that came this way thousands of years ago.

Speeding along the Autobahn, it might all look a bit dull. But leave the main highways to find empty tree-lined secondary roads that twist and turn through forests and fen to come unexpectedly upon pretty villages with neat brick barns, ponds with the statutory quota of ducks and, more often than not, a traditional Gaststätte serving beers and improbably large portions of pork with dumplings. At some of the best such hostelries, look for local freshwater fish, notably pike-perch or carp, and off-dry Müller-Thurgau wines from Eastern Germany. Against all odds, decent white wines are produced in the region south-west of Berlin, and though rarely found in the capital, they often pop up in the countryside.

Some of the finest scenery is about 70 kilometres (43 miles) north of the city in an arc from Rheinsberg via Furstenberg to Templin. But travel out of Berlin in any direction to find exquisite unspoiled forests and lakes, and, at the right time of year, storks that preside majestically over a village from a manicured nest on a vantage point. On minor roads, expect ferries rather than bridges at the major river crossings, and even the odd stretch of gravel or dirt highway too.

Even without a car, it's perfectly feasible to get a flavour of Berlin's hinterland. The **Ostdeutsche Eisenbahn Gesellschaft** (ODEG) (www.odeg.info) runs modern comfortable glass railcars that afford panoramic views from its routes heading out of the city to the east. The OE36 leaves hourly from Berlin-Lichtenberg (U5, S5, S7, S75) and Schöneweide (S8, S9, S45) to Frankfurt-an-der-Oder. The full journey takes two and a half hours, and traverses some of Germany's most beautiful scenery. Break the trip midway at Wendish-Rietz for a boat excursion (from Easter until the end of October) on the Scharmützelsee (schedules on www.scharmuetzelsee.de/schiffahrt). In Frankfurt there's lots of DDR-era architecture and the pleasure of wandering over the river into Poland. Those with a real appetite for train travel can return to Berlin on ODEG's other main route, OE60, which loops north through the hills of the Oderbruch to rejoin the capital from the north-east. This alternative route runs once every two hours, also takes two and a half hours, and terminates at Berlin-Lichtenberg.

The fares aren't expensive – you can get a day ticket for the whole network for €19, and it's even cheaper with a €26 Brandenburg-Berlin-Ticket, which allows up to five people to travel together on the same ticket. Information is at www.vbbonline.de.

composer is buried in the chancel and his statue stands outside the church. Opposite the church in the Bosehaus is the **Bach-Museum**. Documents, instruments and furniture from Bach's time illustrate the work and influence of the great man.

South from the Thomaskirche towards the south-west corner of the ring road is the **Neues Rathaus** (New Town Hall), whose origins are 16th century, though the current buildings are only about 100 years old.

Back at the Altes Rathaus, immediately behind it is the delightful little chocolate box of the **Alte Börse** (Old Stock Exchange), built in 1687, and fronted by a statue of Goethe, who studied at Leipzig University. Follow his gaze towards the entrance to **Mädler Passage**, Leipzig's finest shopping arcade, within which is **Auerbachs Keller** (*see p286*), one of the oldest and most famous restaurants in Germany. It was in Auerbachs, where he often used to drink, that Goethe set a scene in *Faust* – Faust and Mephistopheles boozing with students before riding off on a barrel.

North of the Alte Börse is Sachsenplatz, site of the city's main outdoor market, and new home of the **Museum der bildenden Künste** (Museum of Arts Picture Gallery).

Just south-east of here is the **Nikolai**, Leipzig's proud symbol of its new freedom. This medieval church, with its baroque interior, is the place where regular free-speech meetings started in 1982. These evolved into the Swords to Ploughshares peace movement, which led to the first anti-DDR demonstration on 4 September 1989 in the Nikolaikirchhof.

West of here, on the edge of the ring road, is the **Museum in der 'Runden Ecke'** (Museum in the 'Round Corner', nickname of the building that once housed the local Stasi headquarters and now has an exhibition detailing its nefarious methods). North of here, outside the ring road, is **Leipzig Zoo**. All the usual family favourites are here: lions, tigers, polar bears and hippos.

In the south-east corner of the ring road rises the drab tower block of **Leipzig University**. Rebuilt in 1970 to resemble an opened book, this modern monstrosity is ironically one of Europe's oldest centres of learning. Alumni, besides Goethe, include Nietzsche, Schumann and Wagner. The university runs the **Äyptisches Museum**; nearby is the **Grassi Museum für Angewandte Kunst**.

The university tower stands at the south-eastern corner of Augustplatz, a project of DDR Communist Party leader Walter Ulbricht, himself a Leipziger. Next door are the brown glass-fronted buildings of the **Gewandhaus**, home of the Leipziger Gewandhaus Orchester,

Thomaskirche.

one of the world's finest orchestras. On the square's northern side stands the **Opernhaus Leipzig** (opened in 1960), which also has an excellent reputation. Tours of the building can be booked in advance.

Ägyptisches Museum

Goethestrasse 2 (0341 973 7010, www.uni-leipzig.de/~egypt). **Open** 1-5pm Tue-Sat; 10am-1pm Sun. **Admission** €5; €3 reductions. **No credit cards**.

Bach-Museum

Thomaskirchhof 16 (0341 913 7202, www.bach-leipzig.de). **Open** 10am-6pm Tue-Sun. **Admission** €6; €4 reductions.

Gewandhaus

Augustusplatz 8 (0341 127 0280, www.gewandhaus.de). **Open** *Box office* noon-6pm Mon-Fri; 10am-2pm Sat. **Tickets** vary.

Grassi Museum für Angewandte Kunst

Neumarkt 20 (0341 973 0770, www.museenim grassi.de). **Open** 10am-6pm Tue-Sun. **Admission** €5; €3.50 reductions. **No credit cards**.

Leipzig's Museum of Applied Art was founded in 1874. Labelling is in English, and guided tours in

English are available by advance booking. Also here are the Museum für Völkerkunde (Ethnography Museum) and the Museum für Musikinstrumente (Museum of Musical Instruments).

Leipzig Zoo

Pfaffendorfer Strasse 29 (0341 593 3500, www. zoo-leipzig.de). **Open** *Nov-Mar* 9am-5pm daily. *Apr* 9am-6pm Mon-Fri; 9am-7pm Sat, Sun. *May-Sept* 9am-7pm daily. *Oct* 9am-6pm daily. **Admission** €17; €10-€14 reductions. **No credit cards**.
Now with the brand new Gondwanaland, the zoo's also home to world-famous oppossum Heidi.

Museum der bildenden Künste

Katarienenstrasse 10 (0341 2169 9910, www.mdbk.de). **Open** 10am-6pm Tue, Thur-Sun; noon-8pm Wed. **Admission** €5; €3.50 reductions; free 2nd Wed of mth. *Temporary exhibitions* €6-€8; €4-€5.50 reductions.
The Museum of Arts Picture Gallery's 2,200-strong collection stretches from 15th- and 16th-century Dutch, Flemish and German paintings to expressionism and DDR art. Artists featured include Dürer, Rembrandt and Rubens.

Museum in der 'Runden Ecke'

Dittrichring 24 (0341 961 2443, www.runde-ecke-leipzig.de). **Open** 10am-6pm daily. *Guided tours* 3pm daily. **Admission** free. *Guided tours* €3; €2 reductions. **No credit cards**.
An interesting look at the Stasi's frightening yet ridiculous methods – collecting scents of suspected people in jars, say – and a hilarious section on Stasi disguises. There's no English labelling, but it's worth a visit nonetheless.

FREE Nikolaikirche

Nikolaikirchhof 3 (0341 960 5270, www. nikolaikirche-leipzig.de). **Open** 10am-6pm Tue, Thu, Fri; 10am-4.45pm Mon, Wed; 10am-3.30pm Sat; 1-3.30pm Sun. **Admission** free.

Opernhaus Leipzig

Augustusplatz 12 (0341 12610, www.oper-leipzig.de). **Open** *Box office* 10am-7pm Mon-Fri; 10am-6pm Sat; 1hr before performances Sun. **Tickets** vary.

Stadtgeschichtliches Museum

Altes Rathaus, Markt 1 (0341 9651 340, www.stadtgeschichtliches-museum-leipzig.de). **Open** 10am-6pm Tue-Sun. **Admission** €3; €2 reductions. **No credit cards**.
Special exhibitions are housed in the Neubau, at nearby Böttchergässchen 3.

FREE Thomaskirche

Thomaskirchhof 18 (0341 2222 4100, www.thomaskirche.org). **Open** 9am-6pm daily. **Admission** free.

Where to stay

The **Precise Hotel Accento Leipzig** (Taucher Strasse 260, 0341 92620, www. precisehotels.com, from €85 double) has stylish rooms and polite staff. **Adagio Minotel Leipzig** (Seeburgstrasse 96, 0341 216 699, www.hotel-adagio.de, from €87 double) features individually furnished rooms and a central location. For art nouveau luxury, try the **Seaside Park Hotel** (Richard-Wagner-Strasse 7, 0341 98520, www.park-hotel-leipzig.de, €130 double).
The Leipzig Tourist Service (*see below*) can help with budget options.

Where to eat

Apels Garten (Kolonnadenstrasse 2, 0341 960 7777, mains €5.50-€17) is a pretty restaurant with imaginative German cooking. **Auerbachs Keller** (Mädlerpassage, Grimmaische Strasse 2-4, 0341 216 100, set menus €10-€40), located in a 1525 beer hall, has a gourmet menu and a cheaper version: both serve classic Saxon cuisine (schnitzel, dumplings, pork and sauerkraut). **Barthels Hof** (Hainstrasse 1, 0341 141 310, mains €11-€22) offers hearty Saxon cooking in a cosy panelled *Gasthaus*. **El Matador** (Friedrich-Ebert-Strasse 108, 0341 980 0876, closed Sun, mains €8-€16) serves decent Spanish food.

Nightlife

With its major university, Leipzig is a party town: wander the streets around Markt for late-night quaffing. For dancing, try **Distillery** (Kurt-Eisner-Strasse 4, 0341 3559 7400) or **Schauhaus** (Bosestrasse 1, 0341 960 0596). **Moritz-Bastei** (Universitätsstrasse 9, 0341 702 590) features live jazz and blues. **Velvet Club** (Körnerstrasse 68, 03442 303 2001) is a gay/mixed after-hours venue with hip hop and R&B.

Getting there

By train

Regular trains from Berlin Hauptbahnhof take only an hour to reach Leipzig.

Tourist information

Leipzig Tourist Service

Katharinenstrasse 8 , (0341 710 4260/4265, www.ltm-leipzig.de). **Open** *Mar-Oct* 9.30am-6pm Mon-Fri; 9.30am-4pm Sat; 9.30am-3pm Sun. *Nov-Feb* 10am-6pm Mon-Fri; 9.30am-4pm Sat; 9.30am-3pm Sun.

ESCAPES & EXCURSIONS

Directory

Getting Around

ARRIVING & LEAVING

By air

Until the new **Berlin Brandenburg Willy Brandt Airport** is ready in summer 2012, Berlin is served by two airports: **Tegel** (TXL) and **Schönefeld** (SXF). Information in English on all three airports (including live departures and arrivals) can be found at www.berlin-airport.de. Both Tegel and **Schönefeld** will shut as soon as BER opens, just south of the **Schönefeld site**.

Flughafen Tegel (TXL)

Airport information 0180 5000 186, www.berlin-airport.de. **Open** 4am-midnight daily. **Map** p316 C1.
The more upmarket scheduled flights from the likes of BA and Lufthansa use the compact Tegel airport, just 8km (5 miles) north-west of Mitte.

Buses 109 and X9 (the express version) run via Luisenplatz and the Kurfürstendamm to Zoologischer Garten (also known as Zoo Station, Bahnof Zoo or just Zoo) in Western Berlin. Tickets cost €2.30 (and can also be used on U-Bahn and S-Bahn services). Buses run every 5-15 minutes, and take 30-40 minutes to reach Zoo. At Zoo there are rail and tourist information offices (*see p299*), and you can connect to anywhere in the city (same tickets are valid).

From the airport you can also take bus 109 to Jacob-Kaiser-Platz U-Bahn (U7), or bus 128 to Kurt-Schumacher-Platz U-Bahn (U6), and proceed on the underground from there. One ticket can be used for the combined journey (€2.30).

The JetExpressBusTXL is the direct link to Berlin Hauptbahnhof and Mitte. It runs from Tegel to Alexanderplatz with useful stops at Beusselstrasse S-Bahn (connects with the Ringbahn), Berlin Hauptbahnhof (regional and inter-city train services as well as the S-Bahn), Unter den Linden S-Bahn (north and south trains on the S1 and S2 lines). It costs €2.30, runs every 10 or 20 minutes between 4.30am-12.30am (5.30am-12.30am at weekends), and takes 30-40 minutes.

A taxi to anywhere central will cost around €20-€25, and takes 20-30 minutes.

Flughafen Schönefeld (SXF)

Airport information 0180 5000 186, www.berlin-airport.de. **Open** 24hrs daily.
The former airport of East Berlin is 18km (11 miles) south-east of the city centre. It's small, currently working with only one runway, and much of the traffic is to Eastern Europe and the Middle and Far East. But budget airlines from the UK and Ireland also use it – EasyJet flies in from Bristol, Gatwick, Glasgow, Liverpool, Luton and Manchester; Ryanair from Dublin, East Midlands, Edinburgh and Stansted.

Train is the best means of reaching the city centre. S-Bahn Flughafen Schönefeld is a five-minute walk from the terminal (a free S-Bahn shuttle bus runs every ten minutes between 6am-10pm from outside the terminal; at other times, bus 171 also runs to the station). From here, the Airport Express train runs to Mitte (25 minutes to Alexanderplatz), Berlin Hauptbahnhof (30 minutes) and Zoo (35 minutes) every half hour from 5am-11.30pm.

You can also take S-Bahn line S9, which runs into the centre every 20 minutes (40 minutes to Alexanderplatz, 50 minutes to Zoo) stopping at all stations along the way. The S45 line from Schönefeld connects with the Ringbahn, also running every 20 minutes.

Bus X7, every 10 or 20 minutes from 4.30am-8pm runs non-stop from the airport to Rudow U-Bahn (U7), from where you can connect with the underground. This is a good option if you are staying in Kreuzberg, Neukölln or Schöneberg. When it's not running, bus 171 takes the same route.

Tickets from the airport to the city cost €3, and can be used on any combination of bus, U-Bahn, S-Bahn and tram. There are ticket machines at the airport and at the station.

A taxi to Zoo or Mitte is pricey (€30-€35), and takes around 45 minutes.

Berlin Brandenburg Willy Brandt airport (BER)

This will become Berlin's only airport when it opens in 2012 next door to the Schönefeld site. Limited information was available at press time, but the airport's operators promise a fast train shuttle will transport passengers to the city centre in just 20 minutes. For up-to-date information see: www.berlin-airport.de.

Airlines

Air Berlin *0180 573 7800, www.airberlin.com*
Air France *0180 583 0830, www.airfrance.de*
Alitalia *0180 507 4747, www.alitalia.de*
British Airways *0180 526 6522, www.britishairways.com*
EasyJet 01805 666 000, *www.easyjet.com*
German Wings 0906 294 1918, www.germanwings.com
Iberia *0180 544 2900, www.iberia.com*
Lufthansa *01803 803 803, www.lufthansa.de*
Ryanair *0900 116 0500, www.ryanair.com*

By rail

Berlin Hauptbahnhof
0180 5 99 66 33, www.bahn.de. **Map** p318 K5
Berlin's central station is the central point of arrival for all long-distance trains, with the exceptions of night trains from Moscow and Kiev, which usually start and end at Berlin Lichtenberg (S5, S7, S75).

Hauptbahnhof is inconveniently located in a no-man's land north of the government quarter, and is linked to the rest of the city by S-Bahn (S5, S7, S9, S75), and with the new U55 underground line that runs to the Bundestag and the Brandenburger Tor only (connecting there with the S-Bahn lines S1, S2, S25). Eventually the line will extend to connect to the U5 at Alexanderplatz, but not until at least 2014.

On their way in and out of town, inter-city trains now also stop at Gesundbrunnen, Südkreuz and Spandau, depending on their destinations.

By bus

Zentraler Omnibus Bahnhof (ZOB)
Masurenallee 4-6, Charlottenburg (Information 301 0380,

www.iob-berlin.de). **Open** 6am-9pm Mon-Fri; 6am-3pm Sat, Sun. **Map** p320 B8.
Buses arrive in Western Berlin at the Central Bus Station, opposite the Funkturm and the ICC. From here, U-Bahn line U2 runs into the centre.

PUBLIC TRANSPORT

Berlin is served by a comprehensive and interlinked network of buses, trains, trams and ferries. It's efficient and punctual, but bear in mind that it's not particularly cheap.

With the completion of the inner-city-encircling Ringbahn in 2002, the former East and West Berlin transport systems were finally sewn back together, though it can still sometimes be complicated travelling between Eastern and Western destinations. But services are usually regular and frequent, timetables can be trusted, and one ticket can be used for two hours on all legs of a journey and all forms of transport.

The Berlin transport authority, the BVG, operates bus, U-Bahn (underground) and tram networks, and a few ferry services on the outlying lakes. The S-Bahn (overground railway) is run by its own authority, but services are integrated within the same three-zone tariff system (*see below* **Fares & tickets**).

Information

The **BVG** website (www.bvg.de) has a wealth of information (in English) on city transport, and there's usually someone who speaks English at the 24-hour **BVG Call Center** (194 49). The S-Bahn has its own website at www.s-bahn-berlin.de

The **Liniennetz**, a map of U-Bahn, S-Bahn, bus and tram routes for Berlin and Potsdam, is available free from info centres and ticket offices. It includes a city centre map. A map of the U- and S-Bahn can also be picked up free at ticket offices or from the grey-uniformed *Zugabfertiger* – passenger assistance personnel – who wander about the larger U-Bahn and S-Bahn stations.

Fares & tickets

The bus, tram, U-Bahn, S-Bahn and ferry services operate on an integrated three-zone system. Zone A covers central Berlin, Zone B extends out to the edge of the suburbs and zone C stretches into Brandenburg.

The basic single ticket is the €2.30 *Normaltarif* (zones A and B). Unless going to Potsdam or Flughafen Schönefeld, few visitors are likely to travel beyond zone B, making this in effect a flat-fare system.

Apart from the *Zeitkarten* (longer-term tickets, *see below*, tickets for Berlin's public transport system can be bought from the yellow or orange machines at U- or S-Bahn stations, and by some bus stops. These take coins and sometimes notes, give change and have a limited explanation of the ticket system in English. You can often pay by card, but don't count on it (if you do, don't forget to collect your card – infuriatingly, the machines keep the card until the tickets are all printed, making it very easy to forget).

Once you've purchased your ticket, validate it in the small red or yellow box next to the machine, which stamps it with the time and date. (Tickets bought on trams or buses are usually already validated.)

There are no ticket turnstiles at stations but if an inspector catches you without a valid ticket, you will be fined €40. Ticket inspections are frequent, and are conducted while vehicles are moving by pairs of plain-clothes personnel.

Single ticket (Normaltarif)
Single tickets cost €2.30 (€1.40 for children between the ages of six and 14) for travel within zones A and B, €2.70 (€1.80) for zones B and C, and €3 (€2.10) for all three zones. A ticket allows use of the BVG network for two hours, with as many changes between bus, tram, U-Bahn and S-Bahn as necessary travelling in one direction.

Short-distance ticket (Kurzstreckentarif)
The *Kurzstreckentarif* (ask for a *Kurzstrecke*) costs €1.40 (€1.10 concessions) and is valid for three U- or S-Bahn stops, or six stops on the tram or bus. No transfers allowed.

Day ticket (Tageskarte)
A *Tageskarte* for zones A and B costs €6.30 (€4.50 reductions), or €6.80 (€5.10) for all three zones. A day ticket lasts until 3am the morning after validating.

Longer-term tickets (Zeitkarten)
If you're in Berlin for a week, it makes sense to buy a *Sieben-Tage-Karte* ('seven-day ticket') at €27.20 for zones A and B, or €33.50 for all three zones (no concessions).

A stay of a month or more makes it worth buying a *Monatskarte* ('month ticket'), which costs €72 for zones A and B, or €88.50 for all three zones.

U-Bahn

The U-Bahn network consists of ten lines and 170-plus stations. The first trains run shortly after 4am; the last between midnight and 1am, except on Fridays and Saturdays when most trains run all night in 15-minute intervals. The direction of travel is indicated by the name of the last stop on the line.

S-Bahn

Especially useful in Eastern Berlin, the S-Bahn covers long distances faster than the U-Bahn and is a more efficient means of getting to outlying areas. The Ringbahn, which circles central Berlin, was the final piece of the S-Bahn system to be renovated, though there are still disruptions here and there.

Buses

Berlin has a dense network of 150 bus routes, of which 54 run in the early hours. The day lines run from 4.30am to about 1am the next morning. Enter at the front of the bus and exit in the middle or at the back. The driver sells only individual tickets, but all tickets from machines on the U- or S-Bahn are valid. Most bus stops have clear timetables and route maps.

Trams

There are 21 tram lines (five of which run all night), mainly in the East, though some have been extended a few kilometres into the Western half of the city, mostly in Wedding. Hackescher Markt is the site of the main tram terminus. Tickets are available from machines on the trams, at the termini and in U-Bahn stations.

Other rail services

Berlin is also served by the Regionalbahn ('regional railway'), which once connected East Berlin with Potsdam via the suburbs and small towns left outside the Wall. Run by Deutsche Bahn, it still circumnavigates the city.

For timetable and ticket information (available in English), go to Deutsche Bahn's website at www.bahn.de.

Travelling at night

Berlin has a comprehensive *Nachtliniennetz* ('night-line network') that covers all parts of town via over 50 bus and tram routes running every 30 minutes between 12.30am and 4.30am.

Maps and timetables are available from BVG kiosks at stations, and large maps of the night services are found next to the normal BVG map on station platforms. Ticket prices are the same as during the day. Buses and trams that run at night have an 'N' in front of the number.

On all buses traveling through zones B and C after 8pm, the driver will let you off at any point along the route via the front door. Truncated versions of U-Bahn lines U1, U2, U3, U5, U6, U7, U8, and U9 run all night on Fridays and Saturdays, with trains every 15 minutes. The S-Bahn also runs at 30-minute intervals.

Boat trips

Getting about by water is more of a leisure activity than a practical means of navigating the city, but the BVG network has a handful of boat services on Berlin's lakes. There are also several private companies offering tours of Berlin's waterways. *See also p97* **Boat Trips.**

Reederei Heinz Riedel
Planufer 78, Kreuzberg (693 4646, www.reederei-riedel.de).
U8 Schönleinstrasse. **Open** varies, check website for details. **No credit cards. Map** p323 P9.
A tour through the city's network of rivers and canals costs €4.50-€18.

Stern und Kreisschiffahrt
Puschkinallee 15, Treptow (536 3600, www.sternundkreis.de). S8, S9, S41, S42 Treptower Park.
Open *Apr-5 Oct* (exact date varies slightly) 9am-6pm Mon-Fri; 9am-2pm Sat.
Around 25 cruises along the Spree and around the lakes. A 3hr 30min tour costs €18.50.

Taxis

Berlin taxis are pricey, efficient and numerous. The starting fee is €3.20 and thereafter the fare is €1.65 per kilometre for the first seven kilometres, and €1.28 per kilometre thereafter. The rate remains the same at night. For short journeys ask for a *Kurzstrecke* – up to two kilometres for €4, but only available when you've hailed a cab and not from taxi ranks. Taxi stands are numerous, especially in central areas near stations and at major intersections. You can phone for a cab 24 hours daily on 261 026. Most firms can transport people

with disabilities, but require advance notice. Cabs accept all credit cards except Diners Club, subject to a €1.50 charge.

If you want an estate car (station wagon), ask for a *combi*. As well as normal taxis, Funk Taxi Berlin (261 026) operates vans that can carry up to seven people (ask for a '*grossraum Taxi*'; same rates as for regular taxis) and has two vehicles for people with disabilities.

DRIVING

Despite some congestion, driving in Berlin presents few problems. Visitors from the UK and US should bear in mind that, in the absence of signals, drivers must yield to traffic from the right, except at crossings marked by a diamond-shaped yellow sign. Trams always have right of way. An *Einbahnstrasse* is a one-way street.

Breakdown services

ADAC
Bundesallee 29-30, Wilmersdorf (0180 222 2222). **No credit cards.**
24-hour assistance for about €65/hr.

Filling stations

Both of the places below are open 24 hours a day.

Aral
Holzmarktstrasse 12, Mitte (2472 0748). **Map** p323 P7.
Kurfürstendamm 128, Wilmersdorf (8909 6972). **Map** p320 B9.

Parking

Parking is free in Berlin side streets, but spaces are hard to find. On busier streets you may have to buy a ticket from a nearby machine. Without a ticket, or if you park illegally, you risk getting your car clamped or towed.

There are some long-term car parks at Schönefeld and Tegel airport, and many *Parkgaragen* and *Parkhäuser* (multi-storey and underground car parks) around the city, open 24 hours, that charge around €2/hr.

Vehicle hire

Car hire is not expensive and all major companies are represented in Berlin. There are car hire desks at all of the city's airports.

CYCLING

West Berlin is wonderful for cycling – flat, with lots of cycle paths, parks

and canals to cruise beside. East Berlin has fewer cycle paths and more cobblestones and tram lines.

Cycles can be taken on the U-Bahn (except during rush hour, 6-9am and 2-5pm), up to a limit of two at the end of carriages that have a bicycle sign. More may be taken on to S-Bahn carriages, and at any time of day. In each case an extra ticket (€1.50 for zones A and B) must be bought for each bike. The *ADFC Fahrradstadtplan*, available in bike shops (€6.90), is a good guide to cycle routes. There are also a selection of routes on the Berlin senate website: www.stadtentwicklung.berlin.de/ verkehr/mobil/fahrrad/radrouten/

Berlin's bike rental scheme, **Call-A-Bike**, is only open to registered users. Only operational in summer, the bikes are parked in designated docking stations. You can register at the docking station terminal, via the website (www.callabike-interaktiv.de, in German only) or by calling 07000 5225522. There's a one-off fee of €12 to register and a charge of 0.8c per minute up to a maximum of €15 per 24 hours. The *Pauschal* annual subscription (€36) allows unlimited journeys of up to 30 minutes for free, and make sense for those making longer visits.

The companies below rent bikes:

Fahrradstation
Dorotheenstrasse 30, Mitte (2838 4848, www.fahrradstation.de).
U6, S1, S2, S5, S7, S9, S75 Friedrichstrasse. **Open** 10am-7.30pm Mon-Fri; 10am-6pm Sat; 10am-4pm Sun. **Rates** from €15 per day; €35 3 days. **Map** p318/p327 M6.
Other locations Bergmannstrasse 9, Kreuzberg (21 51 566); Auguststrasse 29a, Mitte (2250 8070); Leibzigerstrasse 56, Mitte (6664 9180), Goethestrasse 46, Charlottenburg (9395 2757), Kollwitzstrassee 77, Prenzlauer Berg (9395 8130).

Pedalpower
Grossbeerenstrasse 53, Kreuzberg (7899 1939, www.pedalpower.de).
U1, U7 Möckernbrücke. **Open** 10am-6.30pm Mon-Fri; 11am-2pm Sat. **Rates** from €10 per day.
No credit cards. Map p322 L10.
Other locations Pfarrstrasse 115, Lichtenberg (5515 3270).

WALKING

Berlin is a good walking city, but it's spread out. Mitte is most pleasant on foot, but if you then want to check out Charlottenburg, you'll need to take a bus or train. .

Resources A-Z

TRAVEL ADVICE

For up-to-date information on travel to a specific country – including the latest on safety and security, health issues, local laws and customs – contact your home country government's department of foreign affairs. Most have websites with useful advice for would-be travellers.

AUSTRALIA
www.smartraveller.gov.au

CANADA
www.voyage.gc.ca

NEW ZEALAND
www.safetravel.govt.nz

REPUBLIC OF IRELAND
foreignaffairs.gov.ie

UK
www.fco.gov.uk/travel

USA
www.state.gov/travel

ADDRESSES

German convention dictates that the house/building number follows the street name (eg Friedrichstrasse 21), and numbers sometimes run up one side of the street and back down the other side. Strasse (street) is often abbreviated to Str, and is not usually written separately but appended to the street name, as in the example above. Exceptions are when the street name is the adjectival form of a place name (eg Potsdamer Strasse) or the full name of an individual (eg Heinrich-Heine-Strasse).

Within buildings: EG means *Erdgeschoss*, the ground floor; 1. OG (*Obergeschoss*) is the first floor; VH means *Vorderhaus*, the front part of the building; HH means *Hinterhaus*, the part of the building off the *Hinterhof*, the 'back courtyard'; SF is *Seitenflügel*, stairs that go off to the side from the *Hinterhof*. In big, industrial complexes, stairwells are often numbered or lettered. Treppenhaus B, or sometimes just Haus B, would indicate a particular staircase off the courtyard.

AGE RESTRICTIONS

The legal age for drinking in Germany is 16; for smoking it is 16; for driving it is 18; and the age of consent for both heterosexual and homosexual sex is 16.

BUSINESS

Conferences

Messe Berlin
Messedamm 22, Charlottenburg (303 80, www.messe-berlin.de). U2 Theodor-Heuss-Platz. **Open** 10am-6pm Mon-Fri; 10am-2pm Sat. **Map** p320 A8/B8.

The city's official trade fair and conference organisation can advise businesses or individuals on setting up small seminars and congresses, or big trade fairs.

Couriers

A package of up to 5kg (10kg in Germany) delivered within Germany costs about €7; to the UK about €17; and to North America about €35. The post office runs a cheaper express service (*see p397*).

DHL
Linkstrasse 10, Tiergarten (0180 5345 2255, www.dhl.de). U2, S1, S2, S25 Potsdamer Strasse. **Open** 9am-6pm Mon-Fri; 9am-noon Sat. **No credit cards. Map** p322 L8.
DHL delivers to over 200 countries worldwide.

Translators & interpreters

See also **Übersetzungen** in the *Gelbe Seiten* (*Yellow Pages*).

Kehila Übersetzungsdienst
Langenscheidtstrasse 9, Schöneberg (781 7584). U7 Kleistpark. **Open** varies. **Map** p322 K10.

Intertext Fremdsprachendienst
Greifswalder Strasse 5, Prenzlauer Berg (4210 1777, www.intertext.de). Tram M4 Am Friedrichshain. **Open** 8am-4.30pm Mon-Fri. **Map** p325 R2.

Useful organisations

American Chamber of Commerce
Charlottenstrasse 42, Mitte (2887 8920, www.amcham.de) U2, U6 Stadtmitte. **Open** 9am-6pm Mon-Fri. **Map** p318/p327 M6.

American Embassy Commercial Dept
Pariser Platz 2, Mitte (83050, www.germany.usembassy.gov). S1, S2 Unter Den Linden. **Open** (phone enquiries) 8.30am-5.30pm Mon-Fri. **Map** p318/p327 L6.

Berlin Chamber of Commerce
Fasanenstrasse 85, Charlottenburg (315 100/ihk-berlin.de). **Open** 8am-5pm Mon-Thur; 8am-4pm Fri. **Map** p321/p328 F8

British Embassy Commercial Department
Wilhelmstrasse 70, Mitte (204 570, www.britischesbotschaft.de). S1, S2 Unter den Linden. **Open** 9-1pm, 2pm-5.30 Mon-Fri. **Map** p318/ p327 L6.
The British Embassy's Commercial Department can offer basic advice for British businesses.

CUSTOMS

EU nationals over 17 years of age can import limitless goods for personal use, if bought with tax paid on them at source. For non-EU citizens and for duty-free goods, the following limits apply:

● 200 cigarettes or 50 cigars or 250 grams of tobacco
● 1 litre of spirits (over 22 per cent alcohol), or 2 litres of fortified wine (under 22 per cent alcohol), or 2 litres of non-sparkling and sparkling wine
● 50 grams of perfume
● 500 grams of coffee
● Other goods to the value of €175 for non-commercial use

Travellers should note that the import of meat, meat products, fruit, plants, flowers and protected animals is restricted and/or forbidden.

DIRECTORY

DISABLED

Only some U- and S-Bahn stations have wheelchair facilities; the map of the transport network (*see p334*; look for the wheelchair symbol) indicates which ones. The BVG is improving things slowly, adding facilities here and there, but it's still a long way from being a wheelchair-friendly system.

Public buildings and most of the city's hotels have disabled access. However, if you require more specific information about access, try the **Beschäftigungswerk des BBV** or the **Touristik Union International**.

Beschäftigungswerk des BBV

Bizetstrasse 51-5, Weissensee (927 0360, www.bbv-tours-berlin.de). S4, S8, S10 Greifswalder Strasse then bus M4 to Antonplatz. **Open** 9am-8pm Mon-Fri, 10am-6pm Sat. **Map** p325 S2

The Berlin Centre for the Disabled provides legal and social advice, together with a transport service and travel information.

Touristik Union International (TUI)

Markgrafenstrassse 46, Mitte (200 58550, www.tui.com). U6 Französische Strasse. **Open** (by appointment) 9am-8pm Mon-Fri; 10am-6pm Sat. **Map** p318/p327 M6.

The Touristik Union International provides information on accommodation and travel in Germany for the disabled.

DRUGS

Berlin is relatively liberal in its attitude towards drugs. In recent years, possession of hash or grass has been effectively decriminalised. Anyone caught with an amount under ten grams is liable to have the stuff confiscated, but can otherwise expect no further retribution. In addition, joint-smoking is tolerated in some of Berlin's younger bars and cafés. A quick sniff will usually tell whether you're in one. Anyone caught with small amounts of hard drugs will net a fine, but is unlikely to be incarcerated.

For *Drogen Notdienst* (Emergency Drug Service), *see p293*.

ELECTRICITY

Electricity in Germany runs on 220v. To use British appliances (240v), change the plug or use an adaptor (available at most UK electric shops, and probably at the airport). US appliances (110v) require a converter.

EMBASSIES & CONSULATES

Australian Embassy

Friedrichstrasse 200, Mitte (880 0880). U6 Französische Strasse. **Open** 8.30am-5pm Mon-Thur; 8.30am-4.15pm Fri. **Map** p322/ p327 M7.

British Embassy

Wilhelmstrasse 70, Mitte (204 570, www.britischesbotschaft.de). S1, S2 Unter den Linden. **Open** 9-11am Mon, Wed, Fri. **Map** p318/p327 L6.

Irish Consulate

Friedrichstrasse 200, Mitte (220 720). U2, U6 Stadtmitte. **Open** 9.30am-12.30pm, 2.30-4.30pm Mon-Fri. **Map** p322/p327 M7.

US Consulate

Clayallee 170, Zehlendorf (83051200 /visa enquiries 0190 850 055). U3 Oscar-Helene-Heim. **Open** *Consular enquiries* 2pm-4pm by phone (and with appointment) Mon-Thur. *Visa enquiries* 7am-8pm (phone enquiries) Mon-Fri.

US Embassy

Pariser Platz 2, Mitte (83050, www.germany.usembassy.gov). S1, S2 Unter Den Linden. **Open** 8.30am-5.30pm Mon-Fri (phone enquiries). **Map** p318/p327 L6.

EMERGENCIES

See also *p293* **Helplines**.
Police 110.
Ambulance/Fire Brigade 112.

GAY & LESBIAN

Help & information

Lesbenberatung e.V.

Kulmer Strasse 20A, Schöneberg (215 2000, www.lesbenberatung-berlin.de). U7, , S2, S25 Yorckstrasse. **Open** 10am-5pm Mon, Wed, Fri; 10am-7pm Tue, Thur. **Map** p322 K10.

Offers counselling in all areas of lesbian life as well as self-help groups, courses, cultural events and an "info-café".

Mann-O-Meter e.V.

Bülowstrasse 106, Schöneberg (216 8008, www.mann-o-meter.de). U2, U3, U4 Nollendorfplatz. **Open** 5pm-10pm Tue-Fri; 4pm-8pm Sat, Sun. **Map** p322 J9.

Drop-in centre and helpline. Advice about AIDS prevention, jobs, flats, gay contacts, plus cheap stocks of safer sex materials. English spoken.

Schwulenberatung

Mommsenstrasse 45, Charlottenburg (office 2336 9070, counselling 194 46, www. schwulenberatungberlin.de). U7 Adenauerplatz. **Open** 9am-8pm Mon-Fri. **Map** p320 D8.

The Gay Advice Centre provides information and counselling about HIV and AIDS, crisis intervention and advice on all aspects of gay life.

HEALTH

EU countries have reciprocal medical treatment arrangements with Germany. EU citizens will need the **European Health Insurance Card** (EHIC). From the UK, this is available by phoning 0845 606 2030 or online from www.ehic.org.uk. You'll need to provide your name, date of birth and national insurance number. It does not cover all medical costs (for example dental treatment), so private insurance is not a bad idea.

Citizens from non-EU countries should take out private medical insurance. The British Embassy (*see above*) has a list of English-speaking doctors and dentists, as well as lawyers and interpreters.

Should you fall ill in Berlin, you can take your EHIC to any doctor or hospital emergency department and get treatment. All hospitals have a 24-hour emergency ward. Otherwise, patients are admitted to hospital via a physician. Hospitals are listed in the *Gelbe Seiten* (*Yellow Pages*) under Krankenhäuser/ Kliniken.

Accident & emergency

The following are the most central hospitals. All have 24-hour emergency wards.

Charité

Schumann Strasse 20-21, Mitte (450 50, www.charite.de). U6 Oranienburger Tor. **Map** p323 O10.

Klinikum Am Urban

Dieffenbachstrasse 1, Kreuzberg (130 210www.vivantes.de/kau/). U7 Südstern/bus M41. **Map** p323 O10.

St Hedwig Krankenhaus

Grosse Hamburger Strasse 5, Mitte (23110, www.alexius.de). S5, S7, S9, S75 Hackescher Markt or S1, S2 Oranienburger Strasse. **Map** p319/p327 M5.

Complementary medicine

There is a long tradition of alternative medicine (Heilpraxis) in Germany, and your medical insurance will usually cover treatment costs. For a full list of practitioners, look up *Heilpraktiker* in the *Gelbe Seiten* (*Yellow Pages*). There you'll find a complete list of chiropractors, osteopaths, acupuncturists, homoeopaths and healers of various kinds. However, note that homeopathic medicines are harder to get hold of and much more expensive than in the UK, and it's generally more difficult to find an osteopath or a chiropractor.

Contraception & abortion

Family-planning clinics are thin on the ground in Germany, and generally you have to go to a gynaecologist (*Frauenarzt*).

The abortion law was amended in 1995 to take into account the differing systems that had existed in East and West. East Germany had abortion on demand; in the West, abortion was only allowed in extenuating circumstances, such as when the health of the foetus or mother was at risk.

In a complicated compromise, abortion is still technically illegal, but is not punishable. Women wishing to terminate a pregnancy can do so only after receiving certification from a counsellor. Counselling is offered by state, lay and church bodies.

Feministisches Frauengesund-heitzentrum (FFGZ)

Bamberger Strasse 51, Schöneberg (213 9597, www.ffgz.de). **Open** 10am-1pm Mon, Tue, Thur, Fri; 5-7pm Thur. **Map** p321 G10.
Courses and lectures are offered on natural contraception, pregnancy, cancer, abortion, AIDS, migraines and sexuality. Self-help and preventative medicine are stressed. Information on gynaecologists, health institutions and organisations can also be obtained.

ProFamilia

Kalkreuthstrasse 4, Schöneberg (2147 6414, www.profamilia-berlin.de). U1, U2, U3 Wittenbergplatz. **Open** 3-6pm Mon, Tue, Thur; 9am-noon Sat. **Map** p321 H9.
Free advice about sex, contraception and abortion. Call for an appointment.

Dentists

Dr Andreas Bothe

Kurfürstendamm 210, Charlottenburg (8826767). U1 Uhlandstrasse. **Open** 8am-2pm Mon, Wed, Fri; 2-8pm Tue, Thur. **Map** p321/p328 F8.

Doctors

If you don't know of any doctors in Berlin, or are too ill to leave your bed, phone the Emergency Doctor's Service (*Ärztlicher Bereitschaftdienst* 310 031). This service specialises in dispatching doctors for house calls. The charges vary according to the treatment required by the patient.

The British Embassy (*see p292*) can provide a list of English-speaking doctors, although you'll find that most doctors speak some English. All will be expensive, however, so be sure to have either your EHIC or your private insurance documents at hand (*see p292*) if seeking treatment. The doctors listed below all speak excellent English.

Dr Joseph Francis Aman

Franzisksus Krankenhaus, Budapester Strasse 15-19, Tiergarten (2638 3503). U1, U2, U3 Wittenbergplatz. **Open** 8am-1pm, 3-6pm Mon, Tue, Thur; 8am-1pm Fri. **Map** p321 H8.
Dr Aman is an American GP with a practice in the Roman Catholic hospital that is opposite the Intercontinental Hotel.

Dr Christine Rommelspacher

Bochumerstr 12, Tiergarten (392 2075) U9 Turmstrasse. **Open** 9am-1pm, 3-6pm Mon, Tue, Thur; 9am-Fri. **Map** p317 G5.

Pharmacies

Prescription and non-prescription drugs (including aspirin) are sold only at pharmacies (*Apotheken*). You can recognise these by a red 'A' outside the front door. A list of the nearest pharmacies open on Sundays and in the evening should be displayed in the window of every pharmacy. You can get a list of *Notdienst-Apotheken* (emergency pharmacies) online at www.apo110.de.

HIV & AIDS

Berliner Aids-Hilfe (BAH)

Büro 15, Meinekestrasse 12, Wilmersdorf (885 6400/advice line 194 11, www.berliner-aidshilfe.de). U1, U9 Kurfürstendamm. **Open**
noon-6pm Mon; noon-2.30pm Wed; noon-3pm Thur, Fri. *Advice line* 1noon-10pm Mon, Tue, Wed. **Map** p321/p328 F9.
Information is given on all aspects of HIV and AIDS. Free consultations, condoms and lubricant are also provided.

HELPLINES

Berliner Krisendienst

Mitte, Friedrichshain, Kreuzberg, Tiergarten & Wedding 390 6310. Charlottenburg & Wilmersdorf 390 6320.
Prenzlauer Berg, Weissensee & Pankow 390 6340.
Schöneberg, Tempelhof, Steglitz 390 6360.
All *www.berlinerkrisendienst.de.* **Open** 24hrs daily.
For most problems, this is the best service to call. It offers help and/or counselling on a range of subjects, and if they can't provide exactly what you're looking for, they'll put you in touch with someone who can. The phone lines, organised by district, are staffed 24 hours daily. Counsellors will also come and visit you in your house if necessary.

Drogen Notdienst

Ansbacher Strasse 11, Schöneberg (2191 6010, www.drogen notdienst.de). U1, U2, U3 Wittenbergplatz. **Open** 9am-10pm daily *Phone line* 24hrs daily. **Map** p321 G9.
At the 'drug emergency service', no appointment is necessary if you're coming in for advice, and the phone line is staffed 24 hours daily.

Frauenkrisentelefon

615 4243. **Open** 10am-noon Mon, Wed, Thur; 7-9pm, 3-5pm, 7-9pm Tue, 5-7pm Sat, Sun,
Offers advice and information for women on anything and everything.

ID

By law you are required to carry some form of ID, which, for UK and US citizens, means a passport. If police catch you without one, they may accompany you to wherever you've left it.

INTERNET

For internet access, there are cybercafés all over town. There is free wireless access in the Sony Center at Potsdamer Platz. For long stays, try www.snafu.de or www.gmx.de.

DIRECTORY

Sidewalk Express Internet Point

Dunkin' Donuts, Sony Center, Tiergarten (www.sidewalk express.com). U2, S1, S2, S25 Potsdamer Platz. **Open** 7am-1am Mon-Fri; 8am-1am Sat. **Map** p322/p327 K7/L7.

Dozens of computers, no staff, mechanised system to buy time online, and plenty of doughnuts to hand. Some other branches are similarly lodged with Dunkin' Donuts.

Other locations Potsdamer Platz Arkaden, Potsdamer Platz; Bahnhof Alexanderplatz Dunkin Donuts; Bahnhof Zoologischer Garten; Bahnhof Friedrichstrasse (ground floor, and Dunkin Donuts basement); Hauptbahnhof Burger King.

LEFT LUGGAGE

Airports

There is a left luggage office at **Tegel** (*see p288*; 0180 5000 186; open 5am-10.30pm daily) and lockers at **Schönefeld** (*see p288*; in the Multi Parking Garage P4).

Rail & bus stations

There are left luggage lockers at Bahnhof Zoo, Friedrichstrasse, Alexanderplatz, Potsdamer Platz, Ostbahnhof and Hauptbahnhof. In addition, Zentraler Omnibus Bahnhof (ZOB; *see p288*) also provides left-luggage facilities.

LEGAL HELP

If you get into legal difficulties, contact the British Embassy (*see p292*): it can provide you with a list of English-speaking lawyers in Berlin.

LIBRARIES

Berlin has hundreds of *Bibliotheken/Büchereien* (public libraries). To borrow books, you will be required to bring two things: an *Anmeldungsformular* ('Certificate of Registration'; *see p299*) and a passport.

Amerika-Gedenkbibliothek

Blücherplatz 1, Kreuzberg (9022 6105, www.zlb.de). U1, U6 Hallesches Tor. **Open** 10am-8pm Mon-Fri; 10am-7pm Sat. **Membership** *Per year* €10; students €5. **Map** p322 M9.

This library only contains a small collection of English and American

literature, but it has an excellent collection of English-language videos and many DVDs.

Staatsbibliothek

Potsdamer Strasse 33, Tiergarten (2660, www.staatsbibliothek-berlin. de). U2, S1, S2, S26 Potsdamer Platz. **Open** 9am-9pm Mon-Fri; 9am-7pm Sat. **Map** p322 K8.

Books in English on every subject are available at this branch of the State Library, which you may recognise from Wim Wenders' film *Wings of Desire*.

Staatsbibliothek

Unter den Linden 8, Mitte (2660, www.staatsbilbiothek-berlin.de). U6, S1, S2, S5, S7, S9, S75 Friedrichstrasse. **Open** 9am-9pm Mon-Fri; 9am-5pm Sat. **Map** p318 M6.

A smaller range of English books than the branch above, but it's still worth a visit, not least for its café.

LOST/STOLEN PROPERTY

If any of your belongings are stolen while in Germany, you should go immediately to the police station nearest to where the incident occurred (listed in the *Gelbe Seiten/Yellow Pages* under *Polizei*) and report the theft. There you will be required to fill in report forms for insurance purposes. If you can't speak German, don't worry: the police will call in one of their interpreters, a service that is provided free of charge.

If you leave something in a taxi, call the number that's on your receipt (if you remembered to ask for one), and tell them the time of your journey, the four-digit Konzessions-Nummer that will be stamped on the receipt, a number where you can be reached, and what you've lost. They'll pass this information to the driver, and he or she will call you if they have your property.

For information about what to do concerning lost or stolen credit cards, *see p296*.

BVG Fundbüro

Potsdamer Strasse 180,, Schöneberg (194 49). U7 Kleistpark. **Open** 9am-6pm Mon-Thur; 9am-2pm Fri. **Map** p322 J10.

You should contact this office if you have any queries about property lost on Berlin's public transport system. If you are robbed on one of their vehicles, you can ask about the surveillance video.

Zentrales Fundbüro

Platz der Luftbrücke 6, Tempelhof (90277 3101). U6 Platz der Luftbrücke. **Open** 9am-2pm Mon; Tue, Wed, Fri; 1pm-6pm Thur. **Map** p322 M11.

This is the central police lost property office.

MEDIA

Foreign press

A wide variety of international publications are available at larger railway stations and Internationale Presse newsagents around town. Book retailers **Dussmann** and **Do you read me?** (for both, *see p180*) also carry international titles. The monthly *Exberliner* magazine offers listings as well as articles on cultural and political topics in English.

National newspapers

BILD

www.bild.de
The flagship tabloid of the Axel Springer group. Though its credibility varies from story to story, *BILD* leverages the journalistic resources of the Springer empire and its three-million circulation to land regular scoops.

Financial Times Deutschland

www.ftd.de
Since hitting newsstands in 2000, the FTD's circulation has been steadily increasing, and though it's not likely to dethrone *Handelsblatt*, its success proves there's room for different approaches within the business trade market.

Frankfurter Allgemeine Zeitung

www.faz.net
Germany's de facto newspaper of record. Stolid, exhaustive coverage of daily events, plus lots of analysis, particularly on the business pages.

Handelsblatt

www.handelsblatt.com
The closest thing Germany can offer to the Wall Street Journal, the *Handelsblatt* co-operates with that paper's European offshoot. Competition from the *Financial Times Deutschland* has shaken *Handelsblatt* out of its complacency and energised its reporting.

Süddeutsche Zeitung

www.sueddeutsche.de
Based in Munich, the *Süddeutsche* blends first-rate journalism with enlightened commentary and uninspired visuals. On Mondays there is an English-language feature supplement called *The New York Times International Weekly*.

die tageszeitung
www.taz.de
Set up in rebellious Kreuzberg in
the 1970s, the '*taz*' attempts to
balance the world view of the
mainstream press and give
coverage to alternative political
and social issues.

Die Welt
www.welt.de
Once a lacklustre mouthpiece of conservative, provincial thinking, *Die
Welt* has widened its political
horizons, though it's still thought of
as a yuppy paper. Not very popular
in Berlin.

Local newspapers

Berliner Morgenpost
www.morgenpost.de
This rather staid broadsheet is the
favourite of the petty bourgeois.
Reasonable local coverage, and
it's gained readers in the East
through the introduction of
neighbourhood editions, but
there's no depth on the national
and international pages.

Berliner Zeitung
www.berliner-zeitung.de
This East Berlin paper has passed
through the hands of a number of
owners since it was relaunched in
the early 1990s. Though it is
profitable and its journalistic
ambitions less sullied than its
West Berlin competitor *Der
Tagesspiegel*, it remains a local
read, with a circulation largely
confined to the Eastern districts.

BZ
www.bz-berlin.de
The daily riot of polemic and
pictures hasn't let up since it
was demonised by the left in the
1970s – but its circulation has.

Der Tagesspiegel
www.tagesspiegel.de
Owned by the conservative
Holzbrinck publishing empire
from West Germany, this paper
has fallen from the pre-eminent
position it once held in West
Berlin. The paper has dumbed
down to boost circulation, losing
the intellectual underpinnings
which once attracted well-educated,
up-market readers.

Weekly newspapers

Jungle World
www.jungle-world.com
Defiantly left, graphically
switched-on and commercially
undaunted, this Berlin-based
weekly can be relied on to mock
the comfortable views of the
mainstream press. Born of an

ideological dispute with the
publishers of *Junge Welt*, a former
East Berlin youth title, it lacks
sales but packs a punch.

Die Zeit
www.zeit.de
Every major post-war intellectual
debate in Germany has been carried
out in the pages of *Die Zeit*, the
newspaper that proved that a
liberal tradition was alive and
well in a country best known
for excesses of intolerance. The
style of its elite authors makes a
difficult read.

Freitag
www.freitag.de
'The East-West weekly paper'
is a post-1989 relaunch of a GDR
intellectual weekly. Worth a look
for its political and cultural articles.

Magazines

Focus
www.focus.de
Once, its spare, to-the-point articles,
four-colour graphics and service
features were a welcome innovation.
But the gloss has faded, and *Focus*
has established itself as a non-
thinking man's *Der Spiegel,* whose
answer to the upstart was simply
to print more colour pages and
become warm and fuzzy by
adding bylines.

Der Spiegel
www.spiegel.de
Few journalistic institutions in
Germany possess the resources
and clout to pursue a major story
in the way that *Der Spiegel* can,
making it one of the best and
most aggressive news weeklies
in Europe. After years of firing
barbs at ruling Christian
Democrats, *Der Spiegel* was
caught off guard when the Social
Democrats were elected in 1999,
but remains a must-read for
anyone interested in Germany's
power structure. Substantial
English content on their website.

Stern
www.stern.de
The heyday of news pictorials may
have long gone, but *Stern* still
manages to shift around a million
copies a week of big colour spreads
detailing the horrors of war, the
beauties of nature and the curves of
the female body. Nevertheless, some
say its reputation has never really
recovered from the Hitler diaries
fiasco in the early 1980s.

Listings magazines

Berlin is awash with free listings
magazines, notably *[030]*

(www.berlin030.de; music,
nightlife, film) and *Partysan*
(www.partysan.net; a pocke
club guide) and their gay cousins
Siegessaeule (www.siegessaeule.de)
and *Blu* (www.blu.fm). These can be
picked up in bars and restaurants.
Two newsstand fortnightlies, *Zitty*
and *tip*, come out on alternate weeks
and, at least for cinema information,
it pays to get the current title.

Exberliner
www.exberliner.com
Berlin's current English-language
monthly is a lively mix of listings,
reviews and commentary, mostly
written by youngish American

expatstip
www.tip-berlin.de
A glossier version of *Zitty* in every
respect, tip gets better marks for
its overall presentation and
readability, largely due to
higher quality paper, full colour
throughout and a space-saving
TV insert.

Zitty
www.zitty.de
Having lost some countercultural
edge since its foundation in 1977,
Zitty remains a vital force on the
Berlin media scene, providing a
fortnightly blend of close-to-
the-bone civic journalism,
alternative cultural coverage
and comprehensive listings. The
Harte Welle ('hardcore') department
of its Lonely Hearts classifieds
is legendary.

Websites

www.iloveberlin.de
Enthusiastic blog about all
things Berlin.
berlin.unlike.net
Frequently updated city guide
with reviews of all the latest bars
and clubs.
www.bangbangberlin.com
Full of features on Berlin fashion,
nightlife, clubs and music.

Television

Germany cabled up in the late
1970s, so there is no shortage of
channels. But television has never
been viewed as an art form. That
means programming revolves
around bland, mass market
entertainment, except for political
talk shows, which are pervasive,
but often very good.

At its worst, there are cheesy
'erotic' shows, vapid folk-music
programmes with studio audiences
that clap in time, and German
adaptations of reality TV and
casting shows such as *Big Brother*

DIRECTORY

and *Star Search*. Late-night TV, in particular, is chock-a-block with imported action series and European soft porn, interspersed with finger-sucking adverts for telephone sex numbers.

There are two national public networks, **ARD** and **ZDF**, a handful of no-holds-barred commercial channels, and a load of special-interest channels. ARD's daily *Tagesschau* at 8pm is the most authoritative news broadcast nationally.

N-tv is Germany's all-news cable channel, owned partly by CNN, but lacking the satellite broadcaster's ability to cover a breaking story. **TVBerlin** is the city's experiment with local commercial television but is still catching up with ARD's local affiliate **RBB** (a merger of Berlin and Brandenburg stations SFB and ORB), which covers local news with more insight.

RTL, **Pro 7** and **SAT.1** are privately owned services offering a predictable mix of Hollywood re-runs and imported series, plus their own sensational magazine programmes and sometimes surprisingly good TV movies.

Special interest channels run from **Kinderkanal** for kids to **Eurosport**, **MTV Europe** and its German-language competitors **Viva** and more offbeat **Onyx**, to **Arte**, an enlightened French-German cultural channel with high-quality films and documentaries.

Channels broadcasting regularly in English include **CNN**, **NBC**, **MTV Europe** and **BBC World**. British or American films on **ARD** or **ZDF** are sometimes broadcast with a simultaneous soundtrack in English for stereo-equipped TV sets.

Radio

Some 29 stations compete for audiences in Berlin, so even tiny shifts in market share have huge consequences for broadcasters. The race for ratings in the greater metropolitan area is thwarted by a clear split between the urban audience in both East and West and a rural one in the hinterland. The main four stations in the region have their audiences based in either **Berlin (Berliner Rundfunk**, 91.4; **r.s.2**, 94.3) or Brandenburg (**BB Radio**, 107.5; **Antenne Brandenburg**, 99.7). No single station is able to pull in everyone.

Commercial stations **104.6 RTL** (104.6), **Energy 103.4** (103.4) and **Hundert.6** (100.6) offer standard chart pop spiced with news.

RadioEins (95.8) is the most adventurous, playing mostly new and old indie music, while **Fritz** (102.6) plays things a little safer. Jazz is round the clock on **Jazz Radio** (101.9). Information-based stations such as **Info Radio** (93.1) are increasing in popularity. The **BBC World Service** (90.2) is available 24 hours a day.

MONEY

One euro (€) is made up of 100 cents. There are seven banknotes and eight coins. The notes are of differing colours and sizes (€5 is the smallest, €500 the largest) and each of their designs represent a different period of European architecture. They are: €5 (grey), €10 (red), €20 (blue), €50 (orange), €100 (green), €200 (yellow-brown), €500 (purple).

The eight denominations of coins vary in colour, size and thickness – but not enough to make them easy to tell apart. They share one common side; the other features a country-specific design (all can be used in any participating state). They are: €2, €1, 50 cents, 20 cents, 10 cents, 5 cents, 2 cents, 1 cent. At the time of going to press, the exchange rate was £1 = €1.15 and US$1 = €0.70.

ATMs

ATMs are found throughout the centre of Berlin, and are the most convenient way of obtaining cash. Most major credit cards are accepted, as well as debit cards that are part of the Cirrus, Plus, Star or Maestro systems. You will normally be charged a fee for withdrawing cash.

Banks & bureaux de change

Foreign currency and travellers' cheques can be exchanged in most banks. *Wechselstuben* (bureaux de change) are open outside normal banking hours and give better rates than banks, where changing money often involves long queues.

Reisebank AG

Zoo Station, Hardenbergplatz 1, Charlottenburg (881 7117, www.reisebank.de). U2, U9, S3, S5, S7, S75 Zoologischer Garten. **Open** 8am-21pm daily. **Map** p321/p328 G8.

The *Wechselstuben* of the Reisebank offer good exchange rates, and can be found at the bigger stations.

Other locations Bahnhof Friedrichstrasse, Mitte (2045 5096); Berlin Hauptbahnhof, Tiergarten (2045 3761); Ostbahnhof, Friedrichshain (296 4393).

Credit cards

Many Berliners prefer to use cash for most transactions, although larger hotels, shops and restaurants often accept major credit cards (American Express, Diners Club, MasterCard, Visa).

In general, German banking and retail systems are less enthusiastic about credit than their UK or US equivalents, though this is gradually changing.

If you want to draw cash on your credit card, some banks will give an advance against Visa and MasterCard cards. However, you may not be able to withdraw less than the equivalent of US$100. A better option is using an ATM.

Lost/stolen cards

If you've lost a credit card, or had one stolen, phone one of the 24-hour emergency numbers listed below.
American Express
0180 523 2377.
Diners Club
0180 5070 704
MasterCard/Visa
0697 933 1910.

Tax

Non-EU citizens can claim back German value-added tax (*Mehrwertsteuer* or *MwSt*) on goods purchased in the country (it's only worth the hassle on sizeable purchases). Ask to be issued with a Tax-Free Shopping Cheque for the amount of the refund and present this, with the receipt, at the airport's refund office before checking in bags.

OPENING HOURS

Most banks are open 9am to noon Monday to Friday, and 1pm to 3pm or 2pm to 6pm on varied weekdays.

Shops can stay open 6am-10pm, except on Sundays and holidays, though few take full advantage of the fact. Big stores tend to open at 9am and close 8pm-10pm. Most smaller shops will close around 6pm.

An increasing number of all-purpose neighbourhood shops (*Späti*) open around 5pm and close around midnight. Many Turkish shops are open on Saturday afternoons and on Sundays from 1pm to 5pm. Many bakers open to sell cakes on Sundays from 2pm to 4pm. Most 24-hour fuel stations and many internet cafés also sell basic groceries.

The opening times of bars vary, but many are open during the day, and most stay open until at least 1am, if not through until morning.

Most post offices are open 8am to 6pm Monday to Friday and 8am to 1pm on Saturdays.

POLICE STATIONS

You are unlikely to come in contact with the *Polizei*, unless you commit a crime or are the victim of one. There are few patrols or traffic checks.

The central police HQ is at Platz der Luftbrücke 6, Tempelhof (466 40), and there are local stations at: Kruppstrasse 2 Mitte; Charlottenburger Chausee 67, Charlottenburg; Friesenstrasse 16, Kreuzber; Eiswaldtstrasse 18, Schöneberg. But police will be dispatched from the appropriate office if you just dial 466 40.

For emergencies, dial **110**

POSTAL SERVICES

Most post offices (simply *Post* in German) are open from 8am to 6pm Monday to Friday, and 8am to 1pm Saturday.

For non-local mail, use the *Andere Richtungen* ('other destinations') slot in post-boxes. Letters of up to 20 grams (7oz) to anywhere in Germany and the EU need €0.55 in postage. Postcards require €0.45. For anywhere outside the EU, a 20-gram airmail letter costs €1.70, a postcard €1.

Postamt Friedrichstrasse

Georgenstrasse 12, Mitte (0180 233 33). U6, S1, S2, S5, S7, S9, S75 Friedrichstrasse. **Open** 6am-10pm Mon-Fri; 8am-10pm Sat, Sun. **Map** p318 M6.
Berlin has no main post office. However, this branch, which is to be found inside Friedrichstrasse station, keeps the longest opening hours of the Berlin offices.

Poste restante

Poste restante facilities are available at the main post offices of each district. Address them to the recipient 'Postlagernd,' followed by the address of the post office, or collect them from the counter marked Postlagernde Sendungen. Take your passport with you.

SAFETY & SECURITY

Though crime is increasing, Berlin remains a safe city by Western standards. Even for a woman, it's pretty safe to walk around alone at night in most central areas of the city. However, avoid the Eastern working-class suburbs if you look gay or non-German. Pickpockets are not unknown around tourist areas. Use some common sense and you're unlikely to get into trouble.

SMOKING

Many Berliners smoke, though the habit is in decline. Smoking is banned on public transport, in theatres and many public institutions. Many bars and restaurants have closed-off smoking rooms. Smaller, one-room establishments (under 75 square metres) may allow smoking if they want to, but must post a sign outside denoting a '*Raucher-Kneipe*' (smoker pub). There's no problem with smoking at outside tables – which means that even in winter there are now lots of places with outside tables.

STUDY

Germany's university system is currently in a state of flux. Under the Bologna Process (the EU's initiative to create a unified standard of education throughout Europe), the traditional Magister degree – which lasts between nine and 12 terms, during which time students can take a wide variety of courses – is being replaced by internationally recognised bachelors and masters degrees. Confusion reigns among lecturers and the gradual changeover has created a two-tiered system, with students on different courses at the same university receiving discrepant levels of education. Magister students are often favoured by employers because of the length and depth of the degree compared to the three-year bachelor.

Berlin retains its pull on scholars from across the world. There are currently almost 150,000 students in the city – approximately ten per cent of whom are foreigners – divided between four universities and 16 subject-specific colleges.

Language classes

Goethe-Institut

Neue Schönhauser Strasse 20, Mitte (259 063, www.goethe.de). U8 Weinmeisterstrasse or S3, *S5, S7,, S75 Hackescher Markt.* **Map** p319/p326 O5.
Although considerably more expensive than most of its competitors (a four-week course costs €1,040, or €1,470 with accommodation), the Goethe-Institut offers the most systematic and intensive language courses in the city. Enrolled students can benefit from extra-curricular conversation classes, as well as a Cultural Extension Programme that organises regular cinema, theatre and museum visits. Exams can be taken (with certificates awarded) at the end of every course.

Tandem

Bötzowstrasse 26, Prenzlauer Berg (441 3003, www.tandem-berlin.de). U2 Eberswalder Strasse. **Map** p319/p328 O3/P3.
For a single payment of €5 Tandem will put you in touch with two German speakers interested in conversation exchange. Formal language classes are also available at €540 a month.

Universities

Freie Universität Berlin

Central administration, Kaiserswerther Strasse 16-18, Dahlem (info 838 700 00, www. FU-Berlin.de). U3 Dahlem-Dorf.
Germany's largest university was founded in 1948, after the Humboldt fell under East German control. Centre of the 1969 student movement, the FU was for a long time a hotbed of romantic left-wing dissent. Sadly, though, not much of this idealism remains. Since the Wall came down the FU lost much of its prestige and influence to its fierce rival, the newly restructured Humboldt, and the vast, anonymous campus is embroiled in the same bureaucratic structures as any other modern (and German) university. The FU got one up on the Humboldt with its new 'elite university' status. The resulting €21 million a year for proposed new research projects is welcome in the strapped-for-cash capital.

Humboldt-Universität zu Berlin (HUB)

Unter den Linden 6, Mitte (20930, www.hu-berlin.de). U6, S1, S2, S3, S5, S7, , S75 Friedrichstrasse. **Map** p318-9/p327 N6/M6
Founded in 1810 by the humanist Willem von Humboldt, Hegel and Schopenhauer both taught there, Karl Marx was a student, and other

DIRECTORY

...ts have included the Albert Einstein, Werner ...nberg, Heinrich Heine and ...ax Planck. The HU entered a dark period in the 1930s, when Professors and students joined enthusiastically in the Nazi book-burning on Bebelplatz. After 1945 the university fell into decline under communism. Since 1989, the HU has regained much of its former reputation and a variety of new courses are being offered.

Technische Universität Berlin (TU)

Strasse des 17. Juni 135, Tiergarten (3140, www.TU-Berlin.de). U2 Ernst-Reuter-Platz. **Map** p321 F7.

The TU began life in 1879 and is strong in chemistry, engineering and architecture. In the 1930s the emphasis on development, business and construction made the TU a priority for the Nazi government, which allocated it more funds than any other university in the country. After the war, the TU was reopened under its current name and expanded to include philosophy, psychology and the social sciences. It is now (with some 30,000 students, 19 per cent of whom are foreigners) one of Germany's largest universities. A new library was recently built.

Sprach- und Kulturbörse an der TU Berlin

Raum 1503, Franklinstrasse 29, Charlottenburg (314 22730, www.skb.tu-berlin.de). U2 Ernst-Reuter-Platz. Map p317 F6.

The TU's Language and Cultural Exchange Programme for foreigners, the SKB, is open to students from any university in Berlin. It offers a range of services, including language courses and seminars on international issues.

Universität der Künste Berlin (UdK)

Hardenbergstrasse 33, Charlottenburg (318 50, www.udk-berlin.de). U2, U9, S3, S5, S7, S75 Zoologischer Garten. **Map** p321/ p328 F7.

Formerly the Hochschule der Künste (a name most Berliners still use), and founded in 1975 as a single vocational academy comprising the former Colleges of Art, Drama, Music and Printing. The range of subjects has been further broadened over the years, and courses are now offered in everything from Fashion Design to Experimental Film and Media. The

eclectic variety of artistic and academic disciplines, along with the appointments of some high-profile teachers, have secured the UdK a well-deserved reputation as one of the best establishments of its kind in Europe.

Useful organisations

Studentenwerk Berlin

Behrenstrasse 40-41, Mitte (939 3970, www.studentenwerk-berlin.de). U6 Französische Strasse. **Open** *InfoPoint* 8am-4pm Mon-Wed, Fri; 10am-6pm Thur. **Map** p321/p328 F7.

The central organisation for students in Berlin will give advice and provide information about accommodation, finance, employment and various other essentials.

Other Locations *InfoPoints* Hardenbergstrasse 34, Charlottenburg; Otto-von Simson-Strasse 26, Dahlem.

TELEPHONES

All phone numbers in this guide are local Berlin numbers (other than those in the Escapes & Excursions chapter). However, readers should note that numbers beginning with 0180 have higher tariffs, and numbers beginning 016 or 017 are mobiles. To call a Berlin number from outside the city, *see below*.

Dialling & codes

To phone Berlin from abroad, dial the international access code (00 from the UK, 011 from the US, 0011 from Australia), then 49 (for Germany) and 30 (for Berlin), followed by the local number.

To phone another country from Germany dial 00, then the appropriate country code:

Australia 61;
Canada 1;
Ireland 353;
New Zealand 64;
United Kingdom 44;
United States 1.

Then, dial the local area code (minus the initial zero) and the local number.

To call Berlin from elsewhere in Germany, dial 030 and then the local number.

Making a call

Calls within Berlin between the hours of 9am and 6pm cost €0.10 per minute. Numbers prefixed 0180 are charged at €0.14 per minute.

A call from Berlin to the United Kingdom or Ireland costs €0.13 per minute, to the US and Canada €0.13 per minute and to Australia €0.79 per minute.

Both local and international calls can be a lot cheaper if you simply dial a prefix before the international code. There are various numbers and they change from time to time. Look in local newspapers or visit www.tariftip.de.

Public phones

Most public phones give you the option of cards or coins, and from Telekom phones (the ones with the magenta 'T') you also can send SMSs. Phonecards can be bought at post offices and in newsagents for various sums from €5 to €50.

Operator services

For online directory enquiries, go to www.teleauskunft.de.

International directory enquiries
11834.
Operator assistance/German directory enquiries
11833 (11837 in English).
Phone repairs/ Störungsannahme
080 0330 2000.
Time (Zeitansage)
0180 4 100 100 (automated, in German).

Mobile phones

German mobile phones networks operate at 900MHz, so all UK and Australian mobiles should work in Berlin (so long as roaming has been activated in advance). US and Canadian cell phones users (whose phones operate at 1,900MHz) should check whether their phones can switch to 900MHz. If they can't, you can rent a 'Handy', as the Germans call them, via www.edikom-online.com. They'll deliver to your hotel and pick it back up from there when you're going.

TIME

Germany is on Central European Time – one hour ahead of Greenwich Mean Time.

When summer time is in effect, London is one hour behind Berlin, New York is six hours behind, San Francisco is nine hours behind, and Sydney is nine hours ahead.

Germany uses a 24-hour system. 8am is '8 Uhr' (usually written 8h),

DIRECTORY

noon is '*12 Uhr Mittags*' or just '*12 Uhr*', 5pm is '*17 Uhr*' and midnight is '*12 Uhr Mitternachts*' or just "*Mitternacht*'. 8.15 is '*8 Uhr 15*' or '*Viertel nach 8*'; 8.30 is '*8 Uhr 30*' or '*halb 9*'; and 8.45 is '*8 Uhr 45*' or '*Viertel vor 9*'.

TIPPING

A 10 per cent service charge will already be part of your restaurant bill, but it's common to leave a small tip too. In a taxi round up the bill to the nearest euro.

TOILETS

Coin-operated, self-cleaning 'City Toilets' are becoming the norm. The toilets in main stations are looked after by an attendant and are pretty clean. Restaurants and cafés have to let you use their toilets by law and legally they can't refuse you a glass of water either.

TOURIST INFORMATION

BerlinHauptbahnhof
Europa-Center, Budapester Strasse, Charlottenburg (250 025/0). U2, U9, S3, S5, S7, S75 Zoologischer Garten. **Open** 10am-7pm Mon-Fri; 10am-6pm Sat, Sun. **Map** p321 G8. Berlin's official (if private) tourist organisation. The Brandenburg Gate branch is open 10am-6pm daily.

EurAide
DB Reisezentrum, Hauptbahnhof, Tiergarten (www.euraide.de). S5, S7, S9, S75 Hauptbahnhof. **Open** May-Aug 10am-7pm daily. *Sept-Dec, mid Feb-Apr* 11am-6pm Mon-Fri. **Map** p318 K5. Staff advise on sights, hostels, tours and transport, and sell rail tickets.

VISAS & IMMIGRATION

A passport valid for three months beyond the length of stay is all that is required for UK, EU, US, Canadian and Australian citizens for a stay in Germany of up to three months. Citizens of EU countries with valid national ID cards need only show their ID cards. Citizens of other countries should check with their local German embassy or consulate whether a visa is required. As with any trip, confirm visa requirements well before you plan to travel.

Residence permits

For stays of longer than three months, you'll need a residence

permit. EU citizens, and those of Andorra, Australia, Canada, Cyprus, Israel, Japan, Malta, New Zealand and the US can obtain one by doing the following.

First you need to register at your local *Anmeldungsamt*. There is one in the Bürgeramt of every district. A list can be found at www.berlin.de/buergerberatung. You don't need an appointment, but expect to wait. Bring your passport and proof of a Berlin address. You'll be issued with an *Anmeldungsbestätigung* – a form confirming you have registered at the *Anmeldungsamt*.

At this point, take your *Anmeldungsbestätigung* to the Landesamt für Bürger und Ordnungsangelegenheiten Ausländerbehörde in the Moabit district of Tiergarten. Also bring your passport, two passport photos and something to read. There are always huge queues and it takes forever – people start queuing hours before the office opens – but all you can do is take a number and wait. Eventually you will be issued with an *Aufenthaltserlaubnis* – a residence permit. If you have a work contract, bring it – you may be granted a longer stay.

If you're unsure about your status, contact the German Embassy in your country of origin, or your own embassy or consulate in Berlin (*see p292*).

Landesamt für Bürger und Ordnungsangelegenheiten Ausländerbehörde
Friedrich-Krause-Ufer 24, Tiergarten (info 90269 0, www.berlin.de/labo/auslaender/ dienstleistungen). S41, S42, S45, S46, S47 Westhafen. **Open** 7am-2pm Mon, Tue; 7am-6am Thur (or by appointment via email). **Map** p317 H3

WHEN TO GO

Berlin has a continental climate, hot in summer and cold in winter. In January and February Berlin often ices over. Spring begins in late March/April. May and June are the most beautiful months.

Public holidays

On public holidays (*Feiertagen*) it can be difficult to get things done in Berlin. However, most cafés, bars and restaurants stay open – except on the evening of 24 December, when almost everything closes.

Public holidays are: **New Year's Day** (1 Jan); **Good Friday** (Mar/Apr); **Easter Monday** (Mar/Apr); **May/Labour Day** (1 May); **Ascension Day** (May/June; ten days before Whitsun/Pentacost, the 7th Sun after Easter); **Whit/Pentacost Monday** (May/June); **Day of German Unity** (3 Oct); **Day of Prayer and National Repentance** (3rd Wed in Nov); **Christmas Eve** (24 Dec); **Christmas Day** (25 Dec); **Boxing Day** (26 Dec).

WOMEN

See also p293 **Helplines** and *p291* **Health**.

Women's centres

EWA Frauenzentrum
Prenzlauer Allee 6, Prenzlauer Berg (442 5542, www.ewa-frauenzentrum.de). U2 Senefelderplatz. **Open** 11am-11pm Mon-Thur, Fri; varies Sat. **Map** p319 P4.

WORKING IN BERLIN

The small ads in the magazines *Zitty, tip* (*see p295*) and *Zweite Hand* are good places to look for work. Teaching English is popular: there is always a demand for native English speakers.

If you're studying in Berlin, try the Studenten Vermittlung Arbeitsamt (Student Job Service). You'll need your passport, student card and a *Lohnsteuerkarte* (tax card), available from your local *Finanzamt* (tax office – listed in the *Gelbe Seiten*). Tax is reclaimable. Students looking for summer work can contact the Zentralstelle für Arbeitsvermittlung.

The German equivalent of the British Job Centre is the *Arbeitsamt* (Employment Service). There are very few private agencies. To find the address of your nearest office in Germany, look online or in the *Gelbe Seiten* under *Arbeitsämter*.

EU nationals have the right to live and work in Germany without a work permit.

Studenten Vermittlung Arbeitsamt
Hardenbergstrasse 34, Charlottenburg (93939-9033 , www.studentenwerk-berlin.de). U2 Ernst-Reuter-Platz. **Open** 8am-6pm Mon-Fri. **Map** p321/p328 F7. **Other locations** Thielallee 38, Dahlem.

Vocabulary

PRONUNCIATION

z – pronounced ts
w – like English v
v – like English f
s – like English z, but softer
r – like a throaty French r
a – as in father
e – sometimes as in bed,
sometimes as in day
i – as in seek
o – as in note
u – as in loot
ch – as in Scottish loch
ä – combination of a and e, like
ai in paid or like e in set
ö – combination of o and e,
as in French eu
ü – combination of u and e,
like true
ai – like pie
au – like house
ie – like free
ee – like hey
ei – like fine
eu – like coil

USEFUL PHRASES

Greetings

hello/good day – guten Tag
goodbye – auf Wiedersehen
goodbye (informal) – tschüss
good morning – guten Morgen
good evening – guten Abend
good night – gute Nacht

Basic words & requests

yes – ja; (emphatic) jawohl
no – nein, nee
maybe – vielleicht
please – bitte
thank you – danke
thank you very much –
danke schön
excuse me – entschuldigen
Sie mir bitte
sorry! – Verzeihung!
I'm sorry, I don't speak
German – Entschuldigung, ich
spreche kein Deutsch
do you speak English? –
sprechen Sie Englisch?
can you please speak
more slowly? –
können Sie bitte langsamer
sprechen?
my name is… – ich heisse…
I would like… – ich möchte…
how much is… ? –
wieviel kostet… ?

can I have a receipt? –
darf ich bitte eine Quittung
haben?
can you call me a cab? –
können Sie bitte mir
ein Taxi rufen?
open/closed – geöffnet/
geschlossen
with/without – mit/ohne
cheap/expensive –
billig/teuer
big/small – gross/klein
entrance/exit – Eingang/
Ausgang
cashier/ticket office/
box office – die Kasse
currency exchange –
der Geldwechsel
bureau de change –
die Wechselstube
help! – Hilfe!

Directions

left – links
right – rechts
straight ahead –
gerade aus
far – weit
near – nah
street – die Strasse
square – der Platz
city map – der Stadtplan
how do I get to… ? – wie
komme ich nach… ?
how far is it to… ? –
wie weit ist es nach… ?
where is… ? – wo ist… ?

Travel

arrival/departure –
Ankunft/Abfahrt
airport – der Flughafen
railway station – der Bahnhof
ticket – die Fahrkarte,
der Fahrschein
airline ticket – die Flugkarte, der
Flugschein
passport – der Reisepass
petrol – das Benzin
lead-free – bleifrei
traffic – der Vehrkehr

Health

I feel ill – ich bin krank
doctor – der Arzt
dentist – der Zahnarzt
pharmacy – die Apotheke
hospital – das Krankenhaus
I need a doctor – ich brauche
einen Arzt

please call an ambulance –
rufen Sie bitte ein Krankenwagen
please call the police – rufen Sie
bitte die Polizei

NUMBERS

0 null; 1 eins; 2 zwei; 3 drei;
4 vier; 5 fünf; 6 sechs; 7 sieben;
8 acht; 9 neun; 10 zehn; 11 elf;
12 zwölf; 13 dreizehn; 14
vierzehn; 15 fünfzehn; 16
sechszehn; 17 siebzehn; 18
achtzehn; 19 neunzehn; 20
zwanzig; 21 einundzwanzig;
22 zweiundzwanzig; 30
dreissig; 40 vierzig; 50
fünfzig; 60 sechzig; 70
siebzig; 80 achtzig; 90 neunzig;
100 hundert; 101 hunderteins;
110 hundertzehn; 200
zweihundert; 201 zweihunderteins;
1,000 tausend; 2,000
zweitausend

DAYS & TIMES OF DAY

Monday – der Montag
Tuesday – der Dienstag
Wednesday – der Mittwoch
Thursday – der Donnerstag
Friday – der Freitag
Saturday – der Samstag
der Sonnabend
Sunday der Sonntag

Morning – der Morgen
Noon – der Mittag
Afternoon – der Nachmittag
Evening – der Abend
Night – die Nacht
Today – Heute
Yesterday – Gestern
Tomorrow – Morgen

EVERYDAY IDIOMS

ich verstehe nur Bahnhof –
I understand only station
(I didn't catch a single word)
Schwein/Pech haben –
to have pig/pitch (to be lucky/
unlucky)
bleib auf dem Teppich –
stay on the carpet (keep
your cool)
mein lieber Herr
Gesangsverein! –
my dear Mr Singing Club!
(I am surprised!)
mir ist wurst –
it's all sausage to me
(I couldn't care less)

Further Reference

BOOKS

We've chosen for quality and interest as much as availability. Most are in print, but some will only be found in libraries or second-hand. Date is that of first publication in English.

Fiction

Baum, Vicki
Berlin Hotel (London 1946)
Written in 1944, this pulp thriller anticipates the horror of the collapsing Reich via the story of a German resistance fighter trapped in a hotel with a lurid cast of Nazi bigwigs.
Deighton, Len *Berlin Game, Mexico Set, London Match* (London 1983, 1984, 1985)
Epic espionage trilogy with labyrinthine plot set against an accurate picture of 1980s Berlin. The next six books aren't bad either.
Döblin, Alfred
Berlin-Alexanderplatz (London 1975)
Devastating expressionist portrait of the inter-war underworld in the working class quarters of Alexanderplatz.
Eckhart, Gabriele *Hitchhiking* (Lincoln, Nebraska 1992)
Short stories viewing East Berlin through the eyes of street cleaners and a female construction worker.
Grass, Gunther
Local Anaesthetic (New York 1970)
The angst of a schoolboy threatening to burn a dog in the Ku'damm to protest the Vietnam War is firmly satirised, albeit in Grass's irritating schoolmasterly way.
Harris, Robert
Fatherland (London 1992)
Alternative history and detective novel set in a 1964 Berlin as the Nazis might have built it.
Isherwood, Christopher
Mr Norris Changes Trains, Goodbye To Berlin (London 1935, 1939)
Isherwood's two Berlin novels, the basis of the movie Cabaret, offer finely drawn characters and a sharp picture of the city as it tipped over into Nazism.
Johnson, Uwe
Two Views (New York 1966)
Love story across the East-West divide, strong on the mood of Berlin in the late 1950s and early 1960s.
Kaminer, Wladimir
Russian Disco (London 2002)

Best-selling collection of short tales from Russian emigre and DJ.
Kerr, Philip
Berlin Noir (London 1994)
The Bernie Gunther trilogy, about a private detective in Nazi Berlin.
McEwan, Ian
The Innocent (London 1990)
A naive young Englishman is recruited into Cold War plotting with tragi-comic results.
Nabokov, Vladimir *The Gift* (New York 1963)
Written and set in 1920s Berlin, where impoverished Russian émigré dreams of writing a book very like this one.
Porter, Henry
Brandenburg (London 2005)
Decent fall-of-the-Wall spy thriller, even if the author does get some of the street names wrong.
Regener, Sven
Berlin Blues (London 2003)
Irresponsibility and childhood's end in the bars of late 1980s Kreuzberg – a western version of ostalgic thinking.
Ryan, Robert
Dying Day (London, 2007)
Readable espionage thriller with the Berlin Airlift as backdrop.
Schneider, Peter
The Wall Jumper (London 1984)
Somewhere between novel, prose poem and artful reportage, a meditation on the absurdities of the Wall.

Children

Kästner, Erich *Emil and the Detectives* (London 1931)
Classic set mostly around Bahnhof Zoo and Nollendorfplatz.

Biography & memoir

Anonymous *A Woman in Berlin* (New York, 1954)
Extraordinary diary of a woman fighting to survive at the end of World War II in the ruins of Berlin.
Bielenberg, Christabel
The Past Is Myself (London 1968)
Fascinating autobiography of an English woman who married a German lawyer and lived through World War II in Berlin.
Funder, Anna
Stasiland (London 2003)
Brutal stories of individuals and the East German state,

reconstructed through the author's conversations with friends..
Newton, Helmut *Autobiography* (London 2003)
Begins with an absorbing account of growing up Jewish in Weimar Berlin, and Newton's apprenticeship with fashion photographer Yva.
Parker, Peter *Isherwood* (London, 2004)
Enormous biography includes a well-researched section on the author's Berlin trouble.
Rimmer, Dave *Once Upon A Time In The East* (London 1992)
The collapse of communism seen stoned and from street level – tales of games between East and West Berlin and travels through assorted East European revolutions.
Schirer, William L
Berlin Diaries (New York 1941)
Foreign correspondent in Berlin 1931-1941 bears appalled witness to Europe's plunge into Armageddon.

History

Beevor, Antony *Berlin: The Downfall 1945* (London, 2002)
Bestselling narrative history of the Third Reich's final, desperate collapse.
Friedrich, Otto
Before The Deluge (New York, 1972)
Vivid portrait of 1920s Berlin, based on interviews with those who survived what followed.
Gaines, James *Evening in the Palace of Reason* (London 2005)
Fascinating essay on music, politics and the Enlightenment built around the 1747 Potsdam encounter of Bach and Frederick the Great.
Garton Ash, Timothy
We The People (London 1990)
Instant history of the 1989 revolutions by on-the-spot academic.
Kellerhoff, Sven Felix
The Führer Bunker (Berlin 2004)
The bare facts about Hitler's last refuge and what became of it.
Levenson, Thomas
Einstein in Berlin (New York 2003)
Absorbing account of the historical deal between physicist and city.
Metzger, Rainer
Berlin in the 20s (London 2007)
A wonderful pictorial record – photos, posters, paintings – of Berlin's most creative era.

DIRECTORY

Read, Anthony and **Fisher, David** *Berlin – The Biography Of A City* (London 1994)
Readable, lightweight history.
Richie, Alexandra *Faust's Metropolis* (London 1998)
Best one-volume history of Berlin.
Taylor, Frederick *The Berlin Wall* (London 2006)
Now the definitive history of the notorious border. Taylor's book on Dresden is well worth a read, too.

Architecture

Ladd, Brian *The Ghosts Of Berlin: Confronting German History In The Urban Landscape* (Chicago, 1997)
Erudite and insightful look into the relationship between architecture, urbanism and Berlin's violent political history.

FILM

Cabaret (Bob Fosse, 1972)
Liza Minelli as Sally Bowles, the very definition of the Berlin myth.
Christiane F. (Uli Edel, 1981)
To hell and back in the housing estates and heroin scene of late 1970s West Berlin, with Bowie soundtrack.
A Foreign Affair (Billy Wilder, 1948)
Marlene Dietrich sings 'Black Market' among the romantically rendered ruins of post-war Berlin.
Funeral In Berlin (Guy Hamilton, 1966)
Adaptation of Len Deighton's novel: Michael Caine in entertaining, puzzling Cold War yarn.
Good bye, Lenin! (Wolfgang Becker, 2003)
Ostalgia, the movie – a comic eulogy for the GDR, in which socialism gets a different kind of send-off.
The Good German (Steven Soderbergh, 2006)
Clooney and Blanchett are old flames in a black and white pastiche of Wilder and Reed set in a cynical 1945.
It's Not The Homosexual Who Is Perverse But The Situation In Which He Lives (Rosa von Praunheim, 1973)
The best of the flamboyant von Praunheim's films, a laundry list of the follies of Berlin's gay population.
The Legend of Paul And Paula (Heiner Carow, 1974)
Cult GDR love story banned by the unromantic regime. Soundtrack by the also legendary Pudhys.
The Lives of Others (Florian Henckel von Donnersmarck, 2006)

Stasi agent watches writer and silently changes sides in this award-winning thriller
M (Fritz Lang, 1931)
Paedophilia and vigilantism as Peter Lorre's child murderer stalks an expressionistic Weimar Berlin.
The Man Between (Carol Reed, 1953)
James Mason stars in the *The Third Man's* Berlin cousin.
Olympia (Leni Riefenstahl, 1937)
In filming the 1936 Olympics, the Nazis' favourite director invented the conventions of modern sportscasting.
One, Two, Three (Billy Wilder, 1961)
James Cagney is brilliant as the Pepsi exec whose daughter falls for East Berlin Communist Horst Buchholz.
Possession (Andrzej Zulawski, 1981)
Sam Neil and Isabel Adjani star in cult psychosexual horror flick which uses its West Berlin backdrop to compellingly weird effect.
The Spy Who Came In From The Cold (Martin Ritt, 1965)
Intense atmosphere, excellent Richard Burton performance, and an ending that shatteringly brings home the obscenity of the Wall.
Westler (Wieland Speck, 1985)
Low-budget gay romance between West and East Berliners and all you need know about the Wall in one checkpoint strip-search scene.
Wings of Desire (Wim Wenders, 1987)
Bruno Ganz in love, Peter Falk in a bunker, Nick Cave in concert, and an angel on the Siegessäule – Wenders has never surpassed his (double) vision of the divided city.

MUSIC

AG Geige *Raabe?* (Zensor)
One of the first post-1989 discs to emerge from the East Berlin underground came from a bizarre electronica outfit rooted in The Residents and Die Tödliche Doris.
Ash Ra Tempel *Join Inn* (Temple/Spalax)
The 1972 hippy freakout incarnation of guitarist Manuel Göttsching, before he was reborn as techno's most baffling muse.
Meret Becker *Noctambule* (Ego)
Actress/chanteuse Becker restages Weimar alongside Berliner Krankheit classics like Neubauten's Schwarz.
The Birthday Party *Mutiny/The Bad Seed EP* (4AD)
Nick Cave and cohorts escaped to early 1980s Berlin to record their

two most intense EPs, here compressed into one volatile CD.
David Bowie *Heroes* (EMI)
In which Bowie romanticises the Wall and captures the atmosphere of (misspelt) Neuköln.
David Bowie *Low* (EMI)
Begun in France, completed at Hansa Studios, the album that soundtracked Bowie's new career in a new town.
Caspar Brötzmann/FM Einheit *Merry Christmas* (Blast First/ Rough Trade Deutschland)
Guitarist son Caspar is no less noisy than père Brötzmann, especially on this frenzy of feedback and distortion kicked up with ex-Neubauten man-mountain FM Einheit on, er, stones.
Peter Brötzmann *No Nothing* (FMP)
Uncharacteristically introspective recording from the sax colossus of German improvisation for Berlin's vital Free Music Production label, which he co-founded 30 years ago.
Ernst Busch *Der Rote Orpheus/Der Barrikaden Tauber* (BARBArossa)
Two-CD survey of the revolutionary tenor's 1930s recordings covers Brecht, Eisler and Weill.
Nick Cave *From Her To Eternity* (Mute)
Cave in best Berlinerisch debauched and desperate mode, with a title track later featured in *Wings of Desire*.
Comedian Harmonists *Ihre grossen Erfolge* (Laserlight)
Sublime six-part harmonies from the Weimar sensations whose career was cut short during the Third Reich.
Crime & The City Solution *Paradise Discotheque* (Mute)
Underrated Berlin-Australian group's finest disc (1990) is an oblique commentary on the heady 'neo-black market burnt-out ruins' amorality of the immediate post-1989 era.
DAF *Kebabträume* (Mute)
Exhilarating German punk satire of Berlin's Cold War neuroses, culminating in the coda 'We are the Turks of tomorrow'.
Marlene Dietrich *On Screen, Stage And Radio* (Legend)
From 'I Am The Sexy Lola' through to 'Ruins Of Berlin', the sultry Schöneberg songstress embodies the mood of decadent Berlin.
Einstürzende Neubauten *Berlin Babylon Soundtrack* (Zomba)
More Neubauten 'Strategies Against Architecture' accompanying a highly watchable

documentary about the changes in Berlin's landscape and the movers and shakers behind them.

Alec Empire *The Geist Of…* (Geist)
Wonderful triple CD compilation of ATR mainman Empire's less combative electronica explorations for Frankfurt brainiac label Force Inc/Mille Plateaux.

Manuel Göttsching *E2-E4* (Racket)
Great lost waveform guitar album by ex-Ash Ra Tempel leader.

Malaria! *Compiled* (Moabit Musik)
With suffocating synth swirls, heavy-stepping beats and songs like 'Passion' and 'Death', Malaria! was '80s girl-pop, Berlin-style.

Maurizio *M* (M)
Essential CD compilation of Basic Channel mainman Moritz Von Oswald's vinyl releases, which lights up Chicago house with streaming beats diverted from the Berlin-Detroit techno grid.

Modeselektor *Happy Birthday* (Bpitch Con)
Out on Berlin techno's leftfield, idiosyncratic duo are joined on second mischievious album by guests such as Thom Yorke and Maximo Park.

Monolake *Hongkong Remastered* (Monolake)
Robert Hencke's post-techno pulses in some vast acoustic space, creating a cityscape ambience with urban samples.

Barbara Morgenstern *Vermona ET-61* (Monika)
Morgenstern's everywoman voice, simple lyrics and clever accompaniment on a GDR home organ grow after repeated listenings, but the achingly beautiful instrumentals are the true highlights.

Iggy Pop *The Idiot* (Virgin America)
With Bowie in the producer's chair, Iggy begins to absorb the influence of early German electronica and the city of bright, white clubbing.

Iggy Pop *Lust For Life* (Virgin America)
Way back in West Berlin, Iggy the passenger cruises through the divided city's ripped-back sides and finds himself full of lust for life.

Rhythm & Sound w/ the artists (Indigo)
Techno meets reggae at the mixing desk of Mark Ernestus and Moritz von Oswald. Eight singles (and vocalists) compiled on this and companion b-side CD, the versions.

Stereo Total *My Melody* (Bungalow)
Demented chansons with cheesy lounge backing – Mitte's kitsch aesthetic plus a Francophone spin.

Tangerine Dream *Zeit* (Jive Electro)
Where cosmic consciousness and electronic minimalism first met by the Wall.

Ton Steine Scherben *Keine Macht Für Niemand* (David Volksmund)
Ernst Busch reincarnated as the early 1970s rock commune which provided Kreuzberg's anarchists with their most enduring anthems.

U2 *Achtung Baby!* (Island)
It took Zoo station and post-Wall Berlin to inspire the U2 album for people who don't like U2.

Christian van Dorries *Wagnerkomplex* (Masse und Macht)
Spooky examination of 'music and German national identity' carried out in the shell of the Palast der Republik using live and recorded orchestral and techno elements, electronic treatments and the building's acoustics.

Various *Das Beste Aus Der DDR Parts I-III* (Amiga)
Three-part DDR rock retrospective, divided into rock, pop and 'Kult', including Ostalgia stalwarts like Puhdys, Silly and Karat plus Sandow's alt anthem 'Born in the GDR' and an early Nina Hagen ditty.

Various *Berlin 1992* (Tresor)
On the first of several Tresor compilations, Berlin techno is captured in its early, apocalyptic phase. Includes Love Parade anthem 'Der Klang der Familie' by 3Phase (at that time, Dr Motte & Sven Röhrig).

Various *Berlin Super 80* (Monitorpop)
CD/DVD/book set documenting the West Berlin underground 1978-83. Features all the usual musical suspects, plus scratchy Super 8 celluloid from Jörg (Nekromantic) Buttgereit, among many others.

Various *Die Grosse Untergangshow: Festival Genialer Dillentanten* (Vinyl-On-Demand)
Double LP/CD and DVD set from the 1981 Tempodrom show that launched the likes of Neubauten, Gudrun Gut, Die Tödliche Doris, Mark Reeder.

Various *Hotel-Stadt-Berlin* (Hausmusik/Kompakt/Indigo)
Label showcase bodes well for the future, with local electronica musicians exploring paths off the beaten track of techno and trance.

Various *Pop 2000* (Grönland/Spiegel Edition)
Eight-CD companion to TV chronicle of postwar German culture in East and West. 'Ostrock'

is under-represented, but otherwise an engaging compilation of the obvious and the obscure.

Various *Russensoul* (Trikont)
Wladimir Kaminer and Yuriy Gurzhy's survey of Russian and east European emigré musical activity in Berlin, with the likes of Leonid Soybelman, Volga Volga and Rotfront, as viewed from their Kaffee Burger DJ console.

Various *Tranceformed From Beyond* (MFS)
Compilation that defined Berlin trance. Selection includes Cosmic Baby, Microglobe, Effective Force.

Westbam *A Practising Maniac At Work* (Low Spirit)
Summarises the peak of Berlin's best-known DJ, veering from stomping techno to twisted disco.

WEBSITES

Alt-Berliner Stadtplan-Archiv *www.alt-berlin.info*
Archive of searchable historic Berlin maps, from 1738 to 1989.

Berlin Info *www.berlin-info.de*
Essentially a hotel booking site, but also contains information for visitors and lots of links. Operated by the official tourist board BTM and oriented to upmarket tourism.

Berlin.de *www.berlin.de*
Berlin's official site – run by the tourist board (BTM) – is inevitably not its most objective but is nonetheless well written.

BVG *www.bvg.de*
Online timetable and public transport information for Berlin/Brandenburg, in English and German. Includes a searchable version of the BVG atlas.

Leo Dictionary *http://dict.leo.org*
Simply the best English-German online dictionary.

Ost-Berlin *www.ostberlin.de*
Everything you wanted to know about life in the former East Berlin, Hauptstadt der DDR.

SMB *www.smb.museum*
Smart bilingual site with detailed information on around 20 major Berlin museums run by the Staatlichen Museen zu Berlin.

Time Out *www.timeout.com/travel/berlin*
General information and history, plus shop, restaurant, café, bar and hotel reviews, written by residents.

Tip *www.tip-berlin.de*
Zitty's competition, offering similar German-only listings and search functions.

Zitty *www.zitty.de*
The online sister of one of Berlin's two listings fortnightlies. In German only.

DIRECTORY

Content Index

INDEX

Venue Index

INDEX

INDEX

INDEX

Advertisers' Index

Please refer to the relevant pages for contact details.

Maps

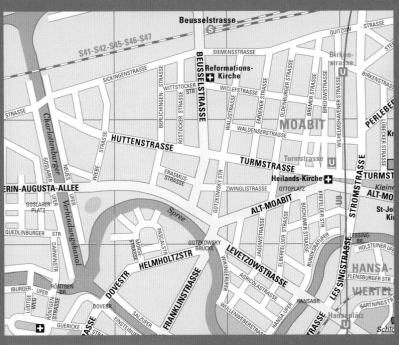

Legend	
Place of interest and/or entertainment	▮
Railway station	▮
Park	▮
Hospital/university	▮
Pedestrian Area	▮
Autobahn	═
Main road	
Airport	✈
Church	✚
S-Bahn Station	Ⓢ
U-Bahn Station	Ⓤ
S-Bahn line	S1
U-Bahn line	U1
District boundary	
Course of Wall	▬
Area	MITTE

Berlin & Around

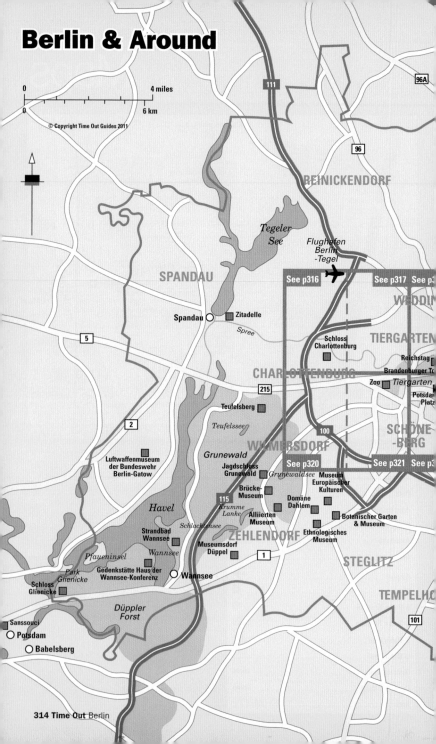

0 ——— 4 miles

0 ——— 6 km

© Copyright Time Out Guides 2011

111

96A

96

Tegeler See

REINICKENDORF

Flughafen
Berlin
-Tegel

SPANDAU

See p316 See p317 See p3

WEDDIN

Spandau ○ ■ Zitadelle

Spree

Schloss
Charlottenburg ■

TIERGARTEN

5

CHARLOTTENBURG

Reichstag ■
Brandenburger To

215

Zoo ■ *Tiergarten* ■

Potsdar
Platz ■

2

Teufelsberg ■

Teufelssee

WILMERSDORF

100

SCHÖNE -BERG

Grunewald

Luftwaffenmuseum
der Bundeswehr
Berlin-Gatow ■

See p320 See p321 See p3

Jagdschloss
Grunewald ■

Grunewaldsee

Museum
Europäischer
Kulturen ■

Havel

115

Brücke-
Museum ■

*Krumme
Lanke*

Domäne
Dahlem ■

Botanischer Garten
& Museum ■

Schlachtensee

Alliierten
Museum ■

Ethnologisches
Museum ■

Strandbad
Wannsee ■

ZEHLENDORF

STEGLITZ

Museumsdorf
Düppel ■

1

Pfaueninsel

Wannsee

*Park
Glienicke*

Gedenkstätte Haus der
Wannsee-Konferenz ■

○ **Wannsee**

TEMPELHO

Schloss
Glienicke ■

*Düppler
Forst*

101

Sanssouci ■

○ **Potsdam**

○ **Babelsberg**

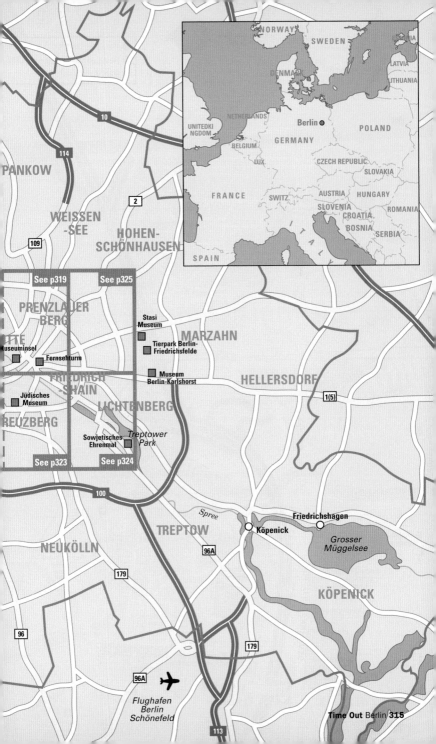

PANKOW

WEISSEN
-SEE

109

HOHEN-
SCHÖNHAUSEN

2

10

114

NORWAY

SWEDEN

DENMARK

LATVIA

LITHUANIA

NETHERLANDS

UNITEDKI
NGDOM

Berlin

POLAND

BELGIUM

GERMANY

LUX.

CZECH REPUBLIC

SLOVAKIA

FRANCE

SWITZ.

AUSTRIA

HUNGARY

SLOVENIA

ROMANIA

CROATIA

BOSNIA

SERBIA

SPAIN

ITALY

See p319   See p325

PRENZLAUER
BERG

Stasi
Museum

MARZAHN

ITTE

Museuminsel

Fernsehturm

Tierpark Berlin-
Friedrichsfelde

HELLERSDORF

FRIEDRICH
-SHAIN

Museum
Berlin-Karlshorst

1(5)

Jüdisches
Museum

LICHTENBERG

REUZBERG

Sowjetisches
Ehrenmal

Treptower
Park

See p323   See p324

100

Spree

Friedrichshagen

TREPTOW

Köpenick

Grosser
Müggelsee

96A

NEUKÖLLN

179

KÖPENICK

96

179

96A

113

Flughafen
Berlin
Schönefeld

A

B

C

D

0   800 m

0   800 yds

© Copyright Time Out Group 2011

Flughafen Berlin -Tegel

1

SINGDROSSELSTEIG

Hohenzollernkanal

SAATWINKLER DAMM

HINCKELDEY -BR

SAATWINKLER DA

2

Volkspark Jungfernheide

Jungfern heide

Werner-von- Siemens Park

Jungfern- heideteich

SCHUCKERTDAMM

HECKERDAMM

QUELLWEG

GOEBEL- STRASSE

HALEMWEG

KURT-SCHUMACHER DAMM

KURT-SCHUMACHER DAMM

REICHWEINDAMM

HECKERDAMM

GRENZWEG

3

JUGEND PLATZ JUGENDWEG

TOEPFERSTRASSE

U7

Halemweg

Jakob- Kaiser-Pl.

POPITZWEG

Siemens- damm

SIEMENSDAMM

SIEMENSSTADT

HELLMANNRING

JAKOB- KAISER- PLATZ

WERNERWERKDAMM

4

ROHRDAMM

Jungfern -heide

Jungfern -heide

Gustav-Adolf Kirche

OLBERSSTRASSE

LISE-MEITNER-STRASSE

5

Sportplätze Westend

CHARLOTTENBURG

BRAHE-

KAMMINER STR.

KEPLERSTRASSE

Maria- Himmelfahrt Kirche

Mierendorff PLATZ

Merendor

Kaiser-Wilhelm Gedächtnis Kirchhof

FÜRSTENBRUNNER WEG

Max-Bürger Zentrum

Karpfen -teich

OSNABRÜCKER STRASSE

MINDENER STRASSE

TEGELER WEG

NORDHAL STRASS

Luisenkirchhof III

E26

HEUBNERWEG

SOPHIE-CHARLOTTEN-STRASSE

Schloss- garten

MIERENDORFFSTR

SOMMERINGSTRASSE

WINTERSTEINSTR.

U7

6

SPANDAUER DAMM

ESCHENALLEE

AKAZIENALLEE

DRK-Kliniken Westend

S41·S42·S45·S46·S47

Schloss Charlottenburg

Museum für Vor- und Fruhgeschichte

Sammlung Berggruen

SCHLOSSBR.

CHARLOTTENBGR UFER

CAPRIVIBR.

EOSANDERSTR

OTTO-SUHR-ALLEE

Richa Wag V

NUSSBAUMALLEE

WESTEND

See p320

SPANDAUER DAMM

Westend

Bröhan Museum

KLAUSENER PLATZ

DANCKELMANNSTR.

NEHRINGSTR.

DISTMAR STRASSE

SCHLOSSSTR.

GIERKE- PLATZ

SCHUSTERHUS- STRASSE

BEHAIMSTR.

316 Time Out Berlin

BRANITZER PLATZ

ULMENALLEE

EICHENALLEE

CHRIST- STRASSE

HAUBACHSTR.

E **F** **G** **H**

Rehberge Ⓤ

GLASGOWER STRASSE

MÜLLERSTRASSE

BARUSSTRASSE EDINBURGER STRASSE

TOGOSTRASSE

OTAWISTRASSE

SANSIBARSTRASSE

LUDERITZSTRASSE

Ⓤ U6

1

ALLEE C. ST SAENS

Volkspark
Rehberge

AFRIKANISCHE STRASSE

GUINEASTRASSE

KAMERUNER STRASSE

KONGOSTRASSE

TOGOSTRASSE

SEESTRASSE

2

TRANSVAAL STRASSE

SENEGALSTRASSE

WEDDING

ANTWERPENER STRASSE

SAATWINKLER DAMM

Hohenzollernkanal

DOHNAGESTELL

Goethepark

Zücker-
Museum

Anti-Kriegs-
Museum

BRUSSELER

OSTENDER STRASSE

Plötzensee

SEESTRASSE

AMRUMER STR

LIMBURGER STRASSE

RIEDEMANNWEG

FRIEDRICH-OLBRICHT-DAMM

HÜTTIGPFAD

**Gedenkstätte
Plötzensee**

Amrumer Strasse Ⓤ

SYLTER STRASSE

NÖRD.
SEESTRASSEN-
BRÜCKE

Schiffahrtskanal

U9

NÖRD. UFER

FÖHRER STR

TORGSTRASSE

FEHMARNER STRASSE

3

LUDW. HOFFM-
BRÜCKE

Westhafen Ⓤ

NÖRD. UFER

PUTLITZBRÜCKE

FRIEDRICH - KRAUSE - UFER

Westhafenkanal

Westhafen Ⓢ

See
p318 ▶

Beusselstrasse Ⓢ

QUITZOW - STRASSE

STEPHAN- STRASSE

4

S41-S42-S45-S46-S47

SIEMENSSTRASSE

Birken-
strasse Ⓤ

BIRKENSTRASSE

PERLEBERGER STRASSE

WILSNACKER

SICKINGENSTRASSE

**Reformations-
Kirche**

WICLEFSTRASSE

BEUSSELSTRASSE

BERLICHINGEN

WITTSTOCKER STR

ROSTOCKER STRASSE

WALDSTRASSE

EMDENER STRASSE

OLDENBURGER STRASSE

BREMER STRASSE

BREDOWSTRASSE

WILHELMSHAVENER STRASSE

LÜBECKER STRASSE

**Krankenhaus
Moabit**

BANDELSTRASSE

HUTTENSTRASSE

WIEBE- STRASSE

NEUES UFER

MOABIT

WALDENSERSTRASSE

Charlottenburger

TURMSTRASSE

Turmstrasse Ⓤ

TURMSTRASSE

5

Kleiner Tiergarten

AUGUSTA-ALLEE

GOSLARER UFER

ERASMUS-
STRASSE

GOTZKOWSKY STR

ZWINGLISTRASSE

Heilands-Kirche ✚

OTTOPLATZ

STROMSTRASSE

ALT-MOABIT ✚

St-Johannis-
Kirche

WILSNACKER STRASSE

GOSLARER
PLATZ

Verbindungskanal

Spree

ALT-MOABIT

KREFELDER STR

BOCHUMER STRASSE

U9

LESSING-
BR.

KIRCHSTRASSE

THOMASIUS STRASSE

96

NBURGER STR

DARWINSTR

PASCALSTR

GOTZKOWSKY
BRÜCKE

LEVETZOWSTRASSE

ELBERFELDER STRASSE

BUNDESRATUFER

HOLSTEINER UFER

MOABITER
BRÜCKE

HELGOLANDER UFER

CALVINSTR

ER- UFER

RÖNTGEN-
STR

HELMHOLTZSTR

MÖRSE STRASSE

WIKINGERUFER

AGRICOLASTRASSE

LES SINGSTRASSE

FLENSBURGER STR

**HANSA-
VIERTEL**

BARTNINGSTRASSE

Bellevue Ⓢ

LÜDTGE
WEG

RÖNTGEN-
STRASSE

DOVESTR

DOVEBR.

FRANKLINSTRASSE

SALZUFER

WULLENWEBERSTRASSE

HANSA-UFER

HANSABR.

BACHSTRASSE

**Akademie
der Künste**

ALTONAER

GER- UFER

GUERICKE STRASSE

EINSTEINUFER

MARCH-
BR.

SALZUFER

See
p321 ▼

Hansaplatz Ⓤ

Schlosspark Bellevue

6

*Lietzow-
kirche* ✚

UERSTRASSE

MARCH STR

ARBBSTR

BACHSTRASSE

Time Out Berlin **317**

*Englischer
Garten*

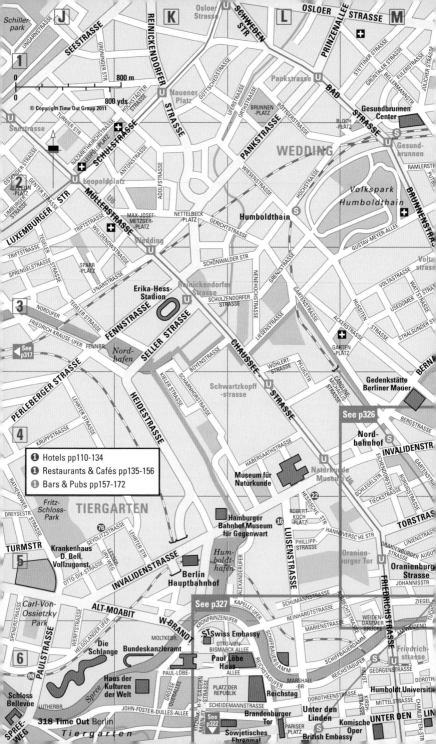

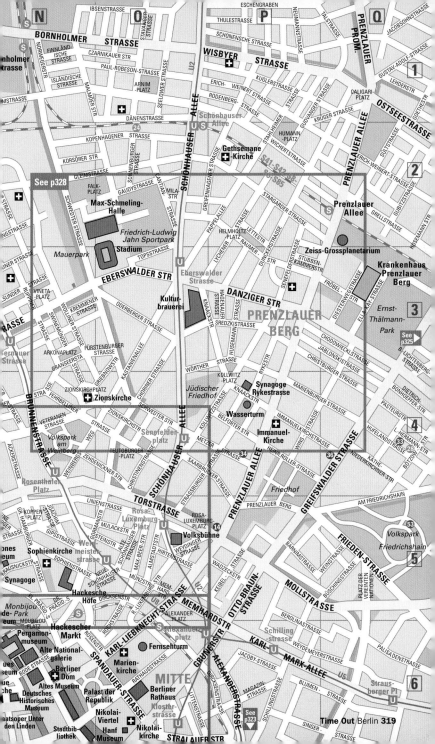

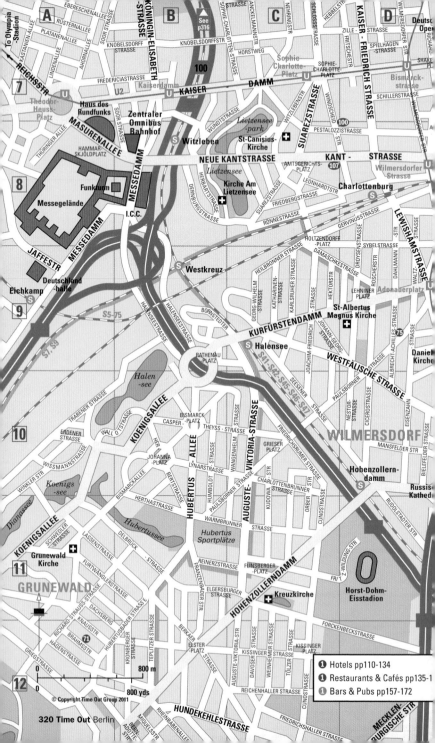

See p316

A | **B** | **C** | **D**

To Olympia-Stadion

REICHSSTR

7

EBERESCHENALLEE
RÜSTERNALLEE
PLATANENALLEE
KASTANIEN ALLEE
LINDENALLEE
AHORNALLEE
KNOBELSDORFF STRASSE
SOOR STRASSE
FREDERICIASTRASSE
Kaiserdamm

KÖNIGIN-ELISABETH-STRASSE

100

KNOBELSDORFFSTR
HORSTWEG
SOPHIE-CHARLOTTEN-STRASSE
WINCKELMANNSTR
NEHRINGSTR

SCHLOSSSTRASSE
HEBBELSTR
ZILLE STR
WILMERSDORFER STR

KAISER - FRIEDRICH STRASSE
SPIELHAGEN STRASSE
FRITSCHSTR

Deutsch Ope

Sophie Charlotte-Platz
SOPHIE-CHARLOTTE-PLATZ

SHAKE
Bismarck-strasse
SCHILLERSTRASSE

Theodor-Heuss-Platz

KAISER DAMM

Haus des Rundfunks

MASURENALLEE

Zentraler Omnibus Bahnhof

THÜRINGER ALLEE
HAMMAR-SKJÖLDPLATZ

8

Funkturm

Messegelände

I.C.C.

MESSEDAMM

SOOR STRASSE
MESSEDAMM

Witzleben
S

NEUE KANTSTRASSE
Lietzensee
Lietzensee-park
St-Canisius-Kirche

Herbartstrasse
DERNBURGSTRASSE
Kirche Am Lietzensee

SUAREZSTRASSE
WITZLEBENSTR
WUNDSTRASSE
MUNDTSTRASSE
WUNSCHED

KANT - STRASSE
AMTSGERICHTS-PLATZ
LEONHARDSTR
SUAREZSTRASSE
FRIEDBERGSTRASSE
RÖNNESTRASSE

PESTALOZZISTRASSE
100
107
Charlottenburg
S

Wilmersdorfer Strasse
U

GERVINUSSTRASSE
HOLTZENDORFF-PLATZ
HEILBRONNER STRASSE
DAMASCHKESTRASSE
DROYSENSTRASSE
SYBELSTRASSE
DAHLMANN
ROSCHERSTR
LEWISHAMSTRASSE
WALTZ

JAFFESTR

Eichkamp
S

Deutschland-halle

Westkreuz
S

S5-75
S7, S9

HALENSEESTRASSE
BORNSTEDTER

KURFÜRSTENDAMM
GEORG-WILHELM-STRASSE
KATHARINEN-STRASSE
KARLSRUHER STRASSE
HEKTORSTR
LEHNINER PLATZ

St-Albertus Magnus Kirche

Adenauerplatz
ALBRECHT-ACHILLES-STRASSE
S 75
Daniel Kirche

9

Halensee
S
Halen-see

RATHENAU-PLATZ

JOACHIM-FRIEDRICH STRASSE
JOHANN-GEORG-STRASSE
SEESENER STRASSE

WESTFÄLISCHE STRASSE
PAULSBORNER STRASSE
NESTOR-STRASSE
CICEROSTRASSE
EISENZAHN
PAULSBORNER
ALBRECHT-ACHILLES

WILMERSDORF

10

TRABENER STRASSE
ERDENER STRASSE
WISSMANNSTRASSE
WINKLER STR

WALL OT STRASSE
KOENIGSALLEE

BISMARCK-PLATZ
CASPER
THEYSS - STRASSE
HER
JOHANNA-PLATZ
BERTISTRASSE

HUBERTUS ALLEE
WANGENHEIM STR
LYNARSTRASSE
HUMBOLDT
PAULSBORNER STR

VIKTORIA-STRASSE
GRIESER PLATZ
CHARLOTTENBRUNNER STRASSE
KUDOWA
ORBER STR

FRIEDRICHSRUHER STRASSE
CUNOSTRASSE

MANSFELDER STR
Hohenzollern-damm
BIELEFELDER STRASSE

Russis Kathed

RUDOLSTADTER STR

Koenigs-see

BISMARCKALLEE
HERTHASTRASSE

Hubertussee
DELBRÜCK - STRASSE
WARMBRUNNER STRASSE

AUGUSTE-VIKTORIA-STRASSE

Hubertus Sportplätze

Dianastr
KOENIGSALLEE
SCHWEDLER STRASSE
LASSENSTRASSE
FURTWÄNGLERSTRASSE

REINERZSTRASSE
FRANZENSBADER STR

FLINSBERGER-PLATZ
ELGERSBURGER STRASSE

HOHENZOLLERNDAMM
FRITZ WILDUNG STR

Horst-Dohm-Eisstadion

11

Grunewald Kirche

GRUNEWALD

RICHARD-STRAUSS-STRASSE
DACHSBERG
KNAUSSTR
BRAHMSSTR
HAGENSTRASSE
GRIEGSTRASSE

HUBERTUSBADER STRASSE
KRONBERGER STRASSE
TEPLITZER STRASSE

BERKAER STRASSE
ELSTER-PLATZ

71

Kreuzkirche

AUGUSTE-VIKTORIA-STR
KISSINGER STRASSE
DAVOSER STRASSE
WEINHEIMER STRASSE
TÖLZER STRASSE
KISSINGER PLATZ

FORCKENBECKSTRASSE

MECKLEN-BURGISCHE STR

0   800 m
0   800 yds

© Copyright Time Out Group 2011

12

❶ Hotels pp110-134
❶ Restaurants & Cafés pp135-1
❶ Bars & Pubs pp157-172

320 Time Out Berlin

HUNDEKEHLESTRASSE
REICHENHALLER STRASSE
CUNOSTRASSE
RHEINBABENALLEE
MIQUELSTR
ABOTT-STR
BERN-STR
FRIEDRICHSHALLER STRASSE
RHEINBABENALLEE

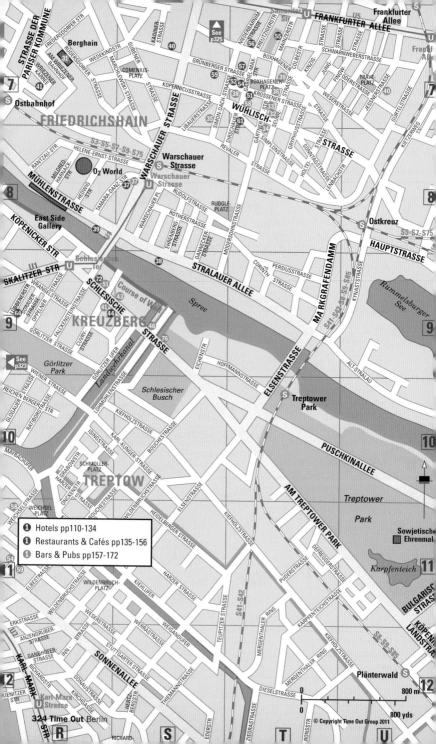

STRASSE DER PARISER KOMMUNE

7

S Ostbahnhof

FRIEDRICHSHAIN

Berghain

MÜHLENSTRASSE

8

East Side Gallery

KÖPENICKER STR

SKALITZER STR

SCHLESISCHE

KREUZBERG

9

STRASSE

Görlitzer Park

Schlesischer Busch

10

TREPTOW

1

❶ Hotels pp110-134
❶ Restaurants & Cafés pp135-156
❶ Bars & Pubs pp157-172

2

Karl-Marx Strasse

WARSCHAUER STRASSE

Warschauer Strasse

O₂ World

Warschauer Strasse

STRALAUER ALLEE

Spree

FRANKFURTER ALLEE

Frankfurter Allee

WÜHLISCH-STRASSE

7

8

Ostkreuz

S3-S5-S7-S9-S75

S5-S7-S75

HAUPTSTRASSE

Rummelsburger See

9

MARKGRAFENDAMM

ELSENSTRASSE

Treptower Park

PUSCHKINALLEE

AM TREPTOWER PARK

Treptower Park

Sowjetisches Ehrenmal

10

11

Karpfenteich

Plänterwald

BULGARISCHE STRAS

KÖPENI LANDSTRA

S8-S9-S85

12

0   800 m

0   800 yds

© Copyright Time Out Group 2011

R   **S**   **T**   **U**

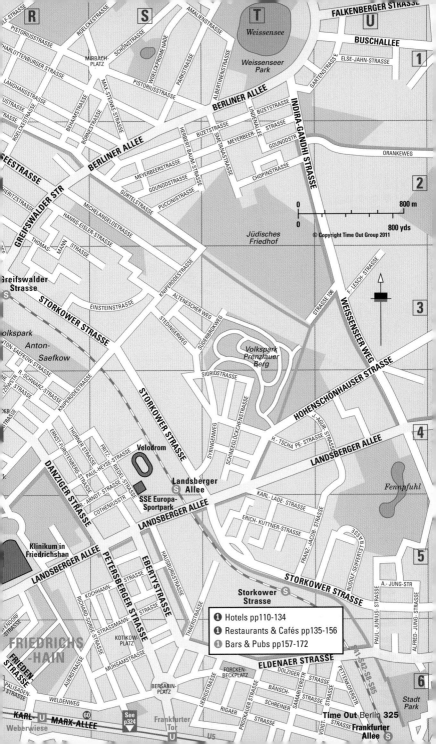

1 Hotels pp110-134

1 Restaurants & Cafés pp135-156

1 Bars & Pubs pp157-172

Time Out Berlin **325**

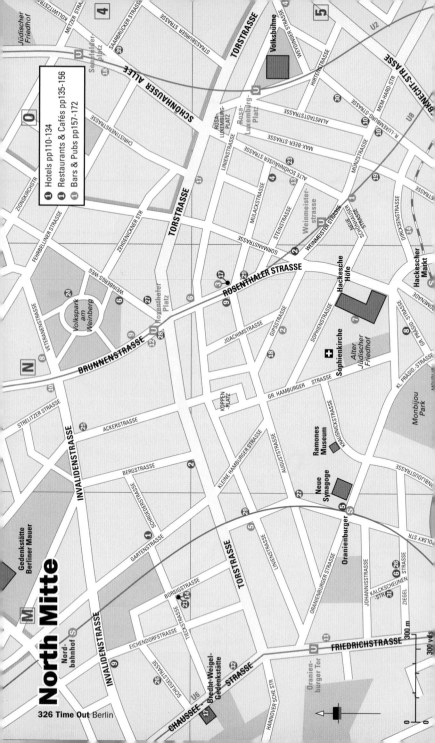

North Mitte

M Nordbahnhof S

326 Time Out Berlin

O
1 Hotels pp110-134
1 Restaurants & Cafés pp135-156
1 Bars & Pubs pp157-172

Gedenkstätte Berliner Mauer

Volksbühne

Hackesche Höfe

Hackescher Markt S

Volkspark am Weinberg

Sophienkirche

Alter Jüdischer Friedhof

Ramones Museum

Neue Synagoge

Monbijou Park

Oranienburger S

Oranienburger Tor

Brecht-Weigel-Gedenkstätte

Jüdischer Friedhof

Senefelder Platz

Streets/labels: KOLLWITZSTRASSE, METZER STRASSE, SAARBRÜCKER STRASSE, STRASSBURGER STRASSE, TORSTRASSE, WEINBERGS WEG, SCHÖNHAUSER ALLEE, CHRISTINENSTRASSE, ZIONSKIRCHSTR, FEHRBELLINER STRASSE, ZEHDENICKER STR, VETERANENSTRASSE, STRELITZER STRASSE, BRUNNENSTRASSE, INVALIDENSTRASSE, ACKERSTRASSE, BERGSTRASSE, GARTENSTRASSE, SCHRÖDERSTRASSE, BORSIGSTRASSE, EICHENDORFSTRASSE, TIECKSTRASSE, SCHLEGELSTRASSE, HANNOVERSCHE STR, CHAUSSEE STRASSE, FRIEDRICHSTRASSE, ORANIENBURGER STRASSE, TORSTRASSE, LINIENSTRASSE, JOHANNISSTRASSE, KALCKSCHEUNEN STR, ZIEGEL STRASSE, KRAUSNICKSTRASSE, AUGUSTSTRASSE, KLEINE HAMBURGER STRASSE, KÖPPEN PLATZ, GR. HAMBURGER STRASSE, SOPHIENSTRASSE, GIPSSTRASSE, JOACHIMSTRASSE, ROSENTHALER STRASSE, Rosenthaler Platz, WEINMEISTER STRASSE, GORMANNSTRASSE, STEINSTRASSE, MULACKSTRASSE, ALTE SCHÖNHAUSER STRASSE, LINIENSTRASSE, MAX-BEER-STRASSE, ROSA-LUXEMBURG-PLATZ, ROSA-LUXEMBURG-STRASSE, MÜNZSTRASSE, ALMSTADTSTRASSE, HIRTENSTRASSE, R.-LUXEMBURG-STRASSE, MEM.-HARD.-STR, WEINBERG STRASSE, B.-KNECHT-STRASSE, DIRKSENSTRASSE, KL. PRÄSID.-STRASSE, GR. PRÄSID.-STRASSE, PROMENADE, MONBIJOUSTRASSE, POLSKY STR, GROSSE PRÄSIDENTENSTRASSE

N (compass)

4 **5** (grid markers)

300 m
300 yds

Prenzlauer Berg

N
FALKPLATZ
GLEIMSTRASSE
GAUDYSTRASSE
ANTONSTR
MILA-STR
GREIFENHAGENER ST
ALLEE
P
STARGARDER STRASSE
Q
19
Prenzlauer Allee S
2

Max-Schmeling-Halle
Friedrich-Ludwig Jahn Sportpark
Mauerpark
Stadium
Zeiss-Grossplanetarium

SCHWEDTER STRASSE
PAPPELALLEE
HELMHOLTZ-PLATZ
35 30
LETTESTRASSE
LYCHENER STRASSE
DUNCKERSTRASSE
RAUMER
SEELOWER STRASSE
STUBBEN-KAMMERSTR
PRENZLAUER
FRÖBEL
STRASSE
23
Eberswalder Strasse U

TOPSTRASSE
400 m
400 yds
© Copyright Time Out Group 2011

EBERSWALDER STRASSE
20

DANZIGER
STRASSE
47

Kultur-brauerei
26
40
25
44
27
ODERBERGER STRASSE
37

1 Hotels pp110-134
1 Restaurants & Cafés pp135-1
1 Bars & Pubs pp157-172

KREMMENER STRASSE
BERNAUER STRASSE
VINETA-PLATZ
KASTANIENALLEE
SREDZKISTRASSE
HAGENAUER STRASSE
HUSEMANN
KNAACKSTRASSE
50
34
WÖRTHER
KOLLWITZ-PLATZ
STRASSE
CHRISTBURGER ST

ARKONAPLATZ
FÜRSTENBURGER STRASSE
48

SWINEMÜNDER STRASSE
RUPPINER STRASSE
WOLLINER STRASSE
CHORINER STRASSE
GREIFSWYGER
GRANSEER STR
SCHÖNHAUSER ALLEE
49
46
Synagoge Rykestrasse
38
22
36
21
45
42
MARIENBURGER STRASSE
WINS
ZIONSKIRCHSTR
Zionskirche
16
20
Jüdischer Friedhof
Wasserturm
Prenzlauer Berg Museum
KNAACKSTRASSE
RYKESTRASSE
PRENZLAUER ALLEE
DIESTERWEGSTR
STRASSE

ANKLA
MEER STRASSE
FEHRBELLINER STRASSE
VETERANEN STRASSE
SCHWEDTER STR
KOLLWITZSTRASSE
BELFORTER STRASSE
32
Immanuel-Kirche
IMMANUELKIRCHSTRASSE
33

Volkspark am
ISENBERGSTRASSE
SCHÖNHAUSER ALLEE
Senefelder-platz U
METZER STR

Charlottenburg

E
F
Universität der Künste
102
STEIN-PLATZ
G
Z
Zoologischer Garten
S
Bahnhof Zoo

HARDENBERGSTRASSE
Museum für Fotographie

400 m
400 yds
© Copyright Time Out Group 2011

PESTALOZZISTRASSE
105 101
Ludwig-Erhard-Haus

1 Hotels pp110-134
1 Restaurants & Cafés pp135-156
1 Bars & Pubs pp157-172

GROLMANSTRASSE
KNESEBECKSTRASSE
CARMERSTRASSE
70
SAVIGNY-PLATZ
61
Theater des Westens
Zoologischer Garten U

LEIBNIZSTRASSE
Savignyplatz S
BLEIBTREU
99
SAVIGNY PASSAGE
KANTSTRASSE
113
110
Kant-Dreieck
112 72
Kaiser-Wilhelm Gedächtnis-Kirche
8
BREITSCHEID PLATZ

NIEBUHRSTRASSE
68
Ku'damm U
106
BLEIBTREUSTRASSE
69
59
Jüdisches Gemeindehaus

MOMMSENSTRASSE
109
WIELANDSTRASSE
SCHLÜTERSTRASSE
78
60
U
Uhlandstr U
111
AUGSBURGER
STRASSE
55

56
SYBELSTRASSE
KURFÜRSTENDAMM
UHLANDSTRASSE
103
66
JOACHIMSTALER STRASSE
MEINEKESTRASSE
RANKE
EISLEBENER STRAS

BLEIBTREU
GEORG-GROSZ-PLATZ
57
Käthe-Kollwitz-Museum
67
70

63 64
OLIVAER PLATZ
LIETZENBURGER STRASSE
FASANEN-PLATZ
9

ALBRECHTST
PARISER STRASSE
SCHAPERSTRASSE
78

Street Index

STREET INDEX

Street Index

STREET INDEX

Berlin Liniennetz *Routemap*

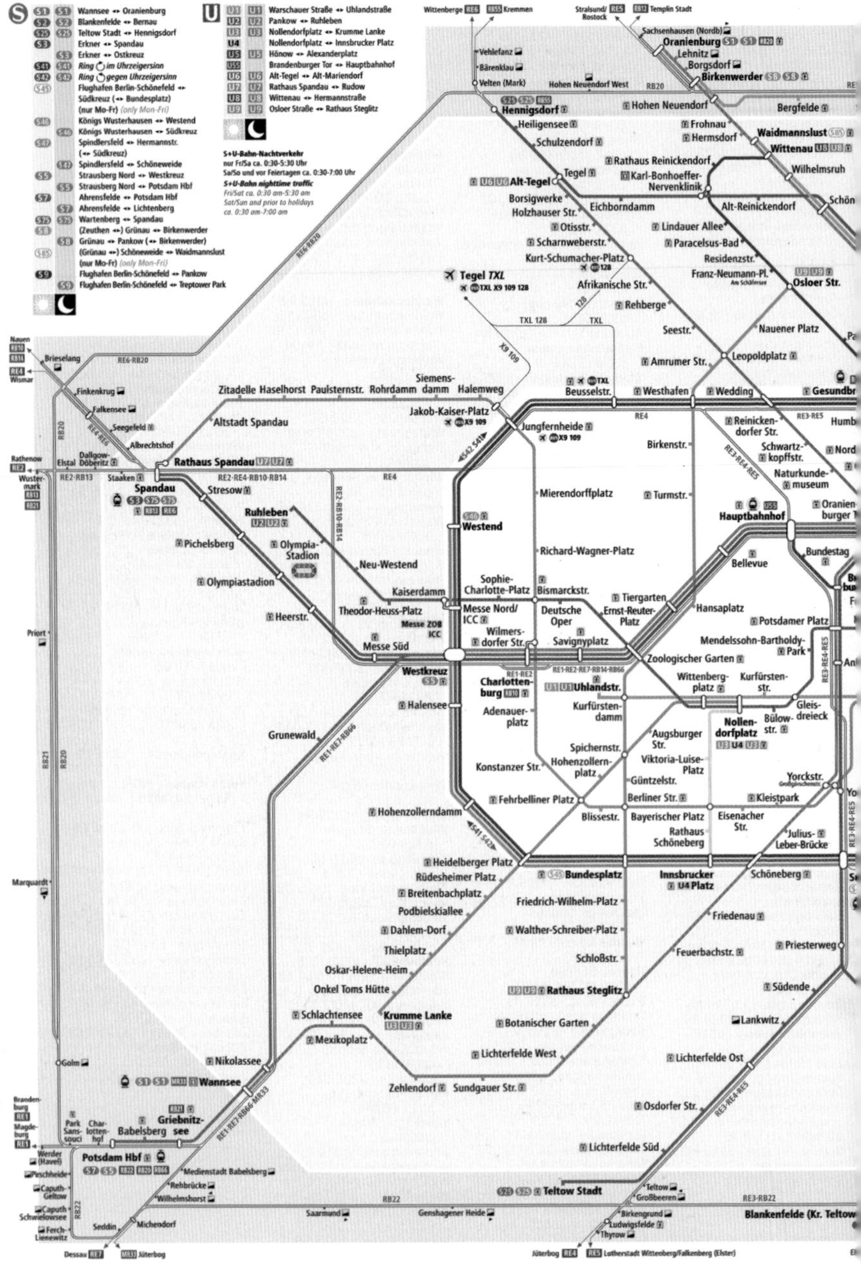

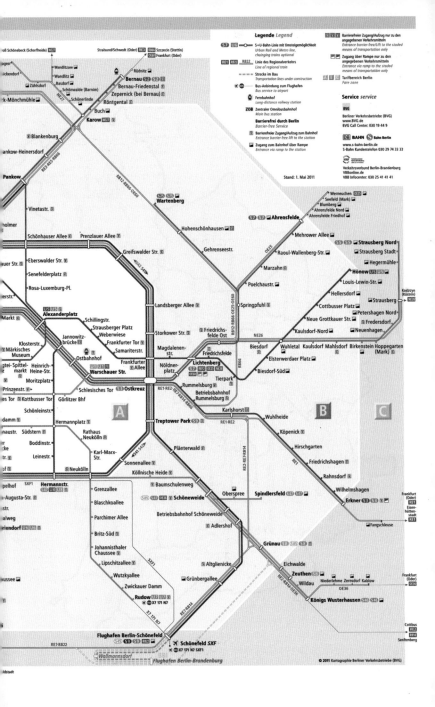

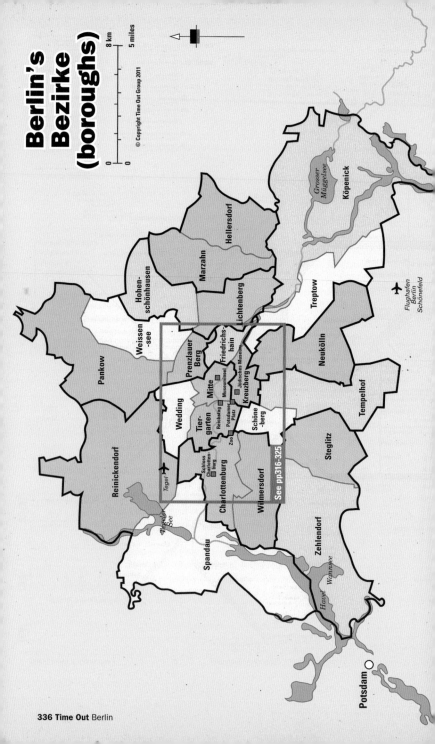

Berlin's Bezirke (boroughs)

© Copyright Time Out Group 2011

0   8 km
0   5 miles

Köpenick

Grosser Müggelsee

Hellersdorf

Marzahn

Hohen-schönhausen

Lichtenberg

Treptow

Flughafen Berlin Schönefeld

Weissen-see

Pankow

Prenzlauer Berg

Friedrichs-hain

Neukölln

Wedding

Mitte

Museumsinsel

Jüdisches Museum

Kreuzberg

Tempelhof

Reinickendorf

Tiergarten

Reichstag

Potsdamer Platz

Schöne-berg

Zoo

Steglitz

Tegel

Schloss Charlotten-burg

Charlottenburg

Wilmersdorf

See pp316-325

Tegeler See

Spandau

Zehlendorf

Havel

Wannsee

Potsdam